Does federal funding threaten state control of education?

What is the best way for states to allocate money for education?

Should teachers control the state standards boards?

Are school choice and tax credits the answer to school funding inequities?

What is society's responsibility to students at risk?

How can children in poor neighborhoods get better schools?

Do programs like Title I perpetuate underachievement?

Does the school-to-work concept have any drawbacks?

Should states mandate that all school districts provide sex education?

Can schools prevent substance abuse by students?

What is multicultural education?

Do alternative culture-based curricula encourage separatism?

How do cultural factors affect cognitive development?

Do boys and girls use different kinds of moral reasoning?

Are single-sex schools the answer to gender bias in the classroom?

What does it take to make inclusion work?

To what extent should the curriculum reflect local interests and values?

What kind of curriculum is in the national interest?

To what extent should teachers and professional associations determine the curriculum?

Is peer-mediated instruction as effective as teacher-mediated instruction?

Can creativity be taught?

What ethical considerations should guide testing and grading practices?

Can teachers use physical punishment on a child?

Can students ever be denied the right to due process of law?

Is posting grades an invasion of students' privacy?

Can a teacher be dismissed for private conduct?

When can a teacher be sued for negligence?

Do school boards have the power to ban textbooks?

Are schools liable for educational malpractice?

Can students who are victims of sexual harrassment sue for damages?

Does Japan have a better educational system than the United States?

Would other countries' solutions for multilingual education work for the United States?

Will accountability for national standards cause schools to "teach to the test"?

How far should schools go in attempting to ensure gender equity?

How far should schools go in teaching moral values?

Should schools make service learning mandatory?

Could the Internet have a negative impact on education?

Can collaborative networks contribute to the professionalization of teaching?

Foundations of Education

Foundations of Education

The Challenge of Professional Practice

SECOND EDITION

Robert F. McNergney

University of Virginia

Joanne M. Herbert

University of Virginia

Allyn and Bacon

Boston · London · Toronto · Sydney · Tokyo · Singapore

Senior Editor: Virginia Lanigan
Editorial Assistant: Kris Lamarre
Senior Marketing Manager: Kathy Hunter
Senior Developmental Editor: Mary Ellen Lepionka
Production Administrator: Susan Brown
Editorial-Production Service: Thomas E. Dorsaneo
Text Designer: Deborah Schneck
Cover Administrator: Linda Knowles
Cover Designer: Susan Paradise
Composition Buyer: Linda Cox
Manufacturing Buyer: Suzanne Lareau
Compositor: Seventeenth Street Studios
Separator: R. R. Donnelley

Library of Congress Cataloging-in-Publication Data

McNergney, Robert F.
    Foundations of education / Robert F.
McNergney, Joanne M. Herbert. —2nd ed.
        p.   cm.
    Includes bibliographical references (p.   ) and
index.
    ISBN 0-205-27009-3
    1. Teaching—Vocational guidance—United
States.   2. Education—United States. I. Herbert,
Joanne M. II.   Title.
LB1775.2.M32   1998
371.1'002373—dc21   97-15153
                                                       CIP

Copyright © 1998, 1995 by Allyn & Bacon
A Viacom Company
160 Gould Street
Needham Heights, MA 02194-2310

Internet: www.abacon.com
America Online: Keyword: College online

Printed in the United States of America
10 9 8 7 6 5 4 3 2 1   RRDW   02 01 00 99 98 97

PHOTO CREDITS

Will Hart: pp. 1, 27, 83, 157, 170, 178, 216, 278, 296,
304, 311, 329, 362, 374, 394, 404, 415, 497, 501, 519;
Brian Smith: pp. 20, 177, 263 (left), 267, 307, 349; Will
Faller: pp. 21, 182, 196, 235, 259, 384, 400, 442, 493;
Vanessa Vick/Photo Researchers: p. 35; North Wind
Picture Archive: pp. 42, 45, 49, 51, 55, 57, 58, 62, 68,
72, 90, 94, 129, 133, 135, 137; The Granger Collection:
pp. 59 (top), 65; Lyrl Ahern: pp. 59 (bottom) 103, 104
(bottom),147; AP/Wide World Photos: pp. 81, 224,
461; The Library of Congress: pp. 88 (both), 95 (both);
Courtesy of the Dalton Public Libary: p. 104 (top);

Courtesy of NASA: p. 106; Robert Harbison: pp. 111,
245, 372, 421; National Library of Medicine: pp. 143,
145; Courtesy of Special Collections/Morris Library
Southern Illinois University at Carbondale: p. 150;
Stephen Marks: p. 241; Jim Pickerell: p. 263 (left);
Stephen Shames/Matrix: pp. 264, 286; Mike
Yamashita/Woodfin Camp & Associates: p. 428;
Steven Rubin/Imageworks: p. 455; Jon Burbank/
Imageworks: p. 470; Courtesy of Jeffery P. Harper:
p. 473, 478, 480; John Coletti: p. 522.

TO OUR PARENTS

Quentin and Thelma McNergney

AND

Elmore and Arvilla May

WITH LOVE

BRIEF CONTENTS

CONTENTS

PREFACE

Professionals, regardless of their fields, use knowledge to solve problems and to capitalize on opportunities. Teachers, physicians, lawyers, and others face the challenge of professional practice by acquiring and learning how to apply specialized knowledge. Even then, professionals often work in situations where their knowledge is tentative and incomplete. They must do the best they can with the knowledge they possess.

THE PLAN OF THE BOOK

The book's organization reflects our conception of teaching as a profession. To us, professionals possess foundational knowledge others do not possess and are able to apply that knowledge to do things others cannot do. Professionals in all fields can explain why they behave as they do. They also have the capacity to reflect on or evaluate their actions and thus to continue to progress professionally. These abilities set the professional apart from other people.

Professional teachers perceive problems that need to be solved and opportunities to learn as they interact with students. They recognize when their own values and the values of others influence education. Professional teachers know about teaching, about students, about learning, and about content so they can improve their chances for successful practice. Because professional teachers are always reinforcing and extending their foundational knowledge, they can act in timely fashion and evaluate or reflect on their actions to advance their development.

Many people have a stake in our educational systems. Because we have a society of ethnic, racial, religious, and social diversity, we also have a tradition of pluralistic thought and action with respect to educational matters. The book reflects this tradition of working together to make a better place for everyone.

This second edition of the book contains 13 chapters. We have written to acknowledge the interdependence of knowledge in the disciplines and knowledge from the education profession. We also have incorporated some very useful ideas and suggestions from readers of the first edition.

Chapter 1 communicates the theme of professionalism. Chapters 2 through 4 place education in historical and philosophical contexts. Chapter 5 explores the many meanings of the concept of school. Chapter 6 examines the governmental and economic contexts in which education for children occurs. Chapters 7 through 9 describe the challenges of meeting students' diverse educational needs. Chapter 10 explores curriculum and instruction. Chapter 11 explains the major legal issues before the education community. Chapter 12 stretches beyond our own borders to consider international and global education. Chapter 13 anticipates an exciting future for educators in an increasingly interdependent world.

How the Second Edition Differs from the First

This edition incorporates the following major changes suggested by our readers and those we thought would help us when we used the book in our own teaching:

- We have combined the chapters on school governance and education finance into a single chapter, excluding some of the interpretation in the first edition and highlighting the essential information.

- We have combined the curriculum chapter and the instruction chapter into one chapter by crafting the concepts into a conceptual whole.

- Given strong expressions of interest in material in the first edition, and the changing reality of American education, we have added a new chapter on comparative and global education.

- We have infused material on multicultural education and technology throughout the text to communicate how and why these concepts are stretching across foundational areas.

- By either deleting old material or adding new information, we have updated the references by 40%.

- As we explain below, we have also strengthened existing features and added some new ones.

AIDS TO UNDERSTANDING

This second edition includes features in each chapter to help you understand and remember the material. We have retained features from the first edition that worked well, enhanced others to capitalize on strengths that our readers found especially helpful, and added new ones to reflect the challenges facing professional educators.

- **Overviews** set the stage for the material presented in the chapter.

- **Professional Practice Questions** have been revised to communicate from the outset, and throughout the chapters, exactly what material will be presented, and why it is important.

- **URLs (Uniform Resource Locators)**, World Wide Web sites, or Web addresses now appear in every chapter. They point you to valuable online information relevant to key concepts in the text. While these addresses are likely to change over time, typically old sites direct you to new addresses. Also we will monitor the URLs in the text and update them on our own Web page (which you can find at Allyn and Bacon's Web site: http:www.abacon.com) from time to time. You can check our site for new and revised information.

- **Benchmarks** represent important conceptual points in time and appear in each chapter.

- **Terms and Concepts** denoted by bold print in the body of the text appear alphabetically at the end of each chapter.

- The **Glossary** at the end of the book defines the terms and concepts.

- **Figures and Tables** communicate in shortened form current theory, research, and background information noted in the text.

- **Foundations-in-Action** features located at strategic points throughout the text demonstrate how the material that precedes them can be applied to real teachers in real classrooms across the nation. These correspond to the **videocases**—real-life classroom and school episodes from multicultural settings across the United States—that accompany your instructor's edition of the text.

- **Cultural Awareness** features highlight the influences of culture, variously defined, on teaching and learning.

- **Voices** proved so popular in the first edition that we have doubled the number of these first-hand accounts, reportage, and professional writings. Critical Thinking questions guide your thinking about these excerpts.

- A **Summary** reiterates the main points made in each chapter.

- A **Reflective Practice** exercise at the end of each chapter takes the form of a "mini case" of real life that encourages you to apply knowledge from the chapter. As you engage in the exercise you will identify issues, problems, dilemmas, opportunities; perceive others' points of view; call up knowledge to inform actions you might take if you were in the situation, and forecast how you might evaluate your actions.

- The **Online Activity** at the end of each chapter points you toward resources and useful professional connections on the World Wide Web.

INSTRUCTOR SUPPLEMENTS TO ACCOMPANY THIS TEXT

Contact your Allyn and Bacon representative for more information about any of the following supplements.

- **Instructor's Resource Manual** containing graphic organizers, transparency masters, teaching suggestions, case-based activities supported by handout masters, and other resources for teaching each chapter.

- A 1300-item **Test Bank** with answer feedback, which includes multiple choice, essay, and application items as well as a component for authentic assessment.

- **Computerized Test Bank** for IBM and Macintosh computers
- **Allyn and Bacon Introduction to Teaching/ Foundations of Education Transparency Package**, containing over 100 ready-to-use acetate transparencies.
- A **Digital Image Archive** of text-specific electronic transparencies.
- A set of four **Videocases** with a comprehensive **Guide**, providing an in-depth look at teaching and learning in multicultural classrooms in the Midwest, the Washington DC area, and New York City.
- A **CD-ROM**, "Educational Border Culture in New Mexico," designed for in-depth exploration of multicultural/multilingual issues in education.
- Our own **Web page** within the Allyn & Bacon Web site (http://www.abacon.com).

Acknowledgments

We thank the many people who gave generously of their time and energy to help produce this book. The following reviewers offered valuable suggestions on various drafts of the manuscript: Ann Batchelder, Northen Arizona University; Rick A. Breault, University of Indianapolis; Richard A. Brosio, Ball State University; Larry Daniels, University of Southern Mississippi; Frank Guldbrandsen, University of Minnesota; Grace C. Huerta, Utah State University; Rosemary Barton Tobin, Emmanuel College; Stephen J. Virgilio, Adelphi University; John Mack Welford, Roanoke College.

The Allyn and Bacon team supported our every move on this second edition. Nancy Forsyth, Editor-in-Chief, marshaled the forces with her usual wit and decisiveness. Once again, we feel very lucky to have worked with our Editor, Virginia Lanigan—truly one of the best in the business. Virginia's support and ideas kept us moving forward. Kris Lamarre, Virginia's assistant, rushed to our aid on numerous occasions. Mary Ellen Lepionka, developmental editor extraordinaire, brought her skills and energy to bear to make this revision a special offering.

For the past eight or nine years, The Hitachi Foundation has provided financial and moral support for our work with cases—much of which is reflected in this volume. Early on, Felicia Lynch encouraged us to begin making videocases. As time has passed, Delwin Roy, President, Laurie Regelbrugge, Vice President, Renata Hron, Program Officer, Roger Nozaki, Program Officer, and Joseph Getch, Comptroller, have been instrumental in shaping our work. Two colleagues associated with the Virginia State Education Department— Ernest Skinner, videographer, and Edward Damerel, sound technician— recorded and edited the videocases that go with the book.

Our colleagues at the University of Virginia helped us many ways. Librarians Betsy Anthony and Kay Cutler led us through the technological labyrinth to find valuable information. Chandlee Bryan performed with skill and grace to accomplish a variety of research, editing, and Web-searching tasks. Peggy Marshall and Karen Dwier typed, taped, and checked references with speed and skill.

Special thanks are due Todd Kent, a valued colleague and friend who has carried the inappropriate title of graduate student. Todd taught us about the power of technology to educate teachers. He also headed a team, composed of Valerie Larson and Frank Becker, to design the CD-ROM entitled "Educational Border Culture in New Mexico" that accompanies the book. We believe this learning aid will set the standard against which others will be judged.

Our families gave us the support and understanding we needed to complete this edition of the text. We could not have done it without them.

RFM
JMH

1

Teachers and Teaching

This chapter frames a concept of the teacher as professional—a concept that has much in common with concepts of professionals in other fields yet is uniquely suited to the work that teachers perform. We consider both group and individual characteristics of the people who call themselves teachers. We also explore why people choose to become teachers, the routes they take to prepare themselves to enter the classroom, why some decide to leave teaching, and what ultimately encourages most who enter to stay and build careers as professional educators.

In this chapter we present information on how to obtain teaching certification, how much money teachers can expect to earn, and how to understand the processes of teacher evaluation and of the distribution of rewards. Because the conditions of teaching in schools and the processes of educating teachers are changing, we use teacher education reform proposals to predict the future of the teaching profession.

PROFESSIONAL PRACTICE QUESTIONS

1 What does it mean to be a teacher?

2 Why do people choose to teach?

3 Why do people leave teaching?

4 Who are America's teachers today?

5 What factors affect the teaching job market?

6 How do people become teachers?

7 How are professional programs accredited and approved?

8 How is teaching performance evaluated and rewarded?

9 What reform proposals are leading to changes in teacher education?

10 What reforms have been initiated?

WHAT DOES IT MEAN TO BE A TEACHER?

Teachers are professionals. **Professional teachers** are people who possess specialized knowledge and skills about education. They have been selected to enter professional programs, their knowledge and skill have been evaluated during their general and professional studies, they have met requirements for graduation from an institution of higher education, and they have fulfilled requirements for **certification**—recognition by the state that they have met minimum standards for competent practice.

In a comparative study of teaching with other occupations, sociologist Brian Rowan (1994) noted that prestige and earnings that accrue to an occupation depend to a significant extent on the complexity of the work performed by members of that occupation.

From this perspective, teaching's claim to professional status, and its quest to attract and retain able recruits through increases in prestige and earnings, can be seen as more than an expression of hollow "professionalism." Instead it is grounded in the following reality: Teaching children and adolescents is complex work, and successful performance of this work requires high levels of general educational development and specific vocational preparation. (Rowan, 1994, p. 13)

Gary Fenstermacher (1990) describes some ways in which teaching is different from other professions:

It is a popular profession in that its practice is open to all who wish to struggle to achieve its ideals and master its requirements for competent practice. It is an egalitarian profession in that its practitioners use expertise and specialization not as instruments of status and control but as a shared resource of the group. It is a demanding profession in that it requires the reflective exercise of knowledge and skill, while being intensely engaged in the complex, perhaps greatly disadvantaged lives of one's students. . . .To think of teaching in this way is to think of it as a fundamentally moral undertaking. (p. 148)

Is teaching a full profession?

Educators hold many opinions about what constitutes the knowledge base—the teaching knowledge, skills, and values that yield student learning. Unlike other professions, teaching lacks consensus on what constitutes the knowledge base. Multiple acceptable opinions are reflected in the more than 1,200 institutions of higher education that maintain teacher education programs and in the thousands of inservice programs in elementary and secondary schools.

Teaching is different from other professions also in that teachers do not control their own entry into the profession. Physicians, lawyers, accountants, and other professionals control who enters their professions: that is, they set minimum standards for professional practice. People other than teachers typically control decision making in matters of teachers' professional practice, decide what teachers must do to progress as professionals, and prepare curricula for students. Teachers often participate in these decisions, but they do not control them. Other professions often command higher salaries, but public school teachers' salaries and perceptions of teachers' capabilities have shown steady increases in recent years.

Despite these differences from other professions, teachers are regarded as professionals because of how they think and behave. A theme of this text is that when teachers reflect on their work—as they teach and in retrospect—they develop their abilities to behave in ways that distinguish them from nonprofessionals.

A Professional Way of Thinking and Acting

Teachers are problem solvers. They plan for, they initiate, and they assess education in its many forms. Teachers continue to learn from the challenges they face on the job. They do so through a five-step process of reflective teaching, represented in Figure 1.1.

FIGURE I.I

Reflective Teaching Process

It is important for teachers to be able to reflect on their work so they can develop their professional knowledge and skills over time. Why is it also important for teachers to be able to explain their methods and the reasons underlying their behaviors?

Note. From "Cooperation and competition in case-based teacher education," by R. F. McNergney, J. M. Herbert & R. E. Ford, 1994, *Journal of Teacher Education,* 45(5), pp. 339–345. Adapted by permission.

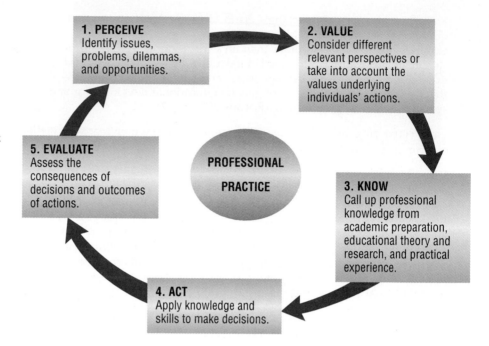

Step 1 of reflective practice involves teachers' awareness of the educational life surrounding them—the actions and interactions of students, the demands of curriculum, the influences of colleagues, and other sights and sounds that affect the ebb and flow of classroom activity. Teachers must be able to *perceive* instructional issues, problems, and opportunities as they arise if they hope to maximize their chances for behaving in ways that make a difference in their students' lives. Teachers' awareness of people and situations, then, is prerequisite to all other professional behavior.

In Step 2, professional teachers consider their own and others' points of view. What might be a compelling instructional problem to one teacher may be of little or no importance to another. When teachers pause to consider a student's or a parent's or a colleague's perspective, they may find that their own concerns are not well formulated and that *valuing* the issues the other individual deems important might be wise. When teachers take into account their own and others' values, the definition of what constitutes a problem or an opportunity can change.

Values and knowledge guide practice. In Step 3, teachers call up the professional *knowledge* they possess in preparation for using that knowledge to take action. As professionals, teachers have specialized knowledge and skills acquired from long, intensive academic preparation and from practical experience in the classrooms. Knowledge from theory, research, and practice informs teachers' decisions. Figure 1.2 suggests the complexity of the professional knowledge base on which teachers draw when they make decisions about teaching.

In Step 4 of reflective teaching, teachers use what they know to *take action.* They apply their knowledge and skills imaginatively and deliberately as needed. If called upon to do so, they can articulate why they behave as they do. In other words, teachers' actions are based on knowledge and reason.

FIGURE 1.2

Foundations of Education: A Teacher's Professional Knowledge Base

Compare the items in this figure with the chapter titles in this textbook. How will your course on the foundations of education help you think and behave professionally?

In Step 5, teachers *evaluate* the consequences of their actions. Professional teachers are equipped intellectually and emotionally to reflect on their work and thus to learn from what they do. Professional teachers develop their expertise over time—a hallmark of professionals in all fields. This final step of evaluation leads back to Step 1 of the reflective practice; that is, what teachers learn from reflecting on their work enhances their abilities to perceive issues and opportunities as they arise in the future. Taken together, then, the five steps of reflective teaching—perceiving, valuing, knowing, acting, and evaluating—form the foundation of professional teaching.

A Teacher's Workweek, Work World

Day-to-day life in elementary and secondary schools is remarkably the same when it comes to how teachers spend their time. Surveys suggest that while teachers are typically required to spend 33 hours each week in school, they actually spend 45–50 hours per week on school-related work (U.S. Department of Education, 1996a). (See Figure 1.3.)

In other ways, however, daily life in schools is restricted only by participants' powers of imagination. Like Picasso, who challenged human perception with his cubist paintings, a teacher can invite students to perceive their educational world in unique and personal ways. When this happens, every day in school is truly different.

FIGURE 1.3

The Teachers' Workweek

Redraw this graph to show what, if anything, you would change about the way teachers use their time during a typical workweek. What are your reasons?

Note. From "Dimensions: The Teacher's Workweek," by *Education Week*, p. 3 February 7, 1990. Copyright 1990 by Education Week. Reprinted by permission.

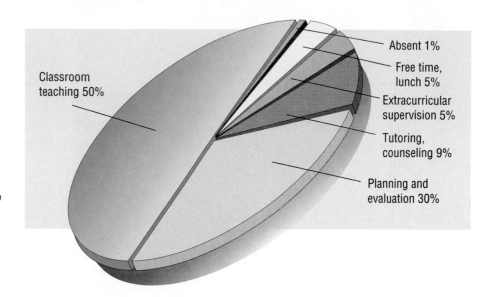

Classroom teaching 50%

Absent 1%

Free time, lunch 5%

Extracurricular supervision 5%

Tutoring, counseling 9%

Planning and evaluation 30%

Society's Expectations of Teachers

Society expects teachers to be all and do all—a mission impossible, of course, but one that often has the effect of bringing out the best in those who accept it. Teachers succeed by exhibiting extraordinary commitment to students, to ideals about professional behavior, and to plain old hard work.

As Edward Ducharme (1993) observes, teachers often expect themselves to meet the challenge of doing important work.

> I went into junior high school teaching. An urban, inner-city school. I did it for a weird reason. I had student taught in a suburban school which was close to where I lived. One of my professors told me that this junior high school (the urban school) was one of the two most difficult junior high schools in which to teach in Pennsylvania. My student teacher supervisor's wife taught there. I wanted to try it and see what I could do in that environment. I loved it; and I succeeded. (p. 28)

Teachers are held accountable for possessing specialized knowledge and applying it when conditions warrant. Knowing and knowing how, then, are explicit attributes of teachers who are professionals. Also, the most successful teachers often are perceived as caring deeply about the people they serve and about the work they perform. Passion for teaching and learning are characteristics thought to distinguish the best teachers.

Teachers are public people; they are always on display. Teachers serve as models for children and adults as they teach and as they live their lives both inside and outside schools. In recent years, the model teacher has increasingly been cast by reformers and the media in terms of being a bright, liberally educated, street savvy professional. This model teacher is solidly grounded in one or more disciplines and works intelligently to make knowledge accessible and useful

Can teachers meet society's expectations of them?

to students. The image this teacher portrays is of a person who can help all students succeed, regardless of their needs, abilities, or circumstances.

People look for more in teachers than the abilities to transmit content and to teach skills to students. Through their words and deeds, teachers demonstrate what it means to be enlightened, hardworking, virtuous—indeed, what it means to be an educated person. Teachers both shape and are shaped by this public image.

Teachers' Organizations

As is true of people in other professions, teachers' identities are shaped in part by the associations to which teachers belong and by the people and organizations that represent teachers publicly. Professional organizations and associations also serve to educate members, provide a forum for discourse, lobby Congress and state legislatures on education issues, and offer a range of professional services.

Teachers, counselors, administrators, and others in education often belong to professional associations closely allied with their particular disciplines. These associations offer a variety of services—journals, conferences, action committees—designed to provide opportunities for interacting with others who have similar interests and to promote continuing professional development.

The largest, most visible, and most powerful teachers' organizations are the National Education Association (NEA) and the American Federation of Teachers (AFT), often referred to as **teacher unions**. Like labor unions, teacher unions protect members' rights to **collective bargaining** (negotiation of the professional rights and responsibilities of teachers as a group) in, for example, contract disputes.

Teacher unions are controversial and are frequently criticized by outsiders for shielding their members from scrutiny and for maintaining the status quo. They are also praised, however, for exercising considerable power for the improvement of public education. Both the NEA and the AFT have helped shape conditions of schooling that promote child welfare. Both have fought for and won increases in teachers' salaries and improvements in working conditions. Both have heightened public awareness about the importance of involving teachers in decision-making processes and of cultivating concepts of teachers as professionals.

Do teacher unions have a positive or a negative impact on education?

The **National Education Association** was founded in 1857 to advance the professionalism of teaching. It now boasts 2.2 million members, including teachers, school administrators, college and university faculty and students, guidance counselors, and librarians, as well as school secretaries, bus drivers, and custodians. Negotiating teacher salaries, reporting educational research, and supporting teachers' professional development are among the many services the NEA provides. The NEA is one of the most effective lobbying organizations in the nation, stating views of educational matters to legislators in Washington, D.C., in state capitols, and in communities across the country.

VOICES

On Student Discipline and Academic Standards

For more than three decades, Albert Shanker, head of the American Federation of Teachers, was a vigorous, out-spoken leader in public education. Shankar died February 22, 1997. He made headlines when he launched a new AFT campaign called "Lessons for Life: Responsibility, Respect, Results," which calls for a get-tough approach to student discipline and academic standards:

Policymakers and reformers have gotten caught up in faddish and radical schemes for improving the schools, and they ignore what is obvious to people who work in the schools and to parents who send children there: Unless you have order and civility, no learning will go on. And unless there are high academic standards, which students are expected to meet and helped to meet, school programs become trivial and meaningless; they do not prepare students to become responsible and productive members of society. Focusing on safe and orderly schools and high academic standards makes common sense, it works and it's long overdue . . . .

Teachers, and the AFT, have supported high standards of conduct and achievement for a long time . . . . Parents and the public, across all demographic groups, have also said for a long time that safe and orderly schools and high standards in the core academic subjects are their priority . . . But individual parents and citizens, . . . have not been able to get school districts, their elected representatives and reformers to make high standards of conduct and achievement a priority. Acting together, however, we can get the job done. And that's what the AFT's national campaign is about.

To see AFT's Bill of Rights and Responsibilities go to the Web (**http://www.aft.org/page19.htm**).

CRITICAL THINKING

Why might people, liberals and conservatives alike, praise Shanker for this kind of talk? Why might others be troubled by his attention to matters of "high academic standards," "safe and orderly schools"?

Source: Shanker, A. (1995, September 10). *The New York Times, CXLIV* (50,180), Section 4, p. 8.

In 1916 the **American Federation of Teachers** was founded from a merger of 20 small teacher unions that had begun to form after the turn of the century. More so than the NEA, the AFT has been closely allied with industrial labor unions and affiliated with the AFL-CIO (American Federation of Labor–Congress of Industrial Organizations). Like the AFL-CIO, in contract disputes the AFT has sometimes advocated withholding professional services through job actions such as work slowdowns, sickouts, or strikes. Today the AFT has more than 800,000 members, mostly in urban areas.

Although the AFT and NEA have a long history of competition for members and a record of disagreement on various issues, they have grown philosophically more compatible in recent years. NEA leaders have increasingly advocated political action on job issues, and AFT leaders have spoken out on issues of professional competence. After two years of serious negotiations to merge the two organizations, however, talks broke off in 1995.

Voting policies, terms of office, and other differences in structure stalled the discussions . . . . Observers also say the unions were concerned about how local and state affiliates would divide their powers under a new national organization. Traditionally, the NEA has had a strong presence at the state level, while the AFT's power has been concentrated in its local affiliates. (*Teacher Magazine,* 1995a, p. 11)

You can learn more about the NEA and the AFT at their Web sites: **http://www.nea.org** and **http://www.aft.org/index.htm/**. An alternative to the NEA and the AFT is the Independent Professional Education Associations, a loose coalition of independent educators and private schoolteachers with an anti-union stance ("A New Voice," 1992, p. 10).

WHY DO PEOPLE CHOOSE TO TEACH?

Teachers have a variety of reasons for their career decisions. Dan Lortie (1975, p. 30) described five themes, or what he called "attractors to teaching," that remain current in the minds of many teachers: (1) the interpersonal theme—feelings of wanting to work with people, (2) the service theme—the desire to perform a special service for society, (3) the continuation theme—the opportunity teaching offers of staying in school, (4) the material benefits theme—job security and steady income, and (5) the time compatibility theme—the attraction of vacations and appeal of on-the-job hours.

Table 1.1 contains more specific information about why people enter teaching. Many teachers attribute their original decision to enter the field to the influence of another teacher.

The U.S. Department of Education (1996b) reports that teachers seem to be happier about their choice of profession than they were in the early 1980s. In 1981, 46% of public schoolteachers said that they certainly or probably would be willing to teach again, a decline from 1971. By the 1990s, however, the percentage of satisfied teachers had increased to about 60%. The reasons for teacher satisfaction relate to both the intrinsic rewards and the practical benefits of teaching. In a recent survey 72% of teachers said that love of teaching is the reason they stay in the profession (Louis Harris and Associates, Inc., 1995). When asked why she was a teacher, Marcia Miller explained:

> This is the best job I could ever have, despite the low salary. I could never sit behind a desk like you do at other jobs. Here I get to work with children, which is fun. It's hard to be in a bad mood when you are with them. Also, my day goes quickly, and I'm never bored. (Herbert & Keller, in press)

Another intrinsic reward is the satisfaction of helping others. At a 1994 gathering of 51 outstanding teachers from the 50 states and the District of Columbia, one teacher who had 29 students in her classroom remarked,

> I really felt good that I was part of each child's life. I taught at a school that had an 80 percent turnover rate. At the beginning, my kids didn't like school and were bored with it. At the end, they left excited to go to the third grade and told me, "Oh, we want a teacher just like you." (Daugherty, 1995, p. 2)

Beyond a desire to develop a career, to work with children and young people, and to help others succeed, there are practical reasons for continuing one's work as a teacher. Figure 1.4 reveals teachers' thoughts about their jobs in 1995.

TABLE 1.1 Principal Reasons Why Teachers Stay in Teaching
Which of the factors listed below do you think are most important?

1995 Teachers Compare Teaching versus Other Occupations

Question: We'd like you to rate some of the aspects of teaching compared to the most recent job you were considering. From what you know, is/are the (read each item) better in teaching or better in the other occupation?

Base: 411 teachers who seriously considered leaving for some specific new occupation

Aspects in Which Teaching is Rated Better or Equal	Better in Teaching	Better in Other Occupation	Same, No Difference (Voluntary)	Not Sure
	Percentage			
Job Security	77	13	8	2
Vacation Benefits	71	23	4	2
Personal Satisfaction	71	13	10	6
Caliber of the Colleagues You Work With	58	20	16	6
Intellectual Challenge	58	29	11	2
Retirement Benefits	52	34	7	8
Health Insurance Benefits	52	29	14	5
Your Control Over Your Own Work	48	42	7	3

Note. From *The Metropolitan Life Survey of the American Teacher, 1984–95: Old Problems, New Challenges* (p. 63) by Louis Harris and Associates, Inc., 1995, New York: Metropolitan Life Insurance Company.

States and localities have increasingly moved to recognize the close tie between teacher quality and teachers' salaries and benefits. As shown in Table 1.2, public schoolteachers nationwide earned an average of $37,868 in 1994-1995 (U.S. Department of Education, 1996b)—3.1% more than in the previous year. Average annual salaries reflect considerable regional variation but also mask variation within states. In Missouri and Illinois, for example, the highest paid teachers earn more than twice as much as the lowest paid teachers.

Wealthy communities—those with a solid tax base—can afford to pay higher salaries to attract and to retain teachers than can low-income districts. Some states are attempting to reduce wide discrepancies in salaries. Tennessee, for example, has been ordered by the courts to equalize teachers' salaries (Richardson, 1995a). At the same time, however, variation in the cost of living can level differences in teachers' salaries from district to district and from state to state.

Job security is another practical benefit of teaching. Teacher **tenure** was originally conceived as protection for good teachers against capricious administrative action, including attempts to fire teachers thought to be too outspoken or too expensive. Tenured teachers can be released only when just cause can be demonstrated. Tenure, sometimes referred to as continuing contract, can be achieved in all states within 2 to 5 years of successful teaching experience.

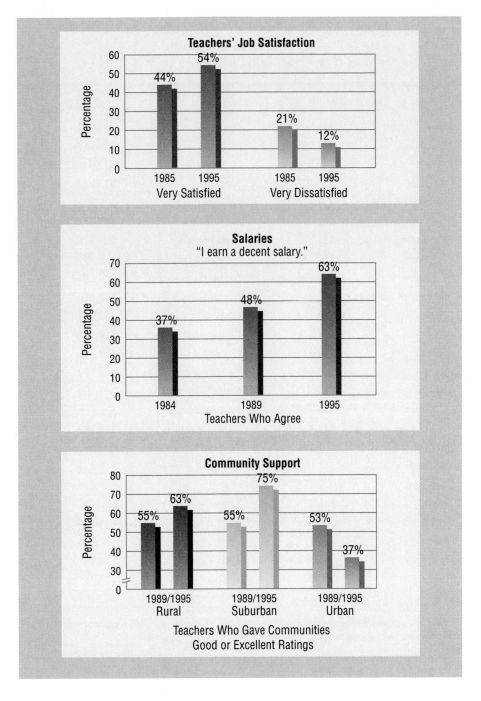

FIGURE 1.4

What Teachers Think About Their Jobs

Describe teachers' overall job satisfaction in 1985 and in 1995. Examine teachers' thoughts about salaries and about community support between these two dates. What factors might affect community support?

Note. From *The Metropolitan Life Survey of the American Teacher, 1984–1995: Old Problems, New Challenges* (pp. 10, 18, 21), by Louis Harris and Associates, Inc., 1995, New York: Metropolitan Life Insurance Company.

Although requirements vary from state to state, school boards typically grant tenure to teachers on the basis of principals' and superintendents' recommendations. These administrators base their judgments on numerous criteria, including classroom observations of teachers at work.

In recent years sentiment has grown in some parts of the country for the modification of tenure policies and, in some instances, for complete abolishment of the practice. The retention of ineffective and unmotivated teachers has

TABLE 1.2 Estimated Average Annual Salary of Teachers in Public Elementary and Secondary Schools, By State: 1994–1995

State	Dollars	State	Dollars
United States	$37,868	Missouri	$32,092
Alabama	$32,046	Montana	$29,619
Alaska	$49,340	Nebraska	$31,818
Arizona	$33,107	Nevada	$35,845
Arkansas	$29,772	New Hampshire	$35,726
California	$42,268	New Jersey	$47,422
Colorado	$35,572	New Mexico	$29,316
Connecticut	$51,495	New York	$48,991
Delaware	$40,208	North Carolina	$31,685
District of Columbia	$44,966	North Dakota	$27,090
Florida	$33,532	Ohio	$37,868
Georgia	$33,578	Oklahoma	$28,988
Hawaii	$39,634	Oregon	$39,708
Idaho	$30,646	Pennsylvania	$45,799
Illinois	$40,573	Rhode Island	$41,909
Indiana	$37,851	South Carolina	$31,156
Iowa	$32,424	South Dakota	$26,747
Kansas	$35,656	Tennessee	$33,418
Kentucky	$33,191	Texas	$32,127
Louisiana	$27,228	Utah	$29,924
Maine	$32,898	Vermont	$36,432
Maryland	$41,839	Virginia	$34,983
Massachusetts	$43,396	Washington	$37,198
Michigan	$48,732	West Virginia	$32,869
Minnesota	$36,989	Wisconsin	$38,839
Mississippi	$27,595	Wyoming	$32,191

Note. From *Digest of education statistics, 1996* (p. 85) by U.S. Department of Education, 1996, Washington, DC: U.S. Government Printing Office.

been blamed on the tenure system. California Governor Pete Wilson's Secretary of Child Development and Education, Maureen DiMarco, has argued that tenure does not work to ensure educational quality: "We check on the people who cut your hair more than the people who have your children's future in their hands" (Richardson, 1995b, p. 13). Jewel Gould, director of research for the AFT, calls attempts to end tenure a "cheap slap at quality"

Should teacher tenure be abolished?

meant to divert attention for a school system's responsibility to provide professional development early in teachers' careers. Tenure, Gould argues, is nothing more than the right to due process that is found in any workplace (Richardson, 1995b, p. 13).

Many teachers view the school calendar as a practical benefit. Summer vacation, even though it is unpaid, appeals to teachers who want to share time with their families and to continue professional studies. Many teachers have learned that they can do a year's work in 10½ months but not in twelve; that is, the summer vacation refreshes them, allowing them to be more productive than they would be without it. The school calendar becomes more important to teachers the longer they stay in teaching (National Education Association, 1992).

At all times of the year, teachers can benefit from many opportunities to continue their professional development. They do so to maintain their certification, to invest in themselves as professionals and as persons, and for the sheer pleasure such opportunities provide. Teachers take college courses and inservice courses offered by their schools, teach in alternative education programs in the summers and during the academic year, work at part-time jobs outside education, and participate in a range of informal development activities—reading, writing, performing, and the like. To be a teacher is to be a learner.

The most promising professional development activities appear to share a set of common attributes (Corcoran, 1995). These activities are

- linked to school initiatives to improve practice;
- based on teachers' ideas as well as school or district aims;
- grounded in knowledge about teaching;
- organized to give teachers opportunities to explore, question, and debate ideas and practices;
- designed to promote intellectual, social, and emotional engagement with ideas, materials, and colleagues;
- planned to demonstrate respect for teachers as professionals;
- organized to provide sufficient time and follow-up support; and
- viewed as an integral part of teachers' work rather than as privileges.

WHY DO PEOPLE LEAVE TEACHING?

Most teachers (75%) do not plan to leave the profession (Louis Harris and Associates, Inc., 1995). For them, education is a long-term career choice. Many do eventually leave, however, for various reasons, particularly low salaries, discipline problems, and low status.

Finding and keeping very talented teachers is a challenge. "Greater intellectual and financial incentives to stay in teaching may be needed to attract and retain talented teachers from minority groups, as well as European-American teachers, in the profession" (Darling-Hammond & Dilworth, 1996, p. 31). Attracting talented and culturally diverse teachers is only half the battle; school systems must work to keep them.

Cultural Awareness

Salary may be more critical to job decisions made by African- and Hispanic-American women than by European-American women because of economic realities: a greater proportion of their families are headed by women, and African- and Hispanic-American women contribute a larger share to two-salary incomes than do European-American women (Dilworth, 1990). As seen in the table that follows, discipline may be more of an issue for prospective teachers who belong to minority groups. Many more of them have been educated in urban and low-income schools sometimes associated with discipline problems than have prospective European-American teachers, who often come from and intend to return to smaller or more affluent school systems.

Teachers' Most Important Reasons for Leaving/
Not Entering Teaching, by Race/Ethnicity

Reasons	White	African American	Hispanic
Low salaries	73/44%	75/74%	68/62%
Discipline problems	62/23%	75/53%	60/43%
Burnout/exhaustion	44/12%	26/29%	34/30%
Frustration	25/27%	17/42%	28/32%

Note. From *Reading Between the Lines: Teachers and Their Racial/Ethnic Cultures* (p. 32) by M.E. Dilworth, 1990, Washington, DC: ERIC Clearinghouse on Teacher Education and American Association of Colleges for Teacher Education. Adapted by permission.

In the next 5 to 10 years, about 40% of the public school student population will come from racial and ethnic minority groups. At the same time, the number of teachers from minority groups could drop to 5% of the teaching force. New teacher recruitment programs reflect this reality. The University of Arizona College of Education's Summer Institute for Careers in Education, for example, encourages interest in teaching among high school students, particularly those who are members of minority groups. University faculty spend the summer working with approximately 50 high school juniors from 35 schools across the state. Nearly 60% of the students belong to minority groups. Students take mock classes in education and do fieldwork at nearby year-round schools. They work in teams with college students to prepare lessons in areas of interest, which they later present to their peers and to their parents (P. Douglas, personal communication, June 26, 1996).

Stress and burnout account for many teachers leaving the field. Like other professionals, teachers may experience considerable stress in their work. If the stress becomes severe, it can lead to low morale, and, in turn, to burnout—a general psychological state of exhaustion affecting those who work too hard and give too much of themselves (Freudenberger, 1975). Teachers who experience burnout often choose to leave their jobs.

Burnout is a serious problem for any teacher who experiences it, but it can also become a problem for students. "Very simply, if you aren't well you can't teach well" (Gold & Roth, 1993, p. 3). Frequently cited reasons for burnout are (a) lack of administrative support, (b) lack of parental and community support, (c) workload, (d) low student motivation, and (e) discipline problems. When teachers and administrators address such concerns, the problems seem less severe. "Teachers who have stronger coping mechanisms, communication skills, interpersonal relations, are emotionally secure, or feel intellectually stimulated and have a balance in personal and professional satisfaction, are much better able to deal with these same problems" (Gold & Roth, 1993, p. 9).

Teachers also leave the profession to have and raise children, and a large proportion later return to carry on with their careers. Others leave the classroom to acquire more education and to pursue careers in other fields. There is also a constant and natural flow of people out of education due to retirement. In reality, a teacher's education is a capital investment in herself or himself, one that often can be developed and used elsewhere.

WHO ARE AMERICA'S TEACHERS TODAY?

Teachers are amazingly diverse as individuals but can be characterized as a group (Feistritzer, 1996). Individual teachers develop their professional identities, in part, by thinking about themselves in relation to others and to the teaching force as a whole.

By the year 2001, the number of teachers in classrooms across the country is expected to increase to 3.2 million (Ogle, Alsalam, & Rogers, 1991). The number of men in teaching has increased as sex-role stereotypes have broken down, the status of teaching as a profession has risen, and trends in employment have opened doors in other careers to women (Warren, 1989). While women still hold most classroom positions in public schools, however, men hold most of the administrative positions.

Why do men and minorities make up such a small proportion of the teaching force?

At the turn of the 20th century, about 5% of teachers were African American at a time when they composed about 11% of the population, and one in four teachers in the total teaching force were first- or second-generation immigrants. By 1980, African Americans' representation in the teaching profession had reached 10% (Warren, 1989).

Cultural Awareness

Teachers as a group have the following characteristics
(U.S. Department of Education, 1995; National Education Association, 1995):

Number of teachers in the U.S.	2,939,659
Number of public schoolteachers	2,561,294
Number of private schoolteachers	378,365
Teachers' median age	42
Percentage of teachers married	78
Median years of teaching experience	15
Percentage of public schoolteachers with 10 or more years of full-time teaching experience	65
Average number of days of classroom teaching per year	180
Percentage of teachers by highest degree earned	
bachelor's degree	52.0
master's degree	42.0
doctorate	0.7
no degree	0.6
associate (two-year) degree	0.2
Percentage of African-American teachers in public schools	7
Percentage of Hispanic-American teachers in public schools	4
Percentage of Asian-American or Pacific-Islander teachers in public schools	1
Percentage of Native-American and Alaskan-Native teachers in public schools	0.01
Percentage of public elementary school teachers who are women	85
Percentage of public secondary school teachers who are women	55

In public schools today, students who are members of minority groups outnumber teachers from minority groups, proportionally, by more than two to one, but the composition of the group of aspiring teachers is changing (Lewis, 1996). Figure 1.5 shows the percent of increase of student enrollments in teacher education programs over a five-year period.

WHAT FACTORS AFFECT TEACHER SUPPLY AND DEMAND?

The availability of teaching jobs is affected by two interrelated factors: the number of properly qualified teachers available and the demand for those teachers. Both supply and demand, in turn, are subject to other influences in society. Factors that determine the demand for elementary and secondary teachers in any school year include enrollment changes, class size policies,

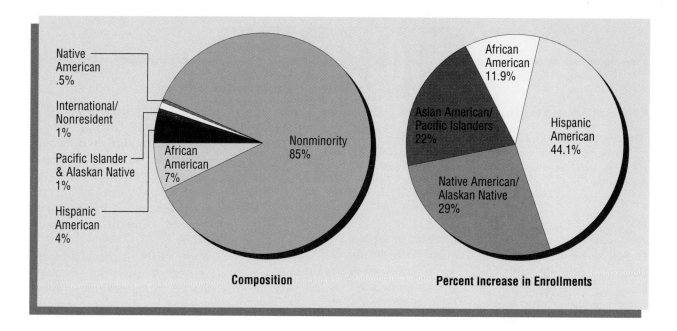

Composition   **Percent Increase in Enrollments**

budget considerations, changes in methods for classifying and educating special education students, and job turnover due to retirement or attrition. These factors influence decisions about hiring new teachers.

Factors that determine the supply of teachers include salaries, educational and licensure requirements, interest in specific disciplines and geographical areas, the cost of living in some states, and other quality-of-life issues. The demand for teachers has gradually increased during the 1990s (Gerard & Hussar, 1991).

▇ Teacher Shortages

Teacher shortages are felt most acutely in the nation's large cities. Why? The work is challenging, the working conditions often are difficult, and teaching opportunities in other settings often pull teachers away from cities. For example, 56.6% of public school administrators in Washington, D.C., reported difficulty in finding qualified applicants (Choy, et al., 1993). The South and Southwest also have unmet needs for teachers. Population growth in these sections of the United States has increased the national demand for teachers.

The need to provide bilingual education and special education services can also influence the demand for teachers. This demand varies, sometimes markedly, by state, and by locality. Demand for special education teachers is affected by the number of students with disabilities entering and leaving school systems and by changes in the criteria used to define specific disabilities. Demand for teachers is so great in some areas and in some specialties that school districts have offered cash bonuses, higher salary schedules, and other types of pay increases to attract and keep new teachers. These incentives have been designed to attract people to less desirable geographical locations and into subject areas that have experienced shortages.

About 15% of the nation's teachers are employed in private schools, including parochial (sectarian) schools affiliated with religious groups and

FIGURE 1.5

Race/Ethnicity of Students in Teacher Education Programs, 1989–1991

What seems to be the relationship between minority enrollments in teacher education programs and the composition of the teaching force? How might you explain this difference?

Note. From *"Supply and Demand of Teachers of Color"* by M. S. Lewis, February 1996, ERIC Digest Washington, DC: ERIC Clearinghouse on Teaching and Teacher Education.

VOICES

On Being a Student Teacher

In a letter to a student teacher, Margaret Metzger—a teacher at Massachusett's Brookline High School for 25 years—explains that teachers have to take care of themselves:

Dear Christine,

As you have begun to notice, some problems repeat themselves endlessly. This is probably true in all fields of work. As Annie Dillard observed about a bumbling church service, "You would think after 2,000 years, we could work the kinks out." We've been doing schools for centuries, and we still haven't worked out the kinks.

As soon as you see a repeating problem, think of a policy that is fair both to you and to the student. Just to help you along, here are a few inevitable problems: absenteeism, late papers, careless proof-reading, missing homework, cheating, record-keeping. What happens when one group finishes group work before the others? How can you maintain discipline while you hold individual conferences?

You will exhaust yourself if you try to think of a solution to each problem individually. Your first year of teaching will be such a whirlwind that you won't be able to step aside and calmly write policy statements. You will barely survive. But notice what bothers you most or what is most easily solved, and write the policies covering those problems over the summer. Knock off the problems one at a time. Don't spend a lifetime complaining about the same issues. . . .

Insist on your own rights in the classroom. What do you need in order to maintain your own life and sanity? Although I hate dealing with late papers, my students may turn in one paper per quarter that is two school days late. I don't even want to hear the excuse, unless it is hysterically funny. My students receive no penalty for the first late paper. However, in exchange for the extra time that they get for the writing, I must get extra time as well. Otherwise, I will resent late papers. Thus I do not write a comment on any late paper; I merely give the paper a holistic letter grade. Late students get extra time, and so do I.

Here are four final bits of advice. I've failed at all of them for years—except the last one, which

independent (nonsectarian) schools. Catholic schools employ more teachers than any other type of private school because the Catholic system is larger than any other private system.

Although states do not require teachers in private schools to meet the same level of certification as public school teachers, most private school teachers are fully certified. Operating without tax support, private schools are free from many state regulations governing curriculum and teaching. At the same time, because private schools are supported by private funds, average teaching salaries are far below teaching salaries in public schools. The average base salary for a teacher with a bachelor's degree in a private school is $21,968 (U.S. Department of Education, 1996b).

Some people with education degrees take jobs outside the school system. Employers in business and industry and various government agencies hire people with education degrees for various jobs. Strong educational programs that combine liberal arts and professional studies prepare people for a variety of technical and human service positions.

has kept me sane. When I follow my own advice, my teaching life feels happier.

1. Sign up for season tickets to cultural events; otherwise you'll think you are too tired to attend anything. Schedule regular social events with friends, even if it's only lunch in the cafeteria every week with your two favorite colleagues in the school.

2. Hunt for a place to work. Some schools spill over with technology, while others have no telephones or copying machines for teachers. Many schools don't provide desk space for teachers. Beg for some space in the school for yourself, even if it's an old closet. Try to get your own classroom. Moving all your belongings every 50 minutes will make you crazy. Imagine any office worker changing desks every hour!

3. Try to stay out of petty politics. There is more squabbling in schools than you can imagine. . . .

4. Find a friend with a sense of humor . . . who can laugh with you [about daily events]. . . .[Y]ou cannot be a good teacher unless you are reading

books, going to the movies, spending time alone, and maintaining a life. In order to give to others, you must take care of yourself. Teachers who generously support other people's growth also need to nurture themselves. Take care of yourself.

Love,

Margaret

CRITICAL THINKING

Metzger seems to argue that there are healthy and unhealthy ways for teachers to address problems and sources of stress. How might you recognize the differences between the two? Can you think of ways you might involve students in finding solutions to daily problems? What might be the upside and the downside of doing so? Do you agree with Metzger's advice? What other strategies might you add for your own situation?

Note: From "Maintaining a Life" by M. Metzger, 1996, Phi Delta Kappan, 77 (5), pp. 346–351.

Projected Student Enrollments and School Budgets

Enrollment trends vary for elementary and secondary schools. In elementary schools, student numbers have been increasing steadily since the mid-1980s as a result of the "echo effect" as the offspring of the baby-boom generation began entering school. Projections suggest that enrollment in kindergarten through eighth grade will continue to increase up to the year 2002. In secondary schools, student numbers began declining in 1976, reaching a low of 12.4 million in 1990. Since that time, enrollment has steadily increased as the baby boomers' children grew older. Forecasters project enrollment in secondary schools to increase to 15.2 million by the year 2002 (U.S. Department of Education, 1996b).

Between 1990 and 2002, enrollment patterns will look different across regions, states, and communities. The greatest increases in public school enrollment will show up in the northeastern states, particularly New Hampshire and New Jersey. Increases are also likely in the South, as previously

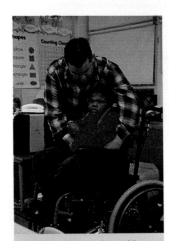

Why might teachers like this one be more in demand in some states and localities? What other factors influence teacher supply and demand? How do these factors relate to you as a prospective teacher?

mentioned; in the western part of the country—Arizona, California, Hawaii, and New Mexico; and in Alaska.

The federal government reports that by 2002 the student–teacher ratio in the nation's schools will be approximately 18:1 at the elementary level and 15:1 at the secondary level. These figures are lower than actual class size, however, because they are calculated by counting all the adults in schools, including many specialists who do not meet regularly with full classes. In 1993, for example, when the pupil–teacher ratio was a little over 17 to 1, average class size was 24 (U.S. Department of Education, 1996).

School budgets determine the school's capacity for hiring personnel. Personnel costs compose the largest category of expenditures in education budgets. Philosophy and mission drive budgets, but, when times are financially lean, boards of education and school administrators often tend to fall back on pocketbook considerations, choosing to eliminate positions through attrition or layoffs. The term *reduction in force*, or *RIF* for short, became familiar to public school employees during the 1980s.

> **Is job security a feature of teaching as a profession?**

HOW DO PEOPLE BECOME TEACHERS?

Formal teacher preparation first appeared in America in 1839 in the form of institutes designed to raise the quality of the teaching force (Stinnett, 1969). Today most teachers obtain a teaching certificate of minimal professional competence by completing a teacher education program approved by the state department of education. Many of these preparation programs are undergraduate level, but there is continued interest in making teacher preparation a 5-year or 5th-year graduate education experience. . . .

Teacher education programs in the United States have typically consisted of general studies or courses in arts and sciences—some required, some elective; professional studies in schools, colleges, or departments of education; and a period of clinical practice or field experience designed to provide opportunities to practice in the classroom. But pressure to reform teacher training has given rise to alternative paths to teaching.

Extended Teacher Education and Induction Programs

Students are not officially admitted to most teacher education programs until their third year of college, and professional studies are taken during the third and fourth years. In these programs, the first 2 years of course work are devoted entirely to general studies. In recent years, however, some colleges and universities have begun to institute 5-year programs of teacher education. These programs spread general, professional, and clinical studies across a student's college career. Students earn a bachelor's or master's degree upon successful completion of the program. The general philosophy underlying these programs is that producing the best teachers requires longer study that integrates general and professional courses and includes periodic application of skills and knowledge in schools.

In programs with fifth- or sixth-year studies, students earn a bachelor's degree in a discipline and then apply for admission to professional studies. Students take no professional education courses until they are in a master's program, which is completed in 1 or 2 years. These programs are driven philosophically by the perceived need for teachers to be firmly grounded in a discipline before they work with children.

Different program patterns have various strengths and limitations from students' points of view. Four-year programs cost less, students do not lose an

How much education should prospective teachers receive?

extra year or two of earning power, and they remain members of the cohort of students with whom they entered college. Longer programs offer opportunities for strengthening one's preparation before assuming a job and often lead to a master's degree, thus allowing graduates to begin teaching at a higher step on a salary schedule. Some people also believe that graduating with a master's degree enhances employability. Others fear that more expensive beginning teachers might be less attractive to employers. Such fear seems unfounded, however, in all but the most financially hard-pressed schools.

Collaboration between institutions of higher education and elementary and secondary schools to prepare teachers makes sense. Collaboration often occurs with regard to the structure and delivery of field experiences—classroom observation, student teaching, and internships—for prospective teachers in schools. Inservice teachers, school administrators, and college or university faculty all have a stake in new teachers' success, and they are recognizing that all should be involved in designing programs for professional development.

In every state, accredited teacher education programs include on-site practice teaching. Recent wider use of internship and induction programs highlights the importance of on-site support for new and prospective teachers.

One example of collaborative field experience for beginning teachers is the **induction program**. This type of program provides special assistance, mentoring from experienced colleagues, and feedback on teaching performance to beginning teachers in their first 1 to 3 years on the job.

Student Teaching

Student teaching—planning, organizing, and providing instruction to students full time over a period of weeks—typically occurs at or near the end of a preservice teacher's program. To prepare preservice teachers for student teaching, most programs require students to engage in a variety of field experiences. The types of assignments vary, but they are generally structured to help preservice teachers become familiar with various contexts in which teaching and learning occur.

Preservice teachers may be asked to maintain a journal in which they record information about students' needs and abilities (e.g., reading levels, mathematics proficiencies, personal interests), classroom rules and routines, and the flow of instructional activities. Preservice teachers also may be expected to conduct one-on-one tutoring sessions or to assist the teacher with classroom activities. Field experiences are usually supervised by the classroom teacher and college instructor to whom the preservice teacher is assigned.

As preservice teachers separate from their previous roles as students and begin their careers as professional educators during student teaching, they gradually assume more classroom responsibilities. They grade papers, teach parts of lessons designed by the classroom teacher (sometimes referred to as the supervising or cooperating teacher), plan for and engage in whole-class instruction for one or two class periods, and eventually assume responsibility for the whole day's instruction.

Because of the demands of student teaching, preservice teachers seldom enroll in academic courses during their field placements. Many teacher education programs, however, require student teachers to attend weekly seminars held on the college or university campus or in classrooms of student teachers. The seminars offer preservice teachers opportunities to discuss problems and issues of teaching and to share ideas about more and less effective teaching strategies.

Cultural Awareness

Some student teaching programs offer field placements in other countries. In a study of four student teachers in international settings, researchers found that teaching abroad can help beginning teachers develop sensitivity to cultural diversity (Jarchow, McKay, Powell, & Quinn, 1996).

- Students develop a broader understanding and appreciation of cultural differences when they become part of the host community culture and interact positively with host families.

- Students who proactively observe and interact with people of another culture test their personal perspectives, construct new ones, and thereby deepen their understanding of cultural diversity.

- International student teachers report concerns similar to their domestic counterparts. Students who explore the multiple dimensions of schooling develop an appreciation for collegiality both within and across cultures.

- As student teachers recognize their own development as teachers, they become more aware of cultural influences on curriculum, instruction, and learning.

Teacher Certification

Requirements for teacher certification are established and monitored by the states. **Certification**, or **licensure**, is granted when teachers have met basic requirements and standards for becoming a practicing teacher. Certification is not meant to convey the idea that a teacher is an expert or even exceptionally well qualified. Processes of certification are controlled by state governments to protect the public from harmful teaching practice backed by false claims of professional expertise.

Teaching certificates are typically granted in two ways: transcript assessment and program approval. The transcript assessment process requires the candidate to submit his or her college transcript directly to the state education department. The department then compares the transcript to the state requirements and grants or denies the request for certification. The program approval approach requires that teacher education programs be approved or accredited by the state. Approved programs submit transcripts of all graduates, and the state grants certification.

Reciprocity Agreements   Certification requirements for teachers differ from state to state. When a college or university student graduates from an approved teacher education program, he or she receives certification to teach in the state where the program is located. But many states recognize one another's certification; that is, states have **reciprocity agreements**, or pacts by which licensure in one state ensures eligibility for licensure in another state.

Because states sometimes change their certification requirements, the list of states having reciprocity agreements can change. Even when one state does not recognize another's certification, however, the additional requirements to obtain a state's certification often can be fulfilled fairly easily by taking some college coursework.

Alternative and Emergency Certifications   In recent years, several states have vigorously promoted the concept of **alternative certification**, or approval to teach without having participated in a traditional, state-approved teacher education program. New Jersey's alternative route into teaching, for example, allows people with college degrees but no formal education training to assume teaching positions and to take education courses as they teach. This alternative certification program offers supervisory assistance to people as they learn to teach on the job.

Emergency certification—certification granted temporarily until requirements are met—is another avenue into the classroom. When school superintendents are unable to find a certified teacher to fill a position, they petition their state departments of education to hire an uncertified person on an emergency basis. This strategy buys time for the person to become certified or for the school district to find another teacher who possesses valid certification.

> **Should people without teacher education or certification be allowed to teach?**

Despite the appeal of alternative certification programs for the ease with which candidates can enter and exit, they have been roundly criticized for providing too little support to prospective teachers.

> Newly launched alternative certification programs include some that provide only a few weeks of training for entering teachers, skipping such fundamentals as learning theory, child development, and subject matter pedagogy and placing recruits in classrooms without previous supervised clinical experience. And over 10 percent of individuals enter on emergency and temporary certificates, without any preparation at all. Studies show that these teachers are less able to address students' needs and less effective in helping students learn. (Darling-Hammond, 1995, p. 2)

Internships for Uncertified Teachers   Another alternative route into teaching is represented by the Metropolitan Multicultural Teacher Education Program. In response to the critical need for excellent teachers in inner-city schools, Martin Haberman of the University of Milwaukee has worked with the American Federation of Teachers and several private foundations to develop a program leading to certification in Wisconsin. The program emphasizes on-the-job training and careful candidate selection (Gursky, 1992).

The program Teach for America (TFA) provides college graduates who do not have teacher education backgrounds the opportunity to become teachers. Wendy S. Kopp's senior thesis at Princeton University stimulated the founding of this national teacher corps in 1989. Early funding from foundations and corporations has enabled TFA recruits to earn from $15,000 to $29,000 as beginning teachers (Lawton, 1991).

The Teach for America program began with 500 recruits from across the nation, who were trained for 8 weeks before assuming teaching responsibilities. TFA quickly grew to several thousand recruits with an annual budget of $8.5 million. Corporate and foundation sponsors liked the idea of putting bright young people into classrooms full of at-risk students and bypassing what they perceived as traditional and ineffectual teacher education programs. Others, however, have criticized TFA for putting ill-prepared teachers with students most in need of professionally strong teachers (Darling-Hammond, 1995). Because of increasing difficulty in attracting outside support, TFA reorganized itself in 1995 to seek support from local education agencies (Teacher Magazine, 1995a). Learn more about Teach for America on the Web (**http://www.teachforamerica.org/**).

National Teacher Examinations

More than 30 states require a national teacher examination as a test of teacher competency before granting initial certification. Although most states do not require people to reach minimum scores for certification, Kentucky, New Mexico, Montana, and Rhode Island do require some minimum level of performance on a nationally marketed test for initial licensure (Tryneski, 1996).

The **Praxis Series**—a battery of tests developed and sold by the Educational Testing Service (ETS)—assesses skills and knowledge at each stage of a beginning teacher's career, from entry into teacher education to actual classroom performance. It measures teachers' basic skills in reading, writing, and mathematics, as well as professional education and subject matter knowledge. Teaching skills assessed include planning instruction, teaching, classroom management, and assessment of student learning. (See Appendix for more information on Praxis or visit the ETS Web site at **http://www.ets.org**).

HOW ARE PROFESSIONAL PROGRAMS ACCREDITED AND APPROVED?

Since 1927, teacher education programs have been subject to **accreditation,** that is, to processes of program review by outside experts. From 1927 to 1952, the American Association of Teachers' Colleges (forerunner of the American Association of Colleges for Teacher Education, or AACTE) performed this function. The National Council for the Accreditation of Teacher Education (NCATE) now conducts program reviews.

NCATE's mission is to provide professional judgment on the quality of the education unit (school, college, or department responsible for teacher education) and to encourage continuous improvement of the unit. Thus, accountability and improvement in teacher preparation are central to the mission of NCATE. NCATE-accredited institutions are

- required to provide quality professional education that fosters competent practice in graduates; and

- encouraged to meet rigorous standards of excellence developed by the profession. (NCATE, 1995, p. 2)

NCATE tries to accomplish its mission by judging, according to a set of established standards and accompanying criteria, teacher education programs that voluntarily apply for such review. NCATE's 20 standards and 69 indicators address four categories: (1) design of professional education, (2) candidates, (3) faculty, and (4) the unit (governance and resources).

NCATE has about 500 accredited member institutions; another 50 or so are in the process of application (W. Wiggins, personal communication, June 25, 1996). Passing an NCATE accreditation review, however, does not determine public acceptance of a program:

> The adequacy of standards is continually under debate. . . . Prestigious universities have withdrawn from NCATE, apparently with impunity. NCATE accreditation has not been required for . . . state program

accreditation (less than half of the state-accredited programs are accredited by the NCATE). . . . Consequently, non-NCATE institutions are able to retain claims to legitimacy in teacher preparation. (Clark & McNergney, 1990, p. 103)

Teacher education programs also are approved through state professional standards boards. All states now have permanent boards or commissions to establish standards for teacher education program approval and to take other professional regulatory actions. However, the makeup of each board, the process of selection for membership, and the authority of board members varies greatly from state to state.

Most states' guidelines for the approval of teacher education programs have been influenced by standards developed by the National Association of State Director of Teacher Education and Certification (NASDTEC, 1992). The NASDTEC standards are statements about expectations for coursework and experiences that are thought to constitute professionally acceptable programs of teacher education.

More recently, the Interstate New Teacher Assessment and Support Consortium (INTASC), a program of the Council of Chief State School Officers, has crafted model standards for licensing new teachers. These standards are meant to represent a common core of teaching knowledge and skills that will prepare students for teaching in the 21st century. The INTASC standards are also intended to be compatible with efforts to create national certification for teachers (INTASC, 1996). National certification is explained further later in this chapter.

Should all teacher education programs be subject to accreditation?

How is Teaching Performance Evaluated and Rewarded?

Evaluation of teachers is used mainly to help teachers grow professionally or to determine whether they meet minimum levels of competence (Duke & Stiggins, 1990). The first type of evaluation, called **formative assessment**, is done to shape, form, and improve teachers' knowledge and behavior. Formative assessment is not concerned with making judgments about salary status, or tenure; instead, it is a helping process that provides data to teachers for making decisions about how they can improve their teaching techniques. Evaluators concerned with formative assessment often concentrate on teachers' in-class performance by collecting data on teacher–student interactions during instruction and by helping teachers perceive what is happening during instruction. Formative assessment is based on the philosophical belief that (a) professional teachers constantly strive for continued individual excellence; (b) given sufficient information, professional teachers can and will evaluate themselves and modify their performance as well as or better than others; and (c) the evaluation procedures provide feedback designed to assist teachers in making judgments about how they can best improve their teaching. (Barber, 1990, p. 217)

Evaluating teachers' competence and teaching outcomes are examples of **summative assessments**, in which data is collected and interpreted at the end of a specified period of time. Results are used to make decisions about teachers on matters such as hiring, compensation, status, tenure, and termination.

Performance Evaluations and Portfolios

Performance evaluations increasingly use observations and evidence that provide an **authentic assessment** of teachers' knowledge and skills. Such assessment is directed toward producing information about teachers' abilities to perform their jobs in context. Authentic or realistic assessments are meant to augment or replace standardized assessments, such as examinations of subject matter and professional knowledge. Analysis of teaching performance on videotapes is an example of authentic assessment.

A **teacher portfolio**, a collection of artifacts that communicate a teacher's abilities to perform his job, is another example of an authentic assessment approach. A portfolio might contain tests and homework assignments the teacher gives students, samples of students' work, lesson plans, a videotape of a lesson, and so forth (Campbell, Cignetti, Melenyzer, Nettles, & Wyman, 1997). Teacher portfolios provide opportunities for teachers to have input into their evaluations, but they are difficult to use in comparing teachers to one another.

According to the reports by a national sample of public school teachers of kindergarten through grade 6, the practice of evaluating teachers is well established in the nation's schools. Evaluation of performance occurs for both formative and summative purposes.

> Evaluation criteria are known by most teachers prior to the process of performance evaluation, and most teachers are evaluated by their school principal, chiefly through formal and informal classroom observation. A large majority of teachers receive both written and verbal feedback following their evaluation, and most can submit a written response or file an appeal at their school. (U.S. Department of Education, 1994, p. 14)

Competency Testing

All states require some form of competency testing for teachers. These tests provide perspectives on the effects of teacher education beyond that provided by teacher education programs. If prospective teachers do well on competency tests, teacher education programs can claim some of the credit for identifying and developing teaching talent. Likewise, when prospective teachers perform poorly on these tests, programs must take some of the responsibility.

How might this teacher's performance be evaluated? For what purposes are formative and summative assessments of teachers made? How is excellence in teaching recognized and rewarded?

Control of teacher education through teacher competency tests is subtle but potentially quite powerful. As teachers exit their professional programs, they must demonstrate the knowledge, skills, and attitudes such tests purport to measure. Teacher education programs will continue to experience pressure to make sure that beginning teachers excel on these tests. In a very real sense, the tests will influence the curriculum of teacher education. States no longer rely strictly on schools, colleges, and departments of education to provide evidence of program quality. Competency tests provide alternative measures.

> **Should teachers be required to pass minimum competency tests for recertification?**

Career Ladders and Merit Pay

Excellence in teaching is recognized and rewarded in a number of ways. **Career ladder** programs are examples of incentive programs for teachers, offering advancement of status, increased responsibility, and extra pay for exemplary teaching practice. In theory, career ladder programs are based on the assumption that "the secret to improvement lies in bringing a change of focus into what one is doing" by motivating teachers to scrutinize their teaching, by encouraging them to think about alternative ways of teaching, and by focusing on what students are learning (Brandt, 1990, p 222). Career ladders usually are designed to acknowledge differences in teachers' levels of accomplishment, as, for example, between beginners and master teachers. These programs come and go with the availability of funds to support them. In the 1980s career ladders failed largely because they were poorly designed; that is, they were not linked to the organizational needs of effective schools (Kelley & Odden, 1995).

Like career ladders, **merit pay** was conceived as an incentive program—a program for encouraging teachers to strive for outstanding performance by rewarding such practice. The idea of merit pay for teachers began in the 1920s. Essentially, merit pay plans are intended to augment the lock-step progression of salary increases that characterize typical salary schedules by awarding either bonuses (one-time cash awards) or raises (financial increases added to teachers' base salaries). Various plans for awarding merit pay have been instituted and usually discarded through the years.

Merit pay plans have faltered most often for three reasons. First, processes of identifying meritorious teachers are difficult to design and implement. Second, until recently, teacher unions have opposed merit plans because they believed that paying some teachers more would mean paying other teachers less. Third, in difficult financial times, money has not been forthcoming for merit pay plans.

School systems often reward excellence informally through investment in professional development. Public recognition of teaching excellence is provided through state and national teacher-of-the-year programs, private organizations, grant foundations, and the mass media.

> **Should teachers be paid on the basis of merit?**

WHAT REFORM PROPOSALS ARE LEADING TO CHANGES IN TEACHER EDUCATION?

Criticism of education is part of American life. Many people level criticism directly at teachers. Others argue that the people who select, prepare, and place teachers in schools—the teacher educators—hold the power to improve teachers, teaching, and opportunities for learning, and must therefore improve themselves. These same critics would reform teacher education before or at the same time as setting out to remedy problems in schools.

In the late 1980s, a host of organizations called for the reform of teacher education, advancing both compatible and competing ideas. Some of the more influential groups pressing for reform included the American Association of Colleges for Teacher Education (AACTE), the Holmes Group, the Task Force of the Carnegie Forum, the Association of Teacher Educators (ATE), and the National Governors' Association (NGA). These organizations' reform reports are especially important to beginning teachers, because they forecast a set of long-term scenarios for the profession.

In 1996, the National Commission on Teaching & America's Future issued its report calling for a "dramatic departure from the status quo" (1996, p. vi). The Commission, composed of representatives from public schools, business, government, colleges and universities, and leading educational associations, was funded by the Rockefeller Foundation and Carnegie Corporation of New York and led by former North Carolina Governor James B. Hunt. Figure 1.6 shows the five recommendations offered by the Commission.

American Association of Colleges for Teacher Education (AACTE)

In 1985 an AACTE commission described its vision of change for teacher education in a document entitled *A Call for Change in Teacher Education*. The AACTE (1985) organized its recommendations around the following five themes:

1. **Supply and demand for quality teachers.** The AACTE recommended rigorous academic and performance standards for program entry and exit, financial incentives to recruit teachers, and special guarantees to ensure that qualified members of minority groups would not be barred from teacher education programs because of cost.

2. **Programs for teacher education.** The AACTE recommended upgrading the quality of the liberal and professional curricula, requiring a 1-year internship of provisional certification, and encouraging experimental models of teacher education.

3. **Accountability for teacher education.** The AACTE recommended that certification and program approval continue to be state responsibilities, that teacher education programs continue to be located in colleges and universities, and that programs begin to consider national accreditation.

FIGURE 1.6

National Commission on Teaching & America's Future Recommendations

If you were to rank the five points at right in terms of their importance, in what order might you place them?

Note. From National Commission on Teaching & America's Future (1996.) *What matters most: Teaching for America's future.* New York: National Commission on Teaching & America's Future.

I.   Get serious about standards, for both students and teachers.

- Establish professional standards boards in every state.
- Insist on accreditation for all schools of education.
- Close inadequate schools of education.
- License teachers based on demonstrated performance, including tests of subject matter knowledge, teaching knowledge, and teaching skill.
- Use National Board standards as the benchmark for accomplished teaching.

II.   Reinvent teacher preparation and professional development.

- Organize teacher education and professional development programs around standards for students and teachers.
- Develop extended, graduate-level teacher-preparation programs that provide a yearlong internship in a professional development school.
- Create and fund mentoring programs for beginning teachers, along with evaluation of teaching skills.
- Create stable, high-quality sources of professional development.

III.   Fix teacher recruitment and put qualified teachers in every classroom.

- Increase the ability of low-wealth districts to pay for qualified teachers, and insist that districts hire only qualified teachers.
- Redesign and streamline district hiring.
- Eliminate barriers to teacher mobility.
- Aggressively recruit high-need teachers and provide incentives for teaching in shortage areas.
- Develop high-quality pathways to teaching for a wide range of recruits.

IV.   Encourage and reward teacher knowledge and skill.

- Develop a career continuum for teaching linked to assessments and compensation systems that reward knowledge and skill.
- Remove incompetent teachers.
- Set goals and enact incentives for national board certification in every state and district. Aim to certify 105,000 teachers in this decade, one for every school in the United States.

V.   Create schools that are organized for student and teacher success.

- Flatten hierarchies and reallocate resources to send more dollars to the front lines of schools: Invest more in teachers and technology and less in nonteaching personnel.
- Provide venture capital in the form of challenge grants to schools for teacher learning linked to school improvement and rewards for team efforts that lead to improved practice and greater learning.
- Select, prepare, and retain principals who understand teaching and learning and who can lead high-performing schools.

4. **Resources for teacher education.** The AACTE advocated establishing a National Academy for Teacher Education, to which promising teacher educators could be nominated for postgraduate traineeships.

5. **Conditions necessary to support the highest quality of teaching.** Finally, the AACTE tackled the issue of improving the conditions of teaching by recommending, among other things, higher salaries for teachers, staff development opportunities, differentiated staffing (jobs that differ in tasks, qualifications, pay, etc.), and incentives to pursue additional college work.

Go to the Web and learn more about AACTE: **http://www.aacte.org/**.

The Holmes Group

In 1986 the Holmes Group recommended (a) making the education of teachers more solid intellectually; (b) recognizing differences in teachers' knowledge, skill, and commitment to education, certification, and work; (c) creating standards of entry to the profession that are professionally relevant; (d) connecting institutions of higher education to schools; and (e) making schools better places for teachers to work and learn. The Holmes Group advocated the following reforms in teacher education:

1. Establish a three-tier system of teacher licensing: instructors (beginners with nonrenewable certificates); professional teachers (people who have demonstrated their competence through work, examinations, and further education); and career professionals (outstanding teachers who show promise as teacher educators).

2. Eliminate the undergraduate major in education.

3. Require all teacher education students to complete an academic major and program of liberal studies.

4. Reform undergraduate education to achieve greater coherence and dedication to liberal education.

5. Organize academic course requirements so undergraduate students can understand the intellectual structure of their discipline.

6. Revise educational studies to focus on the study of schooling; knowledge of pedagogy; skills of classroom teaching; dispositions, values, and ethics of education; and the integration of professional studies with clinical experiences.

Task Force of the Carnegie Forum

In 1986 the Task Force of the Carnegie Forum issued its report, placing greater emphasis on reforming schools and processes of schooling than did the Holmes Group. The following eight points of the Carnegie reform proposal are ordered to permit a comparison with similar proposals offered by the Holmes Group.

1. Restructure the teaching force, introducing a new category of Lead Teachers, who have proven ability to provide active leadership in redesigning schools and in upholding high standards of teaching and learning.

2. Create a National Board for Professional Teaching Standards (NBPTS), organized with a regional and state membership structure, to establish high standards for what teachers need to know and be able to do and to certify teachers who meet those standards.

3. Require a bachelor's degree in the arts and sciences as a prerequisite for the professional study of teaching.

4. Make teachers' salaries and career opportunities competitive with those in other professions.

5. Relate incentives for teachers to schoolwide student performance, and provide schools with technology, services, and staff essential to teacher productivity.

6. Develop a new professional curriculum in graduate schools of education, leading to a Master in Teaching degree, based on systematic knowledge of teaching and including internships and residencies in the schools.

7. Restructure schools to provide a professional environment for teachers, freeing the teachers to decide how best to meet state and local goals for children while holding teachers accountable for student progress.

8. Mobilize the nation's resources to prepare minority-group children for teaching careers (Carnegie Forum, 1986).

The Carnegie Corporation established a **National Board for Professional Teaching Standards (NBPTS)** in 1987. The goal of NBPTS has been to create a system of **national certification** for individual teachers who represent the best and the brightest in the profession. The NBPTS develops assessments as alternatives to paper-and-pencil tests that measure teachers' abilities to apply professional knowledge in their fields of specialization. As described previously, these alternative assessments take the form of teacher portfolios, which may contain a variety of products, such as the tests teachers produce and videotapes of their teaching.

In January 1995, 81 middle school teachers from 23 states became the first teachers to earn national certification (Teacher Magazine, 1995b). The teachers were selected from 289 candidates who had completed a field test of the NBPTS assessment for generalists who work with young adolescents. The NBPTS intends to offer certification eventually in more than 30 teaching fields. (For information about national certification, call 1-800-22-TEACH.) You can learn more about the programs sponsored by the Carnegie Corporation by viewing their Web site: **http://www.carnegie.org/**.

Association of Teacher Educators (ATE)

In 1986 the ATE fashioned its reform report—*Visions of Reform: Implications for the Education Profession*—by examining the Holmes report, the Carnegie report, and *NCATE Redesign*, a description of the reform of teacher education program accreditation from the National Council for Accreditation of Teacher Education. The ATE task force viewed some recommendations for structural change of teacher education with alarm (ATE, 1986).

1. The task force rejected the idea, advanced by Holmes and Carnegie, of eliminating 4-year teacher education programs. Task force members reasoned that teachers' salaries and working conditions were not attractive enough to justify the cost of an extra year or two of schooling.

2. The task force viewed the National Board for Professional Teaching Standards proposed by Carnegie as a problem for states, local education agencies, and teacher education programs. The task force thought that national certification might increase competitiveness among state colleges and universities to produce Board-certified teachers. ATE also was concerned that national certification would lead teacher educators to "teach to the test" and would standardize preparation programs.

Among the ATE task force's recommendations were the following:

1. Establish a National Network of States for the Teaching Profession to determine goals and priorities for the teaching profession, set standards for professional practice, and provide direction and support for the profession.

2. Revise the professional curriculum for teachers based on a strong liberal arts and subject-matter background. The induction phase into teaching would be structured as an internship designed and monitored collaboratively by schools and colleges.

Which proposals for teacher education reform should be adopted?

3. Have three-tiered licensure: instructor, teacher, career teacher. Certification would be separate for early childhood, middle, and secondary school levels.

4. Organize and manage schools in ways that emphasize collegiality, individualized instruction for students, and more technological support.

The ATE home page can be found at this Web site: **http://www.siu.edu/departments/coe/ate/**.

National Governors' Association (NGA)

The NGA gave top priority to defining the body of professional knowledge and practice that teachers must have to be successful. The following recommendations were included in the NGA's response to the question, "What do we do to attract and keep the able teachers?"

1. Define the body of professional knowledge and practice that teachers must have.

2. Create a national board to define teacher standards. This board would define what teachers need to know and be able to do, administer a voluntary system to assess professional capacity, and award nationally recognized certificates to qualified candidates.

3. Rebuild the system of teacher education.

4. Redesign the organization of schools to create more productive working and learning environments.

5. Redesign the structure of the teaching career to provide advancement without moving outside the classroom.

BENCHMARKS

Teacher Education Reports and Reforms of the 1980s and 1990s

1985	A Call for Change in Teacher Education, National Commission for Excellence in Teacher Education of the American Association of Colleges for Teacher Education (AACTE)
1986	Tomorrow's Teachers, the Holmes Group
1986	A Nation Prepared: Teachers for the 21st Century, Task Force on Teaching as a Profession, the Carnegie Forum on Education and the Economy
1986	Time for Results: The Governors' Report on Education, the National Governors' Association (NGA)
1986	Visions of Reform: Implications for the Education Profession, the Association of Teacher Educators (ATE)
1987	National Board for Professional Teaching Standards (NBPTS) established
1989	National Education Goals issued from the White House after first Education Summit in Charlottesville, Virginia
1989	National Goals of Education issued from the White House
1996	President Clinton, 40 governors, and chief executive officers of major corporations meet for second Education Summit in Palisades, New York

6. Recruit able teacher candidates—including members of minority groups.

7. Improve teacher compensation.

8. Align teacher incentives with schoolwide student performance.

9. Improve teacher mobility (National Governors' Association, 1986).

▪ National Education Goals Panel

In September 1989 former president George Bush and the nation's governors met in Charlottesville, Virginia, at the first Education Summit, to craft **National Education Goals** for public education. Equally important, they established a target date for achieving these goals: the year 2000. The group's intent was to "capture the attention and resolve of Americans to restructure our schools and radically increase our expectations for student performance"

How can we achieve the National Education Goals?

(Romer, 1991, p. 1). To make sure their pledge was not an empty gesture, in July 1990 the group established the National Education Goals Panel—a unique bipartisan body of federal and state officials—to assess state and national progress toward achieving the Goals. Panel members include eight governors, four members of Congress, four state legislators, the U.S. Secretary of Education, and the president's domestic policy adviser. By 1994 the original six National Goals, with the addition of two more, were formalized into law with the passage of the Goals 2000: Educate America Act. A summary of the Goals appears in Figure 1.7. In 1996 President

1 Readiness for School. By the year 2000, all children in America will start school ready to learn.

2 High School Completion. By the year 2000, the high school graduation rate will increase to at least 90 percent.

3 Student Achievement and Citizenship. By the year 2000, all students will leave grades four, eight, and twelve having demonstrated competency over challenging subject matter including English, mathematics, science, history, foreign languages, civics and government, economics, arts, and geography; and every school in America will ensure that all students learn to use their minds well, so they may be prepared for responsible citizenship, further learning, and productive employment in our modern economy.

4 Teacher Education and Professional Development. By the year 2000, the nation's teaching force will have access to programs for the continued improvement of their professional skills and the opportunity to acquire the knowledge and skills needed to instruct and prepare all American students for the next century.

5 Science and Mathematics. By the year 2000, U.S. students will be first in the world in science and mathematics achievement.

6 Adult Literacy and Lifelong Learning. By the year 2000, every adult American will be literate and will possess the knowledge and skills necessary to compete in a global economy and exercise the rights and responsibilities of citizenship.

7 Safe, Disciplined, and Alcohol- and Drug-Free Schools. By the year 2000, every school in America will be free of drugs and violence and the unauthorized presence of firearms and alcohol, and will offer a disciplined environment conducive to learning.

8 Parental Participation. By the year 2000, every school will promote partnerships that will increase parental involvement and participation in promoting the social, emotional, and academic growth of children.

FIGURE 1.7

The National Education Goals

Research and present statistical data that justify each of the eight National Education Goals.

Note. From *U.S. Senate-House Conference Report* 103–446 Goals 2000 Educate America Act, March 21, 1994.

Clinton, the governors, and chief executive officers of major corporations met at the second Education Summit to discuss progress toward the National Education Goals and to fund programs that were taking steps toward accomplishing the Goals. Additional information about Goals 2000 can be found on the Web (**http://www.ed.gov/pubs/goals/summary/goals.html**).

The future projected by the National Goals and teacher education reforms is pulling people in new directions. Certainly, teachers' jobs will increasingly demand that they demonstrate broader and deeper knowledge, exercise more skills at higher levels, and be more creative than at any other time in history. Professional teachers will collaborate more closely with one another and with people in the communities they serve to redefine what it means both to teach and to learn.

SUMMARY

What does it mean to be a teacher?

1 The profession of teaching lacks consensus on what constitutes the knowledge base; teachers do not control their own licensing, as do other professionals; and teacher salaries typically are not as high as those of other professionals. Yet the complexities of their work demand that teachers think and behave like professionals, demonstrating their abilities to recognize issues, perceive values, apply knowledge, take action, and reflect on performance so that they can improve.

2 About half of the 50 hours per week teachers devote to their jobs is spent in classroom instruction.

3 Society expects teachers to be knowledgeable, caring, and passionate about teaching and learning—to be models of the educated person.

4 The National Education Association (NEA) and the American Federation of Teachers (AFT) are unions that represent teachers' interests. Other professional associations focus on subject areas, grade levels, educational specialties, and professional development.

Why do people choose to teach?

5 People decide to teach for many reasons, including love of teaching; desire to work with children, young people and adults; desire to perform a service to society; opportunity for further education; job security, steady income and benefits; and job hours and the school year calendar. Many attribute their decision to be a teacher to the influence of another teacher.

Why do people leave teaching?

6 People leave education to relieve stress and burnout, improve salaries, have and raise children, further their education, pursue other careers, and retire.

Who are America's teachers today?

7 Women constitute about 70% of teachers in public schools. Only about 20% of public school teachers are members of minority groups.

What factors affect teacher supply and demand?

8 Demand for elementary and secondary teachers is affected by enrollment changes, class size policies, budget considerations, changes in methods for classifying and educating special education students, and job turnover due to retirement or attrition.

9 The supply of teachers is affected by salaries, educational and licensure requirements, interest in specific disciplines and geographical areas, the cost of living in some states, and other quality-of-life issues.

How do people become teachers?

10 People enter teaching by completing 4- to 6-year programs approved or accredited by their state governments. The programs may or may not be accredited by an independent agency, such as NCATE.

11 Teachers are certified or licensed to practice by state governments. Typically certification is granted automatically upon successful completion of a state-approved program. In many states, teachers can become certified through alternative routes, such as alternative and emergency certifications or internships. Reciprocity agreements allow states to accept teachers certified in other states.

12 Most states require teacher competency tests, such as the Praxis Series.

13 Some colleges and universities have instituted longer teacher education programs that result in more liberal studies and sometimes a master's degree.

14 Induction programs match new teachers with experienced mentors.

15 Student teaching allows aspiring teachers to assume gradually the responsibility for professional practice.

How are professional programs accredited and approved?

16 State governments and organizations independent of state governments accredit teacher education programs. Independent accreditation by an agency such as NCATE typically is done on a voluntary basis.

How is teaching performance evaluated and rewarded?

17 Teachers are evaluated for two purposes: to help them improve (formative evaluation) and to make summary judgments about hiring, promoting, rewarding, or terminating (summative evaluation).

18 All states require some form of competency testing for teachers. Performance evaluations and portfolios are authentic methods of teacher evaluation.

19 Efforts to reward teachers using career ladders and merit pay have been largely unsuccessful.

What reform proposals are leading to changes in teacher education?

20 During the 1980s, several professional organizations and governmental groups called for the reform of teacher education and the schools. The AACTE, Holmes Group, Task Force of the Carnegie Forum, ATE, NGA, and National Education Goals Panel focused greater attention on the development of teaching as a profession. The most visible fruits of reform have been national certification and the establishment of the National Education Goals. Goals are becoming a focal point for national and state action in education.

TERMS AND CONCEPTS

accreditation, *p. 25*
alternative certification, *p. 23*
American Federation of Teachers (AFT), *p. 8*
authentic assessment, *p. 27*
career ladder, *p. 28*
certification, *p. 2*
collective bargaining, *p. 7*
emergency certification, *p. 24*
formative assessment, *p. 26*
induction program, *p. 22*
license, *p. 23*
merit pay, *p. 28*
National Board for Professional Teaching Standards (NBPTS), *p. 32*

National certification, *p. 32*
National Education Association (NEA), *p. 7*
National Education Goals, *p. 34*
Praxis Series, *p. 25*
professional teachers, *p. 2*
reciprocity agreement, *p. 23*
student teaching, *p. 22*
summative assessment, *p. 27*
teacher portfolio, *p. 27*
teacher union, *p. 7*
tenure, *p. 10*

REFLECTIVE PRACTICE

Janet Littlefield stood by the window watching droplets of rain roll down the panes as the last of the guests ran cackling to their cars in a flurry of umbrellas. For many students, she guessed, the end of the second year of college was supposed to be a time to decide on careers. But Janet's interactions with her family and friends that night had left her far from confident.

She had discussed the possibility of entering the education school, but they had said virtually nothing to help her clarify her thinking. Oh, everyone had been generally supportive, but that's not what Janet was looking for. She wanted strongly positive or negative comments that might galvanize her beliefs so she would feel certain about her decision. All she got was the kind of reaction her parents always gave her: "You do what is right for you and what makes you happy, dear." It was almost as if nobody really heard her.

In the quiet of the now empty room, Janet thought not so much about teaching as a career choice but about how she would feel standing before a classroom full of students. Did she have the right stuff to face them day in, day out? How would she know if the contract she signed was a good one? What might she find rewarding and discouraging about the work? Could she have a decent life, materially speaking, given her salary? Would someone be there to help her when she was unsure of herself? How would she know, once she took a job, if she was really succeeding? Would she find colleagues she would like as much as her college friends?

Issues, Problems, Dilemmas, Opportunities

What issues might be most important to Janet as she decides (1) whether to enter a program of teacher preparation and, eventually, (2) whether to stay in teaching or to leave?

Perceive and Value

How might Janet's view of the teaching as a career be similar to and different from her parents' views? How might Janet's view of herself as a teacher be likely to change over time?

Know and Act

If you were Janet, what would you want to know about a teacher education program and about teaching as a career before you decided whether to enter an education school? How might you go about finding answers to your questions before you made a decision?

Evaluate

How might you decide if a career in teaching is a good idea for you? What factors might be most important to you as you considered a career in teaching?

ONLINE ACTIVITY

On the Pathways for School Improvement home page, look for information on professional development for teachers: **http://www.ncrel.org/sdrs/**. If you look within the Pathways Web site for specific information on the critical issue of creating learning communities, you will find the following definition for such a community: "school staff members taking collective responsibility for a shared educational purpose, and collaborating with one another to achieve that purpose" (p.1). What can you learn at the Web site about the conditions that must exist if school staff are to behave in this manner?

Can anyone be a teacher? David G. Imig, Chief Executive Officer of the American Association of Colleges for Teacher Education (AACTE), doesn't think so. Read his essay "Not Everyone Can Teach" on the Web (**http://aacte.org/c4usaedt.html**).

CASE I

Mary Anne Reed-Brown

For some reason, students' lack of immediate cooperation was really getting to me today. Maybe it was because I was exhausted. I felt extremely testy. I really hate losing my patience like that.

Even good teachers can tire and lose their patience. But true professionals learn from these experiences. Failure and success alike prepare them to teach again, better equipped today than they were yesterday.

Mary Anne Reed-Brown, a second-year teacher working outside Washington, D.C. in Northern Virginia, teaches a culturally diverse group of fifth-graders. She is a real person. In some ways she behaves like all beginning teachers who make mistakes and express regret. In other ways, Ms. Reed-Brown exhibits qualities that set her apart as an exceptional beginning teacher. She can reflect on her own behavior and learn from it. Here she is reflecting on her behavior in a videotape of her teaching performance.

Even though Reed-Brown cannot always be certain about underlying causes, she can **recognize issues or problems** that arise in the course of teaching.

Then I have Tony, who really has a hard time in class. I can't pinpoint his problem, so it's been difficult for me to figure out ways to address his needs. In that small group situation, I was trying to get Tony to work on his social skills, to talk in turn. I wanted him to realize that other people have things to say, that he can calm down and listen to others.

At the same time, Mary Anne Reed-Brown is developing her capacity to **take others' perspectives.** When she does so, the "problems" that emerge in teaching can be quite important and not obvious to the casual observer.

Douglas is bilingual. When you are bilingual, a lot of times you are trying to think in two languages, and that's a hard thing to do. It's sort of like driving; you're in drive and then all of a sudden you have to reverse and go

another way. You're in drive in Spanish at home, and then all of a sudden you pull on the reverse real fast, and you're at school, and your thinking has to be done in English. The written language is difficult for most of my bilingual students, and it shows up in the testing, it shows up in the writing, and you just have to address their needs.

Many untrained adults, of course, can recognize educational challenges, and many have the ability to perceive others' perspectives. But teachers are uniquely prepared to **use professional knowledge** to inform their actions. For example, after reading *Ra and His Children* to the class, Ms. Reed-Brown demonstrates her knowledge of the importance of linking new information to students' prior learning.

Reed-Brown: Now how do we relate our study of ancient Egypt with this story I just read to you? Does it help you understand the history of Egypt by reading folklore? Nhung?

Nhung: Yes. I say yes because you would know about their beliefs.

Reed-Brown: What story have you heard that you can relate to this one?

Nhung: Well there's this Vietnamese story about how the world was made. There was a dragon that married an angel . . . .

Teachers possess much knowledge of teaching and learning. But professionals do not simply acquire and possess knowledge like some commodity to be traded for a grade on a test, they use knowledge to **take action**.

Reed-Brown shows students a cookie sheet and asks them to predict how many graham crackers are needed to cover the surface.

Reed-Brown: All right, Leroy, what's your prediction? Lucia? Kevin? (She records student responses, then allows each student to place a cracker on the cookie sheet.) Okay, let's count to see how many we have so far. Do we need to count?

Student: No, we can multiply.

Ultimately teachers must be able to **evaluate** the results of their work if they are to improve their practice. Judging the consequences of one's actions can be especially challenging when a teacher wants to encourage students to take command of their own learning.

CASE APPLICATION

- In what ways does Mary Anne Reed-Brown's approach to teaching reflect principles of professional practice?
- What are some of the complexities of what teachers know and do as professionals that the case of Reed-Brown reveals?
- In what ways is Reed-Brown a role model for students? What are some implications of being models for teachers?
- What rewards of teaching, do you think, does Reed-Brown enjoy?
- How might Reed-Brown respond to the question, What does it mean to be a teacher?

2

Historical
Foundations
of Education,
1600 to 1865

In this chapter we describe American education from the arrival of European settlers in the 1600s to the end of the Civil War in 1865. We set the stage by noting the influence of European thinkers and events in history that influenced education. We also describe variations in educational opportunities extended to or denied different peoples living in America—opportunities that depended on people's ethnicity, gender, religion, wealth, and geographical location.

For many years, informal education—homeschooling, apprenticeships, and other educational activities outside school walls—were more important and more prevalent than formal processes of schooling. Formal education developed unevenly over time and across geographical regions. We examine both the structure and functions of education, broadly defined, in America during this period.

Finally, we describe early reform movements that led to a universal tax-supported system of free schools and increased educational opportunities for women. During this time, people debated what a "good education" should be. As they struggled to define curriculum, people also considered the meanings of educational success and failure.

PROFESSIONAL PRACTICE QUESTIONS

1 What European thinkers influenced early American education?

2 How did Americans rely on informal education before the Civil War?

3 How did Americans view the aims of education?

4 How did formal education develop in America before the Civil War?

5 What curricula and textbooks shaped a uniquely American education?

6 How were educational success and failure evaluated?

WHAT EUROPEAN THINKERS INFLUENCED EARLY AMERICAN EDUCATION?

Although colonists were located far from England and Europe, immigration and overseas trade allowed for the exchange of goods and ideas between America and the larger world. America's formal educational system was influenced heavily by European intellectuals.

Comenius

John Amos Comenius (1592–1670), a Czech theologian and philosopher, viewed education as the primary means for improving society. All children—rich or poor, male or female—were to be instructed "thoroughly" by methodically trained teachers using quality textbooks in schools supported financially by state and city governments and the clergy. Educational programs were to be divided into four distinct "grades": the nursery school (birth to age 6), the elementary or national school (ages 6 to 12), the Latin school or gymnasium (gifted children ages 13 to 18), and the Academy (gifted youths ages 19 to

24). Children in each grade were to meet in a special school for 6 years. For such children, the process of education would be "easy and pleasant" if the following conditions were met: (a) education began early, before a child's mind was "corrupted"; (b) a child's mind was "prepared" to receive instruction; (c) instruction moved from the general to the specific; (d) tasks were arranged from the easy to the more difficult; (e) the number of subjects studied was manageable for children; (f) teachers maintained a reasonable lesson pace; (g) instruction was age appropriate; (h) everything was taught through the senses; (i) material being learned was constantly before the children's eyes; and (j) a single method of instruction was employed at all times. To attain universal peace and progress, Comenius also advocated universal textbooks and schools, as well as a universal college and a universal language (Edwards, 1972; Ulich, 1968).

Locke and Rousseau

John Locke (1632–1704), an English philosopher, argued convincingly that the human mind at birth is a blank slate (tabula rasa), not a repository of innate ideas placed there by God. He proposed that children should not simply read books but should also interact with the environment, using their five senses to accumulate and test ideas. Teachers should tailor instruction to the individual aptitudes and interests of each child; they should encourage curiosity and questions; and they should treat children as "rational creatures." Through reason, people might unlock life's mysteries. These ideas were consistent with the Age of Enlightenment, a period when application of reason was recognized as a virtue.

According to Locke, children learned through imitation; a good teacher taught by example and suggestion, not by coercion (Gay, 1964). Locke's belief in the essential goodness of people foreshadowed the development of a benevolent view of the kind of education children should receive if they were to grow and prosper. To learn more about Locke's views, visit this Web site: **http://swift.eng.ox.ac.uk/jdr/locke.html/**.

Jean Jacques Rousseau (1712–1778), a Swiss philosopher, criticized educational methods that he believed ignored children's ways of thinking, seeing, and feeling. He contended that schools ignored the natural conditions of a child's growth, imposing books and abstract ideas on minds and bodies not yet ready to deal with such demands.

In *Emile*, Rousseau described the development of a human being from infancy to maturity—one who was educated in the country, away from the "vice and error" of contemporary social life. Emile's tutor provided experiences in harmony with the natural conditions of Emile's growth. From infancy through age 11, Emile's tutor dispensed a "negative" education, removing any obstacles that might impede development. Emile explored the environment with his senses, learning through trial and error and experiencing joy and pain from naturally occurring experiences. Between ages 11 and 14, Rousseau argued, education should become more intellectual, as Emile was introduced to geography, astronomy, and his first book, Daniel Defoe's *Robinson Crusoe*. Emile also learned carpentry, a practical skill that might serve him later in life. During adolescence, Emile began to compare himself with others, make abstractions, and probe secrets of the universe. Because his tutor had respected his human nature, removing obstacles that might hinder his development, Emile began to understand the meanings of love, justice, and duty as he entered into a deeper unity with the universe (Boyd, 1962; Ulich, 1968).

Johann Pestalozzi

Pestalozzi and Herbart

Rousseau's ideas contributed to the child-study movement and to efforts to create child-centered schools. Johann Heinrich Pestalozzi (1746–1827), a Swiss educator, tested Rousseau's ideas with teachers and students at two schools for boys established in Germany. Pestalozzi (1898), like Rousseau, decried educational conditions that stifled children's playfulness and natural curiosity:

> At age five we make all nature . . . vanish from before their eyes . . . [and] pen them up like sheep, whole flocks huddled together, in stinking rooms; pitilessly chain them for hours, days, weeks, months, to the contemplation of unattractive and monotonous letters. (pp. 60–61)

Like Rousseau, Pestalozzi believed that children pass through a number of stages and that optimal growth occurs only when children fully master experiences and tasks of the previous stage. Such learning is facilitated by kind and loving educators who provide an array of sensory experiences when teaching concepts and skills rather than relying heavily on verbal instruction (Gutek, 1968). Pestalozzi wrote about his experiments with teaching and learning so parents and teachers might understand his simple methods for developing the inner capacity of the child. In *How Gertrude Teaches Her Children*, a book written for mothers, Pestalozzi (1898) illustrated why it was important to "always put a picture before the eye":

> It was inevitable, for instance, when [the teacher] asked, in arithmetic, How many times is seven contained in sixty-three? The child had no real background for his answer, and must, with great trouble, dig it out of his memory. Now, by the plan of putting nine times seven objects before his eyes, and letting him count them as nine sevens standing together, he has not to think any more about this question; he knows from what he has already learnt, although he is asked for the first time, that seven is contained nine times in sixty-three. So it is in other departments of the method. (p. 97)

Pestalozzi's "object lessons" served as models for ways to facilitate step-by-step learning of abstract concepts. His ideas challenged educators in Germany and America to rethink methods of instruction that relied on repetition and memorization.

Johann Friedrich Herbart (1776–1841), a German philosopher, psychologist, and educational theorist, believed that a primary goal of education was to respect a child's individuality while conveying the discipline and consistency necessary to develop moral strength of character. A teacher should cultivate a child's interests while also introducing the child to a variety of human knowledge and experiences necessary for understanding and appreciating fundamental values of civilized societies. Herbart proposed several "steps of instruction" for developing a child's ability to concentrate, retain ideas, and participate in learning: (a) "clearness" (understanding of content); (b) "association" (connecting new ideas with previously learned content); (c) "system" (the analysis of new ideas and their relation to the purpose of the lesson); and (d) "method" (the ability to apply newly acquired knowledge to future problems). By the 19th century, teacher education programs stressed Herbart's methods of instruction (Ulich, 1968).

> **What elements of colonial experience exist in American education today?**

Froebel

Friedrich Froebel (1782–1852), a German philosopher of education, established the first kindergarten in 1837 at Blankenburg. Froebel's **kindergarten** was not a school in the traditional sense but a "general institution" where young children could learn through the use of educational games and "occupations" (activities). A large portion of a child's school day was spent on gardening, an activity intended to help children see the similarity between the growth of plants and their own development (Downs, 1978).

Unlike Herbart, who explained the workings of the human mind as either associating or conflicting representations, Froebel viewed mental life as "the outgrowth of the incessant creativeness of the Divine" (Ulich, 1968, p. 287). To Froebel, a person's senses, emotions, and reason were the critical attributes necessary for learning to occur. Quality early childhood experiences that focused on play, music, and art allowed children to reveal their internal nature. Children were not "lumps of clay" to be molded; instead they were like plants and animals, which need time and space to develop according to natural law. Froebel recognized play as an important facet of learning and as the child's first sign of purposeful activity (Downs, 1978).

In 1855, Margaretta Schurtz, a German immigrant and one of Froebel's former students, established one of the first kindergartens in America in Watertown, Wisconsin. Schurtz's kindergarten was conducted in German, as were others founded by German immigrants. These early kindergartens were primarily meant to ensure that children would learn to speak German and to guarantee the preservation of their German heritage. The first kindergarten conducted in English was founded in Boston in 1860 by Elizabeth Peabody. By 1868 the first public kindergarten was opened in St. Louis, Missouri. It was a remarkable success and was thus imitated widely.

HOW DID AMERICANS RELY ON INFORMAL EDUCATION BEFORE THE CIVIL WAR?

European settlers who arrived on the shores of the New World in the 1600s had to adapt European ideas to their new environment as they struggled with themselves, with each other, and with outside forces in their efforts to survive and prosper. Education both reflected and shaped people's values as they established their settlements along the eastern coast of America.

Cultural Awareness

Students, young men called "scholars," were educated through a system of tutelage, in which the quality of education often depended entirely on the quality of the "master." In colonial times the schoolmaster typically was a member of the clergy and a prominent figure in the community. The purpose of education was to prepare young men for the ministry and for leadership. In their recollections, Meriwether Lewis, who later explored the Northwest Territories on the famous Lewis and Clark Expedition, and his younger cousin and classmate, Peachy Gilmer, complained about one of their schoolmasters and praised another. Lewis and Gilmer studied under Dr. Charles Everitt, of whom Gilmer said he was

> afflicted with very bad health, of an atrabilious and melancholy temperament; peevish, capricious, and every way disagreeable. . . . He invented cruel punishments for the scholars. . . . His method of teaching was as bad as anything could be. He was imparient [sic] of interruption. We seldom applied for assistance, said our lessons badly, made no proficiency, and acquired negligent and bad habits. (Ambrose, 1996, p. 27)

Lewis transferred in 1790 to Reverend James Waddell, who was a great contrast to the ill-tempered Everitt. Lewis called Waddell "a very polite scholar." He wrote to his mother in August,

> I expect to continue [here] for eighteen months or two years. Every civility is here paid to me and leaves me without any reason to regret the loss of a home or nearer connection. As soon as I complete my education, you shall certainly see me. (Ambrose, 1996, p. 27)

Education in the Southern Colonies

People who settled in the southern colonies of Virginia, Maryland, Georgia, and the Carolinas typically lived on large plantations where there were rigid class distinctions. A plantation was like a small community where crops such as tobacco, sugar, or cotton were raised. The owner's home often was at the center of the plantation and surrounded by a kitchen, smokehouse, stable, and sometimes a school, where a hired tutor taught the landowner's children. Around the periphery were tobacco fields and barns and cabins in which lived slaves from Africa and indentured servants from Europe. These people were the backbone of plantation life. They were trained as field workers, household workers, and skilled artisans—cobblers, carpenters, tailors, blacksmiths. Plantation owners were powerful people, directing both the lives of their servants and the lives of the numerous small farmers in the South.

Small farmers were isolated. Although they worked for themselves, their livelihood was often affected by plantation owners' willingness to purchase or sell surplus crops, rent their lands, and loan money. Farmers' decisions about where to settle were based mainly on the lay of the land, the quality of the soil, and the proximity of water. For these people who struggled to eke out a living from the land, there was no community of any sort, nor were there nearby schools or churches. For the most part, education was informal. Skills that boys and girls needed to learn were taught by the family. Families also taught their children to read and often conducted their own worship services until the middle of the 18th century, when itinerant missionaries began to minister to people in the backcountry.

Education in the Middle Atlantic Colonies

People in the Middle Atlantic colonies (New York, New Jersey, Pennsylvania, and Delaware) were more diverse than were settlers in the Southern colonies. Although most Middle Atlantic colonists spoke English, there were also Dutch-, German-, French-, and Swedish-speaking families whose religious orientation varied greatly from one another. Among others, there were Catholics, Mennonites, Calvinists, Lutherans, Quakers, Presbyterians, and Jews, all diligent in their efforts to preserve their languages and beliefs. To do so, different groups established their own parochial schools. English, Irish, Welsh, Dutch, and German Quakers, for instance, who settled mainly in Pennsylvania, stressed the importance of formal education focused on religion, mathematics, reading, and writing. They also offered some vocational training to children. Teachers viewed children as inherently good and rejected use of corporal punishment. Their schools were open to everyone, including Native Americans and slaves (Bullock, 1967).

> **Why were educational practices so diverse in the American colonies?**

Education in the New England Colonies

In the New England colonies of Massachusetts Bay, Rhode Island, New Hampshire, and Connecticut, there was less divergence in ideas and values, which made possible the establishment of town schools. Two school laws were instrumental in moving New Englanders in this direction. The Massachusetts Act of 1642 required that efforts of parents and master craftsmen who trained novices be monitored to ensure that children were learning to read and understand religious principles. The Massachusetts Act of 1647, sometimes referred to as the Old Deluder Satan Act, required towns to provide for the education of youth so that they might thwart Satan's trickery. To produce Scripture-literate citizens, every town of 50 households was required

VOICES

On Being an Apprentice

The tradition of **apprenticeships**—practical work experiences under the supervision of skilled workers in trades and the arts—also shaped the development of formal schooling and curricula in Britain's American colonies. Sometimes children as young as 7 years of age were sent to live with masters to learn a particular trade, and where law required it, to learn to read and write. Benjamin Franklin's early experiences as an apprentice in various trades led to his successful apprenticeship as a printer under an older brother:

At ten years old, I was taken to help my father in his business of a tallow chandler [candlemaker] and soap boiler, a business to which he was not bred, but had assumed on his arrival in New England, because he found that his dyeing trade, being in little request, would not maintain his family. Accordingly, I was employed in cutting the wick for the candles, filling the molds for cast candles, attending the shop, going on errands, etc.

I disliked the trade, and had a strong inclination to go to sea, but my father declared against it; but, residing near the water, I was much in it and on it. I learned to swim well and to manage boats; and when embarked with other boys, I was commonly allowed to govern, especially in any case of difficulty; and upon other occasions I was generally the leader among the boys and sometimes led them into scrapes. . . .

Through formal apprenticeships the children of early colonists added technical skills to any basic literacy skills they learned at home.

To return: I continued thus employed in my father's business for two years, that is, till I was twelve years old; and my brother John, who was bred to that business, having left my father, married and set up for himself at Rhode Island, there was every appearance that I was destined to supply his place and become a tallow chandler. But my dislike to the trade continuing, my father had apprehensions that if he did not put me to one more agreeable, I should break loose and go to sea, as my brother Josiah had done, to his great vexation. In consequence, he took me to walk with him, and see joiners, bricklayers, turners [a person who uses a lathe], braziers [a person who works in brass], etc., at their work that he might observe my inclination and endeavor to fix it on some trade that would keep me on land . . . . My father determined at last for the cutler's trade, and placed me for some days on trial with Samuel, son to my uncle Benjamin, who was bred to that trade in London and had just established him in Boston. But the sum he exacted as a fee for my apprenticeship displeased my father, and I was taken home again. . . .

CRITICAL THINKING

How did masters during Franklin's time judge an apprentice's suitability for a craft or trade? How did Franklin judge his own suitability and the performances of his teachers?

Note. From *Memoirs of Benjamin Franklin* (Vol. I) (pp. 21–25) by B. Franklin, 1842, New York: Harper & Brothers.

to employ a teacher of reading and writing, and every town of 100 households was to provide a grammar school to prepare youth for study at Harvard University.

Many settlers were Puritans who followed the teachings of John Calvin, a Swiss religious reformer. Calvin believed that God was omnipotent and good, while human beings were evil and helpless, predestined for either salvation or eternal torment. The role of schooling was to produce literate, hardworking, frugal, and respectful men and women who might resist the temptations of the world. Children, perceived as savage and primitive creatures, were to be trained and disciplined for a life of social conformity and religious commitment.

Colonists living in northern cities experienced a lifestyle very different from other colonists. Cities were densely populated and built on trade. Merchants, who were key people in the community, made available an array of goods and services not found in other parts of the country. Cities also contained skilled craftsmen, barbers, wigmakers, and an abundance of schoolteachers better educated than those in other parts of the country. Ships arriving at port brought both goods and ideas from England and Europe. This meant city dwellers on the eastern seaboard were among the best informed and sometimes the most influential of the colonists (Blum et al., 1989).

Education for Nationhood

Literacy was essential for democracy to work. Weekly newspapers and literary and political essays and verse were popular reading matter. The colonists understood how government worked, but they did not always agree on how it should work. Some colonists argued that they should rip themselves free from England; others counseled people to reconcile their differences with England and to remain a colony. The struggle for people's loyalties, both on and off the battlefield, shaped the talk and writings of the day. By the middle of the 18th century, almost every colony had a printing press churning out a daily newspaper containing not only local news and news from abroad but also literary and political essays. Printers also produced almanacs, flyers, and books. Thomas Paine's *Common Sense*—a compelling case for independence—sold 100,000 copies in its first 3 months of publication in 1776 and captured the minds and hearts of the delegates to the Continental Congress and of many others outside Philadelphia (Cremin, 1970). As Figure 2.1 shows, independence was one of several developments that significantly affected the development of an American system of education.

As the country grew, competing forces continued to shape Americans' views of themselves and others. Plantation owners in the South protected their virtually self-sufficient communities with their permanent labor force, while abolitionists in the North battled covertly and openly to destroy the system of slavery that supported the plantations. The Cherokee, Creek, Iroquois, and others fought to preserve their lands and their physical and spiritual wellbeing, while European Americans took land by trickery and force to improve their own lives and to fulfill what they believed was their divine destiny.

Between 1800 and 1840, the value of American agricultural products grew remarkably, largely due to westward expansion. The number of farmers

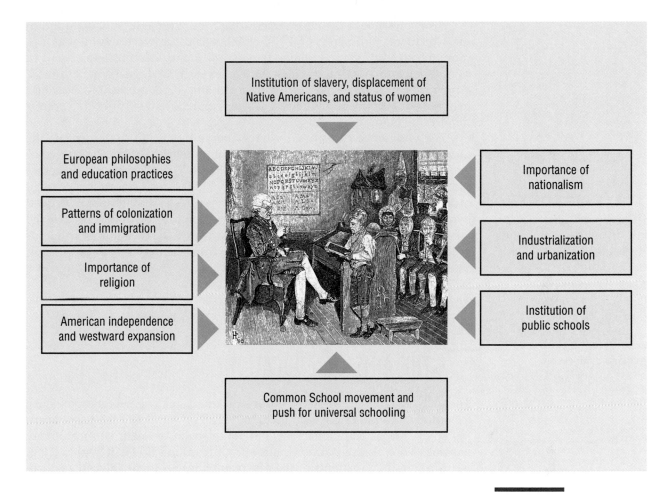

Institution of slavery, displacement of
Native Americans, and status of women

European philosophies
and education practices

Patterns of colonization
and immigration

Importance of
religion

American independence
and westward expansion

Importance of
nationalism

Industrialization
and urbanization

Institution of
public schools

Common School movement and
push for universal schooling

FIGURE 2.1

Some Factors Affecting American Education Before the Civil War

As you read, identify people whose contributions you might add to this figure under the heading "Influential American Educators and Their Ideas."

increased from about 5 million to 15 million during this time. Only about one seventh of the American people lived west of the Appalachians in 1810, compared with one third after 1840 (Blum et al., 1989).

The nation's founders believed that education was the best hope for the Republic. Freedom had to be tempered by the responsibility to maintain social order. Education would prepare good citizens. The virtuous, the disciplined, the intelligent would know how to participate responsibly in a democracy. Noah Webster in Connecticut, Benjamin Rush in Pennsylvania, and Thomas Jefferson in Virginia argued that the ability to read, write, and cipher would make the people and the nation strong. Jefferson (1931) viewed education as the key to advancing civilization:

> Education . . . grafts a new man on the native stock, and improves what in his nature was vicious and perverse into qualities of virtue and social worth. And it cannot be but that each generation succeeding to the knowledge acquired by all those who preceded it, adding to it their own acquisitions and discoveries, and handing the mass down for successive and constant accumulation, must advance the knowledge, and well-being of mankind, not *infinitely*, as some have said, but *indefinitely*, and to a term which no one can fix and foresee. (p. 250)

1 mile

6	5	4	3	2	1
7	8	9	10	11	12
18	17	16	15	14	13
19	20	21	22	23	24
30	29	28	27	26	25
31	32	33	34	35	36

FIGURE 2.2

A Precedent for Public Education

Under the Northwest Ordinance of 1785, the sixteenth square mile of a township's land grant was reserved for town-supported education.

An expression of the desire to educate for nationhood may be found in the Northwest Ordinance of 1785, which sliced the Northwest Territories (now the states of Ohio, Indiana, Illinois, Michigan, Wisconsin, and part of Minnesota) into townships of 36 square miles each. As depicted in Figure 2.2, a township provided a section of land to be used for education. This first national education legislation established the precedent for financing education through **land grant schools**.

The Ordinance constituted what historians typically recognize as the greatest accomplishment of the government under the Articles of Confederation, or the governing principles established by the Continental Congress that preceded the United States Constitution. In fact, fear stimulated passage of the Ordinance—fear on the part of leaders in the East that those who lived in or moved to the Northwest would become less civilized than people on the East coast. The framers of the Ordinance wanted to be certain that residents of the Northwest did not undo democracy from their corner of the country. Education meant socialization.

HOW DID AMERICANS VIEW THE AIMS OF EDUCATION?

The main goal of education for European Americans was salvation of souls. Schooling began at home with the family. Father laid down the rules, keeping an eye on the King James Bible in doing so, and Mother enforced them. Formal schooling was patterned after English schools. In New England, legislatures reminded parents of their responsibility for their children's education, but laws were not well enforced. When families and communities organized themselves to provide schooling for their children, they sent them to inexpensive **dame schools**, or schools run by women, in the area. Dame schools offered training in rudimentary skills of reading, writing, and calculating. Schools were private, although some received town support. Attendance was voluntary. Wealthy Americans sent their children abroad for their education.

The term *educated* evolved rapidly to mean more than learning God's law, as people began to view education as a means for personal advancement. Moreover, government leaders promoted education as a way to develop informed, wise, and honest people who would help the fledgling democracy succeed. However, education for personal advancement and civic participation was rarely extended to women and to non-European populations such as Native Americans, Africans, and Mexicans. As the nation industrialized and urbanized, aims of education gave precedence to occupational training for immigrants and low-income citizens.

The Role of Religion

A majority of colonists, particularly in the South, were Protestant and believed that the Scriptures were key to understanding God's will, as well

Why is religion in the schools an issue in American education today?

as to self-determination. To them, education should help save souls. As early as 1619, Virginia law made religious study on Sunday afternoons standard practice. The Bible typically was the medium for instruction; interpretations of God's will figured prominently in the formative years of the Republic.

The King James Bible and other devotional literature instructed people on how to live and how to die. Written in the 1670s, *The Poor Man's Family Book* taught colonists how to attend to their private duties, family duties, church duties, and duties to rulers and neighbors. Early writers often taught by telling stories and applying religious and moral principles to particular situations. Children's schoolbooks reinforced these principles. Educators' methods of writing and teaching, a sort of case-method approach to divinity, was called "casuistry" (Cremin, 1970, p. 45).

Except in the New England colonies, where church, state, and school were closely related, there generally was a separation of church and state. Nonetheless, church leaders greatly influenced people's thinking. Some, like Cotton Mather, were among the most prolific writers in America, and some, like Michael Wigglesworth, enjoyed wide readership. Between 1662 and 1701, Wigglesworth's *The Day of Doom*, an account of the Last Judgment, went through five editions (Blum et al., 1989).

In the 1740s religious experiences were brought to thousands of people in every rank of society when George Whitefield, a traveling English preacher, prompted the Great Awakening with his religious revivals. Whitefield journeyed from the Carolinas to New England teaching the word of God to rich and poor, old and young, educated and ignorant. Whitefield combined Calvinism and showmanship as he dramatized in vivid detail the pain awaiting sinners, urging his audience to confess their sins and submit to God.

Jonathan Edwards, a minister from Northampton, Massachusetts, who was a staunch defender of the Awakening, preached an even stricter Calvinism. Edwards's Calvinist theology suggested that children were inherently evil and in need of strict discipline. His notions encouraged harsh treatment of children at home and at school (Blum et al., 1989).

By the 19th century the hard tenets of orthodox Calvinism began to soften, and Americans adopted more rationalistic and humanistic views. Many challenged the traditional methods of education and demanded secular curricula. Transcendentalist philosophers Henry David Thoreau, Bronson Alcott, and Ralph Waldo Emerson were among those who advocated the radical reform of education. They were concerned, in particular, with the stifling nature of education. According to Emerson (1884),

> Education has so cold, so hopeless a sound. A treatise on education, a convention for education, a lecture, a system, affects us with slight paralysis and a certain yawning of the jaws. . . . Education should be as broad as man. Whatever elements are in him that should foster and demonstrate. If he be dexterous, his tuition should make it appear; if he be capable of dividing men by the trenchant sword of his thought, education should unsheathe and sharpen it; if he is one to cement society by his all-reconciling affinities, oh! hasten their action! If he is jovial, if he is mercurial, if he is great hearted, a cunning artificer, a strong commander, a potent ally,

ingenious, useful, elegant, witty, prophet, diviner,—society has need of all these. The imagination must be addressed. (p. 133)

The Impact of Industrialization

Forces of urbanization and industrialization shaped the character of America in the Northeast in the late 18th and early 19th centuries. After 1830, factories grew larger and more complex. As roads and shipping improved and as transportation costs decreased, Americans distributed their goods to mass markets. Hard work, inspiration, luck, and education all combined to influence these developments.

The Northeast had waterpower for factories and mills, iron and coal in Pennsylvania, and entrepreneurs ready to make the region the manufacturing center of the nation. The Erie Canal, an engineering marvel, symbolized Americans' technical capabilities and the people's passion for economic prosperity. American law permitted people to patent their inventions, and many capitalized on this fact and on their inventiveness to pursue their fortunes.

As colonists migrated westward into Alabama, Mississippi, and Louisiana, King Cotton dominated southern agricultural life. Once Eli Whitney's cotton gin—a machine that separated seeds from cotton fibers—was invented in 1793, cotton production jumped from about 10,000 bales to about 500,000 bales in the 1820s (Blum et al., 1989). While the North propelled itself toward industrialization, the South remained rural and dependent on agriculture for its economic well-being.

American industrialization in the early 19th century led to an increasing emphasis on practical rather than theoretical learning. At the same time, demands for cheap, reliable labor had a direct effect on schools' enrollment. Women and children met the increased demands for labor in the Northeast by working long hours under extremely difficult conditions. Infant schools, a concept devised by a Welsh cotton-mill owner and social reformer named Robert Owen (1771–1858) to give child factory workers a minimal education, provided much-needed care for young children of working women. Such schools were designed to meet the mental, physical, and moral development needs of children not yet old enough to work in the factories.

The Education of Slaves

When the Civil War began in 1861, there were 7 million slaves in the southern and western states. By the time the war ended in 1865, there were about 4 million, about 5% of whom could read and write (Blum et al., 1989). In the early 1600s, when the American slave trade began, English clergy had expressed interest in providing religious training for slaves and had made some progress in achieving their goal. Presbyterians went a step further, providing formal training to African Americans to prepare them for religious leadership. In 1740 Hugh Bryan, a wealthy and pious Presbyterian, opened his school for African Americans in Charleston, South Carolina. By 1755, Presbyterian schools had extended to Virginia, where slaves were being taught to read and write. In an experiment to test African Americans' abilities to succeed in college, Presbyterians sent John Chavis of North Carolina to Princeton University. Chavis graduated and established a school in the South only to find that European Americans would not allow non-European-American children to attend.

Slavery more than anything made the cultures in northern, Middle Atlantic, and southern colonies different from one another. In the northern states, many people, especially the Quakers, decried human bondage. By the early 19th century, antislavery groups had produced enough pressure to achieve abolition of slavery in the northern states. In the South, however, slavery continued to flourish. Slavery was recognized by the federal Constitution as a local institution within the jurisdiction of individual states; it was also a profitable fact of life for European-American planters in the South. The practice provided a reliable pool of field hands, miners, craftsmen, and domestics. In the 1850s nearly half the populations of both Alabama and Louisiana were African slaves; more than half of Mississippi's population were slaves. Most slaves were owned by a relatively few people; three fourths of southern European-American families never owned slaves (Blum et al., 1989).

In the South teaching slaves constituted a violation of the law, although teaching one or two was not regarded as a serious crime. Teaching slaves in schools was another matter entirely; this practice typically was limited to household servants or to free African Americans. But some courageous Southerners did dare to teach slaves.

> Naturally, more care had to be exercised in the selection of students and in the dissemination of information concerning the schools, but there were blacks and whites who were willing to run the risk of legal prosecution and social disapprobation in order to teach slaves. Negro schools are known to have existed in Savannah, Georgia; Charleston, South Carolina; Fayetteville, New Bern, and Raleigh, North Carolina; Lexington and Louisville, Kentucky; Fredericksburg and Norfolk, Virginia; and various other cities in Florida, Tennessee, and Louisiana. (Franklin, 1980, p. 146)

European-American missionaries and free African Americans established African schools and black academies in the North and the South during the 1800s. Christopher McPherson, a free African American, started a Richmond, Virginia, African school in 1811 to teach other free African Americans and slaves. From dusk until 9:30 each night, a European-American teacher he had hired taught English, writing, arithmetic, geography, and astronomy for about $1.25 per month. Flush with success, McPherson ran an advertisement for his school in the newspaper. Southerners in positions of authority were not quite as enthusiastic about his efforts: They closed his school, proclaiming it a public nuisance, and sent McPherson to the Williamsburg Lunatic Asylum (Berlin, 1974).

In some southern colonies, such as South Carolina, laws forbade teaching slaves to read and write. Some colonists justified such laws by persuading themselves that slaves were incapable of

Informal, often illegal, education for slaves became a hidden passage to freedom for some African Americans.

learning any more than was required to perform their menial jobs. Others believed that education would produce a leadership that would encourage slaves to rebel against a life of bondage. In fact, such leadership did evolve. David Walker of Wilmington, North Carolina, for example, published his widely read *Appeal*, a spirited attack on slavery, in 1829. (Bullock, 1967)

Slave owners and African-American preachers were also sources of education for slaves. Some slave owners placed their slaves under the tutelage of master craftsmen and even helped slaves establish small businesses to help them buy their freedom. Some slaves who did not receive formal education learned informally from their associations with literate European Americans. When assigned to houses, domestic workers might learn to read from the personal libraries of their masters and from studying recipes, music, and the Bible. Slave children also learned from their masters' children as they played school with one another, hidden from public view.

Frederick Douglass learned the alphabet from his Maryland mistress until his master discovered that she was teaching the young slave. Douglass's master said, "If he learns to read the Bible it will for ever unfit him to be a slave. He should know nothing but the will of his master, and learn to obey it" (Douglass, 1974). Douglass (1882) became more determined than ever to learn to read:

> The plan which I mainly adopted, and the one which was most successful, was that of using my young white playmates, whom I met in the streets, as teachers. I used to carry almost constantly a copy of Webster's spelling-book in my pocket, and when sent on errands, or when playtime was allowed me, I would step aside with my young friends and take a lesson in spelling. I am greatly indebted to these boys—Gustavus Dorgan, Joseph Bailey, Charles Farity, and William Cosdry. (1882, p. 2)

Later, as an escaped slave, Douglass became one of the most eloquent orators against slavery in the United States. In his speeches and his newspapers, he advocated the destruction of slavery in the South and the achievement of voting and other rights for African Americans in the North. To help slaves overcome their lack of formal education, Douglass also ran a Sunday school in barns or outdoors (Bullock, 1967).

Some owners taught their slaves because they wanted to protect and enhance their investments; others educated slaves out of respect and caring. Henry Bullock (1967) called these educational activities the **hidden passage** to freedom—literacy helped slaves to escape bondage and to make lives for themselves after the Civil War.

Fear about educating slaves mounted in the years just before the Civil War. Well-educated, vocal freed men and escaped slaves were in a position to demand equal rights and privileges. In the 1840s fearful citizens created a list of "safe" books that reflected the Southern viewpoint. The South Carolina Legislature made it a misdemeanor "to learn a slave to write, subject to fine and imprisonment" (*The Sun*, 1833a, p. 2). Later safe reading lists included a Confederate edition of the New Testament. Many European immigrants in Northern cities also feared and resented Africans and non-European immigrants, perceiving them as threats to their jobs and way of life.

Why might regional differences in students' academic achievement exist today?

Education for Native Americans

In Revolutionary times many settlers believed that Native Americans should be "civilized," or taught the ways of European Americans. Thomas Jefferson expressed the view that European Americans should intermingle with Native Americans and become one people. Paradoxically, he also believed that African Americans did not possess the mental capabilities to achieve equality with European Americans and should probably be resettled elsewhere. Jefferson wrote of Native Americans in 1803,

> In truth, the ultimate point of rest and happiness for them is to let our settlements and theirs meet and blend together, to intermix, and become one people. Incorporating themselves with us as citizens of the United States, this is what the natural progress of things will of course bring on, and it will be better to promote than retard it. (Cremin, 1980, pp. 231–232)

Assimilation—the process of educating and socializing a group to make it similar to the dominant culture— integration, and intermarriage with European Americans was rare, however. Some Native Americans who were self-educated in the European manner in turn advanced the European-style education of their people. In 1821 a Cherokee named Sequoyah devised an 86-character phonetic Cherokee alphabet. A press using Sequoyah's type churned out stories, hymns, and even a Bible in Cherokee. A newspaper, *The Cherokee Phoenix*, did much to advance literacy and knowledge among the tribe. Education of this sort, however, did not protect the Cherokees from the forced relocation and genocide that affected all Native-American tribes and nations during the 19th century.

During the early 19th century, Protestants and Catholics established **mission schools** among the Native Americans to teach English and to inculcate Christianity. One example was Brainerd Mission, established among the Cherokees in Georgia. Brainerd Mission tried to prepare the Cherokees for assimilation into the dominant culture. The schoolmaster even gave each child a new English name. The Mission became a self-sufficient society, producing nearly everything students needed to live. By 1830 there were eight such schools. The Brainerd Mission became the most common model for educating other eastern tribes and nations.

As far as the larger society knew, such schools were the best answer to "the Indian problem." The *Sun* newspaper carried this report in 1833:

> There is . . . an Indian School under the superintendence of Col R.M. Johnson, in Scott Co. which has one hundred scholars from the Choctaws, Creeks, Potawatomies, and Miamies, and supported chiefly by their own funds. This interesting school was established at the house of Col. Johnson, by the Choctaws, some years ago. It is very flourishing, and will do good. (*The Sun*, 1833b, p. 3)

Traditionally, Native-American elders taught children by example, explanation, and imitation (Cremin, 1980). Schooling for Native Americans thus was a continuation of their education, not a beginning (Barman, Hebert, & McCaskill, 1986). Families bore the primary responsibility for education, but they assumed this responsibility in ways markedly different from European settlers. Native-American children were surrounded by educators and caregivers—father and mother, grandparents, older siblings, uncles and aunts,

Sequoyah

other adults, and specialists, such as weavers, potters, warriors, and shamans (Coleman, 1993).

Cultural Awareness

The roles of observation, practice, and self-discipline in traditional Native-American education are evident in this account of learning beadwork by Zitkala-Sa (1921), a Nakota (Yankton Sioux):

> Close beside my mother I sat on a rug . . . with a scrap of buckskin in one hand and an awl in the other. This was the beginning of my practical observation lessons in the art of beadwork. . . . It took many trials before I learned how to knot my sinew thread on the point of my finger, as I saw her do. . . . The quietness of her oversight made me feel strongly responsible and dependent upon my own judgment. She treated me as a dignified little individual as long as I was on good behavior; and how humiliated I was when some boldness of mine drew forth a rebuke from her! . . . Always after these confining lessons I was wild with surplus spirits, and found joyous relief in running loose in the open again. (pp. 18–21)

Education in Spain's American Colonies

Santa Fe (now New Mexico) was founded by the Spanish in 1609, only 2 years after the English settled Jamestown in Virginia. In 1790, in addition to many Native Americans, there were about 23,000 Spanish-speaking people in what is now the southwestern United States; they had migrated north from Mexico, the seat of the Spanish conquest. Most were of mixed Native-American and Spanish descent, with a heritage that had come to be dominated by the Spanish language, religion (Catholicism), and social and political organizations. The Church and its missionaries provided what little formal education existed for Mexican Americans in those early years (Manuel, 1965).

Formal education was basic and heavily religious, conducted mainly by older men for younger men. Upper-class women, such as Sor Juana Ines de la Cruz (1648-1695), also had access to education:

> I was not yet three years old when my mother sent an older sister of mine to be taught to read at a school. . . . Moved by affection and a mischievous spirit, I followed her; and seeing her receive instruction, such a strong desire to read burned in me that I tried to deceive the teacher, telling her that my mother wanted her to give me lessons. . . . (Hahner, 1976, pp. 22–23)

Roman Catholic missions and a class system based on racial origins shaped the educational experiences of Native Americans and Africans in the Spanish colonies.

Sor Juana Ines later studied Latin and became a nun and a writer (Flynn, 1971). Her intellectual abilities made her a favorite of the Spanish viceroy and his wife in Mexico City, and she served as a court poet, successfully debating teachers from the university.

Spanish colonization of the Southwest fulfilled more than one purpose. Priests established mission schools to convert Native Americans to Catholicism, to effect a sort of peaceful conquest of the indigenous people (Fogel, 1988). But the missions also served to capture and hold territory and resources for Spain, while impeding any interests France and Britain might have had in these areas. Junipero Serra, a Franciscan priest, established missions in California territory in the 1770s.

> The missions were far more than religious outposts: They were social institutions, designed to transform the Indians from scattered hunting and gathering peoples into disciplined farmers, ranchers, and cloth weavers clustered around, and faithful to the church. (Fogel, 1988, p. 53)

From the outset, the Spanish-speaking and English-speaking peoples in the Southwest fought for control of the land. English-speaking Texans achieved their independence from Mexico in 1836. The United States, in turn, annexed Texas in 1844. In 1846, the United States and Mexico commenced the Mexican War, which ended 2 years later with Mexico's defeat and the addition of California, Utah, New Mexico, and other Western territories to the United States.

■ Education for Women

During colonial times women played a relatively insignificant role in the formal education of children. In just about every colony, however, there are records of one or more women having been employed as teachers. Most often, they instructed the younger children, and in many instances children of the poor, in dame schools, or schools run by local women. Generally, women taught during the summer months (April to September) and men taught during the winter. The Quakers in Pennsylvania did not discriminate against women to the degree that other religious sects did. While they were not compensated as well as Quaker schoolmasters, Quaker women accounted for a large proportion of the teachers in Pennsylvania (Elsbree, 1939).

Emma Willard

Benjamin Rush's 1787 speech "Thoughts Upon Female Education" marked a turning point in the education of women in the colonies. Rush contended that male heads of families were increasingly occupied with their roles outside the home and thus were unable to serve as primary educators of their sons and daughters. Women, who would necessarily assume such roles, were ill-prepared for the task.

Emma Willard was among several educators who developed programs for women that were more academically focused than schools of the past had been. In her speech to the New York legislature in 1819, Willard advocated the formation of schools that would teach geography, science, domestic skills, music, and other courses to women. Willard opened such a school in 1821 in Troy, New York. Her efforts stimulated others, such as Catherine Beecher, Zilpah Grant, Mary Lyons, and George B. Emerson, also to establish institutions expressly for the purpose of educating women (Deighton, 1971).

Catherine Beecher

VOICES

On Educating Women

On July 28, 1787, Benjamin Rush presented his "Thoughts Upon Female Education" at a meeting of the Visitors of the Young Ladies' Academy in Philadelphia. The gist of his presentation, which he later described as "contrary to general prejudice and fashion," offered a rationale for the education of women and outlined recommended areas of study:

The state of property, in America, renders it necessary for the greatest part of our citizens to employ themselves, in different occupations, for the advancement of their fortunes. This cannot be done without the assistance of the female members of the community. They must be stewards, and guardians of their husbands' property. That education, therefore, will be most proper for our women, which teaches them to discharge the duties of those offices with the most success and reputation. . . .

The equal share that every citizen has in the liberty, and the possible share he may have in the government of our country, make it necessary that our ladies should be qualified to a certain degree by a peculiar and suitable education, to concur in instructing their sons in the principles of liberty and government. . . .

The branches of literature most essential for a young lady in this country, appear to be,

I. A knowledge of the English language. She should not only read, but speak and spell it correctly. . . .

II. Pleasure and interest conspire to make the writing of a fair and legible hand, a necessary branch of female education. . . .

III. Some knowledge of figures and bookkeeping is absolutely necessary to qualify a young lady for the duties which await her in this country. There are certain occupations in which she may assist her husband with this knowledge; and should she survive him, and agreeably to the custom of our country be the executrix of his will, she cannot fail of deriving immense advantages from it.

IV. An acquaintance with geography and some instruction in chronology will enable a young lady to read history, biography, and travels, with advantage; and thereby qualify her not only for a general intercourse with the world, but, to be an agreeable companion for a sensible man. To these branches of knowledge may be added, in

During the mid-1800s Catherine Beecher borrowed concepts from Swedish gymnastics to introduce young women to calisthenics in order to improve their health, beauty, and strength (Steinhardt, 1992).

Cultural Awareness

The literature of the early 19th century, as Patricia Mayer Spacks (1995) has argued, reinforced the "normalization of boredom" for women. Charles Bathurst wrote of young British women, who were emulated by women in upper-class American society, that their natural liveliness and feelings ought not to be encouraged. After all, "passion was passion"—one thing could lead to another.

some instances, a general acquaintance with the first principles of astronomy, and natural philosophy, particularly with such parts of them as are calculated to prevent superstition, by explaining the causes, or obviating the effects of natural evil.

V. Vocal music should never be neglected in the education of a young lady. Besides preparing her to join in that part of public worship which consists of psalmody, it will enable her to soothe the cares of domestic life. . . .

VI. Dancing is by no means an improper branch of education for an American lady. It promotes health, and renders the figure and motions of the body easy and agreeable.

VII. The attention of our young ladies should be directed, as soon as they are prepared for it, to the reading of history —travels—poetry—and moral essays . . . . [W]hen a relish is excited for them, in early life, they subdue that passion for reading novels, which so generally prevails among the fair sex. . . .

VIII. It will be necessary to connect all these branches of education with regular instruction in the Christian religion. . . . A clergyman of long experience in the instruction of youth informed me, that he always found children acquired religious knowledge more easily than knowledge upon other subjects; and that young girls acquired this kind of knowledge more readily than boys. . . .

CRITICAL THINKING

What curriculum did Rush propose for the education of women, and why? Why might Rush have prefaced his remarks by suggesting that they were controversial or "contrary to general prejudice and fashion"? What might the prevailing opinions have been at the time he wrote this speech?

Note. From *Thoughts upon female education: Accommodated to the present state of society, manners, and government in the United States of America* by B. Rush, July 28, 1787, Philadelphia: Richard & Hall.

We often see girls . . . affect that behaviour which shows liveliness and quickness, even of temper, as well as of affectionate feeling, rather than sense and quietness; cultivate (in plain English) passion, feelings, and emotions, and what is called animation; not always meant to be confined to the kindly and affectionate feelings, but to nurse up, heighten, and exaggerate both likings and dislikings of any sort; as opposed to a cool, calm, peaceful state of mind, suited to reason, consideration, patience, and self-control. (Spacks, 1995, p. 184)

In studies of the foundations of education, the contributions of women traditionally have been downplayed or ignored. To see how history looks different when the contributions of women are included, visit this Web site: **http://www.nwhp.org/**.

◼ Education for People with Disabilities

The object of many superstitions, people with physical or mental disabilities were relegated to lives of confinement and idleness or were subjects of scapegoating and exploitation. The first permanent, state-supported school in the United States built expressly for the mentally retarded was opened in Syracuse, New York, in 1854. Clergymen and physicians were among the leaders in providing care and training for people with disabilities.

> The assumption of the leaders in special education was that *all* handicapped persons could and should be provided with residential care that would cure their behavioral deficits and make them useful and productive citizens or at least improve their condition and skills markedly. (Kauffman, 1981, p. 5)

Lester Mann (1979) and others credit Jean-Jacques Rousseau for the ideas that stimulated the development of special education as it has become operationalized in modern times. Rousseau championed the idea of encouraging children to achieve the potential they possess inherently. He wrote of the importance of sensory–motor development in young children, followed by higher intellectual development in their later years. His ideas stimulated Jean-Marc Itard (1775–1838) and Edouard Seguin (1812– 1880) in France, Johann Pestalozzi (1746–1827) in Switzerland, Friedrich Froebel (1782–1852) in Germany, and Maria Montessori (1870–1952) in Italy to fit education to a child's development.

How long-standing are American concerns about equal educational opportunity?

Samuel Gridley Howe and Thomas Gallaudet both left the United States during the early 1800s to study abroad before establishing programs in the United States to educate children with disabilities. Howe taught Laura Bridgmen, a person without sight, hearing, or speech, and achieved international fame. He also taught Anne Sullivan, who later became Helen Keller's teacher. Gallaudet founded the first residential school for the deaf in Hartford, Connecticut. Named after the pioneer in education for people with hearing impairments, Gallaudet College for the Deaf in Washington, D.C., is the only college for the deaf in the world (Hewett & Forness, 1984).

Daniel Hallahan and James Kauffman (1997) contend that the development of education programs specially fitted to people's needs is deeply rooted in the past. Many of today's special education practices can be traced to ideas expressed much earlier, including prescribing instruction based on the child's characteristics, carefully sequencing tasks from simple to complex, emphasizing stimulation of the child's senses, and tutoring in functional skills.

Thomas Gallaudet

How did formal education develop in America before the civil war?

Being a teacher in colonial America was much like being a lawyer: Neither required formal training. Academic qualifications of teachers, most of whom

Cultural Awareness

In 1829 Louis Braille adapted a system used by the French army for the exchange of messages by touch in war zones at night. Braille's raised-line system is a code that uses a six-dot cell to represent 63 alphabetical, numerical, and grammatical characters. By the end of the nineteenth century, "braille" was the universally accepted means of teaching blind people to read and write.

Grade 1 Braille grade 1 uses full spelling and consists of the letters of the alphabet, numbers, punctuation signs, and composition signs which are unique to braille.

capital   Y O U R   F R I E N D   I S   S T A N D I N G   H E R E .   period

Grade 2 Braille grade 2 is a contracted system much like shorthand. It consists of grade 1 braille plus 189 contractions and short-form words.

capital   Y R   F R   I S   (ST) (AND)(ING)   (HERE) .   period

Note. From *"Special adaptations necessitated by visual impairments"* by M. D. Orlansky & J. M. Rhyne, 1981, in J. M. Kauffman & D. P. Hallahan (Eds.), Handbook of special education (pp. 552–575), Englewood Cliffs, NJ: Prentice-Hall, Inc.

were men, ranged from mere ability to read and write to the scholarly attainments of a college graduate. The more rural the school, and the younger the children, the lower were the qualifications for a teaching position. In the North, particularly in Massachusetts, communities at the doorstep of Harvard were more selective, typically giving preference to college-trained men. For the most part, however, communities were not as interested in a candidate's scholastic preparation as in his character and religious orthodoxy. The Quakers of Pennsylvania, for example, stressed morality and membership in the Society of Friends. The Scotch–Irish in Pennsylvania insisted that schoolmasters be intelligent and sufficiently pious to teach the principles of Calvinism. In 1750, Pennsylvania Lutherans required the following qualifications:

> **How have the image, status, and roles of teachers changed since colonial times?**

That the schoolhouse shall always be in charge of a faithful Evangelical Lutheran schoolmaster, whose competency to teach Reading, Writing, and Arithmetic, and also to play the organ (Orgelschlagen) and to use the English language, has been proved by the pastor; special regard being had at the same time, to the purity of his doctrine and his life. He shall be required to treat all his pupils with impartial fidelity, and to instruct the children of other denominations, and of the neighborhood generally. He shall not allow the children to use profane language either in or out of school; but shall carefully teach them how, both in church and in school, and in the presence of others and upon the highway, to conduct themselves in a Christian and upright manner, and not like the Indians. (Elsbree, 1939, p. 39)

Benjamin Rush expressed another popular view of the roles of school-masters and their pupils:

Rush believed that the teacher should be an absolute monarch. "The government of schools . . . should be arbitrary," wrote Rush. "By this mode of education we prepare our youth for the subordination of laws, and thereby qualify them for becoming good citizens of the republic. I am satisfied that the most useful citizens have been formed from those youth who have never known or felt their own wills till they were one and twenty years of age. . . ." (Tyack, 1967, p. 88)

The Colonial Schoolhouse

Besides their teaching duties, schoolmasters were expected to perform a variety of duties outside school. In New England, some of the more common tasks included conducting religious services, leading the church choir, sweeping out the meetinghouse, ringing the bell for public worship, and digging graves (Elsbree, 1939). Schoolmasters usually juggled teaching and extra duties with one or more other jobs, ranging from surveying to innkeeping to artisanship. Teaching was often a stepping stone for other careers, particularly the ministry; hence, teacher turnover was often quite high (Rury, 1989).

Teaching meant making children memorize facts. To do so, children had to sit quietly in their seats until called upon by the teacher to recite. Teachers relied on whole-group instruction and choral responses in mixed-ability classes. The entire system depended on repetition and drill, helped along with a more-than-healthy dose of punishment (Kaestle, 1983).

When students misbehaved, the teacher punished them swiftly and often severely. Teachers used whipping, ear boxing, hand caning, and other terror tactics to control their charges. Although some educators expressed qualms about such brutality, most defended the use of corporal punishment. Punishment was an extension of authoritarian child-rearing practices and religious dictates.

Use of corporal punishment was widespread. Eliphalet Nott, who grew up in Connecticut in the 1780s, said, "If I was not whipped more than three times a week, I considered myself for the time peculiarly fortunate." In 1819, six-year-old James Sims was sent to a boarding school in South Carolina where new boys were always flogged, usually "until the youngster vomited or wet his breeches." (Kaestle, 1983, p. 19)

Why is corporal punishment an issue in many American schools today?

During the mid-1800s teacher brutality decreased. Historians attribute this change to a number of events: (a) graded schools that separated older children from younger children evolved so that teachers who had once dealt with as many as 100 students now dealt with smaller groups; (b) women began entering the teaching profession; (c) educators such as Pestalozzi set out to enlighten teachers about the benefits of teaching students to behave in certain ways instead of beating or coercing them into submission; and (d) some school systems, particularly those in the cities, passed ordinances prohibiting harsh punishment. In 1867 Syracuse, New York, was one of the first cities to do away with corporal punishment (Elsbree, 1939; Kaestle, 1983).

The Monitorial Method and the American Lyceum

Children started school at different ages. Abecedarians—beginners at school—often started as young as age 3. This meant, of course, that teachers often faced very large groups of students, composed of as many as 40 or 50 children, who differed markedly in abilities (Kaestle, 1983). The Lancasterian or **monitorial method** of teaching provided one response to this challenge.

Before graded schools were established in the cities, there were so many students crowded into a room that one teacher could not deal with all of them at once. In the 1820s Joseph Lancaster, a Quaker, found these urban classrooms to be fertile ground for the monitorial method of teaching used in Europe. In this educational pyramid scheme, the master teacher served as a "silent bystander" and "inspector." He instructed the monitors, and they, in turn, instructed the younger children. The older students also monitored attendance and kept order in the classroom. The approach made reading, writing, and arithmetic available to large numbers of children, and it was cheap. Lancaster also offered extensive and explicit directions on how to teach. If teachers followed his system, Lancaster argued, they could not fail (Reigart, 1969).

The monitorial system was one of the most successful and widely used educational methods of the first 30 years of the 19th century. Efficient, and easy to use, the monitorial method enabled voluntary associations to extend educational opportunities to increasing numbers of children from low-income families. Reformers concerned with the moral training of the poor believed that the system might inculcate in these children obedience, industry, and promptness. At the same time, the Lancasterian system's use of monitors allowed for the training of future teachers (Kaestle, 1983).

Other types of schooling that developed during the 19th century included the **lyceum**. In 1826 a wealthy Connecticut farmer, Josiah Holbrook, founded the American Lyceum, an organization devoted to the advancement of education for children and adults. Holbrook wanted to provide an economical and practical education to American youth and to encourage the application of science and education in everyday life. People belonged

Lancaster's monitorial method of instruction addressed the challenge of overcrowded, understaffed, ungraded classrooms in the rapidly expanding cities of the early nineteenth century.

to a lyceum for $1 a year. Some lyceums were reading circles, some debating clubs, and some concerts bands.

The first branch of the American Lyceum was in Millbury, Massachusetts. By 1829 the lyceum had spread across the country. Ralph Waldo Emerson, a frequent lecturer on the lyceum circuit, considered the American Lyceum a new form of education and a broad cultural movement. This first formal adult and community education movement thrived in the late 1820s and 1830s and faded in the years following the Civil War.

The Latin School and the English Academy

The **Latin grammar school**, the first formal type of secondary school in the colonies, was established in Boston in 1635. Boys entered the grammar school at age 9 or 10, if they could read and write English, and attended for 4 to 5 years. Although Latin grammar schools often offered arithmetic, geography, algebra, trigonometry, or rhetoric, their hallmark was the teaching of Latin and Greek and associated literatures. In other ways, the Latin grammar school was a conceptual leap backward to Europe, where money and social status meant power and privilege. The very few students who prepared to enter college went to these schools. Girls were not admitted.

In the belief that a more practical education was needed, Ben Franklin created an English-language academy in Philadelphia in 1749 (Best, 1962). Franklin recognized the need to prepare young people for highly skilled occupations and for the world of commerce. The classics were not neglected entirely, but the **English academy** emphasized the acquisition and application of practical knowledge thought to be most useful to the modern man.

The school originally taught practical subjects such as penmanship, arithmetic, and bookkeeping. Unlike in the Latin grammar school, English was the language of instruction, but students could study other languages related to their needs. Prospective merchants studied French, Spanish, or German. Prospective clergy studied Latin or Greek. Franklin's academy also taught many other practical skills, such as farming, carving, shipbuilding, carpentry, and printing.

The Development of Public Schools

Perhaps most significant was the development of schooling based on the concept of free public education for all Americans. This idea had its roots in the early Republic. Jefferson believed that it was to society's benefit to educate all of its citizens so they might provide leadership and support for the country. As a member of the Virginia Assembly's Committee to Revise the Laws of the Commonwealth from 1776–1779, Jefferson drafted the Bill for the More General Diffusion of Knowledge, a bill he considered one of his finest pieces of work (Cremin, 1980).

The bill proposed the establishment of **common schools**, tax-supported schools for reading, writing, arithmetic, and history, which all boys and girls could attend free for 3 years and pay thereafter. The bill also proposed the establishment of 20 grammar schools, in which Latin, Greek, English grammar, and advanced arithmetic would be taught. The brightest students from the lower schools who could not afford to pay tuition would attend these grammar schools at public expense; children whose families could afford to pay would do so. From the grammar schools, 10 scholarship students would go on to the College of William and Mary for 3 years at public expense. Through such a system of education, Jefferson believed, society could safeguard liberty. To succeed, democracy needed the participation of educated citizens both to support and to restrict the power of its leaders. Although successful in establishing a public university, Jefferson did not live to realize his dream of publicly-supported schools for Virginia's children (Cremin, 1980, pp. 440–441).

> **Why might some Americans have opposed the establishment of a common school?**

Benjamin Rush was also an advocate for the common school. He argued that education should be organized to help prepare people to function effectively in a democratic society, which meant that education should encourage public over private interests. Moreover, education should be uniquely American, that is, practical and forward looking, particularly in light of the emerging sciences (Cremin, 1980).

The spread of common schools led to sweeping educational reform on a national scale. In the 1830s reformers in the common school movement pressed for a variety of measures: (a) taxation for public education (Horace Mann embarrassed Massachusetts towns into improving funding for education by publishing an annual list of all towns ranked by per-pupil expenditures); (b) longer school terms; (c) a focus on getting particular groups of nonattenders enrolled in schools, particularly those living in urban slums and factory tenements and the children of free blacks; (d) hierarchical school organizations (e.g., state education agencies headed by a superintendent, schools headed by a "principal teacher," graded schools); (e) consolidation of small school districts into larger-scale school units so that per-pupil expenditures would be more uniform from district to district; (f) standardization of educational methods and curriculum; and (g) teacher training (Kaestle, 1983).

Primary-school enrollment rates increased over time. In the late 18th and early 19th centuries, school attendance was higher in rural areas than in the cities. More girls began to go to school, particularly in the Northeast (Kaestle, 1983). Signs of literacy—such as the number of people able to sign their names and the number of newspaper subscriptions—pointed to rapid social change during this period (Cremin, 1970). From the 17th through the early 20th century, however, no more than 10% of eligible school-age children ever went beyond elementary school.

The public high school emerged in Boston in the 1820s as an alternative to the Latin grammar school and the English academy. High schools did not become important in American education, however, until the late 1800s, when courts ruled that people could raise taxes to support such schools (Krug, 1964). The high school was a public institution that provided an English or a classical secondary education. Lawrence Cremin (1980) described this early high school as one that "reproduced under public auspices the upper reaches of the academy, making available to day students at modest cost or gratis what had formerly been available to boarding students at more substantial cost" (pp. 389–90).

Leaders in the Movement for Universal Education

A universal tax-supported system of free schools developed in the 3 decades before the Civil War. The Jeffersonian ideal of **universal schooling**, educating all citizens for the common good, came close to reality in the common schools intended to serve all of the children in an area. The primary mission of common schools was to teach reading, writing, and arithmetic to young children of any and all social classes. The schools were to give children the skills they would need to get and hold jobs. Common schools were to inculcate a set of values that guided children to get along with one another and to become good, productive citizens.

Even with the advent of the common school, most people of African, Native-American, and Hispanic descent were denied access to formal education. During this time, however, women became the backbone of the American educational system. First through their own schooling and then by assuming roles as teachers themselves, they capitalized on new and socially acceptable opportunities to assert their independence. Women benefited from the chance to fill jobs that men, for a number of reasons related to the expanding economy, no longer wanted.

Horace Mann   As secretary to the Massachusetts State Board of Education from 1837 to 1848, Horace Mann (1796–1859) aggressively promoted public schools for all children. Mann believed that tax support of education was a key to improving the school facilities and equipment needed for quality education. In his mind, the health of society depended on well-educated citizens, and citizens had a right to expect good secular or nondenominational education supported by public funds.

> **Why and how did teaching evolve into "women's work"?**

Horace Mann also was instrumental in establishing public teachers' colleges, called **normal schools** (from the French *école normale*), in Massachusetts. Largely due to Mann's efforts, the state legislature passed a resolution accepting his proposal, and the first public normal school in the United States was opened in Lexington on July 3, 1839 (Elsbree, 1939).

In 1844, Mann promoted the idea of encouraging women to become teachers, although he did so with somewhat less than a ringing endorsement of their talents:

> There are thousands of females amongst us, who now spend lives of frivolity, of unbroken wearisomeness and worthlessness, who would rejoice to exchange their days of painful idleness for such ennobling occupations [as teaching]; and who, in addition to the immediate rewards of well-doing, would see, in the distant prospect, the consolations of life well spent, instead of the pangs of remorse for a frivolous and wasted existence. (p. 1317)

Normal schools were educational programs dedicated solely to training teachers so that they could perform according to high standards, or "norms." Such institutes had existed in Germany for about 100 years and in France and England since the early 1800s. By 1850, there were a handful of normal schools in the United States, mainly in the Northeast, preparing young

Horace Mann

women to become teachers. The curriculum consisted of courses in the history and philosophy of education, instructional principles and teaching methodology, and a period of practice teaching (Elsbree, 1939; Kaestle, 1983).

Henry Barnard With Horace Mann, Henry Barnard (1811–1900) was a leading proponent of the common school. A journalist by training, Barnard was secretary of the Connecticut Board of Education (1838–1842), state commissioner of the public schools in Rhode Island (1845–1849), chancellor of the University of Wisconsin (1858–1860), and U.S. commissioner of education (1867–1870). He wrote about public education and European educational reformers such as Pestalozzi and Froebel in the *Connecticut Common School Journal* and the *American Journal of Education*.

Barnard extolled the virtue of teaching civic values and basic skills, but to him the most important subject was the English language. He recognized the need for strong teacher preparation and for paying people enough to get them into teaching and to keep them there. This meant, of course, that he also perceived the importance of building public support for such actions: "The right beginning of this work of school improvement is in awakening, correcting, and elevating public sentiment in relation to it" (Barnard, 1857).

Henry Barnard also did much to promote the concept of the public high school. He argued that primary schools were not up to the task of providing the intellectually rigorous education that students needed. He also believed that by reaching out to students over a larger geographical area than did private schools, the high school would better serve the public. The high school "must make a good education common in the highest and best sense of the word common—common because it is good enough for the best, and cheap enough for the poorest family in the community" (Barnard, 1857, p. 185).

◼ The Proliferation of Parochial Schools

Although Protestants were the dominant religious group during colonial times, there was great diversity in religious preferences. Of the 260 churches existing in 1689, 71 were Anglican, 116 Congregational, 15 Baptist, 17 Dutch Reformed, 15 Presbyterian, 12 French Reformed, 9 Roman Catholic, and 5 Lutheran. There were also loosely organized groups of Quakers, Mennonites, Huguenots, Anabaptists, and Jews (Cremin, 1970). Depending on their religious beliefs, different groups had unique ideas about the education of children and so established **parochial schools**, or private schools with religious affiliations.

German Lutherans, for example, wanted to protect their language and way of life. By 1840 there were more than 200 Lutheran parochial schools in Pennsylvania. In 1856, in return for a rent-free house, firewood, a salary of $12 per month, and extra pay for baptisms and marriages, Lutheran minister Edmond Multanowski preached and taught members of his congregation for 6 hours a day, nearly 11 months a year in Carlinville, Illinois (Cremin, 1980). Groups such as the Amish and Mennonites also educated their own children, holding them out of the common schools. Parents were fearful that outside influences might corrupt their sons and daughters.

In the 1840s, Catholic leaders protested the use of the King James Bible in the common schools. They also fought against the religious and ethnic slurs aimed at Irish Catholics in particular in the common schools. The climate was right for the establishment of their own alternative school system—one that has grown to be the largest alternative to public education in the world. John Hughes, Bishop of New York, admonished his parishioners "to build the schoolhouse first, and the church afterwards" (Lannie, 1968). By 1865, Catholic schools were teaching 16,000 students, or about one third of the Catholic school population, in New York (Dolan, 1985).

Why might some Americans have viewed parochial schools as a threat to democracy?

Catholics, Lutherans, Amish, Mennonites, and others wanted to protect their children and their ways of life, as did the general public. Reformers in the common-school movement viewed parochial schools as the greatest possible threat to democracy. In their minds, "the goals of a common-school system—moral training, discipline, patriotism, mutual understanding, formal equality, and cultural assimilation—could not be achieved if substantial numbers of children were in independent schools" (Kaestle, 1983, p. 116).

The Growth of Institutions of Higher Education

The colonists modeled their new colleges on Oxford and Cambridge. Only 6 years after the Puritans landed in Massachusetts, they founded the college that later assumed the name of its first benefactor, John Harvard (see Figure 2.3). Harvard students studied the liberal arts and sciences: Latin, Greek, Hebrew, mathematics, logic, rhetoric, astronomy, physics, metaphysics, and philosophy. Prospective ministers prepared for their callings only after they had graduated. The other colonial colleges also promoted the idea that higher education prepared young men for lives of leadership.

Teachers typically did not attend college. Most prepared to learn on the job in schools. They served as apprentices to teachers who had instructed them. Occasionally, they would read a textbook or attend a teachers' institute meant to transmit some new bit of scientific knowledge about teaching and learning. The first of these institutes, established by Henry Barnard at Hartford, Connecticut, in the autumn of 1839, provided 6 weeks of instruction focused on instructional strategies and curriculum to 26 young men (Cremin, 1980; Elsbree, 1939).

Private **seminaries**—academies for girls—were the primary means for advancing the skills of future teachers. In 1823 Samuel R. Hall opened a seminary with a model school at Concord, Vermont. That same year Catherine and Mary Beecher, sisters of Harriet Beecher Stowe, opened a seminary for young women in Hartford, Connecticut, that eventually became the Hartford Female Seminary. They taught grammar, geography, rhetoric, philosophy, chemistry, ancient and modern history, arithmetic, algebra, geometry, theology, and Latin (Cross, 1965). In 1827 James G. Carter, with the help of local citizens, established a teachers' seminary at Lancaster, Massachusetts. At about the same time, James Neef founded the New Harmony Community School in New Harmony, Indiana, where he introduced Pestalozzi's ideas about teaching and learning (Elsbree, 1939).

Founding of the Colonial Colleges

1636	Harvard
1693	William and Mary
1701	Yale
1746	Princeton
1754	Columbia
1755	Pennsylvania
1766	Brown
1766	Rutgers
1769	Dartmouth

FIGURE 2.3

Founding of the Colonial Colleges

How was teacher education different from college education in 18th-century America?

In response to the need for more teacher training programs, state-subsidized seminaries and academies began to evolve. Gradually private and semi-private institutions gave way to public normal schools.

The growth of higher education was stimulated by the passage of the Morrill Act in 1862. The Morrill Act provided federal assistance for the establishment of public colleges of agriculture and the mechanic or industrial arts. The act granted each state 30,000 acres of public land for each of its congressional representatives. The income from the grant went to support at least one land-grant college in the state, which was devoted to agricultural and mechanical instruction. The Morrill Act emphasized the importance of applied science and made higher education accessible to millions of people in the years that followed. Like the Northwest Ordinance of 1785, it was also a precursor of federal involvement in education. Learn more about the Morrill Act and land-grant colleges at this Web site: **http://www.uky.edu/ CampusGuide/land-grant.html/**.

WHAT CURRICULA AND TEXTBOOKS SHAPED A UNIQUELY AMERICAN EDUCATION?

Until about 1830, the curriculum, or what was to be learned, was driven by unswerving interpretations of God's preferences and the three R's. The Old and New Testaments, which were readily available in print, served as the main reading books in the late 18th and early 19th centuries. Arithmetic students learned from what was around them. Dealing with money, for example, reinforced the importance of numeracy skills. Many children studied whatever books their families sent to school with them—books that were jealously guarded. Sometimes teachers had to contend with as many different books as they had children in their schools (Kaestle, 1983).

Students learned to read by first learning their ABC's. They moved on to memorizing vowel sounds, such as "ab, eb, ib, ob, ub," then one-syllable words, and then longer words and sentences. They practiced on slates and worked their way up to quill pens and copybooks.

Hornbooks, Primers, and Almanacs   The **hornbook** was the first reader for many students. It was a single piece of parchment imprinted with the alphabet, vowels, syllables, the doctrine of the Trinity, and the Lord's Prayer. To increase its durability, the parchment was covered with a transparent sheet of cow's horn, and the two were tacked to a board. The hornbook was eventually replaced with more elaborate books of several pages.

The *New England Primer* appeared in the late 17th century and was the prototype for **primers**—textbooks designed to impart rudimentary reading skills—used widely in the colonies through the 18th century. The *Primer* was a collection of rhymes for the letters of the alphabet, adorned with woodcut drawings. Each rhyme, an admonition or prayer, reflected the religious values of the colonies (Ford, 1899).

Benjamin Franklin left his imprint on the curriculum in the 18th century, as he did so often on anything in which he took an interest. His *Poor Richard's Almanack* extolled the virtues of thrift, hard work, and creativity. The

FROM THE NEW ENGLAND PRIMER.

The *New England Primer* reflected the grim Puritan outlook and focus on religion as the point of education. Later, early American textbooks reflected the importance of moral charcter and national pride.

Almanack, which became a mainstay in the classroom, served as a sort of philosophical touchstone for the self-made colonist.

Geographies, Spellers, and Dictionaries   Jedidiah Morse provided an opportunity for children to think about their cultural identity as Americans when he produced his *Geography Made Easy* in 1784. The book focused on the geography of the United States rather than on that of Europe or Britain. Much like Franklin's *Poor Richard's Almanack,* it contained patriotic and moralistic themes.

In the late 1700s and early 1800s, Noah Webster promoted a common English language—one that was uniquely American. Webster's *American Spelling Book,* sometimes referred to as the **Blue-Backed Speller**, was first published in 1783; by 1837, 15 million copies had been sold. Webster's magnum opus, the *American Dictionary,* first published in 1825, became the authoritative source on information about American English words. Webster believed that power and prestige as a nation distinct from Britain would never come to the United States until it established its own distinctive vocabulary, spelling, and usage.

When and how did education based on European models become truly American?

McGuffey Readers   William Holmes McGuffey, a clergyman and professor of philosophy, produced his legendary reader in 1836. It was the most widely used reading book in America in the 19th century. **McGuffey Readers** taught literacy skills and sought to advance the Protestant ethic through stories and essays that imparted values of thrift, honesty, and diligence. By including speeches of the nation's founders, McGuffey also used his book to promote patriotic nationalism. McGuffey Readers are still produced and sold. See samples at the following Web site: **http://www.thomson.com/sp/ mcguffey.html/**.

HOW WERE EDUCATIONAL SUCCESS AND FAILURE EVALUATED?

Kaestle (1983) argues that before the Revolution and up until about 1840, local communities viewed their schools as quite successful. Because communities still depended on family and church to teach moral values and on work to train young people for occupations, schools did what they were supposed to do: provide rudimentary education in basic skills at low cost.

When and how did education based on European models become truly American?

School is much more a part of American life today than it was in earlier times. From the arrival of the colonists until the Civil War, few people went to school. Those who attended public schools got a dose of reading, writing, calculating, and the Protestant ethic, and then went their own way. Most acquired the knowledge necessary to survive and prosper from their families, churches, and work.

When the young Frenchman Alexis de Tocqueville came to America in 1831 to see the new democracy in action, he observed that Americans influenced or taught one another informally and routinely through newspapers and voluntary associations. Tocqueville (1840) believed that the press, in particular, had great educational power:

> Nothing but a newspaper can drop the same thought into a thousand minds at the same moment. . . . I shall not deny that in democratic countries newspapers frequently lead the citizens to launch together into very ill-digested schemes; but if there were no newspapers there would be no common activity. The evil which they produce is therefore much less than that which they cure. (p. 116)

The narrowly defined and severely delivered education in early America helped those children who attended—most of whom were white, Protestant, and male—to learn the three R's and to assimilate Protestant or Catholic values. For other young people—Native Americans, African Americans, immigrants, and those living in poor, rural places—schooling, if it existed at all, was at best a mixed blessing. Public schools saved some from illiteracy but simultaneously reinforced the idea that one's worth was measured in terms of race and social class.

As the nation grew, people debated what it meant to be American. As Riesman (1954) observed, in the early days, the idea of America as the melting pot of nations was valuable. It forced people to think about equality and hospitality to culturally diverse peoples. But the early arrivals to our country narrowed the idea to try to produce a uniform variety of American, "freed of all cultural coloring, maladjustment, or deviation" (p. 60). This trend continued and even accelerated in the early 20th century. Heavy immigration from southern and

BENCHMARKS

Historical Foundations of American Education, Colonial Times to 1865

1500s–1600s	Spanish conquer Native American peoples in Mexico and the American Southwest. Dutch, English, and French settle the Atlantic seaboard and explore North America. Dutch traders bring African slaves to plantations in the southern colonies. Such actions shape the people who will educate and be educated and will influence both individual and collective educational goals for many years to come.
1620–1630	Puritans and Pilgrims settle in New England, establishing the pattern of education for the New England and Middle Atlantic colonies.
1635–1636	Latin grammar school is established in Boston as a college preparatory school for young men. Harvard College is founded.
1642–1647	Massachusetts Act of 1642 makes citizens responsible for the education of their children and sets a precedent for the development of compulsory education. The Massachusetts Act of 1647, known as the Old Deluder Satan Act, is passed.
1788	U.S. Constitution is ratified. The framers of the constitution give the power to establish schools and license teachers to the individual states rather than the federal government.
1803	Thomas Jefferson doubles the size of the United States with the Louisiana Purchase. During the next 100 years, Americans go west, building one-room schoolhouses across the country to preserve traditions of education.
1810–1811	The Shawnee under Tecumseh establish a confederacy of tribes to preserve their lands and way of life.
1819	Emma Willard asks the New York legislature to extend educational opportunities to women. First public high school opens in Boston.
1824	Federal government establishes the Bureau of Indian Affairs.
1825	First edition of Noah Webster's *The American Dictionary* is published.
1827	Massachusetts becomes the first state to require every town with 500 or more families to establish a public high school.
1833	First "penny press," the New York Sun, makes newspapers available to almost everyone. Popular literature aids the spread of literacy.

Historical Foundations of American Education, Colonial Times to 1865 (cont.)

1836	First of the McGuffey Readers is published. About 122 million copies of the series are sold after this date.
1836–1837	Wesleyan College in Georgia and Oberlin College in Ohio become the first chartered colleges for women.
1837–1848	Horace Mann, secretary of the Board of Education in Massachusetts, calls for sweeping reforms based on the principle of universal free education for all citizens and the belief that teaching is a profession.
1839	First public normal school (teachers college) in the United States is established in Lexington, Massachusetts.
1848	Education issues are aired at the Women's Rights Convention in Seneca Falls, New York.
1852	Massachusetts enacts the first compulsory school attendance law.
1854	Lincoln University, the nation's first college for free African Americans, is established in Pennsylvania.
1855	Henry Barnard founds the *American Journal of Education*, the first educational journal in the United States.
1855	First kindergarten in the United States is established by Margaretta Schurtz in Watertown, Wisconsin.
1857	In the Dred Scott decision, the U.S. Supreme Court rules that African Americans, free or slave, are not citizens. The National Education Association (NEA) is established as a professional organization for teachers.
1860	Elizabeth Palmer Peabody opens the first English-speaking kindergarten in Boston.
1862	Morrill Land Grant College Act passes. Emancipation Proclamation passes.
1865	Civil War ends.

eastern Europe and growing industrialization helped give rise to what Ezra Pound referred to as the "white alabaster cast," or the cultural mold that was used to produce Americans.

When compared to education in other societies, however, education broadly defined in early America was remarkably successful. The nation's literacy rate climbed, industries flourished, people's standards of living increased, and governments usually changed hands peacefully.

SUMMARY

What European thinkers influenced early American education?

1 Although colonists were located far from England and Europe, America's formal education system was influenced heavily by European theorists such as Comenius, Locke, Rousseau, Pestalozzi, Herbart, Froebel, and Spencer.

How did Americans rely on informal education before the Civil War?

2 Education both reflected and shaped people's values as they established their settlements along the eastern coast of America.

3 Education in the southern colonies was done on plantations by hired tutors and on small farms by the family.

4 Colonists in the middle colonies were more diverse than were settlers in the southern colonies. To preserve their language and beliefs, different groups established their own parochial schools.

5 In the New England colonies, the similarity of colonists' ideas and values made possible the establishment of town schools. Many settlers were Puritans who followed the teachings of John Calvin, a Swiss religious reformer.

6 Informal education for all people in early America meant learning from the family and from others in social situations and while at work in apprenticeships. People learned from each other as they interacted. As books and newspapers became available, people also learned from one another by reading.

7 As the country became industrialized and the population grew, the strength and diversity of American beliefs forced new meanings on schooling. Schools began slowly to broaden their focus from serving God, family, and narrowly defined communities to preparing greater numbers and more culturally diverse children for secular lives in the new nation.

How did Americans view the aims of education?

8 Most colonists, particularly in the South, were Protestants who believed that the Scriptures were key to understanding God's will. To them, education should help save souls.

9 People began to view education as a means for personal advancement, primarily for European-American men.

10 American industrialization in the early 19th century led to an increasing emphasis on practical rather than theoretical learning.

11 Religious groups played a major role in extending educational opportunities to oppressed groups, for whom individuals such as Frederick Douglass, Sequoyah, Sor Juana Ines de la Cruz, and Catherine and Mary Beecher were sources of inspiration.

12 Missionaries, freed blacks, religious groups, and slave owners were a source of education for slaves. The education of Native and Hispanic Americans took place at home and in mission schools established by priests who wanted to convert students to Catholicism. Until the 1800s, when formal schools were established for women, females were mainly educated at home or in dame schools, where they learned a variety of rudimentary skills. Clergymen and physicians, including Braille, Howe, and Gallaudet, developed educational programs for people with disabilities.

How did formal education develop in America before the Civil War?

13 During colonial times, academic qualifications of teachers, most of whom were men, ranged from bare ability to read and write to the scholarly attainments of a college graduate. Most often, teaching meant making children memorize facts. Teachers relied on whole-group instruction and choral responses in mixed-ability classes. In such settings, teachers frequently administered harsh corporal punishment.

14 In the 1820s, Joseph Lancaster, a Quaker, introduced to the United States the European monitorial method of teaching, an educational pyramid scheme in which the master teacher served as a "silent bystander" and instructed monitors, who in turn instructed small groups of children.

15 The spread of lyceums, common schools, land-grant schools, Latin grammar schools, English academies, and high schools expanded formal education at the primary and secondary levels.

16 The common-school reform program that began in the 1830s affected greatly the quality of education in the United States. Henry Barnard and Horace Mann were among those who aggressively promoted public schools for all children. Taxation for public education, longer school terms, and the emergence of teacher training programs were among significant outcomes of reform efforts.

17 Private parochial schools attracted many colonists who wanted to preserve their languages and their religious and cultural beliefs. Educational reformers viewed such schools as a threat to democracy.

18 Within 6 years after the Puritans landed in Massachusetts, they founded the first American college (Harvard), and by 1769 eight additional colleges had been established to prepare young men for lives of leadership. The Morrill Act of 1862 expanded educational opportunities even further by providing federal assistance for the establishment of public colleges of agriculture and colleges of mechanical or industrial arts.

What curricula and textbooks shaped a uniquely American education?

19 The Bible served as the main reading book in the 18th and 19th centuries. Hornbooks, primers, almanacs such as Franklin's *Poor Richard's Almanack*, geographies, spellers and McGuffey Readers were also used widely. These texts often contained patriotic and moralistic themes.

How were educational success and failure evaluated?

20 When schools provided rudimentary education in basic skills—reading, writing, and arithmetic—and religious ethics at low cost, they were usually deemed to be successful.

21 Those who were excluded from schools because of their race, gender, or social class may well have judged educational success and failure in other ways.

TERMS AND CONCEPTS

apprenticeships, *p. 49*
assimilation, *p. 57*
Blue-Backed Speller, *p. 72*
common school, *p. 66*
dame school, *p. 52*
English Academy, *p. 66*
hidden passage, *p. 56*
hornbook, *p. 71*
kindergarten, *p. 46*
land-grant school, *p. 52*

Latin grammar school, *p. 66*
lyceum, *p. 65*
McGuffey Reader, *p. 72*
mission school, *p. 57*
monitorial method, *p. 65*
normal school, *p. 68*
parochial school, *p. 69*
primer, *p. 71*
seminary, *p. 70*
universal schooling, *p. 68*

REFLECTIVE PRACTICE

In the 19th and early 20th centuries, when people used the monitorial method to teach reading, a school was divided into eight classes. The classes focused on different topics: letters of the alphabet, words and syllables of two letters, words and syllables of three letters, words and syllables of four letters, reading lesson of one syllable, reading lesson of two syllables, the new Testament, and the Bible. A group of 10 children in the class, who were to receive instruction on the alphabet, sat at a table equipped with trays of sand. This table faced a large board or alphabet wheel that displayed the letters to be studied. Monitors then proceeded as follows:

> [E]ach scholar has a stick given to him about the thickness of a quill, and four inches long, with which he is to write the letters on the sand. The alphabet is divided into three parts, viz., the perpendicular letters, I H T L E F i and l, form the first lesson; the triangular letters, A V W M N Z K Y X v w k y z and x form the second; and the circular letters, O U C J G D P B R Q S, a b o d p q g c m n h t u r s f and j, form the third class. These are in succession placed before the class, which is under the direction of a monitor, who, with an audible voice, desires them to form the first letter; each scholar now makes his best effort, which, perhaps, is a very awkward one; but the monitor pointing out the defects and occasionally printing the letter for them, teaches them to retrace it; after repeated trials upon the same letter, the class is soon able to form it readily, and with neatness . . . . The monitor then points to the first letter, and asks aloud, "What is that?" The boy at the head of the class answers first, when, if he should make a mistake, the question is put to the second boy, and so on until some one in the class answers aright; in which case the boy takes precedence in the class. This exercise soon perfects them in the knowledge of their letters and is also a pleasing relaxation. (Reigart, 1969, pp. 41–42)

Issues, Problems, Dilemmas, Opportunities

As we noted earlier in the chapter, many who promoted Lancaster's monitorial method believed that children would learn obedience, industry, and promptness. Whether or not they were right, what other outcomes might reasonably be expected from such a process of teaching and learning?

Perceive and Value

After reading some early accounts of schooling, one might imagine that monitors in these classrooms could easily have grown into self-important bullies. The chance to "be in charge" has corrupted more than a few people. But despite some pitiful historical and contemporary examples of misanthropic behavior, there is an ethic of caring that is alive and well in our public schools today that has evolved from the beliefs and practices of many early educators. Assume that some of the monitors did make school a valuable learning experience and a "pleasing relaxation" for all those present. What might these monitors have thought, what might they have felt about their fellow students and their teacher, that enabled them to perform their tasks effectively? In your own experience, specifically where and when have you encountered people with similar ideals?

Know and Act

The monitorial method is an excellent early example of a kind of "cross-age tutoring." If you wanted to learn more about other methods of encouraging students to work together—beyond your local library—where might you turn for information?

Evaluate

When it was used, the monitorial method's success was judged at least in part by how much it cost to deliver basic instruction and by how well participating students learned to read. Do you think these outcomes are more or less important today than they were in the 19th century? If you were to judge the monitorial method or some other cross-age tutoring program today, would you still be interested in these outcomes? What, if any, other outcomes might be of interest to you?

ONLINE ACTIVITY

We often ignore primary sources of information because they are too difficult to locate, or we are unwilling to exert the energy to find them. This activity will put you in touch with some primary sources that allow you to step back in time to learn more about how people thought about education prior to the Civil War. To find this information, go to the home page for the Library of Congress at **http://lcweb.loc.gov/homepage/lchp.html** and click on "American Memory Collection." If you select "documents" and search on the word "education," you will have access to more than 1,000 documents. For example, you will find a review of two lectures entitled "Hints to a Young Woman" that were delivered by Horace Mann in 1852. You can also read a report from the Board of Education for Freedmen that describes the creation and sustaining of the first public schools for children of freed slaves in and around New Orleans in 1864. Search through the list of documents for other readings pertinent to education before the Civil War. Discuss your findings with your colleagues.

3

Modern U.S. Education History, 1865 to the Present

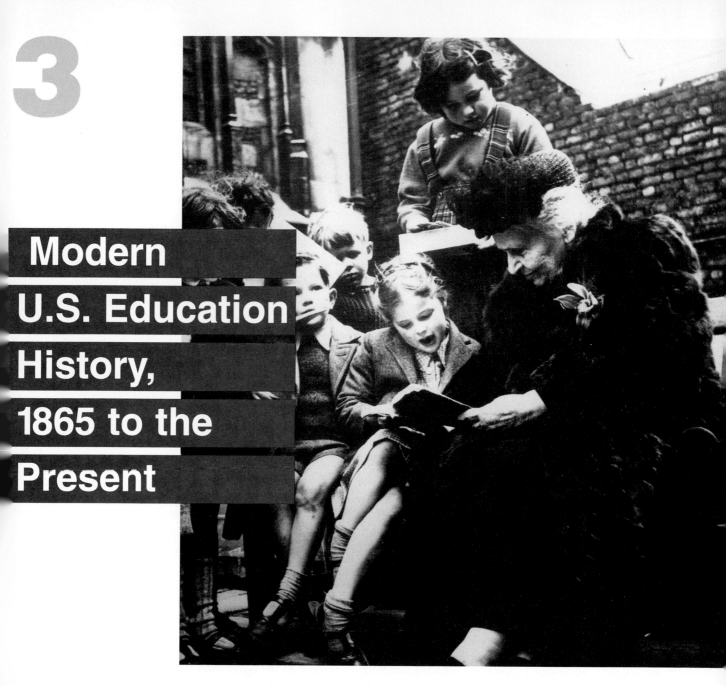

In this chapter we describe education in the United States from 1865 to the present. We provide a historical overview of slavery and the reconstruction of the South after the Civil War, of calls for educational and social reform, of the influences of science, philanthropy, and the mass media on education, and of federal involvement in schooling.

We also discuss the nature of the various types of people who were teachers and students in this society, drawing attention to similarities and differences among these groups. Also noted are the gradual changes in how schools defined themselves and their missions as their leaders faced the demands of progress in its many forms.

Finally, we consider the evolution of teaching and curriculum. As curriculum and teaching have changed during this time, so too have society's expectations for educational success.

As society became more complex in the post-Civil War era, opportunities for education increased dramatically. What factors influenced Americans' abilities to take advantage of these opportunities?

PROFESSIONAL PRACTICE QUESTIONS

1 What changes after the Civil War affected the American system of education?

2 Who are "We the People"?

3 How did teaching change after the Civil War?

4 How did schools change during the modern era?

5 How did opportunities for higher education expand?

6 What issues arose in curriculum development?

7 How do people typically judge educational success and failure?

WHAT CHANGES AFTER THE CIVIL WAR AFFECTED THE AMERICAN SYSTEM OF EDUCATION?

The end of the Civil War left people in the North and South seeking ways to build a nation. Slavery had ended and with it a set of social mores that had governed people's conduct. The nature of the Union was settled, but there was no blueprint for how that Union was to be operationalized in everyday lives. Leaders and ordinary citizens defined education by their actions both inside and outside schools. As illustrated in Figure 3.1, several events and reform efforts changed the nature of American education.

▓ End of Slavery and Reconstruction of the South

Passion for intellectual freedom and civil liberties widened and deepened after the Civil War. The Thirteenth, Fourteenth, and Fifteenth Amendments to the U.S. Constitution changed race relations legally by ending slavery,

End of Slavery

Constitutional Amendments

Landmark Supreme Court Decisions

Progressive Social & Educational Reforms

Research on Human Behavior, Psychology, & Learning

Professionalization of Teaching

Industrialization & Urbanization

New Immigration & Greater Cultural Diversity

Greater Federal Involvement in Education

Developments in Science & Technology

Philanthropy & the Mass Media

Consolidation & Bureaucratization of Schools

Reconceptualizations of Schooling, e.g.:

   Preschools

   Middle Schools

   Comprehensive High Schools

   Adult Education

National & International Events, e.g.:

   Great Depression

   World Wars

   Civil & Equal Rights Movements

   Space Race & Cold War

Curriculum Reforms, e.g.:

   Standardization

   Diversification

   Innovation

FIGURE 3.1

Some Factors Affecting American Education in the Modern Era

Which factors do you think have had the greatest impact on your schooling?

defining citizenship, and forbidding states to deny the right to vote, but the customs of segregation and discrimination remained entrenched. Northerners moved to reconstruct the South, often by trying to reeducate the vanquished. Not surprisingly, Southerners detested and resisted these actions.

The Bureau of Refugees, Freedmen, and Abandoned Lands, commonly known as the **Freedman's Bureau**, established 1 month before the end of the war, provided food, medicine, and seed to destitute Southerners. The Bureau secured legal rights for freed slaves and extended educational opportunities to them. Hundreds of northern teachers went south to teach African-American children and adults. Despite opposition, the Freedman's Bureau succeeded in establishing and operating more than 4,000 primary schools, 74 normal schools, and 61 industrial schools for former slaves and, in so doing, strengthened the role of the federal government in education (Degler, 1959).

Anxious to keep "Negroes" in an inferior position, Southerners constructed the so-called **black codes** of conduct. These codes, or "halfway stations back to slavery," allowed African Americans to hold property, to sue and be sued, and to marry, but forbade them to carry firearms, to testify in court in cases involving European Americans, and to leave their jobs (Degler, 1959, p. 211).

The end of the Civil War did not end violence toward African Americans. Although precise numbers are impossible to determine, between 1865 and 1900, there were approximately 2,500 known lynchings, mainly of African Americans. Between 1900 and the start of World War I in 1914, more than 1,100 African Americans are known to have been lynched—mostly in the South but also in some midwestern states (Franklin, 1967). Although rare, lynchings continued into the 1950s. In 1934 the **National Association for the Advancement of Colored People (NAACP)**, the first nationwide special interest group for African Americans, lobbied for an antilynching bill, which failed. Antilynching bills failed to pass throughout the Roosevelt and Truman administrations. Learn more about the NAACP (**http:www.naacp.org**).

Calls for Educational and Social Reform

The push for universal education that began in the 1830s and 1840s gained momentum as the country moved toward the 20th century. Largely as a result of pressure from the National Teachers Association, organized in 1857, Congress created a Department of Education in 1867. President Andrew Johnson appointed Henry Barnard to assume the position of commissioner of education and to run the department. The commissioner collected statistics and facts on education and tried to promote the cause of education throughout the country.

By the beginning of the 20th century, critics initiated what was to become a sustained attack on public schools, particularly in the cities. Social reformers, sometimes called "muckrakers," bemoaned what they saw as mechanical teaching and learning, administrative ineptitude, and parent's lack of interest in their children's welfare. Joseph Mayer Rice (1969), for instance, thought that the environment of the New York City schools was nothing short of pernicious:

> It is indeed incomprehensible that so many loving mothers whose greatest care appears to be the welfare of their children are willing, without hesitation, to resign the fate of their little ones to the tender mercies of ward politicians, who in many instances have no scruples in placing the children in class-rooms the atmosphere of which is not fit for human beings to breathe, and in charge of teachers who treat them with a degree of severity that borders on barbarism. (pp. 10–11)

Leonard Ayres's *Laggards in Our Schools* (1909) presented what he claimed was scientific evidence that the schools were filled with retarded children, or children who were overage for their grade. He blamed this consequence on the schools for creating programs for unusually bright children and ignoring the slow or average children.

In the early 20th century, many problems played themselves out in schools: an anti-evolution crusade, anti-immigration movements, organized campaigns against Roman Catholics, and increases in anti-semitism, to mention but a few. Urban poverty and the exploitation of children as cheap labor in the rapidly expanding industrial economy fueled the development of public schools and the organization of American labor; that is, schools protected children and prepared them for work later in life. In doing so, schools kept children out of the labor market, thus protecting jobs for adults.

Influence of Science and Philanthropy

Education reformers in the early 20th century placed their faith in science to solve education and social problems. Frederick Taylor's studies on scientific management, or a system for getting greater productivity from human labor, appealed to businessmen who ran the school boards who, in turn, hired the superintendents who ran the schools (Callahan, 1962). Spurred on by grants from private foundations, leaders in school administration—including Elwood Cubberley, Frank Spaulding, and George Strayer—encouraged educational specialization and scientific management (Tyack & Hansot, 1982).

The seeds of basic research on teaching and learning also began to take root in American schools at the turn of the century. James Cattell introduced "mental tests" to assess individual differences and encouraged counseling agencies and schools to incorporate such measures as part of their routine procedures. The work of Alfred Binet, Lewis Terman, and, later, Edward L. Thorndike on the measurement of intelligence was hailed as a great practical advance for schools (Travers, 1983). Psychologist Charles Judd emphasized the importance of viewing teaching and learning as social constructs, that is, as ideas that derive meaning from their use in everyday life. In contrast, John Watson's view of behavior and learning as mechanical phenomena—elements to be manipulated continually by outside sources—prompted a revolution in the way people thought about human behavior. Although strikingly different in philosophical persuasions, these researchers shared a belief in the power of science to improve the human condition.

If, as Walter Lippman argued in the popular press, science was our best weapon against ignorance, others recognized that there was money to be made from applying science to teaching and learning. Survey research and personality assessment centers sprang up in business and industry in the 1930s and 1940s and did much to shape people's thinking about what counted in life. For instance, Dale Carnegie (1936) reported that

> Investigation and research uncovered a most important and significant fact . . . about 15 percent of one's financial success is due to one's technical knowledge and about 85 percent is due to skill in human engineering—to personality and the ability to lead people. (p. 16)

He used this claim to build a case for teaching others how to win friends and influence people. Carnegie sold about 1 million copies of his book in its first 2 years of publication.

From the late 19th century on, schools were embedded in a society that demonstrated in many ways the increasing value of education. In the 1870s fine-art museums first opened—the Metropolitan Museum of Art in New York and the Museum of Fine Arts in Boston. The Library of Congress opened its Jefferson Building in 1897, permitting wide public access to its collection (Cole, 1979). By 1900 more than 45 million volumes were housed in the more than 9,000 public libraries across the country (Blum et al., 1989). Philanthropists such as Andrew Carnegie and Andrew Mellon donated money for promoting public access to books and art and for establishing philanthropic foundations. To upgrade educational conditions in the South, funding for the Southern Education Board (SEB), a philanthropic agency, was provided by northern capitalists, such as merchant Robert Ogden, railroad man William Baldwin, and oil magnate John D. Rockefeller.

Influence of the Mass Media

The press grew more powerful as an instrument of social education in the 20th century. Newspapers and magazines no longer served only the educated middle and upper classes; they now catered to the masses. The sensationalism of the "yellow press" of New York City—so called because the front pages of special editions were printed on yellow paper to catch the potential reader's eye—led by William Randolph Hearst and Joseph Pulitzer, shaped American opinion on education and many other matters, including its views of foreigners.

In the 15 years preceding the turn of the century, the number of periodicals published increased by 2200. By 1905 there were twenty 10¢ monthlies, with a combined circulation of 5.5 million (Blum et al., 1989). From 1920 to 1940, newspapers and magazines "continued to rival schools and churches as the chief instruments of mass education and the dissemination of ideas" (Link & Catton, 1963, p. 295).

By 1930, Americans were experiencing an economic depression. At the same time, new communications technology was fast becoming a part of daily life. Motion picture theaters spread across the country. About 23,000 theaters existed with a combined seating capacity of more than 11 million (Link & Catton, 1963). The entertainment value of the big screen was apparent immediately. The lure of escaping everyday troubles was too powerful to ignore. The more subtle educational influences of the movies—their power to compose the texts by which people lived or wished to live—would become an enduring national issue.

Radio captured the collective imagination of Americans in the 1920s, 1930s, and 1940s. The first broadcast was made in 1920. By 1922 there were 220 radio stations, and, by 1923, there were some 2.5 million radios in the country. Approximately 80% of American families had radios in their homes by 1937 (Link & Catton, 1963).

While radio educated by delivering live voices of famous people into listeners' homes, television added images to those voices. The educational effects of seeing and hearing people and events that were discussed in school were profound. By January 1960, 9 out of 10 homes had television sets, competing with, contradicting, and complementing other sources of information, including teachers and parents. One study found that typical fourth-graders today watch between two and six hours of television daily. (Daily Report Card, 1996). By high school graduation, some children have spent more time watching television than they have spent in school.

Impact of Federal Involvement

Direct federal involvement in education increased after the 1950s, when the Supreme Court ruled that school racial segregation was unconstitutional. Schools became front-page news in the 1960s as battlegrounds in the war on poverty and the quest for racial equality. The federal government exerted its influence with money, legislation, and exhortation in many arenas: desegregation, aid to schools serving children of low-income families, legislation guaranteeing racial and sexual equity, new entitlements for students with disabilities, bilingual–bicultural programs, and career education. The compensatory and early intervention programs emanating from Washington, D.C., were aimed at meeting the basic needs of children living in poverty.

The most dramatic example of federal involvement was the **Elementary and Secondary Education Act (ESEA)** of 1965 (renamed the **Improving American Schools Act**, or **IASA**, in 1994). The ESEA changed the center of policy-making power from states and localities to the federal government and provided funds to alleviate the effects of poverty through a variety of programs. It supported school libraries, the purchase of textbooks and other instructional materials; guidance, counseling, and health services; and remedial instruction. The ESEA also established research centers and laboratories to advance educational practice.

> **Did increased direct federal involvement after the 1950s have a negative impact on education?**

Explore, for example, the Smithsonian Museum's offerings for elementary and secondary schools on the Web (**http://www.si.edu/**). See also A Teacher's Guide to the U.S. Department of Education (**http://www.ed.gov/pubs/ TeachersGuide/**).

The New Federalism of the 1980s returned to states and localities both power and financial responsibility for educational programs. As federal support for education shrank in terms of real dollars, the rhetoric of educational reform increased. National, state, and local commissions and task forces issued a spate of reports that called for changes in everything from how public schools are organized and schoolbooks are written to how teachers and students are taught and tested. Joseph Murphy (1990) described these reforms in terms of three goals: raising performance standards for students and teachers; decentralizing school management; and providing aid, such as preschool and nutrition programs to children in poverty-stricken areas.

As we enter the turn of the century, federal involvement in public education means maintaining existing programs and attempting to improve educational practice via performance standards and other structural reforms. Federal education policy—and, for that matter, education policy at state and local levels—has not yet provided coherent, effective guidance on how to improve instruction (Consortium for Policy Research in Education, 1996).

WHO ARE "WE THE PEOPLE"?

Concepts of federalism, the defining attributes of American unity, have grown richer and more plentiful through the years. America is one nation out of many peoples—*e pluribus unum*. The American people are similar because they are different (Fuchs, 1990). Nearly one in four Americans in the United States is a member of an ethnic or racial minority group.

After the Civil War, the population of the United States grew rapidly, most noticeably in the cities and industrialized areas. In the 1890s about 30% of the population of 63 million lived in cities; by 1988, 75% of the country's 245 million people lived in urban areas (U.S. Bureau of the Census, 1990). Although the population of the United States grew 200% between 1859 and

1914, the number of workers in manufacturing increased 650%. (U.S. Bureau of the Census, 1975)

In 1910 about one half of men and women in the labor force lived in poverty. They worked long hours for meager wages, and their children often left school to work in factories. Only one third of the enrolled children finished primary school; less than one tenth finished high school. Jacob Riis, a photographer who had an agenda for social reform, found poverty and ignorance wherever he pointed his camera. In New York City's East Side, in a tenement building reported to house 478 tenants, Riis (1890) commented that the truant officer could find only seven children who said they attended school (p. 180). See the Jacob A. Riis collection of historical photographs online (**http://www.mcny.org/m28.html**).

Cultural Awareness

Jacob Riis's 1890 photograph (left) shows people crowded into an urban slum in New York City. Although usually staged, as was customary in those times, Riis's photographs show the conditions in which migrant farmers and European immigrants lived in cities in the East. In other parts of the country, conditions for many African-American, Chinese-American, and Native-American children were as difficult or worse.

Walker Evans's 1930 photograph (right) shows children from rural tenant farm families, or "sharecroppers," in Alabama during the Great Depression. As the 20th century wore on, social scientists and reformers talked about having discovered a new culture—a way of life shared by many people old and young, urban and rural, European and non-European in origin. They called it the culture of poverty.

Young social workers, nearly all women, took active roles in improving the deplorable living and working conditions of low-income people in New York City. Some ran charity nurseries, such as New York's Five Points Mission and the Five Points House of Industry. By 1890, an estimated 60,000 children had received assistance from these two institutions (Riis, 1890).

Other agents of change investigated sweatshops and tenements and established settlement houses in poor neighborhoods to help immigrants adjust to life in a new country. The first of these houses was established in 1886 in New York City; by 1910, there were 400 such houses (Carlson, 1975). Jane Addams's Hull House in Chicago had an education program that included playgrounds, a nursery, and a library.

Life was difficult in the rural areas as well, particularly where the tenant farmer population was large. The census of 1930 indicated that tenants constituted 64% of the population in Alabama and 66% in Georgia (Dabney, 1969). James Agee's account of the lives of three tenant farm families in Alabama, accompanied by Walker Evans's photographs, created a classic documentation of the period. Agee (Agee and Evans, 1960) described the families' educational needs:

> They learn the work they will spend their lives doing, chiefly of their parents, and from their parents and from the immediate world they take their conduct, their morality, and their mental and emotional and spiritual key. One could hardly say that any further knowledge or consciousness is at all to their use or advantage, since there is nothing to read, no reason to write, and no recourse against being cheated even if one is able to do sums. (p. 268)

Native Americans

After the Civil War, military supremacy, the destruction of the buffalo, the expansion of railroads, confinement on reservations, and efforts to encourage individual rather than tribal ownership of land further eroded the traditional cultures of Native Americans. As Helen Hunt Jackson noted, the official abuse and neglect of Native Americans shaped *A Century of Dishonor.* Writing in the late 19th century, Jackson (1880/1977) estimated that 250,000 to 300,000 Native Americans lived in the United States, excluding those in Alaska:

> There is not among these . . . one which has not suffered cruelly at the hands either of the Government or of white settlers. The poorer, the more insignificant, the more helpless the band, the more certain the cruelty and outrage to which they have been subjected. . . . There are hundreds of pages of unimpeachable testimony on the side of the Indian; but it goes for nothing, is set down as sentimentalism or partisanship, tossed aside and forgotten. (pp. 337–338)

Government efforts to educate Native Americans were administered through the **Bureau of Indian Affairs (BIA).** Off-reservation boarding schools were meant to ensure the survival of Native Americans but were also instrumental in their destruction. These federal boarding schools took children away from their families and attempted—by way of food, dress, regimented schedules, religion, and job and language training—to impose on them the values and customs of the dominant European-American culture. Students were compelled to learn English and to "breathe the atmosphere of a civilized instead of a barbarous or semi-barbarous community" (U.S. Bureau of Indian Affairs, 1974, p. 1756). One such school, the Carlisle Indian School, established in 1879 by a young army officer named Richard Henry Pratt, educated approximately 4,000 children over a period of 24 years.

Boarding schools immersed Native-American youngsters in the ways of a culture totally foreign to them.

> The first thing to do was to clean them thoroughly and to dress them in their new [military] attire. . . . [then] everything except swallowing, walking, and sleeping had to be taught; the care of person, clothing, furniture, the usages of the table, the carriage of the body, civility, all those things which white children usually learn from their childhood by mere imitation, had to be painfully inculcated and strenuously insisted on. In addition to this, they were to be taught the rudiments of an English school course and the practical use of tools. (U.S. Bureau of Indian Affairs, 1974, p. 1749)

Reservation schools had similar aims, which many Native Americans of the time accepted as valid. In the late 19th century, Princess Sara Winnemucca founded a school in California for Piute children. She taught them to spell, read, write, and calculate in English. She also taught drawing and sewing (Peabody, 1886).

The Dawes Act of 1887 also had the effect of undermining tribal authority by breaking up reservation land into smaller parcels and allotting them to individual Native Americans. These land allotments—most unsuitable for farming, particularly by people who had not been farmers—were initially held in trust and later transferred to individuals. Four out of five individuals were bilked of their property or lost it in other ways (Blum et al., 1989). Read the text of The Dawes Act or General Allotment Act of 1887 (**http://www. csusm. edu/projects/nadp/adawes.htm**).

The "Indian Wars" as they came to be known were a series of bloody encounters between white settlers—sometimes with the aid of troops, sometimes without—and Native Americans. The gradual but deadly certain conclusion of these Wars was twofold: the death or subjugation of Native-American peoples and their displacement from desirable lands.

Indian boarding schools were conceived as a humanitarian way to help Native-American children assimilate, but they often imposed cruel hardships. Students were expected to reject and despise their identities as Indians, their families, and their way of life.

VOICES

On Assimilation

In the late 1800s, the responses of Native-American peoples to schooling on federally administered reservations varied widely. Some resisted, but many had come to believe—and were supported in that belief—that the dominant European-American culture was superior to their own. In a letter to the school trustees of Inyo and to Dr. Lyman Abbot, editor of the *Christian Union*, Sarah Winnemucca appealed to Piutes to send their children to school to address the need for self-determination in the face of perceived cultural inadequacy:

Hearing that you are about to start a school to educate your children, I want to say a word about it. You all know me; many of you are my aunts or cousins. We are of one race,—your blood is my blood,—so I speak to you for your good. I can speak five tongues,—three Indian tongues, English, and Spanish. I can read and write, and am a school teacher. Now, I do not say this to boast, but simply to show you what can be done. When I was a little girl, there were no Indian schools; I learned under great difficulty. Your children can learn much more than I know, and much easier; and it is your duty to see that they go to school. There is no excuse for ignorance. Schools are being built here and there, and you can have as many as you need; all they ask you to do is send your children. You are not asked to give money or horses—only to send your children to school. The teacher will do the rest. He or she will fit your little ones for the battle of life, so that they can attend to their own affairs instead of having to call in a white man. A few years ago you owned this great country; today the white man owns it all, and you own nothing. Do you know what did it? Education. You see the miles and miles of railroad, the locomotive, the Mint in Carson, where they make money. Education has done it all.

CRITICAL THINKING

Winnemucca's letter contains six arguments for education. What are they? Why might Piutes have rejected the idea of formal schooling? What assumptions does the letter reveal about the power of education to change people's lives? How might Native Americans respond today to the viewpoint the letter expresses?

Note. From *Sarah Winnemucca's practical solution of the Indian problems: A letter to Dr. Lyman Abbot of the "Christian Union"* (pp. 5–6) by E. P. Peabody, 1886, Cambridge, MA: John Wilson and Son.

Some historians have marked the conclusion of the Indian Wars at 1890 with the massacre at Wounded Knee, South Dakota. Among the Sioux, there had been a revival of ghost dancing (collective dancing that was supposed to bring back to life all the dead warriors and kin and all the dead buffalo and wild horses). Viewing these dances as a sign of resistance, the army was ordered to arrest and imprison any fomenters of disturbances. On December 15, 1890, a Native-American policeman killed Chief Sitting Bull, and on the 29th, the cavalry surrounded Chief Big Foot at Wounded Knee Creek and slaughtered between 150 and 300 Lakota, or Sioux, men, women, and children. Native-American resistance was crushed.

Native Americans were not considered citizens of the United States until passage of the Citizenship Act of 1924. At about the same time, the Meriam Report—a study conducted by the Brookings Institute—revealed the poor condition of education programs provided by the Education Division of the Bureau of Indian Affairs.

Cultural Awareness

Susette La Flesche Tibbles (1854–1903) was a teacher who spoke out in support of Native-American rights. She was born in a village of the Omaha tribe near what is today Bellevue, Nebraska, and grew up on a small reservation nearby. When she was 8 years old, she attended a Presbyterian mission school. After graduating from a girls' seminary, the Elizabeth (New Jersey) Institute, in 1873, she returned to the Omaha reservation and taught school.

In 1877 the federal government removed some Native Americans, the Ponca people, from their lands. As the controversy mounted, La Flesche served as an interpreter to the Ponca chief. Soon she became part of a group that toured the East to publicize the wrongs that had been inflicted upon the Poncas.

As La Flesche toured the country, she met many influential people, including Edward Everett Hale, Senator Henry L. Dawes, novelist Helen Hunt Jackson, Alice M. Longfellow, and Louis Brandeis. These citizens and others sympathetic to the Poncas' plight lobbied Washington and demanded change. With the help of La Flesche, Congress passed legislation in 1887 called the Dawes Severalty Act. This law authorized the allotment of reservation land with citizenship rights to individual Native Americans. (Equity Newsletter, 1995)

The 1930s and early 1940s were a period of gain for Native Americans. John Collier, commissioner of Indian affairs for Franklin Roosevelt, began to encourage preservation of Native-American culture by permitting reservation schools to offer instruction in Native-American languages and culture. Collier also promoted the idea of local self-government, hired Native Americans in his agency, and channeled millions of dollars into improving Native-American lands. Passage of the Indian Reorganization Act of 1934 returned self-government to Native Americans, eliminated allotment policies that had reduced tribal land holdings, and prompted the study of ways to improve the poor economic, health, and social conditions of Native Americans.

Coinciding with the onset of World War II, reduced funding for educational programs and a resurgence of assimilationist policies had a deleterious effect on the struggle for Native-American autonomy. The National Congress of American Indians, founded during the war, was aggressive in its efforts to improve the lot of Native Americans. The American Indian Movement of 1968—composed mostly of militant urban Native Americans— resorted to violence. As Native Americans continued to press their case, Congress reversed its decision to terminate federal reservations and in 1975 passed the **Indian Self-Determination and Educational Assistance Act.**

> **Why might Native Americans as a group trail in levels of educational attainment today?**

Native-American cultures are tremendously diverse. As a group, however, Native Americans are trailing others statistically in terms of income, life expectancy, and level of education. Unemployment is much greater than that for the total population, and poverty is rampant—particularly among widowed, divorced, and aged women (Goodman, 1985).

European Americans

After the Civil War, the population of the United States grew increasingly heterogeneous due to immigration. From 1880 to 1924, the majority of immigrants came from southern, central, and eastern Europe. Many settled in American cities and took jobs in industry. In Chicago in 1910, for example, 75% of the residents were immigrants or the children of immigrants (Cremin, 1988). In the 1930s and 1940s, Europeans fled the totalitarian regimes of Italy and Germany for the freedom and safety of the United States, and after them

Cultural Awareness

From 1892 to 1954, some 12 million immigrants from many middle and eastern European countries entered America under the gaze of the Statue of Liberty in New York harbor. Emma Lazarus's (1888) poem "The New Colossus," inscribed at the base of the statue, welcomed all who arrived:

> Give me your tired, your poor,
> Your huddled masses yearning to breathe free,
> The wretched refuse of your teeming shore.
> Send these, the homeless, tempest-tost [sic] to me,
> I lift my lamp beside the golden door.

Lazarus's belief in the power of religious and ethnic tolerance, shaped in part by her own Jewish heritage, did not, however, convey the nation's long-standing ambivalence between accepting and rejecting foreign nationals. Many new immigrants met with the hostility of those who had preceded them. Nativism—formal policies and informal actions designed to favor the existing culture over immigrants— flourished. For example, a committee of the Fiftieth Congress appointed to investigate immigration viewed many immigrants with disdain:

> They are of a very low order of intelligence. They do not come here with the intention of becoming citizens; their whole purpose being to accumulate by parsimonious, rigid, and unhealthy economy a sum of money and then return to their native land. They live in miserable sheds like beasts; the food they eat is so meager, scant, unwholesome, and revolting that it would nauseate and disgust an American workman, and he should find it difficult to sustain life upon it. Their habits are vicious, their customs are disgusting, and the effect of their presence here upon our social condition is to be deplored. (Lodge, 1891, p. 33)

in the 1950s followed survivors of the Holocaust. The impact of new immigration on education was twofold: schools had to provide basic education to more people, and they had to socialize these new arrivals to American ways. Assimilation, therefore, again became a major goal of education.

As the population increased, then, it also diversified by religion and ethnicity. Differences in language and culture among the new arrivals, and between the immigrants and native-born Americans, made assimilation slow, difficult, and sometimes seemingly impossible.

Although many immigrants retain their ethnic identities through the years, many others willingly or unwillingly shed these identities. Based on a carefully selected sample of 524 households, Richard Alba (1991) found that almost no ethnic people were fluent in the language of their ancestral group. About 2% had ever received help in business endeavors from other members of their group. Only 2% were members of ethnic social clubs, while 1% ate ethnic foods daily, and 11% lived in neighborhoods having concentrations of their own ethnic group.

African Americans

After the Civil War, African Americans began to take advantage of the citizenship they had gained via the Fourteenth Amendment by participating more fully in society, including attending public schools. In 1860, less than 2% of all school-age African-American children were enrolled in school; by 1900 the figure had risen to 31%. Furthermore, illiteracy dropped from 82% in 1870 to 45% in 1900 (U.S. Bureau of the Census, 1990).

Emancipated slaves and European Americans established Sunday schools and universal public education during Reconstruction. Churches and ministers in African-American communities often formed the nucleus from which educational campaigns spread. By 1868 the African Methodist Episcopal Church had already enrolled 40,000 pupils in Sabbath schools; by 1885, there were 200,000. African-American teachers offered almost all the instruction. At its height, the Freedman's Bureau operated more than 4,000 primary schools, 74 normal schools, and 61 industrial schools for African Americans. Thousands of "Yankee school marms" ventured south to teach in needy schools established for African Americans (Degler, 1959).

Booker Taliaferro Washington was among the many African Americans who flocked to normal schools to gain an education that would enable them to be effective leaders of their people. Washington attended and later taught at Hampton Normal and Agricultural Institute in Virginia. In 1881 he went to Macon County, Alabama, to become principal of the newly created state normal school for African Americans, Tuskegee Institute. Washington built programs at Tuskegee in academics, agriculture, industrial arts, health, religion and music. His first students were public school teachers from Macon Country. He even created a mobile school on a horse-drawn cart that delivered basic education to ex-slaves' door steps.

Booker T. Washington

Through Washington's leadership, the Tuskegee Institute became a national model for educating African-American teachers, farmers, and industrial workers.

Washington believed that vocational or industrial education was the best way for African Americans to gain financial self-sufficiency and better their lives. According to Washington (1907),

> Mental development is a good thing. Gold is also a good thing, but gold is worthless without an opportunity to make itself touch the world of trade. (p. 77)

The development of Washington's ideas about the need for practical rather than academic education is evident in his autobiography, *Up From Slavery*. In response to his own times and experiences, he discouraged African Americans from seeking education to become lawyers, doctors, or politicians. He believed that achieving respectability as a trained worker contributing to the economy not upsetting the social order, was the key to advancement. Washington was working in a time when African Americans were perceived as inferior in ability, and an educated African-American citizenry was perceived as a potential threat to white supremacy.

Which view, Washington's or DuBois's, is a better model for African-American education today?

W. E. B. DuBois

An opposite view was taken by Washington's severest critic, W. E. B. DuBois, an African-American sociologist with a PhD from Harvard. DuBois (1904) argued that African Americans would never achieve civil and political equality with industrial education alone and instead advocated a more academic approach to "train the best of the Negro youth as teachers, professional men, and leaders" (p. 240).

DuBois advocated political activism and challenged the ideas of both African and European Americans, helping to found the Civil Rights movement that continued through the 1970s. As editor of *The Crisis*, the journal of the National Association for the Advancement of Colored People, DuBois helped formulate the educational policy of that body, which was that all American children and youth should have an equal opportunity to pursue an education.

Individuals such as Mary McLeod Bethune were also instrumental in promoting education. Bethune believed, as did other African-American leaders of the time, that education was the means to better lives for all children. As an educator concerned with practical training for upward mobility and as a political activist, Bethune may be seen as representing a combination of the views of Booker T. Washington and those of W. E. B. DuBois. Learn more about Mary McLeod Bethune by visiting the Bethune Foundation Collection online (**http://www.us.net/upa/newtitle/bethune.htm**).

In 1904 Bethune founded the Daytona Normal and Industrial School for Training Negro Girls, which was expanded in 1923 to become Bethune-Cookman College. During the Depression and World War II eras, she served in the administrations of Franklin Roosevelt and Harry Truman as director of the National Youth Administration and adviser to the United Nations.

Mary McLeod Bethune

The efforts of leaders such as DuBois and Bethune gave rise to the Civil Rights movement that grew over the next 50 years and beyond, for in the early 20th century, despite the efforts of the new leadership, education did little to improve economic opportunities or to create political and social equality. Because of segregated housing and voting districts, schools for African

Americans were funded from separate tax bases, and African Americans' comparative poverty meant that their schools were usually underfunded.

In 1896, in *Plessy v. Ferguson*, the Supreme Court ruled that public facilities for European and African Americans could be separate but equal, which served to legalize school segregation. By 1917 the discrepancy in financial resources for European-American and African-American schools had jumped to four to one in favor of European-American schools. In some rural areas, schools for European-Americans received 15 times more support. In Georgia in 1928 to 1929, for example, 99% of the money budgeted for teaching equipment went to European-American schools, even though African Americans composed 34% of the population (Bond, 1934).

By 1900, African Americans outnumbered European Americans in several southern cities, including Charleston, South Carolina; Savannah, Georgia; and Shreveport, Louisiana. African Americans had few opportunities for employment, however. Jim Crow—the colloquial name for laws and customs supporting racial segregation—sharply restricted opportunities. In 1907 in Alabama, for example, European-American teachers were paid roughly five times more money than were African-American teachers.

At the same time, in 1900, southern states spent an average of $9.72 per pupil, compared with $20.80 per pupil in the north-central states. Publicists such as Walter Hines Page admonished Southerners for such inequities and urged citizens to support increases in state and local taxes to narrow the gap. Although such efforts did not equalize funding for schools, between 1902 and 1910, appropriations for schools in the South doubled, enrollment of European-American students increased by almost a third, and school terms increased from 5 to 6 months. Illiteracy among European Americans declined from 11.8% in 1900 to about 5.5% in 1920; during the same time period, illiteracy among African Americans 10 years of age or older declined from 44.5% to about 22.9% (Link & Catton, 1963).

Poverty forced many African Americans to live in squalor. As industrialization advanced in the post–Civil War period, many African Americans migrated north, hoping to find work and to avoid what they perceived as a trend toward economic reenslavement in the South. For instance, after the Civil War, approximately 6,000 freed slaves left Louisiana, Mississippi, and Texas for Kansas in what was called the "Kansas Fever Exodus." These "exodusters" and other African Americans leaving the South prized education and sought educational opportunities as well as land in Kansas, in the West, and in northern cities (Painter, 1977).

African Americans continued to struggle for equality and were heard. President Harry Truman acted to integrate the armed forces in 1948 and 1949. Many members of minority groups capitalized on their opportunities to go to college with expenses paid by the G.I. Bill. Thurgood Marshall of the NAACP argued constitutional cases, including the landmark **Brown v. Board of Education of Topeka, Kansas** in 1954. In this case, the Supreme Court ruled that segregation of students by race is unconstitutional and that education is a right that must be available to all Americans on equal terms. Martin Luther King, Jr. and others led the nationwide civil rights movement into the 1960s.

The economic, political, social, and educational conditions of African Americans have improved over the years. Although the physical separation of African-American students is not legally sanctioned today as it was before

Cultural Awareness

Despite hardships, freedom in northern cities brought a burst of creativity. In New York City following World War I, a group of African-American writers, artists, jazz and blues musicians, and other performers shaped what became known as the Harlem Renaissance, a period of artistic expression that celebrated African-American culture and protested against social and economic injustices. Among the leading writers were James Weldon Johnson, Countee Cullen, and Langston Hughes. For further readings on the Harlem Renaissance, visit the Web (**http://cpl.lib.uic.edu/001hwlc/litlists/harlemren.html**).

Brown v. Board of Education, some people argue that public schools are being resegregated by economic and demographic factors, particularly in the cities. In Detroit's schools, between 1975 and 1996, for example, African-American enrollment increased from 71% to about 94% (Harris, 1984; Kunen, 1996). In 1979 Linda Brown-Smith, who was 5 years old when her father filed the historic *Brown* case on her behalf, went back to court on behalf of her own child to charge that the Topeka, Kansas, public schools remained segregated—a consequence that years of forced busing to promote integration has not cured.

Today, many African Americans remain at the lower end of the economic scale, have more health problems, have a shorter life expectancy, and are statistically more prone to youth unemployment, teenage pregnancy, drug use, and violence. The percentage of high school graduates enrolling in college has consistently remained lower than that for European Americans. In 1976, 9.6% of the college population was African American. By 1995, this figure had risen only slightly to 11.7%. (U.S. Department of Education, 1996a)

Hispanic Americans

Hispanic Americans constitute the fastest growing ethnic group in America. The term **Hispanic** means having Spanish colonial origins or being Spanish-speaking. Hispanics include people of Native-American, African, and European descent. People from Puerto Rico, Cuba, Central and South America, and Mexico have come to the United States to work and, in some cases, to find a haven from war and political repression.

Some groups in the American Southwest prefer the name *Latino* (feminine: *Latina*) or *Chicano* (feminine: *Chicana*) to *Hispanic*, which originally described immigrants to urban areas of the eastern United States.

Most Cubans arrived in the United States as political refugees after Fidel Castro overthrew the Cuban dictatorship of Fulgencio Batista in 1959. Puerto Ricans, on the other hand, have migrated freely between the United States and Puerto Rico since 1917, when Puerto Rico became a possession of the United States with commonwealth status and its citizens became U.S. citizens. As pointed out in Chapter 2, Mexican Americans were absorbed into the United States through conquest and later through annexation of their lands. For decades Mexican nationals have attempted border crossings to the more affluent United States in search of economic opportunities. Today Hispanic peoples—Mexican Americans, Mexican nationals, Puerto Rican Americans, and Central Americans—constitute more than 70% of the migrant workforce, which is made up mainly of farm workers (Bennett, 1990).

Like other immigrant groups, Hispanic Americans have had to struggle to overcome prejudice and discriminatory practices directed against them. Their struggles for civil rights and political representation during the 1960s resulted in four Mexican Americans winning election to Congress. By the 1980s, Hispanic Americans were seen as an emerging political force as they elected members of Congress, a governor in New Mexico, and mayors in Denver, San Antonio, Miami, Tampa, and Santa Fe.

In some states, such as California, Texas, and Florida, Hispanic Americans constitute the majority of public school enrollees. Overall, educational levels of Hispanic Americans have ranked somewhat lower than those of other groups. Comparisons of dropout rates indicate that while only 10.8% of European-American and 12.4% of African-American 14- to 24-year-olds dropped out of school in 1988, 29.7% of Hispanic-American youths failed to complete school (U.S. Bureau of the Census, 1990). Income levels for Hispanic Americans averaged slightly higher than those of African Americans in 1994, but 41% of Hispanic-American children younger than age 18 were living in poverty (U.S. Department of Education, 1996).

Some Hispanic and non-Hispanic Americans, including educators, have emphasized the need for bilingual education, in which children are taught in their native tongue as well as in English. Overall, research on the efficacy of bilingual education has yielded mixed results. Some studies conclude that students learn English at a much faster rate in bilingual classes, while other studies suggest that too many students languish in bilingual education too long, making little or no progress. (Daily Report Card, 1995). Public debate centers on whether bilingual education leads to a lack of unity in American society or represents the best chance for immigrant students to succeed.

Does bilingual education slow down the assimilation of immigrants? Should all immigrants be expected to want to assimilate?

Sometimes public debate results in legislative action. In California, passage of Proposition 187 called for school districts to verify students' legal residency or citizenship status. Proposition 187 was aimed primarily at Hispanic students and their families who have entered the United States illegally and to maintain limited education resources for U.S. citizens and legal immigrants. Opponents characterized the law as racist, protectionist, and harmful to children. The aftermath of the passage of Proposition 187 has been an ambiguous snarl of legal challenges. See A Teacher's Guide to the U.S. Department of Education—Fall 1995 and visit the Office of Bilingual Education and Minority Languages Affairs online (**http://www.ed.gov/offices/OBEMLA/index.html**).

Cultural Awareness

People from Africa, the Middle East, and the Indian subcontinent are among more recent immigrants to the United States. Events and conditions of the 1940s through the 1990s—such as the partition of India, the creation of the state of Israel, the Iran–Iraq War, the Persian Gulf War, and widespread drought and famine—have brought Indians, Pakistanis, Palestinians, Egyptians, Lebanese, Chaldeans, Saudis, Ethiopians, and many others to the United States. Among the largest groups are Arabs—people from around the world who have their cultural origins in the Arabian Peninsula and who speak Arabic. This group includes Muslim, Christian, and secular Arabs. Between 1948 and 1958 more than 330,000 Arabs immigrated to the United States (Orfalea, 1988). Bob McGruder (personal communication, September 3, 1996) estimates that in Detroit alone there could be as many as 250,000 Arab Americans.

Asian Americans

Chinese immigrants began entering the United States in large numbers during the 1850s. Many of them settled in the West, where there was an acute labor shortage. They labored in gold mines and helped build the first transcontinental railway. Most of these early immigrants, typically men who planned to better their lot and then return to China, often lived in "China-towns," where they continued their traditional customs and cultural practices. Attempts by Protestant and Catholic missionaries to Americanize the Chinese were unsuccessful and prompted others to use forceful means—burning Chinatowns and cutting off the customary long braids of Chinese men—to try to destroy their "clannish" ways (Carlson, 1975).

Although these immigrants who seemed so resistant to assimilation composed less than 1% of the total population in 1870, Americans grew increasingly distrustful of them, particularly as union leaders began to paint the Chinese as "part of a diabolical plot to deprive white Americans of their rightful jobs and bleed the West of its wealth" (Brown & Pannell, 1985, p. 203). Congress passed **exclusion acts** based on race to stop unwanted immigration. The Chinese Exclusion Act was passed in 1882.

Japanese immigrants stepped readily into a number of agricultural jobs in California and Hawaii. Despite the fact that the Nipponese Empire of Japan and the United States were allies at the turn of the century, by 1924 the flow of Japanese into this country was halted with the passage of the Orien-tal Exclusion Act. With the onset of World War II, Asian immigrants—particularly those of Japanese descent—suffered the ire of Americans: more than 100,000 Japanese Americans were driven from their homes and placed in temporary assembly centers, relocation centers, and internment camps, and their property was confiscated. Many people believed that this was the worst domestic wartime mistake, but it was not until 1990 that the federal government officially apologized and offered Japanese Americans restitution for the internment.

Since the Korean and Vietnam wars, many immigrants from Korea and Southeast Asia have made America their home. The first Korean immigrants came to Hawaii and then the United States early this century. Most Korean Americans, however, are post-Korean War immigrants or their descendants, coming to the United States after 1970. Koreans have typically left their country for greater economic opportunities in the United States. More than 40% of Korean Americans live in the West, most notably in Los Angeles. Large Korean communities exist in New York, Philadelphia, and other cities.

Vietnamese Americans, one of the larger Asian groups to enter our country recently, represent only 8.4% of the total Asian population (U.S. Bureau of the Census, 1990). The first arrivals "were generals and peasants, schoolteachers and spies, physicians and fishermen, . . . [who] became in America a poignant symbol of the refugee's will to succeed" (Efron, 1990). Making up about one third of the current Vietnamese-American population, these early Vietnamese immigrants have generally done well by American standards. By 1980, their household incomes equaled the U.S. average, and, for the most part, their children were quite successful in American schools. Vietnamese who have been immigrating since the fall of Saigon in 1975, however, have not fared so well. The majority live in poverty, are poorly educated, and have less upward mobility than their predecessors (Efron, 1990).

Cambodians, Laotians, and Thais have also immigrated to the United States, but not in so many numbers as the Vietnamese. These tribal peoples were deeply affected by the war in Vietnam. In addition to facing physical separation from their homelands, they have had to adjust to a society that relies on the power of science and technology to solve human problems, educational and otherwise—a society that is truly foreign in character to that which they left behind.

In the 1950s the United States government began to lift restrictions on immigration by race. In 1965 Congress abolished the quota system that based annual numbers of people allowed to enter the United States on the basis of the proportion of their relatives who were already here.

By the late 1980s and early 1990s, Asian-American students were being called the new "whiz kids." In 1994 to 1995, Asian-American students as a group had the highest SAT scores in the nation (U.S. Department of Education, 1996a). If college admissions had not been influenced in part in recent years by racial and ethnic quotas, artificially depressing the numbers of Asian-Americans admitted, they would have become a majority in some universities.

The size of the Asian-American population is also increasing. The U.S. Bureau of the Census estimates that Asian and Pacific-Islander populations in the United States will grow at a rate exceeding 2% until the year 2030. In comparison, even at the peak of the baby-boom era, the total U.S. population never grew by 2% in a year. The rate of growth of the population with Asian origins will be exceeded only by that of people with Hispanic origins. This growth is occurring not only on the east and west coasts but in other parts of the country (Nifong, 1996).

Why might Asian-American students as a group have the highest SAT scores in the nation?

Exceptional Learners in America

Efforts to meet the educational needs of students with exceptional abilities or disabilities developed during the 1800s (Kauffman, 1981). Physicians, clergymen, educators, and social reformers such as Dorothea Dix were leaders in this movement. Between 1817 and the Civil War, their crusade resulted in the establishment of residential schools for people who were deaf, blind, mentally retarded, or orphaned. After the Civil War, many of these schools were deemed unsavory places—overcrowded, impersonal, and sometimes quite inhumane. At about the time that reformers were calling for an end to such institutions, several states began to include special classes for students with disabilities in their public schools, and a number of professional organizations were formed to improve the care and treatment of children with disabilities.

Why are people with disabilities being more fully integrated into American society today?

The early 20th century also saw an upsurge in the scientific study of children, the scientific classification and measurement of types of disabilities, the establishment of the Children's Bureau in 1912, an increase in public school classes and resource programs for exceptional learners, and the emergence of new professional organizations and training programs for teachers. At the same time, the widespread institutionalization of people with disabilities in isolated special-care facilities led to social isolation and abuses, which sparked humanitarian reform movements in the 1950s and civil rights reform in the 1970s and 1980s.

Through federal involvement during the 1960s, a Bureau for the Handicapped was added to the United States Office of Education, which is now the Office of Special Education and Rehabilitative Services in the U.S. Department of Education. As Hallahan and Kauffman (1997) note, the field of special education has been changing dramatically in the 1980s and 1990s. Increasingly, people with disabilities are being integrated with the larger, nondisabled society. Greater emphasis is being placed on early intervention. And greater emphasis is being given to preparing people with disabilities for their transition from secondary school to adulthood.

American Women

Women's place in society in the early 20th century remained restricted and confused. Some, following in the footsteps of Emma Willard—touted as having done more in the 19th century for the education of women than anyone in America—were determined that women should enjoy the privilege of education no less than men (Raven & Weir, 1981). These women and others fought for and won an amendment to the U.S. Constitution granting women the right to vote in 1920. The suffragettes, as they were called, included Susan B. Anthony, a teacher; Elizabeth Blackwell, the first woman in the United States to qualify as a physician; Margaret Fuller, a teacher and foreign correspondent for the *New York Tribune*; and Elizabeth Cady Stanton, one of the organizers of the 1848 Seneca Falls Women's Rights Convention.

Women did not participate fully in society simply by virtue of winning formal recognition. During the Depression of the 1930s, they were often laid off from their jobs before men were, had greater difficulty finding jobs, and were rarely considered for supervisory positions. When World War II created a labor shortage, women were suddenly pulled into previously male-dominated jobs—and were just as suddenly discouraged from having careers when the war ended and the men came home.

After Congress passed an equal employment act in 1964, many types of job discrimination against women were eliminated. Women gradually moved out of what had become traditionally female-dominated jobs of teaching and nursing and into nearly all professional and occupational roles, including those traditionally held by men, such as firefighting, law enforcement, and military combat. In 1970, women accounted for approximately 5% of law school graduates; in the late 1980s, they constituted about 40% (Blum et al., 1989). **Title IX** of the Education Amendments Act, passed in 1972, guaranteed that "no person in the United States shall, on the basis of sex, be excluded from participation in, be denied the benefits of, or be subjected to discrimination under any education program or activity receiving federal financial assistance" (Title IX, Education Amendments of 1972). The greatest impact of Title IX has been on school athletic programs, which states that girls may not be excluded from any sport and must be given equal access to coaching and equipment. You can read the full provisions of Title IX at the Department of Labor Web site (**http://dol.gov/dol/oasam/public/regs/statutes/titleix.htm/**).

The **Women's Educational Equity Act (WEEA)** of 1974 was a comprehensive attack on sex discrimination in education and had far-reaching impact on curriculum and instruction in the nation's schools. The law expanded programs for females in mathematics, science, technology, and athletics; mandated nonsexist curriculum materials; implemented programs for increasing the number of female administrators in education and raising the career aspirations of female students; and extended educational and career opportunities to minority-member, disabled, and rural women. Visit the Women's Educational Equity Act Publishing Center online (**http://www.weber.edu/MBE/clearinghouse/W/WomenEqAct**).

> **Did the feminist movement help or hurt the struggle for equal educational opportunity for women?**

The struggle for equal rights for women has continued through the feminist movement and efforts to amend the Constitution. Meanwhile, women have been nominated for vice president of the United States; elected as mayors, governors, state legislators, and members of Congress; and appointed as ambassador to the United Nations, heads of cabinet posts, and heads of federal agencies. At the same time, sex discrimination and sexual harassment suits against school districts, corporations, and government agencies have increased, and education researchers in the 1990s have reported the widespread persistence of subtle gender bias in classroom interaction on the part of both male and female teachers.

Many women continue to battle poverty. Indeed, there appears to be what some have referred to as a "feminization of poverty." Between 1960 and 1980 the number of female-headed households increased twofold. By 1985 approximately 10 million children lived in such homes; about 6 million of them were with mothers whose incomes were less than $10,000. Today, on average, women earn about 73¢ for every $1 earned by men (National Center for Education Statistics, 1995).

HOW DID TEACHING CHANGE AFTER THE CIVIL WAR?

Following the Civil War most teachers were young, poorly paid, and rarely educated beyond elementary subjects. Teaching was not considered a desirable job, and the teacher turnover was high.

Discourse on teaching often reflected the traditional image of the teacher as a mentor, model of virtue, and disciplinarian, whose principal concern was the character of her pupils. Efforts to professionalize teaching began during the 19th century, as expectations of teachers broadened to include less subjective qualifications. By the 20th century teachers were supposed to be scientific experts with a mission to educate.

As thousands of immigrants streamed into urban schools in the late 19th century, teachers sometimes found themselves with classes of 70 pupils speaking dozens of different languages. The children often were poor, unbathed, and hungry (Tyack & Hansot, 1982).

Shifts in the Status of Teachers

By 1920, 86% of teachers were women but men controlled public education. In the early 1900s, women began to protest publicly about administrative edicts and the effects of decision making on life in schools. Women teachers fought for better working conditions and for pay that was equal to that received by men teachers.

Women such as Margaret Haley and Catherine Goggin, leaders of the Chicago Teachers Federation (CTF), an all-female teacher organization founded in 1897, drew attention to discrepancies in salaries between administrators and teachers. They also challenged the old male guard in the NEA and tried to force the association to focus on concerns of women teachers, who made up the majority of the teaching profession. (Tyack & Hansot, 1982). The NEA reacted by offering symbolic gains, such as appointing a female president every other year. Ella Flagg Young, a brilliant scholar and leader in the women's movement, spoke against the psychological control that management exerted on teachers, in a sense treating them like "mere workers at the treadmill" (Tyack & Hansot, 1982, p. 181).

Margaret Haley

Although women gained positions as teachers during this time, they lost positions as school administrators. Decisions about who might be the best candidates for various administrative positions were less often based on performance records than on gender. Women were generally appointed to posts that men did not desire to fill. The absence of requirements for special credentials for school administrators continued until the 1930s.

Marriage typically was a liability for women in education but an asset for men. Even by 1940 only 22% of female teachers were married. In 1928 the NEA found that about three fifths of urban districts prohibited hiring married teachers, and half forbade married teachers from continuing in their jobs. The situation grew worse during the Depression, as thousands of districts passed new bans against employing married women.

The Progressive Movement

Between 1920 and 1945, educators were influenced by the progressive movement in American politics and social life. **Progressivism** called for the application of human and material resources to improve Americans' quality of life. Applied to education, progressive ideals meant that the needs and interests of students rather than of teachers should be the focus of everything that happens in schools. Progressive teachers relied more on class discussions, debates, and demonstrations than on direct instruction and rote learning from textbooks. Teachers also experimented with individualized instruction and curricula that involved students in practical experiences and relevant learning outside the classroom. Students were responsible for maximizing their own potential, with the teacher's role being that of a helper and guide.

In 1921, to encourage students' creativity, decision making, and independent thinking, Helen Parkhurst implemented what was to become known as the Dalton Laboratory Plan in Dalton, Massachusetts. The Dalton Plan organized the school day into subject labs. Students from 5th through 12th grades set their own daily schedules. Officials turned off the bells, eliminated schedules, and disbanded traditional classrooms. The plan gave students some control over their learning and relied on their interests to promote learning (Edwards, 1991; Parkhurst, 1922).

The greatest proponent of progressive education was John Dewey (1859–1952), whose Laboratory School at the University of Chicago scientifically tested child-centered curricula and instructional approaches. As will be discussed in the next chapter in connection with educational philosophy, Dewey wanted to avoid teaching subjects in isolation, favoring the idea of integrating them during social activities, such as cooking, sewing, or building a playhouse, so that students might learn about cooperation among human beings (Kliebard, 1986).

Teachers practicing progressive techniques were not united by a single cohesive educational philosophy. After 1945 and until about 1960, critics expressed dissatisfaction with progressive education because it lacked a common set of principles and a body of knowledge. Some people said that progressivism risked pandering to individual happiness at the expense of intellectual rigor and placed Americans at a disadvantage in international competition. Nevertheless, the concept of child-centered education remained and has been revived in educational reforms of the 1990s.

Helen Parkhurst

John Dewey

Why did progressivism enjoy a revival in the 1990s? Does the culture of teaching really discourage change?

Despite the progressive movement, innovations often were abandoned for more traditional instructional behavior. Industrial education, for example, was supposed to help students appreciate the philosophy and methods at the heart of industrial society; instead, it rapidly became vocational education, concentrating on transmitting skills. Activities intended to make learning concrete soon became substitutes for academics (Crein, 1988).

Contemporary critics claim that teachers and teaching have been, and continue to be, virtually impervious to change. Larry Cuban (1984) wrote,

> I have been in many classrooms in the last decade. When I watched teachers in secondary schools a flash of recognition jumped out of my memory and swept over me. What I saw was almost exactly what I remembered of the junior and senior high school classrooms that I sat in as a student and as a teacher in the mid 1950s. This acute sense of recall about how teachers were teaching occurred in many different schools. How, I asked myself, could teaching over a forty-year period seem . . . almost unchanged? (p. 1)

Cuban outlined three reasons for the durability of teacher-centered instruction: (a) schools are a form of social control and sorting; (b) the organizational structure of the school and classroom drives teachers to adopt instructional practices that change little over time; and (c) the culture of teaching tilts toward stability and a reluctance to change.

Education in the National Interest

World War II caused an exodus of men and women from teaching. By 1945 more than one third of the teachers employed in 1941 had left for more lucrative professions in business, industry, and government. Approximately 109,000 individuals employed on emergency teaching certificates assumed some of those positions. Some schools were closed completely or open only for short terms. Some subjects had to be eliminated from the curriculum because there were no qualified staff to teach them.

David Brinkley (1988) describes life in the Washington, D.C., public schools during World War II as a difficult and somewhat unprofessional situation:

> The District School Board ordered its teachers to serve as wardens to protect their school buildings at night. But no one was sure what the buildings were to be protected from or what to protect them with. One teacher was ordered to remain in the school all night and maintain communication with her principal through a telephone inside a locked closet to which she was denied a key. The buildings being unheated at night, the teachers were told to report for duty with blankets and heavy coats. One teacher spent the nights in a chair on the front steps of Eastern High School bundled in blankets, a shotgun in her lap and a German shepherd lying on each side. Another, ordered by her principal to report for duty, agreed and politely asked what she was to do. His response, in tones of some tough drill sergeant he must have seen in the movies: "This is war. It is not the time for subordinates to ask questions." (p. 98)

From 1940 to 1960, many critics expressed dissatisfaction with American education by focusing on progressive education techniques that generally

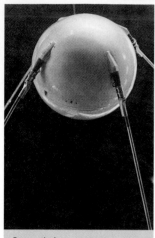

Sputnik I

attempted to make education "practical" and relevant to daily life. Walter Lippmann, for instance, argued that progressive education had no common principles, no common body of knowledge, and no common moral and intellectual discipline (Adams, 1977). In 1957, the Soviet Union's launch of the first satellite, Sputnik, was taken as evidence of our intellectual and moral flabbiness and led to intensified efforts to beef up education in the United States. Schools, critics charged, simply had not been teaching students to think. What we needed was greater emphasis on mathematics, science, and foreign languages.

In the **National Defense Education Act (NDEA)**, passed in 1958, the federal government took the lead in improving schools. The NDEA provided funds for upgrading the teaching of mathematics, science, and foreign languages, as well as for the establishment of guidance services. It also provided low-interest loans to college students. Not since the establishment of the National Science Foundation in 1950 had the federal government moved so decisively in education policy. The passage of the NDEA marked the beginning of a pattern of federal leadership in education. The Vocational Education Act (1963), the Elementary and Secondary Education Act (1965), the Higher Education Act (1965), the Education Professions Development Act (1967), and other federal legislation and programs emphasized our national commitment to progress in education.

In 1979 President Jimmy Carter and Congress split the Department of Health, Education, and Welfare into two federal departments: Health and Human Services and the Department of Education. President Carter appointed Shirley M. Hufstedler as the first Secretary of Education, thus raising the Department of Education to Cabinet level. As early as 1983, President Ronald Reagan was trying to dismantle the Department of Education, and in particular the National Institute of Education. Political conservatives aimed to curtail the federal government's involvement in education matters they believed were better left to states and localities. President George Bush's Education Summit, planned and carried out in cooperation with the National Governors' Association, signaled that public education was to be largely a state, not a federal, matter.

How does American partisan politics affect education?

According to Michael Kirst, policy researcher at Stanford University, President Clinton tried to expand the federal role (Kirst, personal communication, September 5, 1996). He created a new unit called the National Education School Improvement Council (NESIC) and charged the agency to promulgate and certify curricular content, student performance standards, and opportunity-to-learn standards. Congress passed Goals 2000 and the Improving American Schools Act (formerly the Elementary and Secondary Education Act) and created a National Skills Standards Board to address vocational education. These actions were intended to encourage states and localities to address (1) what was to be taught in schools, (2) how student success was to be judged, and (3) how schools would be funded to create learning opportunities for children. Education was a key issue for both Republicans and Democrats in the 1996 presidential campaign.

How did Schools Change During the Modern Era?

The number of schools rose dramatically after World War I, but resources for funding schools rose and fell with the economy. The early Depression years (1929–1932) had a profoundly negative effect on funding for schools and colleges. By 1933–34, school expenditures had dropped more than 30% in many states. School funding in Michigan and Mississippi fell 41% and 52% respectively. This meant that some rural schools' budgets were reduced by one fifth to one half. Teachers' salaries were cut, and some teachers were even paid in 4-year-maturity state bonds rather than by cash or check. Colleges and universities also were hurt by the Depression, particularly state-funded institutions, whose funding was cut by about one third. Between 1931 and 1934 total enrollment in higher education declined by 8.5% (Link & Catton, 1963). Changes in the modern era aimed to make schools more efficient and cost effective while extending public education further and creating educational alternatives.

Consolidation and Bureaucratization

Most schools were small and rural until a program of consolidation began after World War II. Typically, one teacher taught all ages of students in the same room, and each student progressed at his own pace. Rural one-room schools were ungraded until about the 1920s, when they began to fall by the wayside as school districts were combined to concentrate resources and centralize administration. The number of separate school districts was reduced from about 130,000 in 1930 to fewer than 15,000 in 1995 (U.S. Department of Education, 1996). This consolidation meant that students had to be bused to central locations, such as huge regional high schools, often over long distances.

As consolidation increased in rural areas, bureaucratization became the hallmark of urban schooling. Boston, Massachusetts, and New York City developed complex networks of schools with distinct roles and rules, standardized curricula and procedures for each grade level, and administrative ideologies bent on efficiency, rationality, precision, and impartiality. Large cities patterned their school systems on the factory model: the single superintendent with a few foremen to supervise hundreds of operatives (Tyack & Hansot, 1982).

At the same time, many people within the system struggled against bureaucratization. Leonard Covello, teacher and principal in New York's East Harlem, for example, worked to connect schools to communities. He was among the pioneers of bilingual education, storefront schools, community advisory committees for schools, multicultural education, programs to prevent school dropouts, school-based community service, and political action programs. He also criticized the misapplication of IQ tests to culturally different populations (Tyack & Hansot, 1982).

Cultural Awareness

Schools were embedded in communities, but as Marcus Foster demonstrated in the mid-1960s and 1970s, relationships between the two could be both nurturing and calamitous. Foster was a teacher and principal in Philadelphia, Pennsylvania, and then superintendent of the Oakland, California, schools. An African American, Foster worked with militant community leaders to try to make schools more responsive to the needs of the people they served. His success in helping others succeed is legendary. Foster instituted honors courses with scholarships for college-bound students, expanded vocational courses and tied them to employment, sponsored Philadelphia's first course in African-American history, built an educational and recreation center in the community, and generally mobilized people to get involved with their schools. On November 6, 1973, as he left the weekly meeting of Oakland's Board of Education, Foster was murdered. The Symbionese Liberation Army (SLA), a small radical organization, claimed credit for the shooting.

New Links Between Schools and Communities

A sociological view of connections between schools and communities gained credence in the 1960s and 1970s. A survey conducted in 1965 by James S. Coleman, then of Johns Hopkins University, and Ernest Q. Campbell of Vanderbilt University suggested that disparities in students' academic achievement scores were due more to the racial composition of a school than to school facilities, teacher salaries, and per-pupil expenditures. The 1965 Civil Rights Commission found that 75% of African-American urban elementary students were in all-African-American schools, while 83% of European-American urban elementary students were in all-European-American schools. Another finding was that African-American students performed better in desegregated schools than in those that were "racially isolated" (Cremin, 1988).

> **Is equal educational opportunity the key to economic and social equality?**

As technological progress accelerated, people perceived more links between schools and society, specifically, the world of work. In 1986 the Carnegie Forum on Education and the Economy argued that weak schools threatened America's ability to compete in world markets: "Large numbers of American children are in limbo—ignorant of the past and unprepared for the future. Many are dropping out—not just out of school but out of productive society" (p. 2).

Schools that did work were thought to be alike in several ways (Bossert, 1985):

- They had climates that were safe and free of disciplinary problems.

- Teachers expected that students could achieve and communicated these expectations publicly.

- The schools emphasized basic skills with plenty of time for students to work.

- School personnel monitored and evaluated student progress.

- Successful schools had strong principals who served as program leaders.

By 1987, 39 million students were enrolled in elementary and secondary schools and more than 12 million in institutions of higher education. As in the past, the majority of these students attended public schools. In 1996, there were 46 million K–12 students in the public schools, another 6 million in private schools, and 14 million students in post-secondary institutions (U.S. Department of Education, 1996b).

Rise of Preschools

The preschool movement began anew in the United States in the 1920s and rapidly diversified. The American version of the nursery school, patterned on the earlier experiences of the British, stimulated interest in educating the whole child instead of simply providing custodial care. Inspired by the work of Rachel and Margaret McMillan in England, some farsighted teachers, such as Patty Smith Hill of Columbia Teachers College, created models that would guide the development of more schools.

By the depths of the Depression, the country needed good child care, and unemployed teachers needed jobs. Financial support from the federal government in the early 1930s stimulated the formation of many more nursery schools throughout the nation. By 1937 the Works Progress Administration (WPA) was responsible for 1,472 nursery schools with an enrollment of 39,873 children. At the same time, the WPA sponsored 3,270 parent education classes with an enrollment of 51,093 (Cremin, 1988).

During World War II the WPA programs were phased out and replaced by programs that were more oriented to child care than to education. By 1946 the majority of these child care centers closed when federal funds were withdrawn. As women continued to enter the workforce, the need for child care prompted the establishment of many private preschools. Today, enrollment in private prekindergartens continues to exceed that in public preschool programs.

When President Lyndon Johnson launched his war on poverty during the 1960s, education programs such as Head Start were the weapons he chose. Since its inception, **Head Start** has had a dual focus: to stimulate the development and academic achievement of 4- and 5-year-olds from low-income families and to involve parents in the education of their children. Head Start remains one of the most popular preschool programs. In 1995 the Clinton administration proposed spending $4 billion for Head Start, an increase of $700 million over 1994 and a 45% increase since 1993. Head Start served

Why has the demand for preschool education increased dramatically in recent years?

about 840,000 children and their families in 1995, up from 621,000 in 1992. You can find information about Head Start (**http://www.latech.edu/tech/rural/grants/health/health01.html**).

The growing interest in early childhood education and the success of experimental public kindergartens prompted many school districts to establish programs for 5-year-olds. At the beginning of the 20th century, there were 225,394 kindergartners in the United States, 58% of whom were in public schools (Cremin, 1988).

In contrast to the declining elementary and secondary enrollments during the 1970s and early 1980s, preprimary education enrollment grew substantially. Between 1970 and 1980, preprimary enrollment of 3- to 5-year-olds rose by 19%; between 1980 and 1995 it increased by another 32%. With the increase in the number of preprimary students has come an increase in full-day programs for these children. In 1995 about 48% of preschoolers attended school all day, compared with 32% in 1980 and 17% in 1970 (U.S. Department of Education, 1996).

The Middle School Movement

The housing of grades kindergarten through 8 in elementary school and grades 9 through 12 in secondary school, or the 8-4 pattern, was for many years the most common organizational scheme for schools in the United States. During the early 1900s, however, some school systems began to experiment with other ways of grouping their students. Although several organizational patterns were tested, the 6-3-3 pattern, or clustering of grades 7 through 9 in a junior high school—first tried in the cities of Columbus, Ohio, and Berkeley, California—proved to be quite popular in the years following World War I. By the 1950s and 1960s, many school districts began moving 9th-graders back into high schools and replacing their junior high schools with intermediate or middle schools (Cremin, 1988). Today many school systems continue to group 9th-graders with high school students in a 4-4-4 pattern. But their middle group of students (5th- through 8th-graders) are clustered in a variety of ways with both the primary and high school grades. The middle-school movement has resulted in significant changes in curriculum and instruction for students in transition between late childhood and early adolescence.

Comprehensive High Schools

After the 1870s private academies declined in number and were replaced by public high schools. A court case in Kalamazoo, Michigan, validated the right of school districts to establish and support public high schools with tax monies. By 1890 about 203,000 students were enrolled in public high schools, and 95,000 were enrolled in private academies. Together, these two groups made up less than 6% of the population of students 14 to 17 years of age, yet they constituted the entire potential pool of college entrants. In contrast, by 1995 more than 93% of 14- to 17-year-olds were enrolled in secondary schools. Twelve and a half million were enrolled in public secondary schools and 1.3 million in private schools (U.S. Department of Education, 1996).

Although every high school is unique, they all share a common feature—a multiplicity of course offerings for a student body having diverse needs, interests, and abilities. High schools are designed to be comprehensive in their offerings. Arthur Powell, Eleanor Farrar, and David Cohen (1985) liken the comprehensive high school to a shopping mall "governed by consumer choice" (p. 309). They see high schools wanting to maximize their holding power by satisfying consumers. In this metaphor, teachers are salespeople, classrooms are stores, students are customers. This outlook has led to a variety of course offerings, or "specialty shops" for high achievers, students with special needs, troublemakers, students with vocational and technical interests, athletes, and others.

What factors have contributed to the growth of the homeschool movement? Why do critics oppose homeschooling?

Homeschooling

An educational process reminiscent of colonial times, homeschooling is an alternative to on-site public education. Most states allow children to be taught at home, but, as will be explained in Chapter 11, such arrangements are regulated in various ways. Typically, parents must demonstrate that the education their children receive at home is equivalent to what they would receive in the public schools in terms of the books used, tests given, and time spent on studies.

Like private schools, home schools have grown in number for both pedagogical and ideological reasons. Estimates of the numbers of students served in such environments range from 200,000 to 300,000. The majority of these students tend to be from middle-class European-American families located in the western and southern parts of the United States. The curriculum services used by homeschoolers indicate that the majority of families exercising the homeschool option do so for religious reasons.

Not surprisingly, homeschooling appears to have gotten a boost from the telecommunications industry. A quick tour on the Web will reveal hundreds of sites related to homeschooling. For example, see **http://www.ici.net/ cust_pages/taadah/taadah.html** for one view of Islamic homeschooling.

Adult Education

Adult education took many forms in industrial America. Factories taught safety. Settlement houses taught immigrants and their children English and the skills needed to survive in a foreign culture. And beyond the cities, agricultural extension agents helped farmers improve their methods of growing crops and raising livestock.

The **Chautauqua movement** was the preeminent adult education movement of its time. What began as a Methodist Sunday School Institute in 1874 at Lake Chautauqua, New York, flourished as a secular educational institution through World War I. It was not "a single, unified, coherent plan, developed and directed by one man or a group of men. It was, fundamentally, a response to an unspoken demand, a sensitive alertness to the cravings of millions of people for 'something better'" (Gould, 1961, p. vii). Through the years, the Chautauqua movement pioneered the establishment of civic music associations, correspondence courses, lecture-study groups, youth groups, and reading circles. It responded to a vast need for adult education, particularly in rural areas of the United States. The movement may also have been, however, yet another indication of the American preoccupation with self-fulfillment and social advancement. Explore the history of the Chautauqua Institution online (**http://www.chautauqua-inst.org/**).

Public schools and adult education became intertwined at the turn of the century. Progressives strengthened the philosophical and practical connections between community and school, perhaps most notably via the Gary Plan. After 1907, William Wirt, a school administrator in Gary, Indiana, worked to make public schools the centers of life in Gary neighborhoods. His intent was to unify the general, vocational, intellectual, and moral education of youth. By adhering to a "platoon system" of organization, students could be at gymnasiums, playgrounds, and assembly halls, as well as at schools. Gary schools could then accommodate twice as many students as did traditional schools (Cremin, 1988). By 1929 the Gary Plan had spread to more than 200 cities in 41 states. The plan faded a few years later when people opposed it as a form of cheapened education for their children.

More important than introducing progressive philosophy, the hard times of the 1930s forced people to use every resource at hand to help young and old alike work their way out of the Depression. Many programs made it appropriate for adults as well as children to congregate at school. The federally funded community education project associated with the Tennessee Valley Authority (TVA) in the mid-1930s, for example, tried to improve life in the rural TVA area by providing educational opportunities that directly related to community needs, and that served the entire community not just its youth (Minzey & LeTarte, 1979). This meant helping adults learn basic literacy and job skills.

Adult education will likely become more important as we move into the 21st century. In the private sector, more and more corporations offer incentives for job-related education and for postsecondary adult education. Volunteer efforts such as Literacy Volunteers of America, Reading Is Fundamental, and AmeriCorps also underscore the importance of adult education. AmeriCorps, a national service program for adults initiated during the first Clinton administration, had 20,000 members by 1995. AmeriCorps programs address education, public safety, environmental, community, and human needs. In exchange for a year's service, members receive a living allowance, health insurance, child care services, and a cash benefit for further education.

Opportunities for Higher Education

Ongoing pressures of industrialization in the North, the need for postwar development in the South, and the Morrill Act of 1862 combined to stimulate higher education in America. The higher education system offered a variety of alternatives for people who wanted to continue their education beyond high school. Technical training produced graduates for occupations and trades, while colleges and universities educated people for the professions, research, business and industry, and virtually every field that people would want to explore. Although higher education remained largely a man's world, by 1890 about 2,500 women a year were graduating from college.

The desires of the growing middle class for upward mobility stimulated colleges and universities to produce experts, specialists, and managers having greater skills and more degrees. Consequently, new professional schools—in dentistry, architecture, business administration, engineering, mining, forestry, education, and social work—emerged alongside the older professions of law, medicine, and theology and the newer professions of psychology, economics, and political science.

Why has the demand for higher education and adult education steadily increased?

The formation of the Association of American Universities in 1900 marked the beginning of nationwide efforts to raise academic standards in postsecondary education. Slightly fewer than 1,000 colleges and universities existed in 1900, with a combined enrollment of 238,000 students. By 1920 there were 1,041 institutions of higher education, but enrollment had more than doubled to nearly 600,000 students. The prosperity of the 1920s saw increases in state aid to public universities, colleges, and junior colleges, which made possible improvements in facilities for graduate and specialized training and technical education. (Link & Catton, 1963).

The years 1940 to 1960 yielded phenomenal growth in higher education. Enrollment increased from 1.5 million students to about 3.5 million. After World War II, with the passage of the Servicemen's Readjustment Act of 1944 (G.I. Bill of Rights), enrollment increased further. The McCarthy Era—so named for the anticommunist movement led by Senator Joseph McCarthy of Wisconsin—had a negative impact on academic freedom. In 1948 and 1949, many states imposed loyalty oaths on teachers and established committees to examine textbooks for subversive materials. Kansas, Massachusetts, and Pennsylvania authorized schools to dismiss teachers for disloyalty. Maryland, New York, and New Jersey forbade teachers to join certain organizations thought to be subversive.

Many Americans took advantage of higher education in the 1960s, 1970s, and 1980s. In 1994, there were 15.4% more students enrolled in all institutions of higher education than there were in 1981; 40.8% of those students were enrolled in public 4-year institutions (U.S. Department of Education, 1996).

The ratio of average annual earnings of college graduates compared to high school graduates indicates that postsecondary education remains a good investment. The U.S. Department of Education (1996b) reports that in 1994, the median annual income of adults ages 25 to 34 who had completed at least a bachelor's degree was substantially higher than those who had only completed high school (52% and 86% higher for males and females, respectively).

WHAT ISSUES AROSE IN CURRICULUM DEVELOPMENT?

Advocates for common schools after the Civil War tried to encourage citizens to send their children to public schools. But deep divisions along class, religious, and ethnic lines made the task difficult. No single philosophy seemed broad enough to permit the integration of all Americans into the schools. Social changes in the late 19th century—the growth of cities, popular journalism, and railroads—forced previously isolated, self-contained communities to live in a bigger world. As we shall discuss in Chapter 10, these conditions stimulated the struggle for control of American curricula. Figure 3.2 presents a sampling of influential books of the 20th century that stimulated debate about what and how students should be taught.

Standardization of the Curriculum

In 1893 the **Committee of Ten on Secondary School Studies** (established by the National Education Association in 1892) attempted to standardize high school curricula. Chaired by Charles Eliot, president of Harvard University, the Committee of Ten prescribed four different academic courses of study for high school students: classical, modern languages, English, and Latin-scientific. The committee urged high schools to provide 4 years of English and 3 years each of history, science, mathematics, and a foreign language. Although the avowed intent of the curriculum was to put modern academic subjects and classical ones on an equal plane, not to sort students, critics viewed it as a program for failure for all but the college-bound student.

In 1895, the **Committee of Fifteen** took on the curriculum of elementary schools. The chairman of the committee was William Torrey Harris, U.S. Commissioner of Education, who had established the first successful public school kindergarten in St. Louis in 1873 and gave America the graded school (Kliebard, 1986). Harris expressed strong belief in the value of a curriculum that focused on "the five windows of the soul"—grammar, literature and art, mathematics, geography, and history. Harris recommended that knowledge of Western cultural heritage be transmitted to students via standard literary works. He viewed the role of school as an efficient transmitter of cultural heritage through a curriculum that was graded, structured, and cumulative.

Diversification of the Curriculum

Efforts to diversify the curriculum paralleled efforts to standardize it. While some educators were out to safeguard tradition, others, such as G. Stanley Hall, pressed for making the curriculum responsive to stages of human development and to the process of learning. Social efficiency experts—David Sneddon, Ross Finney, and Franklin Bobbitt, for example—advocated training for specialized skills, much like industrial training. Social

John Dewey, *The Child and the Curriculum* (1902)

W. E. B. DuBois, *The Souls of Black Folk* (1904)

Booker T. Washington, *The Future of the American Negro* (1907)

Maria Montessori, *The Discovery of the Child* (1913)

John Dewey, *Democracy and Education* (1916)

H. Parkhurst, *Education on the Dalton Plan* (1922)

George S. Counts, *Dare the School Build a New Social Order?* (1932)

William C. Bagley, *Education and the Emergent Man* (1934)

Robert M. Hutchins, *The Higher Learning in America* (1936)

Harold Benjamin, *The Saber-Tooth Curriculum* (1939)

Ralph Tyler, *Basic Principles of Curriculum and Instruction* (1949)

Arthur Bestor, *Academic Wastelands* (1953); *The Restoration of Learning* (1955)

Theodore Brameld, *Toward a Reconstructed Philosophy of Education* (1956)

James B. Conant, *The American High School Today* (1959)

Hyman G. Rickover, *Education and Freedom* (1959)

Jerome S. Bruner, *The Process of Education* (1960)

A. S. Neill, *Summerhill: A Radical Approach to Child Rearing* (1960)

Paul Goodman, *Growing Up Absurd* (1960)

John W. Gardner, *Excellence: Can We Be Equal and Excellent Too?* (1961)

Robert M. Hutchins, *A Conversation on Education* (1963)

John Holt, *How Children Fail* (1964)

B. F. Skinner, *The Technology of Teaching* (1968)

Jean Piaget, *Science of Education and the Psychology of the Child* (1969)

Herbert R. Kohl, *The Open Classroom* (1969)

W. Glasser, *Schools Without Failure* (1969)

Alvin Toffler, *Future Shock* (1970)

Paulo Friere, *Pedagogy of the Oppressed* (1970)

Ivan Illich, *Deschooling Society* (1971)

B. F. Skinner, *Beyond Freedom and Dignity* (1971)

Charles A. Silberman, *Crisis in the Classroom* (1971)

John Holt, *How Children Learn* (1972)

Jonathan Kozol, *Free Schools* (1972)

Maxine Greene, *Landscapes of Learning* (1978)

Mortimer Adler, *Paideia Proposal* (1982)

Michael Apple, *Education and Power* (1982)

Diane Ravitch, *The Troubled Crusade* (1983)

John I. Goodlad, *A Place Called School* (1984)

Philip Coombes, *The World Crisis in Education* (1985)

A. G. Powell, E. Farrar, and D. K. Cohen, *The Shopping Mall High School* (1985)

Theodore R. Sizer, *Horace's Compromise* (1985)

Elliot W. Eisner, *The Educational Imagination* (1985)

Allan Bloom, *The Closing of the American Mind* (1987)

E. D. Hirsch, Jr., *Cultural Literacy* (1987)

Maxine Greene, *The Dialectic of Freedom* (1988)

Phillip C. Schlechty, *Schools for the 21st Century* (1990)

Jonathan Kozol, *Savage Inequalities* (1991)

Should the curriculum preserve traditional culture or be an instrument for change?

meliorists such as Lester Frank Ward viewed the curriculum as an instrument for producing social change.

Progressives, such as John Dewey, sought expanded, differentiated curricula; individualized school programs; and the use of schools to solve various social and political problems, such as those of racial, ethnic, class, and gender equality (Cremin, 1988). Progressive concerns were fueled by studies suggesting that the standard

FIGURE 3.2

Some Books that Influenced the Development of Education in the 20th Century

How might you use these resources to understand the curriculum you plan to teach?

curricula did not fit the needs of increasingly heterogeneous classrooms. Dewey and others called for pluralism in curricula, meaning that all students were to learn a common culture, but other cultural views were to be both accepted and encouraged. By the late 1880s eight states had statutes permitting bilingual instruction in German and English in public schools. In 1872 Oregon legalized monolingual German schools (Tyack & Hansot, 1982).

Americanization efforts began to intensify in 1914 at the start of World War I and continued into the early 1920s. Schools treated southern and eastern European immigrants as a special group requiring a special, nonacademic education. The curriculum emphasized American government, home economics, and vocational training. During World War I, German was eliminated from the curriculum, and schools began to give report card grades not just for academic achievements but also for students' behavior. Citizenship grades were thought to be a "measure of [students'] dedication to the creation of a happy harmonious America" (Carlson, 1975, p. 123).

The Smith–Hughes Act, signed by President Woodrow Wilson in 1917, promoted job-skill training in public schools. The bill permitted federal funds to be used to train and pay teachers of agricultural, trade, industrial, and home economics subjects. Some saw Smith–Hughes as a natural link to the world of work. But Dewey, Harris, DuBois, and others argued that predetermining courses of study for students could restrict their choices and their natural potential.

The NEA's Commission on the Reorganization of Secondary Education in 1918 set a new direction for high schools. Its Cardinal Principles of Secondary Education called for comprehensive institutions that served all social groups and trained for many occupations (Commission on the Reorganization of Secondary Education, 1918). High schools were no longer to be just for the college bound. As the curriculum diversified, students took different courses and different programs depending on their abilities and interests, and schools assumed more responsibilities for student welfare and vocational training.

Core Curricula and Censorship

As the curriculum increasingly focused on progressivists' concerns with developing life skills, more people began to take the school curriculum to task for its lack of coherence. Robert Maynard Hutchins, president of the University of Chicago from 1929 to 1945, for example, advocated a core curriculum emphasizing grammar, rhetoric, logic, and mathematics. He also encouraged the study of the great books of the Western world so as to provide a common core of knowledge. This theme of a common core resurfaced periodically throughout the century in debates over what schools should teach.

Curriculum reformers in the 1930s disliked what they perceived as colleges' domination of the high school curriculum, a curriculum heavy on traditional academic subjects. The Progressive Education Association launched the Eight-Year Study to examine what was being taught in high schools. This investigation, directed by Ralph Tyler, involved 3,600 students in matched pairs—1 student from an experimental secondary school and 1 from a traditional high school—from 29 high schools. The results were published in 1942 and 1943 and suggested that students in experimental secondary schools (those having a more progressive or functional orientation) achieved as well in college as did students from traditional high schools. The eight-year study stimulated educators to modify the core curriculum to prepare students for "the duties of life." It also encouraged the use of behavioral objectives (statements describing what students should know or be able to do at the end of a lesson) when developing curricula. Such objectives were to have "a lasting and profound effect on the future course of curriculum development" (Kliebard, 1986, p. 220).

Innovation and Reaction

By the 1950s critics grew vitriolic in their attacks on education in America. Arthur Bestor's *Educational Wastelands* (1953) decried the anti-intellectualism he associated with education for "life adjustment." He advocated intellectual training for the masses, not just for college-bound students (Kliebard, 1986). Life adjustment education and other progressive strategies were blamed for America's perceived intellectual failures, following upon the USSR's launch of Sputnik. Critics such as Vice Admiral Hyman G. Rickover, credited with developing the atomic submarine, attacked what they believed was America's neglect of gifted and talented students. To Rickover, education was not rigorous enough to help the United States win the Cold War.

The 1960s and 1970s spawned a host of innovative curricula and instruction methods: School Math Study Group (SMSG), Man A Course of Study (MACOS), Physical Science Study Committee (PSSC), Harvard Project Physics, Biological Science Curriculum Study (BSCS), Chemical Education Materials Study (CHEM Study), Project English, audio-lingual language laboratories, and many more. Most of these efforts tried to involve students actively in their own learning by de-emphasizing teacher-centered instruction while concentrating on methods of inquiry.

What might Vice Admiral Hyman Rickover have said about American education today?

Despite the creativity of many such programs, students—particularly low-income and minority students—seemed to be learning less in school year

Cultural Awareness

Was God or Charles Darwin to be part of the common core? William Jennings Bryan led an anti-evolution crusade in the 1920s. Bryan was concerned about the possibility of atheistic evolutionists posing as teachers in public schools and undermining the Christian faith of American school children (Link & Catton, 1963). The 1925 Scopes trial in Dayton, Tennessee, upheld states' rights to ban the teaching of evolution. Although the forces of science would prevail in transmitting this Darwinian concept, to this day the teaching of evolution in the public schools remains a contentious issue.

by year, while various estimates of the dropout rate climbed. As the country flirted with the possibility of becoming a second-rate economic power in the 1980s, everybody seemed to offer proposals for reform. The National Commission on Excellence in Education (1983) warned of a "rising tide of mediocrity." Many reform reports and proposals offered to fix public education.

How do people typically judge educational success and failure?

Despite the implication that continual reform means continual failure, American education has improved dramatically during the modern era. Schools today educate and provide a variety of services to millions of children every year. Progress has been uneven across regions of the country and across time, but there is no doubt that schools are better today than they were at the turn of the century.

Typically, judgments about educational success and failure have been guided by three factors: (a) the inputs into education, or, in a sense, the raw materials from which educated citizens are produced; (b) what occurs in schools and classrooms, or the processes of education; and (c) some measures of student learning. People have not always considered all three factors at once when judging education but traditionally they have relied on these concepts as indications of educational quality. For instance, the person who says the following is concentrating on inputs: "We have a good school. We built a new building, paid big salaries to hire the best teachers, and bought the newest books and equipment." Students' characteristics, like those of teachers, constitute another important input into the system. One who evaluates education in terms of processes might say: "The teachers and students in our school work together as inquirers. The curriculum is geared toward helping them identify important problems, collect information, and propose solutions. Teachers are always doing interesting things; it is a great school." Processes of schooling have most commonly been characterized in terms of effective teaching and delivery of the curriculum.

> **Should judgments about measuring up as a nation rest on standardized test scores?**

And the person who extols the virtues of schools because of "students' high test scores, winning football teams, and students' affection for the teachers" is judging success by outcomes. The quintessential measure of educational output is the standardized achievement test score. Joseph Rice developed the first educational achievement test in the United States in 1895. His spelling test, which he administered to more than 16,000 pupils in grades 4 to 8, consisted of 50 words. Stone's arithmetic reasoning test and Thorndike's scale for evaluating pupils' handwriting followed quickly. The Stanford Achievement Test, referred to as a "test battery," was published in

VOICES

On Being a Student in Lawrence

Author Jeanne Schinto describes educational life in Lawrence, Massachusetts, in a way that forces us to consider not how bad or good, responsive or unresponsive we believe schools are but how schools are perceived by the students who inhabit them. These students, with strong roots in other countries and other cultures, often describe their schools and their places in them more vividly and generously than would many outside observers.

When I first visited Terri Kelley at Lawrence High School a couple of years ago, her students had already left for the day, but during class time she had asked each of them to write me a letter saying all the things they wanted me to tell my readers. I have read these letters many times. They were written by immigrants and the children of immigrants from Hungary, Korea, Lebanon, Vietnam, Cambodia, Puerto Rico, and the Dominican Republic, as well as by a few descendants of the first immigrant wave. Sometimes they fill me with hope, sometimes with despair. I'm hopeful because the students themselves sound that way; on the other hand, I want to see these young people get every opportunity, and I'm afraid not all of them will.

The letters also make me proud, however—of Lawrence. It's doing a job the whole country takes credit for, but Lawrence is doing most of the work. All of America's Lawrences are. Here is one letter that is fairly typical:

Dear Ms. Schinto: I came to Lawrence in March 1990 [from Fitchburg, Massachusetts, having been born in Puerto Rico in 1977], scared to death about the rumors I heard about this beautiful city, but when I started school I loved it. I had never seen such a quiet school. I made friends quicker than I did in any other school outside the city. None of the garbage I heard was true. I was prejudiced of Lawrence just like many people are now. In fact, all most people see is drugs, violence, and all the negativity of the city. What most people fail to see is the talent hidden inside this beautiful city. Many don't see the talent of the Lawrence High School Girls Ensemble, the Honor Students who work hard every day to make it in this competitive world, or the greatness of having many races in a school where everyone is treated equally. We are privileged to be able to live in a place where we don't have to travel to another country in order to learn its customs because it's right next door.

CRITICAL THINKING

What developments in U.S. life and education following World War II affect Terri Kelley and her students? What problems and opportunities face the student who wrote to Jeanne Schinto about being a student in Lawrence, Massachusetts? In what ways might your personal history help you understand how the past influences the present?

Note. From *Huddle fever: Living in the immigrant city.* (pp. 297–298) by J. Schinto, 1995, New York: Alfred A. Knopf.

1923. It was designed as a group of survey tests in different content areas standardized on the same elementary school population. The Iowa High School Content Examination was published in 1925. Other test batteries, such as the Metropolitan Achievement Test and the California Achievement Test, followed shortly thereafter.

In the 1930s standardized aptitude and achievement tests and formal measures of school performance became the inexpensive and seemingly

BENCHMARKS

Modern U.S. Education History, 1865 to the present

1865	Thirteenth Amendment to the Constitution abolishes slavery.
	Freedman's Bureau is established.
1868	Fourteenth Amendment grants citizenship to African Americans and guarantees that "No state shall make or enforce any law which shall abridge the privileges or immunities of citizens of the United States; nor shall any state deprive any person of life, liberty, or property without due process of law; nor deny to any person within its jurisdiction the equal protection of the laws."
1870	Fifteenth Amendment grants African-American males the right to vote.
1874	Kalamazoo, Michigan, case specifies that states may establish and support public high schools with tax funds, which contribute to the secondary school movement and eventually to compulsory high school attendance laws.
1881	Booker T. Washington is named head of Tuskegee Institute in Alabama.
1890	Sioux men, women, and children are massacred by the U.S. Cavalry at Wounded Knee, South Dakota, which breaks Native-American resistance to forced assimilation.
1893–1895	The Committee of Ten on Secondary School Studies and the Committee of Fifteen on Elementary School Studies attempt to standardize public high school and elementary school curricula, respectively.
1896	In Plessy v. Ferguson, the Supreme Court rules that states can provide separate but equal public facilities, legalizing racial segregation.
1898–1900	A period of American imperialism and statecraft exists, in which Cuba, Puerto Rico, the Philippines, Hawaii, Alaska, and Pacific islands such as Midway, Guam, and Samoa become possessions of the United States.
1909	First junior high schools are established in Berkeley, California, and Columbus, Ohio. The NAACP is founded through the efforts of African-American leaders such as W. E. B. DuBois.
1910	Ella Flagg Young, PhD, the first female superintendent of schools of a large city (Chicago), becomes president of the National Education Association (NEA).
1914–1918	World War I and revolutions in Russia swell the ranks of immigrants from western, central, and eastern Europe to American cities and schools.
1916	American Federation of Teachers is formed as a labor union for classroom teachers.

1917	Congress passes the Smith-Hughes Act, which provides federal matching funds for vocational education in public high schools.
1919	Progressive Education Association is established to promote the educational philosophy of John Dewey and his followers.
1920	Nineteenth Amendment grants women the right to vote.
1925	Trial of John Scopes in Dayton, Tennessee, known as the Monkey Trial, upholds the right of states to ban the teaching of Darwin's theory of evolution.
1929–1936	Stock market crash precipitates the Great Depression. Franklin Roosevelt's New Deal provides federal aid for education of the unemployed and for school construction.
1939–1946	World War II era: Citizens of Japanese ancestry are dispossessed of their property and confined to relocation camps. Holocaust survivors and other war refugees come to the United States from southern and eastern Europe and from other countries touched by war.
1944	GI Bill provides financial aid for veterans to attend college.
1946–1953	The McCarthy Era, Korean War, and beginning of the Cold War period: The House Un-American Activities Committee (HUAC) abridges academic freedom and blacklists artists and intellectuals seen as communist sympathizers.
1950	National Science Foundation is founded.
1954	The Supreme Court rules in Brown v. Board of Education of Topeka, Kansas, that separate but equal schooling is unconstitutional on the grounds that segregated schools generate feelings of racial inferiority and are inherently unequal.
1957	President Eisenhower orders federal troops to Little Rock, Arkansas, to enforce the Supreme Court's ruling against school segregation. The Soviet Union's successful launch of Sputnik I, the first artificial satellite, sparks a race for space and a movement for curriculum reform in the United States.
1958	National Defense Education Act (NDEA) provides federal funds to improve the teaching of science, mathematics, and modern foreign languages and to help schools provide guidance services.
1959-1961	Communist revolution in Cuba brings new wave of immigration; President Kennedy and Soviet Premier Khrushchev bring the world to the brink of nuclear war over the Cuban Missile Crisis and the Berlin Wall.

Modern U.S. Education History, 1865 to the present (cont.)

1963	President Kennedy is assassinated in Dallas, Texas.
1964	The Civil Rights Act of 1964 authorizes the federal government to compel compliance with school desegregation through lawsuits and by withholding federal funds from school districts that continue to discriminate. The era of busing to end racial segregation begins. President Johnson's War on Poverty begins to increase federal funding for school programs.
1965	Elementary and Secondary Education Act (ESEA) and subsequent amendments provide funding to aid students from low-income families through programs such as Title I (Chapter I). The Economic Opportunity Act of 1965 creates Head Start as a compensatory education program.
1965–1973	Vietnam War era brings new waves of immigrants from Southeast-Asian countries. The antiwar movement leads to the "Kent State Massacre" in 1970 and profoundly affects curriculum and instruction in schools and on campuses across the United States.
1968	Dr. Martin Luther King, Jr., and Senator Robert F. Kennedy are assassinated. Bilingual Education Act enacted into law to address the special needs of students whose first language is not English.
1969	American Neil Armstrong becomes the first person to walk on the moon.
1972	Title IX of the Education Amendments Act prohibits sex discrimination in schools receiving federal funds. Indian Education and Self-Determination Act gives Native Americans more control over their schooling.
1974	Richard M. Nixon resigns the presidency of the United States as a consequence of the Watergate scandal.

objective basis for making judgments about educational success or failure. Critics pointed out that the tests contained cultural biases and limited students' chances to demonstrate their true abilities. In addition, tests could be used to drive or control curriculum, instruction, teacher assessment, and school evaluation. The 1980s and 1990s saw renewed interest in comparing students, schools, and communities nationally and internationally. The **National Assessment of Educational Progress (NAEP)**—a battery of achievement tests administered nationwide—is used as a means of charting student progress, or the lack thereof, state by state.

Modern U.S. Education History, 1865 to the present (cont.)

1975	Education of the Handicapped Act (EHA) increases federal commitment to the education of children with disabilities and establishes a basis for subsequent special education legislation.
1979–1980	Department of Education is established; the U.S. Secretary of Education becomes a Cabinet-level post.
1981	Educational Improvement and Consolidation Act (EICA) gives states greater power in allocating federal funds through block grants.
1983	National Commission on Excellence in Education issues a report, *A Nation at Risk*, which leads to new calls for educational reform to eliminate illiteracy and raise SAT scores.
1984	Perkins Vocational Education Act upgrades vocational programs in the schools.
1989	Carnegie Foundation's report, Turning Points: Preparing American Youth for the Twenty-First Century, calls for the elimination of tracking and creation of learning communities in the schools. Presidential Summit Conference on Education held in Charlottesville, Virginia, attended by President Bush and the 50 governors, who agree that "Good education makes good politics, good business, and good sense."
1992	Supreme Court rules that officially sanctioned prayers or invocations in public schools are unconstitutional.
1994	President Clinton and Congress cooperate to pass Goals 2000: Educate America Act.
1996	Second Education Summit held in Palisades, New York, attended by President Clinton, the nation's governors, and business leaders.

SUMMARY

What changes after the Civil War affected the American system of education?

1 Passion for intellectual freedom and civil liberties increased greatly when the Civil War ended. Passage of constitutional amendments changed race relations legally by ending slavery, defining citizenship, and forbidding states to deny the right to vote. Nonetheless, the customs of segregation and discrimination remained entrenched. Intellectuals and ordinary citizens led organized efforts to combat racial, ethnic, and gender discrimination wherever they existed, including in schools. The federal government exerted its influence to educate ex-slaves and to reconstruct a war-ravaged nation.

2 By the beginning of the twentieth century, critics initiated what was to become a sustained attack on public schools, particularly in the cities. Increasingly educators looked to science for answers to their problems, engaging in research on teaching and learning and using techniques of scientific management to run the schools.

3 From the late 19th century on, schools were embedded in a society that demonstrated in many ways the increasing value of education. The increasing availability of newspapers, books, and magazines stimulated and supported people's desires to learn. The development of radio, motion pictures, television, and other forms of mass communication made informal or out-of-school education more pervasive than ever before.

Who are "We the People"?

4 After the Civil War, the population of the United States grew rapidly, most noticeably in the cities and industrialized areas. As Fuchs (1990) observed, because America was meant to be inclusive of all, the country became a kaleidoscope of race, ethnicity, and civic culture. Schools were supported to shape the pieces into a coherent social design—a design that included Native Americans, European Americans, African Americans, Hispanic Americans, Asian Americans, other Americans, exceptional learners, and women.

How did teaching change after the Civil War?

5 Following the Civil War, most teachers were young, poorly paid, and rarely educated beyond elementary subjects. Teaching was not considered a desirable job, and teacher turnover was high. Efforts to professionalize teaching began during the 19th century, as expectations of teachers broadened to include less subjective qualifications. Teachers also gained a measure of economic independence. At the same time, they lost managerial and curricular control of schools and schooling.

6 Between 1920 and 1945, educators were influenced by the progressive movement. Progressive teachers served as helpers and guides, relying more on class discussions, debates, demonstrations, and individualized learning than on direct instruction and rote learning from textbooks. Nonetheless, innovations often were abandoned for more traditional instructional behavior.

7 In the 1960s, schools served as battlegrounds in the War on Poverty, in desegregation, and in the quest for racial equality. The federal government exerted its influence to end segregation, to support the needs of children living in poverty, to promote racial and sexual equity, to secure entitlements for students with disabilities, to promote bilingual–bicultural programs, and to provide career education opportunities. The New Federalism of the 1980s returned to states and localities both the power and financial responsibility for educational programs. This trend has continued in the 1990s.

8 The Progressive Movement flourished in American education from about 1920 to 1945. Progressive teachers were not united by a single philosophy, but in general they tried to make the needs of students the focus of their instruction. They relied less on lectures and rote learning and more on class discussions, demonstrations, and other practical methods to encourage learning.

9 With the conclusion of World War II, a booming economy and the continuing spirit of nationalism fueled human and material investment in public education. The federal government exerted strong and continuing support for elementary and secondary schools and for a host of post-secondary and community education programs.

10 "Civilization" spread across the frontier in the form of one-room schools. As time passed and communities grew, people expected schools not only to eradicate ignorance but also to minimize differences among people and to ameliorate the effects of poverty and discrimination. Schooling was viewed as a way to get ahead.

11 Rapid industrialization in post–Civil War America created immense demands for workers who were willing and able to produce goods cheaply and quickly and to offer services efficiently. Public school teachers and school administrators taught immigrants, members of minority groups, and those from impoverished circumstances skills of literacy and numeracy as they transmitted the work ethic.

How did schools change during the modern era?

12 Wars and economic depressions have had dramatic effects on both the adults and the young in schools. Prior to World War II, for example, one teacher taught all ages of students in the same room, and each progressed at his or her own pace. These one-room schools began to fall by the wayside as school districts were combined to concentrate resources and centralize administration. Consolidation meant that students had to be bused to central locations, such as huge regional high schools, often over long distances.

13 The concept of school developed continually over time. Preschools acknowledged the special needs of young children. Middle schools were structured to help young people make the transition between childhood and early adolescence. Comprehensive high schools were established to meet the diverse needs, interests, and abilities of older students. Interest in home-schooling emerged in large part out of parents' desires to instill their own religious values in their children. Adult education grew and flourished as more and more people recognized needs for training and education that were not being met by traditional colleges and universities.

14 With technological advances, people have perceived more links between schools and the world of work. The 1986 Carnegie Forum on Education and the Economy argued that weak schools threatened America's ability to compete in world markets. Schools that worked were thought to be alike in several ways: (1) They were safe and free of disciplinary problems. (2) Teachers expected that students could achieve and communicated these expectations publicly. (3) They emphasized basic skills. (4) School personnel monitored and evaluated student progress. (5) They had strong principals who served as program leaders (Bossert, 1985).

15 Higher education has grown continually, providing increasingly varied access to adults. Institutions of higher education provide technical training in occupations and trades and academic preparation in the professions, research, business and industry, and a variety of other fields.

What issues arose in curriculum development?

16 School curriculum has often reflected the nation's moods and values as well as its knowledge. Public schools, as defined in terms of teachers and curriculum, have been criticized routinely for trying to be and to do too much. Efforts to standardize the curriculum, to diversify course offerings, and to integrate different cultural views in course materials have been among major concerns.

How do people typically judge educational success and failure?

17 Those having responsibilities for regulation and control of public education have come to view educational success and failure in terms of what goes in, what goes on, and what comes out of schools.

TERMS AND CONCEPTS

black codes, *p. 83*
Brown v. Board of Education of *Topeka, Kansas, p. 96*
Bureau of Indian Affairs (BIA), *p. 89*
Chautauqua movement, *p. 111*
Committee of Fifteen, *p. 114*
Committee of Ten on Secondary School Studies, *p. 114*
Elementary and Secondary Education Act (ESEA), *p. 87*
exclusion act, *p. 99*
Freedman's Bureau, *p. 83*
Head Start, *p. 109*
Hispanic, *p. 97*

Improving America's Schools Act (IASA), *p. 87*
Indian Self-Determination and Educational Assistance Act, *p. 92*
National Assessment of Educational Progress (NAEP), *p. 122*
National Association for the Advancement of Colored People (NAACP), *p. 84*
National Defense Education Act (NDEA), *p. 106*
Plessy v. Ferguson, p. 96
progressivism, *p. 104*
Title IX, *p. 102*
Women's Educational Equity Act (WEEA), *p. 102*

REFLECTIVE PRACTICE

The psychologist William James, professor at Harvard, was asked by the Harvard Corporation to give several public lectures on psychology to Cambridge Teachers. The passage below was taken from one of his talks to teachers.

In the general activity and uprising of ideal interests which every one with an eye for fact can discern all about us in American life, there is perhaps no more promising feature than the fermentation which for a dozen years or more has been going on among the teachers. In whatever sphere of education their functions may lie, there is to be seen among them a really inspiring searching of the heart about the highest concerns of their profession. The renovation of nations begins always at the top, among the reflective members of the State, and spreads slowly outward and downward. The teachers of this country, one may say, have its future in their hands. The earnestness which they at present show in striving to enlighten and strengthen themselves is an index of the nation's probabilities of advance in all ideal directions. The outward organization which we have in our United States is perhaps, on the whole, the best organization that exists in any country. The State school systems give a diversity and flexibility, an opportunity for experiment and keenness of competition, nowhere else to be found on such an important scale. The independence of so many of the colleges and universities; the give and take of students and instructors between them all; their emulation, and their happy organic relations to the lower schools; the traditions of instruction in them, evolved from the older American recitation-method (and so avoiding on the one hand the pure lecture-system prevalent in Germany and Scotland, which considers too little the individual student, and yet not involving the sacrifice of the instructor to the individual student, which the English tutorial system would seem too often to entail),—all these things (to say nothing of that coeducation of the sexes in whose benefits so many of us heartily believe), all these things, I say, are most happy features of our scholastic life, and from them the most sanguine auguries may be drawn (James, 1899, pp. 3–4).

Issues, Problems, Dilemmas, Opportunities

If you were asked to identify the one or two factors in society that have most influenced change in the education system James described, what might they be?

Perceive and Value

If you had ancestors who were educated in American schools at the turn of the century, do you think they might have agreed with James about the superiority of American schools? Why or why not? If some of your ancestors were in the United States at that time but were largely unschooled, what might they have thought about his perceptions?

Know and Act

How might you respond to someone who argues that the problems we face in public education today are not a result of changes in the schools over the last 100 years or so but rather the *lack* of change in schools? Where might you look for evidence to buttress your argument?

Evaluate

If we take James's remarks at face value, then we must conclude that he believed the American educational system was without peer. He seems to make that judgment based on several criteria. Can you identify his bases for the claim of

American superiority? Which, if any, of these claims are made routinely today? Which, if any, seem hopelessly out-of-date, and why?

ONLINE ACTIVITY

One's view of history often depends on where one stands. If you are stuck in one place, you might want to use the Web to help you take another perspective. We suggest that you stand at the site of the National Women's History Project (**http://www.nwhp.org/**) and examine history from that vantage point. When you get there click on the button provided to learn more about exemplary programs for women's studies, a network of scholars in women's history, and even a quiz of your own knowledge of the issues.

When you dig deeper in the "Ideas to Use" section, you will find suggestions for making women's history come alive in the classrooms. How might you use National Women's History Month to stimulate reflection on the history of women's contributions to society? Where can you get videos that highlight women's contributions? How might you have students examine their textbooks for attention to women's issues, and what might they do with the results of their work? What alternatives to the tried-and-true book report might you offer students as they explore historical influences on present practices? You will find possible answers to these questions and, in the process, perhaps reconsider the intellectual and practical value of studying history from different points of view.

4

Philosophical Foundations in Action

Philosophies live in people's minds and hearts and are made evident through their behavior. Although people rarely stop to notice, philosophy saturates their personal and professional existences. In this chapter we provide an overview of major philosophies that have influenced thought and behavior through the ages and that have special relevance for educators.

Francis Fukuyama (1992) has contended that people in the Western world have reached "the end of History," or the point at which all the really big philosophical questions have been settled. While communism is in decline and liberal democracy enjoys popularity, the increasingly complex problems and opportunities that present themselves in everyday life clamor for philosophical attention. No less than those who have preceded them, people today seek to understand who they are and who they might become.

Besides describing classical thought that is relevant to teachers and teaching, we focus on ways philosophies are reflected in schools and through teachers. We also explain why it is important to understand how people think about the means and ends of education and provide specific examples of ways in which different views have been defined through personal and social action. Finally, we describe how you can begin to articulate your own personal philosophy of education and to shape it over time.

PROFESSIONAL PRACTICE QUESTIONS

1 What is philosophy, and what does it have to do with you as a teacher?

2 What are the roots of American educational philosophies?

3 What philosophies influence Western education?

4 What non-Western philosophies influence American education?

5 What factors influence teachers' personal philosophies of education?

WHAT IS PHILOSOPHY, AND WHAT DOES IT HAVE TO DO WITH YOU AS A TEACHER?

Philosophy can be defined as a set of ideas about the nature of reality and about the meaning of life. Ideas about being, knowledge, and conduct have evolved over time as philosophers have pondered such questions as, What is basic human nature? What is real and true about life and the world? What is knowledge? What is worth knowing or striving for? What is just, good, right, or beautiful? Every individual has some notion about the answers to these questions, about the world and the nature of the people who inhabit it.

In the preface to a collection of essays, G. K. Chesterton, 19th- and 20th-century author, poet, social and literary critic, wrote,

> There are some people—and I am one of them—who think that the most practical and important thing about a [person] is still his view of the universe. We think that for a landlady considering a lodger it is important to know his income, but still more important to know his philosophy. We think that for a general about to fight an enemy it is important to know the enemy's numbers, but still more important to know the enemy's philosophy. (cited in James, 1907, p. 17)

As Chesterton suggests, there are some practical reasons why philosophy is important. If we know a lodger's or a general's or a teacher's or a student's philosophy, then we have some indication of how that person will behave, and why. It is the propensity for action inherent in one's philosophy that gives it practical importance. John Dewey (1916) was more direct when he argued that, "Whenever philosophy has been taken seriously, it has always been assumed that it signified achieving a wisdom which would influence the conduct of life" (p. 378).

The Place of Philosophy in Education

Philosophy influences daily educational life in many ways. Parents may choose or reject a school for their children because they believe that the school's philosophy will be translated into desirable or undesirable educational experiences. Principals run schools in keeping with their thoughts about managing people and administering programs—sometimes like businesses or factories, sometimes like churches, sometimes like colleges, sometimes like football teams. Teachers plan lessons, interact with students, and judge students' performances according to their views of knowledge, which may depend heavily on their memories of being a student and their idealized conceptions of the role of teacher. A professor requires teacher education students to learn a particular set of instructional methods to use with pupils in classroom settings based on her view of acceptable professional practice. Philosophy shapes the writing of curricula, the preparation and scoring of tests, and the architecture of school buildings.

The Importance of Putting Educational Philosophies in Perspective

The potential for conflict in this philosophical potpourri is great. And from time to time, some person or some group tries to claim hegemony—the philosophical upper hand, the one best way to view the universe. But the one-best-way people do not seem to last long in public education. Public schools appeal to the general public for support. Sooner or later, extreme ideas are recognized as being unacceptable to the majority of people the schools are meant to serve.

Philosophies, or one's principles, as Nel Noddings (1984) warned in her treatise on caring, can be wielded as bludgeons:

> Wherever there is a principle, there is implied its exception and, too often, principles function to separate us from each other. We may become dangerously self-righteous when we perceive ourselves as holding a precious principle not held by the other. The other may then be devalued and treated "differently." (p. 5)

Philosophical wars in education have become almost routine. People who adhere rigidly to philosophies often neglect to reexamine their views in light of changing conditions. Actions become habitual, out of touch with the present, and limited as expressed visions of the future.

For example, we build educational systems with a view of the "typical," "average," or "ordinary" person in mind and then put considerable resources and energy into maintaining these systems while they are becoming populated by "extraordinary" people. Martin Haberman (1995) argued persuasively that the education of inner-city children and teachers in the United States has suffered from this phenomenon. Colleges and universities are guided by philosophies fitted to suburban America as they recruit, select, and educate teachers to teach the nation's children. These philosophies, however, are radically out of line with life in urban and rural schools and communities.

> **Do educational philosophies relate to the realities of American life today?**

There are other reasons the study of philosophy is important. A philosophy, particularly that which is different from one's own, forces a person to examine his thinking in a new light. Someone who calls herself an "idealist," cannot help but grow from a serious consideration of a "realist" view, and vice versa. There is almost always some room to change one's mind, but change is unlikely if people are unaware of the options. Big minds have room to consider more than one point of view; they are not constricted by real or imagined pressure to be philosophically correct. Many educators, for example, favor eclecticism—they select what appears to be the best from various doctrines, methods, or styles. Others are more pluralistic, that is, they are guided at different times by different philosophies based on their perceptions of learners' needs and educational goals.

WHAT ARE THE ROOTS OF AMERICAN EDUCATIONAL PHILOSOPHIES?

A number of philosophies, or systems of ideas, have developed through the ages. As we describe below, efforts to address life's questions have informed thinking about the education of children. By understanding how these educational philosophies translate into practice, teachers can form their own personal philosophies about teaching and learning.

Western philosophies originated with the classical Greeks, who used a systematic method for addressing life's questions. Figure 4.1 shows how Greek thinkers divided philosophy into three branches:

1. **Metaphysics** and its two corollary areas deal with the study of reality. **Ontology** explores issues related to nature, existence, or being; while **cosmology** is concerned with the nature and origin of the cosmos, or universe.

2. **Epistemology** is concerned with the nature of knowledge or how we come to know things. We develop knowledge of truth through thought from observations and from logic—by reasoning deductively from a general proposition to a particular case and by reasoning inductively from a set of particulars or facts to a general principle. We also develop knowledge from scientific inquiry, intuition, and our senses.

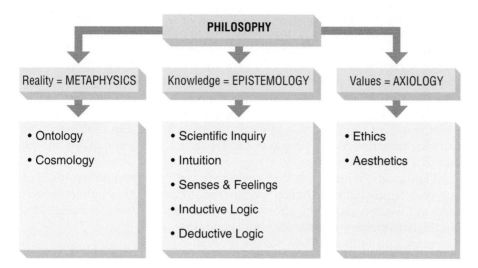

FIGURE 4.1
Summary of Branches of Philosophy
How might each branch of philosophy be embedded in your role as a teacher?

3. **Axiology** seeks to ascertain what is of value. More specifically, **ethics** explores issues of morality and conduct, while **aesthetics** is concerned with beauty.

Our education system has its roots in the philosophies described in the following sections.

Idealism

Idealism is a philosophy that suggests that ultimate reality lies in consciousness or reason. The progenitor of idealism, Plato (427?–347 BC), student of Socrates and citizen of Athens, imagined a society driven by the pursuit of knowledge. To search for truth, justice, and beauty in the world was to seek meaning in one's own life and in the collective life of the community. Plato envisioned this exploration as a shift of the mind away from the immediate physical world of what we can see, feel, smell, hear, and taste and toward a world of enduring ideas. Plato believed that it was the place of philosophy and philosophers to help people think clearly about these important ideas and to aid people in governing themselves wisely. Perfect knowledge of the ideal resided outside humans as an absolute, or as God.

In his writings Plato explained his vision through imaginary conversations between Socrates and his students. These discussions, or dialogues were written as poetry, science, and philosophy. They have guided thought and action in Western civilizations since the fourth century AD, when Socrates died from drinking hemlock at about age 60. He had been convicted of corrupting the young and of not believing in the gods.

In the dialogues, Socrates asks questions of students that force them to examine critically their notions about life, truth, beauty, and justice. As they interact with Socrates, students discover the errors in their thinking and formulate clearer, more accurate ideas about life's questions. The **Socratic method**, then, is one of teaching through inquiry and dialogues in which students discover and clarify knowledge.

Plato

The Republic is Plato's most celebrated dialogue. In it he described his ideal society—how people were to think, to value, to behave, to teach, and to organize and govern society. Plato knew that this utopia was unattainable. Yet for him, and for the idealists who followed, such visions of perfection serve as goals toward which we should strive in our own lifetimes and as benchmarks against which we should judge human progress over many lifetimes.

Plato, like Socrates, believed that people are born with knowledge and that the task of the teacher is to elicit this knowledge. The dialogues were teaching tools that forced people to consider ideas in relation to one another and to some idealized state.

Plato promoted the idea of an aristocracy, not one based on wealth, brute power, or family influence but on wisdom and goodness. Although he believed men and women should be afforded opportunities to learn, he thought few would demonstrate the wisdom and goodness necessary to rule their fellow citizens. In Plato's utopia those tried and tested individuals who remained healthy, who thought clearly, and who were of high moral character would govern. They might arise from any segment of society, but in the end, the most talented among them would serve as philosopher kings.

> **Does truth exist independently of our idea of it?**

An intermediate class of well-trained soldiers would safeguard the community. And a broad base of farmers, traders, and manufacturers would undergird society.

> In short, the perfect society would be that in which each class and each unit would be doing the work to which its nature and aptitude best adapted it; in which no class or individual would interfere with others, but all would cooperate in difference to produce an efficient and harmonious whole. That would be a just state. (Durant, 1961, p. 32)

For Plato, then, education was the vehicle of social mobility. It was also the key to creating and perpetuating the ideal society. Philosophers would train people to think clearly, and processes of education would screen people for their assignments to social classes. Plato's curriculum for this idealized society was straightforward, rigorous, and lifelong. He envisioned a kind of moral education that would make citizens realize they had responsibilities to one another.

Realism

Realism is a philosophy based on the idea that objects of sense or perception exist independently of the mind. Aristotle (384–322 BC), a student of Plato, differed markedly from his teacher in philosophical views. Plato, the idealist in search of truth, had turned away from the physical world toward the world of ideas. Aristotle sought truth by investigating the real world around him. His work reflected the philosophical orientation called realism and forms the basis for the scientific method.

Aristotle established a vast library of manuscripts, a collection of zoological and botanical specimens, and a lyceum in Athens, where he taught many young scholars. A staff of assistants helped him record raw observational information and synthesize the knowledge of the day. Despite the lack of scientific equipment and basic knowledge of the laws of nature, Aristotle pushed science forward by acting on the belief that the study of matter would lead to a better understanding of ideas. Aristotle and his students performed much of the intellectual spadework for Mendel's genetic theory, Darwin's theory of evolution, the science of embryology, and the disciplines of biology and psychology.

Aristotle

For Aristotle, Plato's ideals were real only insofar as they were actualized in material objects. He believed that everything sought to fulfill its potential, or to take the form of what it was meant to be. He characterized this movement from potential to actual as involving four causes. If marble (material cause) was determined by the sculptor to be a statue of a woman (formal cause), and was shaped by the sculptor (efficient cause) to take the form of a woman (final cause), then the potential of the marble would be actualized. This same logical progression of causes, according to Aristotle, held for the development of humans.

Aristotle believed that humans learn through their senses. As individuals experience the world, they develop and refine concepts about objects through direct experience. Unlike idealists, for whom truth resides within an individual, waiting to be discovered, realists believe that knowledge exists independent of human knowing. The role of education, then, is to teach students about the world in which they live.

Aristotle believed that happiness is the ultimate goal in humans' lives. Unlike Plato, he believed that goodness and wisdom were means to this end, not ends in themselves. People traversed the path to true happiness by stretching their minds to the fullest of their capabilities. "Virtue, or rather excellence, will depend on clear judgment, self-control, symmetry of desire, artistry of means" (Durant, 1961, p. 60). People were thought to demonstrate virtue through the achievement of experience; they did not simply possess virtue because of their intent or innocence.

> **Is happiness the ultimate aim of education?**

But if excellence is desirable, excess is taboo. Aristotle counseled people to seek the middle ground, or Golden Mean, in matters of life: ". . . between cowardice and rashness is courage; between stinginess and extravagance is liberality; between sloth and greed is ambition" (Durant, 1961, p. 60). Indeed, to Aristotle, the middle ground was fertile territory where training could make excellence flourish. As people practiced thinking and behaving in productive ways, they developed habits that would lead them to excellence.

Like Plato, Aristotle believed in government by an aristocracy of talented people. A government-run education system would emphasize balance in assigning people to the work of society and teaching responsibility to the state.

Thomism

Thomism is a philosophical orientation that relies on faith and reason as complementary sources of truth. Thomism may rightfully be considered the religious form of realism (O'Neill, 1981). Named after Saint Thomas Aquinas (1225–1274), a Dominican theologian who taught at the University of Paris,

Thomism is based on the belief that there is a knowable independent reality that is the creation of God, Christianity's supreme power. Like Aristotle, Aquinas believed that human beings use their senses and reason to understand the world. Aquinas also believed that all people have a soul, and that the ultimate goal in life is to experience eternity with God. Truth, then, is both natural and spiritual. Natural truth is knowledge about the physical world gained through reason. Attainment of spiritual or supernatural knowledge is also dependent on reason:

> Supernatural knowledge is *nonrational*, but it is not irrational. Ideally, the teachings of faith should be presented through reason, as a logical inference from the known. When this is done, the supernatural pronouncements of faith become convincing beyond all doubt, because (a) they are the logical outgrowth of man's innate powers of rational inference and (b) they reflect a vision of reality that is so overwhelmingly meaningful as to be rationally irresistible. (O'Neill, 1981, p. 164)

To grasp truth, people combine reason with faith in the perfect knowledge that comes directly or indirectly from divine revelation or from the authority of the Church. The role of education is first and foremost to train individuals to understand the religious truths necessary for spiritual salvation. Secondary aims are to develop the intellectual, social, religious, and physical skills that will enable students to be effective and contributing members of society. Most often this is achieved through direct rather than indirect instructional methods; that is, information is conveyed through drill, lecture, recitation, teacher-directed questioning, and highly structured discussions. Catholics have used catechisms to teach students to reach their goals.

Thomism is the historical and philosophical foundation of Roman Catholic education, according to Nancy Lesko (1988). Prior to 1965, religion was the first subject of the day in Catholic high schools. "The class's prominent place in the schedule was intended to reinforce the preeminent position of religion in school and in a student's life" (Bryk, Lee & Holland, 1993). Many Catholic schools today do not adhere strictly to the principles of Thomism but have turned their attention instead to secular issues common to the middle class:

> [R]eligious training is becoming secondary in Catholic schools; that is, these schools have become centrally concerned with preparing Catholic youth for contemporary life, i.e., facilitating their educational and social mobility. Catholic school administrators and board members are also prompted to emphasize the academic side of their schools as they develop strategies for the schools' economic survival. (Lesko, 1988, p. 18)

Humanism

Humanism is a philosophy that, in terms of education, calls for respect and kindness toward students and developmentally appropriate instruction in liberal arts, social conduct, and moral principles. This orientation is grounded in the writings of Erasmus (1466?–1536), Martin Luther (1483–1546), and Jean Jacques Rousseau (1712–1778).

During the Renaissance in Europe, Erasmus advanced an enlightened view of the essential goodness of children. He advocated that the young be taught with kindness and gentleness. Children were to be nurtured, not scolded and abused.

Luther and others associated with the Protestant Reformation inspired the idea of public-supported education—education meant to prepare people to take responsibility for their own lives—so that people could read and interpret the Bible for themselves. As people defined the ways they would worship God, then, they also began to define how they would educate for character. Education was an essential ingredient in stimulating and sustaining both the Reformation and the Renaissance. Education empowered people to make their own decisions, thereby determining their own destiny on earth and thus in the afterlife.

Rousseau enriched Erasmus's humanistic perspective on the needs of children and the aims of education. He suggested children not be viewed as blank slates, or as miniature adults but as individuals possessing natural goodness and needing continual support (see Chapter 2).

In the 1950s, 1960s, and 1970s, humanistic psychologists, including Alfred Adler, Carl Rogers, Paul Goodman, and Abraham Maslow, extended humanist philosophy to education and schooling. They wrote and spoke often about the assumptions upon which a humanistic education should be based. Humanists

Jean Jacques Rousseau

Is the basic nature of children good or bad?

believed students should not be forced to learn; they would learn what they needed and wanted to know. Processes of learning were thought to be at least as important as the acquisition of facts and skills. Students were assumed to be capable of evaluating themselves and so did not need to be judged by teachers or other adults. Students' emotional well-being was of critical importance in the learning process. Schools had to be free from threat if students were to take responsibility for their learning and to enjoy what they did. Self-fulfillment was the principal aim of education.

The work of Paulo Freire, a humanistic Brazilian educator, swept the developed world in the 1960s and 1970s. He encouraged the teaching of illiterate, indigent workers in the developing world. With the abilities to read and write, Freire believed, people would become aware of their own essential humanness and their social situation. Education, Freire (1970) wrote, would empower people to better their own lives and the lives of others:

> [W]hile both humanization and dehumanization are real alternatives, only the first is man's vocation. This vocation is constantly negated, yet it is affirmed by that very negation. It is thwarted by injustice, exploitation, oppression, and the violence of the oppressors; it is affirmed by the yearning of the oppressed for freedom and justice, and by their struggle to recover their lost humanity. (p. 28)

	IDEALISM	REALISM	THOMISM	HUMANISM
Philosophers	**Plato**	**Aristotle**	**Thomas Aquinas**	**Erasmus**
Metaphysics	Reality is an unchanging world of perfect ideas and universal truths.	Reality is observable events, objects, and matter independent of human knowing.	Reality is an ordered world created by God that people can come to know. People strive for eternity with God.	Reality is also humanity's creation. People strive for personal meaning in their experience and interpretation of life on earth.
Epistemology	Knowledge is obtained when ideas are brought into consciousness through self-examination and discourse.	Knowledge is obtained when students are taught ideas that can be verified and skills that enable them to know objects they encounter.	A combination of reason and faith enables students to acquire and use bodies of knowledge.	Exploration, questioning, and critical thinking enable students to discover or construct and use knowledge.
Axiology	Wisdom of goodness; discipline, order, self-control; preservation of cultural heritage of the past.	Self-control; clear judgment and rational thought; personal excellence; balance and moderation.	Knowing, loving, and serving God.	Knowing and loving God; serving humanity.

FIGURE 4.2

Philosophies on Which Western Education Is Based

How might teachers who are idealists, realists, Thomists, and humanists differ in their philosophies of education, relationships with students, and approaches to teaching?

FIGURE 4.3 *(opposite)*

Philosophical Orientations in Education Today

What combination of philosophical orientations best matches your own beliefs and values?

To learn more about humanism, visit the Library of Congress Vatican Exhibit at **http://www.ncsa.uiuc.edu/SDG/Experimental/vatican.exhibit/**.

Through the years classrooms have been influenced by idealism, realism, Thomism, and humanism. Each philosophy, as can be seen in Figure 4.2, reveals itself in educationally recognizable ways.

What modern philosophies influence Western education?

Educational philosophies have their roots in idealism, realism, Thomism, and humanism. They also have been influenced by modern philosophies such as existentialism, Marxism, and others, as well as by philosophical orientations toward learning, such as behaviorism and cognitivism. The following sections describe modern philosophical orientations in education today, which are summarized in Figure 4.3.

	Goal of Education	Role of Students	Role of Teachers	Teaching Methods	Subjects Studied
Existentialism	Develop authentic individuals who exercise freedom of choice and take responsibility for their actions.	Develop independence, self-discipline; set challenges and solve problems.	Encourage students to philosophize about life and to recognize and fulfill personal freedom.	Discussion and analysis, examination of choice-making in own and others' lives.	Drama Art Literature Social Sciences History
Marxism	Shape people and institutions; change material conditions of society, producing classless society.	Live and work harmoniously with others, acquire and use knowledge that will enable them to transform natural and social world.	Lead and advocate change.	Scientific methodology, practical activity (problem solving).	Emphasis on science and history.
Behaviorism	Engineer environments that efficiently maximize learning.	Respond to environmental and behavioral stimuli; become self-regulated.	Manipulate the learning environment and present stimuli, using conditioning and social learning to shape student behavior.	Programmed instruction that provides feedback on performance behavioral contracts, reinforcement.	Learning tasks in which behavior can be directly observed, measured, and evaluated.
Cognitivism	Develop thinking skills for lifelong self-directed learning.	Construct meaningful knowledge through experience and interaction.	Stimulate cognitive development; mediate student learning and monitor thought processes.	Use of manipulatives and real-life learning opportunities relevant to students' prior experiences.	Integrated curricula; emphasis on thinking and critical thinking skills, study skills, and problem solving skills.
Pragmatism	Develop and apply practical knowledge and skills for life in a progressive democratic society.	Active learning and participation.	Teach inductive and deductive reasoning, the scientific method, and the powers of observation and practice.	Hands-on curricula; group work; experimentation.	Emphasis on citizenship, knowledge and skills applicable to daily life, and career or job preparation.
Perennialism	Acquisition of timeless principles of reality, truth, and value; learning for the sake of learning.	Receive knowledge and academic skills.	Guide to the classics; teach basic skills.	Teacher-centered direct instruction.	Emphasis on Great Books and core curricula in the arts and sciences.
Essentialism	Acquisition of culture; cultural literacy for personal benefit.	Receive knowledge; demonstrate minimum competencies.	Deliver a standard curriculum.	Subject-centered direct instruction.	Uniform curriculum for all students that emphasizes the essence of traditional American culture.
Social Reconstructionism	Solve social problems and create a better world.	Inquire, apply critical thinking skills, and take action.	Ask questions; present social issues and problem-solving challenges; serve as organizer and information resource.	Stimulate divergent thinking and group investigation.	Emphasis on social studies, social problems, global education, and environmental issues.

Existentialism

Sören Kierkegaard (1813–1855) is considered the originator of **existentialism**, a philosophy that emphasizes the subjectivity of human experience and the importance of individual creativity and choice in a nonrational world. Friedrich Wilhelm Nietzsche (1844–1900), Martin Heidegger (1889–1976), Jean-Paul Sartre (1905–1980), Albert Camus (1913–1960), Paul Tillich (1886–1965), Martin Buber (1878–1965), and others have developed existentialist thought by attempting to describe reality not as separate from or beyond the comprehension of humans, but as the result of individual passion and life experience.

Existentialists believe that the physical universe has no inherent meaning apart from human experience. The world and forces of nature exist, but they are not ordered in some grand scheme in which humans play their appropriate part. Human life, too, exists; we are here, but we are only what we make of ourselves. Sartre's (1947, p. 28) often-quoted phrase states that "Existence precedes essence." We owe our existence to nature, but we define ourselves through our actions.

Nietzsche (1924, 1961) revealed the dark side of this view. He characterized life as a grim battle in which one requires strength, pride, and intelligence just to survive. Sensitivity, kindness, and consideration were signs of weakness. There was no God of mercy who ruled benevolently and rewarded the worthy with eternal life in heaven. Indeed, there was no God at all. And if there ever had been, He was surely dead. Nietzsche believed that we should strive not to better the majority of people, who were mostly worthless, but to promote genius and to develop superior personalities. From an aristocracy of talent and power—one cultivated by those who choose to restrain and discipline themselves—would arise the superman.

Do we have free will to choose who we will be?

For existentialists, choice is a critical concept. People choose who they will be. Some allow others to decide for them, but exercising this default option is also a choice. Although existentialists do not reject morals or norms of behavior, they repudiate habitual adherence to them. Existentialists encourage people faced with a difficult conflict of values to concentrate seriously on their own situations and to choose what is right for them. When we are cut loose from restrictions, we assume responsibility for our own actions. We cannot simply rely on what we are told to do or on what some scripture directs us to do. And when we are free to choose our directions, we prize that freedom for others.

Martin Buber, existentialist and Hasidic Jew, assailed theologians' talk of God and their pretensions about knowing God. In *I and Thou* (1970), Buber did not try to prop up religion or to argue that God was present in all things. Instead, he raised the possibility that life without religion lacked an important dimension. Buber proclaimed that the secular was sacred and that God is present when people encounter one another in honest dialogue. Human relationships are central in creating meaning in our lives. Buber and other existentialists influenced the development of humanistic psychology, in which relationships, free thinking, and action lead to self-actualization, or personal fulfillment.

VOICES

On the Existentialist Teacher

George F. Kneller, philosopher of education formerly at the University of California at Los Angeles, argued that if teachers were to adopt an existentialist view, their choices would be important and difficult and their pedagogical strategies would be clear.

If we accept [existentialism as a world view] . . . as free men and free teachers we must seek to expose and combat all those forces in culture and society that tend to dehumanize men by denying their freedom. We must repudiate the subordination of the person to economic "laws," the tyranny of the majority over the dissenting minority, and the stifling of individuality by social conformism. We must urge our students to recognize and fulfill the freedom that is theirs as persons. What we urge we must also practice by respecting their freedom as we value our own.

Most choices we make are admittedly trivial and inconsequential—choice of a necktie, choice of a restaurant, choice of a movie. A serious choice is a choice between actions involving fundamental values. It calls for deep concentration, a looking into oneself. However, I must not be content merely to apply an abstract moral principle. This is a weak choice, reliance on a rule rather than on myself. I should choose the course of action that seems uniquely right in this particular situation. I should seek not the way but my way. The hardest choices to make are often those between alternative goods. Two courses of action seem to have an equally good claim on us—which course do we take?

If I am an existentialist teacher, I urge the student to take responsibility for, and to deal with, the results of his actions. To act is to produce consequences. He must accept that these consequences are the issue of his choice, but at the same time he must not submit to them as unalterable, for this is to assume that freedom is exhausted in a single act. Freedom is never exhausted, and each consequence poses the need for further choice. I would teach him that his life is his own to lead and that no one else can lead it for him. It is pointless to blame his failures on environment, family, temperament, or the influence of others. These conditions are for choice to challenge. Whatever may have happened to the student in the past, the future is his to make.

Does this attitude lead to a ruthless disregard for others, to my fulfillment at the expense of yours? Not at all. True freedom implies not egoism but communion. The egoist is driven by a narrow self-interest. With him choice is not self-fulfillment but self-limitation. Freedom, open and dynamic, longs for other centers of freedom, other persons. It does not calculate but gives. The fulfillment of freedom is communion with others.

If as a teacher I assume the style and gestures for which convention calls, I may touch only surfaces of my students' lives. I must go beyond familiarity and open myself to them. I must come to them unreservedly, creating the trust from which springs communion and true self-fulfillment.

CRITICAL THINKING

How might a classical idealist such as Plato respond to Kneller's declaration? How might a classical realist such as Aristotle respond? What examples of "dehumanizing" and "stifling" conditions in school cultures might Kneller accept as evidence of his claim? To what teacher "styles" and "gestures" might Kneller refer when he suggests that teachers risk touching only the "surfaces of students' lives"? How might teachers "open themselves" to students to create communion or mutual participation in educational life? How might "schools without walls" and "democratic classrooms" reflect values implicit in the philosophy of existentialism?

Note. From *Introduction to the Philosophy of Education* (2nd ed.) by Kneller, George F., © 1971. Reprinted by permission of Prentice-Hall, Inc., Upper Saddle River, NJ. New York: John Wiley & Sons. (pp. 72-76)

A. S. Neill's Summerhill in England is a famous application of the existentialist/humanistic philosophy to schooling. Under Neill's direction, teachers encouraged students to philosophize about life, using their personal experiences as bases for examining individual choice making. Through dialogue with peers and instructors, students attempted to perceive and solve problems. The goal is to help students become cognitively equipped, "authentic" individuals having a deep commitment to the creation of a better world. Summerhill school continues today under the leadership of Neill's wife and daughter. (See **http://ourworld.compuserve.com/ homepages/summerhill/**.)

◾ Marxism

Marxism is a philosophy based on the belief that the human condition is determined by forces in history that prevent people from achieving economic freedom and social and political equality. Karl Marx (1818–1883) was a historian, philosopher, and social theorist born to Jewish parents in Germany. In the main, his work was not taken seriously until after his death.

As a university student Marx was influenced greatly by the idealist Georg Wilhelm Friedrich Hegel (1770–1831), who at the time was the grand master of German philosophy. Although Marx grew to reject Hegel's political philosophy, he was influenced greatly by Hegel's thought, particularly his development of the concept of the dialectic, or the process by which human thought and human history progress.

The dialectic is a constant intellectual movement from thesis, to antithesis, and finally to synthesis. Movement in thought occurs, for example, when one plays a thesis or idea against its opposite, which for Hegel was the reality of nature. Thought moves along a continuum by way of the dialectic process to richer, more complex syntheses. Hegel argued that ultimately this process would reach the Absolute Idea, or an idea that bore close resemblance to idealists' conceptions of truth. He rejected the realist view that truth is independent of our minds. People become and remain alienated, according to Hegel, until they understand that they are thinking beings and that truth is a function of this self-realization.

> **Are our consciousness and progress shaped by material conditions?**

The process, Hegel maintained, works also for history. Civilization progresses along a continuum toward richer, more complex syntheses. Culture moves forward, building on what has come before. To Marx, progress meant revolution. Marx thought of the dialectical process as a clash of economic forces in which the capitalist system exploited the worker. The ruling class seized workers' productive capacities and offered money in return, making workers subservient to the system.

Within this context, Marx saw progress as a mixed blessing. In capitalist society, the forces of production continually increase. Simultaneously, people create a more oppressive social organization as they characterize society by unequal classes. Capitalists, Marx contended, accumulate great wealth, but they create inequalities and dehumanize people. Marx thought that in time the exploited would rise up and overthrow the ruling class.

Marx recognized the value of science as a way to acquire knowledge. For Marx, human perception is based on sense experience of the material world, and this perceptual experience shapes one's knowledge. The social order, therefore, is not fixed. Human nature is malleable—people and social institutions can be shaped and formed. A person's social class is a matter of education and circumstance. The aim of Marxism, then, is to change the material conditions of society. When these conditions change, consciousness changes; when consciousness changes, ideology changes, and the perfect, classless, communistic society will result.

In the 20th century, Marxism has been articulated and developed intellectually most notably by people referred to as the Frankfurt School—a school of thought based on Marxist assumptions about the social world, including Max Horkheimer, (1895–1973), Theodor Adorno (1903–1969), Herbert Marcuse (1898–1979), and Jürgen Habermas (born 1929). Habermas in particular has exerted considerable influence on educational theory (Ewert, 1991). Critical theorists such as Habermas attempt to reveal the covert values in schooling and society, claiming that schools alienate students and "deskill" them by establishing the goals of education instead of encouraging students to set their own goals. The process of schooling thus breeds dependency on authority, promotes top-down communication, and advances a distorted view of history (Apple, 1995).

Behaviorism and Cognitivism

Behaviorism is a philosophical orientation based on the belief that human behavior is determined by forces in the environment that are beyond our control rather than by the exercise of free will. Behaviorism stands in stark contrast to **cognitivism**, a philosophical orientation based on the belief that people actively construct their knowledge of the world through experience and interaction rather than through behavioral conditioning. Several names are associated with the development of behaviorism—Ivan Pavlov (1849–1936), John Watson (1878–1958), and E.L. Thorndike (1874–1949)—but none is more prominent than that of B. F. Skinner (1904–1990).

Skinner was a psychologist who concentrated on scientific experimentation and empirical observation. Although he made his reputation with tightly controlled laboratory experimentation, he could let his mind roam freely over complex social problems. Skinner (1971) viewed our failure to solve social problems as a failure of the knowledge of human behavior:

> Physics and biology have come a long way, but there has been no comparable development of anything like a science of human behavior. Greek physics and biology are now of historical interest only . . ., but the dialogues of Plato are still assigned to students and cited as if they threw light on human behavior. Aristotle could not have understood a page of modern physics or biology, but Socrates and his friends would have little trouble in following most current discussions of human affairs. And as to technology, we have made immense strides in controlling the physical and biological worlds, but our practices in government, education,

B. F. Skinner

and much of economics, though adapted to very different conditions, have not greatly improved. (pp. 5–6)

Skinner would have placed science in the hands of those who would work for a peaceful and more just world. Science could be used to shape morality. To behaviorists, education conditions people to behave in more and less civilized ways.

Behaviorism is sometimes characterized as an "empty organism" theory of behavior; that is, behaviorists view the immediate world in terms of stimuli and responses to these stimuli without acknowledging what, if anything, happens in a person's mind. John Watson was extremely influential in this regard. In some of his experiments, he conditioned his son to fear small animals and then deconditioned him. Watson repudiated completely the value of introspection in psychology. He thought that because free will could not be measured, it did not exist.

Like other realists, then, behaviorists rely on knowledge derived from the physical world. To understand this world in relation to human behavior, they examine patterns of environmental influences on patterns of human responses to these influences.

The educational applications of behaviorism to enhance achievement and to improve conduct are many and varied. Schools use programmed instruction, both computer-based and print materials, to teach mathematics, reading, and other subject matter. These curricula are organized into discrete, sequentially ordered units of study, accompanied by unit tests, opportunities for feedback on performance, and chances to practice skills. Educators also advocate the use of behavioral contracts or contingency management schemes to influence student behavior. These are organized as "if . . ., then . . ." agreements between teachers and students: If you do your homework correctly, then you can spend the end of the class period reading whatever you wish in the library.

The language of education is rife with behavioral terminology—*reward, punishment, contingency, reinforcer, shaping, fading.* Teachers speak of "reinforcing desirable behavior." They try to "ignore inappropriate behavior." People want student motivation to become "intrinsic" rather than "extrinsic," and so forth.

Many educators use the words and phrases of behavioral engineering. They have incorporated the ideas, the language, and some of the practices into their own professional repertoires without abandoning strongly held beliefs about the importance of students' thoughts and feelings (Cohen & Hearn, 1988). When students are not learning, behaviorists think there must be something wrong with the educational program. The way to solve the problem is to break down the program into its component parts and to fix the pieces that are broken, or to scrap the program altogether and try a new one. The challenge, then, is to engineer environments that produce desired results. This outlook has heavily influenced both the lay public's and educators' perceptions of educational problems and solutions.

> **To what extent are we the products of behavioral conditioning?**

Alternatives to the behaviorist outlook take a variety of forms, loosely called cognitivism, from *cognition*—the process of thinking and knowing. On the basis of research on thinking, cognitive psychologists assert that people are not passively conditioned by the environment but rather are active learners. They mentally construct their knowledge of the world and beliefs about reality through their own direct experiences and interactions, and then they act upon those constructs. Cognitivists therefore focus on thought, which cannot be observed directly, while behaviorists focus on behavior that is observable and measurable.

Like behaviorism, cognitivism is a philosophical orientation having implications for education. Educators who favor teaching models based on cognitivism often choose student-centered learning experiences. They assist students by teaching them study skills, thinking skills, and problem-solving skills. They try to provide conceptual bases or **scaffolding** upon which students construct meaning or make sense of information for themselves. In education, the movement to modify curriculum and instruction to reflect the cognitivist outlook is called **constructivism**.

Pragmatism

Pragmatism is a philosophical method that defines the truth and meaning of ideas according to their physical consequences and practical value. An Englishman, Charles Sanders Peirce (1839–1914), is acknowledged as the originator of modern pragmatism. But pragmatism is so readily equated with the quality people refer to as "common sense" that many would claim it as the unofficial American philosophy. In the last 100 years or so, William James (1842–1910), John Dewey (1859–1952), and, most recently, Richard Rorty (born 1931) have used pragmatism to try to strike a philosophical balance between the realism of the natural sciences and the beliefs of idealists as expressed in art, religion, and politics (Rorty, 1991).

Like other philosophers, early pragmatists concerned themselves with the dualism of mind and matter: A subjective reality exists in our minds, an objective reality exists in the physical world around us. They agreed with the realists that a world exists and is not merely a figment of our imagination. In the objective/subjective dichotomy, however, objective reality has meaning only insofar as people ascribe meaning based on the consequences of the object. The goal of pragmatists, then, has been to seek wisdom, or truth, by examining the consequences of holding particular beliefs and acting on them.

William James emphasized the right of individuals to create their own reality. He (James, 1907) described the pragmatic method as a way to settle metaphysical disputes:

> Is the world one or many?—fated or free?—material or spiritual?—here are notions either of which may or may not hold good of the world; and disputes over such are unending. The pragmatic method in such cases is to try to interpret each notion by tracing its respective practical consequences. What difference would it practically make to any one if this notion rather than that notion were true? If no practical difference whatever can be traced, then the alternatives mean practically the same thing, and all dispute is idle. Whenever a dispute is serious, we ought to be able to show some practical difference that must follow from one side or the other's being right. (p. 42)

William James

Other pragmatists have argued that the correspondence between human beliefs and physical objects is unimportant. If we believe with good reason that something is true, and there is some gap between our beliefs and truth, we can always improve our beliefs as new evidence becomes available. Truth is what is good for us to believe (Rorty, 1991). For all practical purposes, if something works, it is true.

John Dewey linked pragmatism to educational preparation for life in a democracy. When people are educated democratically, Dewey argued, they are prepared for life. And when education concentrates on real-life problems, that education prepares people for living fully and effectively in a democracy. Dewey believed that ordinary people possess the intelligence to govern themselves and to direct their own actions; the function of education is to enhance human potential.

> **To what extent should education focus on relevance and utility?**

Pragmatists thus believe that children should be encouraged to learn to make difficult decisions by considering the consequences their actions might have on others. Because democracy permits people to consider multiple points of view, pragmatic action and democracy complement each other. Education never ends—it is a process that continues throughout one's lifetime. People are instruments of change, capable of experiencing, experimenting, and testing their beliefs. Dewey believed that people can interpret the practical consequences of their actions; democracy demands as much (Westbrook, 1991).

Dewey criticized American public education as mechanical, mindless, and practically irrelevant—as little more than indoctrination. His progressive views (see Chapter 3) led him to argue for education that helps students realize their capacities to engage in activity that calls for genuine thinking and problem solving. According to Robert Westbrook (1991),

> The youngest children in [Dewey's] school, who were four and five years old, engaged in activities familiar to them from their homes and neighborhood: cooking, sewing, and carpentry. The six-year-olds built a farm out of blocks, planted wheat and cotton, and processed and transported their crop to market. The seven-year-olds studied prehistoric life in caves of their own devising while their eight-year-old neighbors focused their attention on the work of the seafaring Phoenicians and subsequent adventurers like Marco Polo, Magellan, Columbus, and Robinson Crusoe. Local history and geography occupied the attention of the nine-year-olds, while those who were ten studied colonial history, constructing a replica of a room in an early American house. The older groups of children . . . [focused on] scientific experiments in anatomy, electro-magnetism, political economy, and photography. The search of the debating club formed by the thirteen-year-old students for a place to meet resulted in the building of a substantial clubhouse, which enlisted children of all ages in a cooperative project. (pp. 101–102)

Explore the Center for Dewey Studies at Southern Illinois University on the Web at **http://www.siu.edu/~deweyctr/**.

Perennialism

A modern educational philosophy that looks backward through history and forward in time to shape thought about the goals and processes of education is called **perennialism**. Perennialists exalt the great ideas and accomplishments of Western civilization for their own sake and also for what Western classical writings can offer to future generations. Perennialists believe that the purpose of schools is to develop students' intellectual capabilities.

Perennialists contend that there are principles of education so important, so central to the development of culture that they cannot be ignored, such as the universality of truth, the importance of rationality, and the power of aesthetics and religion to encourage ethical behavior. Much like realists, Perennialists believe that such enduring principles exist in the physical world and demand the attention of teachers and students. Culture is not relative, perennialists argue. That which is rational and intellectually self-disciplined is most desirable.

This philosophical view of what is important in education has been articulated most notably by Robert Maynard Hutchins (1899–1977) and Mortimer Adler (1902–). They have argued that in every important way, people are basically the same, regardless of where they live and who they are, thus all people need the same basic education. This education should consist of a fundamental grounding in history, language, mathematics, science, literature, and humanities.

Robert Maynard Hutchins

Hutchins and Adler introduced perennialism in the 1930s in reaction against progressive educational approaches that stressed the importance of change in society and the dynamics of teaching and learning. Progressives thought that education should be tailored to the times, the people, and the places it was offered. They advocated active learning, child-centered teaching, and problem solving as opposed to knowledge acquisition.

The perennialists, on the other hand, contended that people are rational animals having free will who learn to exercise self-control when their minds are disciplined by knowledge acquisition through basic education. Education implies teaching, teaching implies knowledge, knowledge is truth, truth is the same everywhere: therefore education should be the same everywhere (Hutchins, 1936).

Perennialists aver that schools are supposed to prepare students by putting them in touch with the classics of Western culture. A contemporary curriculum that disregards the classics does students and society a disservice. One must know the past if one is to be prepared to participate fully in the present and to contribute in the future. This view led to the development of the Great Books program at the University of Chicago in the 1950s.

Mortimer Adler's *Paideia Proposal* (1982), a more recent expression of perennialism, calls for a one-track system of public schooling. This single track would promote the same three learning objectives for all students. The first deals with mental, moral, and spiritual self-improvement. The second concerns civic education. The third addresses adults' needs to earn a living. In Adlerian language, these objectives are translated into goals. The goals and the means to their achievement are described in Figure 4.4.

The practical implications of perennialism for schooling are numerous. Perennialists prefer teacher-centered education; the teacher is the authority

	A	B	C
Goals of Education →	Acquisition of organized knowledge	Development of intellectual skills and skills of learning	Enlarged understanding of ideas and values
	by means of	*by means of*	*by means of*
Means to Goals →	Didactic instruction, lectures and responses, textbooks and other aids	Coaching, exercises, and supervised practice	Socratic questioning and active participation
	In three areas of subject-matter	*In the operations of*	*In the*
Areas, Operations, and Activities →	Language, literature, and the fine arts	Reading, writing, speaking, listening	Discussion of books (not textbooks) and other works of art and
	Mathematics and natural science	Calculating, problem solving, observing, measuring, estimating	Involvement in artistic activities, e.g., music, drama, visual arts
	History, geography, and social studies	Exercising critical judgment	

FIGURE 4.4

Adler's Recommended Course of Study

What might be some advantages and disadvantages of Adler's curriculum for a one-track system of public schooling?

who must possess both the knowledge and responsibility necessary to teach a core curriculum to young people. Moral education, including Bible study, is important for what it communicates about self-control and social responsibility. Concepts of academic tracking and gifted education are acceptable to perennialists.

Essentialism

Essentialism is a philosophical orientation that claims the existence of a body of knowledge that all people must learn if they are to function effectively in society. Like perennialists, essentialists acknowledge the timeless quality of great works, but they do not base their views on realist principles, and they do not agree on what constitutes the "essentials" that educated people should know. Essentialists agree that such essentials exist and that they ought to be represented in the curriculum. Like perennialists, essentialists have been criticized for defining the essentials in terms of Western history and culture. But unlike perennialists, essentialists want students to study great works not for their own sake but to become better prepared to solve contemporary problems. The sciences, too, are useful and central to the process of knowing and improving one's world.

William Bagley (1874–1946) founded the Essentialistic Education Society as a reaction against progressive, pragmatic trends in education. Like the perennialists at the end of World War II, Bagley and his colleagues feared what they saw as an erosion of moral and intellectual standards in the young. To remedy this situation, they advocated that schools transmit a common essential core of knowledge to all students.

Essentialist Arthur Bestor (1879–1944), for example, also criticized the lack of rigor in American education. Bestor (1985) wrote,

> To put the matter bluntly, we regard schooling as a mere experience, delightful to the recipient but hardly valuable to society. The school or college has become, to our minds, merely a branch of the luxury-purveying trade. Like the club car on a passenger train, it dispenses the amenities of life to persons bound on serious errands elsewhere. (p. 2)

In contrast to perennialists, essentialists place less emphasis on learning for learning's sake. They concentrate instead on the power of knowledge for solving contemporary problems and for preventing such problems from arising in the future.

How would essentialists encourage societal progress? They would have teachers instill in students the old-fashioned values of discipline, self-control, and hard work. Because essentialists view children as incapable of directing their own learning, teachers would direct it by structuring and pacing students' mastery of subject matter. Because much knowledge is abstract, practical problem solving, or "learning by doing," would not apply. Essentialists

Cultural Awareness

A criticism of Hirsch's work and that of perennialists and essentialists generally is that it is **Eurocentric**—that is, it is centered on the history and cultures of Europe. Such a curriculum is said to consist mainly of works by "dead white males." Cultural literacy becomes an exclusionary concept, one that does not include knowing the history and culture of non-European peoples. Defenders of essentialism, such as Allan Bloom in his book *The Closing of the American Mind* (1987), say that this is as it should be: "One should conclude from the study of non-Western cultures that not only to prefer one's own way but to believe it best, superior to all others, is primary and even natural—exactly the opposite of what is intended by requiring students to study these cultures" (p. 36). Michelle Fine (1987) and Henry Girous (1984) contend that such an approach silences talk about instances of social, economic, and educational discrimination experienced by minority and low-income students. For these students, school "disconfirms rather than confirms their histories, experiences, and dreams" (Girous, 1984, p. 189). In the United States, members of minority cultures are among those who bitterly oppose the essentialist interpretation of what is worth knowing. The countermovement of Afrocentrism makes the history and cultures of Africa and African Americans the focus of the curriculum.

might well argue that details get in the way of seeing the big picture (Clive, 1989).

Essentialist curricula are rarely as specific as the recommendations of E. D. Hirsch (1987; Hirsch, Rowland, & Stanford, 1989). Hirsch argues that society cannot function properly without communication among its members, and communication cannot occur in the absence of literacy. But true literacy, Hirsch (1996) contends, is more than mechanical performance of the skills of reading and writing; it depends on people's shared information, or common knowledge of their culture.

Hirsch referred to this shared common knowledge as **cultural literacy** and developed an elaborately prescribed curriculum for students. He delineated exactly what he believed children need to know by the end of sixth grade in such categories as literature, religion and philosophy, history, geography, mathematics, science, and technology.

> **Should all students learn the same curriculum? What should a common curriculum include?**

Social Reconstructionism

Social reconstructionism is a philosophy based on the belief that people are responsible for social conditions and can improve the quality of human life by changing the social order. Theodore Brameld (1904–1987) and George Counts (1889–1974) were instrumental in articulating social reconstructionism which advocates education as a means of preparing people to create a new society. Stimulated by progressivism, Brameld, Counts, and others pushed for rapid, sweeping changes throughout society to effect a new world order. Whereas the progressives and pragmatists of Dewey's day were politically moderate, urging gradual change, the social reconstructionists were provocative in advocating systemic change.

For example, social reconstructionists might attack the governance of schools to reorganize decision-making power, as they did in Chicago in the 1920s (Counts, 1928). They argued that every major legitimate interest in the city should be represented on the school board and that teachers should prepare themselves professionally to meet their responsibilities and guard their right to perform professional functions. Counts (1928) and other social reconstructionists argued that rebuilding public education was not going to be easy but was possible through courageous leadership and modern science. The optimism of early social reconstructionists was based on faith in the power of science to solve human problems, a faith others criticized as unjustifiable.

> Unless the profession can develop a superior type of social leadership, a leadership at least equal in intelligence, courage, and power to the leadership in other fields of interest with which it must contend, the profession will find itself unable to incorporate in the systems of public education the findings of educational science. (p. 361)

The same kinds of arguments made by early social reconstructionists are advanced today to restructure schools and redesign professional education for teachers.

George Counts

From the 1930s to the 1960s, social reconstructionists saw a world where confusion and crisis reigned. The Great Depression, World War II, the Nuclear Age, and the Cold War era stimulated and sustained concerns about world order. Rather than bemoan world conditions, social reconstructionists sought to define opportunities to build a good and just society. People cannot sit comfortably in their safe homes holding tightly to the good life while others less fortunate sit on the outside looking in. People have to act to bring the have-nots into a better society.

Therefore Brameld thought that the future could be bleak or promising: the choice belonged to all. People can take control of their lives and behave in ways that improve the human condition. But the education system itself needed to be reconstructed as a tool for transforming individuals' lives and shaping a new social order. Like the Platonists, social reconstructionists were utopian. As Brameld (1950) noted,

> The common denominator of [social reconstructionism's] beliefs is a passionate concern for the future of civilization. It centers attention, therefore, upon clear-cut cultural goals, which, because they are idealizations of human and especially social potentialities, are in the historic stream of utopian philosophy. (p. 407)

How can education make the world a better place?

The spirit of social reconstructionism has been nurtured in the United States over the years by individuals and groups intent on creating change through social activism. The work of Saul Alinsky (1909–1972), Ivan Illich (1926–), and others embodied this spirit. Social reconstructionists of the late 20th century press for schools to address many societal problems that occur because of ignorance, poverty, lack of educational and employment opportunities, and the like. This multiple-causation view of problems dictates a multifaceted approach to solving them. Social reconstructionists conceive of education, then, not so much as a linear response to a particular need but as the means to address an interdependent set of intellectual, emotional, personal, and social needs. Social reconstructionists' views of the interconnectedness of problems and solutions and of people's responsibility to society shape educational programs today.

WHAT NON-WESTERN PHILOSOPHIES INFLUENCE AMERICAN EDUCATION?

Eastern and Middle Eastern philosophies, religions, and cultures are gradually beginning to influence schools in the United States as the number of people having roots in Eastern and Middle Eastern countries grows. In cities across the country, there are many first-, second-, and third-generation American and foreign national public school students who have Asian and Middle Eastern backgrounds. Groups such as Buddhist-Vietnamese Americans in Los Angeles, Islamic-Arab Americans in Detroit, and Hindu-Indian

Americans in New York often maintain private schools and educate children and adults through cultural festivals and religious celebrations.

In some nonsectarian private schools, students are guided in an exploration of world religions. Students are encouraged to develop secular spirituality, a personal ethical system, and inner peace. New multicultural curriculum materials also provide access to past and present ideas and expressions of spirituality, and in some alternative private schools, non-Western philosophies play a significant role. F. Robinson (1990) reported about one such school in the affluent community of Chevy Chase, Maryland:

> The Oneness school in Chevy Chase is one of a handful of non-sectarian schools in the metropolitan area whose curriculum includes a "spiritual" component . . . A copy of the Koran sits on a book case in front of a poster celebrating the fourth centenary of the death of Teresa of Avila. Nearby were Native American sand paintings used by medicine men, statues of Shiva, Buddha, and St. Francis, crucifixes from South America and a wooden plaque of the Virgin Mary from Yugoslavia. (pp. 9–10)

The school, dedicated to world peace, was founded in 1988 on the belief that "peace begins with the individual and personal growth goes hand-in-hand with academic achievement" (A. Kutt, personal communication, September 5, 1996). To accomplish their goals, faculty encourage students of all ages to work and play together during the school day.

In general, Western ways encourage people to look outward toward what they hope lies ahead in their personal and professional lives. One's sense of progress is rooted in work and one's place in society. Attendance at church or temple, the latest self-help book, or some traumatic event prompts people to think about "meaning" in their lives, but introspection may occur rarely for many. Non-Western philosophies can remind people that a long, focused gaze inward, often undertaken with the help of a spiritual guide or teacher, is essential if a life is to be fully lived.

Hinduism

Hinduism is a religion, a philosophy, and a way of life:

> Hinduism is a spectrum of beliefs and practices ranging from the veneration of trees, stones, and snakes in villages scarcely out of the Stone Age to the abstract metaphysical speculations of sophisticated urban intellectuals whose attainments have been recognized [widely]. (Organ, 1974, p. 1)

Major Hindu writings began to appear in the form of hymns and chants, or mantras, about 1200 BC to AD 200. The three basic Hindu texts—the Vedas, the Upanishads, and the Epics—reveal a way of life that has evolved to guide believers through the years. The Vedas present a vision of the universe consisting of the earth, the atmosphere, and heaven. Vedic believers worship many gods, ascribing human characteristics to nonhuman things. Varuna, for example, is thought to control the changes in seasons. The Upanishads, or secret teachings, recognize a single god, Brahman, and established laws to govern conduct. These laws laid down rules for personal conduct and promoted the caste system. This system of social hierarchy, now outlawed, put the Brahmin, or priests, teachers, and other thinkers, at the top and relegated the Sudras, or "untouchables," to the bottom.

The Epics, which contain among other writings the Bhagavad-Gita, were written between 200 BC and AD 200. The Bhagavad-Gita is a poem of more than 700 verses that depicts a compassionate god who opens salvation to all devoted, dutiful souls. The Bhagavad-Gita also describes yoga as a means of uniting one's soul with the Absolute. Through yoga's teaching of right posture, correct breathing, and control of the senses, one learns to concentrate so as to free the mind and to attain enlightenment.

Mohandas Gandhi, a member of the Jain sect of Hinduism, was known as the Mahatma (the Great). His influence on Western thought included his advocacy of nonviolence as a means to social reform. Martin Luther King, Jr. (1964) wrote about the use of Gandhian nonviolent political action during the bus boycott in Montgomery, Alabama: "For Gandhi love was a potent instrument for social and collective transformation. It was in this Gandhian emphasis on love and nonviolence that I discovered the method for social reform that I had been seeking for many months" (p. 79).

To characterize Hindus as a single group having a monolithic set of beliefs is inaccurate and misleading. "Diversity is perhaps the first and most important feature of Hindu worship to be noted" (Rambachan, 1992). The beliefs, customs, and religious practices of Hindus vary widely from sect to sect and place to place. The life of a Bengali woman in rural India, for instance, can differ markedly from that of a Hindu woman in Calcutta, and even more so from the life of a Hindu woman in New York.

Buddhism

Having its roots in Indian Vedic culture, Buddhism is meant to help people recognize truth for themselves:

> Buddhism is not a fundamentalist religion. Its teachings are not dogmas or articles of faith that have to be blindly accepted at the cost of suspending reason, critical judgment, common sense or experience. Quite the contrary, in fact; their basic aim is to help us gain direct insight into the truth for ourselves. (Snelling, 1987, p. 51)

Buddha, or the Enlightened One, was born as Siddhartha Gautama (563–483 BC) to wealthy parents in Nepal. Although Gautama enjoyed a sheltered, opulent existence until age 29, tradition teaches that his life was immutably altered by three events. He saw an old man bent over a walking stick, a diseased man suffering with fever, and a corpse being carried to a funeral pyre. These experiences compelled him to seek a spiritual inner peace with which to face the ravages of old age, sickness, and death.

Gautama left his wife and son and lived an austere life of study concentrated on human suffering and its cure. The doctrine, or dharma, he taught consisted of four truths: life is full of suffering and dissatisfaction; suffering emanates from desire; suffering will cease when desire stops; and the cessation of desire can be accomplished through eight steps. These eight steps are right views, right aspirations, right speech, right conduct, right livelihood, right effort, right mindfulness, and right contemplation.

Buddhists think of life as a flowing stream. They believe in Hindu reincarnation, that is, rebirth in which people assume a new physical form and status depending on the quality of their deeds (karma). They also believe that with progress along Buddha's eight-fold path people will reach *nirvana*, a state of serenity and wisdom in which they can escape the cycle of endless rebirth. Although Buddha did not believe in an Absolute or God, after his death he became revered as a god.

Zen, a sect of Buddhism, took root in Japan in the 12th century. Shinto, the traditional religion of Japan prior to the introduction of Buddhism and Confucianism from China, focused on worshipping nature and family ancestors (Holtom, 1984). Shinto philosophy encourages feelings of reverence toward all life, past and present. In feudal, patriarchal Japanese society, Zen Buddhist monks stressed the dignity of physical labor, the arts, swordsmanship, and the tea ceremony, emphasizing stern discipline, selflessness, and spontaneity. Zen beliefs and rituals became integral to Japanese culture.

Islam

Islamic philosophy is based on the writings of the Koran (Quran), the holy or sacred book of Muslims. Muslims believe that the word of God, or Allah, was revealed to Muhammad by the angel Gabriel. Abu-Bakr, Muhammad's father-in-law, collected Muhammad's words in the Koran. Muhammad (570–632), then, was a prophet, like Christ, who described Allah's will. Muhammad foretold of a world where Allah would come on the Last Judgment to appraise all souls by their abilities to live according to Allah's will. To those who succeeded, eternal reward would be granted in paradise; those who failed would be condemned to suffer the pain of eternal fire. The religion of Islam thus was rooted in both Judaism and Christianity and was strongly influenced by the Old and New Testaments (Corbin, 1993; Fakhry, 1983).

Al-Kindī (died after 870) expressed Islam's view of God as an absolute, transcendent being and the idea that revealed truth (that which emanated from philosophy and religion) and rational truth are the same thing. Al-Fārā bī (875–950) expressed the Islamic view that the goal of humankind is to attain immortality through education or the development of one's intellect.

In the ancient world Muslims made important advances in science and medicine. The physician ibn-Sina (980–1037), known as Avicenna, described concepts of matter, form, and existence in a way that allowed for a Necessary Being, or God, who was distinct from the world. To ibn-Sina, the prophets were teachers who used religion as philosophy for the masses to reveal symbolic truth—a kind of truth that helped people approach absolute truth, or God.

African and Native-American Philosophies

According to M. K. Asante, African and African-American philosophies differ from European philosophies in important ways. Western thought is rational (I think, therefore I am), whereas African thought is based on feeling and sociality (I feel, and I relate to others, therefore I am) (Asante, 1987).

Cultural Awareness

During the 1960s Islam gained large numbers of converts in the United States among African Americans, particularly among urban African-American males, principally because Islam is nonracist. The Koran, which includes both Judaic and Christian writings in addition to those of Muhammad and his disciples, expressly forbids discrimination in thought or deed on the basis of race. Submission to Allah and strict adherence to Islam's five pillars of faith guarantee automatic brotherhood and equality. In 1965 Malcolm X, an influential "Black Muslim," wrote bitterly about the need for Islam at a time when many African Americans felt disappointed that the civil rights acts of the late 1950s and early 1960s had not yet made much of a difference in people's lives.

> I am in agreement one hundred per cent with those racists who say that no government laws ever can *force* brotherhood. The only true world solution today is governments guided by true religion—of the spirit. Here in race-torn America, I am convinced that the Islam religion is desperately needed, particularly by the American black man. (p. 369)

In 1995 Louis Farrakahn, leader of the U.S. Nation of Islam, led African Americans in a Million Man March on Washington, D.C., as a protest against racism in America.

Likewise, Christine Sleeter and Carl Grant (1993) describe a "synergetic" way of thinking among some African Americans—a preference for working cooperatively rather than independently and a desire to integrate personal relationships into learning tasks (p. 54).

This holistic view is expressed by the African writer Chinua Achebe. While no single scholar can claim to represent the African perspective, Achebe's *Things Fall Apart* (1968) has been translated into 50 languages and sold 50 million copies. He has "held fast to an African vision of the role of art, one that rejects the Western tradition of seeing the artist apart and alienated from society. In Africa's communal culture, 'art is intended to help society.'" (Winkler, 1994, p. A9).

Asante (1992) writes of the importance of understanding an African-American philosophy and its bearing on educational life in America. He advocates a curriculum that acknowledges African history and culture.

> The African-American children in your classrooms are not a black version of white people. They have different cultural and historical experiences that must be looked at and examined in a different way. To give an obvious example, African Americans did not come to America on the Mayflower. We recognize the Mayflower as part of the American experience, but our experience was different: We crossed the ocean packed in boats with as many as 1,000 other people, with only 18 inches of space between us and the deck above, and chained from neck to ankle. (p. 21)

Traditional Native-American thought also emphasizes holistic, nonrational being and social relations. Reason and logic, for example, are not seen as superior to other explanations of events. Like African traditions, Native-American traditions encourage spiritualism based on animism—belief in the presence of active supernatural forces in the natural world—and on the ideal of harmonious coexistence with nature. Truth comes not from great books or scientific inquiry but from personal introspection, oral traditions, and the values and knowledge handed down from ancestors.

Native-American philosophies stress personal dignity, moral responsibility, and the mutual interdependence of all the people in a society or group. Group identity and well-being take precedence over individual needs and abilities. Traditional social values encourage silent reflection over verbalizing, cooperation over competition, stability over change, and continuity over progress (Banks, 1994).

African and Native-American thought, like the religious and secular philosophies of the Middle East, India, and Asia, influence the development of educational philosophies in the United States in two main ways: They broaden people's minds and they enlighten changes in curriculum and instruction that are designed to meet the needs of all students in our culturally diverse society.

WHAT FACTORS INFLUENCE TEACHERS' PERSONAL PHILOSOPHIES OF EDUCATION?

Individual educators draw upon various philosophies, both purposefully and casually, to fashion their own unique views of teaching and learning. Teachers are idealists, realists, pragmatists, cognitivists, and the like. They reveal their philosophical roots, both knowingly and unknowingly, through their interactions with students, parents, administrators, and others. Some hold classical positions on the nature of knowledge and of being—we think of a New York teacher we met who spoke a dozen languages and expresssed a personal commitment to helping his students discover the universal truths we share as human beings. Others, like a teacher we encountered in New Mexico, describe the importance of their work almost strictly in terms of the practical value it yields in the lives of students. If asked to do so, many teachers might well articulate their philosophies as some amalgam of classical positions.

> As a person, a teacher is changing and developing, advancing and regressing, experiencing the joys and disappointments of life just as all adults do. At the same time, a teacher is a powerful adult in a world of children. For most schoolchildren, their teacher is the adult with whom they have the greatest amount of daily contact. Teachers therefore have significant opportunities to influence the personal development of their impressionable students. Teachers act as potential role models of responsible adult behavior, attitudes, and values. And the teacher is the architect of the social system of the classroom with its rules, norms, sanctions and rewards. The social system of the classroom sets the tone and context

for human interaction for an entire school year. And the personality and values of the teacher are clearly reflected in how life in a classroom is lived out. Parents of schoolchildren know that who the teacher is as a person has a profound effect on the quality of education that their children experience (Clark, 1995, p. 4).

Since the mid-1970s educational researchers and cognitive psychologists have explored teachers' beliefs, judgments, and decisions for clues to the "mental lives of teachers" (Clark & Peterson, 1986, p. 255). Much of the work has been aimed at portraying the psychology of teaching so as to guide policymakers, curriculum developers, and teacher educators, but research on teachers' thought processes also has revealed the philosophies and habits of mind that shape and are shaped by life in classrooms.

Why does this teacher need to know her own philosophy of education? How can she develop a personal educational philosophy to guide her professional practice as a teacher?

Teachers' Theories and Beliefs

Clark and Peterson (1986) offer a model that attempts to account for the relationships between teachers' thought and action. In Figure 4.5, the first circle depicts what goes on inside teachers' heads, the unobservable. In this circle the terms *preactive, postactive,* and *interactive* refer respectively to thoughts before, after, and during teaching. Teachers' theories and beliefs derive from these thoughts and also from their ideas about the nature of children as learners (metaphysics), ways of knowing (epistemology), and right content and conduct (axiology). The second circle—teachers' behaviors, students' behaviors, and students' achievements, such as test scores—represents the observable in classrooms. This circle is the domain where teaching actually occurs.

The arrows in the model show how teachers' thought processes and actions interact. For example, teachers' theories and beliefs affect their planning and their thoughts during teaching, which in turn, affect their theories and beliefs.

Effective teachers are more predisposed than are others to look for meaning in the events of teaching and learning. They are openminded and sensitive to new ideas. They resist simple explanations for complex problems and try instead to understand acts in the contexts in which they occur. They might be said to be more philosophical or theoretical than other teachers; they might also be said to be more practical.

Should you teach from an educational philosophy or from a personal philosophy?

How do teachers develop their habits of thinking, their personal philosophies? Although there are no simple answers, David Hunt (1987), an instructional psychologist at the Ontario Institute for Studies in Education, has provided some intriguing leads. Hunt observes that most new ideas in philosophy, psychology, education, and social sciences are presented in orthodox

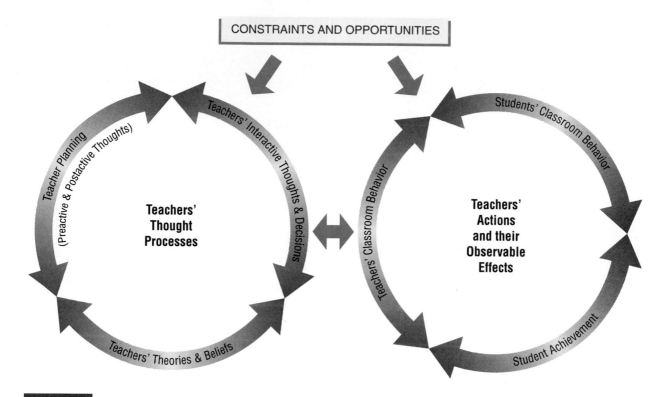

FIGURE 4.5

Teachers' Thought Processes in Relation to Teachers' Actions

In what ways might teachers' thought processes constrain teachers' actions? In what ways might teachers' thought processes provide opportunities for enhancing the effects of teachers' actions?

Note. From "Teachers' Thought Processes" by Christopher M. Clark and Penelope L. Peterson. Reprinted with permission of Macmillan Publishing Company from *Handbook of Research on Teach* (3rd. ed.) Merlin C. Wittrock, Editor. Copyright 1986 by the American Education Research Association.

fashion by making cases for them based on research results or on theoretical grounds. Teachers, for instance, take college courses designed to present them with the latest research and thinking on human behavior. They, in turn, are supposed to translate this knowledge into action with their students. Most of the time, then, teachers begin with someone else's ideas and try to make sense out of them in their own situations, a logical progression from philosophy to practice.

Hunt argues, however, that viewing the development of knowledge this way cuts people off from their own experiences. In effect, they must take information from outside themselves and try to integrate it, or to put it inside themselves. Hunt believes that people should begin constructing their philosophical and professional knowledge by examining their own personal beliefs. For teachers this means making explicit their own beliefs and values about teaching and learning by consciously considering their ideals about the nature of children as learners, what is worth knowing, and the purposes of education.

Teachers' Personal Life Experiences

Personal life experiences profoundly affect a teacher's educational philosophy. Gerber (1992) investigated the life of a teacher with learning disabilities, TJ, during his first year on the job. TJ's assignment was as a resource room teacher—a special education teacher who works with students in small groups. This role was new to the rural school district where TJ taught, so he

VOICES

On Thoughtful Teaching

Teachers must deal regularly with truth, lies, honesty, dishonesty, cheating, and fair play. In his book entitled *Thoughtful Teaching*, Christopher Clark shares a teacher's reflection on honesty as told by Canon Farrar more than 100 years ago.

At Harrow, two boys brought me [Canon Farrar] exercises marked by the same grotesque mistakes. It seemed certain that those exercises could not have been done independently. Both boys assured me that there had been no copying. One whom I had considered a boy of high morale assured me of this again and again with passionate earnestness. I said to him, "If I were to send up these two exercises to any jury in England, they would say that these resemblances could not be accidental, except by something almost like a miracle. But you both tell me that you have not copied. I cannot believe that you would lie to me. I must suppose that there has been some extraordinary accident. I shall say no more." Years after, that boy, then a monitor, said to me: "Sir, do you remember that exercise in the fourth form?" "Yes", I said. "Well, sir, I told you a lie. It was copied. You believed me, and the remembrance of that lie had remained with me and pained me ever since." "I am inclined to think," says Canon Farrar, "that boy was more effectually taught and more effectually punished than if I had refused to accept his protests."

CRITICAL THINKING

If you were a teacher and faced with a situation similar to the one described above, would you feel compelled to behave in some particular way, or would you simply ignore the situation? Do you think that your propensity to act in a particular way, or to not act at all, would be influenced more by values you acquired from your parents, by some religious beliefs, by some philosophical ideal, or by some other influence? Can you imagine having to modify your own philosophy of teaching in some way if you had to face increasing numbers of students who cheated? If so, how might you change your outlook and your behavior as a teacher?

Note. From *Thoughtful teaching* by C. M. Clark, 1995. London: Cassell. (pp. 77–78).

faced the additional challenge of helping others understand how resource teachers function.

The way he decorated his classroom walls was an indicator of TJ's beliefs about people with learning disabilities:

> From the first moment that one enters TJ's classroom several messages become abundantly clear. They are—it is okay to have a learning disability, and you must work hard in order to succeed. Moreover, when you are learning disabled you are entitled to basic rights granted to persons with disabilities. An article complete with pictures from *Psychology Today* informs the reader that George Patton, Auguste Rodin, Leonardo Da Vinci, Albert Einstein, Tom Cruise, and Stephan Cannell (television writer and producer) were learning disabled. The LD Bill of Rights is thumbtacked next to it. It states that when one has a learning disability certain accommodations are permitted such as extended time limits for testing, tests read by a reader, presentation of material so it can be

understood, access to a resource room, and the right to an appropriate education. (p. 219)

TJ's student teaching experience was fraught with problems. His university supervisor even suggested that he would not make it as a teacher. The negative feedback "made him feel like he wasn't worth a plug nickel" (p. 17). When Gerber observed TJ in the classroom, however, he saw a very different teacher—one who was self-confident and supportive of his students.

Estimates of teacher attrition vary from 20% to 40% during the first 5 years on the job. If you are a teacher with a disability, discouragement can be part of the territory. Members of the Council for Exceptional Children recognized as much when they passed the "Resolution of Special Educators with Disabilities, which supports the recruitment, training, and employment of individuals with disabilities" (Council for Exceptional Children, 1996, p. 11). For individuals such as TJ, this support, coupled with a healthy philosophy, can make all the difference.

TJ stayed in teaching the first year and returned again the following fall. His philosophy of teaching, realistically formed by collecting information from both sides of the teacher's desk, weighted the importance of success and personal satisfaction heavily:

> The satisfaction of witnessing the learning of his students is exhilarating. As TJ explained, "My experiences have really helped me with the students. If I had to do it all over again, I'd do it all over again. Because when I feel I'm with my students and things are clicking—that's a great high." (Gerber, 1992, p. 224)

Teacher Reflection and Problem Solving

Researchers also have explored how teachers think on the job. As illustrated in Figure 4.6, Greta Morine-Dershimer (1990) has noted that teachers think about teaching in a variety of ways.

First, some teachers base their thoughts on organized structures of knowledge that represent relationships among concepts. For example, sometimes they think in terms of scripts that summarize typical classroom routines. They envision scenes to organize information about people and objects in recurring classroom events. They also formulate propositions to summarize factual knowledge about students, subject matter content, and teaching strategies. Morine-Dershimer (1990) believes that this line of work "provides a very positive image of the mental functioning of teachers" (p. 5). Studies of experts and novices indicate that experienced teachers have acquired and systematically stored much useful information and can access this information when they need it (Clark & Peterson, 1986).

Second, teachers' thinking has been characterized in terms of artistry, or as reflecting in and reflecting on action. Reflection in action has been compared to having a conversation with a situation (Schön, 1987). During *reflection*, a teacher perceives a problem, thinks about other past similar events,

How do teachers achieve professional excellence?

Conceptualizations	Types of information emphasized	Notable transformations of information	Ideal state	Possible use in teacher education
Thinking through schemata	Routines/scripts Classroom organizations/schemes Activity structures	Reorganization of new information according to existing schemata	Teacher manages flow of information to track pupil understanding of lesson content	Prospective teachers learn classroom routines
Reflecting in/on practice	Classroom events recalled from prior situations "Backtalk" of pupils in immediate situation	Reframing an ambiguous or problematic situation	Teacher reconceptualizes the situation and resolves the problem	Prospective teachers acquire experience in a variety of settings
Formulating pedagogical content	Subject matter content Pedagogical processes Pupils' common misconceptions of subject matter Pupils' real life experiences related to subject matter	Transforming subject matter for presentation to pupils	Teacher uses appropriate analogies and varied examples to develop pupil understanding of concepts, and relates topic to pupils' own experiences	Prospective teachers learn many alternative analogies and examples appropriate for use with basic concepts
Perceiving practical arguments	Experiential knowledge (situational premises) Propositional knowledge (principles of practice; empirical premises) Normative knowledge (value premises)	Recognizing "subjectively reasonable beliefs" and reformulating to arrive at "objectively reasonable beliefs"	Teacher's actions are consistent with objectively reasonable beliefs (research and "warranted practice")	Prospective teachers explore own beliefs in relation to research

FIGURE 4.6

Comparing Conceptualizations of Teacher Thinking

Note. From *To Think Like a Teacher* by G. Morine-Dershimer, 1990. Vice Presidential address presented to the annual meeting of the American Education Research Association, Boston. Reprinted with permission.

interprets the problem in light of this past knowledge, and takes action. The problem "talks back" by yielding information that causes the teacher to reframe the problem and to make another move. And so on. In contrast, reflection on action is after-the-fact analysis—that is, once an event has occurred, a teacher might think back on what he or she might have done differently and what effects such action might have produced. Such reflection is disconnected from present action. Because there is no need for a quick response, reflection on action is a more analytical process.

Vivian Paley (1979) demonstrated this type of thinking after a colleague accused her of reinforcing stereotypes. She reported, in *White Teacher*, how a

BENCHMARKS

Developments in Western Intellectual Thought and Their Influence on American Education

The Classical Period **500 BC–500 AD**	Greeks and Romans define the branches of philosophy and basic ideas on which Western intellectual thought is based. Socrates and Plato define idealism; Aristotle, realism. Quintillion establishes the Roman school system from which the American school system is descended.
The Middle Ages **500 AD–1300**	Arab scholars preserve the Greco-Roman intellectual traditions after the fall of Rome. Arab mathematicians, geographers, physicians, and scientists, such as Ibn-Sina (Avicenna), Ibn-Rushid (Averroes), and Ibn-Battuta contribute to Western learning. In Charlemagne's empire, Alcuin establishes a prototype curriculum of seven "liberal arts." The first universities are established in medieval Spain, France, and England. Thomas Aquinas formalizes scholasticism, later known as Thomism, an educational philosophy based on the logical study of beliefs of the Church. Thomism becomes the basis of Roman Catholic parochial education.
The Renaissance **and Reformation** **1300-1700**	Humanism revives the classical philosophies of human nature. The humanist philosopher Erasmus calls for respect and kindness toward students and developmentally appropriate instruction in liberal arts, social conduct, and moral principles. Developments in printing-press technology increase the availability of books and public demand for literacy. To the curriculum of humanism, Johann Comenius adds the study of science and the use of textbooks written specifically for students. Martin Luther launches the Protestant Reformation, a reaction against some of the teachings of the Roman Catholic Church based on the idea that people should read and interpret the Bible for themselves. Luther and other Protestants call for universal state-supported liberal education. Ignatius of Loyola founds the Society of Jesus (Jesuits), and Jean Baptiste de la Salle founds the Brothers of the Christian Schools, teaching orders devoted to furthering the cause of the Church and counteracting the Protestant Reformation. In *Essay Concerning Human Understanding and Some Thoughts on Education*, John Locke expresses the realist view that reality and thought are separate. He describes a child's mind as a blank slate (tabula rasa) on which teachers must imprint an education.

middle-aged, Jewish woman learned to think about her own thinking as she interacted with her African-American kindergarten students:

> "[T]he black girls" were, in fact, five separate girls who played together and copied each other a great deal. I could name five white girls who played together, but I did not call them "the white girls." I was starting to realize, with help of a good friend, that thinking of Ayana, Rena, Karla, Joyce, and Sylvia as "the black girls" kept me from seeing them always as individuals. (p. 135)

The 1700s	In *Emile*, Jean Jacques Rousseau expresses a humanistic view of education in which children are not blank slates but possess natural goodness and freedom which must be nurtured so that individuals can express their greatest potentials. Educator Johann Pestalozzi puts Rousseau's theory into practice.
	The writings of Voltaire and Descartes help to popularize scientific inquiry and spread commitment to rationalism and empiricism as philosophical orientations to education.
	In his *Critique of Pure Reason*, Immanuel Kant reflects classical idealism in his definition of knowledge as the interaction of reason and experience. German idealist Georg Wilhelm Friedrich Hegel describes reality as a dialectic between thesis (idea), antithesis (nature), and synthesis (mind or spirit).
The 1800s	Karl Marx transforms Hegel's dialectic between ideas, nature, and mind into a dialectic between economic or material conditions and human choices. Dialectical materialism becomes the basis of the political philosophy known as Marxism.
	Educators Johann Herbart and Friedrich Froebel develop Rousseau's philosophy into teaching methods that spread to the United States.
	Charles Darwin's 1859 *On the Origin of Species* focuses attention on heredity, evolution, and natural processes of adaptation and change. His work stimulates the scientific movement and influences the philosophers and educators who come to be known as the pragmatists. Herbert Spencer's theory of Social Darwinism becomes the basis of a movement calling for utilitarian education.
Around the Turn of the Century	Charles Pierce and William James express the philosophy of pragmatism, based on the idea that the purpose of thought is to produce action. Practical knowledge and applied skills become a focus of educational reform.
	Maria Montessori develops an educational philosophy in the humanist tradition that continues today through a system of private schools.

Third, Morine-Dershimer notes that Lee Shulman (1987) suggested that teachers possess a unique form of knowledge, which exists at the intersection of content knowledge and knowledge of teaching or pedagogy, which he calls "pedagogical content knowledge." Shulman has explored how teachers transform content and pedagogy by reading, discussion, observation, and practice into knowledge that is adapted to the abilities of students. TJ, the teacher of learning-disabled students, for example, uses himself as an analogy for his students, adjusting his teaching to meet the needs of students whom he perceives to be much like himself.

Developments in Western Intellectual Thought and Their Influence on American Education (cont.)

1920s and 1930s	John Dewey extends the philosophy of pragmatism in education. His views—that ideas must be tested through experimentation, that people learn best through questioning and hands-on experiences, and that the needs of the child are most important—become known as progressivism. Progressivism becomes the most influential educational philosophy in America until the 1950s. Influenced by events of the Great Depression, Theodore Brameld and George Counts develop the philosophy of social reconstructionism, in which the aim of education is to reform the social order, fulfill democratic ideals, and improve the quality of human life.
1940s and 1950s	Progressivism underlies Jean Piaget's studies of children's cognitive and social development. Opposing Dewey and progressivism, Robert Maynard Hutchins and Mortimer Adler promote the philosophy known as perennialism. They develop Great Books of the Western World, the study of selected classics to uncover enduring basic truths. Other perennialists call for reserving general education for the gifted and including character training and Bible study in the curriculum. Other critics of progressivism, such as William Bagley and Arthur Bestor, promote essentialism, calling for a common core of essential knowledge that changes with the times and rigorous teacher-centered instruction in basic skills so that people can lead productive lives. Influenced by events surrounding World War II, existentialist writers and philosophers such as Sören Kierkegaard, Albert Camus, and Jean-Paul Sartre popularize the idea that reality resides within the individual, that we are free to search for our own meaning in the world, and that we are what we choose to be. Behavioral psychology emerges from experiments by Ivan Pavlov, John Watson, and others. B. F. Skinner improves this earlier work and develops principles based on the idea that behavior is determined by environment and that people are best motivated by rewards and punishments.

And fourth, teachers' thinking about their work has been characterized in terms of Aristotle's concept of "practical argument"—that is, an argument ending in action related to the logic of one's initial proposition. Tom Green (1976) suggested that good teachers can perceive the practical arguments of students. For instance, when students are incorrect or unreasonable, the teacher determines why students think as they do, then helps them reexamine their beliefs so as to formulate better responses. Gary Fenstermacher (1986) also suggests that research on teaching can be used to influence teachers' beliefs, in a sense, to strengthen their practical arguments.

When teachers understand, articulate, and act on their philosophies, they cultivate their own "literacy of thoughtfulness" (Brown, 1991, p. 35).

1960s and 1970s	In Walden Two, B. F. Skinner shows how behavioral engineering—the scientific control of the educative process—might lead to the creation of a utopian society. Behaviorism widely influences educational practice. Humanistic psychology develops from the work of Alfred Adler, Carl Rogers, Abraham Maslow, and others, partly as a reaction against behaviorism, and influences the open school movement. Experimental curricula, such as A. S. Neill's Summerhill, express the humanistic and existentialist views that the aim of education is to promote personal freedom and expression and individual self-fulfillment. Eastern philosophies derived from Hinduism and Buddhism influence curriculum in the United States and educational movements based on existential and reconstructionist philosophies. Social reconstructionism based on Marxist assumptions about the world is expressed in the writings of Herbert Marcuse, Jurgen Habermas, and others.
1980s and 1990s	In Paideia Proposal, Mortimer Adler extends the educational philosophy of perennialism that he and Hutchins developed earlier in the century, calling for one course of study for all. The Back to Basics movement, the Essential Schools movement developed by Theodore Sizer, and E. D. Hirsch's curriculum for cultural literacy revive interest in essentialism. Constructivism and multiculturalism as educational movements have combined roots in the philosophies of humanism, progressivism, existentialism, and reconstructionism.

By example, then, they encourage students to do the same. These consequences, some would argue, are enough to justify the study of philosophy for its own sake. But a teacher's philosophy serves other purposes as well. Philosophy provides the foundation upon which teachers construct knowledge about teaching and learning. Philosophy guides the professional rationale that supports reasoned and reasonable action. Philosophy helps teachers evaluate their work and thus assists them in their pursuit of personal and professional excellence.

SUMMARY

What is philosophy, and what does it have to do with you as a teacher?

1 Philosophy is a set of ideas about the nature of reality and about the meaning of life. Both ancient and modern philosophies influence education today.

What are the roots of American educational philosophies?

2 The three main branches of philosophy are (a) metaphysics, which deals with the study of reality; (b) epistemology, which is concerned with the nature of knowledge; and (c) axiology, which seeks to determine what is of value.

3 Idealists are concerned with goals against which people can judge their own progress and the progress of civilization. Platonian idealists believe that education is the key to creating and perpetuating a society in which talent rises to the top.

4 Realists seek to discover truth in the world around them via methods of direct observation and scientific inquiry. Aristotle believed that excellence would flourish as one sought the middle ground between life's extremes. Realists believe that the role of education is to teach students about the world in which they live.

5 Thomists believe there is an independent reality knowable to man that is the creation of God. A combination of reason and faith enables people to discover truth. Thomists see the primary role of education as training individuals to understand the religious truths necessary for spiritual salvation.

6 Humanists reform people's perceptions of themselves in relation to teaching and learning. They also express their beliefs in the inherent goodness of children. Humanists believe that education should prepare people to take responsibility for their own lives.

What modern philosophies influence Western education?

7 Existentialists believe that people are free to define their lives as they choose. As such, existentialist educators prize individuality and resist social conformism.

8 Marxists believe that the human condition is determined by forces in history that prevent people from achieving economic freedom and social and political equality. When Marxists view public schools in the United States, they see evidence of the ruling elite, or the haves, in a capitalist society dominating the have-nots. This evidence, they contend, is often veiled by a curriculum that assumes the values of the ruling elite are viable for all.

9 Behaviorism explicates relationships between the environment and behavior. In America's schools, both curriculum and teaching reflect behavioristic philosophy in the use of conditioning and modeling techniques.

10 Cognitivism is based on the belief that people actively construct their knowledge of the world through experience and interaction rather than behavioral conditioning.

11 For pragmatists, and progressives, truth is relative, or determined by science or by function. According to their philosophy, people are capable of experiencing, experimenting, and testing their beliefs, changing them if need be.

12 Perennialists and essentialists assert that there are some recurring principles of education so important that they should be learned for their own sake. Because people are basically the same, there must be constancy in the way they are educated. Essentialists also believe that some principles must be taught to all students so that they can solve contemporary problems. For essentialists, science is central to societal progress.

13 Social reconstructionists seek change in society. They would use education to reform not only schools but also the communities in which schools are embedded.

What non-Western philosophies influence American education?

14 Hinduism, Buddhism, and Islam influence contemporary American educational philosophies.

15 African-American and Native-American philosophies, based on feeling and sociality, influence the development of curriculum and instruction.

What factors influence teachers' personal philosophies of education?

16 Educators draw upon Western and non-Western philosophies, both purposefully and casually, to fashion their own unique views of teaching and learning. Teachers' theories and beliefs, personal life experiences, and reflection and problem-solving skills also help to shape their personal philsophies.

TERMS AND CONCEPTS

aesthetics, *p. 133*
axiology, *p. 133*
behaviorism, *p. 143*
cognitivism, *p. 143*
constructivism, *p. 145*
cosmology, *p. 132*
cultural literacy, *p. 150*
epistemology, *p. 132*
essentialism, *p. 148*
ethics, *p. 133*
Eurocentric, *p. 149*
existentialism, *p. 140*
humanism, *p. 136*

idealism, *p. 133*
Marxism, *p. 142*
metaphysics, *p. 132*
ontology, *p. 132*
perennialism, *p. 147*
philosophy, *p. 130*
pragmatism, *p. 145*
realism, *p. 134*
scaffolding, *p. 145*
social reconstructionism, *p. 150*
Socratic method, *p. 133*
Thomism, *p. 135*

REFLECTIVE PRACTICE

Harry Shabanowitz, eighth-grade science teacher at Garfield Junior High School, served as managing editor of *The Garfield Gazette*—the school paper produced by students and faculty as part of an interdisciplinary unit. Shabanowitz thinks that students need to make logical connections between the subject matter and their own lives and to improve their work habits.

I have watched them go through general science and biology, and in elementary chemistry, without understanding why they are here. They can't explain how an experiment relates to a concept in the text, or how a scientific concept in the text relates to a practical example of the concept in our lives. They just go through the motions—even the bright students. The other thing that worries me is their lack of general knowledge and the absence of pride in their work. They can't even keep a lab book so I can read it. Sloppy handwriting. Lousy grammar. They exhibit a casual disregard for self-discipline that would prevent them from ever being admitted to a decent college or university, let alone getting and keeping a job.

Steve Keegan, history teacher and entertainment editor for *The Garfield Gazette*, sees his teaching world in different terms.

Our task is more than teaching our subject matter in interrelated ways. The kids come in here not knowing what they are going to do with their lives. They are too young really to know. But some are already failing—they are goofing up their chances for any kind of academic success in high school and probably for later economic success in life. Others are college bound. These students and their parents just naturally assume they will succeed. I think our work should suggest that interdisciplinary studies can help students connect with each other and link school work to real life.

LeRoy, a student who works on the newspaper, got caught in what might be termed a philosophical dispute between Shabanowitz and Keegan.

Scene: *Teachers had rolled back the accordion walls of their four classrooms in the west wing of Garfield Junior High in September and gathered 80 students. They were deep into production of the first issue of* The Garfield Gazette. *Harry Shabanowitz served as managing editor and held a meeting with his student science reporters.*

SHABANOWITZ: Okay, I want all you science reporters to tell me the name of the person you interviewed, the topic of your story, and how many manuscript pages you have written.

LEROY (student): Gretchen Vanderkellen. Astrology. Twelve pages.

SHABANOWITZ: LeRoy, this is supposed to be the science section, not the comics. Are you trying to roll in a story on the occult?

LEROY: You said we could identify a topic we were interested in, Mr. Shabanowitz. Astrologers predicted the future based on the mathematical positions of the sun, moon, stars, and planets. They also kept track of the movement of these bodies. Astrologers were practically worshipped by people. I think they were respected as much as our scientists are today. I read that astrologers even diagnosed diseases and prescribed medicines for the sick. See here, Mr. Keegan showed me how to take some things astrologers might say and to prove that their ideas are not that different from other people's ideas today. [LeRoy pulls a story outline out of his backpack and lays it on Harry Shabanowitz's desk.]

SHABANOWITZ: Look, LeRoy, that's all very interesting. I think I understand where you want to be going with this piece, but it does not belong in the science section. We can't have our readers thinking you believe astrology has the same credibility as physics or chemistry, or even as some social science.

LEROY: But Mr. Shabanowitz, I believe people thought about astrology and astronomy almost the same way for many centuries. You can even find astrology on the World Wide Web. I got this address from my older sister. [LeRoy puts a scrap of paper on the desk that contains the following address: **http://marilyn. metawire.com/stars**]

SHABANOWITZ: Sure, sure, LeRoy, but I think you had better find a new topic or try to convince Mr. Keegan to put your story in the entertainment section.

Note. From *All the news that's fit to teach.* by R. F. McNergney, 1996, Washington, DC: The Hitachi Foundation. Available at **http://teach.virginia.edu/go/casecourse**.

Issues, Problems, Dilemmas, Opportunities

What problems or issues arise when Shabanowitz is talking with LeRoy?

Perceive and Value

Describe the similarities and differences in the views of Harry Shabanowitz and Steve Keegan. How might their personal philosophies influence their interactions with students?

Know and Act

Assume you were the managing editor in this situation. What more might you want to know if you were faced with the decision of running LeRoy's story? What might you do?

Evaluate

What might be the outcomes of publishing and not publishing LeRoy's story? What outcomes emanating from the publication or rejection of LeRoy's story might cause you to change your outlook on what is important for students to learn from their participation in the newspaper unit?

ONLINE ACTIVITY

The American Philosophical Association challenges Web travelers to discern the relevance of philosophy to their lives by exploring their site (**http://www.udel.edu/apa/**). You will find newsletters, electronic texts, Web conferences, and even information on a television show called *No Dogs or Philosophers Allowed*. When you arrive at the site, see if you can find The International Encyclopedia of Philosophy, which contains translations of original texts by philosophers mentioned in this chapter. For example, you might want to read Plato's *Republic* at **http://www.utm.edu/research/iep/text/plato/rep/rep.htm**.

5

Schools

The emergence of the common school marked the beginning of public education in America. Many people such as Horace Mann viewed the common school as a great equalizing force having the potential to eliminate poverty, crime, and ignorance. Although schools have fallen short of these goals in many ways, Americans continue to pin their hopes for a better world on a place called "school."

In this chapter, we describe some of the ways schools differ from one another and what makes some schools more appealing to one group of people than to another. We also present research on more and less effective schools, which focuses on a number of attributes that seem to make a difference in students' performance and their attitudes toward school.

PROFESSIONAL PRACTICE QUESTIONS

1 How is the school a social institution?

2 How is public schooling organized in the United States?

3 What are some schooling alternatives?

4 How are schools administered?

5 What organizational and policy issues do schools face?

6 What makes some schools more effective than others?

How is the School a Social Institution?

The school is first and foremost a social **institution**; that is, an established organization having an identifiable structure and a set of functions meant to preserve and extend social order. Schools are structured to operate as relatively self-contained units, loosely coupled to other schools within a system. Schools have personalities that characterize daily life within their walls. Sometimes these personalities are visible in written mission statements, but more often than not they emerge in interactions with the members of the organization.

As a social institution, a school's primary function is to move young people into the mainstream of society. The curricula, teaching, processes of evaluation, and relationships among people reinforce a public image to which young people are expected to aspire. This image is concerned with preserving our heritage, adapting to social change, and making change happen where it is needed.

More and more people are recognizing the power of the school as a social institution. Recent reform efforts have tried to capitalize on the fact that schools are the places where people come together and stay together for an extended period of time in their lives. In such settings, educators work with parents, children, and outside agencies to ensure the psychological and physical well-being of students and to foster academic success. They also work collaboratively to build students' understanding and acceptance of others.

◼ School Districts

A **school district** is a state-defined geographical area assigned responsibility for public instruction within its borders. During the 1995–1996 academic year, there were 87,110 public schools serving a total of 43,464,916 students in grades prekindergarten through 12 (U.S. Department of Education, 1996a). Sizes of school districts vary from place to place, but generally the largest can be found in the eastern third of the United States. As illustrated in Table 5.1, the largest districts serve more than 28% of the total elementary and secondary school population in the country, yet they account for only 1% of all school districts. The New York City school district, the largest in the country, alone has 1,064 schools, 55,353 teachers, and 1,005,521 students (U.S. Department of Education, 1995).

Big school districts are very different from one another in a number of ways. In Gwinnett County, Georgia, for instance, 6.7% of the students are eligible for free lunch, while 73% of those in Orleans Parish, Louisiana, qualify for the program. Racial/ethnic compositions of school districts also show considerable variation. At least 89% of students in the District of Columbia are African American, while 88% in Jefferson County, Colorado, are European American. In Hawaii, 68% are Asian/Pacific-Islander American, while 73.7% in El Paso, Texas, and 82.2% in San Antonio, Texas are Hispanic American. As noted in Table 5.2, six large school districts, three of which are in Texas, have student bodies composed mainly of three racial/ethnic categories (U.S. Department of Education, 1995).

To find out more about school districts in your area or in an area of the country where you might want to teach, access the Web site **http://www. sunspace.com** and click on "school district profiles." Profiles include information such as how many children attend school in the district, the percent-

TABLE 5.1   Public School Districts and Enrollment by
                Size of District, 1994–1995

Enrollment size of district	Number of districts	Percent of districts	Percent of students
Total	14,772	100.0	100.0
25,000 or more	207	1.4	29.9
10,000 to 24,999	542	3.7	18.6
5,000 to 9,999	996	6.7	15.7
2,500 to 4,999	2,013	13.6	16.1
1,000 to 2,499	3,579	24.2	13.4
600 to 999	1,777	12.0	3.2
300 to 599	2,113	14.3	2.1
1 to 299	3,173	21.5	1.0
Size not reported*	372	2.5	

*Includes school districts reporting enrollment of 0.

Note. From *Digest of Education Statistics*, 1996 (p. 96) by U.S. Department of Education, 1996, Washington, DC: U.S. Government Printing Office.

TABLE 5.2   Variation in Racial/Ethnic Composition of Student Populations in Six Districts, in Percent

School District	Hispanic	African American non-Hispanic	European American non-Hispanic	American Indian/ Alaska Native	Asian/ Pacific
Dade County, FL	48.1	33.9	16.7	0	1.2
Dallas, TX	38.2	44.9	14.8	.4	1.7
Fort Worth, TX	28.0	37.5	29.5	1.6	3.3
Austin, TX	36.7	19.0	41.9	.3	2.1
Denver, CO	41.2	21.8	31.7	1.4	3.9
Boston, MA	22.7	47.6	20.2	.4	9.1

Note. From Characteristics of the 55 largest public elementary and secondary school districts in the United States: 1992–93 (p. 31) by U.S. Department of Education, 1995, Washington, DC: U.S. Government Printing Office.

age of youngsters who are in poverty, the amount of money the district spends on students each year, and the average pupil–teacher ratio.

Types of Schools

Children in the United States have access to many types of public and private schools (see Figure 5.1). Schools are designed for different ages of students, from preschool to college. In many public school settings, there are magnet schools, charter schools, alternative schools, and vocational or trade schools. There are also rural schools, suburban schools, and urban schools. The various schools often differ in structure (organization) and function (programs and services).

An analysis of more than 14,000 parental responses to a survey conducted by SchoolMatch, a data-based information and counseling service in Columbus, Ohio, suggests that many parents consider several attributes when selecting a school. Among respondents, however, low pupil–teacher ratio was the one attribute of schools having universal appeal. The majority (62.7%) wanted "small" or "very small" classes for elementary-age children, and 57% indicated that "average" classes were suitable for junior- and senior-high school students. With regard to academic rigor, only 28.3% wanted their children in schools with the highest range (81st to 99th percentile) of composite scores on standardized tests; 53.2% wanted a school system in the second highest range (61st to 80th percentile). Data suggest that parents want their children to attend school where they can be successful rather than where students have the highest scholastic ranking (Bainbridge & Sundre, 1992).

What do parents want in a school system?

FIGURE 5.1

Examples of the Structure and Types of Schooling in America

You will learn as you read this chapter that it is difficult in many cases to draw solid lines between the three columns in this chart. Develop a hypothesis that you think might explain this difficulty.

PUBLIC SCHOOLS	PUBLIC ALTERNATIVE SCHOOLS	PRIVATE SCHOOLS
Kindergarten (K)	Head Start	Nursery Schools & Preschools
Elementary School (K/1–6 or K/1–8)	Prekindergarten Programs	"Concept School" Alternatives
• Primary (K–2)	Laboratory Schools	• Montessori Schools
• Intermediate (3–6)	Nongraded Schools	• Waldorf Schools
Middle School (5–8)	Magnet Schools	• Steiner Schools
Secondary Schools	Charter Schools	"Ethnic School" Alternatives
• Junior High School (7–8 or 7–9)	Accelerated Schools	• Afrocentric Schools (Black Academies)
• High School (7–12, 9–12, or 10–12)	Cluster Schools	• Reservation Schools
Post-Secondary Schools	Vocational–Technical Schools	Parochial/Religious Schools
• Community Colleges	Professional Development Schools	• Catholic Schools
• State Colleges	Government-Run Schools	• Christian Academies
• State Universities	• Department of Defense Dependents Schools	• Hebrew Schools
	• Native-American Schools	• Islamic Schools
	• Career Academies	College Preparatory Schools
	• Job Corps	Trade Schools
	Home Schooling	Military Academies
		Junior Colleges
		Colleges & Universities
		Adult Education Centers

HOW IS PUBLIC SCHOOLING ORGANIZED IN THE UNITED STATES?

Many children in the United States attend some form of preschool, but, as we explain later in the chapter, enrollment rates vary according to family income and race/ethnicity. Once children reach kindergarten age, nearly 84% enroll in one of the more than 60,000 public elementary schools (U.S. Department of Education, 1996b). Enrollees often are classified as primary (kindergarten through grade 2) and intermediate (grades 3 through 6) students. With increasing frequency, however, students in grades 4 through 6, 5 through 7, or 6 through 8 attend middle schools. In some school districts students in grades 7 through 8 or 7 through 9 are enrolled in junior high schools.

High schools, or secondary schools, usually include grades 10 through 12 or 9 through 12. In some states, such as California, Illinois, and New Jersey, where 4-year high schools are the rule, the high school may function as a separate entity, having its own board of education. For the most part, however, the trend has been to combine elementary, middle, and high schools into a unified district.

Because parents and school leaders want high school students to go on for more education, high schools try to prepare students to move up the academic ladder. As with preschool, however, access to higher education is influenced in large part by the cost of postsecondary education programs to students and their families. Among high school graduates' options are technical or vocation institutions, 2-year colleges, and 4-year colleges and universities.

Early Childhood Education

Many of the first early childhood programs were in day nurseries funded by philanthropic organizations and associated with settlement houses. Today, preschool programs are more diversified and are supported by both public and private interest groups and sponsors. Project Head Start, infant intervention and enrichment programs, nursery schools, public and private prekindergartens and kindergartens, college and university laboratory schools, church-sponsored preschools, and parent cooperatives offer a variety of educational programs for young children. Although enrollment in such programs has gradually increased over time, 4- to 5-year-olds are more likely to receive some type of education on a regular basis than are 3-year-olds. Nonminority-group children also participate in such programs at higher rates than do minority-group children. The majority of students receiving preschool services are enrolled in nursery schools and other types of organized group programs, such as prekindergarten and Head Start (U.S. Department of Education, 1996).

To what extent should preschools be expected to assume child-rearing functions?

With so many agencies sponsoring preschool programs, there is much variation in the types of services offered and in the types of families served. While some preschools offer full-day educational or custodial care, others offer only half-day programs. Preschools also may be restricted to children from low-income families, to children of adolescent parents, or to children with disabilities. Among the different preschools, program goals and philosophies about teaching and learning also vary considerably.

The professional preparation of early childhood education staff and the quality of programs vary greatly. This fact has fueled ongoing debates about whether early childhood programs should be school based or community based. Qualitative differences in programs also spurred the **National Association for the Education of Young Children (NAEYC)**, the largest professional association for early childhood educators, and the National Association of Early Childhood Specialists in State Departments of Education (NAECS/SDE)

Cultural Awareness

Preschools in Reggio Emilia, Italy, are recognized by many American educators as being among the best in the world. At their 1992 annual meeting, NAEYC showcased methods used in the schools to illustrate how preschools may be structured appropriately to cultivate problem-solving, creativity, and cognitive skills in young children. "The Hundred Languages of Children," an exhibit that has been touring Europe and the United States continuously since 1991, features the paintings, sculptures, and other projects of Reggio Emilia preschoolers, who are encouraged to express themselves in the "languages" of art. Many early childhood programs have adopted methods used in Reggio Emilia schools, but as of 1996, only one American program—the Model Early Learning Center in Washington, D.C.—has a formal connection with the Italian schools. Their consultant-teacher, Ameilia Gambetti, taught in Reggio Emilia for 27 years (Kalson, 1996).

to develop guidelines that could be used to ensure quality education of 3- through 8-year-olds (NAEYC & NAECS/SDE, 1991). Visit NAEYC's Web site at **http://www. america-tomorrow.com:80/naeyc/index.html**.

While many people tout the importance of philosophy and curriculum in preschool settings, others contend that increased funding for public preschool programs is crucial. In 1996 the National Center for the Early Childhood Work Force (NCECW) reported that the national average wage for a center-based early childhood teacher was only $6.70 per hour, or $11,700 per year. Such low wages make it difficult to attract and retain qualified staff—and it is staff who ultimately make the difference in what children experience at school (Schweinhart, 1992).

Kindergarten

While the number of students attending kindergarten on a full-time basis has quadrupled since 1969, only 44% of 5-year-olds experience full-time programs (U.S. Department of Education, 1996). In some instances, children old enough to enter kindergarten programs are placed in one of two tracks, the regular kindergarten or a junior kindergarten. Those in junior kindergartens go to school for 1 year before being promoted to a regular kindergarten. This experience is supposed to help get them "ready" for kindergarten.

Placement in either setting is usually determined by students' performance on a variety of screening tests. Although screening policy and practice vary from district to district, low-income males have a tendency to score poorly on screening tests and thus are more likely to spend two years in kindergarten (Walsh, Ellwein, Eads, & Miller, 1991). Boys' lower scores may be due in part to the fact that they develop more slowly than do girls in the early years and also that some cultures' expectations for young boys are not geared toward the development of attributes measured by such tests. Even extra time in kindergarten, however, often fails to improve achievement or to eradicate students' inadequate school readiness (Dennebaum & Kulberg, 1994).

In some kindergarten programs, teachers are oriented to an academic curriculum, which often means extensive time spent in whole-group settings, didactic instruction, use of worksheets, and few opportunities for small-group, individualized, or hands-on activities. Other kindergarten teachers use a curriculum that is more student centered, or "developmentally appropriate," which usually means that students are expected to acquire skills and abilities at their own pace through exploration and free play.

How is early childhood education organized in the United States? What alternatives exist for education at the preschool and kindergarten levels?

Although kindergarten programs may differ from state to state, many kindergartens focus on academics. A survey of 103 public kindergartens randomly selected from different regions of North Carolina, for example, revealed that only 20% of kindergarten classes used a developmental approach. Type of instruction seemed unaffected by region of the state, size of the school, or per-pupil expenditure. Researchers hypothesized that, among other things, differences might be attributed to kindergarten teachers' and principals' beliefs about best practice, parent and community values, and attitudes of and pressures from first- and second-grade teachers (Bryant, Clifford, & Peisner, 1991).

> **To what extent should kindergartens focus on academics?**

Grades K through 6

Schools for elementary students typically have 20 to 25 students working in a self-contained classroom with a teacher and sometimes, particularly at the primary level, with an aide. Classroom teachers usually focus on language arts, mathematics, science, social studies, and health, while specialist teachers offer instruction in art, music, physical education, and special education.

Despite many outward similarities, there are a number of curricular and instructional variations within and among elementary schools. Sometimes students are grouped homogeneously by ability or achievement for instructional purposes. Such grouping can occur within a classroom or across classrooms. In other settings, students work in **nongraded classrooms**, where they are grouped heterogeneously by ability, sometimes with students of various ages. Nongraded programs, also referred to as multiage, multigrade, or family grouping programs, are most prevalent in primary schools.

The popularity of multigrade or nongraded programs has waxed and waned through the years. During the 1950s and 1960s, nongrading was practiced in more than 7% of the schools. The popularity of the concept declined, however, when "back to basics" ideas took hold during the mid-1970s.

What are some advantages and challenges of multiage grouping in elementary schools? How would working in a nongraded classroom affect your role as teacher?

Recently, concerns about the strong correlation between retention in grade and the subsequent dropping out of a growing number of students have stimulated some elementary schools to revert to the one-room schoolhouse notion of multiage groupings of students. One state, Mississippi, passed a law in 1993 that allowed school districts to implement multiage grouping in elementary schools. A year later, 20 school districts won two-year grants from the state to develop such programs (J. Prather, personal communication, June 23, 1996).

Ideally, nongraded programs provide a developmentally appropriate curriculum—curriculum that may be tailored to differences in students' stages of intellectual, emotional, physical, and/or social development—that allows for individualized, continuous progress for young children. Purportedly, this means that, while there are standards of performance to be reached by students, the time taken to reach those standards and methods for doing so will likely vary from student to student. Any grouping for instruction is said to be flexible and based on the abilities, interests, and needs of students. In these programs there is no formal promotion from one grade to the next. Instead, a student stays with a group of students until he has mastered necessary skills (Cushman, 1990).

Should schools use multiage rather than graded groupings?

Research on nongraded elementary schools suggests that they can be quite effective when nongrading is used as a grouping method rather than as a means for individualizing instruction. Positive effects are greatest in situations where students are grouped across age lines in just one subject (usually reading) or in multiple subjects, with students receiving direct instruction for the majority of a class session. Experts agree that groupings should not be stagnant, however. They should be reassessed frequently and changed when student performance indicates a mismatch in instruction and achievement (Gutiérrez & Slavin, 1992).

▮ Junior High Schools and Middle Schools

In the fall of 1909, Columbus, Ohio, opened a new 3-year intermediate school, calling it a "junior high school." This was the first mention of such a school. In 1910, Berkeley, California, opened two 3-year intermediate schools and called them "introductory high schools"—a name that never caught on (Til, Vars, & Lounsbury, 1967). Junior high schools have been an important part of our education system since the 1930s. Junior high school programs are meant to help students make the transition from elementary to high school by concentrating on academic subjects and by exposing students to careers and occupations.

Although there are variations in enrollment patterns for junior high schools, most include students who are in grades 7 through 9. As in elementary schools, instruction occurs mainly in self-contained classrooms. Curriculum at the junior high school level, however, is usually more diversified, that is, there are more types of courses offered. Like their colleagues at the senior high school level, junior high school teachers generally specialize in the content and teaching of a particular subject area. Junior high schools typically use six class periods per day; instruction is usually teacher directed.

Middle schools, which emerged in the 1960s, aim to provide an educational environment less imitative of high school and better suited to the developmental needs of 10- to 14-year-olds in early adolescence. By the 1970s the number of middle schools (usually grades 5 through 8 or 6 through 8) had surpassed the number of junior high schools. Despite their continued popularity, particularly in the suburbs, middle schools for many years have been criticized for tailoring programs similar to the ones they were designed to replace. No doubt the preparation of teachers has been a factor in the way middle schools have operated. A study of the credentials of teachers in four junior high schools that were converting to middle schools (grades 6 through 8) during the 1995–1996 school year revealed that the majority of teachers (66%) were certified in secondary education. Only 21% of the teachers were certified in middle-grades education, and 13% were certified in elementary education (Hadley, 1996).

Advocates for middle schools argue that the special needs of young adolescents require a school that is not as juvenile in its structure and approach as an elementary school and not as impersonal and demanding of independence as a high school. In a middle school, they contend, students should have a chance to mature before being thrust into the high school environment (The Focused Reporting Project, 1995).

Indiana's Harshman Middle School in downtown Indianapolis is an example of a middle school that shaped a program to meet the unique needs of young adolescents. Until 1992 Harshman had been a junior high school for students in grades 7 and 8. At the time, urban junior high schools in Indiana exhibited "violence; high rates of suspensions, expulsions, and absenteeism; low test scores; students with overwhelming social and emotional needs; and a general climate of disrespect for the teaching profession" (Ames, 1996, p. 4). When Indiana implemented its statewide Middle Grades Improvement Program, funded by Lilly Endowment Inc., substantive changes took place in Indiana's middle schools.

Marcia Capuano, the newly hired principal of Harshman (the seventh principal in 5 years), first instituted a host of physical and mental health services for students. Next, she introduced a wide variety of reading initiatives and convinced her colleagues that teachers and students should be clustered in seven "houses," or teams, to create more personal units for teaching and learning. Finally, Capuano attempted to build community support for her programs.

Capuano worked with an existing parent–teacher planning group, Community Council 101, to arrange parent workshops, to create a parent–child reading program, and to sponsor a recognition evening for honor-roll students and their parents. She also started a GED (general equivalency diploma) class at the school. Other bridges to the community were formed through such programs as a buddy system, which linked students with key

How are middle schools different from junior high schools? Why has the middle school movement spread so successfully nationwide?

members of the community, and through "Just Say Grow," a project in which students worked with local residents to plant trees and other shrubs to help beautify the local neighborhood.

As these and other changes occurred at Harshman, attendance went up, and students' standardized scores in reading and math showed modest improvement. In 1993 Indiana reorganized its middle schools, moving sixth-graders in with seventh- and eighth-graders. Harshman continued to flourish —large numbers of students used the on-site health clinic, students were reading and writing more, and community volunteers were making frequent classroom visits. Parents new to the school proclaimed Harshman to be "the best kept secret in the district" (Ames, 1996).

High Schools

High schools vary greatly in size, with enrollment in alternative schools as low as 200 and enrollment in large comprehensive high schools as high as 4,000. As noted in Chapter 3, comprehensive high schools—large high schools having a full range of programs—evolved over time from experimentation with concepts of the Latin grammar school, the academy, and the high school that emerged in the late 19th century. The comprehensive high school as it exists today was popularized in the late 1950s, largely through the efforts of former Harvard University president James B. Conant.

Large high schools are comprehensive in their educational offerings and also in their social mission. They educate in the general sense, they prepare young people for the world of work and for college, and they fulfill the civic mission of working toward the maintenance of a sense of community.

Comprehensive high schools are not without their critics, however. In a study conducted by the Center on Organization and Restructuring of Schools, investigators discovered that large high schools can have deleterious effects on students. In fact, evidence suggests that "students learn more, and learning is distributed more equitably in smaller high schools" (Lee, Smith, & Croninger, 1996, p. 4). Critics also argue that the sense of alienation and purposelessness that plagues minority and other disadvantaged high school students, particularly those in urban areas, only deepens in huge, impersonal school settings. They point to high dropout rates, absenteeism, and classroom disorders as indications of the failure of large schools (Toch, 1991). School size may not cause such problems, but the problems of individual students are more difficult to identify and address in large schools.

Are high schools *too* comprehensive?

In recent years several school districts have reduced the size of their secondary schools. In Columbus, Ohio, for example, educators reorganized several of their 17 high schools, creating "houses" of 250 students, each with an administrator, a team of teachers, and a guidance counselor who stay together throughout students' high school careers.

In New York City, Community School District 4 subdivided Benjamin Franklin High School, a crime-ridden, one-building school, into a progressive elementary program for 220 youngsters, a junior high for 250 advanced seventh- and eighth-graders, and a high school for 1,300 students with average or above-average academic performance (Toch, 1991). Other school districts have instituted magnet programs, or schools within schools, to create a more personal environment. Many high schools in New York City, for example, include "clusters," or groups of programs in related career areas such as business, communications, law, and technology education.

Comprehensive schools can offer a wide variety of curricula fairly economically. They typically provide an array of courses to prepare students for vocational or technical areas and for college, but they also offer other experiences. Besides expecting students to have a certain number of credit hours in core courses, some, like Missouri's Pattonville High School, require students to spend 50 hours performing community service to graduate.

Depending on their academic needs, some high school students take courses at nearby colleges. In Minnesota, where state policy in 1985 enabled high school juniors and seniors to earn both high school and college credits at state expense, the line of distinction between the two institutions has become somewhat blurry. In 1995 about 750 students of high school age and younger took classes at the University of Minnesota (A.S. Huang, personal communication, June 25, 1996).

Higher Education

Between 1980 and 1994 the percentage of high school graduates who enrolled in college immediately after graduation increased from 49% to 62%. Only 45% of graduates from low-income families, as opposed to 77% from high-income families, were among this group. About 21% of graduates attended 2-year colleges, while 41% enrolled in 4-year public or private institutions (U.S. Department of Education, 1996).

Curricular offerings in 2- and 4-year colleges are somewhat different. Two-year colleges typically offer basic undergraduate liberal arts and science courses while providing a wide range of vocational, technical, and adult education programs. They also offer a variety of professional and preprofessional programs. Four-year colleges and universities generally provide a full undergraduate program leading to a bachelor's degree as well as first-professional and graduate programs leading to advanced degrees.

As noted in Chapter 3, adult education programs have allowed many citizens to return to school. The increasing numbers of younger and older adults participating in such programs illustrate the possibilities for lifelong learning in our society. Adult education classes offer opportunities for young and old alike to develop interests and talents and to increase their literacy skills. According to the first report from the National Adult Literacy Survey, adults with higher literacy skills are more likely to work full time, to earn high wages, and to vote (U.S. Department of Education, 1993).

People are never too old to learn. Elderhostels provide educational opportunities for people age 60 and older. A network of some 800 institutions of higher education in the United States sponsors a wide variety of travel and study opportunities in every state and in many foreign countries. Students live in dormitories and study in college classrooms and conference centers. Even though elderhostels do not give college credit, the offerings range from oceanography to space science. The relatively low cost of elderhostels boosts their appeal.

WHAT ARE SOME SCHOOLING ALTERNATIVES?

An **alternative school** is any school operating within the public school system that has programs addressing the specific needs or interests of targeted student groups. Some alternative schools are self-contained structures; others are organized as schools within schools.

Although there are many models of alternative schooling in our country, alternative schools generally share many of the following attributes: small school size, small class size, voluntary membership, absence or minimization of ability grouping and other forms of labeling, school-based management, student involvement in governance, and extended roles for teachers that include counseling and guidance. Many people believe that alternative schools provide nonconforming programs for "at risk" or "bad" students. As we explain below, alternative schools are for all types of students.

Magnet Schools

Magnet schools are alternative schools within a public school system that draw students from the whole district instead of drawing only from their own neighborhoods. Magnet schools emerged in the 1970s, primarily as a means to desegregate schools. The intent was to avoid the divisiveness of mandatory busing by developing schools so appealing that a racial cross-section of students would be drawn voluntarily to the schools. Despite the fact that many enrollees have to travel long distances for a longer and somewhat harder school day than they might have in typical public schools, the appeal of magnet programs is strong enough that schools usually have long waiting lists for enrollment. To visit magnet schools around the country, go to the Web (**http://www.yahoo.com/Education/K_12/Schools/Magnet_Schools**).

Magnet schools typically have three distinct features: (a) an enrollment policy that opens the school to children beyond a particular geographic attendance zone, (b) a student body that is present by choice that meets variable criteria established for inclusion, and (c) a curriculum based on a special theme or instructional method. Built into any level from preschool to senior high school, magnet schools may organize their curricula around mathematics and computers, the arts, the sciences, foreign language, or general academics, such as college preparation and honors courses.

A variety of themes exist for magnet schools. For example, as of 1993 there were more than 24 "micro-society" magnet schools in elementary and middle schools around the country, with the theme of making schooling more relevant to students' lives. To cultivate the skills students need to become good citizens, micro-society schools operate

What are some alternatives to the comprehensive high school model? What are some distinguishing features of magnet schools? What other schooling alternatives exist for students in preprimary grades through grade 8?

miniature civilizations complete with all the trappings of the real world: a legislature, courts, banks, post offices, newspapers, a host of entrepreneurial businesses, and even an Internal Revenue Service. Students hold jobs and are paid salaries in an ersatz currency, which they use to pay simulated taxes and tuition and to purchase a variety of goods and services at the school's marketplace. (Sommerfeld, 1993, p. 8)

A St. Louis magnet program, the Mason Investigative Learning Center, is one of 14 schools in the United States and Canada known as schools for thought. Mason is a science and mathematics magnet school attended by 274 students who are remarkably and intentionally diverse. About one fourth of the student body is formally identified as gifted, and another fourth participates in the Title I remedial education program for disadvantaged low achievers. Twenty-four students commute from affluent neighborhoods, and slightly fewer receive special education services. The school's instructional philosophy is to involve students in the construction of knowledge, rather than to have them read from textbooks and listen to lectures. To develop students' thought

Cultural Awareness

San Antonio, a crossroads between the United States and Mexico, is home for the International School of the Americas, a magnet school housing 231 first- and second-year high school students in a 10-classroom arm of the 2,200-student campus of Robert E. Lee High School. As the school grows to include grades 11 and 12, organizers intend to keep enrollment to fewer than 425 students. Students apply to the International School, but they are chosen by lottery. The principal, Chula Boyle, also recruits foreign-exchange students. About half of the local students are Hispanic, more than a third are European American, and the rest are African American.

The school's mission is to prepare students for a world in which "borders are blurred, speaking English alone won't do, and multicultural savvy is a matter of survival" (Schnaiberg, 1995, p. 31). Besides doing at least B quality work, students are expected to take four years of math and science (unless they can acquire precalculus and physics competence faster) and to stay abreast of international and national news. They are also required to be fluent in Spanish and English and conversant in a third language by graduation.

The school's Latin-American focus was motivated, at least in part, by NAFTA—the North America Free Trade Agreement. Two local Fortune 500 businesses are the school's partners. They have linked the school with the Mexican consulate and the Mexican university system to eventually enable teachers and students to take conversational Spanish and Mexican culture courses through interactive video. Another goal is to create internships, both locally and abroad, for future juniors and seniors.

processes, teachers attempt to build on students' existing knowledge, allowing students to do their own research and work collectively on complex, real-life problems that are anchored in the subject areas they are studying (Viadero, 1996).

Results from a national study conducted by Adam Gamoran in 1996 suggest that magnet schools can be more effective than regular schools at improving student learning. Data collected on 4,000 urban high schools in the 8th and 10th grades revealed that magnet school students made greater gains over two years in reading, social studies, and science than did students who were enrolled in public comprehensive high schools, private schools, or Roman Catholic schools, although Catholic-school students appeared to make more gains in mathematics.

Should all schools be magnet schools?

Vocational–Technical Schools

As the phrase implies, vocational–technical high schools provide an education for students who wish to enter the trades or to develop technical skills for future employment. These schools offer programs in cosmetology; food production, management, and service; law enforcement; horticulture; automotive repair; tool and machine operation; air conditioning and refrigeration; building construction; masonry; graphic and commercial arts; drafting; electronics; data processing; a variety of health-related fields; child care; and many other areas.

Although vocational–technical high schools are designed to prepare people to assume jobs upon graduation, students who attend these schools may go on to community colleges or 4-year institutions. Vocational–technical schools that integrate academic work with technical training are thought to provide the best opportunities for continued development.

There are three general approaches to encouraging such integration (Grubb, 1996). Some schools simply exhort vocational instructors to use more reading, math, or writing in their courses; this is the least effective strategy. Other schools operate as academies, aligning the content of both types of courses so that they reinforce each other. Such approaches are fairly common in Philadelphia, Pennsylvania, and in California and appear to increase enrollments and decrease drop-out rates. The third approach is to organize and deliver academic courses on clusters of related occupations. For example, a manufacturing cluster might include mathematics and writing instruction relevant to future engineers, machinists, and production-line workers.

Dauphin County Technical School in Harrisburg, Pennsylvania, operates on the cluster approach by integrating basic skill training with vocational education. While studying a trade, "in their four years of English, students will work on everything from basic writing skills and comprehension through literature to American literature, job applications, writing of business and personal letters, and development of the resume and cover letter" (Penkowsky, 1991/1992, p. 67).

VOICES

On Going to "Night High"

Manhattan Comprehensive Night High School at Fifteenth Street and Second Avenue in New York City is an academic, accredited, diploma-granting high school that opened in 1989 with 25 students between the ages of 17 and 22. In 1996 Manhattan had 750 students from 32 countries and a waiting list for admission. Classes are offered year-round, Monday through Thursday. Sundays are devoted to athletics and cultural enrichment activities. This alternative high school is a school of choice, open to all New York City residents who have completed one year of high school and are reading at or above seventh-grade level. Before serving as its principal, Howard A. Freedman—the founder—was an English major at Hunter College and a teacher at New York's John Dewey High School and City as School. He also worked for the federally funded National Diffusion Network, helping others around the country start their own schools. Freedman described what makes Manhattan Comprehensive Night High School special:

When I worked at the high school division of City as School, one of the most well-known alternative schools in the nation, I wrote a proposal to create this high school designed to serve many young people who needed real flexibility in terms of time. Many had to support themselves and their children, whether they lived with their children or not. Many others traveled from school to school and never got their diplomas. They felt like they were too old to return to their neighborhood schools. The literature suggested that students over 17 or 18 should be treated differently from younger adolescents. And this moment in their lives was the last chance to educate these youngsters. In New York you can get anything at any hour, why not school?

In the beginning we were open from 5:00 P.M. to 11:00 P.M., Monday through Thursday, and on Sunday afternoon. I could write a book on working out agreements with unions, custodians, and others who were not used to working such strange hours. Now we start at 11:00 A.M. and go until 10:45 at night.

We are a full academic school. We are also an ESL school (about 45% of the students are foreign born), but we are not a bilingual school. Our collaborative relationships are great. We have working relationships with about 30 community-based organizations. Business and community leaders on our nonprofit board helped us raise about $300,000 for our library. A number of architects did a lot of pro bono work on the library too. We also started our student center with donations. It includes job counseling, medical referrals, job readiness training, and other services beyond our academic program. We have about 55 teachers and maybe another 15 or so staff members. We have 140 mentor volunteers. Our next challenge will be to create a dormitory for the homeless students while we raise money for our science program.

CRITICAL THINKING

What are some of the special challenges students at Manhattan face? How might such a school create an environment in which school feels like "home" for its students? Are there specific activities individual teachers might use to foster a sense of community?

Note. From personal interview, Howard A. Freedman, June 24, 1996.

▩ Montessori and Waldorf Schools

Alternative schools, public and private, often reflect all-encompassing philosophies of education. Montessori and Waldorf schools are examples. Montessori preschools focus mainly on the development of children's perceptual, motor, intellectual, and social skills. Programs are based on the ideas of Maria Montessori (1870–1952), a physician who developed preschool teaching methods in the early 1900s focused on students' maturation levels and readiness to learn particular skills. Teachers trained in Montessori methods use a curriculum based on materials specifically designed to help children discover the physical properties of objects. As students interact with materials, such as the "pink tower" (blocks of graduated size), learning is self-directed rather than teacher directed. Teachers act as observers, assisting indirectly by asking questions or providing materials to optimize learning. Given that most instructional materials are graded and self-correcting, students experience liberty within structure in such settings.

Montessori schools can extend beyond preschool to include older children. Sands Elementary School, the first Montessori school (now a magnet school) in Cincinnati, Ohio, enrolls about 700 students between the ages of 3 and 12. Classes are divided into overlapping age-group combinations: 3 through 6, 6 through 9 and 9 through 12. Often teachers organize their curriculum around a theme, such as "workers in the neighborhood," and children of different ages and abilities work as a group, practicing skills at different levels. When doing a theme-related project, for example, an older student might record a story dictated by a younger student, type it, and bind it into a book illustrated by the nonreader, who can then use the book to learn to read. You can learn more about Montessori schools by visiting the Web (**http://www.education-world.com/files/schools/mont_usa.html**).

At the other end of the philosophical spectrum, Waldorf educators oppose a focus on the structured acquisition of specific learning skills. Waldorf education has its roots in the spiritual–scientific research of Rudolf Steiner (1861–1925), an Austrian scientist and educator. According to Steiner's philosophy, young children learn primarily through their senses and respond in the most active mode of knowing: imitation. In Waldorf preschools, creative play is viewed as the critical element in a child's development. Waldorf teachers believe that to draw the child's energies away from creative play to meet intellectual demands will rob the child of the health and vitality she will need in later life. They argue that in the end, premature intellectual demands weaken the powers of judgment and practical intelligence the teacher wants to encourage (Barnes, 1991).

There are about 125 Waldorf schools, most of which are private, in the United States and Canada. Although the majority are elementary schools, there are also a few secondary schools that follow the Waldorf way. All Waldorf schools have a strong spiritual component, though they are nonsectarian. Ideally, teachers remain with the same group of students from 1st through 8th grades. To learn more about Waldorf schools, go to the Web (**http://www.yahoo.com/Education/Educational_Theory_and_Methods/ Waldorf_Method/Schools/**).

Private and Independent Schools

Private, or independent, **schools** are nonprofit, tax-exempt institutions governed by boards of trustees and financed through private funds, such as tuitions, endowments, and grants. Some are religiously affiliated while others are secular. All are accredited by state departments of education, must meet state and local health and safety rules, and must observe mandatory school attendance laws.

Despite many similarities, private schools differ from public schools in several ways:

- Public schools are tax supported while, in the main, private schools are not.

- Private schools can set their own admissions requirements, while public schools must accept all those who come for an education.

- Private school students are enrolled by parental or student choice, while, in the main, public schools serve only students in their districts.

- Private schools have the freedom to craft philosophies that appeal to specific groups of people, while public schools are driven by inclusivity.

As alternatives for schooling have increased, the distinction between public and private education has become increasingly vague. Although not a prevalent practice, the use of public revenues to fund private education has done much to blur the definition of a private school: "Public vouchers are being used to pay for private education, and private firms are operating public schools. Some corporations are underwriting design efforts to transform the public schools; others are investing in for-profit enterprises to compete with them" (Olson, 1992). Other actions obscuring the division between public and private education include (a) state loans of secular textbooks to church schools, (b) state reimbursement of funds for transportation to church schools, and (c) public funding for mandated standardized testing and scoring and for diagnostic, therapeutic, and remedial services in private and parochial schools.

Should distinctions between public and private schooling be dropped?

There are 26,093 private elementary and secondary schools in the United States (U.S. Department of Education, 1996a). The line demarcating public from private schools traditionally has been drawn in the source of funds and in the proscription against religious activity. That line, however, has continually been challenged. Although the number of initiatives to transform schools is small, the acceptance of new ideas about structuring schools seems to be growing. Ideas for private and quasi-private alternatives are based on the idea that market forces and competition will force public schools to improve or change (Kennedy, 1996).

There are a number of nonsectarian private school options in the United States. These schools vary in focus, structure, social organization, and size. Some, such as military schools, emphasize self-discipline while encouraging academic study. Others, such as elite college preparatory schools, place an unusually high premium on academic achievement. Some schools are less easily classifiable, developing their own unique personalities.

For-Profit Schools

In the late 1980s and 1990s, concepts of for-profit schools have gained notoriety as alternatives to public schools. **For-profit schools** do not claim tax-exempt status because they are run by companies to make money. For-profit schools come in various forms, but the idea underlying their creation is that private enterprise can deliver better education to children than can public schools and can do so for the same or less money. Advocates of for-profit schools seek to privatize education, that is, to contract with private enterprise to perform educational services performed typically by public employees.

One of the most visible efforts to mount and sustain for-profit schools is The Edison Project, with headquarters in New York City. In 1995–1996, The Edison Project taught approximately 2,000 students in Boston, Massachusetts; Mount Clemens, Michigan; Sherman, Texas; and Wichita, Kansas. These efforts began at the elementary level and are expanding to the middle grades. The Edison Project plans to contract with more schools in 1996–1997 in Colorado Springs, Colorado; Dade Country, Florida; Lansing, Michigan; and Worcester, Massachusetts (Walsh, 1996).

The Edison Project schools have experimented with school schedules to create a longer school day and longer year. They have also invested heavily in technology, both at school and in student's homes. In Wichita, Kansas, for instance, teachers and students have laptop computers. "Although it took until well into the school year, virtually every home of a 1st- through 5th-grade student now has an Apple Macintosh computer and a modem. Students and their parents can tap into The Edison Project's computer network, called the 'Common'" (Walsh, 1996, p. 10).

> **Should schools be run as profit-making business enterprises?**

Another for-profit enterprise, the Minneapolis-based Education Alternatives, Inc. (EAI), has not fared so well. It signed and later lost contracts to run schools in Hartford, Connecticut; Baltimore, Maryland; and Dale County, Florida. The company started big and lost big. Apparently, EAI failed in Hartford not so much because of its educational program, although company claims of gains in achievement and attendance were not corroborated, but because of conflict over money. The schools and EAI could not agree on how much control a for-profit company should exert over a struggling city's school budget and how much it should be paid (Judson, 1996).

Parochial Schools

As defined in Chapter 2, private schools that are maintained and operated by religious organizations are called parochial schools. Parochial schools vary in terms of their underlying philosophies, structures, and programs. Catholic schools account for the largest number of parochial-school students. The majority of these students attend schools in New York, Pennsylvania, California, Illinois, and Ohio. Other areas of the country where Catholic schools are prominent include New Orleans, Louisiana, and Detroit, Michigan.

Sociologists have described the Catholic school as contributing heavily to the middle-class mores of our society. It teaches "respectability, cleanliness, conformity, ambition, patriotism" (Fichter, 1958, p. 451). A survey conducted by the National Catholic Educational Association (NCEA) indicates that today's teachers, 91% of whom are laypeople, are highly committed to inculcating values and morals. Respondents listed "gospel values" and "parental involvement" as the two most important benefits of a Catholic education. When asked to name five resources that were absolutely necessary for them to do their jobs in the year 2000, teachers named "parental support" first. Other choices were the Bible, finances, computers, and textbooks (Ponessa, 1996). You can visit a number of Catholic schools on the Web by searching on "Catholic Schools," or by going directly to a site (**http://www.oise.on.ca/ %7Ekmalcolm/schools.html**).

About 40% of American Jewish children are currently enrolled in Jewish schools. Supplementary schools, which for years have reached the largest number of Jewish students in the United States, meet at the end of a full day of secular school. Curricula often include instruction in Hebrew or Yiddish, Bible, Rabbinic literature, prayer, religious ritual procedures, and Jewish history, lore, and law (Brown, 1992). Day schools, attended by about 12% of the total Jewish population, generally integrate the secular and religious worlds of American Jews (Commission on Jewish Education in North America, 1991).

Chabad-Hebrew Academy is a parochial Jewish dayschool that focuses on Hebrew and secular studies. The academy was founded in 1969 in Westminster, California. During the 1995 academic year, 400 students were enrolled in nursery-level through 12th-grade classes. Classes at the academy are coeducational through the 9th-grade; classes in grades 10 through 12 are for girls only. According to Rabbi Moishe Engel (personal communication,

Cultural Awareness

Curriculum decisions define parochial education for a host of other religious minorities, such as Muslims and Old Order Amish. In the 1995–1996 school year, there were 701 Amish and Mennonite one-room schools in the United States. Most were rural, and 57% were in Pennsylvania and Ohio (Blackboard Bulletin, 1995). At Meadowbrook School, one of several hundred Old Order Amish schools, 30 children in eight grades sit in a sunny schoolroom heated by a potbellied coal stove.

> Four second-graders are at the recitation bench taking turns reading aloud as the other children work quietly at their desks. The teacher listens to each child read and then, while the third grade comes up to the recitation bench, she calls on the students whose hands are raised . . . . [M]ethods and materials differ little from those of two generations ago. . . . The pupils have no catechism, but together with their teacher they pray the Lord's Prayer and sing hymns. . . . On the walls . . . there are posters and pictures . . . with moral messages that support cooperative attitudes rather than competitiveness. Absent from the school curriculum are books on science, physical education, computer instruction, and sex education. Also absent are organized sports, clubs, career education, guidance counseling, and television. (Hostetler & Huntington, 1992, pp. 1–2)

June 24, 1996), vice principal of the academy, boys in the upper grades either attend public schools or they enroll in yeshivas, private boarding schools that have a more religious atmosphere and a greater emphasis on Hebrew. To learn about other Jewish dayschools, visit the Web site (**http://ramat-negev. org.il/jwsch.htm**).

Other parochial schools—in particular, fundamentalist Christian schools—are growing in number more quickly than are other private schools, in large measure because of the popular appeal of their philosophies and curricula. Melinda Wagner's 1990 study of nine Christian schools in the southeastern United States suggests why this may be so. In examining the schools' philosophies, Wagner found that conservative Christians attempt to create an "ideal" culture to serve as a "crucible of change" for altering the inadequacies and evils in existing culture (p. 20).

Charter Schools

Charter schools are independent public schools supported by state funds but exempt from many regulations. They are based on a contract, or "charter" between a group of school organizers (parents, teachers, or others) and a sponsor (usually a local or state board of education). Organizers generally have the power to hire and fire staff and to budget money as they see fit. In turn, they guarantee to sponsor certain academic outcomes.

Described as the "upstart reform idea of the decade," charter schools represent to some people the means for promoting school accountability and excellence in educational outcomes. According to Ray Budde, the originator of the charter schools concept, charter schools allow organizers autonomy and flexibility when determining how to respond to increasingly varied student needs. Thus they serve as the first real model of local autonomous control (Kennedy, 1996).

Like other reform initiatives, charter schools are meant to be innovative—to reach out to those not being served by the public schools. Metro Deaf School, a charter school in Minnesota, teaches all subjects in American Sign Language to students who are deaf or hard-of-hearing. City Academy, a charter school housed in a local recreation center in St. Paul, Minnesota, has a staff of four teachers, two volunteers, and two teachers' aides delivering individualized and small-group instruction to 30 former dropouts.

In 1991 Minnesota became the first state to approve the concept of charter schools. According to Minnesota law, only certified teachers can contract with local school boards to create charters. While the board has a say in what outcomes charters must meet, it maintains a hands-off posture in their day-to-day operation. Within only 4 years after Minnesota's charter school legislation, at least 19 states had passed initiatives to allow charter schools.

In Philadelphia, funding from the Pew Charitable Trusts allowed for the establishment of several charters in neighborhood schools, many of which were considered troubled institutions. The charters serve heterogeneous groups of 200 to 400 children. In some instances, groups stay with the same teachers for 4 years. Parents are encouraged to be active participants in the program and are paid stipends for attending planning and staff-development meetings. Evidence suggests that such programs are paying off; students in charters have better attendance records and lower drop-out rates than do those in regular programs. An increase in the number of students repeating ninth grade reflects the fact that students are choosing to return to school rather than dropping out (Bradley, 1992).

One of the smallest and perhaps most unique charter schools is the Big Apple Circus's own One-Ring Schoolhouse, a formal independent school in New York state "where no one looks at you funny when you tell them your dad is a ringmaster" (Sommerfeld, 1995, p. 22). The school, an apple-red trailer that travels 5,000 miles a year, has only seven students, ranging in age from 6 to 14 years old, and one teacher. The teacher—Leslie Martin—introduces basic concepts in reading, writing, math, science, and history and also works to incorporate the circus's theme in her lessons. (Sommerfeld, 1995).

For more information about charter schools, visit the home page of the Center for Education Reform (**http://edreform.com/charters.htm**).

Home Schools

About 300,000 primary and secondary students in the United States study at home, or in "home schools," rather than in public or private schools. As described in Chapter 3, the majority of these students are children of ideologists who want to ensure that their religious doctrines are an integral part of daily lessons and values. Many people educate their children at home to avoid what they perceive as lock-step learning practices sometimes used in schools. David Guterson, a homeschooling parent in Bainbridge Island, Washington, whose son didn't learn to read until he was 7 years old, describes his beliefs about homeschooling:

> I'm not trying to make the statement that schools are bad and homeschoolers are good. I'm just trying to make a choice that works for our family and works for our kids. . . . Why did he need to read at 5?. . . We don't worry about comparisons to other kids or to the established norms of each grade. They're not relevant to our thinking. But I certainly would start to be concerned if . . . [my children] got to be about 10 or 11 and they weren't interested in learning to read. It's really great when a kid says [he wants to read] . . . as opposed to school, where it maybe gets rammed down their throats and some kids aren't ready. (Hill, 1993, pp. 16, 21)

Will the charter-school and home-school movements damage public education?

Wisconsin has one of the nation's most lenient homeschooling laws. It requires only that parents submit an annual statement that they plan to educate their children at home. Since 1985 the number of homeschoolers in the state has increased by 20% each year. By 1996 approximately 16,000 Wisconsin students were being educated at home ("Homeschooling," 1996).

(You will find more than 268 home pages for homeschooling on the Web simply by typing "homeschooling" on the Web Crawler or similar search engine.)

How are Schools Administered?

School administrators, from the **superintendent**—chief executive—on down, must operate in a world that has changed dramatically in the past 30 years or so. Today's school administrators have much less flexibility in making decisions than did their predecessors. As you will read in Chapter 6, they must contend with state-aid formulas, government mandates, external standards for educators' and students' performances, and a host of political pressure groups intent on sharing power. Administrators appear caught between the need to build consensus and the necessity to innovate—to raise expectations above the lowest common denominator.

Despite the fact that there are about 85,000 public schools in the United States, surveys indicate that the superintendents and their associates and assistants who compose the **central office staff**, along with principals, tend to view their worlds in remarkably similar fashion. The demands of their jobs and their training, no doubt, contribute to their common outlook. But administrators share other characteristics as well.

The School Superintendent

Superintendents administer school systems organized to carry out line and staff functions. They do so with the approval of the board of education. The typical line and staff organization of public school systems is shown in Figure 5.2.

The superintendency can be an incredibly demanding job. The issues and challenges facing superintendents are many and varied: financing schools, planning and goal setting, assessing educational outcomes, maintaining and enhancing accountability and credibility, evaluating staff and administrators, developing working relations with a school board, administering special education services, obtaining timely and accurate information, negotiating labor contracts, dealing with changing enrollments, and so on (Norton, Webb, Dlugosh, & Sybouts, 1996).

Cultural Awareness

Most superintendents of schools are men (93%), and most are European American (97%). Their mean age nationally is 49.8 years (Glass, 1992). In addition, about 65% of principals in public schools are men and about 84% are European American. More than 93% are over the age of 40 (U.S. Department of Education, 1995b). Some would argue that this pool of people represents a convergence of quality in the characteristics of leadership. In contrast, Emily Feistritzer contends that, "Probably nowhere in America is there a larger bloc that gives more credence to the phrase, 'old boys' club' than public school administrators" (Feistritzer, Quelle, & Bloom, 1988, p. 3).

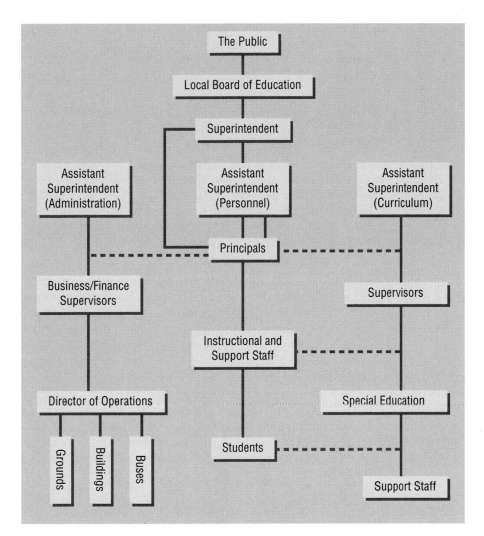

FIGURE 5.2

Typical Line and Staff Organization of Public School Systems

What could you say about the role of principals on the basis of this organization chart?

In large U.S. cities, the superintendency has become an embattled position. There are so many problems, so many constituencies with competing interests, and so few resources that city superintendents stay in their jobs about 2.5 years on average, compared to the U.S. average of 5.5 years. Nathan Glazer (1992) has argued that, because the job is so overwhelming and performed so poorly, we should abolish the position.

The chancellor of the New York City public schools—a sort of super superintendent—presides over 32 community school-district superintendents, 1,000 schools, 100,000 employees, and more than 1 million students. About 6.4% of students are Native American or Alaskan-Native American, 9.5% Asian or Pacific-Islander American, 16.4% European American, 36.4% African American, and 37.3% Hispanic American (New York City Public Schools, 1995).

Should school superintendencies be abolished?

The New York City public school system is the largest in the nation. The chancellor is expected to be (a) an educator well versed in instruction, supervision, and administration; (b) a leader who exhibits decisiveness, shrewdness, powers of consensus building, and a commitment to children; (c) a manager having skills to run a bureaucracy with more than 100,000 employees; and (d) a strategist, good at overcoming institutional barriers (New York City Public Schools, 1992).

No wonder superintendents face great pressure and are often forced out of their jobs. Raymond Callahan's 1962 description of the power of politics in school management still applies today:

> I am now convinced that very much of what has happened in American education since 1900 can be explained on the basis of the extreme vulnerability of our schoolmen to public criticism and pressure and that this vulnerability is built into our pattern of local support and control. This has been true in the past and, unless changes are made, will continue to be true in the future. (Eaton, 1990, p. viii)

Many more superintendents work in small communities than in large ones. About 4,000 districts enroll fewer than 300 students; only 16 districts enroll 100,000 or more students. The superintendents in small communities must, however, fulfill many of the same responsibilities of educational leadership as do those in large districts. In many instances, their small and declining enrollments make opportunities to offer an intellectually rich, high-powered curriculum virtually impossible. Merely staffing the courses they must have to meet minimal requirements can be a major challenge. For rural school administrators to be successful, they must be a good "fit" with their communities (Tift, 1990). "Time and again rural administrators have stressed the necessity of understanding their community" (p. 5). In small towns, educational leaders are not nameless, faceless bureaucrats. People know where to go and with whom they can speak if they are unhappy about educational policies and practices.

Principals and Assistant Principals

Many scholars emphasize the importance of human relationships in successful school administration and programmatic change. Roland Barth (1990) suggests that schools, be they large or small, rise and fall on the strength of human relationships. Human relationships and **collegiality**, or relationships based on a sharing of power, "allow, energize, and sustain all other attempts at school improvement" (p. 32).

If any single individual is key to the everyday operation and tone of a school, it is the **principal**—the person responsible for managing a school at the building level. After formal training, one becomes a principal through a process of socialization, learning on the job (Leithwood, Steinbach, & Begley, 1992). Principals typically administer discipline to students, give guidance to students, deal with staff and faculty on simple to complex issues, locate substitute teachers, implement rules, conduct surveillance of halls, balance the school's budget, and maintain the building and equipment. High school principals may also spend 10 to 15 hours per week attending sporting events, fine arts performances, faculty socials, parent–teacher meetings, and dances (Hoy & Miskel, 1991).

Principals all perform similar everyday activities, such as visiting or observing classrooms, circulating through the building, and monitoring hallways. However, the ways principals interpret these activities can make a big difference in their effectiveness as leaders. More effective principals view everyday activities as opportunities for defining the school's goals, aiding student achievement, praising others' work, and practicing other characteristics of effective leadership.

Building-level administrators' work lives can be defined by the tensions they believe they must resolve but more often must learn to live with. Some questions are never satisfactorily or permanently resolved (Ackerman, Donaldson, & Van der Bogert, 1996). Figure 5.3 identifies seven persisting questions that administrative teams face.

Terrence Deal and Kent Peterson (1991) have described the job of principal as one of shaping the culture by playing several important roles: symbol,

1. The Justice Question

How can we be just to each child, as an individual and as a learner, and create a just and disciplined school as well?

2. The Teaching Question

How can we assure our children and the community that every staff member is performing effectively and value each individual staff member as well?

3. The Purpose Question

How can we produce measurable learning products and develop children who are capable of healthy learning, social, moral, and work processes as well?

4. The Resource Question

How can we encourage constant growth and improvement in our school and acknowledge the realistic limitations on our ability to meet such goals as well?

5. The Change Question

How can we foster improvement and change, and respect and value each staff member and citizen as well?

6. The Ownership Question

How can we honor the perspectives and purposes of multiple constituencies and work toward unified goals that will benefit all children as well?

7. The Autonomy Question

How can we honor teacher creativity and autonomy and share purposes, curricula, and equitable resources as well?

FIGURE 5.3

Persisting Questions that School Administrators Face

How might you answer these questions? Develop a set of guidelines for addressing the question that concerns you the most at this time.

Note. From *Making Sense as a School Leader: Persisting Questions, Creative Opportunities* (p. 7), by R. Ackerman, G. A. Donaldson, Jr., & R. Van der Bogert, 1996, San Francisco: Jossey-Bass Publications.

How are schools administered and managed? In what ways do administrators and administrative teams influence the life of the school and school effectiveness? In what ways do teachers participate in the administrative process?

potter, poet, actor, and healer. The principal's background, lifestyle, communication style, and management style strongly influence the culture of a school both practically and symbolically. Like a potter with a lump of clay, the principal shapes the shared values of the school. She emphasizes various school rituals—the pep rally, the reading of the honor roll, the stories told at public gatherings—to cultivate a sense of community. Like a poet and an actor, the principal expresses to everyone a shared vision of the school's philosophy and mission. Like a healer, the principal mediates among the groups that make up the school and responds to any criticism from the community about school operations or administrative decision making. If the principal has an assistant, the administrative team can reinforce even more effectively the school's values, norms, and goals.

The administrative team's relationship with teachers is a critical dimension of the job. The principal is in a position of middle management—between the superintendent and the teachers and school staff. As such, he must be able to follow and to lead. To lead the teachers and the support staff (guidance counselors, special education teachers, media specialists, librarians, custodians, bus drivers, and others), the principal must involve others in formulating and implementing ideas without sacrificing authority. Ultimately, the principal is responsible for what occurs in and around the school.

For more information about the roles of principals, visit the Web site for the National Association of Elementary School Principals (**http://www.naesp.org**) and the National Association of Secondary School Principals (**http://www.nassp.org**).

Site-based Management

In the 1980s and 1990s, educators have promoted the idea of involving people at the school level more directly in making decisions about teaching and learning, budgeting, and hiring personnel. This relatively new phenomenon in school governance is referred to most often as **site-based management**, sometimes as school-based management, or shared decision making. "For all its guises, site-based management is basically an attempt to transform schools into communities where the appropriate people participate constructively in major decisions that affect them" (David, 1995/1996, p. 4).

Reformers encourage these new governance and management strategies for two reasons. First, proponents believe that people who are most affected by educational decisions ought to be involved in those decisions. This belief is driven not only by a concern for fairness but by a sense that the people most intimately involved may also be most capable of rendering the best decisions. Second, proponents argue that once decisions are made, they are more likely to result in success if those who must live with the decisions helped make them. Or, at least, people who are involved in making the decisions may be less likely to undermine them.

> The composition of site-based management teams varies tremendously: In addition to teachers, parents, and the principal, they may include classified staff, community members, students, and business representatives. Educators may outnumber non-educators, or vice versa. States or districts may list constituencies who must be represented, or simply leave [this decision] to individual schools. (David, 1995/1996, p. 5)

Thomas Guskey and Kent Peterson (1995–1996) note that leaders of site-based management teams often face various problems, including, but not limited to, trying to fulfill an ambiguous mission, finding time for meetings, and motivating involvement. Effective leaders, however, are those who help the group set clear and specific goals, ensure that the decision-making process is not viewed as a goal in itself, and redesign schedules to give people time to participate. Guskey and Peterson suggest that administrators who reward accomplishments and encourage genuine collaboration are more likely to enhance involvement than are those who neglect such opportunities.

The job of leading site-based teams must also include attention to both classroom- and school-level measurement of students' performances (Popham, 1995). Measurement should be decision driven, that is, results should be geared to help administrators and teachers act as a result of what they learn.

> School-site assessment, because it's closer to children than district, state, or national assessment, should have a more decisive instructional payoff. It will succeed, however, only if principals realize that they must learn enough about it to supply the same sort of leadership in assessment that they possess in the realm of instruction. (Popham, 1995, p. 40)

In schools where there is site-based management, teachers have opportunities to serve in leadership roles that allow them to help shape educational programs to meet the needs of students. Some contend that transforming schools into communities where everyone, including the students, has a voice goes "beyond issues of school reform to the heart of our democratic society . . . [and] ultimately benefits not just the school community but our entire society" (David, 1995/1996, p. 9).

Can site-based management really work?

Use a search engine to explore the topic of site-based, or school-based, management [SBM], on the Web. Select government addresses, where you will find, for example, Department of Education and ERIC National Clearinghouse for School-Based Management documents on planning and implementing SBM as part of school restructuring. Or select addresses where you can learn about specific schools' and individuals' ongoing experiences with SBM. For example, see how site-based management is working at various schools across the country (**http://www.ed.gov/pubs/SER/SchBasedMgmt/section4.html**).

VOICES

On Being Assistant Principal

To learn about the experiences of new assistant principals making the transition from teacher to administrator, Gary Hartzell, Richard Williams, and Kathleen Nelson (1995) interviewed approximately 90 first-year secondary principals in California, Washington, and Nebraska. In "Maria's Story" the personal reflections of one principal are revealed as she stands poised to address a group of graduate students enrolled in a class on educational administration.

"Maria Winston" parked her Honda in the green space marked "Reserved for Visitors" outside the Education Building at the university, twisted the rearview mirror toward her face, and assessed the damage from the long Monday at her school. The day showed. Ruefully, she remembered a time when it was important that her lipstick was always fresh, her hair perfectly in place, her clothes wrinkle-free. She sighed, ran her fingers through her short, permed hair, pinched her cheeks for color, and straightened the bow on her suit blouse.

When Professor Simpson had called, asking her to talk to his summer secondary school administration class [at the university] about her first year as an assistant principal (AP) [in an area high school], Maria had hesitated. Of course, she was flattered, but it felt like a lifetime ago that she sat in one of these modern brick and glass classrooms, eagerly offering her opinions on educational reform, convinced that all she needed was a chance to take on the whole job herself. A year's experience had forced changes in some of her most passionately held beliefs about education and educators.

The room quieted as the two of them walked in. There were thirty students, mostly women, mostly in their 30s, an ethnic salad of Whites, African Americans, Latinos, and Asians. Professor Simpson opened the class with a greeting, paused, looked at the students, and said, "Before we begin tonight, I'd like all of you to think about this basic question: Why do you want to be a school administrator?"

He had asked Maria's class the same question, and she remembered responding that she wanted to make a difference, break the old boy network, something like that. But one of the first things she had noticed in her new job was that the teachers, even close friends, treated her differently. They assumed she had become part of the network she'd really hoped to change.

Simpson's students were not sure how to react to his question. A few of them laughed, as if they hadn't really thought about an answer. Someone

WHAT ORGANIZATIONAL AND POLICY ISSUES DO SCHOOLS FACE?

As described earlier, schools have been organized in different ways to try to meet the needs of today's students. Decisions about such things as whether to establish separate grades or to implement multiage groupings shape the unique character of each school. School policies about issues from retention and tracking to class schedules and class size also affect life in classrooms. Regardless of school setting, these and other policies are regularly reviewed or revised. Changes might be prompted by teachers, administrators, parents, and students.

called out, "Money." Others shifted uneasily in their seats. Finally, one man spoke up.

"I want to have some influence over what happens at my school. I'm tired of some of the things that go on, and tired of complaining about administrators."

"You can do as well as the people you work for now? Is that what you're saying?" Simpson asked. The man nodded.

A woman in the back, dressed in green sweats, answered next. "You can't make any decisions at all unless you leave the classroom. I love teaching, but I can't stand how powerless I feel."

"Is it power you're after?" Simpson asked. "Power to do what?"

"Power to change things," she replied.

Another woman, middle-aged, nodded agreement. "I love teaching, too, but I want to do more. People seem so narrow-minded. I want to be an administrator who supports teachers, who places more of a value on instruction than on athletics."

Murmurs of approval greeted this comment, and Maria felt the push-pull of their eagerness and her year of experience that had tempered her own naiveté and blind optimism. She, too, had wanted power, and she had seen herself in the principal's office wielding it.

Simpson smiled at the class as if he couldn't hope for a better warm-up audience. Then he introduced Maria. As he described her background—10 years as a classroom teacher, then several years as an in-service specialist who trained teachers in cooperative learning techniques and the writing process—Maria looked out over the faces in the audience. Because she had been one of them not too long ago, she understood what they needed, but she wasn't too sure she could give it to them. And she wasn't sure they would want to hear, let alone believe, some of the things she was going to tell them.

CRITICAL THINKING

Why, do you think, is Maria concerned about what to say? What will she tell her audience about becoming a school administrator? If you were an administrator with the power and authority to change things in a school, where would you begin? In what ways and to what extent would you seek to share power and authority with others in the school?

Note. From *New voices in the field: The work lives of first-year assistant principals (pp. 1–4)* by G. N. Hartzell, R. C. Williams, & K. T. Nelson, 1995. Thousand Oaks, CA: Corwin Press.

Retention

Flunking, to use the derisive term for failing a course or repeating grades in school—always an issue of concern—has taken on new urgency as education reformers tout the advantages of setting and maintaining high standards. To prevent mediocrity, they argue, educators must practice **retention** and abandon the idea of **social promotion**, or passing children to successive grades to keep them with other children of their age. According to this view, it is only logical—and helpful to individuals and to the system as a whole—to retain children who do not reach set standards (Shepard & Smith, 1989).

Educators disagree on the issue of retention. Like some teachers, Patricia Smith, reading and language arts coordinator at Cypress-Fairbanks

School District in suburban Houston, Texas, argues that "An extra year gives students a shot at success." "Retention is more merciful," adds Shari Iba, coordinator of child development services in Florida's Broward County. "What is more devastating: to be with my peers and know that I am failing, or to be held back one year?" (Nazario, 1992)

But facts do not support retention as a viable strategy. Professor Lorrie Shepard of the University of Colorado points out that repeating a grade actually worsens achievement levels in later years for some 70% of students who have been retained (Natriello, 1990). Results from a study by Russ Rumberger of the University of California also indicate that students who repeat one or more grades are more likely to drop out of school than are their peers (Rumberger, 1995).

Should students who fail be held back?

According to one analysis of the research, flunking students causes more problems than it remedies (Holmes, 1989). Studies also suggest that, instead of forcing academically troubled children to mature, to master deficient skills, and to achieve competence in later grades, retention makes students feel "sad," "bad," "upset," and "embarrassed" (Olson, 1990). These feelings cause students to exhibit behavioral problems and often eventually to drop out of school.

Class Schedule and Class Size

One effort to restructure schools has involved changing factors such as class schedule and class size. Colorado's Wasson High School has altered class schedules so that students have four class periods instead of seven. It now takes only half a year instead of a full year to complete a course. Parents, students, and teachers have responded positively to 90-minute classes. Data suggest that there are fewer discipline problems and greater enthusiasm for learning than there were in the previous system (American Political Network, 1992).

Block scheduling has been successful in many schools attempting to restructure. Ewell S. Aiken Optional School, a school in Alexandria, Louisiana, serving 300 students ages 14 and older who need help in grades 5 through 12, has also drastically changed the typical school day to try to help its at-risk enrollees. Classes are held in 4-hour blocks, with a maximum of 15 students per class. Instruction is computer-assisted and self-paced (R. Yarbrough, personal communication, July 1, 1996).

While fiscal woes prevent some school districts from keeping schools open for more than 7 months, others provide **year-round schools** for their students, or educational programs that run through the summer months as well as during the academic year. In some instances, these programs are used to relieve space and budget concerns. In others, year-round schools are viewed as a means to improve pupil performance. Some 1.58 million students in 2,048 public and private schools attended school year-round during the 1992–1993 academic year. States having the largest year-round enrollments were California, Utah, Florida, and Nevada. According to a survey by the National Association for Year-Round Education, the majority of schools having year-round programs operated on a single-track calendar rather than on overlapping multitrack schedules typically used to save money (Harp, 1993).

One of the more controversial issues in public education—and one over which teachers exert little or no control—is that of class size. How many children should be placed in a single room with one teacher? What happens to teaching and learning when a group becomes larger or smaller? Should the inclusion of one or more students with disabilities or students at risk in a class be weighted more heavily in the calculation of class size? How much does it cost to lower class size? How much money can a system save by increasing class size? What are the political costs to policy makers of increasing and decreasing class size?

Are block schedules and year-round schools the answers to restructuring needs?

In general, research supports the value of smaller classes (22 or fewer students), particularly in the early grades. Younger pupils, especially those who are economically disadvantaged and ethnic minority-group students, have benefited from smaller classes, as demonstrated in reading and mathematics achievement and in terms of their attitudes and behavior (Finn & Achilles, 1990; Pate-Bain, Achilles, Boyd-Zaharias, & McKenna, 1992; Achilles, 1996). Critics are quick to observe, however, that simply lowering class size does not automatically lead to increases in learning (Hanushek, 1995).

Districts vary in the way they report average class size. Surprisingly, just measuring class size can cause problems (Glass, 1988). Dividing the total number of students by the total number of staff (including noninstructional staff members) yields a more favorable **student–teacher ratio** than do calculations based on the number of actual classroom teachers.

Tracking

Should students be grouped homogeneously or heterogeneously based on estimates of their abilities? Assigning students deemed to have similar abilities to certain instructional groups, class sections, and programs of study—a practice referred to as **tracking**—is anathema to many educators and to others is the only reasonable way to handle differences in ability between students.

Many educators and parents believe that tracking contributes to problems youngsters experience in their early adolescent years. Students in middle schools are often grouped homogeneously by ability for at least one subject (Mansnerus, 1992). At Lanier Middle School in Houston (as in all Houston, Texas, schools), students are placed into one of two tracks: the Vanguard program for gifted and talented students or the regular program. The two groups of students meet only during lunch, gym, fine arts, and elective classes (R. Cusack, personal communication, July 1, 1996).

Critics argue that students are tracked on flimsy, often biased evidence. Many assigned to "lower," or nonacademic, tracks may be placed there as much for behavior problems as for academic reasons. Those hurt most severely and most often are disadvantaged, minority-group students (Oakes, 1995). Students often get by in lower-track classrooms because teachers in lower-track classes may expect little or nothing of students. Students, in turn, tend to develop a negative self-concept or lowered self-esteem, poor motivation, and even learned helplessness. Perhaps the most damning charge against tracking is the static nature of the assignments: once a student falls into the lower tracks, he or she seems caught in an academic tailspin from which few pull out (Pool & Page, 1995).

Rudolph Ford, middle school principal, remembers the feeling he had when a teacher helped him break out of the lower track.

> I remember being quietly told in the tenth grade by a blonde, middle-aged guidance counselor that I was college material and would be taken out of the general education track and would be placed in an academic track. . . . I had just been told by a white woman that I was as capable as the white students on the academic track, and that I deserved to be educated among the best children in school. This surprised me, because by tenth grade I had become accustomed to low expectations from school officials for students like myself—black males. I always knew that I was as capable academically as my white schoolmates—to have a white adult confirm this was an uplifting experience. She affected my self-esteem and shaped my later educational development more significantly than anyone else except my parents. (Ford, 1995, p. 161)

Other programs combine tracking with mixed-ability groupings of students. At Louis Armstrong School in Queens, New York, a middle school for grades 5 through 8, students of different abilities have more opportunity to interact. Tracking occurs only in some eighth-grade math and English classes because of state mandates. Otherwise, students work in heterogeneous groups, each classroom taking on the aura of a microcosmic society.

Why does the practice of tracking persist?

Informal tracking occurs even in schools that do not use test scores or grade-point averages to place students in either a straight college preparatory track or a vocational track. Schools offer choices. Counselors and teachers, however, guide students in particular directions, as do prerequisites for upper-level courses. Scheduling also tracks students informally. For example, students who take general mathematics may also be forced to take lower-level English because it is the only course that fits the time slot in their schedule ("The Tracking Wars," 1992). Meanwhile, students selected for gifted and talented programs get the best teachers, bright peers with whom to associate, and the most interesting curriculum.

Many argue that educators need to reconsider how "ability" is to be defined, relying less on standardized aptitude and achievement tests and more on constellations of formal and informal assessments that yield a holistic definition of ability. Also, good teachers resist permanent assignment of students to groups in favor of periodic review and reassignment. Cooperative learning, grouping around curricular themes, cross-age tutoring, and multiage classrooms offer positive alternatives to tracking.

WHAT MAKES SOME SCHOOLS MORE EFFECTIVE THAN OTHERS?

Effective schools, defined generally as those schools that can demonstrate student learning, allow substantial staff development time, some of which takes place during the regular workday. In these schools, improvement goals are sharply focused, attainable, and valued by staff members who receive in-class guidance and support from specialists. School needs, not standardized forms and checklists, guide staff. Methods for reaching goals often are based on techniques and materials that have proven successful in similar situations. Furthermore, a judicious mixture of teacher autonomy and central office control permeates improvement programs in effective schools (Levine, 1991).

Standarized test scores are another criterion for identifying effective schools. When the Sandia National Laboratories in Albuquerque, New Mexico, evaluated student performance on the National Assessment of Education Progress (NAEP) and the Scholastic Aptitude Test (SAT), they found that student scores have steadily improved over time and that gains have not been at the expense of advanced skills. The previously supposed decline in test scores is due not to decreasing student performance but to the fact that more students in the bottom half of their class are taking the exam today than they did in years past. Although every ethnic group taking the test performs better today than it did 15 years ago, minority-group youth still lag behind (Carson, Huelskamp, & Woodall, 1993).

Thus, standardized test scores often reflect factors other than those relating to student demographics and school effectiveness. In the 1994 NAEP scores in reading, for example, the 12th-grade scores reflected a significant decline in overall reading proficiency, but this decline occurred primarily among lower performing students (below the 50th percentile). NAEP scores in reading for the fourth grade were higher for students whose parents had more education, for female students, for students in private schools, for students whose parents read aloud to them or talked to them about literature, and for students who did more homework, read for pleasure at home, and watched less television (U.S. Dept. of Education, 1996c). The many elements that contribute to school effectiveness are summarized in Figure 5.4.

Effective schools are managed by effective leaders—individuals who provide the leadership necessary to create a strong curriculum and a safe environment in which students can achieve academic success. At the same time, effective leaders are concerned with the needs of faculty, promoting teacher recognition, and encouraging professional development. Good leaders also encourage parental, family, and community involvement in school activities (National Association of Elementary School Principals, 1994).

Many school leaders work in environments in which parents and teachers are assuming new and powerful leadership roles. In such situations effective leaders think of themselves as "leaders of leaders," creating conditions under which authority can be transferred to others (Parks & Barrett, 1994). Figure 5.5 identifies some of the attributes effective leaders share.

FIGURE 5.4

Elements that Contribute to School Effectiveness

Identify specific examples for each of the nine elements. What other characteristics of effective schools might you add?

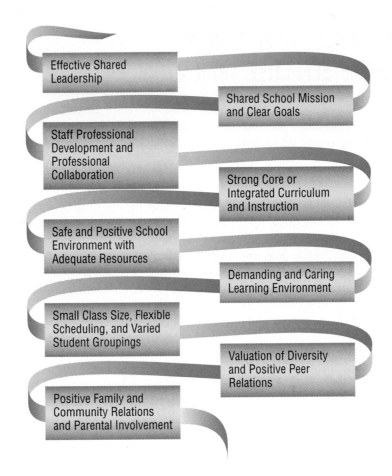

By 1996, 16 elementary schools were part of the Basic School Network—another conception of effective schools. This alliance was established by the Carnegie Foundation for the Advancement of Teaching in partnership with the National Association of Elementary School Principals (NAESP), the American College Testing Program, and the Ewing Marion Kauffman Foundation. These "Basic Schools" were based on Ernest Boyer's (1995) ideas on effective schools. The alliance's goals are to help students communicate effectively, acquire a core of knowledge, and become lifelong learners. Four key components distinguish these schools (Boyer, 1995):

1. The School as a Community—Separate classrooms are connected through a clear and vital mission. Teachers serve as leaders, and the principal acts as lead teacher. Parents are viewed as partners in the learning process.

2. A Curriculum with Coherence—There is an emphasis on language and on core subjects, which are organized around common themes.

3. A Climate for Learning—Class sizes are small, teaching schedules are flexible, and student grouping arrangements are varied. Students are provided with resources ranging from building blocks to electronic tools. They also have access to basic health and counseling services and afternoon and summer enrichment programs.

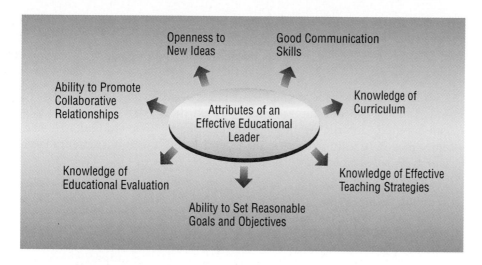

FIGURE 5.5

Some Characteristics of Effective Educational Leaders

In what ways do these attributes contribute to effective leadership? What other attributes might you add?

4. Character Development—The Basic School focuses on seven core values: honesty, respect, responsibility, compassion, self-discipline, perseverance, and giving.

Teachers at David Cox Road Elementary School in Charlotte, North Carolina, suggest that their affiliation with a Basic School has been beneficial in different ways. Melissa Dunlap, a fourth-grade teacher, commented that "The whole school has a common language. We have a common philosophy, common goals, a common belief about children. Everyone does a lot of sharing." Tonya Butts, a third-grade teacher, explained how her experience in a Basic School shaped her teaching:

> When I'm teaching math and other disciplines, I find myself putting more art into it, the language of art, the language of numeracy. That's exciting to me. When I'm teaching a lesson on congruency, I'm thinking of ways I can pick up a picture and discuss with the children the congruent shapes in it. I'm starting to naturally integrate the curriculum. (Raymond, 1996, p. 46)

Positive School Environments

Interviews with 54 representative students from four comprehensive high schools in two California school districts suggest that students' views of positive school environments match those of contemporary theorists. Student measures include the following (Phelan, Davidson, & Cao, 1992):

- the level of visibility and accessibility of the principal,
- the amount of support students receive from teachers and staff members,
- students' perceived degree of personal safety,
- types of interactions between student groups,
- student behavior in general,
- availability of extracurricular activities,

- the physical condition of the school, and
- degree to which students can speak their native language in informal settings and the availability of at least one staff member who speaks the same primary language.

Students' opinions about schools are particularly strong when they have attended more than one high school or when their experiences in middle school are quite different from those in high school. One student who had recently moved to California described vividly how the environment in her former high school compared to her new one:

> They didn't really care if you were in the classroom, they didn't care what you were doing . . . . Only one teacher in the high school had a personal thing with any of the students. It was a very large school, maybe that's why. There were real large classes, but [the teachers] were very distant from everybody, so they didn't know me. I could have done anything. They had no idea who I was.

How should school effectiveness be judged?

> I did very bad in that school. I came here, and I was failing. It was so easy not to do anything. I mean it was, well they don't care, so why should I?

> And then I got here and the teachers that I met, the first day they had my name right. "Wow, this is cool! You know who I am." I was tardy to class once, a couple of minutes late, and that day they called my house to talk to my parents.

> Oh, this is great . . . You go in and you're not there for a day and they notice and say, "Hi, are you tardy?" And they care. (Phelan, Davidson, & Cao, 1992, p. 702)

A report by the National Association of Secondary School Principals (NASSP, 1996) suggests that small school size, or creating small units within a school, is one way to banish anonymity. Teachers' expectations for students, their willingness to be flexible—not equating seat time with learning and extending learning beyond the high school campus—are other factors that the NASSP considers crucial to the success of a school. Two programs that seem in keeping with principals' ideas about effective schools are Ward Melville High on the North Shore of Long Island and Benjamin Mays High in southwest Atlanta. Students at both schools must apply for admission, write an essay, and submit their grades. Mays takes about 175 of 300 applicants and Melville accepts about 35 of 65. Each program sends 100% of its graduates to 4-year colleges. Over the years, each school has also produced two members of the All-USA Academic First Team—students selected for national recognition by *USA Today* (Ordovensky, 1996).

When asked why students at the two schools have been so successful, winners of academic awards offered several reasons that sounded much like the NASSP's recommendations for creating effective schools. One student explained that teachers had high expectations, "paint[ed] pictures of the future," and encouraged students to excel. Another said that teachers allowed students to miss class if they needed to work on a project, for example, rather than "locking" them into class every day for the 50-minute period. Others noted the importance of strong parental support and positive role models who are "concrete examples of people achieving" (Ordovensky, 1996, p. 2D).

Positive Family and Community Relations

Links between homes and schools have become more important in recent years because evidence suggests that connections between home and school help students adjust and learn. Parents influence their children's academic achievement by exposing them to intellectually stimulating experiences, directly teaching them, monitoring homework, and communicating with the school. Parents also strengthen ties by volunteering at the school, attending school conferences, requesting information, and participating in school governance (Eccles & Harold, 1996).

The larger and more diverse schools are, the less likely parents are to be involved. As students are assigned to multiple teachers for various classes in middle and high schools, and as teachers teach large numbers of students in staggered classes, close teacher–student relationships are unlikely to develop (Dornbusch and Glasgow, 1996). Teachers do not get to know their students well. And teachers are unlikely to encourage parental involvement because they find the idea impractical. In these situations, teachers tend to focus on the strongest and weakest students because they seem to require the most attention. The parents of the students of average achievement, then, may be among those least likely to be linked closely to schools (Dornbusch & Glasgow, 1996).

Some parents who live in dangerous or resource-poor neighborhoods have less time, energy, and resources available for parenting and for getting involved with schools. Indeed "family" involvement is probably a more appropriate term than "parent" involvement; in many communities children are raised by people who are not their parents (Decker, Gregg, & Decker, 1995). Children from single-parent families and stepfamilies are more likely than are children from two-parent families to experience school-based problems and are most in need of strong home–school ties (Zill, 1996).

Positive connections between home and school also may be influenced by social networks and social class. The social networks to which parents belong, which may be influenced by their linguistic and ethnic backgrounds, can affect their attitudes and beliefs about schools. Some research suggests that middle- and upper-class parents are more likely to think of education as a joint responsibility of school and home, while parents of lower socioeconomic status are more likely to view education as the teacher's job (Lareau, 1996). As children grow older, their parents become less likely to be involved in school activities. The gap that exists between socioeconomic status and children's academic achievement also widens with age, making it even more difficult for parents from low-income families to get involved (Alexander & Entwisle, 1996).

BENCHMARKS

The Development of American Schools
From 1635 to the Present

1635–1636	Latin Grammar School is established in Boston as a college preparatory school for young men. Harvard College is founded.
1788	U.S. Constitution is ratified. The framers of the constitution give the power to establish schools and license teachers to the individual states rather than to the federal government.
1801	First Roman Catholic school in New York is established.
1819	First public high school opens in Boston.
1824	Rensselaer Polytechnic Institute opens in Troy, New York.
1827	Massachusetts becomes the first state to require every town with 500 or more families to establish a public high school.
1836–1837	Wesleyan College in Georgia and Oberlin College in Ohio become the first chartered colleges for women.
1839	First public normal school (teachers college) in the United States is established in Lexington, Massachusetts.
1855	First kindergarten in the United States is established by Margaretta Schurtz in Watertown, Wisconsin.
1860	Elizabeth Palmer Peabody opens the first English-speaking kindergarten in Boston.
1865	The American Association of School Administrators is organized in Harrisburg, Pennsylvania.
1874	Kalamazoo, Michigan, case rules that states may establish and support public high schools with tax funds, which contributes to the secondary school movement and eventually to compulsory high school attendance laws.

1901	First public junior college is established in Joliet, Illinois.
1907	Maria Montessori founds the first Montessori school in Rome.
1909	First junior high schools are established in Berkeley, California, and in Columbus, Ohio.
1916	The National Association of Secondary School Principals (NASSP) is founded in Chicago.
1917	Congress passes the Smith-Hughes Act, which provides federal matching funds for vocational education in public high schools.
1919	Rudolph Steiner founds the first Waldorf school in Stuttgart, Germany.
1921	National Association of Elementary School Principals (NAESP) is founded in Washington, D.C.
1964	Economic Opportunity Act establishes a Job Corps program and authorizes support of education and training activities and of community action programs, including Head Start.
1966	Adult Education Act (Public Law 89-750) authorizes grants to states for the establishment and expansion of educational programs for adults.
1991	Minnesota enacts the first charter school legislation.
1992	Chris Whittle announces his Edison Project, a plan to create 1,000 for-profit schools to compete with the public school system.
1994	Goals 2000: Educate America Act allows state education agencies to use federal funds for state planning and evaluation activities involving local efforts to contract with private management organizations to reform public schools.

SUMMARY

How is the school a social institution?

1 Schools are organizations having an identifiable structure and a set of functions. Their primary function is to move young people into the mainstream of society. Educators work with parents, children, and outside agencies to ensure the psychological and physical well-being of students and to foster academic success. They also work collaboratively to build students' understanding and acceptance of others.

2 Schools differ in size, structure, and function. Their student populations are also quite diverse in terms of socioeconomic status and racial/ethnic composition.

3 Students have opportunities to attend many types of public and private schools. Parents base decisions about where their children go to school on such variables as class size and a school's scholastic ranking.

How is public schooling organized in the United States?

4 There are many types of preschools in the United States, and the professional preparation of staff and the quality of programs vary greatly. Programs are supported by both public and private interest groups and include Project Head Start, infant intervention and enrichment programs, nursery schools, public and private prekindergartens and kindergartens, college and university laboratory schools, church-sponsored preschools, and parent cooperatives.

5 About 44% of five-year-olds experience full-time kindergarten programs. Kindergarten programs differ, but many focus on academics. About 84% of children in the United States attend public elementary schools. There are many instructional and curricular variations within and among schools.

6 Junior high and middle schools are meant to help students make the transition from elementary school to high school by concentrating on academic subjects and exposing students to careers and occupations. Some critics claim, however, that existing schools are too imitative of high schools and inappropriate to the needs of 10- to 14-year-olds.

7 Sizes of high schools vary, with enrollment in alternative schools being as low as 200 and enrollment in large "comprehensive" schools—high schools offering a full range of programs—being as high as 4,000.

8 In 1993 about 62% of high school graduates enrolled in college immediately after graduation. About 22% attended 2-year colleges, while 40% enrolled in 4-year public or private institutions.

What are some schooling alternatives?

9 There are a number of notable alternative programs that provide educational opportunities for people in the United States. Among these are magnet schools, vocational–technical schools, Montessori and Waldorf schools, private and independent schools, for-profit schools, parochial schools, charter schools, and home schools.

10 As alternatives for schooling have increased, the distinction between public and private education has become increasingly vague. Despite their similarities, public schools differ from private schools in several ways: (a) public schools are tax supported, while, in the main, private schools are not; (b) private schools can set their own admissions requirements; (c) private school students are enrolled by parental or student choice; and (d) private schools have the freedom to craft philosophies that appeal to specific groups of people.

How are schools administered?

11 Among those who are responsible for the administration of schools are superintendents, principals, assistant principals, and site-based management teams. These individuals and groups, from the superintendent down, operate in a world that has changed dramatically in the past 30 years or so. Today's school administrators have much less flexibility in making decisions than did their predecessors. They must contend with state-aid formulas, government mandates, external standards for educators' and students' performances, and a host of political pressure groups intent on sharing power.

What organizational and policy issues do schools face?

12 Schools have been organized in different ways to try to meet the needs of students. Decisions about such things as whether to establish separate grades or to implement multi-age groupings shape the unique character of each school. School policies about a number of other issues, including retention, class schedules, class size, and tracking are regularly reviewed or revised. Changes might be prompted by teachers, administrators, parents, and students.

What makes some schools more effective than others?

13 Students seem to do better in schools where there is effective leadership and a positive relationship between school personnel and parents and other members of the community. Such schools are generally marked by substantial staff development time, a strong curriculum, and a safe environment. Teachers think positively about students' abilities to succeed, set high but reasonable standards for student performance, and maximize students' opportunities to learn.

TERMS AND CONCEPTS

alternative school, *p. 182*
block scheduling, *p. 200*
central office staff, *p. 192*
charter school, *p. 190*
collegiality, *p. 194*
for-profit school, *p. 187*
institution, *p. 171*
magnet school, *p. 182*
National Association for the
    Education of Young Children
    (NAEYC), *p. 175*

nongraded classrooms, *p. 177*
principal, *p. 194*
private school, *p. 186*
retention, *p. 199*
school district, *p. 171*
site-based management, *p. 196*
social promotion, *p. 199*
student–teacher ratio, *p. 201*
superintendent of schools, *p. 192*
tracking, *p. 201*
year-round school, *p. 200*

REFLECTIVE PRACTICE

Pamela Piersol had lobbied the state legislature for 2 years on behalf of Citizens for Charter Schools (CCS). The group wanted the freedom to establish new schools that were free from most, if not all, state regulations but were supported with public funds. Pam and her colleagues contended that the public schools as they were presently run did not deliver the quality of education that students and taxpayers deserved or had a right to expect.

Piersol had taught public school for 6 years and served as a principal for 5 years before leaving to become headmaster of a private school. Her credentials were impeccable. She lobbied with considerable skill and managed to win a state-supported program of experimentation with charter schools funded for 5 years. Groups would write proposals for new charter schools, and, if the program were funded, parents could choose to send their children to one of the charter schools.

The new charter schools could serve any and all levels as the designers saw fit. The schools could not discriminate against students or staff by race, ethnicity, or gender, and they could not value one religion over another. Otherwise charter schools would be free to organize and run themselves in any fashion. Charter schools would not have to hire state-certified or -licensed personnel. They could include or exclude any grade levels. They could create their own admission standards and expel students. Most important, Piersol and her colleagues believed, they could craft their mission broadly or narrowly to shape the schools' structure and functions, which in turn would be used to attract and hold parents and students. At the end of the 5-year period of experimentation, those schools that got and kept students would continue to receive state aid; those that did not demonstrate holding power would lose funding.

Issues, Problems, Dilemmas, Opportunities

Assume Piersol and the CCS were located in your state. What specific problems, if any, might a new charter school be able to address more effectively than an existing public school? What opportunities, if any, might a charter school capitalize on to attract and hold students?

Perceive and Value

How might a proposal to create a new charter school written by a group of private school teachers and parents differ from one written by public school teachers and parents? In other words, how might the values of the people designing the school influence the school mission, its organization, and the activities in which faculty and students engage?

Know and Act

In 50 words or fewer, craft an advertisement that reflects your estimate of the defining characteristics of a charter school that might succeed in your community. Design the advertisement so that the attributes of the new school appear in descending order of importance.

Evaluate

In both the long and short term, a new charter school will be judged by its ability to attract and hold students. Are there other factors that might be used to judge the quality of a newly organized charter school? What might they be? How might you assess a school's ability to attend to these factors?

ONLINE ACTIVITY

The Virtual Schoolhouse

(**http://sunsite.oit.unc.edu/cisco/schools/elementary.html**) contains Web addresses for schools all over the country (even one in Paris, France). These have been designed locally, yet it is possible to identify some concepts that people everywhere use to describe their schools. Look at 6 to 10 different sites and identify some of these common concepts. To do so you must read carefully for the intent of the description, asking yourself what the author hoped to convey. Does one particular site communicate its philosophy more effectively than the others? If so, why do you find it more appealing?

Foundations in Action

CASE 2

Laura Saatzer

When *the students come into my room, they have assigned books that they are reading. I have students choose a fairy tale, or a folktale, read it with a partner, and practice retelling the story. I want them to practice summarizing a story and to communicate orally in a clear way. I also think the whole oral tradition of folktales and fairy tales sometimes has a tendency to be shoved to the side, so I try to emphasize that aspect of language arts.*

Laura Saatzer teaches third grade at Roosevelt Elementary School, a language magnet school, in St. Paul, Minnesota. The school focuses on reading, writing, listening, speaking, and critical-thinking skills. Ms. Saatzer uses history to encourage self-expression and communication among her culturally diverse students. Storytelling is a way of keeping history alive.

While Ms. Saatzer's philosophy dictates that she attend to individual needs, she often finds it difficult to translate this philosophy into practice. She **recognizes issues** that arise that force her to adapt her views and find creative solutions.

My *class is very challenging this year. Sometimes they exhaust my patience, because there are just so many children with so many needs who come from homes where their needs aren't being met. One of my students is classified Emotionally Behaviorally Disordered (EBD). She can be a real challenge at times.*

I know she is acting out anger that she is unable to handle by herself. My heart goes out to her, so I don't mind her behavior so much, but it does disrupt class, and it does take away from the other students' learning.

Ms. Saatzer tries to adapt her teaching by **taking others' perspectives** and also encourages her students to view the world through others' eyes.

With *some students, like Southeast Asian students, it is hard to know what is going on in their minds. At the beginning of the year, I find that they need space, and that they need to establish a comfort level with you.*

Ms. Saatzer uses "Up-Close-and-Personal" boards—posters of family photos created by students—to help them learn about one another. As the class gathers in a corner of the room, Kia interviews Joe about his family:

Kia: Do you like to show your board?

Joe: This is my cousin Greg when he was a year old, last year. And this was my Aunt Vicki at Christmas time and my cousin Shannon at Christmas time. . . .

Like any professional striving to enhance her knowledge and develop her skills, Laura Saatzer uses available **professional knowledge** and professional development to inform her practice.

The first year that I started teaching, I was part of a Compass program—Writers in the Schools—and I worked with a professional author who helped me come up with some lessons and some ways to work with children on writing. I really learned a lot. She stressed the importance of using children's literature and students' own work when teaching skills.

As a professional Ms. Saatzer does not simply possess knowledge, she applies what she knows—**takes action**—to address the problems and opportunities she encounters.

So a couple of years back that was one of my big goals. Instead of pulling out my language book, and saying, "Open it up and do page 4," I wanted to come up with more creative and enjoyable ways for children to learn. . . . When we study quotation marks I can refer to the poem of The Little Old Man. I'm also going to refer to a book we read, "George Washington's Breakfast," that has dialogue in it. I want students to become aware of the dialogue that is in what they read and to see it in what they write.

Laura also tries to understand the consequences of her actions through **evaluation** of the results of her efforts.

Grading students' presentations is always hard. I look for creativity. I also consider students' speaking skills, because I don't want to discourage efforts to improve their oral language.

CASE APPLICATION

- How might Laura Saatzer be influenced by the histories of her students as she plans and teaches?
- How might the school philosophy shape the kinds of instructional activities Laura and her colleagues select?
- If a pragmatist or an existentialist were interested in results or outcomes, what evidence of success might they look for in Laura Saatzer's classroom?
- How can a teacher's selection of literature shape children's views of their past and their future?
- How and why might teachers test the accuracy of their own beliefs about the nature of children as learners?

6

School Governance and Education Finance

This chapter describes governmental influences on education and the characteristics of people who lead and manage public education at federal, state, and local levels. We note the importance of special-interest groups in influencing the structure and functions of public schooling and discuss the subtle interplay of public values and school funding. We also consider continuing problems of increasing demands and decreasing resources, as well as new issues presented by concepts such as site-based management and school choice.

1 What are school governance and education finance?

2 How does the federal government influence education?

3 How is education financed and controlled by the states?

4 How are schools financed and managed at the local level?

5 How are governance and funding related to educational success?

WHAT ARE SCHOOL GOVERNANCE AND EDUCATION FINANCE?

The power to establish and operate public schools is derived from the Tenth Amendment to the U.S. Constitution: "The powers not delegated to the United States by the Constitution; nor prohibited by it to the States, are reserved to the States respectively, or to the people." The power to educate is one reserved to the states; that is, the states are ultimately responsible for **school governance**, or for establishing and overseeing the structure and functions of public education. That does not mean the states must go it alone; they delegate many educational functions to local education agencies. Indeed, over time, a complex network of formal organizations and informal pressure groups at the federal, state, and local levels has made public education what it is today.

The governance system determines how funds are used for public education, and education finance strongly influences school practices. That is, how funds are raised, allocated, spent, and accounted for affects how schools operate and what teachers and students can and cannot have or do. School governance and finance are therefore relevant for teachers. Teachers must be knowledgeable about both the formal systems of governance and finance and the informal influences of special-interest groups if they are to serve their students and the teaching profession effectively.

How Schools Are Run

As you learned in Chapter 5, schools are *managed* or *administered* by school administrators. People tend to use these verbs interchangeably. For some, administration and management have meant decision making (Barnard, 1938; Griffiths, 1959). For others, these actions have been defined "as the process of working with and through others to accomplish organizational goals efficiently" (Sergiovanni, Burlingame, Coombs, & Thurston, 1992, p. 60). Certainly, to administer or to manage schools is to lead others in the fulfillment of a school's mission.

The definition of *leader*, however, is subject to considerable debate. To some, a leader is a person who takes on new tasks and pushes for change, someone who is proactive, not reactive (Zaleznick, 1977). To others, a leader is a system-oriented person who is concerned about production and a person-oriented manager who demonstrates considera-tion for staff members (Stogdill, 1981), or, similarly, a person who is concerned with tasks and people in the organization (Bales, 1954; Bow-ers & Seashore, 1966). Aristotle believed that leaders are born—people either have the capac-ity to lead or they do not, and some modern

> **What is good leadership?**

organizational theorists tend to agree. Yet others think that leadership is largely a function of the situations in which people find themselves (Fiedler, 1967). Kenneth Leithwood (1992) has argued that school leaders are finding themselves more and more in the position of having to create conditions that enable staffs to find their own directions.

These leaders—school board members, superintendents, principals, department heads, and teachers—are responsible for the "governance" of schools: for controlling, directing, and otherwise influencing the actions and conduct of schooling. They do so within a system of institutions, laws, policies, politics, and customs. The leaders are designated and paid to exercise and del-egate power to make the schools work. To get a sense of school leadership today, visit the home page of a group dedicated to supporting leaders—the American Association of School Administrators (**http://www.aasa.org**).

How Schools Are Funded

The total expenditure per pupil in public elementary and secondary school programs in 1995–1996 was $6,993. (U.S. Department of Education, 1996a). As illustrated in Figure 6.1, public schools are financed primarily by localities, states, and the federal government. More than three fourths of the 15,437 school boards in the United States have taxing authority. In economi-cally troubled times, however, few political leaders at any governmental level are willing to risk the ire of voters by raising taxes to support public schools. The chances for success of such a maneuver are diminished even further by the fact that an increasing number of voters no longer have children in the public schools. Those who are retired and on fixed incomes often are less will-ing and less able to support public education. In an unusual move in 1994, Michigan legislators first ruled out property taxes as a source of support for schools and then passed a 2% increase in the state sales tax.

Relationships Between Education and the Economy

Since before the founding of the republic, values and money have shaped public education into the system we have today. Values and money trigger all kinds of questions about the conduct of education. Does "equal" educational opportunity mean the same level of funding for all students, or must some students and localities be afforded extra resources to put them on

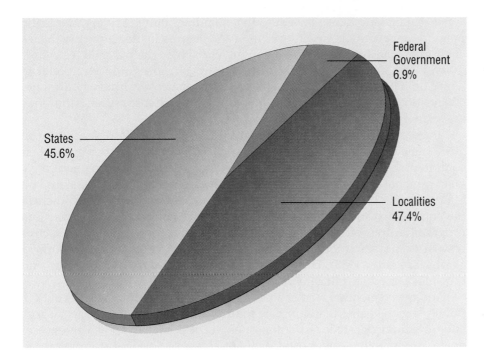

States
45.6%

Federal
Government
6.9%

Localities
47.4%

FIGURE 6.1

**Sources of Revenues
for School Funding**

What factors might alter
the proportion of financial
support that each level of
government provides?

Note. From *School Finance: Trends
in U.S. Education Spending* by
United States General Account-
ing Office, September, 1995,
Washington, D.C.: Government
Printing Office

equal footing with others in their quest for educational success? Why should
and how could low-income communities be helped to provide adequate
facilities and programs for educating their children? At what point do
providers of money for education cross the line from being efficient to being
stingy? Who decides how money will be spent at the school level? Should
parents and localities be allowed to choose what schools their children
attend and use tax dollars to finance these choices? Contemporary leaders
communicate their values through their answers to such questions.

Corporate values also shape education. Today, increasing computerization, the proliferation of services offered by businesses, a growing global
economy, and decentralization of responsibility necessitate that workers
possess a variety of basic and work-related skills (Berryman & Bailey, 1992).
Besides learning reading, communication, and mathematical skills, Americans who progress through the educational pipeline have opportunities to reason, to direct their own work, to cooperate with others, and to adapt to
change. Armed with such skills, workers are better prepared than the
unskilled to understand the requirements of their jobs, to communicate effectively with colleagues, to advance to more challenging positions, and to
make decisions. Because they may not need to defer to supervisors in the
workplace, such individuals make production more efficient.

As people have increased their levels of educational attainment, they also
have increased their work options. The more marketable skills a person has,
the more likely she is to find a job. High employment rates signal reduced
numbers of welfare recipients and possibly more money for education. A
repertoire of sophisticated skills also allows many individuals to seek and
attain high-paying jobs. High salaries, in turn, increase purchasing power for
both goods and services. One service in particular—health care—contributes
significantly to general well-being and productivity.

When making a case for education spending, public leaders frequently point to connections between education and success in life and between lack of education and failure. "Would you prefer to pay to help a child learn how to read," a candidate for public office might ask, "or would you prefer to house an illiterate felon at three or four times the cost?" Illiteracy does not always lead to crime, just as education does not guarantee success, but they are related.

Increased educational opportunities also have made democracy run more smoothly. Knowledge of history, geography, and the nation's and their community's cultural heritage enables people to gain a common perspective on current political and social problems. Development of language skills and interpersonal skills prepares people to communicate and work with others in the community and in the larger world to reach common goals. Education programs convey from generation to generation more and less effective ways for conducting social and political discourse in a free society (Guthrie, Garms, & Pierce, 1988). These outcomes are essential for a democracy, and they make efforts to educate people worth the price.

Today's economists tend to assess the value of education in terms of both public or social benefits and private returns. Many argue that the social benefits of education—reduced crime rates, inculcation of moral values, economic productivity—are most difficult to assess but also most important to achieve. Society as a whole, they contend, must benefit from money spent on public education because it requires redistribution of resources—taking money away from some to provide service to others.

People also view education as a means of developing human capital, much as businesses acquire and develop physical capital, such as buildings and equipment (Becker, 1964; Schultz, 1981). These individuals believe that the returns of education must accrue to both students and society; that is, students should have reason to expect that the time, effort, and money they invest in their education will yield some personal benefit, such as increased earnings and greater job satisfaction. Society should expect that public education will yield productive citizens with some sense of the common good.

What concept of the common good should education provide?

Personal and social gains are not mutually exclusive; education yields both. When people learn, they become more valuable to their neighbors. When all the neighbors are improving themselves, the neighborhood—regardless of whether it is defined locally, regionally, or nationally—is a better place for the individual.

Through the years, the challenge for policy makers has been to strike some balance among four ideals (Guthrie, Garms, & Pierce, 1988). Although the relative importance of these ideals has waxed and waned at different times and in different locales, all have figured prominently in shaping public education:

- *Equality*, or equal educational opportunity, typically has been defined in terms of providing equal access to schooling, making available to every student educational treatment tailored to his strengths and weaknesses and ensuring that all students acquire at least minimum or basic skills.

- *Adequacy* refers to the minimum resources sufficient to achieve some educational result (Clune, 1995).

- *Efficiency* connotes getting the maximum benefit from dollars spent on education.

- *Liberty*, or choice, implies control over where, how, and for what purposes students are educated.

Political and Economic Influences on Public Education

Various individuals, groups, and organizations wield power to shape the course of events in schools. Formal sources of power reside in the organization itself—those in charge have final authority over salaries, make staff appointments, and the like. Increasingly, in restructured schools, this formal authority is being redefined to include parents and teachers. Others exercise power informally by virtue of their personalities and/or the constituencies they represent. Figure 6.2 shows some of the forces influencing education at the national, federal, regional, state, and local levels, which are discussed in this chapter.

Education Lobbies and Special-Interest Groups   Public education, it seems, is everyone's business, and some people are more powerful in influencing its direction than are others. People often coalesce around specific interests and try to exert pressure for the advancement of their cause, hence the terms **special-interest group** and *pressure group*. These terms often are used pejoratively to communicate the idea that group members promote their own narrow point of view. But special-interest groups also educate the public about important issues and offer alternative solutions to problems.

While many education reforms in recent years have been initiated publicly by authorities at the state level, a variety of organizations and special-interest groups have contributed informally to the reforms by working publicly and behind the scenes to shape policy at the local, state, and national levels. For example, the largest volunteer education organization in the United States, the **National Congress of Parents and Teachers (PTA)**, has long supported legislation at the state and national levels designed to benefit children. Professional organizations such as the National School Boards Association, the National Association of State Boards of Education, and the American Association of Colleges for Teacher Education also support in spirit and with funds many education policy initiatives (Campbell, Cunningham, Nystrand, and Usdan, 1990).

Do special interest groups have a negative impact on education?

Interest groups often attempt to influence schools on ideological grounds. The Council for Basic Education, founded in 1956 by Mortimer Smith and Arthur Bestor, advocates curriculum in the liberal arts, much in keeping with Bestor's essentialist ideas (see Chapter 4). Since the 1960s, African Americans and Native Americans have been increasingly active in demanding that schools respond to their needs and facilitate their participation

FIGURE 6.2

Influences on Public Education

How might this figure change if you ranked the levels in terms of their power? Explain your reasoning.

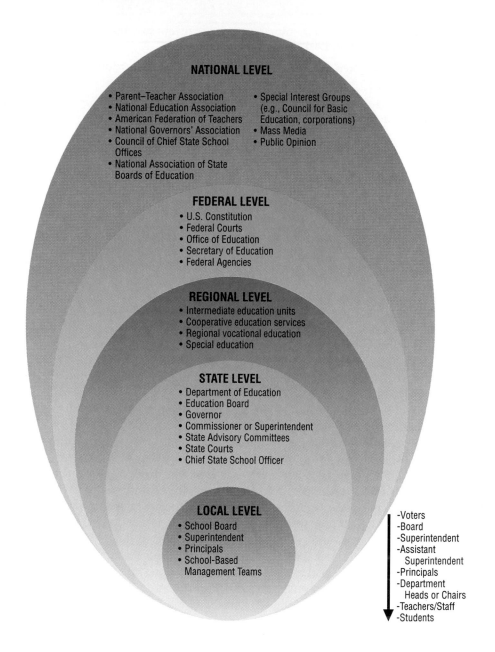

NATIONAL LEVEL

- Parent–Teacher Association
- National Education Association
- American Federation of Teachers
- National Governors' Association
- Council of Chief State School Offices
- National Association of State Boards of Education
- Special Interest Groups (e.g., Council for Basic Education, corporations)
- Mass Media
- Public Opinion

FEDERAL LEVEL

- U.S. Constitution
- Federal Courts
- Office of Education
- Secretary of Education
- Federal Agencies

REGIONAL LEVEL

- Intermediate education units
- Cooperative education services
- Regional vocational education
- Special education

STATE LEVEL

- Department of Education
- Education Board
- Governor
- Commissioner or Superintendent
- State Advisory Committees
- State Courts
- Chief State School Officer

LOCAL LEVEL

- School Board
- Superintendent
- Principals
- School-Based Management Teams

-Voters
-Board
-Superintendent
-Assistant Superintendent
-Principals
-Department Heads or Chairs
-Teachers/Staff
-Students

have tried to establish *unidos,* or unity, among Spanish-speaking peoples to effect change in public schools. Such groups often are stimulated and sustained by their beliefs about school curricula and issues of social justice.

Interest groups advocate a wide range of activities aimed in one way or another at exerting control over curricular, instructional, and governance issues in public education. In 1992, for example, the American Association of University Women (AAUW) issued the results of a national study on gender bias in schools: "How Schools Shortchange Girls" (American Association of University Women and the National Education Association, 1992). As a result of this study, the AAUW made 40 recommendations for action in pub-

result of this study, the AAUW made 40 recommendations for action in public education, including

- strengthened reinforcement of Title IX, which prohibits discrimination against women;
- preparation of teachers, administrators, and counselors to bring gender equity and awareness to every aspect of schooling;
- inclusion in the formal curriculum of the experiences of women and men from all walks of life, with women and girls valued in the material young people study;
- encouragement of girls to pursue mathematics and science careers;
- attention to gender equity in vocational education; and
- support for students to deal with realities of their sexuality and health.

Visit the home page of the AAUW at **http://www.aauw.org/**.

The American Civil Liberties Union (ACLU) has taken public positions on educational issues to defend people against what it has perceived as attacks on their civil liberties. One of its most notable involvements was in the Scopes trial of 1925; in fact, the ACLU stimulated the confrontation between Christian fundamentalists and evolutionists. The ACLU offered counsel to any Tennessee teacher who would test the law that forbade teaching in public schools any theory that denied the account of creation in the Book of Genesis. John T. Scopes took them up on the offer and was defended by Clarence Darrow. The ACLU's home page on the Web contains position statements on education. Visit **http://www.aclu.org/**.

The ACLU also has filed briefs on legal issues as a "friend of the court" for the purpose of educating judges and lawyers; endorsed exempting students from the flag salute when their religion suggests that refusal is appropriate; and opposed the use of public funds for private education.

The Anti-Defamation League (ADL), organized in 1913 to end unjust and unfair discrimination against and ridicule of any religious sect or body of citizens, has 400 staff members in 30 field offices in U.S. cities. Its World of Difference Campaign—a comprehensive educational program for elementary and secondary teachers and students—fosters tolerance through teacher awareness training, youth training, classroom discussion guides, student after-school programs, and weekend awareness retreats. According to ADL figures, it has trained 100,000 teachers and 10 million public, private, and parochial school students. (More information about ADL activities can be obtained from their Web site at **http://www.adl.org/**.)

For more than 100 years, the Daughters of the American Revolution (DAR) has promoted awards and scholarship programs in schools to foster patriotism. The group sponsors the Junior American Citizens program to encourage the teaching of good citizenship and gives Good Citizenship Medals to recognize qualities of honor, service, courage, and leadership. The DAR sponsors the American History Essay Contest for the middle grades, gives scholarships to college and university students in the Reserve Officer Training Corps (ROTC), and recognizes outstanding teachers of American history. See **http://www.dar.org/**.

The Legal Defense and Education Fund (LDEF) of the National Organization for Women (NOW) sponsors a variety of actions to advance women's rights in education systems across the country. In St. Louis, Missouri, for

What effects do organizations such as PTA, NOW, and NAACP have on the governance and finance of American public education? What other interest groups influence public education policy and practice? How would you evaluate the benefits and dangers of these stakeholders' involvement in education?

example, the LDEF fought against the board of education policy to transfer pregnant elementary and junior high school girls to a less desirable school when their pregnancies became obvious. The board changed its policy, allowing girls to choose to remain in regular classes or to transfer (National Organization for Women Legal Defense and Education Fund, 1993, p. 2). For more information on NOW, visit their Web site (**http://now.org/now/**).

Since its founding in 1909, the National Association for the Advancement of Colored People (NAACP) has worked to ensure racial justice for all people and to improve the living conditions of low-income people. The association is the largest and most influential civil rights organization in the country. The NAACP has worked for open housing, job opportunities, prison reform, school desegregation, and education programs for youths and adults. For more information on the NAACP and its influence on education and society, see **http://www.naacp.org**/.

Business organizations also have left their mark on education. The National Association of Manufacturers (NAM), for example, believes that America's economic well-being and ability to compete in global markets depend on the skills of the nation's workforce (National Association of Manufacturers, 1993, p. 29). The NAM and the U.S. Department of Labor have formed a partnership to encourage small, medium, and large manufacturers to attend to training, education, and changes in work organizations to create high-performance work environments.

What other special-interest groups can you identify that have had an impact on American education?

Business–School Partnerships   Partnerships between public schools and private enterprises have existed for years. New York Alliance for the Public Schools, for example, was established in 1979. It includes business, community, and civic leaders, as well as school board members, representatives from the United Federation of Teachers, parents, and others. In the mid-1980s there were some 35,000 such partnerships (McCormick, 1984). By the 1990s the number had increased five-fold. Associations involving private businesses and corporations typically are driven by the idea that good schools yield good citizens, good employees, and good consumers.

> **Is business involvement in education a good thing?**

Business–school partnerships engage in many different activities meant to improve schools. The New York Alliance has sponsored training for school principals and created a data bank to link classrooms with city resources. Houston partnerships have provided career counseling for students and put science equipment and computers in Texas schools. The Minneapolis Public Academy, sponsored by General Mills, started a program in the schools that reduced class size, made teachers accountable for students' scores on standardized achievement tests, and put telephones in classrooms so parents and teachers could communicate directly.

Sometimes partnerships take the form of local education funds (LEFs) that offer money directly to teachers for special projects. LEFs provide teachers with mini-grants ($100 to $900) and sponsor conferences and workshops for teachers on a variety of subjects.

Although business–school programs are becoming increasingly visible, they raise questions even in the minds of some believers. As Joan Richardson, an education writer at the *Detroit Free Press*, suggests, there may be good reasons to be skeptical of the business–school connection:

> What problems might be created when Ford Motor Company designs a curriculum aimed at encouraging teenagers' interest in manufacturing as a career? What conflicts exist when a school uses a local company's laboratories for Saturday morning science classes? Is it appropriate for fourth graders to learn about energy needs from Detroit Edison Company, a company whose profit margin hinges on insuring popular acceptance of nuclear power? . . . Do we want Mazda Corporation footing the bill to take American students to Japan for study programs? Should school districts agree to accept computers from Kroger Company for every $150,000 in Kroger receipts from parents? Do we want Pizza Hut treating first-graders to free pizza if they meet reading goals set by that company? (Richardson, 1992, p. 2)

Others insist that public education demands public involvement. Well-managed partnerships between schools and businesses can break down barriers between disparate groups of people; that is, such partnerships create opportunities for people to work together on common tasks that they want to see accomplished. When stakeholders in the success of public education work together to achieve common goals, the schools are bound to benefit.

Public Media   One cannot ignore the influence of public opinion on processes of governing and managing public education in the United States. The press figures prominently in public opinion both by reporting on the state of the public mind and by suggesting what people ought to think.

> **Do the mass media affect education both positively and negatively?**

One view, expressed by Juan Williams, is that the job of the press is to watch governmental and educational leaders so that they do not cheat the public. This time-honored role of journalism is important. Williams (1992) describes the job of the journalist on the education beat:

> The truth is, reporters and editors and, most important, readers are interested in education only as a function of political power. A major proportion of any jurisdiction's tax dollars goes into schools. Politicians have to make up those school budgets and defend them. The school or university budget has to be both sufficient to the task of educating young people and simultaneously able to withstand charges that it is really a pork-barrel project, wasting the taxpayer's money. Education budgets pay not only for teachers and books but also for construction workers, maintenance people, teachers' aides, administrators, union chiefs, and cooks. In other words, the tax dollars assigned to educate children are a

major source of patronage and power in our society. Newspaper editors, as the public's watchdogs, want to know if the taxpayers are being cheated out of their money. (p. 179)

The press performs not only an informational function in society but a major educational functional as well. Television, newspapers, radio, and magazines touch more people today than at any time in our history, and they will reach more tomorrow than they do today. To make a positive impact, former U.S. Senator Bill Bradley has argued, the media must be more civic minded.

At a time when harassed parents spend less time with their children, they have ceded to television more and more of the all-important role of storytelling, which is essential to the formation of moral education that sustains a civil society. But too often . . . the market acts blindly to sell and make money, never pausing to ask whether it furthers citizenship or decency. (Bradley, 1996, pp. 40–41)

How Does the Federal Government Influence Education?

Although there is no specific mention of public education in the Constitution, the federal government has always had a hand in shaping education. James Guthrie, Walter Garms, and Lawrence Pierce (1988) suggest that the federal agenda for education is shaped by the "Iron Triangle"—the combination of education interests in the executive branch, congressional committees, and interest groups outside government.

The executive branch combines exhortation and programs to influence public education. Presidential staffs and cabinets speak publicly about education issues, encourage states' attention to education reform, and earmark federal funds for reform initiatives. In 1995 fourteen federal departments, including the Office of Education, and more than 22 agencies and programs were involved in the organization of federal programs for education (U.S. Department of Education, 1996b, p. 337).

Congress attends to public education by passing laws and appropriating funds. Although not part of the "Iron Triangle," federal courts also exert influence on the conduct of public education through their decisions. For instance, the courts play a continuing role in ruling on civil rights cases and controversial issues such as prayer in the public schools.

Federal Funding for Education

Since the Reagan presidency there has been a continual shift in spending on education from the federal level to state and local education agencies. Figure 6.3 illustrates trends in total federal support for education between 1965 and 1996. For elementary and secondary schools, for example, support increased by 204% between 1965 and 1975, rose only 1% between 1975 and

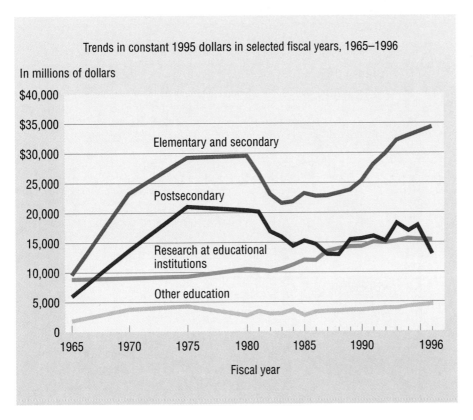

Trends in constant 1995 dollars in selected fiscal years, 1965–1996

In millions of dollars

Elementary and secondary

Postsecondary

Research at educational institutions

Other education

Fiscal year

FIGURE 6.3

Federal On-Budget Funds for Education by Level or Other Educational Purpose 1965 to 1996

Why might support for elementary, secondary, and postsecondary education have declined in the 1980s?

Note. From *Digest of Education Statistics 1996* (p. 380) by U.S. Department of Education, 1996, Washington, DC: U.S. Government Printing Office.

1980, declined 21% between 1980 and 1985, and then rose again 47% between 1985 and 1996.

The **National Center for Education Statistics** (1996b), an arm of the executive branch responsible for collecting and analyzing education statistics for the nation, reported that the total federal support for education in fiscal year (FY) 1996 was $70.9 billion. As illustrated in Figure 6.4, a substantial portion of that money went to elementary and secondary education programs. Specifically, 50% was allocated to elementary and secondary education, 21% to post-secondary expenses, 22% to university research, and 7% to "other" education programs, including libraries, museums, cultural activities, and miscellaneous research. Funds were distributed not only through the Department of Education but via the Departments of Health and Human Services, Agriculture, Defense, Energy, and Labor, as well as through the National Science Foundation.

President Clinton's education reform bill (Goals 2000: Educate America Act) allocated money for a system of national standards and assessments for grades K through 12 and also boosted the Head Start budget in order to eventually provide educational services to all eligible preschool children in the nation. Among other programs for which Clinton sought funding were school clinics; school-to-work programs; a national telecommunications network that would link schools, libraries, and other public institutions with individual homes; and educational research, statistics, and assessment (Miller, 1993; West, 1993). In 1996 the continuing battle over the budget between Congress and the president left the fate of many federally funded education programs in limbo.

FIGURE 6.4

Estimated Federal Education Dollar, 1996

What proportion of the federal budget goes to elementary and secondary education?

Note. From *Digest of Education Statistics* 1996 (p. 381) by U.S. Department of Education, 1995, Washington, DC: U.S. Government Printing Office.

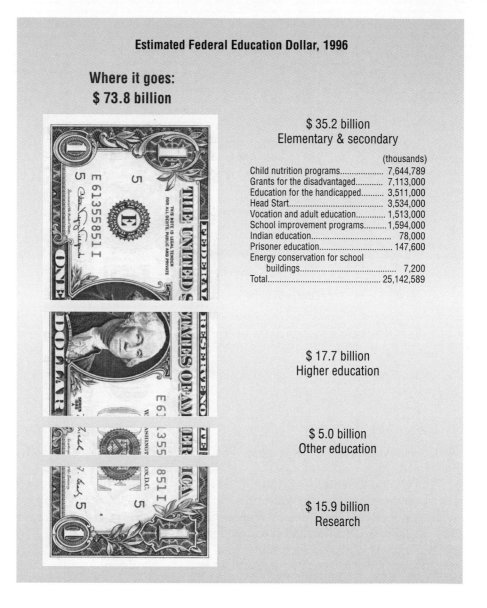

Estimated Federal Education Dollar, 1996

Where it goes:
$ 73.8 billion

$ 35.2 billion
Elementary & secondary

	(thousands)
Child nutrition programs	7,644,789
Grants for the disadvantaged	7,113,000
Education for the handicapped	3,511,000
Head Start	3,534,000
Vocation and adult education	1,513,000
School improvement programs	1,594,000
Indian education	78,000
Prisoner education	147,600
Energy conservation for school buildings	7,200
Total	25,142,589

$ 17.7 billion
Higher education

$ 5.0 billion
Other education

$ 15.9 billion
Research

Federal funding for education takes many forms: (a) major grant programs established through legislation such as the Vocational Act of 1963 (more recently the Carl Perkins Vocational Education Act of 1984) and the Education for All Handicapped Children Act of 1975 (more recently the Individuals with Disabilities Education Act of 1990); (b) aid to localities where there are large federal installations, such as military bases; and (c) **categorical grants** for funding of education programs designed for particular groups and specific purposes, including bilingual education (provided through the Bilingual Education Act of 1972) and compensatory programs for low-income children, such as Project Head Start and Title I.

Sometimes several education programs are grouped together as a **block grant** to localities. Chapter Two of the 1981 **Education Consolidation and Improvement Act (ECIA)** combined 32 previously enacted education programs under one block grant that state and local education agencies could use for general education purposes. With this block grant, funds are allocated to states based on a student population formula. States then prepare a plan for using federal funds based on district enrollment or on measures of student need. Finally, the state gives money to local school districts for use in whichever programs need additional services.

> **Does federal funding threaten state control of education?**

Regardless of what type of federal funding a school district receives, the district is obligated to comply with federal guidelines when spending grant money. In the event that a school district does not comply, that is, either does not spend the money the federal government allocates or misspends the money, one of several things can happen: the school system can be forced to return the money, it can be fined, and/or it can be debarred from receiving any federal funds in the future. States and school districts with educational programs or practices that are found to be in violation of federal laws also lose funding.

National Goals

In the 1980s and 1990s, the federal government has made the National Goals one of the most visible aspects of its attempts to influence education at state and local levels. Secretaries of education in the Reagan, Bush, and Clinton administrations have focused attention on states' performances on a variety of educational measures, including standardized achievement test scores, graduation rates, and teachers' salaries. States' progress toward meeting the Goals is made public through a national "report card" on governors' efforts to reform public education. You can read the Daily Report Card of the National Education Goals Panel online. See **http://www.utopia.com/mailings/ reportcard/**.

Table 6.1 shows how progress in one state, California, was measured in 1995. For example, Goal Five, which calls for improvement in students' mathematics achievement, shows that California moved up slightly over previous years in terms of the number of degrees awarded in mathematics and science.

HOW IS EDUCATION FINANCED AND CONTROLLED BY THE STATES?

State governments exercise more influence on public education than does the federal government. They do so in a variety of ways. Figure 6.5 shows a typical organization of public education at the state level.

State governments influence public education most notably through taxation and distribution of revenues. States also set standards for building schools, educating teachers and school administrators, licensing school personnel, and establishing curriculum, the minimum length of the school term, attendance requirements, and school accreditation. States provide a host of

TABLE 6.1   One State's Progress on the National Goals

California: Measuring Progress Toward a Goal	Baseline	Most Recent Update	Overall Progress
Goal 1—Ready to Learn			
1. Reduced infants born with health risks? (1990, 1992)	—	—	
2. Increased immunizations? (1994)	74%	—	
3. Increased family–child reading and storytelling?	—	—	
4. Reduced the gap in preschool participation?	—	—	
Goal 2—School Completion			
5. Increased high school completion rate? (1990, 1993)	77%	79%	▲
Goal 3—School Achievement and Citizenship			
6. Increased reading achievement?			
• Grade 4 (1992, 1994)	17%	14% ns	↕
7. Increased mathematics achievement?			
• Grade 4 (1992)	13%	—	
• Grade 8 (1990, 1992)	16%	20% ns	↕
Goal 4—Teacher Education and Professional Development			
8. Increased secondary school teachers who held a degree in main teaching assignment? (1991, 1994)	56%	51% ns	↕
9. Increased participation in professional development programs on selected topics? (1994)	94%	—	
Goal 5—Mathematics and Science			
10. Reduced mathematics achievement gap between state and highest scoring country? (1991 and 1992)	21 points	—	
11. Reduced science achievement gap between state and highest scoring country?	—	—	
12. Increased mathematics and science degrees awarded to (1991, 1993):			
• All Students?	43%	45%	▲
• Minorities (Blacks, Hispanics, American Indians/Alaskan Natives)?	43%	45%	▲
• Females?	39%	41%	▲
Goal 6—Adult Literacy and Lifelong Learning			
13. Increased adult literacy? (1992)	53%	—	
14. Reduced the gap in adult education participation?	—	—	
15. Increased postsecondary enrollment? (1992)	50%	—	
Goal 7—Safe, Disciplined and Alcohol- and Drug-free Schools			
16. Reduced marijuana use? (1990, 1993)	—	—	
Reduced alcohol use? (1990, 1993)	—	—	
17. Reduced sale of drugs? (1993)	—	—	
18. Reduced student victimization? (1993)	—	—	
Reduced teacher victimization? (1994)	9%	—	
19. Reduced student disruptions?			
• Student reports	—	—	
• Teacher reports (1991, 1994)	43%	43%	↕
Goal 8—Parental Participation			
20. Decreased schools with minimal parental involvement?			
• Teachers' perspective (1991, 1994)	32%	32%	↕
• Principals' perspective (1991, 1994)	20%	11%	▲
21. Increased influence of parent associations? (1991, 1994)	30%	36% ns	↕

— Data not available.   ns   Interpret with caution. Change was not statistically significant.

Note. From *The National Education Goals Report: Building a National of Learners* (p. 92) by National Education Goals Panel, 1995, Washington, DC: U.S. Government Printing Office.

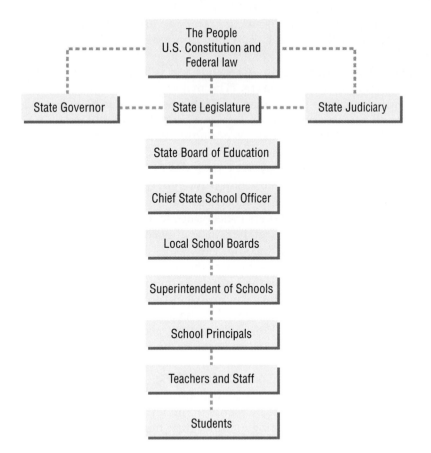

FIGURE 6.5

Typical Organization of Public Education at the State Level

Why are "The People" shown at the top of this figure? In what sense are the top and the bottom of this figure the same?

other special services. While the structure of state bureaucracies and the relative influence of key officers vary from place to place, the role of the state in public education has become increasingly prominent over the years.

The states relate to the federal government in several ways. Education is recognized as a right reserved to the states under the Tenth Amendment to the Constitution. In addition, court cases have defined education as a property right or civil right under the Constitution and thus subject to the Fourteenth Amendment (Section 1: "No State shall make or enforce any law which shall abridge the privileges or immunities of citizens of the United States; nor shall any State deprive any person of life, liberty, or property, without due process of law; nor deny to any person within its jurisdiction the equal protection of the laws."). The Fourteenth Amendment has allowed the federal government to intervene in ways that influence the education of children at the local level.

State Funding

Much of the funding for public schools comes from the state. Between 1920 and 1994 state aid to education increased from an average of 16.5% to 45.2% of total spending (U.S. Department of Education, 1995a). State funds earmarked for education are procured from a variety of sources other than the federal education budget, especially from taxes.

State Sales Taxes   Only Alaska, Delaware, Montana, New Hampshire, and Oregon have no sales taxes. (The majority of their educational funds come from income or property taxes.) The other 45 states have general sales taxes, with rates varying from 3.5% in Colorado and Wyoming to 7% in Rhode Island. Of the 45 states, 31 permitted cities and/or counties to add local sales taxes to state sales taxes. New York City, for example, charged 4.25% in addition to the New York state sales tax of 4% for a total rate of 8.25% (U.S. Advisory Commission on Intergovernmental Relations, 1995).

Sales taxes have great appeal because they are relatively easy and inexpensive to administer. Retailers collect sales taxes at the point of sale, and the state deals directly with retailers instead of collecting from individuals, as in the case of personal income taxes. Sales taxes raise large sums of money. The more money people earn, the more they spend, and the more revenue is collected. To ease the burden on the poor and the elderly, some items, such as food and drugs, can be exempt from sales taxes. Sales taxes on luxury items and so-called sin taxes—taxes on cigarettes and alcohol—are relatively easy to raise. From 1983 to 1987, across the 50 states, taxes on cigarettes were increased 63 times and on alcoholic beverages 32 times (Webb, 1990).

Sales taxes, however, also have drawbacks. As long as the economy expands and more money is generated from retail sales, people come to expect that there will always be plenty of money. When retail sales decline, however, and there is less money rather than more, the downward adjustment in support for all public services, including education, can be painful. In addition, as more necessities are subject to taxation, sales taxes require people with limited incomes to spend a greater percentage of their income on taxes than wealthy people spend. This is referred to as **regressive taxation** (Burrup & Brimley, 1982).

State Income Taxes   State income taxes, both personal and corporate, are another source of revenue for education. Unlike sales taxes, income taxes are a form of **progressive taxation**; that is, people pay more as they earn more. But income taxes are only part of a state's education finance system, which is often a hodgepodge of revenue-producing and revenue-spending strategies.

> **What is the best way for states to raise money for education?**

Every state's financial situation is unique in some way, but in the 1990s, the battle over raising taxes and cutting services has been common to most states. Connecticut provides an especially useful example because it did not have an income tax until 1991. Public debate about establishing this tax helped frame the issues. The necessity of balancing the state budget required, in the minds of the governor, the legislature, and many citizens, a stronger source of income to underwrite basic services —education, roads, prisons, and health care.

In 1992 Connecticut had to face the problem that new money raised from the income tax, combined with cuts in public services, was still insufficient both to meet the demands for basic services and to reduce its budget deficit.

Unlike the federal government, Connecticut could not print more money with which to pay its bills. Like many other states it suffered from the economic recession of the 1980s; less business meant less money collected from all its taxes. Also like other states, Connecticut suffered from diminishing federal aid, yet it had to respond to federally mandated programs, such as Medicaid, that required major commitments of funds. The problem of too much money going out and too little coming in forced state leaders in Connecticut and elsewhere to make difficult choices about where to spend their limited revenues.

State Lotteries and Other Sources Other courses of state aid for education include estate and inheritance taxes, miscellaneous user fees, licenses, severance taxes—fees for the privilege of extracting natural resources from land or water—and lotteries.

Early attempts to establish state lotteries were cumbersome and largely unsuccessful. New Hampshire, a state that had neither a sales tax nor an income tax, established a state lottery in 1964 to support public education and to hold down property taxes. New York followed in 1967. Neither state raised as much money as it had expected because the lotteries were too costly and burdensome to operate. Tickets cost several dollars each, buyers had to register, and drawings were held only twice a year.

In the 1970s other states instituted lotteries having streamlined procedures and more frequent payoffs. By 1996, 36 states and the District of Columbia had lotteries that, combined, put billions of dollars into state coffers. Only a small percentage of this money went for state aid to education.

Lotteries have been criticized as inefficient ways to raise money (Webb, 1990). They are also frowned upon as an immoral way to raise money, even though the cause may be just. After payoffs, however, the profit margin is immense. An average of about 40% of the money collected ends up in the state treasury.

State Aid Plans **Flat grants** are one type of financial aid provided by states to local communities; these grants are either uniform or variable in nature. States that provide flat grants usually give equal amounts of money on a per-student basis to districts, regardless of district needs or financial capacity. States that use variable flat grants try to compensate for differing classroom needs. Typically, these needs are weighted to give more money to schools having more expensive services. For example, high schools with vocational programs can command more money than can elementary schools. Districts having high demands for bilingual or special education classes also may receive more aid.

When using a **foundation program**, the state guarantees a certain amount of money for educational expenditures (by pupil or by classroom) and determines what proportion of that cost, usually based on a mandated property tax rate, should be shouldered by localities. The required local rate is usually expressed in terms of "mills." A millage rate is the amount of property tax dollars to be paid for each $1,000 of assessed valuation. Foundation funding varies inversely with community wealth; that is, in poorer communities, where revenue from property taxes is low, the state contributes more money than in affluent communities, where revenue is high. Local leeway allows school districts to supplement state contributions with local revenues.

Inequalities in **per-pupil expenditures**—that is, money allocated for education services divided by the number of pupils to be served—vary from state to state, as shown in Figure 6.6. Variations in the way states distribute funds to localities depend mainly on money available, demand for services, and cost of living.

Results from the 27th Annual Phi Delta Kappa/Gallup Poll indicate that lack of proper financial support for schools is the second greatest problem (following lack of discipline) facing schools today. Responses also suggest that the public may favor more control at the state level, even if it means that less money is available from the federal government. (Elam & Rose, 1995)

Under a **district power equalization** plan, localities establish the tax rate for educational spending, and the state guarantees a set amount of money proportional to local revenue. As in the foundation program, the state augments local revenue if it comes up short of the state guarantee. This program, then, does not attempt to equalize expenditures on education; it merely equalizes access to funds for expenditures.

> **What is the best way for states to allocate money for education?**

Hawaii, operating as a one-district state, provides **full state funding** for its schools—the state pays all educational expenses through a statewide tax. In this plan, then, all funding is equal and all taxation is equal. Although this plan is the most egalitarian, in other states the desire for local autonomy causes many districts to reject the option of full state funding.

FIGURE 6.6

Expenditure Per Pupil in Average Daily Attendance in Public Elementary and Secondary Schools, by State: 1993–1994

What regional trends do you identify in per-pupil expenditures? What factors might account for differences?

Note. From *Digest of Education Statistics* (p. 164) by U.S. Department of Education, 1996, Washington, DC: U.S. Government Printing Office.

*Unadjusted U.S. dollars.

Total U.S. 1993–1994: $5,767*

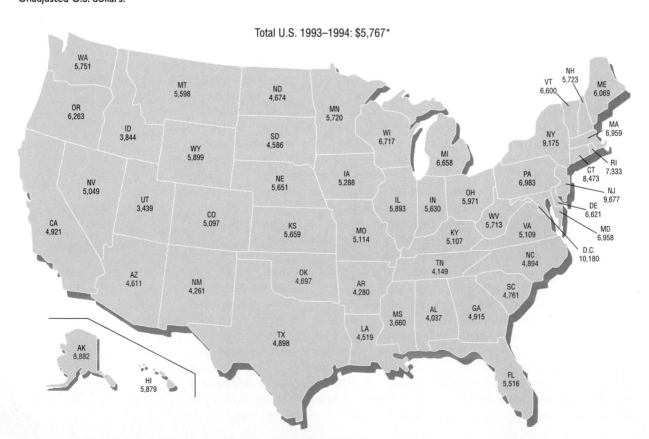

State Education Oversight

State government has the responsibility to ensure that public education truly serves its citizens. The quantity and quality of educational services can and do vary across communities within a state, sometimes quite markedly. State government, however, must oversee educational operations to make certain that all communities receive at least the minimal level of services required to educate state residents. State government fulfills this mission by monitoring resources devoted to public education, design and implementation of educational programs, and results of such programs.

State Boards of Education   **State boards of education** regulate educational practice and advise governors and state legislators about the conduct of educational business. All states except Wisconsin have state boards of education. The majority of states—35, to be exact—allow governors to appoint some or all board members (National Association of State Boards of Education, 1996). Some states have two boards—one for elementary and secondary education, the other for higher education. With the flurry of education reform in recent years, state boards of education often find themselves embroiled in controversy. For example, states establish requirements for homeschooling, creating possibilities for children to avoid ever setting foot inside a school building. Some state boards establish minimal standards for student performance that serve as barriers to student promotion and embarrass educators. State boards of education also regulate what teachers must do to get and keep their jobs, even though professional organizations and local education authorities may disagree with these requirements.

State board members also make momentous decisions about textbook adoption. Adoption procedures vary from state to state, but generally a state board approves a list of textbooks from which local school districts may select. If local districts expect to receive state funds for textbooks, they must buy from the approved list. State board members in densely populated states thus wield great influence by approving some books and banning others.

State board members in the populous states of Texas, California, and Florida influence schools in other states by shaping the content of textbooks that are sold across the nation. For example, when California state board members voice concerns about the lack of literature in elementary reading books or the sparseness of multicultural examples of family life, textbook publishers take notice because these populous states represent a huge volume in potential sales. Soon, the reading textbooks contain more samples of literature and focus greater attention on multicultural life. Often, children in less populous states, such as Montana, Kansas, or Vermont, for better or worse, use textbooks designed for other states.

How do the powers and responsibilities of state governments and the national government differ with regard to the governance and finance of education? How are the responsibilities of local boards of education or local education agencies different from those of state boards of education?

State Education Departments   A state education department (SED) is a bureaucracy organized to carry out a state's education business. An SED may administer programs directly, for example, schools for the deaf or blind. SEDs are directed by a state superintendent, a commissioner, or a **chief state school officer**. The organization regulates or oversees, among other things, the elementary and secondary schools' attention to curriculum and colleges' conduct of teacher preparation programs. An SED advises the executive and legislative branches of state government on a variety of issues, including school finance. It engages in staff development and public relations work for itself and for other governmental and nongovernmental agencies that have a stake in education. Over the years, SEDs have taken on more and more tasks. As laws have been passed and regulations established, SEDs have been expected to monitor schools' compliance. This has meant that the number of employees in SEDs has grown steadily.

Some states are trying to alter the way their state education departments are organized and the way they do their work. Michigan and Iowa, for instance, have moved to reduce the level of services provided at the state level and the number of employees in their state education departments.

State Standards Boards   All states now have **state standards boards** or commissions to regulate professional practice in education. In 13 states these boards have final authority; in the rest they serve only in an advisory capacity to policymakers. In Alabama, for example, the State Advisory Committee on Teacher Education and Certification is composed of about 30 members appointed by the state superintendent. As its name suggests, this Committee advises state policymakers. In contrast, standards boards in Minnesota, Nevada, Kentucky, West Virginia, and North Dakota have final authority concerning certification, entry, and exit standards for teachers, who make up a majority of the members.

> **Should teachers control the state standards boards?**

The National Education Association and others have encouraged the establishment of standards boards to promote a concept of professionalism. Not until teachers control the state policy-making apparatus, it is argued, will teachers be able to control their own professional destiny.

The Governor's Influence   Historically, governors have relied on their appointees to formulate and implement educational policy in the states. Only recently have governors themselves become personally involved in education issues.

The appointed leaders of state departments of elementary and secondary education in the 50 states, the District of Columbia, the Department of Defense Dependents Schools, and 5 U.S. jurisdictions—Virgin Islands, Puerto Rico, Northern Mariana Islands, Guam, and American Samoa—are tied to one another informally by an organization called the **Council of Chief State School Officers**. The Council provides a forum for education leaders and sponsors a series of special programs (international education, technology, national teacher of the year, etc.), a resource center on educational equity, and a state education assessment center. These programs and activities, plus an electronic network, provide opportunities for communication among leaders of state systems of public education.

In recent years the governors themselves have become major players in education reform via the **National Governors' Association (NGA)**, founded in 1908 as a coalition of state chief executives. Many governors have come to believe that good education makes good politics. The problems in education are so intractable and so related to other facets of society that real reform demands strong, visible leadership from the very top of state government.

Cooperation Among School Districts

Some educational services are so expensive, and both human and material resources so lean, that districts must band together to provide such services. Such joint facilities are most often called **intermediate educational units (IEUs)**, educational service agencies (ESAs), or boards of cooperative educational services (BOCESs). For example, every high school in a state cannot provide the kind of vocational training that students need to be competitive in the job market. Several districts may join together to construct and maintain a technical training center for their students.

About three fourths of the states mandate the creation of special units between the state and local levels and provide special support for the maintenance of these units. Special education services, particularly for children with severe and multiple disabilities, represent opportunities for such interdistrict cooperation or even for statewide cooperation.

Sometimes organizational units other than school districts cooperate with one another to increase their power, to reduce uncertainty, to increase performance by ensuring a steady flow of resources, and to protect themselves (Stearns, Hoffman, & Heide, 1987). They do so by sharing information, people, funds, and equipment. Schools contract with state and federal governments, universities, and private corporations to conduct research and to operate innovative educational projects. Projects Head Start and Follow Through are examples of such cooperative arrangements (Hoy & Miskel, 1991).

HOW ARE SCHOOLS FINANCED AND MANAGED AT THE LOCAL LEVEL?

Schools' personalities reflect the dispositions of the communities in which they are embedded. Some are dull, lethargic, and complacent; others bristle with activity and exude hopefulness. Citizen participation in and influence on educational matters are apparent at a variety of events—school board meetings, gatherings of parent–teacher organizations, and high school sporting events. People affect the schools, and the schools, in turn, influence constituents both inside and outside their walls.

Spring (1991) notes that because communities vary in character, they exert different types of influences on the schools and on those who run them.

> In dominated communities, majority power is exercised by a few persons or one person. . . . Factional communities are usually characterized

by two factions competing for power. . . . Pluralistic communities have a great deal of competition between a variety of community-interest groups with no single group dominating schools' policies. . . . And in inert communities, there is no visible power structure and there is little display of public interest in the schools. (p. 167)

At the same time as communities are amazingly diverse in character, individuals within those communities and the organizations they represent also shape schools into the kind of places they are.

Property Taxes

In the majority of states, the local portion of schools' funds is derived almost exclusively from **local property taxes** (mostly taxes on land and improvements). A community's ability to pay for education is dependent on its real assets, that is, on the assessed value of its property. To determine this figure, appraisers estimate the price that property would bring if placed on the market. This market value is then converted to an assessed value by using a predetermined ratio, which, in the majority of states, is now set at 100%.

Use of property taxes as a source of revenue for public schools is a procedure that is widely criticized. One criticism is that homeowners shoulder a disproportionate amount of the cost for funding education. Lack of uniformity in schedules for conducting property assessments creates other inequities. While some communities reassess property every year, others reassess every third or fourth year. If the economy fluctuates greatly from year to year, some taxpayers pay more or less than their fair share of taxes because their property assessments remain the same over a long period of time. Furthermore, when localities within a state use different rates of assessment, a rich municipality having a low assessment rate may raise as much revenue or more than a property-poor area having a higher tax rate. Differences in revenue for education lead ultimately to educational inequalities.

> **Should property taxes be abandoned?**

Another concern about property taxes is that valuation procedures are inexact. When determining the market value of a house in a subdivision, assessors typically set a value based on what the house might sell for if it were on the market. This value is influenced in large part by recent sales of similar homes in the neighborhood. Such a strategy is difficult to use, however, in neighborhoods where houses vary greatly in age, size, and style. Assessment methods are also problematic in high-priced housing areas where real estate activity is minimal. When there are no benchmarks, some properties may be undervalued, thus masking the wealth of some districts (Cohn & Geske, 1990).

Property taxes, of course, are used to meet needs other than educational ones. This may be more problematic in some areas than in others, particularly in cities, where tax-exempt property (e.g., public buildings, churches, government property, and parks) can be a large part of the total. Cities, particularly those in high-crime areas, incur many expenses that suburbs either do not face or face on a more modest scale:

Police expenditures are higher in crime-ridden cities than in most suburban towns. Fire department costs are also higher where dilapidated housing, often with substandard wiring, and arson-for-profit are familiar problems. Public health expenditures are also higher where poor people cannot pay for private hospitals. All of these expenditures compete with those for public schools. So the districts that face the toughest challenges are also likely to be those that have the fewest funds to meet their children's needs. (Kozol, 1991, p. 56)

Cities often provide services funded from property taxes to people who work in the city but live in the suburbs. When it snows, for example, the city must plow the streets so people can get to work. Workers who live in the suburbs benefit from the plowing of city streets, even though they do not support this activity with their own property taxes. While snow removal benefits many people, it uses up money that could be earmarked for inner-city schools.

Rural districts, too, may face considerable financial hardship because of higher per-pupil costs (Appalachia Educational Laboratory, 1990; Verstegen, 1990). When a rural district must build a new school, for example, relatively few taxpayers share the cost of a building. To ease such inequities and the burden on property taxes, the trend in recent years has been to replace declining local revenues with state aid.

Local School Boards

Local school boards are bodies of elected or appointed public servants with responsibility to provide advice and consent on the operation of public schools. Local school boards are one of the most common, visible examples of democracy in action. Because overseeing education is a power reserved to the states, local school boards are agents of the states.

The local school board is generally recognized as the policy-making body for public schools. For the most part, this means that school board members have the right to establish schools, to select the board's executive officer (the local superintendent of schools), to set rules to ensure the smooth running of schools, and to raise and spend tax dollars as they see fit.

Generally, school board members view their schools in much the same way as their constituents do. And, usually, people think that their schools are good. In these times of pressure for increasing accountability, the job of being a board member is anything but worry free. In fact, most board members worry about financial support for schools, size of enrollment, deteriorating school facilities, curriculum development, state mandates, needs of at-risk students, lack of parents' interest in education, crime and violence, and management problems (National Association of State Boards of Education, 1996). Figure 6.7 shows some of the categories of decision making with which local school boards in West Virginia have been involved.

Like all representatives in a republic, school board members try to interpret the public will and to exercise their own personal judgment in governing the public education system. On some issues, board members and the people they represent are out of tune with one another. Results from a survey of school board presidents highlight some of these differences (Feistritzer, Quelle, & Chester, 1989):

Cultural Awareness

Approximately 97,000 American citizens serve on school boards. About 95% are elected to represent their constituents, while the other 5% are appointed. Characteristics of local board members are similar to those of state board of education members. What generalizations could you make about the cultural characteristics of people making decisions about schooling?

Sex:	Male
Age:	41 to 50 years
Race/Ethnicity:	White
Marital status:	Married
Children in school:	One or more
Family income:	$40,000 to $49,999
Community type:	Suburban

(National School Boards Association, 1995)

- About two thirds of school board presidents and superintendents opposed the idea of parents exercising "choice" in where to send their children to school—this is in contrast to three fourths of the general public and parents, who favored the idea.

- The public believed, as they have for many years, that the biggest problems facing schools in their communities were "use of drugs" and "lack of discipline." School board presidents and school administrators overwhelmingly pointed to "lack of financial support" as the biggest problem.

When there is tension between school board members and their constituents, dissatisfaction can result in curtailment of power and, in some instances, complete disbandment of school boards. In Chicago, advocacy groups lobbied successfully for the establishment of popularly elected councils of citizens, parents, and teachers at each school who were given the right to select principals and to decide how discretionary funds should be spent. In New Jersey, dissatisfaction with the quality of education in the public schools resulted in state takeover of the Jersey City and Paterson districts (Olson & Bradley, 1992).

School District Budgets

The best way to understand local finance of public schools is to study a school district budget. Most school boards control the staffing of local schools and types of programs that are offered to students, so the budget represents

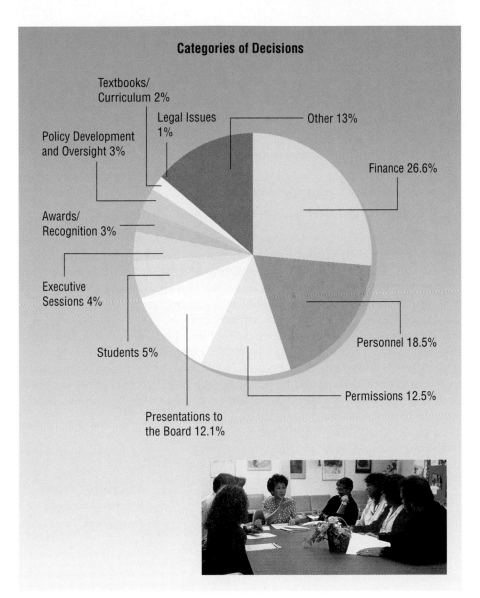

Categories of Decisions

- Textbooks/Curriculum 2%
- Legal Issues 1%
- Policy Development and Oversight 3%
- Awards/Recognition 3%
- Executive Sessions 4%
- Students 5%
- Presentations to the Board 12.1%
- Other 13%
- Finance 26.6%
- Personnel 18.5%
- Permissions 12.5%

FIGURE 6.7

School Board Decision Making

Do you find any parts of this graph surprising? How do the figures compare with your prior assumptions about what school boards do?

Note. From "School Boards at a Glance, Categories of Decisions," April 29, 1992, *Education Week/Special Report*, p. 6. Used by permission.

a concrete statement of local values. To separate rhetoric about educational values from reality, look at the budget.

School districts develop long-term financial plans that represent predictions about the future. District employees craft a new budget for each fiscal year—a 12-month period covered by the annual budget, often corresponding with the state's fiscal year. Once an annual budget is adopted by local officials or approved by the voters, it guides school administrators' actions.

Who makes these plans, and how are they set in place? In most localities the budget-adoption process involves a number of steps (U.S. Department of Education, 1989):

1. District administrators led by the superintendent analyze needs and costs, set policies for the coming year, and plan an initial draft of the budget.

2. District administrators discuss this draft with the school board in one or more meetings.

3. District administrators publish a proposed budget, which is made available for public study.

4. The school board holds one or more public hearings, at which they receive comments from citizens on the proposed budget.

5. The school board adopts an official budget based on the proposed budget but with amendments it deems necessary.

6. In some districts the school board vote is the final decision. In other districts the budget must then be approved by elected officials or by voter referendum.

7. A budget that has received final approval takes effect in the district.

In other areas where site-based management is the norm, people are experimenting with **school-based budgeting**, in which responsibility for allocating resources is fixed at the building level rather than at the level of central administration. Teachers, parents, and principals often are involved in making decisions about how money is spent on hiring staff, professional development for staff, and goods and services.

Advocates of school-based budgeting think that efficiency will improve if decision-making authority is given to those who actually do the work (Levin, 1987). Budgeting, then, becomes responsive to the needs of those most immediately affected. School-based budgeting can also make it easier to hold people accountable for spending and for the results they produce, thereby helping to control costs.

People craft and adopt school budgets through processes of negotiation. Many people (taxpayers, teachers, administrators, and special-interest groups) have a stake in where the money to run schools comes from and where it goes. A school budget, then, represents a balance of values. It is a political document formed from compromise, one that should provide adequately for the educational needs of the school district's constituents.

> **Whose values and needs should a school budget represent?**

When establishing their budgets, school officials sometimes justify only the increase that exceeds the previous year's request. In such instances, what the school district is spending is usually accepted as necessary. On occasion, however, schools must make a case for their entire appropriation request each year. Pyhrr (1973) calls this process **zero-based budgeting**. While zero-based budgeting has not gained widespread use, many districts analyze and report past and budgeted expenditures on a program basis (Hentschke et al., 1986).

Once a budget is set, plans for spending can change for a number of reasons: enrollment figures may be higher or lower than projected, unexpected weather may affect utility bills, and unforeseen events (e.g., flooding of a school gymnasium during a heavy rain) can require emergency maintenance. School administrators sometimes have the authority to transfer dollars from one line item to another to take care of unforeseen needs. In other districts, administrators must first consult with the school board before making changes. When changes in budget are made, however, federal regulations prohibit the removal of money from federal grants designed to benefit specific groups of students or programs.

Most school districts use line-item budgets to explain their financial plans. These budgets include a beginning balance for the year, estimates of revenue by source, planned expenditures, and a projected balance at the end of the year. Sources of revenue may include moneys from federal, state, county or parish, and city government; income from local taxes or from the sale of bonds; payments of fees for meals and for use of sports facilities; and private donations expected during the year. Income often is earmarked for use with specific groups of students (e.g., students with disabilities) or special programs (e.g., library support or school nurse).

Planned expenditures represent the most detailed portion of a school budget. As illustrated in Table 6.2, a school system can incur a number of educational expenditures. In some states, regulations dictate which categories are to be listed in a budget; in other states, local districts can create line items as they see fit. Generally, districts categorize expenses in terms of "functions" (broad categories of purposes, such as instruction and support, to be served by spending) and "objects" (specific things to be paid for, such as personnel salaries and benefits).

Salaries and benefits for both instructional and noninstructional staff (e.g., teachers, administrators, support staff, and maintenance workers) constitute the largest portion of any school budget. Salaries often become sources of irritation in communities across the country.

How do governance and funding relate to educational success?

Public schools exist because of the idea that a child's future ought not to be limited by his parents' wealth and influence. Public education uses public funds to provide access to education for all children. Funds are related directly to educational opportunities—that is, funds can buy equipment, materials, experiences, and the like. But the relationship between funds and learning as measured by standardized achievement tests resists simple explanation.

Eric Hanushek (1989) reviewed 38 research studies and concluded that there is no strong or systematic relationship between school expenditures and student performance. In contrast, Larry Hedges and his colleagues (Hedge, Laine, & Greenvals, 1994) reviewed the same studies using a different method, and they found that expenditures are positively related to school outcomes. Who is right? According to Michael Sadowski (1995), given their methods, both Hanusheck and Hodges are right. The question people should ask is, What do schools do with the money they have? When schools use money to reduce class size so that educators can change how they offer instruction, there are remarkable gains in student learning. In contrast, when decision makers simply reduce class size and hope for the best, while failing to adopt new curricula and methods that meet the needs of students, more money has little effect on student performance.

Unfortunately, more money is not always available. The press of debt and economic recession began to turn the education reforms of the 1980s

TABLE 6.2   A Sample of Actual and Proposed School
Budget Items

	Fiscal Year 1998 proposed budget	Fiscal Year 1997 actual budget
Instruction		
Salaries	$3,085,500	$2,843,500
Benefits	242,000	242,000
Purchased services	60,500	60,500
Supplies	121,000	181,500
Property	363,000	363,000
Total Instruction	3,872,000	3,690,500
Support		
Salaries	1,331,000	1,089,000
Benefits	121,000	121,000
Purchased services	181,500	60,500
Supplies	121,000	181,500
Property	181,500	121,000
Total support	1,936,000	1,573,000
Noninstructional services		
Salaries	60,500	121,000
Benefits	6,050	12,100
Supplies	18,150	36,300
Property	48,400	60,500
Total noninstructional	133,100	229,900
Facilities		
Salaries	181,500	145,200
Benefits	18,150	14,520
Supplies	242,000	145,200
Property	163,350	58,080
Total facilities	605,000	363,000
Total expenditures	$6,546,100	$5,856,400

Note. From Making Sense of School Budgets (p. 15) by U.S. Department of Education, 1989, Washington, DC: Office of Educational Research and Improvement.

into the retrenchment of the 1990s. Even while tax revolt flourished at the state and federal levels in the 1980s, states experimented with a wide range of programs and organizational mechanisms to maximize the effect of the dollars spent on public education. These included site-based management, high-tech classrooms, career ladders for teachers, professional development schools, better and longer educational programs for teachers, innovative curricula, restructured school calendars, and new testing vehicles for both students and teachers.

But innovations can be expensive; they became increasingly difficult for policymakers to justify in the tight economic times of the 1990s, as most states faced serious budget problems. Some people argue that money spent on education is being wasted; that is, the public continues to pay for education, but teachers and students do not produce—test scores do not change. Why spend more money on people and systems that are failing?

David Berliner and Bruce Biddle (1995) and others (Bracey, 1991; Carson, Huelskamp, & Woodall, 1991; Verstegen & McGuire, 1991) take issue with the position that schools are failing and that funding for education is not connected to success. They argue that people interpret test results incorrectly to suggest that student performance and educational quality are declining; moreover, they argue that test results fail to represent accomplishments or aptitudes.

How might this community support its schools? Why might this community have less money for education than other nearby communities or municipalities? Would funding relate to how well the students do? What measures might work to reduce disparities in funding from one school district to the next?

> The highest spending states have, on average, eleven times higher percentages of their students taking the SAT than the lowest spending states. . . . Working under difficult conditions, with a greater at-risk population, the highest spending states posted a loss of up to ten items or about 7 percent of the raw score points on the SAT, but they posted an 1150 percent increase in the percent of high school seniors thinking about going to college. (Berliner, 1992, pp. 22–23)

Berliner and others contend that educational decline, if it exists, is educationally insignificant. While schools need funds to create opportunities for students to learn and to succeed at a variety of challenges, the schools are doing remarkably well given their circumstances.

▪ The Issue of Funding Equity

People make trade-offs when education dollars are limited. Sometimes the tradeoffs exist as choices between educational equity and educational excellence. Some people believe that efforts to promote educational excellence will swamp the poor, the weak, and the minority-group students, while others argue that money spent on equalization could be put to better use capitalizing on the strengths of outstanding students. Allan Odden (1984) contends that such choices are ill conceived, for there are more connections between excellence and equity than many realize:

> On economic grounds, the simultaneous pursuit of excellence and equity is mandatory. If our national strategy for maintaining a competitive edge in the international market is to increase the per capita productivity of the U.S. work force, then all U.S. workers must have better-developed skills than their counterparts in other countries. In other words, it will not be enough for the top 10% of workers in the U.S. to outperform the top 10% of the workers in Japan. . . . The bottom 90% of U.S. workers will have to be better too. . . . (p. 316)

According to James Ward (1992), although the various state funding formulas are intended to provide some standardization of educational quality among communities, formulas are unable to do so for at least two reasons: (a) the level of funding from the state is seldom high enough to level the playing field, and (b) localities have discretion in setting local property tax rates for schools. James Ward contends that in many instances, "politics of privilege and exclusion" (p. 246) get in the way of changing inequalities. More affluent school districts can support high levels of education without much assistance from the state. They are reluctant to shoulder increased state taxes to benefit other districts in the state. Nor do such communities want to give up control of their ability to levy taxes, for to do so potentially reduces their ability to maintain a position of privilege (Ward, 1992, p. 246).

As we noted earlier, there are wide variations in expenditures and revenues among school districts across the country and within states. In some instances the differences between revenues available for education in school districts are so wide that the courts have been involved in settling issues of **funding equity**.

> **How can funding equity be achieved?**

Some schools and school districts have much more money to spend on their students, staff, and facilities than do others. The disparities are so great in some parts of the country that those districts poor in property have had to tax themselves three or four times as heavily as rich districts to raise revenue for their schools. On the average, however, the high-poverty districts receive much more of their revenue from state and federal sources than do low-poverty districts—73% versus 35% (U.S. Department of Education, 1995a).

Even the casual observer of school buildings can recognize poorly funded districts instantly. In New Orleans, for example, nearly half of the district's 124 schools were built before World War II; the oldest was built just before the Civil War began. Only the two newest schools meet fire codes issued by the National Fire Protection Association (Lindsay, 1994). But these New Orleans schools represent only some of the more visible examples of the problems with the nation's public school buildings:

- One of every four school buildings is in inadequate condition, 33% are adequate, and 42% are in good condition, based on information on one half of the nation's public school buildings.

- Of the buildings that are inadequate, 61% need maintenance or major repairs, 43% are obsolete, 42% have environmental hazards, 25% are overcrowded, and 13% are structurally unsound.

- The replacement cost of the nation's 88,021 public school buildings is estimated to be $422 billion. States estimate that the education infrastructure needs an investment of $84 billion in new or retrofitting construction and $41 billion for maintenance and repairs (Education Writers Association, 1989).

Capital construction can be a heavy burden for any school district but especially for the poor district. When considering building a new school, district leaders must engage in an expensive and time-consuming process. This process begins with determining the need for a new building by examining other options, such as remodeling existing facilities, searching for other existing facilities, rescheduling instruction, or consolidating with other districts. A decision to build means determining location by studying possible sites for a new building and acquiring land through negotiation or through condemnation (sometimes referred to as eminent domain).

In the 1960s people thought that inequities in school finance might be corrected by appealing to the courts. The landmark 1971 case of *Serrano v. Priest* was the first case filed in state court (California) that declared unconstitutional a state public school finance system based on taxable wealth. By focusing on the link between educational expenditures and district property wealth, this case stimulated challenges to school district spending inequalities across the nation. William Thro (1990) refers to these cases as the "first wave" of public school finance reform litigation.

In *San Antonio Independent School District v. Rodriguez* (1973), a federal district court had ruled that the San Antonio, Texas, school finance system violated the equal protection clause of the Fourteenth Amendment because large disparities in school district expenditures existed across the state. The United States Supreme Court, however, ruled that education was not a fundamental right under the Constitution and was therefore not protected by the Fourteenth Amendment—a major setback for those who sought to reform school finance.

Thro (1990) noted three landmark school finance reform cases in 1989—cases in Montana, Kentucky, and Texas—in which school finance systems were invalidated in the same year because school funding disparities had grown dramatically. In part, these cases assert that a right to education is fundamental or of extreme importance under state constitutions. Many people believe that these cases will serve as the basis for a revolution in school finance reform.

The Issue of School Choice

Some people believe that **school choice**—the right of parents to choose the schools their children attend instead of being limited to schools in their immediate geographical area—should be common practice. Proponents of school choice argue that competition among schools would improve the public school system. Opponents contend that school choice would destroy the concept of a public education in which children of diverse backgrounds live and learn together. As illustrated in Figure 6.8, in 1996, 59% of public school parents who responded to a national survey indicated that they opposed allowing students and parents to choose a private school to attend at public expense (Elam, Rose, and Gallup, 1996).

In a survey of parents who had "chosen" their child's school, the National Center for Education Statistics (1995b) reported that all parents selected a school primarily for academic reasons. For parents who chose a public school, the second-most important reason was convenience; among those who selected a private school, the second-most important reason was religious preferences.

People oppose concepts of "choice" for many reasons. They believe that if citizens can choose where to send their children to school, schools will become racially segregated, or, at the very least, the gains made by private schools will exacerbate class distinctions. A central purpose of public education is to prepare people to participate in our democracy, and school choice will allow people to opt out, thus subverting this goal (Levin, 1980). Also,

FIGURE 6.8
Public School Parents' Thoughts About School Choice

How might these percentages compare with the attitudes in your community? What is your opinion? What circumstances might make you want to change your opinion?

Note. From "The 28th Annual Phi Delta Kappa/Gallup Poll of the Public's Attitudes Toward the Public Schools," by S. M. Elam, L. C. Rose, & A. M. Gallup, 1996, *Phi Delta Kappan,* 78(1), p. 43.

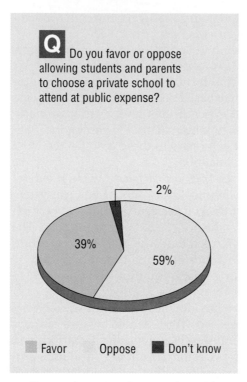

Q Do you favor or oppose allowing students and parents to choose a private school to attend at public expense?

- 2%
- 39%
- 59%

■ Favor   Oppose   ■ Don't know

children who most need their parents' involvement in order to make wise choices will be least likely to get it.

Opponents fear that in a deregulated market—one largely devoid of governmental control—for-profit schools will flourish largely unmonitored, reaping large profits at the expense of consumers (Putka, 1991). Others point out that the money available for most "choice" programs is far below costs—only wealthy individuals who can pay the extra will benefit.

Various plans are at issue in allowing parents to choose schools for their children, including providing for choices among public schools and between public and private schools. Chubb and Moe (1990) have outlined what they believe are the essential attributes for any choice plan. These attributes include defining "public school," monitoring the enactment of choice programs, informing parents about rights and responsibilities, having the freedom to expel students, and eliminating teacher tenure thus allowing for teacher dismissal. These last two factors—student expulsion and teacher dismissal—would enable schools to improve themselves by subtracting negative influences.

Historically, paying for private schooling has been a private matter. If parents wanted their children to be educated in a certain manner, to be inculcated with particular values, and to associate with certain other children, they paid for these privileges out of their own pockets. Those who could afford to send their children to private schools continued to pay their taxes, which in turn supported public schools.

While some private schools have developed and maintained their reputations by appealing to the moneyed elite of society, others have attracted people from across the socioeconomic spectrum. The largest alternative school system in the United States, the Catholic schools, has high- and low-income students. Catholic schools may offer tuition endowments to encourage students from families with low incomes to attend. Other private schools, both religious and nonsectarian, may do so as well. Many parents over the years, even those who could least afford to do so, have been willing to sacrifice economically to send their children to private schools.

Are school choice and tax credit schemes the answer to funding inequities?

In the 1980s and 1990s, the debate about public support for private elementary and secondary schools has taken on renewed vigor, focusing in part on several mechanisms for enacting choice

VOICES

On Choice

Roberta Tovey, a former professor of English at Clark University, is a Boston-based writer, editor, and teacher in the humanities and social sciences. When she looked critically at the literature on school choice, she found reason for concern.

School choice was first advocated by Southern conservatives as a means of thwarting desegregation efforts in the 1960s; the new choice programs of the 1990s, if not carefully monitored, could further that same goal. Though proponents of choice often describe it as a form of voluntary desegregation, as well as an opportunity for low-income and minority students to get a better education tailored to their particular needs, recent research tells a different story. "Choice appears to have a stratifying effect, by race, social class, and ethnicity," says Richard Elmore of the Harvard Graduate School of Education, "even when it is explicitly designed to remedy inequalities on these dimensions."

These new statistics reveal a disturbing trend: families that participate in choice programs often choose schools on the basis of similarity in culture, location, and ethnic mix—factors that tend to perpetuate segregation. Jeffrey Henig of George Washington University studied the Montgomery County

magnet schools and found that "race continues to play a role in shaping parental choices among schools." White students from higher income families were more likely to request transfers into mainly white schools in higher income neighborhoods; students of color were more likely to request transfers into mainly nonwhite schools in lower income areas. The reasons, Henig speculates, may be that the schools' academic programs are not as clearly differentiated as they appear to be, or simply that parents place more importance on the nonacademic qualities of schools, like proximity to home or familiarity.

CRITICAL THINKING

Why do people worry about schools becoming segregated by class and race? Why might parents emphasize nonacademic factors in choosing a school? If you were choosing a school for your child, what factors would you regard as most important?

Note. From "Despite the promises, school choice can worsen racial and social class inequalities" by R. Tovey, *The Harvard Education Letter,* 11(3), 1–3.

plans. The idea of using **vouchers**, or scrip, to purchase public education was first offered by economist Milton Friedman in 1955. He argued that local government ought to create vouchers that provided parents with a sum of money in the form of scrip to pay for each of their children's education. Parents should be free to spend this money at any school they chose, as long as it met minimum governmental standards. "Such schools would be conducted under a variety of auspices: by private enterprises operated for profit, non-profit institutions established by private endowment, religious bodies, and some even by governmental units" (Friedman, 1955, p. 144). In 1993 the voucher notion appeared on the ballot in California and was a central factor in debate about restructuring education finance in Michigan in 1995.

A **tuition tax credit** allows a taxpayer to subtract educational costs from taxes owed. A **tuition tax deduction** allows a taxpayer to subtract educational costs from taxable income before computing taxes. Both credits and deductions resemble vouchers in that they are designed to give parents at least part of the money they spend on private schooling for their children. The appeal is obvious to parents who do so. Opponents contend that credits and deductions may encourage people to flee the public schools, leaving the public system for low-income families, who cannot afford to pay up front for the cost of education and wait to receive a deduction later.

Tuition tax credits, deductions, and vouchers must meet with state approval. Even if states adopt new funding mechanisms, they cannot contravene federal law in the process. For example, if a plan were enacted that denied persons their civil rights, the plan would be ruled unconstitutional by federal courts. If vouchers, deductions, and tuition tax credits continue to be part of the public debate on public and private education in the future, court challenges will surely ensue. Issues of the separation of church and state and of the possible establishment of a religion by allowing public funds to be spent on private schools will continue to make private schools a focus of public interest.

The Issue of Site-Based Management

Increasingly, principals lead site-based management teams composed of teachers and parents—and sometimes students. As noted in Chapter 5, the basic idea is that administrators, teachers, parents, and students best understand the school culture and have the biggest stake in outcomes and so must share responsibility for student learning and school decision making (Darling-Hammond & McLaughlin, 1995).

Reforms to institute site-based management occur most often in places where the schools are perceived as being in crisis. Chicago, Illinois; Dade County, Florida; and Rochester, New York, have tried to move educational decision making and control away from the superintendent's office and toward local schools.

Who could argue with the idea of involving in the formation of educational policies those affected by such policies? The nation's historical commitment to the common school has meant that public education should serve all the people by providing a central knowledge base and by involving people so as to form a community. Site-based, or school-based, management, then, has historical precedent and seems to make sense. But what appears reasonable in theory does not necessarily translate smoothly into practice. Moreover, other reform efforts, such as those aimed at professionalizing education, tend to conflict with participatory decision making.

Attempts to use site-based management to change the basic structure of schools have raised serious questions: Do people agree on the purposes and methods of restructuring schools? Are people clear about redefinitions of the roles of teachers, administrators, professional organizations, parents, and policy makers? Who will make what decisions? How will people decide if the changes are improvements over old ways of operating?

VOICES

On Privatization

Milton Friedman, a senior research fellow at the Hoover Institution, won the Nobel Prize for Economics in 1976. Excerpts from a paper he wrote on vouchers appear below.

Our elementary and secondary educational system needs to be radically reconstructed. That need arises in the first instance from the defects of our current system. But it has been greatly reinforced by some of the consequences of the technological and political revolutions of the past few decades. Those revolutions promise a major increase in world output, but they also threaten advanced countries with serious social conflict arising from a widening gap between the incomes of the highly skilled (cognitive elite) and the unskilled.

A radical reconstruction of the educational system has the potential of staving off social conflict while at the same time strengthening the growth in living standards made possible by the new technology and the increasingly global market. In my view, such a radical reconstruction can be achieved only by privatizing a major segment of the educational system—i.e., by enabling a private, for-profit industry to develop that will provide a wide variety of learning opportunities and offer effective competition to public schools. Such a reconstruction cannot come about overnight. It inevitably must be gradual.

The most feasible way to bring about a gradual yet substantial transfer from government to private enterprise is to enact in each state a voucher system that enables parents to choose freely the schools their children attend. I first proposed such a voucher system 40 years ago.

Many attempts have been made in the years since to adopt educational vouchers. With minor exceptions, no one has succeeded in getting a voucher system adopted, thanks primarily to the political power of the school establishment, more recently reinforced by the National Education Association and the American Federation of Teachers, together the strongest political lobbying body in the United States. . . .

Finally, as in every other area in which there has been extensive privatization, the privatization of schooling would produce a new, highly active and profitable private industry that would provide a real opportunity for many talented people who are currently deterred from entering the teaching profession by the dreadful state of so many of our schools.

This is not a federal issue. Schooling is and should remain primarily a local responsibility. Support for free choice of schools has been growing rapidly and cannot be held back indefinitely by the vested interests of the unions and educational bureaucracy. I sense that we are on the verge of a breakthrough in one state or another, which will then sweep like a wildfire through the rest of the country as it demonstrates its effectiveness. . . .

CRITICAL THINKING

How might you evaluate the success or failure of a voucher program designed to allow parents to send their children to any school of their choice, public or private? Try to synthesize what you have heard and read about vouchers into two crisp paragraphs, one for and one against.

Note. From *Public schools: Make them private* by M. Friedman, 1995. Washington, DC: CATO Institute. You can get Friedman's complete manuscript online at **http://www.cato.org/**.

BENCHMARKS

Examples of Federal Government Involvement in Education, 1785–1996

1785–1890	Northwest Ordinances of 1785 and 1787 and the Morrill Acts of 1862 and 1890 stimulate the establishment of schools through land grants.
	The Department of Education Act authorizes the establishment of the U.S. Department of Education.
1887–1917	The Hatch Act and the Smith-Lever Agricultural Extension Act establish land-grant college extension services across the nation to improve agriculture and industry.
1917–1935	The Smith-Hughes Act marks first federal financial aid to public schools below college level. Funds are earmarked for vocational programs, including homemaking. Other acts fund vocational rehabilitation for veterans of foreign wars.
1935–1944	Congressional acts to cope with the Great Depression fund programs that benefit education, such as the Agricultural Adjustment Act (authorizes using funds for school lunch programs), Civilian Conservation Corps, National Youth Administration, Federal Emergency Relief Administration, Public Works Administration, and Federal Surplus Commodities Corporation.
1944–1964	The G. I. Bill of Rights assists the education of World War II veterans. Benefits are extended to Korean War veterans in 1952 and to Vietnam War veterans in 1966.
	Federal Funding increases for educational programs that contribute to national defense and economic security, such as the Vocational Education Act of 1963, the Manpower Development and Training Act, and the International Education Act. One of the most important is the National Defense Education Act of 1958, which extends financial aid to college students and funds research centers, foreign language study, and experimentation with media.

Like other educational innovations, site-based management must overcome a number of obstacles to succeed. One of the more prominent obstacles is inertia. When people are used to behaving in certain ways, it is difficult to change these patterns. Carol Weiss (1995) notes, for instance, that teachers often resist decisions that require them to make drastic changes in the way they teach. Moreover, Weiss argues, teachers must be convinced that reform is permanent and real and that they can exert some power over events if they are to take collective action.

Do teachers have what it takes to participate in site-based management?

When Chicago began restructuring 32 schools in 1987 to encourage site-based management, teachers and administrators worried about blurring the

1964–1975	Congress funds equal educational opportunity programs and services as part of the Civil Rights Movement and War on Poverty.
	The Civil Rights Act of 1964 authorizes the Commissioner of Education to support educational institutions with problems caused by desegregation.
	The Elementary and Secondary Education Act of 1965 creates grants for schools serving low-income children, strengthening state agencies, and enhancing educational research and development.
	Federal funding also increases for higher education, adult education, elementary and secondary education, special education, and teacher education.
	In 1966 the federal government funds a number of research, training and development, and dissemination agencies: the Office of Educational Research and Improvement (OERI), the Educational Resources Information Center (ERIC), Research and Development Centers, and Regional Education Laboratories.
	In 1970 the Environmental Education Act and the Drug Abuse Act provide for the development of curriculum for schools.
	The Education Amendments of 1974 establish a National Center for Education Statistics to track vital educational information.
1975–1996	The 1975 Education for All Handicapped Children Act (Public Law 94-142) provides a free and appropriate education for children with special needs.
	The Indian Self-Determination and Education Assistance Act of 1975 gives Native Americans more say in the establishment and conduct of their education programs and services.
	The Department of Education Organization Act (1979) creates a Cabinet-level department replacing the former U.S. Office of Education.
	Presidential Education Summits with the nation's governors are held in 1989 and 1996.
	The Goals 2000: Educate America Act establishes a new federal partnership through a system of grants to states and local communities to reform the nation's education system.
	The Appropriations Bill of 1996 continues support for direct student loans, Americorps, and Goals 2000.

distinctions between management and labor. And both were concerned about how to involve parents in decision making at the school level. In 1989 the Illinois legislature created local councils in each of Chicago's 595 schools. These councils were composed of six parents, two other community members, two school employees, and a principal. The councils were to govern the schools, managing the budget and hiring and firing of employees without regard to seniority. These restructured working relationships provided for shared authority and accountability among the stakeholders, but many became mired in the politics of the past and failed to deliver change.

Kentucky began site-based management in 1990 when its supreme court declared the public education system unconstitutional. The move was a bold attempt to reform a system rife with cronyism and nepotism by restructuring the way schools are funded, governed, and operated (Lindle, 1996). School-Based Decision Making (SBDM) councils were established, with authority to make decisions in 16 areas of school operations and policy, including hiring principals, selecting curriculum, assigning staff and students, setting the school schedule, formulating discipline policy, overseeing extracurricular programs, and aligning educational practice with state standards. All schools in Kentucky were required to be engaged in local decision making by July 1996.

SBDM councils are composed of equal proportions of administrators, teachers, and parents. The size of councils varies from 6 to 12 members. In 1994 the legislature mandated that any school with an 8% or greater minority enrollment must elect a minority member to its council. Jan Clark Lindle (1996) contends that the councils have learned that to be effective they must

1. represent their local constituencies;

2. have support of political groups in the community;

3. concentrate on substantive issues and avoid legal wrangling; and

4. operate democratically, that is, accept and plan for conflict, not avoid it.

Regardless of where site-based management occurs, lack of resources can be a serious impediment to effectiveness. With too little money, no matter how it is shared, even schools managed on site can remain dismal places to be. The schools most in need of a new lease on educational life may be least able to afford it. The ultimate intent of restructuring schools to encourage site-based management is to create environments that motivate and teach students to be successful. But as Jonathan Kozol observes, "In many cities, what is termed 'restructuring' struck me as very little more than moving around the same old furniture within the house of poverty" (Kozol, 1991, p. 4).

Real change in how schools are governed, paid for, and operated comes slowly. The participation so necessary to make these organizations work is influenced by opposing forces. The promise of democratically organized schools, however, continues to fire people's imaginations.

SUMMARY

What are school governance and education finance?

1. The power to establish and operate public schools is located in the Tenth Amendment to the U.S. Constitution: "The powers not delegated to the United States by the Constitution; nor prohibited by it to the States, are reserved to the States respectively, or to the people."

2 Governance is the web of laws, rules, guidelines, and procedures by which schools must operate. Education finance is concerned with raising, allocating, spending, and accounting for funds for schools.

3 Educational leaders—school board members, superintendents, principals, department heads, and teachers—shape educational policy and practice. Corporate values also shape education. Increasing computerization, the proliferation of services offered by businesses, a growing global economy, and decentralization of responsibility necessitate that workers possess a variety of basic and work-related skills.

4 Public schools are financed primarily by localities, states, and the federal government. Contemporary leaders communicate their values in the ways they allocate resources for public education. The challenge for policy makers has been to strike some balance in public education among four dominant ideals: equality, adequacy, efficiency, and liberty.

5 There are many political and economic influences on public education. Special-interest groups influence the conduct of public education by lobbying for particular actions and by educating the public. Business–school partnerships can influence the content and delivery of instruction. The public media both reflect and shape public opinion on education.

How does the federal government influence education?

6 The federal agenda for education is shaped by the "Iron Triangle"—the combination of education interests in the executive branch, congressional committees, and interest groups outside government.

7 Federal funding initiatives take many forms: major grant programs, aid to localities, and categorical grants for funding of education programs designed for particular groups and specific purposes. Sometimes several education programs are grouped together as a block grant to localities.

8 The National Goals are one of the most visible aspects of the federal government's attempts to influence education at state and local levels by focusing attention on states' performances on a variety of educational measures.

How is education financed and controlled by the states?

9 State funds for public education emanate from a variety of sources such as sales tax, income tax, lotteries, and various state aid plans. The expenditure of public monies for education is guided and monitored by various oversight groups—state boards of education, state education departments, and the governors themselves.

10 Because of the power reserved to states in the Constitution, state governments influence public education through taxation and distribution of revenues. They also set standards for buildings, personnel, and programs.

11 All states have state standards boards or commissions to regulate professional practice in education.

12 Many states support cooperative educational programs across local districts through intermediate educational units, or organizations that fall between state and local authorities.

How are schools financed and managed at the local level?

13 Communities vary in character and thus exert different types of influences on the schools and on those who run them.

14 In the majority of states, the local portion of schools' funds is derived almost exclusively from local property taxes.

15 Because overseeing education is a power reserved to the states, local school boards are agents of the states. The vast majority of local board members are elected to represent their constituents. These board members exercise power most explicitly through the decisions they make about the budget.

How do governance and funding relate to educational success?

16 Funds relate directly to educational opportunities for students.

17 Some argue there is no strong or systematic relationship between school expenditures and student performance. Others contend that expenditures are positively related to school outcomes. The important issue is how schools use their funds to offer instruction for students.

18 Disagreements over school funding are often couched in terms of two positions: excellence and equity. Others argue that society cannot afford to have one without the other.

19 The idea of allowing parents to choose schools for their children has been a hot topic in the 1980s and 1990s. Advocates argue that competition for students will strengthen schools. Opponents worry that choice will destroy the concept of the common school.

20 Site-based management is an attempt to involve people at the school level more directly in making decisions. Reforms to institute site-based management occur most often in places where the schools are perceived as being in crisis.

TERMS AND CONCEPTS

block grant, *p. 228*
categorical grant, *p. 228*
chief state school officer, *p. 236*
Council of Chief State School
    Officers, *p. 236*
district power equalization, *p. 234*
Education Consolidation and
    Improvement Act (ECIA), *p. 228*
flat grant, *p. 233*
foundation program, *p. 233*
full state funding, *p. 234*
funding equity, *p. 246*
intermediate educational unit
    (IEU), *p. 237*
local property taxes, *p. 238*
local school board, *p. 239*
National Center for Education
    Statistics (NCES), *p. 227*

National Congress of Parents and
    Teachers (PTA), *p. 221*
National Governors' Association
    (NGA), *p. 237*
per-pupil expenditures, *p. 234*
progressive taxation, *p. 232*
regressive taxation, *p. 232*
school-based budgeting, *p. 242*
school choice, *p. 247*
school governance, *p. 217*
special-interest group, *p. 221*
state board of education, *p. 235*
state education department, *p. 235*
state standards board, *p. 236*
tuition tax credit, *p. 250*
tuition tax deduction, *p. 250*
voucher, *p. 249*
zero-based budgeting, *p. 242*

REFLECTIVE PRACTICE

Harley Schumacher was recently elected for the first time to a local school board of a major metropolitan area. His community is economically depressed, and he feels honor bound to keep the promise on which he was elected, that is, to protect the quality of the schools regardless of the cost—within reason. Assuming a minimal level of public support, a new state law allows local school boards to augment the money they receive from local property taxes with local sales tax, local income tax, or local lottery. The tax measures would be add-ons to existing state sales and income taxes; that is, the state would administer the programs and return a percentage of money to the locality. Schumacher believes that he must work to encourage his colleagues on the board to put a proposal for revenue enhancement before the public at the coming election. Two of the board members have expressed their concerns about trying to raise taxes as they face reelection. Schumacher cannot decide on a course of action.

Issues, Problems, Dilemmas, Opportunities

What problems and opportunities do Schumacher and his colleagues face?

Perceive and Value

If you were a retired person in the school district, why might you oppose any attempt to raise additional funds for schools? If you supported any revenue enhancement measure, which one might it be, and why? If you were a beginning teacher, what might your preference be? Why?

Know and Act

List the general types of revenue-raising options the school board might consider putting before the voters, and discuss the pros and cons of each. If Schumacher and his colleagues want to seek public support for their proposal, where might they turn?

Evaluate

Assume that the school board and the voters decided to adopt a local lottery to raise revenue. What factors might you use to judge whether the lottery is successful? Would people's feelings about the morality of gambling enter into your assessment? Why or why not?

ONLINE ACTIVITY

Visit the Web site of the Education Commission of the States (ECS) at **http:// www. ecs.org/**.

The ECS is a national nonprofit organization that offers assistance to state leaders to improve their educational systems. The site contains information about a variety of current issues, policies, and programs. You will find information on school-to-work policies in various states, school governance, and school finance. See, for instance, how states compare in their approaches to establishing policies on school uniforms and dress codes.

Visit the Web site for the American Association of School Administrators (**http://www.aasa.org/**). See "Front Burner Issues" for career advice that the organization offers school administrators. Note in particular the entry by J. Caster on the tactics that school boards use in their superintendent searches. He describes the process in four steps: (1) the announcement of the vacancy, (2) the paper screening, (3) the interviews, and (4) the selection of finalists. He suggests how the process actually hampers the selection of qualified candidates. You might also be interested in seeing superintendents' salaries.

7

Social Issues and the Schools

We are social beings. Some of our problems have the capacity to impinge on every aspect of our lives and, to a great extent, on the lives of those around us. Some problems are shaped in part by who we are—our health, our attitudes, our beliefs, our dispositions. Other problems depend largely on the conditions in which we live—our home, our neighborhood, our community. Many problems are defined by the interplay of intrinsic and extrinsic forces. When we can prevent problems instead of trying to solve them, our energies seem well spent. Schools exist in this reality.

Young people experience many problems, both acute and chronic. Adults express increasing concern about the variety of pressures on today's youth. In this chapter we explore some of society's most urgent problems and consider how they affect children. We describe some of the ways schools have stretched beyond their traditional missions to involve parents, social agencies, and private enterprise to counter threats to young people's lives.

PROFESSIONAL PRACTICE QUESTIONS

1 What are society's expectations for schools?

2 How does poverty place students at risk of school failure?

3 How can schools intervene to help students at risk?

4 How can schools get parents involved in their children's education?

5 How can schools reduce risks that threaten children's health and safety?

WHAT ARE SOCIETY'S EXPECTATIONS FOR SCHOOLS?

For many children, the years they spend in school are the best years of their lives. They interact with people who care about them and for them—people who do whatever they can to help children learn and to feel good about themselves in the process, and who nurture young people's hopes for the future.

In recent years, however, some have argued that efforts to counter children's social problems while also trying to meet their academic needs have created for our schools what amounts to a blueprint for failure. Students attending school from the beginning of kindergarten to the completion of 12th grade will have spent only about 9% of their total time on earth in the classroom (Finn, 1991). Nonetheless, expectations for schools usually exceed the "9% limit," as people look increasingly to schools to solve some of society's most difficult problems (see Figure 7.1).

When young people have problems, society has problems. Typically, different agencies address the plight of children. Because the public supports schools with tax dollars, people expect educators to help students succeed, regardless of circumstances.

The growing number of **at-risk students** who have "little or no hope of success in school or productivity in later life" (Barr & Parrett, 1995, p. 2) present unusually difficult challenges to educators. Generally, these students

- have failed one or more grades;
- have high rates of absenteeism and tardiness;

PUBLIC EXPECTATIONS OF SCHOOLS
- Social problem solving
- Implementation of reform initiatives
- National goals of education

SOCIOECONOMIC PROBLEMS OF FAMILIES AND COMMUNITIES
- Family distress
- Poverty and homelessness
- Violence and crime

EDUCATION OF STUDENTS AT RISK
- Early intervention
- Compensatory education
- Dropout prevention
- Parental and community involvement

HEALTH AND SAFETY ISSUES OF CHILDREN & YOUTH
- After-school care
- Child abuse and neglect
- Substance abuse
- Teen pregnancy
- AIDS and other diseases
- Suicide
- Motor vehicle accidents

EDUCATION OF ALL STUDENTS IN A DIVERSE SOCIETY
- Bilingual education
- Special education

FIGURE 7.1

Some Social Issues that Affect Schools

Think of other items that could be added to this figure. What effects might they have on teaching and learning?

- speak a language other than English;
- are enrolled in special education classes; and/or
- are affected adversely by health-threatening factors, such as poverty, disease, abuse and neglect, substance abuse, teenage pregnancy, and physical violence. (Waxman, 1992; Smith, Polloway, Patton, & Dowdy, 1995)

As these definitions suggest, students can be at risk for failure academically and socially due to intrinsic factors—motivation, ability, disability, and the like—or extrinsic factors—home and community environments.

Eventually, many students at risk drop out of school altogether. Communities across the country have structured schools and have advanced a variety of political initiatives to meet the challenge presented by school dropouts. School choice plans try to stimulate educators to make schools places where students want to stay. In some states, redrawing school attendance zones ("redistricting") is an attempt to prevent some schools from becoming way stations where students pause briefly before assuming a permanent spot on the streets. Efforts to equalize funding for public schools are also undertaken to help schools in poverty areas reduce their dropout and failure rates.

What is society's responsibility to students at risk?

HOW DOES POVERTY PLACE STUDENTS AT RISK OF SCHOOL FAILURE?

Children—one in four of whom go to bed hungry, sick, or cold—are the people hardest hit by poverty (Sidel, 1996). Among the 16 million children who are victims of poverty, about 5.6 million live in families in which one or both parents are employed at least 50 weeks a year yet earn less than the 1994 federal poverty level of $15,141 (U.S. Bureau of the Census, 1996). This figure is calculated as three times the cost of a diet that would meet minimum nutritional requirements for a family of two adults and two children. The figure does not include other living expenses, such as housing, transportation, and health care.

A basic link exists between poverty and learning. Low-income communities mean underfunded school districts and poorer schools on virtually every index of quality. High-poverty schools exhibit diminished capacities to create educational opportunities for students. As Figure 7.2 indicates, students in high-poverty schools have test scores markedly lower than their counterparts in more affluent schools.

Generally, the sooner a child starts school, the longer she stays, and the greater the financial reward later in life. The social conundrum inherent in this statement is that more affluent parents send their children to school sooner and encourage them to stay in school longer.

Most affluent families are two-parent families. As Table 7.1 indicates, the percentage of children living in two-parent households varies greatly across different racial groups. Many single parents cope admirably, but the demands they must face can be formidable. Moreover, those parents most in need of

FIGURE 7.2

Poverty and Performance

According to this graph, how does school poverty appear to relate to student academic achievement?

Note. From Exhibit 49: "Seventh Graders' Grades and Percentile Test Scores: Low- and High-Poverty Schools, 1991" by Abt Associates, 1993, *Reinventing Chapter 1: Final Report of the National Assessment of the Chapter 1 Program* (p. 199), Washington, DC: U.S. Department of Education.

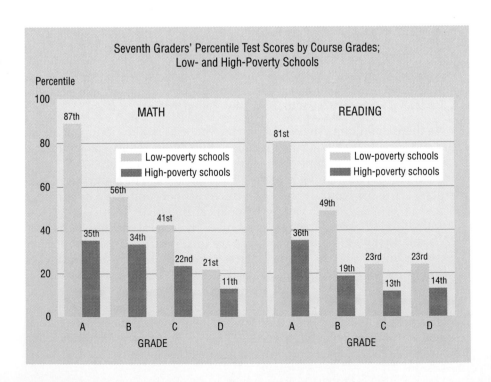

TABLE 7.1   Household Data, 1994 Families with Children

Why might family configurations vary across racial groups?

Why might so few one-parent families be headed by fathers?

	All Races	White	Black	*Hispanic
Family groups with children under 18 years living with:	100	100	100	100
Two parents	69.0	78.5	33.0	63.4
One parent	27.0	18.9	57.1	31.8
Mother only	24.0	15.9	53.4	27.9
Father only	3.0	3.0	3.7	3.9
Other relatives or nonrelatives	4.0	2.5	9.5	4.6

*Persons of Hispanic origin may be of any race.

Note. From *Marital Status and Living Arrangements*: March 1994 (pp. 28–30) by U.S. Department of Commerce, Census Bureau, 1994, Washington, DC: Author.

child care can least likely afford it. In 1993, for example, families below poverty level spent 18% of their weekly income on child care, while more affluent families spent only 7% of their weekly income on child care (U.S. Bureau of the Census, 1996).

How can children in low-income neighborhoods get better schools?

Conditions of life for many low-income families, many of whom are ethnic minorities, can be depressing. But these conditions are by no means characteristic for all minority-group members. It has been estimated that 43% of African-American families and 48% of Hispanic-American families generate incomes of $25,000 or more (U.S. Bureau of the Census, 1994a). Many more European-American than minority group children in the United States live in poverty. Within minority groups, however, percentages of children from low-income families are higher. Socioeconomic status cuts across all group distinctions.

Poverty leaves indelible marks on people. Some are trapped and embittered by it; others are resilient and motivated to defeat the circumstances in which they find themselves. In *Amazing Grace: The Lives of Children*, Jonathan Kozol (1995) describes vividly what he learned in New York City about being poor.

The rate of poverty is higher in rural areas than in inner cities. Regardless of setting, about two thirds of the poor in the nation are white, and most live in families with a wage earner.

The following day, I visit a soup kitchen where more than 200 people, about two thirds of whom are children, come to eat four times a week. The mothers of the children seem competitive, and almost frantic, to make sure their children get their share. A child I meet, a five-year-old boy named Emmanuel, tells me he's "in kiddie garden." His mother says he hasn't started yet, "He starts next year."

"You have to remember," says one of the priests with whom I share my thoughts about these meetings, "that for this little boy whom you have met, his life is just as important to him, as your life is to you. No matter how insufficient or how shabby it may seem to some, it is the only one he has"—an obvious statement that upsets me deeply nonetheless (Kozol, 1995, p. 70).

Explore the concept of poverty by going to **http://www.ncrel.org/sdrs/pathwayg.htm** and searching on the word *poverty*.

HOW CAN SCHOOLS INTERVENE TO HELP STUDENTS AT RISK?

One response to the problem of poverty is to provide money directly to those who need it via some type of cash grant, tax credit, housing assistance, or food stamps. While such assistance can be aimed at families with dependent children, it is difficult to measure how much of the aid touches children directly. Another approach provides assistance indirectly through social or educational services.

We argue throughout this chapter that investing in education can foil the effects of poverty. For example, the U.S. Department of Education (1995b)

Cultural Awareness

More than half of the low-income people in this country are children. About 53% of them are from female-headed families. About half of the mothers were at least 20 years old when the children were born, and most get no welfare payments. Although the percentage of poverty is slightly higher in cities than in rural areas, 16% and 14.2% respectively, a far greater number of low-income children live in rural areas. They may be members of racial minorities, but more likely they are European Americans (Bureau of the Census, 1996).

notes that the availability of free or low-cost education can lead to a reduction in welfare or public assistance programs. People with more education rely less on welfare and public assistance than do people with less education. In 1992 high school dropouts were three times more likely to receive income from Aid to Families with Dependent Children (AFDC) or public assistance than were high school graduates who did not go to college (17% versus 6%).

People who realize that problems facing the young are interrelated and are largely environmental advocate the development of comprehensive integrated approaches to reduce the exposure of young people to high-risk settings—settings characterized by poverty, substance abuse, parental neglect, and violence in many forms. According to the Panel on High Risk Youth (1993), "Reducing the risks generated by these settings is virtually a precondition for achieving widespread reductions in health- and life-compromising behavior by adolescents" (p. 235).

Often, helping students cope with serious social and personal problems falls to school counselors. In general, counselors try to enhance self-esteem, but many also foster career awareness and offer support groups for children affected by divorce or who need work on study skills or social skills. High school counselors, in particular, focus on college or job counseling (Gladding, 1996).

With the passage of the National Defense Education Act (NDEA) in 1964, counseling services moved beyond high schools to include elementary schools. This action acknowledged the importance of helping children succeed early in their educational careers, with "helping" defined increasingly in terms of preventing problems. Counselors typically perform the following functions:

1. provide inservice training and consultation for teachers in preventing serious student problems;

2. work with parents to promote understanding of child development;

3. identify and refer children with developmental deficiencies or disabilities to others who can offer assistance; and

4. help older children make connections between school and work (Gladding, 1996, p. 389).

Cultural Awareness

According to the U.S. Bureau of the Census, about 3.2 million children in the United States lived with their grandparents in the early 1990s (Creighton, 1991). That was an increase of 40% over the previous decade. About 4% of European-American children and 12% of African-American children live with grandparents. At least half of the grandparents are single women who receive, on the average, about one third of the financial support available to foster families. Their payments are less because most grandparents are not licensed caregivers. In Illinois, for example, a licensed foster parent receives $335 per month for an infant and up to $415 for a child age 12 years or older. A grandparent receives $252 per month to care for one child, regardless of the child's age. (H. Darville, personal communication, August 20, 1996)

For many children, these and other school-based interventions make a profound difference in their lives. Patsy Walker, a high school dropout with a family history of abuse and neglect, incest, prostitution, drugs, and incarceration, abandoned a lucrative career as a prostitute, got a job cleaning a store, completed high school, and at age 26 entered graduate school. Patsy Walker described the secret to her amazing turnaround:

> My secret was not so much liking everything we did in school . . . but I did like some of it, and a few of the teachers. Not a lot of them, but you don't need a lot of them. Fact is you only need a few. . . . 'Cause what they both were telling me was, okay, you want to make a secret out of it, that's cool. But we could either forget you and let you fall away like everybody else, or we can, like I say, plant a little seed in you.
>
> That's what both of them did, too, plant little seeds. Took a long, long time for those seeds to grow into something, but they did. . . . What they were telling me, see, was you can play the game, but we want to tell you we'll support you playing a whole 'nother game if there ever comes a time you feel you might be ready. Maybe they were daring me. And the school, see, it stunk like it always stunk. Nothing changed. Wasn't like the day after they spoke with me everything was perfect again, and my mother was all good and my father flew out of prison. No magic. But the seeds. Two funny old ladies, two funny little seeds. So school didn't fail out like everything else. (Garbarino, Dubrow, Kostelny, & Pardo, 1992, 132–133)

Patsy Walker's experience points to the most important interventions that schools provide—caring teachers. These teachers collaborate with parents and other professionals to create conditions necessary for student success.

Providing Early Intervention Programs

Early intervention provides desperately needed opportunities for student success in elementary school and beyond. The National Commission on Children recommended that "all children, from the prenatal period through the first years of life, [should] receive the care and support they need to enter school ready to learn—namely, good health care, nurturing environments, and experiences that enhance their development" (National Commission on Children, 1991, p. 187). The Commission's reasoning emanated from a set of facts that make evident the old adage: An ounce of prevention is worth a pound of cure.

There are many testaments to the value of early intervention. The Perry Preschool Program, begun in 1962 by David P. Weikart in Ypsilanti, Michigan, provided a preschool and home-visit program to 3- and 4-year-olds from economically disadvantaged families. The program captured public attention with results from a follow-up study of its students and a matched control group. Data collected over a 30-year period revealed that, in comparison to the control group, 27-year-old adults born into poverty who participated in the program made more social and economic gains than did adults from similar backgrounds who did not receive preschool services.

Perry Program participants had committed fewer crimes, had better-paying jobs, had been married longer, and were more likely to own their homes than those in the control group. Out-of-wedlock births were high for both groups but were less prevalent among program females (Cohen, 1993). Some people question the generalizability of findings from one study of only 123 individuals, 58 of whom received preschool services in a model program led by highly trained and closely supervised teachers. Nonetheless, the project remains a unique long-term study of preschool effects.

Many programs help disadvantaged students enter school ready to learn. Data suggest, however, that lack of funding prevents such programs from reaching large numbers of children. In 1995, for example, only 26.2% of 3-year-old children from families earning $10,000 or less were enrolled in preschool, compared with 61.2% from families earning $50,000 or more (U.S. Department of Education, 1996).

As noted in chapter 5, Project Head Start, a federally subsidized preschool program for 3- and 4-year-old children from low-income families, tries to provide a curriculum fitted to students as well as deliver health, nutrition, and social services to their families. Head Start promotes parental involvement. Parents participate in program governance and parenting classes, and they also have opportunities to do volunteer work or to be hired as staff members in Head Start classrooms.

What are the goals of early intervention programs? How effective is early intervention and in what ways?

The Head Start Act amendments of 1994, signed into law by President Clinton, extended authority for Head Start through fiscal year 1998. Among other things, the amendments required the Department of Health and Human Services to review, and to revise as needed, performance standards of local Head Start programs and to specify the minimum levels of accomplishment that must be achieved. Amendments also authorized funding for a new initiative—Early Head Start, a program designed to provide comprehensive child development and family support services to low-income families with children younger than 3 and to pregnant women. Funding for fiscal year 1996 was 4% of Head Start's total appropriation of $3.6 billion.

Some states and localities experiment with ways to supplement federal support for nutrition and health care to reach larger numbers of children. The state of Minnesota, for example, funded a pilot program that provides a free breakfast to all students, regardless of family income level. The intent is to help all children be nutritionally ready for learning and to avoid stigmatizing anyone as being low-income. Before the program began at Hans Christian Andersen Open Elementary School in Minneapolis, only 42% of the 760 students who qualified for federally subsidized breakfasts ate them; now 99% participate in the free-breakfast program (Teacher Magazine, 1995).

The younger the child, the more important it is not only to support good nutrition but to encourage opportunities for human interaction—time to talk and listen. Researchers and practitioners agree that early intervention programs, coupled with parent action at home, can make a big difference in children's language skills.

> When parents and preschool teachers read to children and then stop to interpret what they read, when they take children on outings where they hear new vocabulary terms, and when they play fantasy games with children or engage them in mealtime talk that goes beyond "please pass the salt," they provide opportunities for children to exercise certain kinds of oral-language skills. (Viadero, 1994, p. 36)

Researchers have concluded that if children are to enjoy the benefits of parental involvement in their education, professionals must be willing to try different teaching strategies congruent with family beliefs. Parents must be willing to participate in activities that enhance their role as educators of their own children. For example, when researchers studied 19 African-American teenage mothers from low-income backgrounds whose children attended an early intervention program, they found considerable variation in the mothers' beliefs about learning and literacy. The mothers valued educational achievement, security and independence in learning, respect from and for teachers, and information that might help them help their children learn. While they shared such mainstream educational ideals, they also held very specific beliefs about how their children should be educated—beliefs that included the value of working with teachers.

> I'm a friend of Tameika's (her daughter) teacher. She know I'm a single parent and I'm young. She's working with me a lot, but I think that's helping me a lot, the way she teaches me how to. See, I don't have any patience, but she teaches me to 'just sit down, and you do your homework while Tameika does her homework,' and when you're finished you can recite words with her. And we worked it out, the way she told me to do. (Neuman, Hagedorn, Celano, & Daly, 1995, p. 820)

Keeping Students in School

Educators cannot help young people avoid and face problems if they are not in school. Trying to determine who is not there and why, however, are major challenges for school officials. Some districts count as dropouts students who have died, left school to get married, taken a job, gone to vocational school, entered the armed forces, gone to jail, or been expelled. The federal government uses three measures to calculate dropouts: (1) an event rate, or the proportion of students who drop out in a single academic year; (2) a cohort rate, or the number of students who drop out of a specific grade level; and (3) a status rate, or the percentage of people in a certain age range who are not enrolled in school.

> **How can we prevent students from dropping out of school?**

Regardless of the confusion, educators are expected to keep students in school at least through 12th grade, ultimately turning out literate, responsible, productive citizens. **Holding power,** or the ability to keep students in school until they receive a high school diploma or an equivalency certificate, has increased over the decades as youth have spent more and more years in school. Despite this positive trend, by 1994 more than 10% of students between the ages of 16 and 24 failed to complete high school (U.S. Department of Education, 1996a).

Providing Compensatory Education

A number of programs provide children from low-income families with additional educational opportunities beyond those offered in a school's standard program. These **compensatory education programs** attempt to

VOICES

On Holding Power

One of the most important factors in a school's holding power is teachers. Marie Ortiz has taught for more than 20 years at Lewis B. Fox Middle School in an inner-city neighborhood of Hartford, Connecticut. She decided that she wanted to be a teacher when she was in the first grade in Canóvanas, Puerto Rico, where she encountered Mrs. Betancourt.

She was not only a teacher, but a kind of mother to us—so loving to each kid that I can remember almost every single moment of first and second grade (I had her for two years) even though it was more than forty years ago. Every morning, she was waiting for us outside in the school yard. She hugged each kid like we were her long-lost children. Then she would gather us around her, like a mother hen with her chicks, and lead us inside.

And waiting for us would be hot cocoa and soda crackers—she didn't believe we should have to wait for mid-morning snack time; we got our snack first thing. Then she would get us singing, all of us. And her songs were full of tricks to make us learn things even while we were singing and having fun: songs about the alphabet, about animals and numbers. We would get so involved in her projects—drawing, building things, making a doll out of an old sock with buttons for its eyes—that we didn't realize how much we were learning. We knew we had to do schoolwork, but because of her warmth it didn't seem like work, it seemed like fun. . . .

And so I became a teacher, just like that. After a few years, I was offered a chance to come to America and teach for a year. I came to this school, in Hartford, in 1972. And I'm still here. I believe I make a difference not only by helping kids connect math and science to their lives, but also in understanding how to reach their goals in life—how to be somebody. It's strange: in Puerto Rico the kids seem so proud of themselves. But when they come here, they suffer a great blow to their esteem. We have to work very hard to help them convince themselves that their goals still matter, that nothing is impossible, that they can do it, that to be bilingual is to have power.

I don't feel fifty years old. I can still think like a teenager. There are three teachers in Hartford schools who were my students, here at Fox Middle, and another who's at the university, studying to be a teacher. And we owe it all to Mrs. Betancourt.

Note. From *The passionate teacher: A practical guide.* By R. L. Fried, 1995. Reprinted by permission of Beacon Press, Boston.

CRITICAL THINKING

Teachers who feel a sense of self-efficacy can make a difference in the lives of their students. What might help teachers develop and sustain such feelings under especially difficult circumstances?

---

compensate for important educational factors (e.g., teachers, curricula, time, and materials) that may be missing in young people's lives.

Title I Title I, one of the largest federally funded education programs for at-risk elementary and secondary students, began in 1965 as the first bill of President Lyndon Johnson's War on Poverty program. At one time referred to as Chapter 1, the program has provided more than $80 billion to meet the educational needs of low-income, low-achieving students. For the most part, academic assistance to Title I students occurs in **pull-out programs**, that is, Title I children most often receive their services outside the regular classroom. Instruction usually lasts for 30 to 35 minutes and focuses mainly on reading, mathematics, and language arts. While the majority of the nation's school districts receive federal monies for such assistance, there is not enough money to fund instruction for all children who qualify for extra help under Title I guidelines.

Early reports from the first large-scale longitudinal study of Title I indicate that almost one half of the elementary schools that served fewer than 10% low-income children participated in Title I, while one third of the low-performing children in high-poverty schools went unserved (U.S. Department of Education, 1993). Results also suggest that the program has had little or no success in closing the achievement gap between low-income children and other disadvantaged students not in the program.

> **Do programs such as Title I perpetuate underachievement?**

These results may not be as negative as they appear at first glance. University of Chicago researcher Kenneth Wong said, "Given all the constraints these schools face, it is to our surprise that some of the kids—particularly 50 percent or more—are progressing. It gave us hope to come to the tentative conclusion that Title I does have an impact" (Viadero, 1996, p. 10).

Upward Bound   Many older children also need all the help they can get. Upward Bound, a federally funded program, is structured to improve the academic performance and motivational levels of low-income high school students. Participants in the program receive tutoring, counseling, and basic skills instruction. The program encourages students to finish high school and win acceptance into college. At the end of the school year, students participate in a summer residential program focusing on the improvement of study skills and content knowledge. Established in the 1960s, Upward Bound programs continue to operate across the nation.

Success for All   Success for All, a program designed by Johns Hopkins researchers for preschool and elementary children, organizes resources to ensure that every student in a Title I school will be at or near grade level in reading and other skills by the end of third grade and will continue to achieve in later grades. Among elements of the program are one-on-one tutoring for students who are unable to keep up with their peers in reading, daily 90-minute reading periods, frequent assessments, and a family support program that involves parents in the education of their children.

When Success for All was compared to Reading Recovery, a program designed to tutor first-graders who are having difficulty learning to read, both were shown to benefit students. Success for All, however, was more beneficial for special education students. Teachers also liked the program's approach to integrating reading curriculum with family support (Ross, Smith, Casey, & Slavin, 1995).

Providing Before- and After-School Programs

During the past 20 years, women have entered the workforce in increasing numbers, with the sharpest increases being among married mothers of young children. By 1993, 59.6% of mothers with children younger than age 6 and 74.7% of women with children between the ages of 6 and 13 were employed or looking for employment (U.S. Bureau of the Census, 1994b). With more women in the workforce and thus unable to stay at home with their children, traditional roles and responsibilities of parents have changed. In some two-parent families, fathers assume child care responsibilities. In others, parents change their work schedules so that one or the other can be home with their children during the day. Working mothers of children between the ages of 5 and 14 most often hire someone to provide care in the child's home. Although most children under age 4 have some type of supervised care, nonrelatives typically provide this care outside the child's home.

Schools respond to needs for child care in many different ways. Buses transport children to school in the morning and home in the afternoon. Some children arrive early enough each day to receive a hot breakfast they would not get otherwise. For too many, national school breakfast or lunch programs offer the best meal of the day.

Sometimes schools provide after-school programs for students who are at risk for failure. In Mt. Carmel, a rural community in southeastern Illinois, citizens' concerns about the use of alcohol and other drugs by young people prompted the community and schools to work together to try to improve students' experiences inside and outside school. Activities scheduled during and after school hours promote academic achievement and try to improve children's self-esteem, decision-making, and knowledge about healthy and unhealthy life-styles. For example, the high school drama club develops skits that warn about the dangers of using alcohol and other drugs and performs for student and adult audiences. Another program links at-risk preschoolers with senior citizens. A host of after-school, weekend, and summer activities provide healthy options for students who once complained that they had "nothing to do" (S. Schwartz, personal communication, September 28, 1996).

After-school programs across the country offer opportunities for supervised study, play, and participation in sports. In addition, bands and choruses and clubs of every kind meet in the late afternoons, evenings, and weekends. These offerings—billed as services, extracurricular activities, or enrichment programs—also amount to forms of child care. Unless schools provide transportation and equipment for such events, however, low-income children in particular are unlikely to benefit from after-school programs.

> **How can we meet the needs of latchkey children?**

Every day about 1.6 million, or 76.4% of grade school children of employed mothers go home to an empty house. These **latchkey children** may be without adult supervision for several hours each day. Self-care is a more common after-school arrangement among children of single mothers than among children of married mothers (5.1% versus 2%). Older children also are more likely to be in self-care than are younger ones. For both younger and older grade school children, those living in suburban areas are more than twice as likely to be left alone for some time during their mothers' workday than are those living in rural areas (Casper, Hawkins, & O'Connell, 1994).

In recent years, public librarians have witnessed a dramatic increase in the number of latchkey children. Working parents sometimes tell their youngsters to go to the library after school and do homework until they can pick them up after work. The policies of libraries vary with regard to serving children unaccompanied by adults. You can visit the Web for some guidelines for protecting children at the library without discouraging them from going there alone (**http://hkein.ie.cuhk.hk/Education/Kids/Library/Alone.html**).

Offering Incentives and Disincentives

Other tactics used to encourage academic success include **incentive programs**. These programs offer outside incentives—rewards for good attendance and good grades. For example, the Hope Scholarship Program, which is supported entirely by a state lottery, offers a free college education to all Georgia high school students with a B average who choose to attend a public college, university, or technical institute in the state. If students choose a private school, they receive an annual $3,000 scholarship. In 1996 to 1997, the program appropriated $159 million for 124,000 scholarships (Applebome, 1996).

In 1988, in an effort to help young people with little hope of going on to college, Patrick F. Taylor, a Louisiana philanthropist, guaranteed college tuition and fees for 183 seventh and eighth graders at New Orleans' Livingston Middle School who could meet the demands of a rigorous precollege curriculum. By 1991, 126 "Taylor Kids" were still in school, working hard to qualify for Taylor's program. About one half of those children graduated from high school, and one half of those graduates, in turn, entered college (J.W. Smith, personal communication, September 26, 1996).

Taylor stimulated the state legislature to agree in 1989 to pay tuition at state universities for any Louisiana student completing a college-preparatory core curriculum, maintaining a 2.5 grade-point average, and scoring at least 20 out of 36 on the Enhanced American College Test (Mitchell, 1991). By 1996, 13 states (Arkansas, Florida, Georgia, Indiana, Louisiana, Maryland, Mississippi, New Mexico, North Carolina, Oklahoma, Tennessee, Texas, and Virginia) had passed similar bills.

Such inducements, however, are not uniformly successful. Some people question inducement programs for sending the wrong message about motivation and achievement. Why should students be rewarded for achievements commonly expected of all or most students? When students work for the rewards, does the behavior they demonstrate become self-reinforcing, or does it cease when the incentives are removed?

> **Should students be paid for good attendance and good grades?**

In some instances punitive measures have been employed to reduce the dropout rate. Arkansas penalizes students with excessive unexcused absences and school dropouts by revoking their driver's licenses. In a typical 3-month

VOICES

On Teachers' Perceptions of Students' Needs

Ms. Lori DeLuca began her career teaching low-achieving fifth graders who lived in poverty. She describes how another teacher's perceptions of students' needs influenced her own teaching behavior. What seemed to work for her colleague, however, did not work for Lori. She learned to rely on her own perceptions of her students' needs.

When I think of how my view of literacy has changed, I recall my first job with low-achieving fifth graders. As a new teacher, I was assigned to a very regimented veteran teacher who dismissed the ideas I learned in college and stressed instead phonics and vocabulary memorization. I was eager to follow her advice because she had a reputation in the district of getting results and improving her students' reading skills. I began my first year with phonics workbooks and vocabulary notebooks. I also imitated her strict discipline, even though I found it burdensome. By the end of the first month, I was overwhelmed, frustrated, and exhausted. It required so much energy to get my bored students to complete all their wearying work. I did read aloud chapter books and poems, but only after all the work was finished. When I expressed my discontent to the teacher I had emulated, she said, "These kids are tough. You've got to be tough to light a fire under them."

After a month of this, I decided that I was just not equal to the task of working with these students. I expressed my insecurities to my mother, a teacher in a different district. She encouraged me to have fun, to "do my own thing." She said I needed to trust my own ability and discover my own style of teaching. I decided to take her advice to heart, and my classroom changed dramatically. I abandoned many of our workbook pages and encouraged children to respond to literature in a variety of creative ways. We read chapter books, researched topics of interest at the library, discussed books by favorite authors, used the computer to compose original stories, read picture books to the first graders, and went on a poetry picnic. To my surprise, when doing these supposedly less structured activities, I had fewer discipline problems and more on-task behavior from my students. I enjoyed my job so much more, and my students enjoyed reading much more. My sober, teacher-controlled classroom took on more of a workshop atmosphere as students grew motivated to become literate.

CRITICAL THINKING

Compare Lori DeLuca's beginning philosophy with her reformed outlook. How do her expectations for students differ? If you were asked to explain what Ms. DeLuca might have meant by the phrase *teacher-controlled classroom*, what would you say? Why is "having fun," as Ms. DeLuca describes it, as important for teachers as it is for students?

Note. From *Teachers' stories: From personal narrative to professional insight*, pp. 157–158, by M. R. Jalongo, J. P. Isenberg, & G. Gerbracht, 1995. San Francisco: Jossey-Bass Publishers.

period in 1996, the state revoked 78 licenses for these reasons (L. Johnson, personal communication, September 26, 1996).

Since the establishment of Wisconsin's controversial Learnfare program in 1987 and passage of the Family Support Act of 1988, several states have imposed penalties on parents who do not demonstrate "responsible" behaviors, including the completion of school. While the Family Support Act makes welfare payments contingent on parents' efforts to obtain education, training, and employment necessary for breaking the cycle of welfare dependency, Learnfare-type programs such as those in Wisconsin, Maryland, and Oregon cut welfare payments to parents whose children are truant or drop out of school (S. A. Riedasch, personal communication, January 19, 1994).

Ohio's Learning, Earning, and Parenting (LEAP) program blends penalties and rewards to encourage teenage parents to stay in school and graduate. Students can earn a $62 monthly bonus in their welfare benefits for staying in school, an additional $62 for completing a grade level, and a $200 bonus for graduating. LEAP deducts $62 from students' monthly benefits for poor attendance (Simich, personal communication, October 1, 1996).

Providing Mentors and Tutors

Some programs try to enhance the academic success and self-esteem of at-risk students through the use of tutors and **mentoring programs**—efforts to model appropriate behavior in one-on-one situations. For example, in 1994 Donovan Steiner and Judy Mullet of Eastern Mennonite University (EMU) and Carole Groves of Bridgewater College began a tutoring program for high school students who had been suspended from school. For two days a week, these students go to EMU, where they work with college students specializing in education and counseling. They engage in a range of activities designed to enhance their academic success and to improve their attitudes toward learning. For suspended students, the program amounts to a kind of "homeschooling" at a university (Mullet & Groves, 1996).

Pairing younger students with older ones can yield positive results too. Margaret Johnson and Delma Gomez (1995) report that the pairing of "big buddies" and "little buddies" in Lubbock, Texas, fostered caring attitudes in the older students. Ramirez Elementary School, located in a low-income neighborhood, is composed of 60% Hispanic-American, 20% African-American, 12% European-American, and 5% Asian-American and Native-American students. More than 90% of the students receive free or reduced-price lunches.

Johnson and Gomez found that when first-grade and fifth-grade students were paired for tutoring, field trips, and other activities, the fifth graders demonstrated caring behavior with the first graders who, in turn, showered respect and admiration on the fifth graders. These behaviors appeared to carry over to other relationships among children as well. Johnson and Gomez concluded that the relationships reinforced each other because there were regular and frequent opportunities for the students to work together on important tasks. One fifth-grade boy explained his feelings about the buddy program:

> My buddy needs me to help him on anything he needs help on. I teach my buddy so he can be smart, so he can learn more of everything, so when he grows up he can be what he wants to be. (Johnson & Gomez, 1995, p. 12)

■ Linking Home, School, and Work

Other efforts to help students at risk have tried to tighten the links among home, school, and the workplace to influence parents' and children's commitments to education. One of the most noteworthy efforts in recent years has been school-to-work (STW) programs. On May 4, 1994, President Bill Clinton signed the School-to-Work Opportunities Act of 1994. This law provides

> **Does the school-to-work concept have any drawbacks?**

seed money to states and local partnerships of business, labor, government, education, and community organizations to develop school-to-work systems. The law allows states and their partners to integrate efforts at education reform, worker preparation, and economic development to create a system to prepare youth for jobs of the future. Many who will benefit most from STW efforts will be those in poverty-stricken areas. You can learn more about STW programs at **http://stw.ed.gov/general/general.htm**.

Sometimes local businesses and industries view their work with community schools as an investment in people. The Danville, Virginia, school board formed the Industry in Education group to involve local business and industrial leaders in the promotion of educational excellence. The group of about a dozen plant managers and executives uses a variety of means for stressing the value of education. At Goodyear Tire and Rubber Company, the public relations manager devotes one page of the plant's monthly newsletter to accomplishments of employees' children and to other educational issues. Plant employees also work on a volunteer basis in the public schools, speaking to classes, participating in Parent–Teacher Association activities, and tutoring students at the middle school level (K. Wright, personal communication, August 30, 1996).

Some view school-to-work transitional programs with skepticism. They argue that the major goal of public schools should be to prepare students to become informed participants in our democracy, not to produce workers for business and industry. The concentration on school-to-work, they fear, will drive school curriculum to become commercially oriented, while de-emphasizing the importance of a liberal education. Critics also contend that local and regional variations in resources will yield variations in schooling that will only exaggerate differences between more and less affluent communities.

How can schools get parents involved in their children's education?

Parents are teachers, too. To do their jobs well, they must ask good questions. How much television is Johnny watching? How much does he read? What should I do to help him with his homework? Is Johnny getting enough sleep? What does he eat? Parents can make the home-to-school connection an important factor in their child's success. When the link is weak or nonexistent, students' chances for healthy, productive academic lives diminish.

When schools are able to encourage parents to get involved in their children's education, the payoffs can be high. Research indicates that parent

Cultural Awareness

Sandra Balli (1996) relies on the results of a major study of migrant children conducted in 1992 to argue that socioeconomic status need not limit one's aspirations or level of achievement. When children have at least one parent who communicates high expectations for academic achievement, the children stay in school and perform well.

involvement in children's education from birth until they leave home has a major positive impact on children's achievement at school. Students benefit in a variety of ways:

- higher test scores,
- better grades,
- more consistent attendance at school,
- more positive attitudes and behavior, and
- greater participation in effective academic programs. (Macfarlane, 1995, p. 1)

Surveys indicate that many students lack the parental involvement needed to succeed in school. The 1990 National Assessment of Educational Progress (NAEP) of 4th, 8th, and 12th graders indicated a relationship between literacy and school attendance, outside reading, homework, and television viewing (activities parents can control). Secretary of Education Richard Riley (1996) noted, "If all parents in America made it their patriotic duty to find an extra thirty minutes to help their children learn more—each and every day—it would revolutionize American education" (1996, p. 1).

Figure 7.3 shows the percentage of eighth-grade students who said that their parents limited their television viewing. Students with three or more

FIGURE 7.3

Parental Limits on Television Viewing of Students Involved in Misbehavior Incidents

Based on this study, how would you describe the relationship between the amount of students' television viewing and the amount of their misbehavior?

Note. From *Condition of Education* by U.S. Department of Education, 1994.

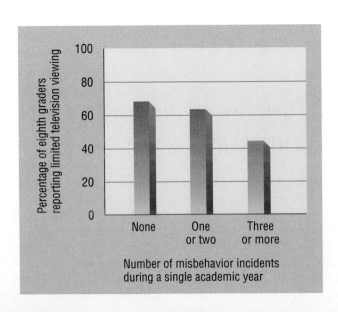

misbehavior incidents were less likely to report that their parents limited their television viewing (or going out with friends) than were students with fewer than three misbehavior incidents (U.S. Department of Education, 1994).

Follow-up surveys conducted since the National Education Longitudinal Study of 1988, which focused on 24,599 American eighth graders, revealed that regardless of subject matter, slightly more than 50% of 1988 eighth graders spent the same amount of time on homework in high school as they had in eighth grade. Of the remaining students, approximately 25% reported doing more homework in high school than in eighth grade and slightly more than 15% said they were doing less. Females, Asian Americans, students in the highest SES (socioeconomic status) quartile, and students scoring in the highest quartile on standardized tests were more likely to have increased their homework time since eighth grade than were other groups of students (U.S. Department of Education, 1995c, p. v).

Implementing Parental Involvement Programs

For some parents, school involvement may seem like a luxury. As Figure 7.4 suggests, parents in poverty worry so much about making money to support their families that they may have little emotional energy left to devote to school activities. This is neither an indictment nor an excuse; poverty and worry are simple but hard facts of life for some people.

Schools have always tried to involve parents in the education of their children, but their efforts seem to have increased in recent years. Common and visible attempts are parent–teacher conferences, school open houses, parent–teacher associations and organizations (PTAs and PTOs), and school advisory councils. PTAs and PTOs vary in size and level of participation. Their goal is to bring parents into school activities to tackle virtually every kind of problem imaginable. In many instances, their fund-raising efforts allow schools to purchase classroom materials and equipment. PTA-generated funds also provide educational opportunities, such as field trips and theatrical performances. But despite its size—nearly 7 million members—the

FIGURE 7.4

Percentage of Parents Who Worry "All the Time" That Their Family Income Will Not Be Enough, By Family Income

Make one generalization based on the information in this graph about the relationship between income and worry. If parents were surveyed today, how might their responses compare to those in this figure?

Note. From *Speaking of Kids: A National Survey of Children and Parents* (p. 23), 1991. Washington, DC: National Commission on Children.

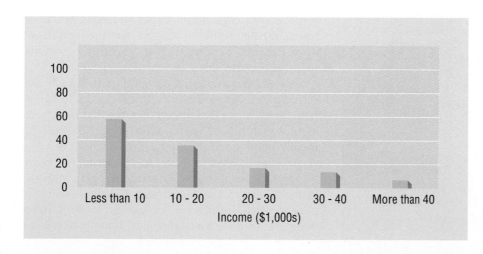

National PTA is not highly visible in debates about school funding, curricula, or school governance issues (Harp, 1994).

Some of the more successful efforts to involve parents in schools have occurred where people might least expect to find them. At Fairbanks Elementary School in Springfield, Missouri, about 50% of the students come from single-parent households, about 88% are eligible for free or reduced-price lunches, and nearly 50% need remedial work on their math and verbal skills. Fairbanks parents tutor students during and after school, serve as classroom aides, participate in evening workshops to learn how to help their children succeed in school, and organize special events (Leighninger & Niedergang, 1995).

> **How can teachers and schools encourage more parental involvement?**

Sandra Balli (1996) offers the following practical suggestions for encouraging parents to become involved in school activities, bearing in mind that some parents may not have had positive school experiences themselves.

- Offer school-sponsored workshops on how to help children with homework.
- Send daily notes to parents with information about how to help their children academically.
- Send parents letters of encouragement about student performance and appreciation for participation in school programs. Write the letters in the language spoken by parents.
- Conduct meetings for parents in their native tongues.
- Invite parents from diverse cultures to share their heritage and cultural artifacts with all students.
- Decorate classrooms using artifacts from students' cultures.
- Involve parents in the planning of school activities.

Why is parents' involvement in their children's education important? How do full-service schools support family-based education?

Parental involvement figures heavily in efforts to reorganize schools. Concepts of parental choice, for example, are based on the idea that when parents can exercise some control over where their children attend school, schools become more responsive to consumers. Other strategies of school restructuring and school-based management draw upon parental participation in governing councils to bring about change in school systems.

Sometimes increased parental involvement is a serendipitous byproduct of another action. In Plainfield, Indiana, for example, when the middle school instituted a no-cut policy with regard to student membership on clubs and teams—anybody who shows up makes the team—parental interest jumped right along with student participation. With 72 cheerleaders and anyone who wants to play football suiting up for games, parents have volunteered their assistance and bought tickets to

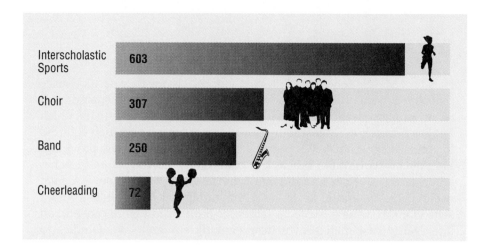

FIGURE 7.5

Plainfield Participation in Extracurricular Activities

How would you describe student participation in extracurricular activities at Plainfield High School? How does the level of participation compare with that in schools you have attended or observed?

games in record numbers. As Figure 7.5 illustrates, students in Plainfield participate in a number of activities in addition to football and cheerleading (G. Bradley, personal communication, November 26, 1996).

Visit the National Parent Information Network [NPIN] online at **http:// ericps.ed.uiuc.edu/npin/reswork.html**. Once there, you will find reviews of books for family support personnel, descriptions of innovative programs for parents, organizations that support parent education, and lists of activities occurring at national, state, and local levels.

Providing Family Services Through Full-Service Schools

As school budgets have dwindled in the past decade, the need to focus limited services has increased. Some health and social service agencies have begun to collaborate with schools to create a kind of one-stop shopping at what are being called **full-service schools** (Dryfoos, 1994). These schools offer a range of services for children and their families while reducing bureaucratic overhead.

The challenges of dealing with students who have a variety of health problems have prompted the establishment of school-based health centers in a

Should schools provide health and social services?

number of states. These centers allow schools to coordinate health care with health curricula emphasizing preventive care. Full-care clinics provide such services as physical examinations, weight and drug counseling, treatment of illness and minor injuries, and testing for pregnancy and sexually transmitted diseases. The first of these full-care centers was established in Dallas, Texas, in 1970. Now most states have such centers.

The success of these and related efforts depends on many people. Teachers, families, administrators, social service providers, health care providers, and others must collaborate to maximize the benefit of their energies. When

Cultural Awareness

Hanshaw Middle School in Modesto, California, is one type of full-service school. The school serves a population of low-income Hispanics and recent immigrants from Cambodia and Laos, many of whom do not speak English proficiently. Many of the families, however, expect their children to go to college. Hanshaw's primary goal has always been on providing high-quality education, but as the community needs become clearer, school leaders began to add social services—a school nurse, a mental health clinician, and aides to assist the immigrant populations. With a state grant, Hanshaw created a center for health and dental care and an interagency case-management team linking students and families to other social services.

Salome Ureña, a middle school in the Washington Heights section of upper Manhattan, is designed to serve as a community center and as a school. The school is zoned to offer different programs and services. In addition to typical course offerings, this full-service school provides after-school programs fitted to children's interests, traditional tutoring in academic subjects, language programs for students and members of the community, and special projects, from performing arts programs to business courses (Carnegie Corporation, 1995).

they do so, children's chances for living and learning in healthy environments are improved. You will find information about full-service schools on the Web (**http://www.ncrel.org/sdrs/areas/issues/students/atrisk/at5full.htm**).

HOW CAN SCHOOLS REDUCE RISKS THAT THREATEN CHILDREN'S HEALTH AND SAFETY?

Although medical advances and extensions of health care coverage have resulted in better health and life expectancy for many Americans, today's children have not fared so well.

Every day in America,

- 3 children and youths under age 25 die from HIV infection.
- 6 children and youths under age 20 commit suicide.
- 13 children and youths under age 20 are homicide victims.
- 15 children and youths under age 20 are killed by guns.
- 35 children and youths under age 20 die from accidental injuries.

- 95 babies die before their first birthday.

- 144 babies are born at very low birthweight (less than 3.5 pounds).

- 255 children and youths under age 18 are arrested for drug offenses.

- 318 children and youths under age 18 are arrested for alcohol-related offenses.

- 327 children and youths under age 18 are arrested for violent crimes.

- 564 babies are born to mothers who had late or no prenatal care.

(Children's Defense Fund, 1995)

At every age, among all races and income groups, and in communities throughout the nation, these and other problems threaten the well-being of young people.

Preventing Child Abuse and Neglect

Many youngsters suffer from physical, emotional, or sexual abuse, and many more may be the victims of neglect by their parents or guardians. In 1974 Congress passed the **Child Abuse Prevention and Treatment Act** to provide financial support to states that implemented programs for identification, prevention, and treatment of child abuse and neglect. Nationally, there are about 3 million reported cases of such abuse each year. Some people contend that the poor treatment of "throwaway" children—or children no one appears to value—is the nation's "secret scandal" (Reynolds, 1993).

Teachers are among those required by law to report instances of suspected child abuse. When teachers fail to do so, one or more things may happen: (a) they may be fined from $500 to $1,000, (b) they may be given prison terms of up to 1 year, (c) civil suits may be brought against them, and (d) they may be disciplined (e.g., demoted or dismissed) by their school system (McCarthy & Cambron-McCabe, 1992).

Problems of child abuse and neglect cut across all socioeconomic strata. According to the National Research Council (1993), however, financial problems may be the greatest contributor to the plight of children:

> [Child maltreatment] is disproportionately reported among poor families. Furthermore, child maltreatment—especially child neglect—is not simply concentrated among the poor, but among the poorest of the poor. Whether this association results from greater stress due to poverty-related conditions that precipitate abuse, or from greater scrutiny by public agencies that results in overreporting, or whether maltreatment is but one characteristic of the pattern of disruption among the poorest of the poor continues to be debated. The link between unemployment and maltreatment is significant in understanding the relationship between poverty and maltreatment. Families reported for abuse often have multiple problems, and the abuse may simply be a part—or a consequence—of a broader continuum of social dysfunctions. (p. 9)

Because the physical and mental health of parents bears directly on the health and well-being of their children, many community-based programs try to provide parents with the skills and knowledge needed to cope more effectively with everyday stress and to care for and nurture their children. Parenting programs can help increase parents' involvement in their children's lives and also teach parents—particularly young, inexperienced ones—how to take care of themselves and their children. Schools often sponsor parenting programs within their own buildings. Some provide day care for infants and preschool children of high school students so the parents can complete their own high school programs and avoid the stunningly cruel conditions of life that breed child abuse and neglect.

Preventing and Responding to Teen Pregnancy

Teenage childbearing correlates negatively with educational attainment, income, and participation in the labor force. Statistics indicate that for teens, having a child out-of-wedlock greatly increases the chance that a young mother and her child or children will live in poverty (Strapp, 1996). Many children of teenage parents wind up as teenage parents themselves, thus perpetuating the cycle of poverty and hopelessness.

In 1993 there were more than half a million births to teenagers, more than 200,000 to girls younger than age 18. Although the 1993 teen birth rate is higher than it was 20 years ago, the birth rate for girls ages 15 to 17 declined 2% between 1991 and 1992 and was unchanged in 1993 at 37.8 births per 1,000. The birth rate for older teens, ages 18 to 19, was down 3% in 1993, to 92.1 per 1,000 (U.S. Department of Health, Education, and Human Services, 1996).

Sex education, the most common method of attempting to prevent teen pregnancy, varies greatly from one school district to another. While approximately 90% of the American public support some form of sex education in schools, there is a great deal of disagreement about the appropriate content of such education (Sanderson & Wilson, 1991). The overwhelming majority of states encourage some type of sex education in schools, but the content and method of courses vary widely. Instruction runs the gamut from advocating abstinence from sexual contact to distributing condoms within the school.

Should states mandate that all school districts provide sex education?

The high dropout rate among young mothers and, in many instances, the poor health of their babies have encouraged many school systems to alter their programs to meet the needs of adolescent parents and parents-to-be. In addition to its standard curriculum, Texas's Spring Independent School District (ISD) offers home instruction to teenage mothers during their 4- to 6-week postpartum period. The Spring ISD program also provides teenage parents with child care, individual and group counseling, health care, parenting education, and vocational training. Over the 6-year history of Spring ISD's Teen Parenting Program, about 85% of participants have remained in school and on track for graduation. Also, the immunizations for all children enrolled in the Teen Parenting Day Care Center are current. Furthermore, screening of infants for growth and development has allowed several infants to receive special services much earlier than would have been possible otherwise (Strapp, 1996).

Preventing the Spread of AIDS and Other Communicable Diseases

Students engaging in sexual relationships and students abusing drugs are especially susceptible to sexually transmitted diseases, including HIV (human immunodeficiency virus)—the virus that causes AIDS (acquired immunodeficiency syndrome). According to data collected by the Centers for Disease Control, 53% of students in grades 9 to 12 have had sexual intercourse. Almost 19% of these teenagers have had four or more sexual partners (Kann, Warren, & Harris, 1993). Although AIDS often has been characterized as a disease confined mainly to homosexual men and intravenous drug users, about 8% of HIV/AIDS cases result from heterosexual intercourse (Centers for Disease Control and Prevention, 1996).

Douglas Tonks (1992/1993) counsels educators to remember two important facts when developing programs to prevent HIV transmission. First, many students experiment with drugs as young as age 12. Sexual experimentation also begins at an early age, even though this may not include intercourse. HIV prevention programs, therefore, must begin in elementary school and continue through high school; they must also be flexible enough to meet the needs of all children.

One study of school-based HIV education programs revealed that the most effective interventions had the following characteristics:

- a narrow focus, emphasizing risk-taking behaviors that could lead to HIV infection;

- opportunities to acquire and practice refusal and communication skills through such activities as role playing and brainstorming;

- acknowledgment of social and media influences on sexual behavior;

- an emphasis on developing values and group norms regarding postponing sex, avoiding unprotected sex, using condoms, and avoiding high-risk partners; and

- inclusion of testimonials from respected peers to encourage a more conservative set of values (Landau, Pryor, & Haefli, 1995).

Childhood diseases also place at risk children who have not received preschool vaccinations on time and therefore enter school vulnerable to disease. Resurgences of preventable diseases such as measles, mumps, pertussis (whooping cough), and rubella are threats to both health and learning (Children's Defense Fund, 1992). The emergence and spread of drug-resistant strains of tuberculosis also threaten the children's well-being (Groopman, 1993). To stem outbreaks of childhood diseases, public health officials have expanded outreach programs to ensure the timely immunization of children. They have also increased several immunization requirements for school-age children. To enable all children to meet these requirements, many districts offer school-based clinics for youngsters.

Preventing Suicide and Accidental Injury or Death

Adolescent suicide is a serious problem in the United States. Data from a national survey of students in all public, parochial, and private schools in grades 9 through 12 revealed that during the 12 months preceding the survey, 29% had thought seriously about attempting suicide, 18.6% had made a specific plan to attempt suicide, and 1.7% had made a suicide attempt that resulted in an injury, a poisoning, or an overdose that had to be treated by a doctor or nurse. Females were significantly more likely than were males to have thought about, planned, and attempted suicide (Kann, Warren, Collins, Ross, Collins, & Kolbe, 1993). An earlier study revealed that a number of factors led students to consider or attempt suicide: family problems or problems at home, problems with friends/peer pressure/social relations, boy/girl relationships, and feelings that no one cared (Gallup Organization, 1991).

Addressing potentially suicidal students and acquaintances of suicide victims requires special attention to young people's concepts of themselves. Single suicides can stimulate imitation, or what some people have referred to as "cluster suicides." School-based programs on suicide prevention and suicide curricula advocate careful training for teachers who offer such programs. For example, the California State Education Department has developed a program of worksheets, quizzes, and simulation games to address directly the threat of suicide. Other programs in other locales also address suicide more indirectly via drug education programs. In many of these programs, adults and students may be taught to understand the myths, signs, facts, and symptoms of suicide. They may also concentrate on identifying the feelings of students at risk, thinking of ways to help students cope with stress and depression, and learning how to respond to a suicide crisis. Figure 7.6 lists some of the warning signs of suicide.

The U.S. Department of Health and Human Services has an online guide for students that offers information about depression. You can access the document on the Web (**http://www.hoptechno.com/book34.htm**).

Motor vehicle accidents are the leading cause of death among teenagers 15 to 19 years old (U.S. Bureau of the Census, 1995). Many fatalities are alcohol related. Moving the minimum drinking age up to 21 in states where it was lower has resulted in a decline in arrests of teenagers for driving while intoxicated.

Cultural Awareness

Some groups of students are more prone to suicide than are others. Data suggest that homosexual adolescents are two to three times more likely to attempt suicide than are their heterosexual peers (Green, 1991). Among ethnic groups, the suicide rates for African-American males have risen dramatically. Between 1980 and 1992 the suicide rate for African-American children ages 10 to 15 more than doubled, increasing from 0.8 to 1.7 per 100,000. For African-American males ages 15 to 19, the rate jumped from 5.6 to 14.8 per 100,000 (Lawton, 1995).

WARNING SIGNS:

- Changing eating and sleeping habits
- Withdrawal from friends, family, and regular activities
- Violent or rebellious behavior
- Running away from home
- Unusual neglect of personal appearance
- Radical change in personality
- Persistent boredom, difficulty concentrating, or a decline in the quality of schoolwork
- Frequent complaints about physical symptoms often related to emotions, such as stomachaches, headaches, or fatigue
- Loss of interest in previously pleasurable activities
- Inability to tolerate praise or rewards

FIGURE 7.6

Some Warning Signs of Suicide

How might you respond to students who persistently exhibit these warning signs? What actions might you take?

Note. From "Counselors Can Make a Difference" by L. Peach and T. L. Riddick, 1991, *The School Counselor, 39*, pp. 107–111. Copyright by ACA. Reprinted with permission. No further reproduction authorized without written permission of the American Counseling Association.

High schools offer driver education programs that precede the granting of a license to operate a motor vehicle. Insurance companies offer incentives to students for high scores in driver safety and to students who do well in academic courses. In combination with health education, driver education can potentially lower the incidence of the lethal habit of drinking and driving. Nonetheless, when school budgets are tight, driver education courses are among the first to be dropped.

Preoccupation with body image threatens the psychological and physical well-being of many students, particularly adolescents. A growing number of females from all races and socioeconomic groups experience anorexia nervosa (self-starvation) and bulimia (binging and purging). Eating disorders not only harm students physically but also contribute to underachievement, interpersonal difficulties, and emotional instability (Phelps & Bajorek, 1991).

Preventing School Violence

Assault, homicide, vandalism, and related violent acts committed by and against young people are on the rise.

Some assaults against young people result from gang warfare. While gangs are not confined to urban areas, big cities in particular experienced growth in gang membership and gang violence in the 1980s. Much of the gang-related violence that seeps into schools results from struggles between gangs for drug-selling "turf."

While some gang and individual acts of brutality seem random and baseless, others are the cold and calculated manifestations of hate against people who are different. "Different" can be defined in terms of religion, sexual preference, race, age, or virtually any characteristic. Attacks are aimed at specific people or perceived types of people.

About one in four students report some kind of social tension or violence in their schools (Louis Harris and Associates, Inc., 1996) including hostile or

Cultural Awareness

Since 1979, more children (60,008) have died from gunfire in the United States than American soldiers died during the Vietnam and Gulf wars and in U.S. engagements in Haiti, Somalia, and Bosnia combined. African-American males ages 15 to 19 have suffered the greatest gun toll among children and teens. They are five times as likely as are European-American males to be gun victims. Gun violence is now the leading cause of death among African-American teens 15 to 19 years old (Children's Defense Fund, 1996, pp. 1–2).

threatening remarks among different groups of students (25%); physical fights among members of different groups of friends (26%); threats or destructive acts other than physical fights (24%); turf battles among different groups of students (21%); and gang violence (26%). The same survey indicates that as students grow older, however, their concern for such problems diminishes. Some 30 to 36% of 8th graders surveyed perceive violence as a very serious problem, compared to just 11 to 15% of 12th graders. Urban students are more like to report having serious problems with hostile remarks, physical fights, threats or destructive acts and gang violence (32 to 36%)

> **How can schools be made safe places where all students can learn?**

than are suburban (20 to 24%) or rural (17 to 20%) students. African-American and Hispanic students are twice as likely as are other students to report experiencing very serious problems with turf battles (32% and 33% respectively, versus 16%) and gang violence (40% and 41% respectively, versus 19%) (Louis Harris and Associates, Inc., 1996).

The central issue for educators is how to ensure children's safety. A number of efforts, many school based, aim to change the odds for children at highest risk.

To deter crime and violence on buses and at school, some localities have turned to metal detectors and video cameras. Some schools employ police officers, sometimes referred to as resource officers, to help maintain order and to prevent nonstudents from going on to school grounds. In 1993 only about 5% of students attended schools equipped with metal detectors. Students attending a public school, a high school, a school located in an urban area, or a school with enrollment above

Children's shocking violence towards other children, including hate crimes and firearm homicides, came to greater national attention during the 1990s.

1,000 were more likely to have metal detectors or security guards in their schools than were students attending other types of schools (U.S. Department of Education, 1996a).

Many schools have educational programs designed to enlist students' cooperation in preventing violence. One program, Helping Our Public Schools (HOPES) is the result of collaboration between principal Ana McLinn of Marvin Avenue Elementary School and the Los Angeles Police Department (LAPD). Goals of HOPES are to improve students' behavior and to build positive relationships between students and police. The Junior Cadet program—a popular component of HOPES—involves about 100 students who are trained by officers in character development, self-pride, and respect. Cadets remind peers about school rules, help supervise hallways and the playground, and "ticket" students for such infractions as running in the halls. Cadets also reward peers for good behavior and, once a week, wear uniforms similar to those worn by LAPD officers. Youths with three or more suspensions are paired with police officers, who serve as mentors and tutors after school hours. Since the program began in 1994, student behavior has improved and criminal activity in the community has declined (Coles, 1996).

Preventing Substance Abuse

As seen in Figure 7.7, surveys conducted between 1975 and 1995 reveal that high school seniors' reported use of alcohol and drugs over a 30-day period had declined somewhat. Nonetheless, because 50.3% of those surveyed

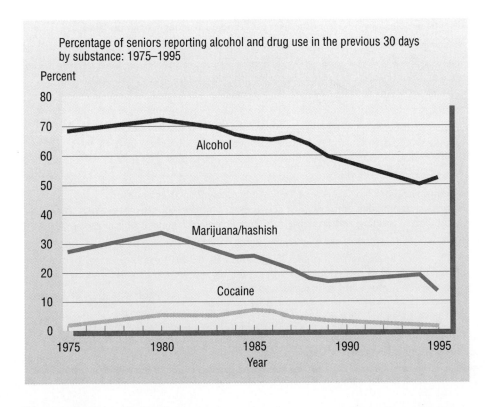

Percentage of seniors reporting alcohol and drug use in the previous 30 days by substance: 1975–1995

FIGURE 7.7

Alcohol and Drug Use Among High School Seniors

Describe the trends indicated on this graph.

Note. From *Digest of Education Statistics,* 1996, by U.S. Department of Education, 1996. Washington, DC: U.S. Government Printing Office. Table 147, p. 141.

BENCHMARKS

Legislation for Student Health and Safety (1946–1996)

1946   National School Lunch Act (Public Law 79-396) authorizes assistance through grants-in-aid and other means to states to assist in providing adequate foods and facilities for the establishment, maintenance, operation, and expansion of nonprofit school lunch programs.

1954   School Milk Program Act (Public Law 83-597) provides funds for the purchase of milk for school lunch programs.

1958   National Defense Education Act (Public Law 85-864) provides assistance to state and local school systems for strengthening many services, including guidance and counseling.

1964   Economic Opportunity Act of 1964 (Public Law 88-452) authorizes grants for college work–study programs for students from low-income families; establishes a Job Corps program and authorizes support for work-training programs to provide education and vocational training and work experience opportunities in welfare programs; authorizes support of education and training activities and of community action programs, including Head Start, Follow Through, and Upward Bound; and authorizes the establishment of Volunteers in Service to America (VISTA).

1965   Elementary and Secondary Education Act of 1965 (Public Law 89-10) authorizes grants for elementary and secondary school programs for children from low-income families; school library resources, textbooks, and other instructional materials for school children; supplementary educational centers and services; state education agencies; and educational research and research training.

Higher Education Act of 1965 (Public Law 89-329) establishes a National Teacher Corps devoted to teaching in the nation's poverty-striken areas.

1970   Drug Abuse Education Act of 1970 (Public Law 91-427) provides for development, demonstration, and evaluation of curricula on the problems of drug abuse.

1974   Juvenile Justice and Delinquency Prevention Act of 1974 (Public Law 93-415) provides for technical assistance, staff training, centralized research, and resources to develop and implement programs to keep students in elementary and secondary schools.

1977   Youth Employment and Demonstration Projects Act of 1977 (Public Law 95-93) establishes a youth employment training program that includes, among other activities, promoting education-to-work transition, literacy training and bilingual training, and attainment of certificates of high school equivalency.

1980   Asbestos School Hazard Detection and Control Act of 1980 (Public Law 96-270) establishes a program for inspection of schools for detection of hazardous asbestos materials and provides loans to assist educational agencies to contain or remove and replace such materials.

1986   Drug-Free Schools and Committees Act of 1986 (Part of Public Law 99-570), part of the Anti-Drug Abuse Act of 1986, authorizes funding for programs for drug abuse education and prevention, coordinated with related community efforts and resources.

1988   The Omnibus Drug Abuse Prevention Act of 1988 (Public Law 100-690) authorizes a new teacher training program under the Drug-Free Schools and Communities Act, an early childhood education program to be administered jointly by the U.S. Department of Health and Human Services and the U.S. Department of Education, and a pilot program for the children of alcoholics.

1990   Children's Television Act of 1990 (Public Law 101-437) requires the Federal Communications Commission to reinstate restrictions on advertising during children's television programs and enforces the obligation of broadcasters to meet the educational and informational needs of the child audience.

National Assessment of Chapter 1 Act (Public Law 101-305) requires the Secretary of Education to conduct a comprehensive national assessment of programs, carried out with assistance under Chapter 1 of Title 1 of the Elementary and Secondary Education Act of 1965.

School Dropout and Basic Skills Improvement Act of 1990 (Public Law 101-600) improves secondary school programs for basic skills improvements and dropout reduction.

1991   A bill making appropriations for the U.S. Department of the Interior and related agencies (Public Law 102-154) amends the Anti-Drug Abuse Act of 1988 to extend the authorization of appropriations for drug abuse education and prevention programs relating to youth gangs and for runaway and homeless youth. Directs the Secretary of Health and Human Services to report annually on the program of drug education and prevention relating to youth gangs.

1994   School-to-Work Opportunities Act of 1994 (Public Law 103-239) establishes a national framework within which states and communities can develop School-to-Work Opportunities systems to prepare young people for first jobs and continuing education. The act also provides money to states and communities to develop a system of programs that include work-based learning and school-based learning. School-to-Work programs provide students with a high school diploma (or its equivalent), a nationally recognized skill certificate, or an associate degree (if appropriate) and may lead to a first job or further education.

Safe Schools Act of 1994 (Part of Public Law 103-227) authorizes the award of competitive grants to local educational agencies with serious crime to implement violence prevention activites, such as conflict resolution and peer mediation.

1995   House Resolution HR 1390—Children's Media Protection Act of 1995 makes the following requirements: *Establishment of Television Violence Rating Code*—In consultation with television broadcasters, cable operators, appropriate public-interest groups, and interested individuals by television broadcast systems and cable systems. *Television that Blocks Programs*—New televisions sold in the United States must (1) be equipped with circuitry designed to enable viewers to block the display of channels, programs, and time slots; and (2) enable viewers to block display of all programs with a common rating. *Prohibition on Violent Programming*—A commission shall . . . initiate a rule-making proceeding to prescribe a prohibition on the broadcast on commercial television and by public telecommunications entities, including the broadcast by cable operators, from the hours of 6 A.M. to 10 P.M., inclusive, of programming that contains gratuitous violence. *Educational and Information Programming for Children*—Broadcast and cable companies are required to provide a specific amount of "children's programming," as defined by the FCC.

reported use of alcohol and 15.6% use of illicit drugs during the 30-day time frame, evidently many youth are engaging in practices considered detrimental to health and safety (U.S. Department of Education, 1996). According to a study by the Center on Addiction and Substance Abuse at Columbia University, girls use drugs at younger ages than ever before. The report suggests that girls today are 15 times more likely than were their mothers to have begun using illegal drugs by age 15 ("Girls' Substance Abuse," 1996).

Concerns about patterns of behavior that put students at risk have prompted parent groups in some school systems to band together to keep teenagers safe. The Boomerang Committee in Ames, Iowa, for example, was established more than 10 years ago. Members of the group sign a pledge, promising that parties held in their homes will be free from alcohol and drug use.

Can schools prevent substance abuse by students?

A variety of school-based programs also attempt to curb substance abuse. Project ALERT, a curriculum developed by the RAND Corporation, and Drug Abuse Resistance Education (DARE), a program that began as a joint effort between the Los Angeles Unified School District and the Los Angeles Police Department, are two examples of programs designed to help elementary and junior high school students resist peer pressure to experiment with drugs and alcohol. Among program goals are helping students learn to make their own decisions, learning drug and alcohol facts, understanding peer pressure, and developing positive self-esteem. While such programs enjoy widespread use, some educators have created their own health education programs to meet their students' needs.

Well-designed drug prevention programs have had positive effects. A 7-year study indicated that seventh and eighth graders in 30 schools in California and Oregon who were taught the Project ALERT curriculum reduced their use of illegal drugs, particularly marijuana, by as much as 50% while enrolled in the program. Once students left the program, however, positive effects all but disappeared. Such results suggest that prevention programs are most effective if they are continued at the high school level (Portner, 1993).

For information on at-risk students—those who experience threats from suicide, gangs, violence, teen pregnancy, drugs, poverty, language barriers, peer pressure, racial tension, and homelessness—visit the Web (**http://chef.sped.ukans.edu/~ks2000/risk.html**).

SUMMARY

What are society's expectations for schools?

I   Americans have turned increasingly to schools to solve some of society's most difficult problems, many of which have devastating effects on children. The demands placed on schools often exceed their resources.

2 Of growing concern to educators is the increasing number of students at risk for failure both academically and socially.

How does poverty place students at risk of school failure?

3 Conditions of poverty or lower socioeconomic status (SES) are strongly and consistently related to school failure. Children from low-income homes often begin school less well-prepared than their peers and have difficulty staying on grade level.

How can schools intervene to help students at risk?

4 Early intervention programs can help disadvantaged students enter school ready to learn. Some programs, such as Head Start, provide comprehensive child development and family support services to low-risk families with young children.

5 Compensatory programs provide children from low-income homes additional educational opportunities beyond those in a school's standard program. Before- and after-school programs can benefit children nutritionally, socially, and academically.

6 Establishing incentive programs; providing mentors and tutors; and linking home, school, and the workplace are other ways schools attempt to improve students' opportunities for success.

How can schools get parents involved in their children's education?

7 Parent–Teacher Associations and Organizations (PTAs and PTOs) provide opportunities for parent participation in school activities. The more successful parent involvement programs, however, are those in schools where parents are encouraged to participate in the education process.

8 Full-service programs and adult education programs also facilitate parental involvement by providing daycare services.

How can schools reduce risks that threaten children's health and safety?

9 The first demand schools face in reducing risks to children is to identify those risks.

10 Schools often are the first line of defense against child abuse; that is, educators have opportunities and responsibilities to identify and report suspected abuse and neglect.

11 Educational programs can make students and parents aware of a variety of risks, including but not limited to teen pregnancy, sexually transmitted diseases, suicide, and accidental injury or death.

12 School violence erupts for a variety of reasons. Increasingly, schools are taking measures to prevent violence at school that is initiated from within and outside school walls. In big cities, gang violence around the drug trade has grown even more vicious as young people have turned to weapons.

TERMS AND CONCEPTS

at-risk student, *p. 260*
Child Abuse Prevention and Treatment Act, *p. 281*
compensatory education program, *p. 268*
early intervention, *p. 266*
full-service school, *p. 279*

holding power, *p. 268*
incentive program, *p. 272*
latchkey child, *p. 271*
mentoring program, *p. 274*
pull-out program, *p. 270*
Title I, *p. 269*

REFLECTIVE PRACTICE

Before she got her doctorate, Ann C. Diver-Stamnes taught English in the Watts section of Los Angeles, an area of the city where for years gang warfare has been frighteningly common. The Crips and the Bloods claim this territory as home. In recent years routine violence in the community has been exacerbated by the drug trade. Combine drugs with the tendency to "come from the pocket," or to use knives and guns to settle scores, and anxiety is a fact of life for everyone within striking distance.

> When I first began to teach in Watts, I taught a senior remedial English class. We were discussing paragraph development one day when I heard a beeping noise. A student stood up and began to sidle toward the door, saying, "I gotta go. No offense. I just gotta go now." He was very polite, attempting to make sure I knew it was not my lesson on paragraphs that caused him to leave the room. I was completely baffled and turned to my class for some explanation. They explained, amused by my obvious confusion, that the student who had left was a gang member and was selling drugs, and the noise I had heard was his pager or beeper. He had probably been paged, they told me, by either his supplier or a customer, either of which required his immediate response.

> This young man, who was charming and warm in class, read and wrote at the fourth-grade level, carried a beeper, and had politely left my classroom to deal with a drug transaction.

Issues, Problems, Dilemmas, Opportunities

Diver-Stamnes notes that some people consider gang members to be expendable or "throwaway kids." Why is this attitude, particularly when held by teachers, a problem in itself? If you taught in a school in a community where drugs and violence were commonplace, beyond everyone's personal safety, what might be your major concerns?

Perceive and Value

Diver-Stamnes argues that the formation and maintenance of gangs is not a simple matter of too many "bad kids" in the same place at the same time. She characterizes gang membership as an almost logical response to a virtually hopeless situation—that is, the situation of being young and caught in the downward spiral of inner-city violence, poverty, and crime. Can you imagine why joining a gang might be viewed as a matter of self-protection? Why might a young person choose to sell drugs instead of working at a minimum-wage job?

Know and Act

If you had students in your classes who wore gang colors and emblems, what more might you want to know about these students? If you were the teacher, how might you respond to the student who excused himself from Ann Diver-Stammes's class to respond to a beeper? Diver-Stamnes described herself as feeling like a member of the "fashion police," always having students remove baseball caps and "rags" (bandannas), confiscating beepers, and instructing students to undo their braids, remove their earrings, or unlace their shoes. Why do schools have such rules?

Evaluate

Rightly or wrongly, we often evaluate people and situations by appearances. Diver-Stamnes describes how appearances affected her one day as she was walking near her school:

> As I walked down the street to the elementary school one day early in my second year at Medgar High, I noticed a large group of young men walking toward me, dressed in standard gangbanger attire. Although I had been given a walkie-talkie to carry on my frequent trips back and forth to the elementary school to drop off and pick up my high school students who worked there with the younger children, I felt foolish using it for more than reporting my arrival at or departure from either school. As the group of young men drew closer, I forced myself to keep walking and to refrain from crossing the street, although I was very nervous. When they drew up in front of me, I gasped as one young man separated himself from the group and launched himself at me. He threw his arms around my neck, and yelled, "Dr. Stamnes! How you doing?!" In an instant, this frightening group of "gangbangers" was transformed into a group of laughing kids, one of whom had been a favored student of mine the previous year. Mingled with my relief was a profound sense of shame that I too had not seen beyond appearances.

Do you think Diver-Stamnes's "reading" of the students was typical of how you or other teachers might view the situation? Was her fear warranted? How might students' appearances influence teachers' judgments of students' capacity for violence and their capacity for success? How might such judgments vary by locale, that is, in inner-city schools, in suburban schools, and in rural schools?

ONLINE ACTIVITY

As we note in this chapter, many projects and programs exist to help children in need of special support. One, the Comer School Development Program, at Yale University, has spawned some 65 related programs across the nation. Another, Edward Zigler's School of the 21st Century, is based on the belief that public schools can help alleviate the stressors associated with poverty and the lack of quality, affordable child care, and can contribute to improving school readiness and academic success. There are now some 300 schools in 14 states implementing Zigler's principles of the School of the 21st Century.

Visit the Yale Child Study Center online (**http://info.med.yale.edu/comer/**). When you arrive at the site, you will find a link to the Comer/Zigler Initiative or CoZi Schools—schools that combine Comer's School Development Program with Edward Zigler's concept of the School of the 21st Century. How does a CoZi School compare to schools with which you are familiar? Given what you have read in this chapter, why might CoZi Schools increase success opportunities for at-risk students?

Influence of American Cultural Diversity

We use this chapter to explore concepts of diversity in society and to speculate about what differences and similarities among the nation's people mean for education. The assumption upon which the chapter is based is that how people view society depends greatly on where they stand; thus the chapter positions readers to perceive different conceptions of the influence of culture on education.

We draw attention to the confusion in the language used to describe concepts of diversity and consider some of the practical implications of this language for schools and society. As we note, Americans have developed some unique ways of living with their diversity. We describe the more prominent ways multicultural education has been defined theoretically and in practice.

Rarely, if ever, has an education concept been surrounded by more contentious debate than has multicultural education. We explore reasons for this state of affairs and the challenges of evaluating multicultural education programs fairly and thoroughly.

PROFESSIONAL PRACTICE QUESTIONS

1 How does diversity affect education in America?

2 How do cultural and ethnic factors influence educational opportunities?

3 How do educators define and implement multicultural education?

4 How do curricular standards influence multicultural education?

HOW DOES DIVERSITY AFFECT EDUCATION IN AMERICA?

Americans, like no other social experimenters in history, have cursed and tolerated and ignored and celebrated their diversity in virtually every way imaginable. As Table 8.1 indicates, when diversity is defined in racial terms, numbers only hint at the richness of our society.

Thoughts about culture in the United States have been dominated by the metaphor of the melting pot. Immigrants, like ingredients, were to be added to the great cauldron (public education) and simmered over low-intensity educational fire until a perfectly blended soup was achieved in which characteristics of the individual ingredients disappeared.

The melting pot metaphor has come under attack, however, by advocates of pluralistic views, who call for the preservation, even celebration, of Americans' cultural diversity. In the pluralist salad bowl (or salsa) metaphor, people in all their crisp, colorful, tangy ways, while tossed together, retain their unique identities and essential differences. In similar fashion, the mosaic metaphor compares different shapes, sizes, and colors of tiles in a conceptual whole to our society.

Is "salad bowl" a more apt metaphor than "melting pot" for American cultural diversity?

TABLE 8.1   Race and Hispanic Origin for the United States: 1996
Are figures lower, higher, or about the same as you would have estimated?

United States	Numbers in thousands	Percent
Total Population	264,966	100
White	194,182	73.3
Black	31,961	12.1
American Indian, Eskimo, or Aleut	1,953	0.7
Asian or Pacific Islander (Chinese, Filipino, Japanese, Asian Indian, Korean, Vietnamese, Hawaiian, Samoan, Guamanian, and other Asian or Pacific Islander	9,014	3.4
*Hispanic Origin (Mexican, Puerto Rican, Cuban, and other Hispanic)	27,856	10.5

Note: Percentages total more than 100% due to rounding error and interaction of race (white and black) and Hispanic origin.
*Spanish origin and race are distinct; thus, persons of Spanish origin may be of any race.

Note. From "Resident U.S. Population by Sex, Race and Hispanic Origin" by U.S. Census Bureau 1996,
http://www.census.gov/

Such metaphors can be useful devices for thinking about culture in creative ways and for communicating social ideals. But a metaphor can become a hindrance when it is used as a prescription for practice. Although public education has educated the public in remarkable fashion, it has not completely met the demands of the melting pot, the salad bowl, or the mosaic metaphors, nor is it likely to do so anytime soon. Who Americans are as a people, and who Americans wish to become, are ideas too complex to be described fully by any metaphor. As a society, we seek a sense of **cultural pluralism**, that is, a state in which people of diverse ethnic, racial, religious, and social groups maintain autonomous participation within a common civilization.

How, then, are educators to view our sprawling, complex society to perceive the talents and needs of the people? There is no fail-safe plan, but the urgency to "decenter," to see and understand society from different points of view, is compelling. For the alternative is to be locked in an **ethnocentric** power struggle for the societal upper hand—a struggle based on the belief of the superiority of one's own ethnic group or culture.

Concepts of Diversity

What do people mean when they speak of the influence of "culture"? To what characteristics does one's "ethnicity" refer, and how is ethnicity different from one's "national origin," if at all? Is "race" a concept with many connotations or only those limited to physical characteristics? When educators mention "minorities," do they intend to refer only to the human attributes of race and ethnicity, or do they also mean gender, sexual orientation, disabilities, giftedness, and social class?

The language of diversity is perplexing because the concepts are defined in terms of both variable and critical attributes. Variable attributes are characteristics, such as preferences or behavioral traits, that may or may not define a person's membership in a group. However, critical attributes, those characteristics necessary to define a concept, such as physical characteristics, can be elusive too. People use ideas and language imprecisely to describe their own and others' racial or ethnic or cultural identities. You can explore online the complexities of American diversity in its many forms. Visit the U.S. Census Bureau at **http://www.census.gov/**.

Race and Ethnicity

Race is defined most often by physical characteristics, especially skin color, but sometimes also by ethnicity—ancestry in terms of national origin. A person of color might refer to himself or herself as black or African American or Hispanic (or Mexican, Cuban, Haitian, or Puerto Rican); but depending on appearances, a Hispanic or a person with African ancestry might just as easily identify himself or herself as white or Caucasian (Banks & Banks, 1997). The term **ethnicity** refers to membership in a group with a common cultural tradition or common national origin. Ethnic groups function as subgroups within the larger society and may share a common language, religion, customs, or other elements of culture. While racial traits are heritable, cultural traits are learned in social contexts. The most important identifying characteristic of an ethnic group is the members' feelings of identification with the group, because ethnicity is largely a matter of self-identification (Banks, 1996).

When people complete forms for school enrollment, job applications, student loans, and the like, they are asked questions about racial or ethnic heritage. Usually students or their parents are asked to check one of four racial categories used by the federal government: American Indian or Alaskan Native, Asian or Pacific Islander, black, or white. They are also asked to note whether they are of Hispanic origin. This information serves many purposes—to monitor equal opportunities in education and employment and to track school desegregation.

> **Should racial designation matter for purposes of education?**

The arbitrariness of racial classification categories is evident in the changes in Census Bureau questions asked since 1790 (Carey & Farris, 1996). In 1790, four categories were used to designate race: Free White Males, Free White Females, All Other Free Persons, and Slaves. In 1970, nine categories were used: white, Negro or black, Indian (American), Japanese, Chinese, Filipino, Hawaiian, Korean, and Other race. In the 1990 census the designation of Mixed Race was added, reflecting demographic realities and public discontent with the standard categories used by the government to collect statistics about the American population.

While the same four categories noted above were used to designate race for 20 years, the population changed dramatically during that time. Immigration surged during the 1980s. Fewer of those immigrants came from Europe and Canada, and more came from Mexico, Central and South America, the Caribbean, and Asia (Harrison & Bennett, 1995). More than 40% of public

VOICES

On Racial Designations

What do you do when you don't fit? "The number of interracial couples in America has increased by 78 percent since 1980. One in every 50 marriages is now between people of different races. In addition to interracial marriages, there were over 8,000 foreign and transracial adoptions in 1992 alone" (Steel, 1995, p. 45).

The use of the four ethnic categories by the federal government has profound implications for voting, housing, employment, and education in this country. But for an increasing number of people who would categorize themselves as multiracial, the present system does not work, as Susan Graham, a European-American woman married to an African-American man in Roswell, Georgia, can attest.

When I received my 1990 census form, I realized that there was no race category for my children. I called the Census Bureau. After checking with supervisors, the bureau finally give me their answer: the children should take the race of their mother. When I objected and asked why my children should be classified as their mother's race only, the Census Bureau representative said to me, in a very hushed voice, "Because, in cases like these, we always know who the mother is and not always the father."

I could not make a race choice from the basic categories when I enrolled my son in kindergarten in Georgia. The only choice I had, like most other parents of multiracial children, was to leave race blank. I later found that my child's teacher was instructed to choose for him based on her knowledge and observation of my child. Ironically, my child has been white on the United States census, black at school, and multiracial at home—all at the same time.

Some estimates suggest that 75 to 90% of the people who now check the Black box on census forms could check Multiracial because of their mixed genetic heritage (Wright, 1994). If only 10 or 15% decided to designate themselves as Multiracial in many sections of the nation, legislative districts would have to be redrawn. Many multiracial people understandably refuse to be categorized as either White or Black. The dilemma, as Lawrence Wright argues, is that if the government were to use the category Multiracial, "we would pull the teeth off the civil-rights laws."

CRITICAL THINKING

How do ethnic categories divide us? How do you categorize yourself, and what criteria do you use? What differences does this make in your life? What difference does it make to others? What facts do you need about students to ensure that all of them feel welcome in your classroom?

Note. From "New Colors: Mixed-Race Families Still Find a Mixed Reception" by M. Steel, 1995, Spring, *Teaching Tolerance*, 4(1), pp. 44–49; and "One Drop of Blood" by L. Wright, 1994, July 25, *The New Yorker*, pp. 46–55.

---

schools report that there are students in their schools who are not described adequately by the current standard federal categories (Carey & Farris, 1996).

Three important facts emerge immediately from a dispassionate examination of terms such as *race* and *ethnicity*. First, as Webster observes, these classification systems are arbitrary—established capriciously or by convention or left generally ill-defined. Second, there may be as much or more variation within a group as there is between or among groups. For example, Matute-Bianchi (1991) found that "Mexican-descent students" as a group are quite diverse in terms of their school performance. Thus the group requires more precise definition to help explain observed differences among Mexican-descent students relevant to their educational achievement. Mexicans tend to perform relatively well in school and, in many cases, outperform nonimmigrant Mexican-American students. A simplistic classification scheme can mask important differences among people. When this happens teachers may be "pulled" to behave in ways that are consistent with that scheme but out of line with students' real needs.

The third fact that emerges from a consideration of the language of diversity, as Brian Bullivant (1993) observes, is that classifications can vary depending on who does the classifying. "The subgroups within a pluralistic society can be distinguished by outsiders, or they can distinguish themselves because of the characteristics their members share" (p. 36). Different perspectives, not surprisingly, often yield dissimilar concepts. When people behave in accordance with their differing expectations, as people often do, misunderstanding and conflict may arise.

Even the process of self-definition, while seemingly a reasonable way out of the semantic maze, can be problematic. For example, for census taking purposes, the federal government defines "American Indian or Alaskan Native" as, "A person having origins in any of the original peoples of North America, and who maintains cultural identification through tribal affiliation or community recognition" (Office of Federal Statistical Policy and Standards, 1978, p. 37). People must define for themselves the meaning of "origins" and "maintains cultural identification."

◾ The Concept and Effects of Culture

Culture can be used in an inclusive or "macro" sense to refer to the sum of the learned characteristics of a people—language, religion, social mores, artistic expression, beliefs and values, and so on. In some cases a culture can be tied to a geographical region, while in other cases a culture exists largely irrespective of geography.

Culture also can be used in a "micro" sense to describe more conceptually discrete groups of people—cultures within cultures, subcultures, or microcultures. Users of illegal drugs are said to be part of the "drug culture" or "drug subculture." Some people with hearing impairments choose to be part of the "deaf culture." Some women consider themselves to be members of the "feminist culture."

Culture is an important concept for educators to understand, because it influences students' lives. Culture teaches; it shapes learners' identities, beliefs, and behaviors. Understanding students' cultures is a prerequisite to valuing diversity and enlisting the force of culture as an instructional ally. To ignore or misunderstand students' cultures is to risk teaching at cross-purposes with them. In recent years, social scientists have begun to explore critically the influence of culture in classrooms.

Educational and psychological research used to be conducted routinely on the American "mainstream"—the dominant ethnic and cultural group, typically composed of Anglo-Saxon Protestant males from middle or higher social classes. When results suggested that certain educational approaches were more or less effective, these results were translated into educational materials and programs for all students, including females, African Americans, and others. These approaches, however, often worked better with European-American males than with females, people of other racial groups, and students from different cultures. Now, instead of assuming research findings hold up across genders and cultural groups, researchers investigate how such differences among people can affect learning and teaching.

Cultural Differences Between Teachers and Students

From interviews with students, Louis Harris and Associates, Inc. (1996) found three factors that influence positive relations in schools: the quality of teachers' relationships with students, the quality of education, and the social skills teachers impart to students. When these factors are present, students perceive social problems in their schools as less serious and express more confidence that people from different backgrounds receive equal treatment by adults in their community. These factors depend heavily on teachers' knowledge of and attitudes toward their students.

Children (and teachers) who grow up in diverse communities have opportunities to learn about others who are different from them and about themselves in relation to others. These opportunities do not always result in social harmony; neither do they inevitably lead to tension and conflict. Without a heterogeneous population of students, however, a school has less human capital upon which to draw when preparing students for life in a diverse world.

What teachers expect from the mix of students they teach and how they act on those expectations are crucial. One way that teachers demonstrate what they expect is through grouping and labeling students. A label sets up expectations in the minds of those who label and those who are labeled; behavior flows from these expectations. These expectations, expressed in the treatment and evaluation of students, underlie discrimination and can come from conscious or unconscious prejudice.

When cultural mismatches between teacher and students occur in the classroom—when teacher and students are different racially or ethnically and operate outside each other's normative cultures—the effects can be hard on teachers and their students. For instance, in low-income inner-city schools with high proportions of racial and ethnic minorities, low-income students, and at-risk learners, mismatches between teachers' and students' experiences and values are common. Such differences can be frustrating to novice teachers:

> My first year was arduous, exhausting, and disillusioning. The progress my class made was not sufficient. My students' environment was the first obstacle I encountered. Poverty dominated their lives: almost all were on welfare, lived in public housing projects and came from single-parent homes. All were African American. Most witnessed violence and drug use in their neighborhoods daily. These problems powerfully affected the children; they came to school angry, upset and scared (Lach, 1992, p. 151).

Mismatches also frustrate students, who believe that teachers do not understand or value them. Too often, "[R]ather than think of minority students as having a culture that is valid and distinct from theirs, [teachers] sometimes think of the youngsters as deficient" (Viadero, 1996, p. 40). Teachers can misinterpret students' responses, believing that students are ignorant or disobedient, for example, when they are only exhibiting subtle and deep-seated cultural differences.

Cultural Awareness

Cultural differences might be as simple as not knowing or not having had experience with guiding educational conversation in classrooms. For example,

> Ms. White, a teacher in an isolated rural community, is teaching her 1st graders how to tell time. She points to a clock, telling her students that 'It's 10 o'clock because the big hand is on the 12 and the little hand is on the 10.'

> 'What time is it?' she asks the students. Many of the white children raise their hands, eager to answer. The black students sit silently. A few give her a puzzled look.

> Ms. White concludes that many of her black students do not know the answer, and she silently makes a note to herself to revisit the concept with them later. . . .

> In the African-American children's families, such questions were posed only when someone genuinely needed to know the answer. 'What is she asking us for?' some of the black children might have wondered. 'She just told us it was 10 o'clock' (Viadero, 1996, pp. 39-40).

Aspects of classroom life that are subject to misunderstandings between teachers and students include verbal communication, patterns of participating and listening, body language and movement, uses of signs and symbols (such as clothing, jewelry, and emblems), modes of relaxing and of paying attention, conceptions of time, social values, peer interaction patterns, values concerning what is worth knowing, and many other areas (Bennett, 1995).

By 2020 more than half the children in public schools will be racial and ethnic minorities. Most teachers will be European Americans. As diversity increases, so too will the possibilities for miscommunication and misunderstanding.

What can teachers do to ensure that cultural differences between them and their students do not have negative effects on student learning and achievement? Knowing students' backgrounds and giving culturally appropriate responses to students is an important first step.

For example, a summary of interviews conducted with 10 Asian-American students (Oei & Lyon, 1996, pp. 54-55) suggests ways teachers can respond appropriately to Asian-American students and welcome student diversity:

1. Call students by their correct names. Ask for help with pronunciation of unfamiliar names, and help classmates learn to say the names correctly. Do not offer to change or shorten children's names or give them nicknames.

2. Ask students how they identify themselves (such as "Asian American," "Korean American," "Chinese," or just "American"). Do not assume a particular nationality or birthplace. Some students' families will have lived in the United States for many generations; others may be recent immigrants.

3. Do not assume that Asian-American students will have particular academic or athletic interests or abilities. Encourage participation in all aspects of school life.

4. Help all students identify and challenge the stereotypes of Asians that might arise in film, literature, textbooks, or TV.

5. If Asian-American students express an interest in their Asian heritages, encourage efforts to bring that cultural connection into the classroom. Integrate appropriate literature, arts, and language into the curriculum, and invite students to describe holiday celebrations and religious observances.

Sensitivity training and cultural awareness programs for both teachers and students are being implemented in schools and communities throughout the nation. For example, the Chicago Children's Museum features an exhibit called "Prejudice Bus," which aims to help children handle discriminatory behavior. The "bus" is a room with enlarged cardboard photos of children sitting on bus seats. People who enter the room hear taped children's voices blurting out racial, ethnic and other epithets aimed to offend virtually every segment of society. The program, called "Face to Face: Dealing with Prejudice and Discrimination" guides children in strategies for responding to name-calling and other discriminatory behavior ("Words that hurt," 1996).

Manning and Baruth (1996, pp. 212-219) offer guidelines such as the following for teachers in diverse classrooms:

-   Recognize and accept diversity of culture, gender, ethnicity, race, social class, and religion.

-   Value diversity as a positive benefit rather than as a problem.

-   Become informed, not only about students, their families, and their community, but about complex relationships between culture and learning.

-   Create a classroom environment that demonstrates acceptance and respect.

-   Encourage students to express diverse views and to take others' perspectives.

-   Encourage cooperation and positive social interactions and relationships among diverse students.

-   Develop the skills to plan and implement curriculum and instruction that reflect student cultural diversity and addresses culturally diverse students' needs.

-   Value objective perceptions of all learners; base all educational decisions on objective evidence with the student's welfare in mind.

-   Expect all students to succeed academically.

Perhaps most important is to provide a culture-fair education and to ensure that all students in your classroom have as many opportunities as possible to demonstrate success.

Prejudice and Discrimination

Providing equal educational opportunity in the classroom is complicated by continuing prejudice and discrimination in the wider society. **Discrimination**—differential treatment associated with labels—gives rise to conflict. People too often report and interpret information about groups as though all members conform to some mythical image of sameness, some average that, in turn, drives educational action. This tyranny of "average thinking" overwhelms good sense about the real people who are assigned to these groups.

Studs Terkel's (1992) description of C. P. Ellis, former Exalted Cyclops of the Durham, North Carolina, chapter of the Ku Klux Klan, demonstrates the kind of thinking that leads to racial prejudice and discrimination and also demonstrates the ever-present potential for changing one's attitudes toward others. Ellis told of growing up in abject poverty and quitting school in the eighth grade so that he could go to work when his father died. The degrading poverty was fertile ground for hate, and hate is the grist for the Klan:

> I began to say there's somethin' wrong with this country. I really began to get bitter. I tried to find somebody. I began to blame it on black people. I had to hate somebody. Hatin' America is hard to do because you can't see it to hate it. You gotta have somethin' to look at to hate. [Laughs.] The natural person for me to hate would be black people, because my father before me was a member of the Klan. As far as he was concerned, it was the savior of the white people. It was the only organization that would take care of the white people. So I began to admire the Klan." (Turkel, 1992, p. 272)

Through the years, Ellis grew to believe that he and other people like him were being used as pawns by white businessmen. His confrontations with an African-American woman named Ann Atwater and his eventual willingness to sit and talk with African Americans under the auspices of a federal program designed to solve racial problems in the schools led gradually to a change of heart.

> One day, Ann and I just sat down and began to reflect. Ann said, 'My daughter came home cryin' every day. She said her teacher was makin' fun of her in front of the other kids.' I said, 'Boy, same thing happened to my kid. White liberal teacher was makin' fun of Tim Ellis's father, the Klansman, in front of other peoples. He came home cryin'.' At this point"—[He pauses, swallows hard, stifles a sob.]—"I begin to see, here we are, two people from the far ends of the fence, havin' identical problems, except her bein' black and me bein' white. From that moment on, I tell ya, that gal and I worked together good. I begin to love the girl, really." [He weeps.] (pp. 275-276)

Because some people are segregated from society—isolated by formal and informal means—they feel frightened, alone, and yet defiant. Nine teenagers experienced these feelings in the fall of 1957, when they entered Central High School in Little Rock, Arkansas, accompanied by 22 troopers from the U.S. Army's 101st Airborne as 350 more

What issues relating to racial and cultural diversity might be played out in this classroom? In what ways might diversity issues affect what, how, and whom you teach?

troopers surrounded the building. Hand picked by the Board of Education, these young people began putting an end to the era of school segregation.

For four decades court-ordered busing plans have signaled the nation's moral resolve to end de jure and de facto segregation (see Chapter 3).

> **Has busing successfully led to school integration?**

Nonetheless, informal or de facto segregation continues today. Many urban systems, such as the Kansas City, Missouri, School District, have lost European-American students to the suburbs in droves, which has made impossible the task of achieving racial balance in the schools (Kunen, 1996).

In 1995 the Supreme Court of the United States ruled in *Missouri v. Jenkins* that the state of Missouri and the school district did not have to pay for a school desegregation plan designed to attract European-American suburban students to Kansas City schools. The Supreme Court held that the ultimate goal was to restore state and local authorities to the control of the school system, not to achieve racial balance. This meant that once the effects of segregation were eliminated, a district could operate schools that were either all European-American or all minority. As Figure 8.1 shows, the effect of this decision has been to stimulate efforts around the country to end busing for racial integration.

FIGURE 8.1

Efforts to Back Away from School Desegregation

What factors and events have contributed to resegregation in some parts of the country?

Note. From "The End of Integration" by J. S. Kunen, April 29, 1996, *Time, 147*(18), pp. 42-43, © 1996 Time Inc. Reprinted by permission.

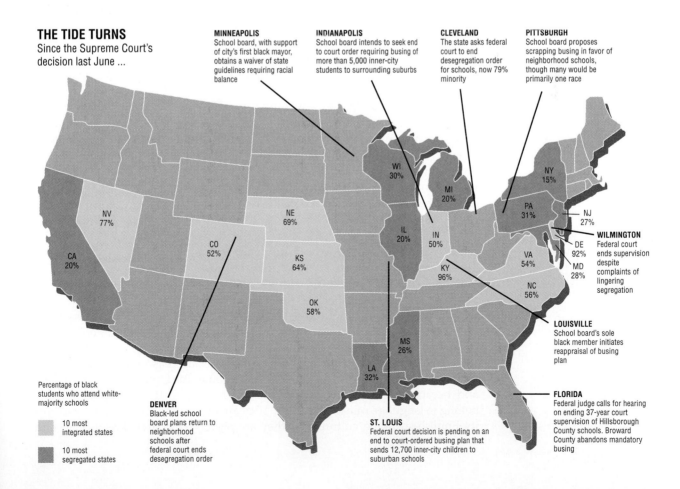

THE TIDE TURNS
Since the Supreme Court's decision last June ...

MINNEAPOLIS
School board, with support of city's first black mayor, obtains a waiver of state guidelines requiring racial balance

INDIANAPOLIS
School board intends to seek end to court order requiring busing of more than 5,000 inner-city students to surrounding suburbs

CLEVELAND
The state asks federal court to end desegregation order for schools, now 79% minority

PITTSBURGH
School board proposes scrapping busing in favor of neighborhood schools, though many would be primarily one race

WILMINGTON
Federal court ends supervision despite complaints of lingering segregation

LOUISVILLE
School board's sole black member initiates reappraisal of busing plan

FLORIDA
Federal judge calls for hearing on ending 37-year court supervision of Hillsborough County schools. Broward County abandons mandatory busing

ST. LOUIS
Federal court decision is pending on an end to court-ordered busing plan that sends 12,700 inner-city children to suburban schools

DENVER
Black-led school board plans return to neighborhood schools after federal court ends desegregation order

Percentage of black students who attend white-majority states

- 10 most integrated states
- 10 most segregated states

NV 77%, CA 20%, CO 52%, NE 69%, KS 64%, OK 58%, WI 30%, IL 20%, IN 50%, MI 20%, KY 96%, MS 26%, LA 32%, VA 54%, NC 56%, NY 15%, PA 31%, NJ 27%, DE 92%, MD 28%

How do Cultural and Ethnic Factors Influence Educational Opportunities?

Knowledge and attitude are inextricably bound—joined in tangled, seemingly inseparable ways. Nowhere is this fact more obvious than in the relationship of what Americans know about race and social status and our attitudes about what we should do to educate people for full participation in society.

A national telephone survey of public perceptions of minorities in America sponsored by *The Washington Post*, the Kaiser Family Foundation, and Harvard University (Morin, 1995) suggests that unfortunately, much of what we "know" often is incomplete, biased by the language we use, or just plain wrong. A total of 1,970 randomly selected Americans were interviewed, including 802 European Americans, 474 African Americans, 352 English-speaking Asian Americans, and 252 Spanish- and English-speaking Hispanic Americans. Remaining interviewees were of other races or declined to identify their race.

In the survey a majority of European Americans said they believed that the average African American is faring as well or better than the average European American in jobs, health care, and education. But government statistics show that European Americans, on average, earn 60% more than do African Americans, are more likely to have medical insurance, and more than twice as likely to graduate from college. Most of those surveyed, regardless of race, also overestimated the number of minority Americans in the United States. African Americans constitute about 12% of the population, but all respondents said that the percentage was about twice that high (Morin, 1995).

The term *minority status* or **minority** carries both a quantitative, or statistical, meaning and a political connotation. Those groups or subgroups in society who are identifiably fewer in number than another group are said to be in the minority. This is a relative term, however. Nationally, African Americans are a minority compared to Anglo European Americans. In some states and cities, however, African Americans constitute a majority of the population.

Minority is also used to describe perceptions of the relative political power or influence that a group exerts in society. For example, because women do not hold public office in the same proportion as their number in the population, women are said to be a minority, that is, they are perceived to exert less influence on the operation of government than do men. The term *minority*, then, is defined comparatively.

> **What groups are to be defined as minorities?**

Some groups are minorities for more than one reason. Because the language of commerce, government, and education in the United States is English, and because most people speak English, those who do not speak English belong to language minority groups. They are fewer in number than the majority English-speaking culture, and they are perceived to exert less influence in society. Minority status is not equivalent to concepts of social or socioeconomic status (SES), described in Chapter 7.

Immigrant Minorities

About 1 million people immigrate to the United States each year (Ungar, 1995). Some 2 million immigrant children enrolled in American schools in the 1980s—more than at any other time since the early years of this century. New immigrants are concentrated in cities in California, New York, Florida, Texas, and Illinois. These newcomers "teach" educators about the need for changes in the schools. For example, many immigrant children have had no formal education but are the ages of sixth, seventh, and eighth graders in U.S. schools. In these situations, immigrants to the United States sense the tension immediately.

> "I want to melt into this country and participate in the life here, but it seems so hard," said Deborah Hsu, 20, a college student in Los Angeles who came to the United States from Taiwan just over a year ago. "People don't give me a chance to make friends with them." (1995, p. A27)

Immigrants' experiences vary widely and differ from those of other minorities. Anthropologist John Ogbu has offered a controversial theory on these differences (Ogbu, 1991). He describes "castelike minorities," or involuntary nonimmigrant minorities, as people who are Americans as a result of slavery, conquest, or colonization. Ogbu contends that in addition to experiencing discrimination from others, involuntary minorities may also defeat themselves through feelings of inferiority.

When Ogbu and colleague Signithia Fordham studied bright African-American students in Washington, D.C., they found that the students did not live up to their potentials. Ogbu and Fordham claimed that these students did not want to be accused by their peers of "acting white"—speaking standard English, adopting certain clothing styles, listening to certain radio stations, or engaging in activities such as studying in the library or going camping (Hill, 1990). Ogbu argues that as members of involuntary minorities, some African Americans, such as these students, see education as a "subtractive process" that forces them to lose their own cultural identity if they are to succeed. Critics denounced the findings as blaming the victims for their failures.

Ogbu contends that, in contrast, voluntary immigrant minorities tend to see education as an opportunity to get ahead and may not equate success in school with losing their culture. Critics point out, however, that many voluntary minorities also resist cultural assimilation. While they may value economic success, they do not view erasing or discarding all signs of native origin and cultural identity as a desirable outcome.

What are some implications of minority status for students and families? For teachers and schools? How might the experiences of immigrants differ from those of other minorities?

Barbara Vobejda (1991) of *The Washington Post* described how life in a Kansas town has evolved in recent years with the arrival of many non-English-speaking immigrants eager for work in the local meatpacking industry.

On the dusty streets outside the diner, their town has a new look and feel: Tornado warnings are posted in three languages, Vietnamese, Spanish and English. The police department is under pressure to hire Hispanics, and farmers look forward to the Asian dragon dance at the Cinco de Mayo parade. The old-timers can't pronounce the name of the new Vietnamese restaurant, Pho-Hoa, but they know they like No. 38 (barbecue pork and noodles). (p. A1)

Cultural Awareness

When Al Kamen (1991) looked out at Lowell, Massachusetts, through the eyes of Cambodian refugees, he saw people working like those who had come before them to make the United States their home. From 1983 to 1991, the Cambodian population in Lowell grew from 150 families to more than 10,000 persons. Social services, jobs, and housing attracted the Cambodians to Lowell and helped them get a start, but the two Buddhist temples and some 100 Cambodian-owned businesses formed the spiritual and economic center that kept them there.

In 1996 the Cambodian population of Lowell had grown to about 20,000 with a combined Southeast-Asian population of about 25,000. The Lowell Public Schools offered full transitional bilingual education to 1,184 Cambodian, 93 Laotian, and 105 Vietnamese students. Another nearly 2,000 Cambodian students were in general academic courses. The system of some 15,000 students employed 164 teachers of transitional bilingual education in addition to its staff of ESL (English as a Second Language) teachers (S. O'Donnell, personal communication, September 3, 1996). In a very short period of time Lowell became an educational and cultural center for Southeast Asians.

Nathan Caplan, Marcella Choy, and John Whitmore (1991) described compellingly the combined power of cultural factors and education in their discussion of "the children of the boat people." In 1981 these researchers began studying Vietnamese, Chinese, and Laotian immigrants to the United States and found among the children "high levels of achievement at the very outset of their formal education in America" (p. 20). Even when they attended low-income, inner-city schools, they earned uniformly high standardized achievement test scores. Kindergarten teachers' anecdotal records showed that the children were eager to learn and took pleasure from their work even before they entered first grade.

Why were these children so successful? The researchers attributed success on scholastic and economic measures to three factors they called "culturally based values, family life-style, and opportunity" (p. 88). The refugee children most broadly successful are those who

> (1) have the strongest respect for their past and its relevance to the present, that is, their cultural heritage; (2) are most willing to face the formidable challenge of seeking out new paths and means of adapting to the demands of different settings; and, having arrived stripped of belongings and lucky to be alive, (3) now are most desirous of physical well-being and freedom from danger." (p. 90)

Language Minorities and Bilingual Education

Language can be a formidable barrier in American society. Interpreting life as a language-minority person might do is something most monolingual, English-speaking Americans never contemplate. Relatively few monolingual English speakers ever find themselves in situations where someone else does not also speak English. But many students who are categorized as **limited English proficient (LEP)** or qualify for instruction in **English as a Second Language (ESL)** view life in American society from behind a language barrier.

According to the U.S. Department of Education (1996), there were dramatic changes in the numbers and characteristics of the non-English-speaking population between 1979 and 1989. The number of people in the U.S. population 5 years old and older who spoke a language other than English at home increased from 9 to 12%. Surprisingly, almost half of all non-English speakers were born in the United States. Spanish was spoken by 58% of all speakers of languages other than English.

About half of the non-English-speaking population has difficulty speaking English. In 1979, 53% of this group were enrolled below their expected grade level. By 1989, 38% were below grade level, compared to 34% for English-only speakers. Making placement decisions is difficult, however, because gauging the progress of students with limited English proficiency is challenging. No standard criteria exist by which specific forms of assessment can be selected or adapted to fit these students' language needs (U.S. Department of Education, 1996).

Students with limited English proficiency receive help in the form of **bilingual education**, or instruction in both English and their native language. Bilingual programs vary in the amount of support they provide. Some offer instruction to students in both English and their native language and culture throughout their school years. Other programs help students make the transition from their native language to English by offering ongoing, intensive instruction in English as a Second Language (ESL) classes. Yet other programs remove students from regular classes to receive special help in English or in reading in their native language. And some programs immerse non-English speaking students in English, sometimes providing an aide who speaks the native language, then place students in English-speaking classes.

Some people believe that teaching non-English-speaking children in their native language, the language they hear most at home, while easing them gradually into English is the only reasonable way to move these children into the mainstream. Make them "competent in two languages," argues Raul Yzaguirre, director of the National Council of La Raza in Washington, D.C., an

VOICES

On Passion

Passions underlying the debate about culture in our nation can be volatile and dangerous; at the same time, they can stimulate genuine human understanding where little or none has existed before. Philosopher Maxine Greene of Teachers College, Columbia University, reaffirms passion's correct place in the dialogue about American cultural diversity.

There have always been newcomers in this country; there have always been strangers. There have always been young persons in our classrooms we did not, could not see or hear. In recent years, however, invisibility has been refused on many sides. Old silences have been shattered; long-repressed voices are making themselves heard. Yes, we are in search of what John Dewey called "The Great Community"; but, at once, we are challenged as never before to confront plurality and multiplicity. Unable to deny or obscure the facts of pluralism, we are asked to choose ourselves with respect to unimaginable diversities. To speak of passions in such a context is not to refer to the strong feelings aroused by what strikes many as a confusion and a cacophony. Rather, it is to have in mind the central sphere for the operation of the passions: "the realm of face-to-face relationships." It seems clear that the more continuous and authentic personal encounters can be, the less likely it will be for categorizing and distancing to take place. People are less likely to be treated instrumentally, to be made "other" by those around.

No one can predict precisely the common world of possibility, nor can we absolutely justify one kind of community over another. Many of us, however, for all the tensions and disagreements around us, would reaffirm the value of principles like justice and equality and freedom and commitment to human rights, since, without these, we cannot even argue for the decency of welcoming. Only if more and more persons incarnate such principles, we might say, and choose to live by them and engage in dialogue in accord with them, are we likely to bring about a democratic pluralism and not fly apart in violence and disorder. Unable to provide an objective ground for such hopes and claims, all we can do is speak with others as eloquently and passionately as we can about justice and caring and love and trust.

We want our classrooms to be just and caring, full of various conceptions of the good. We want them to be articulate, with the dialogue involving as many persons as possible, opening to one another, opening to the world. And we want them to be concerned for one another, as we learn to be concerned for them. We want them to achieve friendships among one another, as each one moves to a heightened sense of craft and wide-awakeness, to a renewed consciousness of worth and possibility.

CRITICAL THINKING

Why might people who interact face-to-face continually and in genuine ways be less likely to categorize one another and to hold each other at a psychological distance? How might we use information we acquire about others not to understand them but to construct conceptions of whom we believe them to be? What guidelines would you develop for yourself to ensure that your classroom is "just and caring"?

Note. From *Freedom's Plow: Teaching in the Multicultural Classroom* (p. 193–194) by M. Greene, 1993, New York: Routledge. Reprinted by permission of the publisher.

umbrella group of several hundred Hispanic organizations (Bernstein, 1990, p. 44). The most prominent concern of bilingual-education advocates is retention of cultural identity. Visit the National Council of La Raza online (**http:// www.hispanic.org/nclr.htm**).

Others believe that teaching children in their native language is bad for them and bad for the country. They contend that bilingual programs hold children back by doing a substandard job of teaching children either in their native tongue or in English. "Bilingual education, they argue, is more likely to prepare minority children for careers in the local Taco Bell than for medical school or nuclear physics" (Bernstein, 1990, p. 44). Bilingual programs vary by the amount of English taught and the rapidity with which it is introduced. Definitions of program and student success vary widely.

Why might some Americans oppose bilingual education?

J. David Ramirez (1992) studied more than 2,000 students for 4 years. After examining data on the children, their families, classrooms, teachers, schools, school districts, and communities, he concluded that the more instruction children receive in their first language, the better they perform in their second language. Ramirez also found that children in all-English and bilingual programs showed comparable performances during the early elementary grades, and the students in immersion and early-exit bilingual programs began to fall behind in the upper grades. Other researchers have reached similar conclusions (Caudell, 1996).

Rosalie Pedalino Porter (1995) offers another view. Based on the findings of a study conducted over 4 years in the New York City schools, she argues there is strong evidence

> [that] the earlier a second language is introduced, the more rapidly it is learned for academic purposes. . . . Apparently, with appropriate teaching, children can learn a new language quickly and can learn subject matter taught *in* that language. Reading and writing skills can be mastered and math can be learned successfully in a second language. (1995, p. 2)

Claims for and against the efficacy of bilingual education interact with feelings of ethnic pride. Some Hispanic Americans, for example, argue that a "white, Anglo" education damages students' feelings of self-worth. Others worry that bilingual education emphasizes differences in language, thus pushing people further apart when they need to come together as Americans. Anglos and Hispanics can be found on both sides of the argument.

Independent of such disputes, schools often have great difficulty delivering bilingual services. There is a shortage of qualified bilingual teachers. Most are needed for Spanish/English classes, because most LEP students are Hispanic Americans. Increasingly, teachers are needed with combined skills in English and other languages. Fewer capable professionals means higher chances for misdiagnosing learning problems as special education concerns and lower capacity for teaching students with language needs. Hiring larger numbers of more highly qualified professionals is, unfortunately, a costly undertaking.

Should this student receive instruction in Spanish? in English only? What issues are involved? What does research suggest is the best way to educate students whose first language is not English?

How do Educators Define and Implement Multicultural Education?

The term *multicultural education* is used in a variety of ways. At its core, however, multicultural education attempts to alter existing education programs to respond more effectively to diversity in the United States:

> **Multicultural education** is a field of study and an emerging discipline whose major aim is to create equal educational opportunities for students from diverse racial, ethnic, social-class, and cultural groups. One of its important goals is to help all students to acquire the knowledge, attitudes, and skills needed to function effectively in a pluralistic democratic society and to interact, negotiate, and communicate with peoples from diverse groups in order to create a civic and moral community that works for the common good. (Banks & Banks, 1995, p.xi)

Geneva Gay (1995) notes that multicultural education is also a "concept, idea, or philosophy." As such, multicultural education both describes the way life is and prescribes what should be done to ensure equal access to education and treatment of diverse groups of students in schools. Diversity typically is addressed in terms of social class, gender, and disability, as well as race and ethnicity.

> **What is multicultural education?**

Christine Sleeter and Carl Grant (1994) note five general educational approaches to multicultural education, shown in Figure 8.2:

1. "teaching the culturally different" involves attempts to assimilate people into the cultural mainstream using transitional bridges in the regular school program;

2. "human relations approaches " try to help students of differing backgrounds understand and accept each other;

3. "single-group studies" encourage cultural pluralism by concentrating on the appreciation of the contributions of individuals and groups;

4. "multicultural approaches" promote pluralism by reforming whole educational programs—altering curricula, integrating staffs, and affirming family languages; and

5. "education that is multicultural and social reconstructionist" promotes active challenge of social inequality.

We examine each general approach in turn below.

Teaching the Exceptional and Culturally Different

This approach attempts to assimilate students of different races, low-income students, and special education students into the "cultural mainstream" as it currently exists (Sleeter, 1993). These efforts may take the form

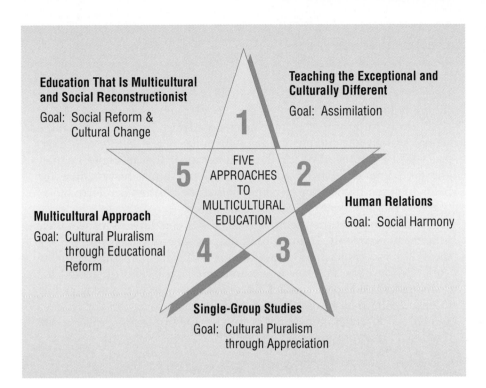

FIGURE 8.2

Five Approaches to Multicultural Education

Think of one clear example of each of the five approaches identified in this figure.

Note. From *Making Choices for Multicultural Education: Five Approaches to Race, Class, and Gender* (2nd Ed.), by C. E. Sleeter and C. A. Grant, 1994, Englewood Cliffs, NJ: Merrill/Prentice Hall.

of organizational or instructional changes intended to match students' learning styles and existing skills (Grant & Gomez, 1996).

For years this was the preferred approach to multicultural education. As immigrants arrived in this country, they were placed in programs designed to transmit the knowledge, skills, and attitudes deemed appropriate for successful life in American society. Such programs often made their goals explicit. For example, students were to learn to read and write English, to master American history, to adopt American social customs, and so on.

Programs and processes of teaching the culturally different, however, have also been characterized by their implicit demands. Teachers' expectations for appropriate behavior, for example, subtly influence students to question their backgrounds or to view themselves negatively.

Human Relations Approaches

Human relations approaches to multicultural education try to help students of differing backgrounds understand and accept each other. Encouraging cooperation and building self-esteem are activities integral to a human relations approach to multicultural education. These approaches take many forms and often are as informal as teachers assigning a "friend" to a new student in class or assigning work or play groups to facilitate understanding and acceptance. Human relations approaches also include formal procedures for accomplishing goals such as the resolution of conflict.

Cultural Awareness

Interpersonal friction between students—often between those from different races and cultures—seems to plague some schools. In El Paso, Texas, for example, trouble has reached such proportions that the school system has established its own police force. While educators must take responsibility for the well-being of the students in their charge, some have tried to make students more responsible for resolving their own disagreements. This strategy often is referred to as "conflict management" or "conflict mediation."

Conflict mediation attempts to teach students how to resolve their differences peaceably. Training programs exist across the country. Since the 1970s, groups such as Educators for Social Responsibility in New York City and San Francisco's Community Board have pioneered the development and use of conflict mediation strategies with young people (Meek, 1992). In an interesting twist, at Cleveland High in California's San Fernando Valley, gang leaders are learning how to be peacemakers (National Education Association, 1993).

Although program goals are the same in conflict mediation, the means for teaching students to reach these goals can differ. David and Roger Johnson advocate that teachers provide opportunities for students to practice skills involved in negotiating and mediating differences among themselves. The Johnsons' approach proceeds through three steps (Johnson, Johnson, Dudley, Ward, & Magnusan, 1995). The first step involves negotiation. Here teachers try to "overteach" all students the skills for negotiating constructively. The intent is to keep these skills from being swamped by emotion when they will be most needed. Students learn to (a) state what they want; (b) state how they feel; (c) state the reasons for their wants and feelings; (d) summarize their understanding of the other person's wants, feelings, and reasons; (e) invent three optional plans to resolve the conflict; and (f) choose one plan and shake hands.

The second step is to teach all students how to mediate the conflicts of their peers. This means asking the students in conflict if they want to solve the problem and not proceeding until both say yes. Then the mediator explains that (a) mediation is voluntary, (b) the mediator will not try to decide who is right or wrong, only to help solve the problem, and (c) each party will have the right to air his side of the problem. The parties to the dispute must agree to solve the problem, not to call each other names, not to interrupt, to be as honest as possible, to abide by the agreement if one is reached, and to keep confidential what is said in mediation.

In step three the teacher chooses two official mediators each day, rotating the assignments throughout the class. Any conflicts students cannot resolve themselves are referred to the mediators. The Johnsons advocate booster sessions from time to time to ensure that the skills are a natural part of a student's social repertoire. Peacemaking in this fashion can help young people learn to settle differences without resorting to violence.

The connection between legal action and education aimed at ending racial strife and promoting understanding has been forged with remarkable clarity by the Southern Poverty Law Center in Montgomery, Alabama. The center publishes and distributes free copies of *Teaching Tolerance*, a magazine that describes resources and ideas to help promote harmony in the classroom.

Single-Group Studies

Single-group studies promote cultural pluralism by concentrating on individual and group contributions, emphasizing the importance of emulating the lives of outstanding people in various cultures. The intent is for young people to study the history of oppression, to feel proud of their heritage, and to recognize that human accomplishment transcends racial and cultural barriers.

Single-group approaches often address affective objectives (objectives aimed at influencing feelings, attitudes, or values), fostering appreciation and respect for other ways of life, or sometimes promoting the value of cultural relativism. In the simplest or most traditional approaches, students present or participate in activities that feature ethnic foods, dress, and customs of foreign countries. Sometimes single-group studies emphasize differences among groups to the extent that pluralism is celebrated over unity. Some curriculum reformers, for example, have taken a centrist, separatist, or particularist tack by emphasizing each of the primary ethnic/racial groups in America in separate courses. Others have advocated pluralist or infusion approaches by integrating information on these groups into all courses at all grade levels (Quality Education for Minorities Network, 1991).

Do alternative culture-based curricula encourage separatism?

Multicultural Approaches

Multicultural approaches attempt to reform education by revising curricula, integrating school staffs, and acknowledging the importance of families and family languages. Advocates of a multicultural approach "recognize, accept, and affirm human differences and similarities related to gender, race, disability, class, and (increasingly) sexual preference" (Sleeter & Grant, 1994, p. 167). In doing so, they encourage students to consider different viewpoints, drawing on content developed through single-group studies. Instructors also involve students actively in thinking about and analyzing real-life situations, attempting to make curriculum relevant to students' experiences and backgrounds. "This approach deliberately fosters equal academic achievement across groups; achievement does not take a back seat to interpersonal relationships" (Sleeter, 1993, p. 56).

Robert Moses, a civil rights activist in Mississippi in the 1960s, teaches algebra to sixth-grade African-American students in the Mississippi delta by drawing on examples from their everyday lives. A firm believer that algebra is the "gatekeeper" to the college prep math sequence, Moses uses a variety of strategies to help students succeed in school and to learn to view themselves as thinkers. He may teach the often-mysterious concept of ratios to students by contrasting rhythms of African drumbeats or by having students construct their own recipes. Or he may teach the concept of negative numbers by riding a make-believe subway and labeling the stops on the line. Kleinfeld (1995) calls this the "A Train approach" to teaching mathematics (after the A train on the New York subway system). Moses's Algebra Project methods are now used coast to coast (Chevigny, 1996).

Cultural Awareness

The Algebra Project is about more than algebra. Dave Dennis and his wife Carolyn head the project's Southern Initiative in places such as Jackson and Indianola, Mississippi.

> "We didn't develop a community structure to take ownership of the program and push it through," Dennis says. "We're learning to start with the kids. Once you get the kids, you can organize parents around their belief in them." The story of the math games proves the point. First Thelma McGee, a gently forceful teacher, invited parents to watch students perform project math games after school. Now an Indianola Math Games League Board of children and parents arrange well-attended tournaments of games like Flagway, built on the factoring of whole numbers. At an evening practice session at Merritt Middle School, I saw children physically perform and write out equations; they told me the tournaments are as thrilling as athletic events. Led to overcome their own fear of algebra, parents participate as scorekeepers, unobtrusively strengthening a culture of educational expectations. (Chevigny, 1996, p. 19)

The A Train approach is appropriate for classrooms containing any mix of ethnic groups. The basic method—drawing on children's background knowledge, incorporating it into the curriculum, and creating concrete experiences for students to think about—is universal (Kleinfeld, 1995).

■ Education That Is Multicultural and Social Reconstructionist

This general approach to educate for diversity actively challenges social inequality and seeks to restructure educational institutions ultimately to change society. According to Sleeter and Grant (1994), teachers who want to achieve these goals use students' life experiences as opportunities to discuss inequities in society. They encourage students to think critically about information in textbooks, newspapers, and other print and media sources in which classism, sexism, racism, or other social issues might be evident. Students are encouraged to consider alternative points of view and to think about ways they might work constructively to achieve social justice for all peoples.

When studying American history, for example, students might investigate how the racial category of "Other" evolved over time. They might begin by reading passages from Christopher Columbus' diary, in which he describes his encounter with the Taino Indians in the Caribbean. Through discussion, students could examine Columbus' perceptions of the Tainos and consider how his thoughts about these new peoples were influenced by European ideas and concepts. According to Banks (1996), one outcome of such a lesson would be to help students understand how Columbus began to think of the Tainos as the Other, "thus forming the basis for Indians to be perceived as a different and inferior race from Western Europeans" (p. 81).

Discussion of excerpts from Columbus' diary could serve as the springboard from which students move on to other activities. For instance, students might draw parallels to views of "others" in their extended families, or in the larger society, who have been characterized in specific ways. Teachers might then encourage students to speculate about personal, social, and civic activities in which they could engage to alter prevailing conceptions of these "others" to create a more democratic and just society.

How do Curriculum Standards Influence Multicultural Education?

The debate about multicultural education is neither new nor faddish. It is part of the larger, continuing dialogue about the meaning of *e pluribus unum*. As one country composed of many states and many peoples, the nation continues to struggle to define itself. How is America to conceptualize and deliver a public education that is appropriate for all of its people? This question arises in many forms and many languages in political forums, churches, social organizations, and schools across the country.

What standards should be applied to multicultural curricular reform?

The appropriateness of multicultural education content and methods is defined most often at national and state levels. National and state initiatives related to multicultural education are numerous and varied. Donna Gollnick (1995) notes that both federal and state education laws are most often concerned with protecting the rights of cultural and ethnic minorities. This legislation is designed, however, to ensure equal educational opportunity, mostly for students with disabilities and culturally diverse students rather than to promote the preparation of all students to function effectively in a culturally diverse society.

At the federal level, this has meant focusing on providing equal educational opportunities for female students, students of different races, LEP students, students from low-income families, and students with disabilities. At the state level, Gollnick notes that 35 states have regulations or policies related to ethnicity, race, class, gender, and other cultural groups. Forty states require schools and/or teacher education programs to include in their curricula the study of one or more ethnic groups, human relations, cultural diversity, multicultural education, and bilingual education.

Through their professional literature, programs, and publications, national educational associations encourage attention to multicultural education, equity, and educational opportunity by advocating direct educational intervention at all levels of the public education system. National accreditation standards for teacher education programs and national certification programs for teachers also acknowledge the importance of multicultural education.

James Banks's (1997) levels of integrating ethnic content into elementary and high school curricula offer a practical guide that teachers might use to judge multicultural approaches (see Figure 8.3). Banks envisions a taxonomy of approaches to multicultural curricular reform, in which the lowest level is represented by "The Contributions Approach" and the highest level is "The Action Approach."

When standards are applied at the local level, the results can stimulate controversy. One of the more visible and controversial attempts to alter whole programs to reflect concern for multicultural education was undertaken by the state of New York. The New York State Social Studies Review and Development Committee (1991) was charged by the New York Commissioner of Education to develop criteria for review of the social studies curriculum, to examine curriculum models showing special promise, and to assess existing syllabi for effectiveness and recommend changes in content, form, or emphasis. Once this was accomplished, the committee was to assist the state education department in the development of changes in syllabi, instructional materials, and staff development.

Upon review, the committee found the syllabi "to contain insensitive language, to draw upon too narrow a range of culturally diverse contexts, and to omit content specific to some groups and areas of the world" (p. 7). The committee advocated a complete overhaul of the social studies curriculum to remedy what they viewed as a series of related needs including the needs for multiple perspectives; for understanding indigenous social, political, economic, and technological structures and the precolonial histories of indigenous peoples; for viewing effects as bidirectional instead of unidirectional (with the European-American participants as the actors); for eliminating language insensitivity; for expanding the range of examples used in teaching; and for encouraging educationally appropriate assessment. The continuing national debate about the formulation of history standards suggests that disagreements such as those in New York will not be settled easily.

◾ Accountability Issues

Multicultural education—education that promotes equity for all students—is subject to the same assessment questions that any educational

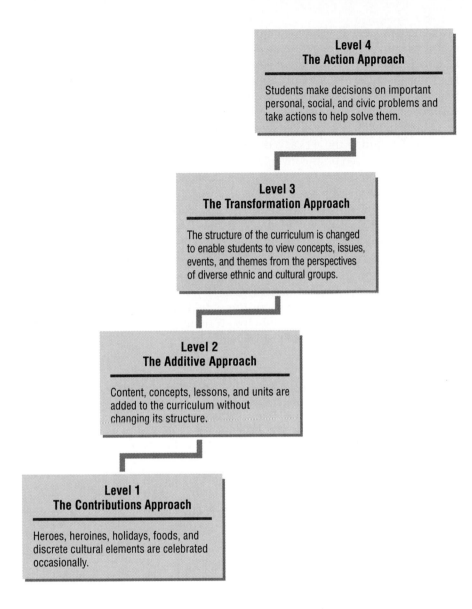

Level 4
The Action Approach

Students make decisions on important personal, social, and civic problems and take actions to help solve them.

Level 3
The Transformation Approach

The structure of the curriculum is changed to enable students to view concepts, issues, events, and themes from the perspectives of diverse ethnic and cultural groups.

Level 2
The Additive Approach

Content, concepts, lessons, and units are added to the curriculum without changing its structure.

Level 1
The Contributions Approach

Heroes, heroines, holidays, foods, and discrete cultural elements are celebrated occasionally.

FIGURE 8.3

Banks's Approaches to Multicultural Curricular Reform

How is Banks' model similar to and different from the five approaches to multicultural education identified by Sleeter and Grant? (See Figure 8.2.)

Note. From "Approaches to Multi-cultural Curriculum Reform" by J.A. Banks, 1997. In J.A. Banks and C.A. Banks (Eds.), *Multicultural Education: Issues and Perspectives*, p. 233, Boston: Allyn & Bacon.

approach must answer: What does it cost; that is, what human and material resources are devoted to multicultural education efforts? What happens during the conduct of educational activities? And what are the outcomes of multicultural educational efforts?

Answers to these questions are judged acceptable or unacceptable by comparing them to program claims, to some other competing program, or to standards that describe what might be expected of any educational effort. Useless answers come in response to the inappropriate question, "Is multicultural education effective?" Useful answers about the overall worth of multicultural education, those that can be fairly judged, come in response to the appropriate question, "Are multicultural programs effective compared to other programs and compared to the goals they were designed to achieve?"

People commonly rely on standardized test scores to judge educational programs, and, through the years, minority-group students have not fared as well on such tests as have majority-group students. There has been considerable within-group variation, however. Overall, the scores of members of minority groups have increased. As Table 8.2 indicates, members of minority groups capitalized on educational opportunities in ways that many had not in the past. Their continued participation is key to learning.

Is multicultural education effective?

Many other outcomes, however, could be examined to judge the efficacy of multicultural programs. These can be as conveniently and inexpensively acquired as test scores, and they can be extremely useful. For example, high-quality paper-and-pencil measures of student satisfaction with programs and with school generally can be obtained and tracked over time. These can be supplemented with interviews of students, parents, and staff to determine what they do and do not like about multicultural offerings. One also could examine figures on school attendance, dropouts, and participation in extracurricular activities to infer program efficacy. The more these assessments reflect real life in the larger, more inclusive culture outside school, the better. Multicultural education succeeds when it helps students use what they have learned in school in other settings and with other people.

Alternative Curriculum and Instruction

In addition to fostering the development of multicultural curricula, diversity issues in education have led to the creation of alternative curricula.

TABLE 8.2   Changes in SAT Scores, by Racial/Ethnic Group
Which two groups showed the greatest improvement in SAT scores between 1975 and 1995?

SAT composite (verbal and math) scores

Group	1975	1995	Point difference
African Americans	686	744	+58
Native Americans	808	850	+42
Asian Americans	932	956	+24
Mexican Americans	781	802	+21
Puerto Ricans	765	783	+8
Whites	944	946	+2
All students	903	910	+7

Note. From *Digest of Education Statistics* (32nd ed.) (p. 127) U.S. Department of Education, 1996, Washington, DC: U.S. Government Printing Office.

In Atlanta, Georgia, for example, nearly all schools and 80% of teachers are using at least some **Afrocentric curricula** (Cooper, 1992), which emphasize African history and culture and the role of African Americans in the making of our nation (Asante, 1991; Y. Winn, personal communication, October 9, 1996). Afrocentrism is intended to counteract bias in books and curricula that are viewed as Eurocentric or that focus exclusively on Europe as the cradle of American civilization.

Afrocentric curricula infuse academic material with cultural examples meant to build students' knowledge and pride. Teachers and students may solve math problems in Swahili, read African folktales, or teach African and African-American history. An example of an Afrocentric approach is found at the Westside Preparatory School in Chicago, a private school founded by African-American teacher and administrator Marva Collins. To counter what she perceives as public schools' low expectations of African-American students, Collins gives high priority to intellectual rigor in her program (Villegas, 1991).

Collins's classroom is organized like a traditional African family, in which the members cooperate with one another, assume collective responsibility for their actions, and are governed by strong adult leadership (Hollins, 1982). Students cooperate instead of compete with each other as in many American public school classrooms. Collins takes charge of curriculum and teaching, but students function autonomously within the structure she provides, knowing the potential consequences of their actions.

Collins links home and school through the use of interaction patterns found in the African-American church. She promotes choral and responsive reading, audience participation, the use of analogies, and the derivation of morals from readings. In so doing, she fosters what might be characterized as "culturally responsive pedagogy."

Cultural Awareness

The All Nations Alliance for Minority Participation (AMP) is an association of 55 educational institutions spanning nine states (Kansas, Michigan, Minnesota, Montana, Nebraska, North Dakota, South Dakota, Washington, and Wisconsin). (See Figure 8.4.)

The overall goal of this alliance is to increase the representation of Native Americans in college degree programs in science, mathematics, engineering, and technology (SMET). Participating Tribal Colleges develop and implement project activities, recruit and select students, track student progress, maintain a comprehensive telecommunications network, establish retention programs, and provide student support services. The AMP integrates input from both the Native-American community and the SMET community to enhance matriculation of Native-American students from high school to college, from two-year colleges to four-year institutions, and from four-year institutions to graduate programs in SMET fields.

FIGURE 8.4

All Nations AMP Alliance Map

The All Nations AMP is an alliance of 55 institutions, spanning nine states: Kansas, Michigan, Minnesota, Montana, Nebraska, North Dakota, South Dakota, Wisconsin, and Washington. For more information on the AMP visit the home page of Salish Kootenai College (**http://skcweb.skc.edu/ skcinfo.html**).

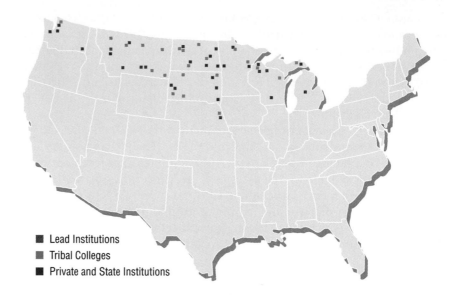

■ Lead Institutions
■ Tribal Colleges
■ Private and State Institutions

Making minority cultures the focus of a curriculum extends to other minority groups as well, as Native Americans and others have given increased attention to their traditional ways of life.

Critics claim that alternative curricula can lead to education that is exclusionary. In its extreme form, for example, Afrocentric education has led to the founding of special schools or academies for African-American males. The Matthew A. Henson School in Baltimore, Maryland, opened in 1989 on the premise that an African-American male teacher "could be a positive role model for black boys who may come from female-headed households and may know black men only as drug dealers and idlers on the street corners" (Cooper, 1992). Attempts to start whole schools for African-American boys in Milwaukee, Wisconsin, and Detroit, Michigan were criticized as both sexist and separatist, however. In Detroit a U.S. District Court judge ruled that the intentional creation of a race-segregated school or class violates existing federal civil rights law.

Other Controversies Concerning Multicultural Education

Education for diversity often sparks disagreement and debate, especially on issues concerning which groups are to be identified as cultures, included in multicultural curricula, or educated separately in alternative or magnet schools. Consider, for example, New York City's controversial Harvey Milk School, opened in 1985 as the first and only high school in the nation for gay and lesbian youth. The school is jointly funded by the board of education and the Hetrick-Martin Institute, a nonprofit organization offering counseling and other services to homosexual youth. Named for Harvey Milk, the gay San Francisco supervisor murdered in 1978, the school is fully accredited and run through the board's Alternative High Schools and Programs division. The school is meant to provide an environment free from violence where gay and lesbian youth can work and learn with adults and peers who will not judge them by their sexual orientation. In 1996 the school had nearly 50 students enrolled.

Gay and lesbian issues seem to draw particularly vehement attacks. When the National Education Association passed a resolution in support of Lesbian and Gay History Month, a group called the Concerned Women for America (CWA) placed advertisements in newspapers around the country, condemning the NEA's action. They billed the resolution as a "threat to morality and decency." CWA's language was so strong that two newspapers in which the ads appeared later apologized for running inappropriate statements (Ponessa, 1995).

Initiatives such as the Harvey Milk School and the NEA resolution have been perceived by some people as responses to narrow and partisan interests in society. African-American historian Shelby Steele (1990) argues that a power base, a "new sovereignty," has been organized around the grievances of some interest groups. In higher education, for example, according to Steele, African Americans, women, Hispanic Americans, Native Americans, Asian Americans, gays, and lesbians press their agendas as "victims" of a racist, sexist, homophobic society to their own and to others' detriment. Separate dormitories, preferential admissions, campus study centers, fiscal aid policies, and faculty hiring quotas, Steele argues, make people concentrate on attributes such as skin color or sexual orientation first, before they assess the content of their own or others' characters.

While those for and against multicultural education wage rhetorical war, some have opined that multiculturalism is a "middle-class movement," largely irrelevant to life in inner-city schools. According to these opponents, the middle class and privileged have the luxury to consider such issues, because they do not have to suffer the indignities of a life unprotected by money:

> [A]dvocates who put their faith for saving the schools in a multicultural social studies program are as mistaken as those who think multiculturalism means the end of Western Civilization. . . . What most teachers need, more than workshops on diversity, are basic supplies—glue, paper, crayons. (Mosle, 1993).

Barbara Sizemore, former superintendent of the Washington, D.C., public schools and dean of the School of Education at Depaul University, warns educators who alter curriculum to teach diversity not to lower their standards.

> What African children who live in poverty need most, she insists, is a highly structured school with firm discipline that is focused on teaching them to take and pass standardized tests. Sizemore . . . is fond of pointing out that students must score 1040 on their SATs to even be considered for admission to her school (Bradley, 1996, p. 36).

Some people believe that efforts to encourage openness to and acceptance of multicultural approaches to teaching and learning have themselves become closed and doctrinaire, yielding what is popularly termed "political correctness." The debate on this point has focused mainly on teaching and learning in higher education, but the issue is as important for elementary and high school teachers, if not more so (Phillips, 1993). John Searle (1993) argues that extreme proponents of multiculturalism often demand that people choose sides in the debate about the place of various cultures in our society, when we should be helping students to understand different positions and accommodate different ideas. Searle also criticizes multiculturalists for focusing on moral and social issues, thereby distracting people from practical problems, such as adequately funding the programs proposed and finding the time to add, integrate, and deliver the new curricula. The questions remain: What content is most important for students to learn? What standards should be applied for the inclusion and exclusion of content? Who is to decide what stays and what goes?

> **Has multiculturalism become just another form of political correctness?**

And so goes the debate, often with little regard for the many ways multicultural education is defined in practice. The challenge has been and continues to be one of finding ways to help all children succeed—not just separately, but together—and to appreciate one another in the process.

SUMMARY

How does diversity affect education in America?

1 The population in the United States is quite diverse. The language of diversity, or the words people use to describe others, is characterized by terms relating to race, ethnicity, culture, and minority status. These classification systems often are arbitrary, ambiguous, and changeable.

2 Three factors often influence positive relations in schools: the quality of teachers' relationships with students, the quality of education, and the social skills teachers impart to students. When teachers and students are mismatched by culture their difference in values can contribute to misunderstanding and frustration on both sides.

3 The term "culture" can be used in a macro sense to communicate the sum of the learned characteristics of a group. In a micro sense "culture" can describe conceptually discrete groups of people or cultures within cultures. There often is as much variation among members of a group as there is variation between groups.

4 Cultural identity and group membership are self-selected by families and individuals. Labels are harmful when they fuel prejudice, justify discrimination, and lead to lowered expectations.

How do cultural and ethnic factors influence educational opportunities?

5 Immigrants' experiences before coming to the United States vary widely and differ from those of non-immigrant minorities. Teachers' knowledge of and

BENCHMARKS

Peak Immigration of Selected Groups as Sources of American Cultural Diversity (1800–2000)

Colonial Era & Early Republic	Spanish, French, English, Dutch, Portuguese, African slaves.
1800–1860	Germans, Irish, African slaves, English, Swedes, Danes, Norwegians, Dutch, Belgians, Swiss, French. Peak immigration of people from western and northern Europe. One million Irish immigrate to the United States between 1847 and 1860. In 1854, Germans compose 50% of all immigrants.
1860–1880	Chinese, Poles, Russians, Hungarians, Serbs, Austrians, Scandinavians, Italians, Greeks, Canadians. By 1880, 4 of 5 New Yorkers are foreign born or first-generation American.
1880–1900	Japanese, Italians, Poles, Russians, Slovaks, Magyars, Czechs, Croats, Greeks. Four million Russians and Poles and 4.5 million Italians immigrate to the United States during these years.
1900–1930	Mexicans, Latin Americans, Canadians, Italians, Russians, Poles. Period of peak immigration from eastern and southern Europe. Puerto Ricans become U.S. citizens in 1917.
1930–1960	Cubans, Mexicans, Koreans. Period of peak relocation of Puerto Ricans. In the 1940s and 1950s, 3.5 million refugees come to the United States from all countries affected by World War II.
1960–2000	Vietnamese, Cambodians, Laotians, Thais, Guatemalans, and other groups from Central and South American countries, Ethiopians, Haitians.

attitudes toward immigrant students can influence their educational experiences in the United States.

6 For students whose first language is not English, language can be a formidable barrier in U.S. schools. Assessing the progress of limited-English-proficient students is difficult because there are no standard criteria.

7 Often students with limited English proficiency receive help in the form of bilingual education. Programs vary greatly in terms of the amount of English taught, and the speed with which English is introduced.

How do educators define and implement multicultural education?

8 There is much confusion about the meaning of multicultural education, yet there is emerging consensus among specialists that multicultural education is a reform movement designed to bring about educational equity for all students from different races, ethnic groups, social classes, abilities, and genders.

9 Multicultural educational approaches have been defined in five ways: (a) teaching the culturally different; (b) human relations; (c) single-group studies; (d) multicultural education; and (e) education that is multicultural and social reconstructionist.

How do curricular standards influence multicultural education?

10 The appropriateness of multicultural education is defined most often at national and state levels in education standards and in legislation meant to provide equal educational opportunities.

11 James Banks has identified four levels of integrating ethnic content into school curricula that can be used to evaluate multicultural education: contributions, additive, transformation, and action approaches.

12 Many outcomes have been used to judge the efficacy of multicultural education—standardized test scores, student satisfaction, school attendance, dropout rates, and participation in extracurricular activities.

13 Education for diversity often sparks disagreement and debate. Critics contend that multicultural education is irrelevant to life in inner-city schools, lowers performance standards, encourages people to choose sides rather than helping them understand points of view, and overloads the curriculum.

14 Most people agree that multicultural education presents opportunities for educators to seek ways for all children to succeed and to appreciate each other in the process.

TERMS AND CONCEPTS

Afrocentric curriculum, *p. 321*
bilingual education, *p. 309*
conflict mediation, *p. 314*
cultural pluralism, *p. 297*
culture, *p. 300*
discrimination, *p. 304*
English as a Second Language (ESL), *p. 309*

ethnicity, *p. 298*
ethnocentric, *p. 297*
Limited English Proficient (LEP), *p. 309*
minority, *p. 306*
multicultural education, *p. 312*
race, *p. 298*

REFLECTIVE PRACTICE

Teachers in the multicultural resource team at Columbus Elementary School—a public school in Columbus, New Mexico—discuss their work concerning parent involvement, family values, and multicultural education (Herbert & McNergney,

1996). Team members work with classroom teachers to enrich multicultural studies in the curriculum. Their school is unusual in that it serves children who live in the United States and children who live in Mexico. Columbus Elementary School is located in a small farming community 3 miles from the United States/Mexico border. As you read the account below, imagine why and how teachers "categorize" the people with whom they work and what effects such categorizations might have on teaching and learning.

CONSUELA: [*Describes parent education program.*] Our parents are coming to visit the computer lab now for ESL at night. I didn't think it was going to work, because some of the parents don't know how to read at all, and this requires some reading. But they don't even want to take a break.

OTHERS: Uh huh. . . . Parents love those computers.

MARIO: They don't even take a break. I know that Consuela tells them, "Okay, time to take a break. She has to tell them a couple of times."

CONSUELA: In both cultures, education is seen as something that is a necessity for the future.

OPHELIA: Education is a little bit different here. . . .

CONSUELA: I think that Anglo parents' expectation of a student is to excel, excel, excel in anything they do. This is from day one.

OPHELIA: The Mexican family, and I don't know if it is true any more, but their expectation is to just get enough education so they can go out there and work. Maybe it is changing a little bit. But in the United States, it is all college-bound. That is all you think . . . college, college.

CONSUELA: It is very evident too that the parents in Mexico take responsibility for the behavior or discipline part of the child's education. In the United States, a lot of parents say while students are in school, you teach them how to behave, you teach them what is right and what is wrong, all of that. In Mexico, I feel that is quite a bit different. Parents expect the child to come to school to learn subject matter. Discipline and behavior patterns are definitely the responsibility of the parent, but mostly of the mother.

Multicultural education takes advantage of a child's language. It is an asset to be able to speak a child's language, because the teacher can get so much more participation from the student if she can relate to the language.

Issues, Problems, Dilemmas, and Opportunities

What problems can arise when teachers expect too little/too much from students and their parents?

Perceive and Value

According to these teachers, how are Mexican/Hispanic and Anglo families similar? How are they different?

Know and Act

According to some of the models of multicultural education described in the chapter, what are some effective ways to integrate students of different cultures into schools? If you were going to teach in Columbus Elementary School and you were not bilingual or bicultural, what sort of information might you want about the students, the school, and the community? Where or from whom might you seek such information? What might you do to encourage parental participation?

Evaluate

One way to think about assessing education is to examine the resources, processes, and outcomes of education. Assume that you teach in a school on the border between the United States and Mexico and you are expected to provide an education for your students that is multicultural. What human and material resources might be useful? What learning activities would you provide, and what student outcomes would you encourage?

ONLINE ACTIVITY

Explore the following ESL site on the Web: **http://www.lang.uiuc.edu/r-li5/esl/**, and locate, for example, "Learning Oral English Online," an online conversation book for intermediate ESL learners. To learn more about multicultural education online, visit the Pathways to School Improvement project (**http://www.ncrel.org/sdrs/pathwayg.htm**) and search on the phrase "multicultural education." You will find a list of articles recommended by different educators that address both the problems and the possibilities of various approaches to multicultural education.

9

Students and Learning

It takes more than ideas, enthusiasm, and love of children to be a successful educator. To create educational environments that work, teachers need to understand young people in ways that inform teaching. This means teachers must study students—read about, think about, and discuss what others have written about students, and perhaps most important, listen to the students themselves.

In chapters 7 and 8, we discussed the types of problems students face and the influence of culture on their lives. In this chapter we focus on ways students are alike and different. Specifically, we describe students in terms of intelligence, cognitive development and academic achievement, moral development, physical development, and "habits of mind"—the shared skills, attitudes, and values transmitted by custom or convention from one generation to the next.

Each person is unique yet like all other people in many ways. Successful teachers understand this maxim and try to learn as much as they can about their students. If teachers want students to make sense of the world around them, to begin to construct knowledge for themselves as they are compelled to do in life, teachers must try to understand the needs of students both generally and individually. Students often suggest, in their own voices, how teachers can be most helpful.

PROFESSIONAL PRACTICE QUESTIONS

1 How do students' intellectual abilities influence learning and teaching?

2 How do perceptions of student learning influence teaching?

3 How do physical and psychosocial development affect children's learning?

4 How does moral development influence learning and teaching?

5 How do students' habits of mind influence learning and teaching?

6 How does gender influence learning and teaching?

7 How do student exceptionalities influence teaching and learning?

HOW DO STUDENTS' INTELLECTUAL ABILITIES INFLUENCE LEARNING AND TEACHING?

As Figure 9.1 shows, intelligence is one of several characteristics of students as learners. Robert Sternberg and Douglas Detterman's (1986) analysis of 24 descriptions of intelligence by leading experts in the field identifies many competing ideas about the nature of intelligence. Intelligence has been defined as a single, general trait and as a multidimensional set of traits that varies from time to time and from situation to situation. Intelligence also has been defined as "error-free transmission" of information through the cortex of the brain and as one's repertoire of intellectual knowledge and skills available at a particular point in time. In another definition intelligence is the combination of cognitive skills and knowledge demanded, fostered, and rewarded by one's particular culture.

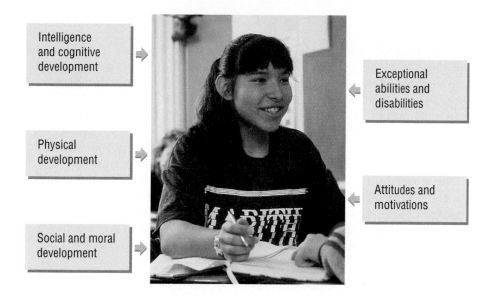

Intelligence and cognitive development

Physical development

Social and moral development

Exceptional abilities and disabilities

Attitudes and motivations

FIGURE 9.1

Some Domains of Student Characteristics

Why is each domain of student characteristics important to you as a teacher?

Psychometric Perspective

Those who view intelligence from a **psychometric perspective** believe that intellectual aptitude can be measured with tests. Measurement is conducted by administering a number of tasks, observing responses to these tasks, and inferring intellectual capabilities from examinees' performances. Efforts to quantify aptitudes in this fashion began in the late 1800s, when Sir Francis Galton (1822–1911) devised a series of tests of reaction time and sensory acuity to assess adults' mental ability. By the early 1890s Alfred Binet (1857–1911) and Theophile Simon (1873–1961) of France had developed intelligence tests designed to discriminate between more and less able students. Test items assessed intellectual abilities such as attention, verbal comprehension, and reasoning.

When Binet's tests were brought to the United States, translated, and revised for use with American children and adults, his detailed profiles of performance across a variety of measures were replaced with a single score, or **intelligence quotient (IQ)**. IQ scores were calculated by dividing an individual's mental age by his chronological age and multiplying the result by 100. Thus, IQ test scores compared individual mental ability to average mental abilities for other people of the same age.

What do intelligence tests measure, a single, general capacity or a combination of multiple abilities? Charles Spearman (1927) studied intelligence tests and determined that there was a "general factor," or g, that all tests shared. He defined g as a general ability to form abstract relationships.

How should intelligence be defined?

More recently, J. P. Guilford (1988), Howard Gardner (1993; 1995), and Robert Sternberg (1988) have argued that there are many cognitive abilities, each slightly different from the next, that constitute one's intellectual ability. Guilford suggests that mental operations (ways of thinking), contents (what people think about), and products (results of thinking) define more and less intelligent people. Gardner contends that individuals possess **multiple intelligences** that include seven types of capacities and abilities: linguistic (verbal), logical-mathematical, musical, spatial, bodily, knowledge of self, and understanding of others. In his triarchic theory of intelligence, Sternberg argues that intelligence is determined by the degree to which individuals demonstrate three processes: metacomponents (mental processes used to plan), performance components (processes used to execute a task), and knowledge-acquisition components (processes used to learn how to solve problems). All three theorists contend that people differ in the strength of these intelligences and in the ways that multiple intelligences are invoked and combined to perform tasks and to solve problems. In recent years, however, Howard Gardner has expressed concerns about inappropriate applications of his work to classroom practice. After viewing videotapes from teachers trying out his ideas, Gardner spoke out:

> One of the things that drove me bananas in these tapes was to have kids crawling around the floor aimlessly and calling it bodily/kinesthetic intelligence. Exercise, of course, is not a bad thing, but random muscular movements have nothing to do with the cultivation of the mind. (Viadero, 1996, p. 24)

Other concerns in the psychometric perspective have to do with the origins of intelligence. Is intellectual ability a result of one's biological inheritance or the product of one's environment? In other words, are people born with their intellectual abilities (endowed with them by nature), or are such abilities nurtured (developed by education and life's experiences)? Although it is impossible to answer the question with certainty, most experts agree that intellectual ability is a product of both nature and nurture. Many studies of twins who have been reared apart show that although genetic factors are strong predictors of intellectual functioning, other influences on intellectual ability, such as parenting and education, cannot be ignored (Bouchard, Lykken, McGue, Segal, & Tellegen, 1990).

Intellectual ability is certainly critical to one's academic success, but family income is also a powerful determinant of intellectual ability, particularly among young children. An analysis of longitudinal data from the Infant Health and Development Program, an eight-site study of low-birthweight babies that was launched in the 1980s, revealed that family income correlates more strongly with IQ at age 5 than do such factors as mother's education, child's ethnicity, or the fact that a child lives in a home headed by a woman. Among the sample of 900 low-birthweight children studied, those living in persistent poverty from birth had IQs about 9 points lower than did those who were not living in poverty during their first few years of life (Cohen, 1993).

Is there a "cognitive elite" in our society?

Intelligence test scores, estimates of scholastic aptitude, and measures of general ability are widely considered good predictors of success in school and in the workplace, yet some people contend that test scores tell us relatively little about intelligence and even less about a person's creativity, wisdom, and intellectual style (Sternberg, 1996). Critics argue that tests unfairly restrict opportunities for growth and advancement (Hilliard, 1990). Employers who have worked with individuals with IQ scores below 100, for example, have found that low-scorers' abilities extend beyond what IQ scores predict (Ceci & Ruiz, 1993).

Robert Sternberg (1996) warns that in society's confusion over concepts of intelligence and desire for simplicity, psychologists and other writers have sometimes taken extreme positions not justified by theory or research. He is especially critical of Richard Herrnstein and Charles Murray's (1994) book *The Bell Curve* in which the authors contend that differences in intelligence have resulted in the formation of a "cognitive elite."

> It is always tempting to value most what we ourselves possess—and, in the process, to scapegoat other groups. It is happening in ethnic wars around the world. And one might argue it happens when Herrnstein and Murray (1994) cheerfully note that most readers of their book are members of the cognitive elite and other elite groups. We need to remember that over time and space, those at the higher rather than the lower end of the various intellectual spectra have been those most likely to be persecuted or scapegoated. However it is defined, intelligence is only one attribute of human beings and one attribute leading to certain kinds of success, but tests of intelligence can at best provide measures of certain cognitive skills (Keating, 1984); they are not measures of human worth. (Sternberg, 1996, p. 15)

Informal Perceptions of Intelligence

Interviews with 71 first, third, and sixth graders suggest that young children think of intelligence as something we are born with, whereas older children believe that experiences are a major determinant of intelligence. Many children also think that the amount of knowledge people have makes the difference between more and less intelligent people (Yussen & Kane, 1985). Other studies indicate that young people conceptualize ability as either fixed or fluid. Those who think that intelligence is fixed are vulnerable to learned helplessness, especially when their confidence is low. Those who think that intelligence is changeable are more willing to take risks and are more resilient when unsuccessful at tasks (Elliott & Dweck, 1988). Such beliefs may be modified through instruction (Bempechat, London, & Dweck, 1991).

Intelligence, however defined, is an important concept for teachers and students. Teachers' perceptions of mental ability and the learning environment they create can greatly affect students' attitudes about themselves as learners and their success in school. Teachers who think of intelligence as a fixed entity may characterize children as "fast" or "slow" learners based on test scores, feedback from their other teachers, or their performance in class. Those children who fall into the "slow" track may find it difficult to climb out. Even if they show improvement on learning tasks, these children may not receive recognition for their achievements and may give up on schoolwork.

On the other hand, teachers who view intelligence as a multifaceted, malleable capacity use estimates of it not only as predictors of success but also as dynamic capacities to be changed. Teachers having such a view are more likely to use multiple methods of assessing achievement rather than to rely on standardized tests and normative comparisons of students. When teachers treat students as intelligent people, students often rise to the occasion.

How do perceptions of student learning influence teaching?

Other theorists and researchers reject the study of intelligence and concentrate instead on learning as a function of children's cognitive development or as a function of the mental processes involved in thinking, remembering, and problem solving. These approaches try to explain not how intelligent people are but how they think and learn. Theories about **cognitive development**—or changes in children's mental abilities as they mature—and theories about **information processing**—or processes by which information is received, analyzed, stored, retrieved, and used—in turn affect what and how children are taught.

Developmental Perspectives

Teachers need to be aware of how students' perceptions of the world change from infancy to adolescence. Theories of cognitive development are based on the work of Jean Piaget (1896–1980), a Swiss psychologist whose lifework was understanding how children at different ages perceive and know the world around them. Piaget believed that children are born with the potential to develop intelligence and that the increasing complexity of children's thinking as they age is caused both by maturational changes in the nervous system and by direct experience as children interact with the physical world and with other people. Changes in cognitive development are based on the child's ability to change her ways of thinking about the world when existing ideas do not match new information and experience.

To explain how children perceive and structure reality at different points in their development, Piaget categorized children's ways of thinking into four qualitatively different stages: sensorimotor (birth to 2 years), preoperational (2 to 7 years), concrete operational (7 to 11 years), and formal operational (11 to 16 years). (See Table 9.1.)

According to Piaget, children may progress through the stages at different rates, but the order in which they do so remains constant. Decisions about a child's stage cannot be made on the basis of age alone, however. Children demonstrate inconsistencies in thinking; that is, a child may demonstrate one level of thinking in one situation and a different level of thinking in another.

TABLE 9.1   Piaget's Stages of Cognitive Development

Age	Stage	Characteristics
0–2	Sensorimotor	Learn primarily through the senses and strongly affected by the immediate environment.
		Begin to follow objects with eyes (visual pursuit).
		Begin to realize objects still exist, even though they are out of sight.
		Movement from reflex actions to goal-directed activities.
2–7	Preoperational	Vocabulary development, especially the ability to understand and use words, increases.
		Tendency to talk at rather than with others.
		Ideas begin to replace concrete experience.
		Have difficulty realizing the reversible nature of relationships.
7–11	Concrete Operational	Ability to solve problems logically through the use of hands-on materials.
		Understand reversible nature of relationships.
		Can classify objects according to color, size, etc.
		Can arrange objects in sequence according to such attributes as size and weight.
		Literal minded.
11–16	Formal Operational	Solve abstract problems in logical fashion.
		Able to hypothesize.
		Can reflect on their ways of thinking.
		Aware that people see and think about situations and ideas differently.

Note: From *Educational Psychology: A Developmental Approach, Fifth Edition* (pp. 102–113) by N. A. Sprinthall & R. C. Sprinthall, 1990, New York: McGraw-Hill, Inc. Used with permission of McGraw-Hill.

Cultural Awareness

Piaget's stage theory does not account for the effects of individual differences such as gender, personality, intelligence (as measured by IQ tests), or culture on students' cognitive development. Although Piagetians contend that the four developmental stages are universal, there is evidence that formal operations, the highest level of thinking, is attained by few adolescents, college students, or adults in the United States, Africa, or Europe (Mwamwenda, 1992). In some non-Western cultures that do not focus on abstract thinking, formal operational thought as defined by Piaget is not present. How quickly children move through the different stages also varies by culture, depending on environmental conditions. According to one researcher, children in Martinique, an island in the West Indies, were 4 years later developing operational thought than were their counterparts in Switzerland. In Tehran, the capital of Iran, children developed similarly to children in Switzerland, but in the rural villages of Iran, children developed 2 years later. (Sutherland, 1992)

The development of cognitive abilities from one stage to another therefore depends strongly on children's interaction with their environment. Classroom applications of the principles of cognitive development include the teacher creating a learning-oriented environment and acting as a facilitator, rather than a director, of students' learning. This might mean, for example, providing opportunities for concrete operational learners to manipulate objects and symbols as an aid to acquiring concepts and skills. **Developmentally appropriate instruction** is the term given to teaching practices based on an awareness of learners' stages of development.

How do cultural factors affect cognitive development?

While Piaget minimized the importance of systematic teaching, other theorists gave more importance to teacher–learner interaction in specific learning contexts. Lev Semenovich Vygotsky (1896–1934), a Russian psychologist, was an influential proponent of the view that stage theories of intellectual development, such as Piaget's, are too limiting (Berg, 1992). According to Vygotsky, rather than focusing on a child's present abilities, teaching should lead development forward to new abilities (Davydov, 1995).

Vygotsky argued that teachers—whether professionals, other adults, or older or more competent peers—are critical in stimulating learners' development. Children need to talk with and listen to others to develop intellectually (Sutherland, 1992). More able "teachers" support learners by assisting them when they are at the threshold of acquiring a new skill or ability. Assistance might be in the form of a demonstration, hint, probing question, or problem-solving strategy. This process of interactive assistance at critical times during learning has come to be known as **scaffolding**.

Information-Processing Perspectives

Cognitive science is a term used for perspectives on learning that focus on information processing rather than on human development. These perspectives have their roots in the physical sciences, systems theory, and computer technology. Researchers in information processing study observable behaviors—such as reaction times to stimuli, verbal recognition, recall of previous learning, and performance on memory tasks and problem-solving tasks—to understand how thinking occurs and how it can be enhanced.

Classroom applications of information-processing perspectives include the direct instruction of thinking skills and problem-solving strategies; among these, methods for directing and monitoring one's own thinking. Teachers help students develop and use these **metacognitive skills** by teaching them, for example, memory strategies, self-questioning scripts, and procedures to follow when they are having difficulty comprehending written material.

An example of a successful program for improving students' thinking skills is called HOTS (Higher Order Thinking Skills), developed by Stanley Pogrow of the University of Arizona. HOTS, a compensatory program for disadvantaged students in grades 4 through 7, is used in more than 2,000 schools in 49 states (Pogrow, 1995). The 2-year program provides scripted computer- and teacher-led activities that help students understand how to understand, using probing questions designed to stimulate students to analyze, apply, evaluate, and synthesize information.

HOW DO PHYSICAL AND PSYCHOSOCIAL DEVELOPMENT AFFECT CHILDREN'S LEARNING?

Children's patterns of physical, psychological, and social development and their individual differences in these areas have important implications for education. Between the ages of 2 and 5, preschoolers' control of their large and small muscles improves greatly. Teachers of young children optimize development of large muscles by providing a variety of activities that improve agility, strength, endurance, balance, rhythm, and speed. Teachers also incorporate diverse materials and activities, such as small-block play, clay manipulation, and puzzles to develop fine motor skills and to improve eye–hand coordination.

Some children develop abnormally because of the environments in which they live. One of the most insidious threats—lead—is present in the paint in many homes. Children who are poisoned by ingesting lead-contaminated dust and chips from lead-based paint may experience lasting developmental and health problems and, in extreme cases, comas, convulsions, mental retardation, even death (Children's Defense Fund, 1992).

VOICES

On Ways of Knowing

Harvard psychologist Jerome Bruner, a noted cognitivist, argues that there are two kinds of cognition. One is scientific, logical, and objective, undertaken to discover truth. The other is intuitive, emergent, and subjective, meant to interpret and construct life. Both have implications for teaching:

Let me begin by setting out my argument as baldly as possible. . . . There are two modes of cognitive functioning, two modes of thought, each providing distinctive ways of ordering experience, of constructing reality. . . . Efforts to reduce one mode to the other or to ignore one at the expense of the other inevitably fail to capture the rich diversity of thought.

Each of the ways of knowing, moreover, has operating principles of its own and its own criteria of well-formedness. They differ radically in their procedures for verification. A good story and a well-formed argument are different natural kinds. Both can be used as means for convincing another. Yet what they convince of is fundamentally different: arguments convince one of their truth, stories of their lifelikeness. The one verifies by eventual appeal to procedures for establishing formal and empirical proof. The other establishes not truth but verisimilitude. (1986, p. 11)

These two modes of thought, as Bruner observed, have different implications for education:

Much of the process of education consists of being able to distance oneself in some way from what one knows by being able to reflect on one's own knowledge. In most contemporary theories of cognitive development, this has been taken to mean the achievement of more abstract knowledge through Piagetian formal operations or by the use of more abstract symbolic systems. And it is doubtless true that in many spheres of knowledge, as in the sciences, one does indeed climb to "intellectually higher ground" (to use Vygotsky's phrase) by this route. One does indeed come to see arithmetic as a special case when one reaches the more abstract domain of algebra. But I think it is perilous to look at intellectual growth exclusively in this manner, for one will surely distort the meaning of intellectual maturity if one uses such a model exclusively.

The idea that any humanistic subject can be taught without revealing one's stance toward matters of human pith and substance is, of course, nonsense.

[T]he language of education, if it is to be an invitation to reflection and culture creating, cannot be the so-called uncontaminated language of fact and "objectivity." It must express stance and must invite counter-stance and in the process leave place for reflection, for metacognition. It is this that permits one to reach higher ground, this process of objectifying in language or image what one has thought and then turning around on it and reconsidering it. (pp. 128-129)

CRITICAL THINKING

What are some examples of scientific and intuitive ways of knowing? What does Bruner mean by his claim that subjects "[cannot] be taught without revealing one's stance toward matters of human pith and substance"? What are some implications of this claim for teachers? How, do you think, might teachers invite reflection and encourage students to create culture? Give some specific examples.

Note. From *Actual Minds, Possible Worlds* by Jerome Bruner, 1986, Cambridge, MA: Harvard University Press. Copyright © 1986 by the President and Fellows of Harvard College. Reprinted by permission of the publishers.

Children experience a rapid increase in both height and weight that begins at about age 8 or 9 in girls and age 10 or 11 in boys. Although boys often are taller and heavier than girls at age 10, by age 13 girls usually surpass boys in height and weight. By age 16, this trend reverses and boys are once again taller and heavier than girls. The growth spurt young people experience during early adolescence is accompanied by a series of changes in all parts of the body as they begin to develop sexually.

Although children begin their school careers very interested in sports, their desire to participate declines over time. Some argue that one reason young people's enthusiasm wanes with age is due to the emphasis placed on winning. The keen competition it takes to produce champions drives off the majority of young people, who also need opportunities to learn about fair play and chances to practice teamwork skills.

Physical Development and Psychological Well-Being

As children grow and change, their body types influence developmental task achievement, self-image, and self-satisfaction. Students who are attractive and athletic typically are popular with adults and peers and are better adjusted than are unattractive students, particularly those who are overweight. Adolescents are particularly sensitive about their physical appearance and often have unrealistic expectations for physical attractiveness. Often **self-esteem**, or the value or sense of worth an individual places on his own characteristics, abilities, and behaviors, is affected by such expectations. In particular, girls who are dissatisfied with the way they look often are self-conscious and may suffer from low self-esteem (Abramowitz, Petersen, & Schulenberg, 1984; Brooks-Gunn, Graber, & Paikoff, 1994). Many teenage girls who are unhappy with their bodies develop eating disorders. Girls who mature early exhibit more eating problems than do average- or late-maturing girls. Early-maturing girls also are at greater risk for depression (Brooks-Gunn, Graber, & Paikoff, 1994; Rierdan & Koff, 1991).

How do perceptions of physical attractiveness relate to academic success?

For the past three decades, the percentage of very overweight children has roughly doubled. For children ages 6 to 11, the incidence of being extremely overweight increased over a 30-year period from 5.2% of the population to 10.8% for boys and 10.7% for girls. For 12- to 17-year-olds, the percentage increased a similar amount, but more dramatically for boys than for girls (Lawton, 1995, p. 6).

Efforts to improve diet and exercise can make a difference in the overall health of young people. Researchers in four states studied the health and behavior of third-grade students over a 3-year period starting in 1991. They changed school lunches and physical education classes at 56 schools. By concentrating on eating habits and promoting exercise, they found that students lowered their fat and cholesterol consumption and increased their physical exercise (Lawton, 1996).

It is essential that adults be sensitive to what children do about their weight and say about their body images. Young people's comments and actions can provide valuable clues about their psychological well-being as well as about their physical health. But one must be careful when reading these clues. For example, what may appear as laziness in the behavior of students may in fact be a manifestation of poor nutrition.

Psychosocial Development

Psychosocial development refers to changes in the way an individual's social and emotional needs are met through relationships with others. Erik Erikson (1902–1994) proposed that individuals have the potential for proceeding through eight stages of personal development, five of which occur during the school years. (See Table 9.2.) Each stage involves a central developmental crisis; how well an individual deals with each crisis determines his progress through succeeding stages.

During the first stage (birth to 2 years), feelings of trust or mistrust are influenced by the quality of care and affection babies experience. Those who experience a world that is dependable and warm have a good chance of resolving the conflict and developing trust.

During the second stage, autonomy versus shame (2 to 3 years), children must establish a sense of autonomy, or ability to stand on their own two feet, or they will experience shame or doubt. How well children resolve this crisis depends on the degree to which parents talk with their children, allow them to initiate activities, support rather than criticize their early language skills, and ask questions that allow children to express their ideas and think for themselves.

The third stage, initiative versus guilt (3 to 6 years), is a time when children learn what kind of people they are, mainly with regard to gender. According to Erikson, children at this stage need to be allowed to express themselves through play without a lot of censoring, which may evoke guilt.

During the fourth stage of personal development, industry versus inferiority (6 to 12 years), children spend more hours away from home than ever before. Neighborhood and classroom cliques (almost always composed of all boys or all girls) become major socializing agents. Besides being faced with the demands of learning many school oriented skills, youngsters develop a sense of personal mastery as they engage in new games and activities. When children are not encouraged in their efforts to master their environment, or when they fail, they may develop a sense of personal inferiority.

The fifth stage of personal development, identity versus confusion, occurs during adolescence, when individuals need to develop a sense of self that will provide a firm basis for adulthood. To overcome confusion adolescents need to differentiate among feelings in self and others, distinguish between objective and subjective reality, see things from another's perspective, and distinguish between literal and symbolic meaning (Sprinthall & Sprinthall, 1990). Ironically, when adolescents first enter this stage, they become egocentric in their thinking. They also become self-conscious and vulnerable to peer pressure, particularly at the junior high school level.

When sense of self is weak, young people develop a condition termed *identity diffusion*. Having no firm direction, they wrestle mentally with who

TABLE 9.2   Erikson's Stages of Psychosocial Development

Birth to age 6:
Trust versus mistrust

Ages 2 to 3:
Autonomy versus shame and doubt

Ages 3 to 6:
Initiative versus guilt

Ages 4 to 12:
Industry versus inferiority

Adolescence (Ages 12–18):
Identity versus role confusion

Young adulthood (Ages 13–25):
Intimacy versus isolation

Ages 25 to 60:
Generativity versus stagnation

Full maturity:
Ego integrity versus despair and disgust

Note. From *Identity and the Life Cycle* (pp. 51–107) by E. H. Erikson, 1980, New York: Norton. Reprinted with the permission of W. W. Norton & Company, Inc. Copyright 1959 by International Universities Press, Inc.

they are and what they want to do with their lives. Young people who do not have satisfying social relationships may experience different degrees of loneliness. A study that examined relationships between loneliness and adolescent health behaviors in a sample of approximately 1,300 senior-high school students revealed that extreme loneliness has adverse effects on young people's health. Lonely adolescents, for example, are more prone to use marijuana than are those who are not lonely. Boys who are lonely tend to engage in fewer physical activities and are more likely to watch television for longer periods of time than are boys who are not lonely. Among females, loneliness often is associated with cigarette smoking, binge eating, purging, and crash diets (Page, 1990).

What are teachers' roles in helping students cope with psychosocial crises?

Some people argue that adolescents' weak sense of identity also can produce a tendency to engage in reckless behavior. This line of reasoning suggests that such behavior is a means of "acting out" in response to a variety of problems adolescents face, an indication of low self-esteem, or a manifestation of depression. Jeffrey Arnett (1994/1995) contends, however, that such explanations can detract our attention from the fact that some adolescents think reckless behavior is fun.

One boy whom Arnett interviewed reinforced this view by describing his adventures in an automobile:

> Ken: I love to drive fast. Going fast, you know, it stimulates you. But after a while driving fast just wasn't doing it any more, so I started driving without the lights on, going about 90 on country roads. I even got a friend to do it. We'd go cruising down country roads, turn off the lights, and just fly. It was incredible. We'd go as fast as we could, (and) at night with no lights it feels like you're just flying. (Arnett, 1994/1995 pp. 1–2)

How does moral development influence learning and teaching?

Moral development, or changes relating to age and intelligence in the way an individual makes reasoned judgments about right and wrong, has always been a concern of public schools. Despite disagreement over the meaning of the term, educators' goal has been to produce good people. Historically, programs in the United States have been structured to help students achieve a kind of American character—the particular variety of which was described early on by Horace Mann in terms of "veracity, probity, and rectitude" (Cremin, 1957, p. 100).

Too often, as Christopher Clark observes, concepts of moral development have been used by adults to describe children's shortcomings. Clark challenges adults to recognize that a young person's moral development depends in no small measure on the context in which the child lives—a context shaped and controlled by adults.

> Our culture of parenting and pedagogy invariably takes the side of the adult and blames the child for what has been done to him or her; for what was done to you and to me, when we were helpless children. Faced with the power of adults and the social conspiracy of denial, we and our children repress our feelings, idealize or excuse those parents and teachers who abused us, and, tragically, perpetuate the victimization of the next generation. (1995, p. 24)

Stages of Moral Development

Character development and moral education have grown less absolute, less propagandistic, and more aligned with students' development. Beginning with his doctoral studies at the University of Chicago and proceeding through his career on the faculty at Harvard, Lawrence Kohlberg (1927–1987) shaped modern thinking about moral development and moral education. Much as Piaget described intellectual development, Kohlberg described moral reasoning in terms of six stages. (See Table 9.3)

TABLE 9.3   Erikson's Stages of Psychosocial Development

Preconventional Morality

Stage 1:   Punishment-Obedience Outlook. Decisions are made on the basis of power. People behave in ways that indicate a desire to avoid severe punishment.

Stage 2:   Personal Reward Outlook. Actions are taken to satisfy one's one personal needs. People make trades and exchange favors but try to come out a bit ahead in the bargain.

Conventional Morality

Stage 3:   Social Conformity Outlook. People make moral judgments to do what is "nice" and what pleases others.

Stage 4:   Law and Order Outlook. People believe laws are right, and they are to be obeyed. They believe people should respect authority and maintain order.

Postconventional Morality

Stage 5:   Social Contract Outlook. Morality is governed by a system of laws based on socially accepted standards. Judgments are not based exclusively on the situation or on a particular rule but viewed in relation to the system.

Stage 6:   Universal Ethics Outlook. Behavior is judged on principles, not necessarily written, of justice, of concern for human rights, and of respect for human dignity.

Note. From *Lawrence Kohlberg's approach to moral education* (pp. 8–9) by F. C. Power, A. Higgins, & L. Kohlberg, 1989. New York: Columbia University Press. Reprinted with permission of the publisher.

Kohlberg reasoned that, given opportunities, people's moral character grows more complex and more comprehensive over time. By studying how people think about moral questions, he recognized that simplistic terms such as *right* and *wrong*, *good* and *bad* did not reflect the full range of people's capacity to judge moral issues. As illustrated in Table 9.3, people at stages 1 and 2, or what Kohlberg called a preconventional level of morality, make decisions based on their own needs. People at stages 3 and 4 (conventional morality) weigh social mores and laws as they make judgments. And those who are at the most complex level of morality (stages 5 and 6, a level of post-conventional morality) consider moral issues in keeping with abstract personal or universal principles. Kohlberg and others have noted that stages 5 and 6 are difficult to separate from each other because both systems are based on similar concepts.

The stories Kohlberg and his colleagues used to assess stages of moral development are presented in the form of moral dilemmas—problems that force choices between unsatisfactory alternative courses of action. People's responses to these problems can be categorized into distinct types that represent the six stages in Kohlberg's theory. The following is an example of a dilemma used for assessment and educational purposes:

Before the junior class trip the faculty told the students that the whole class had to agree not to bring or use alcohol or drugs on the trip. If students were found using drugs or alcohol, they would be sent home. The students knew that without faculty approval they would not be able to have their trip. The students said in a class meeting that they all agreed to these conditions. On the trip, several students ask Bob, a fellow student, to go on a hike with them to the lake. When they get to the lake, they light up a joint and pass it around. What should Bob do? (Power, Higgins, & Kohlberg, 1989, p. 247)

Some social scientists have criticized Kohlberg for what they perceive to have been his bias in favor of males (Gilligan 1982; Gilligan, Attanucci, 1988). Carol Gilligan argued that Kohlberg's scoring system penalized females and that his level of postconventional morality excluded a dimension of human caring—a dimension upon which she believed females would excel. David Hansen (1996) argues, however, that such moral dimensions as justice and caring coexist in individual reasoning and development; they are not gender- or culture-specific but may be regarded as fundamental and universal. Regardless, Gilligan's claims have sensitized others to the importance of compassion as a dimension of morality.

> **Do boys and girls use different kinds of moral reasoning?**

Critics of Kohlberg also have focused on the absence of an explicit relationship in the theory between moral judgment and moral action (Sockett, 1992). Simply because people reason at higher levels of development does not guarantee that they will behave in moral ways.

Most stage theorists, such as Kohlberg and Piaget, hold that people only progress to higher stages when forced to confront situations that are slightly more complex than those with which they are prepared to deal. Generally, teachers who wish to encourage development try to understand how their students reason and to create learning opportunities that gently stretch the students to consider new possibilities.

■ Understanding Students' Moral Development

Young people confront moral questions regularly. If asked to do so, many can describe such confrontations vividly. When understood as intensely personal problems, students' stories can lend direction to teaching. Nona Lyons (1993) provides an example of thoughts from a high school sophomore, Rebecca.

> I just went through a stage where I thought that anyone who came here and violated a rule should be kicked out of school because they couldn't handle it. They couldn't come there and totally stay within the rules, you know. And then I went through the thing: Is it possible to go through here four years without breaking a fundamental rule? And I asked someone, who said, "I don't think so." So, that is something I am going to have to deal with in the future. (p. 147)

As Lyons points out, Rebecca articulates a complex view of rules and their meaning in her life and in her relations with others. If she maintains and exercises her power to choose, this view may continue to evolve, influencing her values and sense of integrity.

When confronted with hypothetical moral issues, even young children display remarkable capacities to reason about justice and compassion. Experimenters in New England studied the reactions of children ages 5 to 13 to two fables—the "Porcupine and the Moles" and the "Dog in the Manger." The "Porcupine and the Moles" fable presents a family of moles who invite a porcupine to share the warmth of their cave. Unfortunately, the porcupine is so large that his sharp quills make the moles uncomfortable. When they courteously ask the porcupine to leave, he declines, because he likes the cave. The "Dog in the Manger" fable describes a hungry ox who returns to his stall after a hard day at work. There he finds a dog on the hay refusing to move aside so the ox can eat. The investigators asked the children how the animals should solve their problems.

Boys and girls tended to reason in similar fashion. As indicated in Figure 9.2, when asked for the best solution to the fables, children preferred "care-oriented responses." Children's ability to see more than one moral orientation depended on their abstract reasoning skills.

While not everyone agrees about what students should be taught to think, many agree that learning how to reason effectively about moral issues should be a high priority. People may favor contemporary moral orientations or prefer traditional values, but teaching children to handle the power to choose falls increasingly to schools and teachers.

HOW DO STUDENTS' HABITS OF MIND INFLUENCE LEARNING AND TEACHING?

Students' intellectual capacities and their abilities to reason morally influence both teaching and learning, but so too do what James Rutherford and Andrew Ahlgren (1990) and Melinda Fine (1995) call students' **habits of mind**. Habits of mind are the shared skills, attitudes, and values transmitted by custom or convention from one generation to the next. Many people other than teachers try to affect students' habits of mind. They do so by writing and selecting curricula, by funding or denying funding for educational programs, by creating employment opportunities for graduates, and by setting college admissions standards. Influencing students' habits of mind is serious business, for this set of values, attitudes, and skills relate directly to a person's outlook on education.

Formal and Informal Influences on Habits of Mind

The habits of mind deemed important by parents, leaders in government and business, professors, and many others appear in public policy statements. The National Goals, for example, contain references to skills, attitudes, and values that various people consider essential. But in many ways the informal, often implicit habits of mind, are those that shape the ethos of a

FIGURE 9.2

Children's Responses to Fables

How do the justice-oriented responses differ from the care-oriented responses?

Note. From *Approaches to Moral Development: New Research and Emerging Themes* (p. 64) by Andrew Garrod, 1993, New York: Teachers College Press. Copyright 1993 by Teachers College, Columbia University. All rights reserved. Reprinted by permission of the publisher.

JUSTICE-ORIENTED RESPONSES

If there's a whole messload of dogs and a whole messload of oxes, they should have a big war to see who gets the hay.
(Boy, age 8)

They should put out a sign and it has a circle and a cross on it and a porcupine in the middle. And maybe they write in red on it that says "No porcupines allowed."
(Boy, age 6)

The porcupine should move because they [the moles] were there first, and if they left it wouldn't be fair, because they were there first. And the porcupine should move because they could hurt him, you know, really bad like that and stuff, and it's their home.
(Girl, age 10)

If you want to be treated nicely, you got to treat the other person nice, too.
(Boy, age 12)

CARE-ORIENTED RESPONSES

The porcupine could make a wall across the cave. 'Cause then they'd both have a home.
(Boy, age 5)

They should cooperate. Maybe like if there was more rock they could try and blast out some more, and they would all help. And a few of 'em, maybe, ought to take care of the babies if they have some.
(Girl, age 6)

They should all go on an expedition for marshmallows on the porcupine's quills and then the moles will really, really, really not get pricked. Then the porcupine would be happy because he could live in the moles' house that suited him just fine and the moles could have tasty tidbits as well as a warm home because of the porcupine's body heat… and all would be happy
(Boy, age 8)

The moles could dig another home for the porcupine. It would be generous of them, and they could make another friend if they did that. The more friends you have usually is the better.
(Girl, age 12)

community. They can be thought of as the attributes of the more abstract concepts that bind us together as one people.

When people discuss education reform, talk turns to students' attitudes. Two attitudes in particular are often characterized as socially desirable: cooperation and competition. Adults argue that students need to cultivate the temperament to cooperate with one another. When they possess cooperative attitudes, and the concomitant skills needed to work together effectively, they will be prepared to compete with our economic rivals.

When young people realize that cooperating and competing involve some personal risks and that working with and against others means not always getting one's own way and maybe losing more often than winning, they realize that the "winning-is-everything" attitude does not work. In fact, striving for success, failing, and coping gracefully with defeat yield an uncommon dignity that is widely admired.

Another attitude thought to be essential in a civilized society is compassion. Teachers encourage children to be kind to one another not because of the school mission statement or curriculum but because civilized people expect as much of each other.

People also expect each other to possess a variety of skills associated with science, mathematics, and technology that will allow them to participate fully in society. These include calculating skills, skills of manipulating and observing, communication skills, and critical response skills. Such skills are also recognized as habits of mind. Every day, particularly on the job, people need to be able to calculate. Simple paper-and-pencil arithmetic skills once were sufficient for most situations, but with the introduction of inexpensive electronic calculators, the workplace has changed. Operators must be able to read and follow step-by-step instructions in calculator manuals; construct simple algorithms for solving problems; determine what the unit (seconds, square inches, dollars per tankful) of the answer will be from inputs; round off answers; and judge whether an answer is reasonable by comparing it to an estimated answer. Each of these skills, in turn, involves other problem-solving skills (Rutherford & Ahlgren, 1990).

What habits of mind should teachers promote?

Mathematically and technologically literate people also must possess skills of manipulation and observation. These skills include distinguishing between observations and speculations; storing and retrieving computer information using standard computer software; using appropriate instruments to measure length, volume, weight, time, and temperature; troubleshooting common mechanical and electrical systems; and comparing consumer products.

Skills of reading, writing, and speaking have traditionally served as the hallmarks of literacy. The skill of listening—always crucial for learning but magnified in importance with the growth of modern technology—must be added to the list. People cannot take advantage of opportunities or advance their position in society without strong communication skills. Our "information society" demands ever-increasing levels of communicative sophistication.

The skills and attitudes society requires are worth little if young people do not develop a set of values. Some argue that public schools reinforce values of obedience and conformity to protect the status quo. Such skepticism expressed about educational intent is a widely accepted value. But the results of schooling as measured in bright, productive people who have emerged from the system stand as testament to the abiding importance of curiosity and openness to new ideas. When coupled with motivation or drive, good people resist being held down.

The habits of mind valued by society are not always transmitted in ways that children from certain cultures are used to seeing and hearing. The style of communication to which they are accustomed is not congruent with that which they find in school. A study of Native-American children, for instance, revealed that much of the formal learning that took place at home was non-verbal in nature. That is, children learned skills and values not from verbal instruction but from observing and sharing directly in the activities of others. While learning through observation and imitation is common across all cultures, Native Americans' predisposition to use this method of learning puts them at a disadvantage in schools, where learning socially desirable habits of mind often means being told (Henry & Pepper, 1990).

Understanding Students' Habits of Mind

Students have much to tell teachers about the skills, attitudes, and values that should and should not be transmitted in schools. Take, for example, their feelings about the connection between caring and boredom.

"'I'm bored,' says Christina Saffell. 'I don't have my book, so it is not very thrilling for me. . . . You know [the teacher] doesn't care about the homework. She never checks it, just goes over the answers.'" (Leff, 1992, p. A1). It's just another day in the life of a student at Bethesda-Chevy Chase High School in Montgomery County, Maryland. The majority of Bethesda-Chevy Chase students go on to college. Still, here, as in many other schools across the nation, a group of students "in the middle" have chosen to cruise mentally, or to work just enough to get by. They can meet teachers' expectations without overexerting themselves, and they are not sufficiently self-motivated to challenge themselves.

"Middle" students are not uniquely susceptible to boredom; it can strike those at the top and bottom too. An investigation into student attendance in eight Louisiana high schools showed that a greater percentage (82.4%) of high-achieving students disliked school than did average and low achievers together (73.2%) (LoVette & Jacob, 1995). When asked why, students cited boring teachers, uninteresting courses, and busywork as reasons. Might we conclude that students value interesting teachers, engaging courses, and meaningful work?

Many students express what they value through their participation in extracurricular activities. When they choose freely to participate, one might conclude that students value the activity itself and/or the other students who participate. Using 1992 data on high school seniors, the U.S. Department of Education (1995a) suggests that when students have access to a full range of extracurricular activities, they differ markedly in what they choose. Individual or team sports appealed to most students, with 42% of the seniors participating. Sports were followed by performing arts and academic clubs. Honor societies, publications, and student government, which have more limited memberships, drew 16 to 18% of the seniors (see Table 9.4).

Participation itself, then, might be a value that many students share. As noted in Table 9.4, despite the wide availability of activities, students with low socioeconomic status (SES) participated less in extracurricular activities than did their high-SES classmates. Nonetheless, low-SES students did participate at fairly high levels. If educators are to reinforce the value of participation, we must better understand how the constraints of poverty and family background and the influence of school community affect student participation.

We also need to understand what motivates students to get involved and stay involved. From

Why do so many students claim they are bored in school? What can be done about it? In what ways can participation in extracurricular activities positively influence students' habits of mind?

TABLE 9.4 Percentage of public school seniors participating in selected extracurricular activivities by SES of student and affluence of school.

		Low SES students		High SES students	
Selected Activity	**All Students**	**Less affluent schools**	**More affluent schools**	**Less affluent schools**	**More affluent schools**
Any extracurricular activity	79.9	74.7	73.0	86.8	87.6
Sports (individual and team)	42.4	34.3	33.2	48.6	53.1
Performing arts	27.5	25.0	20.7	32.0	29.2
Academic clubs	26.2	20.2	20.5	36.2	32.3
Vocational/ professional clubs	20.8	29.2	25.6	16.0	11.8
Honor societies	18.1	10.3	10.0	30.8	29.9
Publications	17.0	17.6	9.5	22.4	20.0
Student government	15.5	12.6	9.9	17.5	20.9
Service clubs	15.2	10.0	9.4	25.0	21.1
Hobby clubs	8.5	8.2	6.9	9.4	9.6

Note. From Educational Policy Issues: Statistical Perspectives: Extracurricular Participation and Student Involvement (p. 2) by U.S. Department of Education, 1995, Washington, DC: U.S. Government Printing Office.

VOICES

On How Great Teachers Influence Students

Teachers strongly influence students' habits of mind. Edward R. Ducharme, editor of the *Journal of Teacher Education* and himself a teacher educator, reflects on his experiences as a student of Muriel Ragsdale, his high school art teacher.

I often find it valuable to speculate on what I call great teachers: what makes them the way they are? How are they alike? What do they have in common? I frequently ask students in teacher preparation classes to write about great teachers they may have had. A number of years ago I wrote about a great teacher I had in high school even more years ago. She remains dear in my memory years later.

I begin by arguing that we should surround our children with great people. In general we have not surrounded kids with great people; nice people, maybe, but not great people. What are great people? They are those with a passion for something, with a high degree of tolerance for all kinds of difficulties, with finely honed talents or skills, people with a desire to engender and help develop the best in others, and with a love for the variety that is humankind.

Let me reflect on Muriel Ragsdale who was my high school art teacher when I was a high school student. She taught an art class in which we started with pencils and sheets of paper when we were in the 10th grade and by the time we graduated three years later we had worked in just about every imaginable medium. Most of us had some degree of competency in our work, so I guess it would have to be said that Muriel Ragsdale was a pretty good teacher of her subject matter of art.

But art became a class in which hundreds of things other than drawing, sketching, and painting went on. Muriel Ragsdale fostered all manner of conversations in that room as we worked on our projects. She talked of the power of dreams, fashions in dress, life in Manhattan (where she'd lived for a while). We did oil paintings of our favorite phobias (mine was falling off cliffs) so as to exorcise them from our consciousness and thus avoid bad dreams (not all schemes of gifted teachers work; I still have that occasional dream of falling!); we played a game inviting any five people in the history of the world to a dinner party and telling the reasons for our choices. I remember inviting Leonardo Da Vinci, Robert Frost, Joan of Arc, Ted Williams, and Franklin Roosevelt. (Now, that would have been some dinner!) I'm not sure I would make many changes if I were asked to play the same game today. We planned school dances sponsored by the Art Club which she advised. She showed slides and copies of famous paintings. To this day, when I walk into a museum like the National Gallery in Washington there is always a moment when I see the original of a painting and I remember Muriel Ragsdale showing us a copy.

Trust and warmth developed among us kids, some of whom saw one another only in this class. One day we talked and laughed and made noise beyond Muriel Ragsdale's tolerance. She asked us to stop and we thought she was kidding, so we continued. She asked again; we kept on. She wept,

the results of an analysis of 96 studies, Judy Cameron and David Pierce (1994) argue that reinforcement (verbal praise) and reward are what hook students and keep them coming back for more. Others (Kohn, 1996; Lepper, Keavney, & Drake, 1996) contend that the effects of rewards and verbal reinforcement are far too complicated to rely on them as simple prescriptions to

looked at us, and left the room. We sat in shame for five minutes or so and then went and got her. I still feel shame recalling that moment when we made her cry through our own callousness and insensitivity.

My favorite art activity was producing sports cartoons. I was pretty good, and by my senior year, I was considering art school. One day I went to Muriel Ragsdale and asked her: "Am I good enough that, with schooling and more training, I can make a living at art?" (Yes, a very practical question; but what do you expect of a French Canadian, callow youth whose parents were limited to 6th and 7th grade education, who worked in a grocery store every day after school and all day Saturday, and saw college only through the images presented in Hollywood musicals of the time?) She looked at me—I am sure I was her favorite student (one instinctively knows that)—a long time and then said: "No. You see, you cannot do with your hands what you see in your head and you probably wouldn't be satisfied with that kind of life." Those of us who teach know what courage it takes to discourage our favorite students from pursuing what we do for a living.

You may now see why I loved Muriel Ragsdale and cherish her memory. She gave us a sense of dignity and importance; she didn't ridicule our occasional adolescent whining and pains. I saw Muriel Ragsdale twice after graduating from high school, the first time when I was a senior in college, majoring in English, not art. The second time was years later; she had retired, and I was a professor at the University of Vermont. She had read what I had written. She said to me, "All those years I taught, I never knew anyone understood what I was doing." I was glad I had written what I had and sad that only in her retirement had she read words of love and praise and understanding.

Children of all ages should have people like Muriel Ragsdale around them. She goaded us, inspired us, wept in front of us. She told jokes, talked about great literature, dared us to be ourselves, and—most importantly—she loved us,

I have walked a long distance since my school days. Many other teachers have taught me; I have taught many teachers; I have taught high school students, undergraduates, masters students, and doctoral students. Always I look in others and in myself for the qualities that made Muriel great as a teacher and as a human being.

All these thoughts reduce to one: schools should have many people in them whom kids would go out of their way to spend time with and still remember years later.

CRITICAL THINKING

What great teachers have you known? How were they similar to and different from Muriel Ragsdale? What characteristics did Muriel Ragsdale possess, if any, that would help her succeed in today's schools? If, sometime, somewhere in the future, one of our former students was writing about you as a teacher, how would you want to be remembered?

Note. From *In Praise of Muriel Ragsdale* by E. Ducharme, September, 1996, Unpublished manuscript, Drake University.

guarantee successful teaching. Teachers must work to know their students' values, interests, and concerns—habits of mind—if they are to stimulate and maintain students' participation in school. Teachers themselves must be motivated if they expect students to be motivated, to care, to participate.

Cultural Awareness

A musician from Chicago, Billy Branch, and his band, Sons of Blues, made the importance of habits of mind—commitment to one's discipline, to cooperation, and to competition—abundantly clear in Charleston, South Carolina (Kuralt, 1992). When a local businesswoman read about Branch's Blues in the Schools program in Chicago, where it originated, she helped bring it south to a predominantly African-American middle school in one of Charleston's lowest income neighborhoods. For 2 hours a day for 3 weeks, students studied the blues. They played and sang the blues, studied the history of the blues, and wrote their own songs.

BRANCH: Anybody remember any of the people I mentioned that recorded Willie Dixon tunes?

UNIDENTIFIED STUDENT #1: Bo Diddley.

BRANCH: WHO?

STUDENT #2: Elvis Presley, Led Zeppelin, The Rolling Stones and Koko Taylor.

BRANCH: See, somebody took notes. Yes. Right! (p. 13)

As a schoolteacher of the blues, Branch does not simply talk about his subject, he jams with his students, teaching them in a demonstrable way how to play together harmoniously and encouraging them to push each other to reach for the best sounds they can produce. Branch listens to students' musical and verbal expressions, which he interprets as indications of their ability to "feel the feel of the blues."

HOW DOES GENDER INFLUENCE LEARNING AND TEACHING?

Girls consistently outscore boys on tests of reading and writing. Even though girls and boys are approximately equal in measured academic ability when they enter school, by age 12, girls perform less well than boys in such areas as higher level mathematics and measures of self-esteem, although the gender differences are declining in some areas such as mathematics (AAUW Educational Foundation & National Education Association, 1992; Pollina, 1995). Such differences may be due in part to **gender bias**—discriminatory treatment, often subtle or unconscious, that unfairly favors or disfavors individuals because they are females or because they are males.

Girls receive less attention from teachers than do boys, and the quality of attention boys get is better (Sadker & Sadker, 1993). The literature also suggests that teachers are prone to choose classroom activities that appeal to boys' interests and to use instructional methods that favor boys. Teachers foster competition, for example, despite the fact that many studies suggest that girls, and many boys, experience greater academic success when they work cooperatively (AAUW Educational Foundation & National Education Association, 1992). Teachers also ask boys more challenging questions, encourage them to work to get a correct answer, offer them more praise and constructive criticism, and acknowledge their substantive achievement more than they do girls (Sadker & Sadker, 1993).

Are single-sex schools the answer to gender bias in the classroom?

Are boys also victims of bias in the schools? Studies indicate that teachers consider boys in general to be significantly more active, less attentive, less dexterous, and more prone to have behavioral, academic, and language problems than are girls. When schools identify children with learning disabilities, mental retardation, and reading disabilities, boys typically are identified more often than girls. A study of 152 preservice teachers at the University of Minnesota during the 1990–1991 academic year revealed that the majority of teachers surveyed attributed disparities in academic achievement between boys and girls to society (87%) and school (71%). Other explanations for differences included family (25%) and genetics (21%) (Avery & Walker, 1993).

Research on the progress of young women and men in areas related to success in the labor market suggests that educational differences matter in their later lives—but not equitably. Female students are as likely as are males to take advanced math and science courses and are more likely to study a foreign language. Females are slightly more likely than are males to make an immediate transition from high school to college. Employment and earnings rates rise with educational attainment for both females and males, but earnings are lower for females than for males with the same education (National Center for Education Statistics, 1996).

Cultural Awareness

Public schools continue to experiment with the idea of single-sex education. Whether these experiments can survive legal challenges remains to be seen. University of Maine professor Bonnie Wood claims that an all-girl algebra class offered at the high school in Presque Isle, Maine, produces girls who are twice as likely to enroll in advanced chemistry and college physics.

Single-sex education also may benefit boys. Marsteller Middle School, in Manassas, Virginia, offers single-sex classes in physics and English, claiming that separating the sexes eliminates distractions. Marsteller boys raised their average language arts scores by one grade after only one term. Robert Coleman Elementary School in Baltimore, Maryland, introduced single-sex classes to instill discipline in the boys.

But legal challenges could be on the horizon. Federal law does not allow segregation by sex in public schools, except for contact sports, human sexuality courses, and remedial classes. One middle school in Ventura, California, won a legal challenge by changing the name of its all-girl math class to Power Learning for Underrepresented Students (PLUS). No boys signed up.

Some critics are concerned that single-sex classes will "set back the cause for gender equity." Others claim that girls and boys must learn to work together in preparation for a coed world. However, some teachers counter that single-sex classes work because they "let kids think with something besides their hormones." "Impressing the opposite sex is a 14-year-old's reason for being. Take away that pressure, and miracles happen." (Daily Report Card, 1996)

How do student exceptionalities influence teaching and learning?

Children have similar needs, interests, and ways of knowing. About 1 in 10, however, also has a special ability or disability that sets him apart from other children (U.S. Department of Education, 1995). More than 5 million **exceptional learners** across the United States possess one or more attributes that greatly affect the experiences they have at home, at school, and in the community.

> **How should exceptionality be defined?**

Through the years, the knowledge of exceptionalities has grown. And with that growth has come public recognition of the importance of attending to exceptionalities in ways that maximize students' chances for success. Learner characteristics that were viewed as "handicaps" just 10 or 20 years ago are now characterized as "disabilities" that need not limit students' chances to advance or to contribute to the greater good.

Types of Exceptionalities

While there is widespread agreement that some children deviate from the norm, the definition of the norm can be debated. *Normal* means what is typically expected or desired in the context of a specific culture. Those who deviate from cultural expectations may possess one or more of the following characteristics.

Giftedness   **Giftedness**, like other types of exceptionality, has been defined in several ways. According to the 1972 Marland definition (Public Law 91-230, Section 806), gifted and talented students are those children capable of high performance who excel in one or more of the following areas: general intellectual ability, specific academic aptitude, creative or productive thinking, leadership ability, ability in the visual or performing arts, and psychomotor ability. Traditionally, however, children have been labeled as gifted if they score above a certain level on an IQ test. A recent national survey indicated that 73% of school districts have adopted the Marland definition, yet few schools use the definition to identify and serve any area of giftedness other than high general intelligence as measured on verbal IQ and achievement tests (U.S. Department of Education, Office of Educational Research and Improvement, 1993).

As noted earlier, some contend that intelligence is not a general characteristic but instead a combination of several capacities and cognitive abilities that cannot all be measured through the usual types of testing (Gardner & Hatch, 1989). Joseph Renzulli (1982) argues that giftedness is determined by high ability, high creativity, and high levels of motivation and task completion. Giftedness also has been described as "a sign of biopsychological potential in whichever domains exist in a culture" (Gardner, 1993, p. 51).

Mental Retardation   As indicated in Table 9.5, **mental retardation** is one of several categories of disability. According to the American Association on Mental Retardation (AAMR), this disability manifests before age 18 and greatly limits personal capabilities. It is characterized by

> significantly subaverage intellectual functioning [an IQ standard score of 70 to 75 or lower], existing concurrently with related limitations in two or more of the following applicable adaptive skill areas: communication, self-care, home living, social skills, community use, self-direction, health and safety, functional academics, leisure, and work. (American Association on Mental Retardation, 1992, p. 5)

Despite their limitations, those with mental retardation who receive appropriate support over a sustained period will generally demonstrate improvement in their life functioning.

Hearing Impairment   **Hearing impairment** is a term used to describe degrees of deafness. While individuals who are hard of hearing can usually process oral language with the use of hearing aid, those who are deaf are unable to do so. Educators who work with hearing-impaired youngsters are concerned with the time in a child's development when hearing impairment

---

TABLE 9.5   Some Categories of Disability

Mental retardation	**Communication disorder**
Sensory impairment	Speech impairment
Hearing impairment	Language disorder
Vision impairment	
Physical disability	**Emotional behavior disorder**
Orthopedic impairment	**Attention deficit disorder**
Health impairment	**Learning disability**
Seizure disorder	

occurred. They may describe hearing-impaired youngsters as "congenitally deaf" (born deaf) or "adventitiously deaf" (acquiring deafness sometime after birth). The main concern is the degree to which speech and language are affected by hearing loss and how best to facilitate communication skills (Hallahan & Kauffman, 1997).

Cultural Awareness

Language and communication reveal the nature of a culture. People with hearing impairments remind the hearing community that systems of communication that are unspoken and unheard also help to define a culture. People who identify themselves as members of the deaf culture advocate the use of sign language rather than mechanical aids. Some argue that mechanical hearing devices, particularly those that are surgically implanted, rob deaf people of their self-respect and their group identity. They would prefer to teach children with hearing impairments to communicate with one another as members of a distinct culture by signing. Others spurn the legitimacy or value of a deaf culture and opt for any chance to help children be more like their hearing peers. Some discourage signing, advocate the use of technology to boost children's chances to hear, and encourage speech therapy for all children with hearing impairments.

American Sign Language (ASL), one of the most common sign languages, consists of hand movements that represent concepts or words rather than isolated sounds or letters. Learning ASL is much like learning a foreign language. People learn signs for whole words and complete thoughts, build their vocabulary, and improve their speech through practice. As Figure 9.3 shows, signs vary regionally, like dialects.

FIGURE 9.3 *(opposite)*

How One Concept Is Expressed in American Sign Language in Different Areas of the Country

Which ASL speakers might have the greatest difficulty in understanding each other?

Note. From *Signs Across America,* (pp. 79-80) by E. Shroyer and S. Shroyer, 1984, Washington, DC: Gallaudet University Press. Copyright 1984 by Gallaudet University. All rights reserved. Reprinted by permission of the publisher.

Visual Impairment   A child who has **visual impairment** may be classified as "legally blind," "partially sighted," or "educationally blind." According to the American Medical Association, a person is considered legally blind when visual acuity in her better eye does not exceed 20/200 with corrective lenses or when her field of vision is limited at its widest angle to 20 degrees or less. Those who are partially sighted have better visual acuity (greater than 20/200 but not greater than 20/70 in the stronger eye after correction.) Children with educational blindness depend on senses other than sight; typically they use braille when reading (Wolf, Pratt, & Pruitt, 1990).

Orthopedic Impairments and Other Health Impairments

Individuals with orthopedic and other health impairments include those with neurological impairment, or damage to their central nervous system; skeletal and muscular disorders; and congenital malformations. About half of the children with physical impairments in the United States have cerebral palsy,

FAINT:
My mother fainted
from the ammonia
fumes.

1 Alabama, Hawaii

2 Arkansas, Florida, Maine
Kentucky, Louisiana, Virginia,
North Carolina, South Carolina

3 California, Illinois, Utah

4 Colorado, Texas (1 of 2)

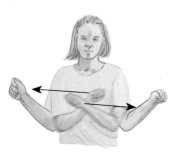

5 Massachusetts

6 Michigan, Ohio

7 Missouri, New Mexico,
Washington

8 New York

9 North Dakota

10 Pennsylvania

11 Texas (2 of 2)

12 Wisconsin

a neurological impairment characterized by weakness, lack of coordination, and/or motor dysfunction. Other neurological impairments include epilepsy (recurrent seizures), spina bifida (an improperly developed spinal cord that often causes paralysis of the lower body), and spinal cord injuries that occur when the spinal cord is traumatized or severed. Skeletal and muscular disorders include arthritis, a disease that causes inflammation around the joints, and muscular dystrophy, a degenerative disease that causes the breakdown of muscle tissues. Congenital malformations are abnormalities of any part of the body, such as the heart or the extremities, that are present at birth.

Speech and Language Disorders   Children with **speech impairments** may have fluency disorders (such as stuttering), articulation disorders (abnormality in the production of sounds), or voice disorders (such as hoarseness or hypernasality—too many sounds produced through the nose). Some children may exhibit delayed speech; that is, they use communication patterns like those of someone of a much younger age (e.g., pointing at something they want rather than verbalizing what they want). Children with **language disorders** may have receptive, expressive, or language-processing problems, as well as combinations of these problems. In some instances they also have difficulty with the meaning of words (semantics), with the sequential organization of words according to their relationships to each other (syntax), or with the purpose of or uses for language (Palmer & Yantis, 1990).

Emotional and Behavioral Disorders   Among terms used to describe those who have emotional, social, and behavioral problems are *behavioral disordered, socially maladjusted, emotionally disturbed,* and *emotionally/behaviorally disordered.* These problems can reveal themselves through behaviors such as phobias or depressions that are directed inward or by behaviors that are directed more at others (Wolf, Pratt, & Pruitt, 1990). The federal definition of "seriously emotionally disturbed" is as follows:

> The term means a condition exhibiting one or more of the following characteristics over a long period of time and to a marked degree, which adversely affects educational performance: (1) an inability to learn which cannot be explained by intellectual, sensory, or health factors; (2) an inability to build or maintain satisfactory relationships with peers and teachers; (3) inappropriate types of behavior or feelings under normal circumstances; (4) a general pervasive mood of unhappiness or depression; or (5) a tendency to develop physical symptoms or fears associated with personal or school problems. The term includes children who are schizophrenic. . . . The term does not include children who are socially maladjusted, unless it is determined that they are seriously disturbed. (U.S. Department of Health, Education, and Welfare, 1977, p. 42478)

Attention Deficit Disorder   **Attention-deficit/hyperactivity disorder (ADHD)** is a neurobiologically based disorder characterized by inappropriate levels of three observable behaviors: inattention, impulsivity, and hyperactivity (Friend & Bursuck, 1996). Attention-deficit/hyperactivity disorder is sometimes referred to as attention-deficit disorder (ADD). Classroom manifestations of the disorder include difficulty in staying on task, focusing attention, and completing work. Children with ADHD appear not to listen or not to have heard what they have been told. They may also display age-inappropriate hyperactive behavior, be easily distracted, and produce sloppy and careless work. Impulsivity can cause difficulty in accomplishing tasks that call for a delayed response, such as raising hands to answer questions, reading or listening to directions, asking questions to clarify information, planning, and organizing.

Learning Disabilities　The National Joint Committee on Learning Disabilities, a group of representatives from eight national organizations that have a major interest in **learning disabilities**, defines the term as follows:

> Learning disabilities is a general term that refers to a heterogeneous group of disorders manifested by significant difficulties in the acquisition and use of listening, speaking, reading, writing, reasoning, or mathematical abilities. These disorders are intrinsic to the individual, presumed to be due to central nervous system disorder, and may occur across the life span. Problems in self-regulatory behaviors, social perception and social interaction may exist with learning disabilities but do not by themselves constitute a learning disability. Although learning disabilities may occur concomitantly with other handicapping conditions (for example, sensory impairment, mental retardation, serious emotional disturbance) or with extrinsic influences (such as cultural differences, insufficient or inappropriate instruction), they are not the result of those conditions or influences. (Hammill, Leigh, McNutt, & Larsen, 1988, p. 217)

Delivery of Services for Gifted and Talented Students

Programs for gifted and talented students have enjoyed varying levels of support over the years. Events such as the launching of Sputnik in 1957 and the publication of *A Nation at Risk* by the National Commission on Excellence in Education in 1983 stimulated Americans to put more emphasis on programs for the brightest students. Between the 1960s and 1970s, however, issues of equity often forced gifted education to take a back seat as educators switched their attention to the needs of below-average and disadvantaged students. With increasingly limited resources for public education, people often chose to curtail or eliminate programs for gifted and talented students.

Currently, every state and many school districts have gifted and talented programs. Gifted and talented students who remain in general education classrooms may be placed in accelerated curricula. They may be pulled out of the general education classroom for special instruction in a resource room. Sometimes gifted and talented students may attend self-contained classes for talented students. They may also skip a grade in school.

When students are selected for gifted and talented programs, studies suggest that economically disadvantaged students are significantly underserved. In 1988 only 9% of students in gifted and talented programs were in the bottom quartile of family income, while 47% were from the top quartile of family income (U.S. Department of Education, 1993). Studies also indicate that disproportionately fewer limited English proficient (LEP) students are included in gifted and talented programs. Although schools provide instructional assistance to these students, many people argue that educational programs do not teach the language or higher-order skills that students need to perform well on placement tests and that many gifted LEP students therefore end up in lower-level classes and even are erroneously placed in special education classes (Schmidt, 1993).

There is sometimes a stigma involved in being labeled a high-achieving student. In a survey of students in three midwestern high schools, students said that they wanted to do well in school but not exceptionally well because they were afraid they would be associated with the "brain crowd" rather than the "in crowd" (U.S. Department of Education, 1993).

The story of one high school student reveals some of the reasons why being bright may be somewhat difficult. In 1993, when Elizabeth Mann was a senior at Montgomery Blair High School in Silver Spring, Maryland, an article in *The Washington Post* bumped her status from "brilliant" to "legendary" (Finkel, 1993). Elizabeth scored 1570 out of a possible 1600 on the SATs, 800 (out of 800) on her achievement test in math, and 800 on her achievement test in physics. Several themes emerged in the story, among them the teachers' near veneration of Elizabeth's talents. The guidance counselor spoke of the "burden" Elizabeth bore because teachers were "absolutely charmed by her" (p. 13). "They are in awe of her. They have set her up as a paragon in their minds, and, I think, in the minds of her peers, which has made her road that much harder" (p. 13).

> **Is there a best way to educate students who are gifted and talented?**

Some spoke of Elizabeth as likely to be among history's greatest mathematicians or among the smartest people of all time. All of this caused Elizabeth to cringe:

> From what I've heard and what I can see, you get the general impression they're all overly enamored of me . . . I guess in and of itself, that's nice. I mean, you can't ever be upset that people like you. So that's fine. The consequences of it are what make me uneasy. (p. 22)

It is not difficult to see why Elizabeth feels this way when a fellow student discusses what he perceives as her favored status:

> If you look at what's happened to Elizabeth in her four years in the magnet, there isn't one example of her being disadvantaged. . . . I have a hard time complaining. I've gotten a lot out of the magnet program. But no one has gotten as much out of it as she has. Let me make it clear. Nobody has gotten as much attention out of the program as her. (p. 22)

Elizabeth's closest friend, Valerie Wang, also offered her perspective: "No one dislikes her, because she's not dislikable, but I think there's a lot of resentment" (p. 22).

After finishing third behind two of her classmates in a highly competitive science fair, Elizabeth sat outside her house the next day and expressed her doubts and dreams:

> I wish I had beautiful hair. . . . I wish I were better at physics and math than I am. I wish I could stay awake 24 hours a day. I wish I had a car. I wish I could figure out why I've lost so much respect from Josh [a fellow student], and what I could do about it, and what I'm doing wrong. I wish teachers wouldn't single out people. I wish I could be respected for my mind and yet liked as a person regardless of what my mind is like. I wish,

well, this is a hard one. I wish people knew about my insecurities, so they wouldn't think I'm conceited, as apparently they do. (p. 27)

Once educators identify giftedness in students, they must decide how to teach them. Some researchers note that participation in gifted and talented programs has positive effects on academic achievement for many gifted and talented students but not for all of them (Marsh, Chessor, Craven, & Roche, 1995). Participation in such programs has negative effects on some gifted students' academic self-concepts. These students suffer from what Marsh and his colleagues call the "big-fish-little-pond effect"; that is, they feel better when they are the most talented students in a class but suffer when they are with others who are equally or more talented.

Do such findings suggest that teachers of the gifted should avoid grouping gifted children together for instruction? Not necessarily:

Of course they get a different view of the world when they are with other bright children—the halos and wings they assumed were their "gift" may seem a little tarnished—this may be a very healthy encounter with reality, but, at the same time, to preserve their sense of power, energy, and effectiveness, they need support in redrawing a healthy vision of themselves. (Marsh, Chessor, Craven, & Roche, 1995, p. 316)

Although the teaching of gifted students defies simple prescriptions, most educators agree on some general guidelines. Definitions of giftedness must be expanded to include criteria other than standardized test scores. Competition is not always conducive to academic and personal growth. Gifted students do better when they pursue projects that are of particular interest to them. They need specific feedback on their performance of tasks, not comparisons of their performances to other students.

Delivery of Services for Students With Disabilities

The law assures individuals with disabilities a right to a free, appropriate education in the least restrictive environment. This means that students with disabilities must be educated in regular classrooms whenever possible. During the 1992–1993 school year, 94% of 3- to 21-year-olds with disabilities were served in regular school buildings alongside students without disabilities. Most often, educators place students with disabilities in regular, resource, or separate classroom environments. The government reports that about 40% are in regular classes; another 30% are in resource rooms, and 24% are in separate classes (U.S. Department of Education, 1995c).

The 1975 Education for All Handicapped Children Act (Public Law 94-142) recognized the rights of students between the ages of 5 and 18 to **equal educational opportunity,** or access to resources, choices, and encouragement so they might achieve to their fullest potential. Education programs were to be fitted to students' individual needs and were to be carried out in the least restrictive environment. The 1990 **Individuals with Disabilities Education Act (IDEA)** amended the **Education for All Handicapped Children Act**, or Public Law 94-142, by changing the term *handicapped* to *with disabilities* and by extending a free and appropriate public education to every individual between 2 and 21 years of age, regardless of the nature or severity of his disability.

How might a classroom teacher and a special education teacher collaborate to teach this student in a general education classroom? What roles might other students in the class take? What might be some advantages and disadvantages of this arrangement?

Schools provide special education services for students with disabilities in a variety of ways. These service options can be described on a continuum ranging from those most physically integrated into general education classrooms to those least integrated.

In some instances the general education teacher meets all the needs of the student. Sometimes a special educator acts as a consultant to the teacher, or an itinerant special education teacher may offer some instruction to a student within the classroom. A student may go to a resource teacher part of the day for specific help. A special education teacher in a center might provide most or all instruction for several days or weeks. When a student is hospitalized, an itinerant general or special educator provides all instruction in the hospital or home before a student returns to school. A student's primary assignment may be to a self-contained special education class, with the student leaving only occasionally to participate in school activities. Sometimes special education students attend separate schools. The least physically integrated arrangement is for a student to be in a residential setting devoted totally to providing a therapeutic environment (Hallahan & Kauffman, 1997, pp. 16–17).

What does it take to make inclusion work?

Some are quick to point out that despite strong legislation, special education students still have not been included in processes of general education as fully or completely as they should be. Reformers propose to create a "new, inclusive system of education for all students" (NASBE Study Group on Special Education, 1992, p. 5). An inclusive system is meant to move beyond mainstreaming, which is the practice of educating exceptional learners in the general education classroom for as much time as possible.

The movement for **full inclusion**—teaching students with disabilities in regular classrooms throughout the day in their neighborhood schools—like busing to end racial segregation, is controversial. Experts in favor of full inclusion argue that present practices of special education do not work and are costly (Gartner & Lipsky, 1989). On the other side, experts argue that to restructure special education would threaten existing support for students with disabilities and would place an unbearable burden on an already overstressed general education system (Kauffman, 1990). There are no simple answers to the question of where and how to teach students with disabilities. The debate about inclusion serves to focus educators and the general public on the need to avoid a unilateral approach and instead to seek the most appropriate placements and instructional methods for students with special needs.

Regardless of where children with disabilities are placed in schools, general and special educators need to work with parents and other professionals to plan an **individualized education program (IEP)** for each child. A child's IEP identifies, for example, current level of performance (strengths and limitations), long- and short-term goals, criteria for success, methods for

BENCHMARKS

Equal Opportunity for Americans with Disabilities

1973   Vocational Rehabilitation Act (Public Law 93-112, Section 504): People with disabilities cannot be discriminated against in any way in any federally funded program.

1974   Educational Amendments Act (Public Law 93-380): Federal funds are provided to the states for implementing programs for exceptional learners, including the gifted and talented. Rights to due process are granted to children with disabilities and their families in special education placement.

1975   Education of the Handicapped Law (Public Law 94-142, Part B, known as the Mainstreaming Law): A free and appropriate public education must be provided for all children with disabilities ages 5 and above. Education must be planned through an individualized education program (IEP) and carried out in the least restrictive environment.

1986   Education of the Handicapped Act Amendments (Public Law 99-457): A free and appropriate education must be extended to all children with disabilities ages 3 to 5, and early intervention programs must be established for infants and toddlers with disabilities.

1988   Technology-Related Assistance for Individuals with Disabilities Act of 1988 (Public Law 100-418): Provides financial assistance to states to develop and implement consumer-responsive statewide programs of technology-related assistance for persons of all ages with disabilities.

1990   Americans with Disabilities Act (ADA, Public Law 101-336): This law is essentially a national mandate to end discrimination against people with disabilities in private-sector employment, public services, public accommodations, transportation, and telecommunications.

          Individuals with Disabilities Education Act (Public Law 101-476), or IDEA, replaces the Education of the Handicapped Act. Special education services are extended to children with autism and traumatic brain injury, and rehabilitation and social work services are included in the definition of special education.

1991   Individuals with Disabilities Act Amendments (Public Law 102-119): This law amends IDEA to extend authorization of appropriations and to revise the early intervention program of services for infants and toddlers with disabilities.

1994   Technology-Related Assistance for Individuals with Disabilities Amendments of 1993 (Public Law 103-218): This law amends the Technology-Related Assistance for Individuals with Disabilities Act of 1988 to authorize appropriations for each of the fiscal years 1994-1998.

assessing mastery of objectives (e.g., observation, testing), amount of time that will be spent in general education classrooms, and beginning and ending dates for special services. One page from an IEP appears in Figure 9.4, which was written for one behavior problem (noncompliance) and one curriculum

FIGURE 9.4

**Sample Excerpt
from an IEP**

How might having an individualized education program
(IEP) help the classroom
teacher and the special education teacher work together
to meet a student's needs?

Note. From *Exceptional Children:
An Introduction to Special Education*
(7th Ed.) (p. 37) by D. P. Hallahan
and J. Kauffman, 1997, Boston:
Allyn and Bacon. Copyright 1997
by Allyn and Bacon. Reprinted
by permission.

INDIVIDUALIZED EDUCATION PROGRAM

Student: *Amy North*   Age: *9*   Grade: *1*   Date: *Oct. 17, 1995*

1. Unique Characteristics or Needs: Noncompliance

Frequently noncompliant with teacher's instructions

Present levels of Performance
Complies with about 50% of teacher's requests/commands

Special Education, Related Services, and Modifications
*Implemented immediately, strong reinforcement for compliance with teacher's
instructions (Example: "Sure I will!" plan including precision requests and reinforcer
menu for points earned for compliance, as described in The Tough Kid Book, by Rhode,
Jenson, and Reavis, 1992); within 3 weeks, training of parents by school psychologist
to use precision requests and reinforcements at home.*

Objectives (Including Procedures, Criteria, and Schedule)
*Within one month, will comply with teacher's requests/commands 90% of the time;
compliance monitored weekly by teacher*

Annual Goals
Will become compliant with teacher's requests/commands

2. Unique Characteristics or Needs: Reading

2a. Very slow reading rate
2b. Poor comprehension
2c. Limited phonics skills
2d. Limited sight–word vocabulary

1. Present Levels of Performance
*2a. Reads stories of approximately 100 words on first-grade reading level at
approximately 40 words per min.*
*2b. Seldom can recall factual information about stories immediately after reading
them*
*2c. Consistently confuses vowel sounds, often misidentifies consonants, and does
not blend sounds*
2d. Has sight–word vocabulary of approximately 150 words

2. Special Education, Related Services, and Modifications
*2a–2c. Direct instruction 30 minutes daily in vowel discrimination, consonant
identification, and sound blending; begin immediately, continue throughout
schoolyear*
*2a & 2d. Sight–word drill 10 minutes daily in addition to phonics instruction and daily
practice; 10 minutes practice in using phonics and sight–word skills in reading
story at her level; begin immediately, continue for schoolyear*

3. Objectives (Including Procedures, Criteria, and Schedule)
*2a. Within 3 months, will read stories at her level at 60 words per minute with 2 or
fewer errors per story; within six months, 80 words with 2 or fewer errors;
performance monitored daily by teacher or aide*
*2b. Within 3 months will answer oral and written comprehension questions requiring
recall of information from stories she has just read with 90% accuracy (e.g., Who
is in the story? What happened? When? Why?) and be able to predict probable
outcomes with 80% accuracy; performance monitored daily by teacher or aide*
*2c. Within 3 months, will increase sight–word vocabulary to 200 words, within 6
months to 250 words, assessed by flashcard presentation*

4. Annual Goals
2a–2c. Will read fluently and with comprehension at beginning-second-grade level.

area (reading) for Amy, a student in elementary school with mild mental retardation.

In some instances, teachers have students in their classrooms who share many of the attributes of exceptional children but who, for one reason or another, are not identified as such. Although teachers are not required to create IEPs for these children, they are obligated to create a learning environment that enables all children to maximize their potentials. When implementing plans, good teachers seek ways to increase students' achievement and to foster positive social relationships between children with disabilities and their nondisabled peers. Just as gifted and talented students may have difficulty winning acceptance by their peers, children with disabilities may also experience social problems.

As P. J. Magik (1995) suggests so vividly, the failures and successes of people with disabilities—and their sense of self-efficacy—depend heavily on the context in which they live and are educated.

> I acquired my disability in the Midwest, an especially good place to get a disability if individual effort brings improvement. In that part of the world there's the "if-you-try-hard-enough-you-can-do-anything" syndrome, as well as the belief in individual responsibility. . . . Doing my best to meet challenges comes naturally and, when I was exhausted, others didn't hesitate to assist. (Magik, 1995, p. 7)

Educators can use such strategies as conflict resolution and cooperative learning to improve interpersonal relationships, to enhance self-esteem, and to maximize students' opportunity to learn. Chapter 10 will describe, in particular, the utility of cooperative learning for helping to change negative stereotypes and for integrating children of all ability levels into the classroom mainstream.

SUMMARY

How do students' intellectual abilities influence learning and teaching?

1 There are competing ideas about the meaning of intelligence. While some experts view intelligence as a unitary trait, others define it as a multidimensional trait that varies over time and from situation to situation. Yet others view intelligence as knowledge and skills deemed important for a particular culture. Young people also view intelligence in different ways, including as a static entity impervious to change and as a dynamic entity that can be affected by teaching.

2 Psychometricians develop tests to assess intelligence. Measurement is conducted by administering a number of tasks and inferring intellectual capabilities from examinees' performances. Scores are used widely to predict success in school and work.

3 Students' thoughts about the nature of intelligence as well as their teachers' perceptions of mental ability can greatly affect students' attitudes about themselves as learners and their success in school.

How do perceptions of student learning influence teaching?

4 Intelligence is sometimes characterized in terms of stages of development, each more complex than the last. Stage theorists suggest that teaching must fit students' levels of development in order to be successful.

5 Theorists with a contextual perspective suggest that systematic teaching can and does influence intellectual development. Vygotsky and others with this outlook recommend that teachers actively intervene to shape intellectual growth rather than assume that such growth will occur merely by placing students in educational environments with certain materials.

6 Theories of information processing describe how information is received, analyzed, stored, retrieved, and used. These theories emphasize the importance of helping learners to acquire bodies of useful information and to develop thinking skills that will allow them to learn on their own.

How do physical and psychosocial development affect children's learning?

7 In healthy individuals, both the mind and body develop together and over time, but not always at the same rate. Different people develop in different ways. Nonetheless, there are identifiable common patterns of physical and mental development from birth to death that have important implications for education.

8 Differences in physical development may be caused by such factors as genetics, amount of stimulation from caretakers, nutrition, and the quality of a child's physical environment.

9 Lead poisoning is one of the most common and devastating housing-related diseases. It can cause severe developmental and health problems for children.

10 As children grow and change, their body types influence developmental task achievement, self-image, and self-satisfaction.

11 Young people's personal and social (psychosocial) development proceeds somewhat systematically and is affected in large part by the people around them.

How does moral development influence learning and teaching?

12 Moral development can be described in terms of developmental stages that have implications for how students are taught. Reasoning becomes more complex, less egocentric, and less absolute at each successive stage.

13 Despite claims to the contrary, males and females appear to make judgments about moral issues in much the same way. Students' thoughts about moral dilemmas can lend direction to teachers as they plan for instruction.

How do students' habits of mind influence learning and teaching?

14 The most powerful habits of mind (the shared skills, attitudes, and values transmitted by custom or convention from one generation to the next) may be the less visible, informal, implicit ones held and modeled by teachers and by members of a community.

15 Teachers who want to stimulate and maintain students' participation in school work need to understand students' habits of mind.

How does gender influence learning and teaching?

16 Differences in students' achievement may be due in part to what students are taught (or not taught) and how they are treated in the classroom. Such differences may be due in part to gender bias.

How do student exceptionalities influence teaching and learning?

17 Although children have similar needs, interests, and ways of knowing, some individuals have special abilities or disabilities that set them apart from other children. These *exceptional* children may possess one or more attributes that greatly affect the experiences they have at home, at school, and in the community at large.

TERMS AND CONCEPTS

attention-deficit/hyperactivity disorder (ADHD), *p. 358*
cognitive development theory, *p. 334*
developmentally appropriate instruction, *p. 336*
Education for All Handicapped Children Act, *p. 361*
equal educational opportunity, *p. 361*
exceptional learner, *p. 354*
full inclusion, *p. 362*
gender bias, *p. 352*
giftedness, *p. 354*
habits of mind, *p. 345*
hearing impairment, *p. 355*
individualized education program (IEP), *p. 362*

Individuals with Disabilities Education Act (IDEA), *p. 361*
information-processing theory, *p. 334*
intelligence quotient (IQ), *p. 331*
language disorder, *p. 358*
learning disability, *p. 359*
mental retardation, *p. 355*
metacognitive skill, *p. 337*
moral development, *p. 342*
multiple intelligences, *p. 332*
psychometric perspective, *p. 331*
psychosocial development, *p. 340*
scaffolding, *p. 337*
self-esteem, *p. 339*
speech impairment, *p. 358*
visual impairment, *p. 356*

REFLECTIVE PRACTICE

Unlike many other teacher education students who attended State University in the early 1990s, Anita decided to get a dual endorsement to teach kindergarten through sixth grade and to teach special education. She spent an extra semester and two summers taking the special education courses necessary to add the endorsement to her teaching certificate. She reasoned that the extra time and money would be well spent, because the dual endorsement would enhance her employability, and if she taught in a regular classroom, she probably would be expected to work with students who had special needs who were mainstreamed for part or all of their instruction.

When Anita landed her first job teaching sixth grade in Middle Town, she was thrilled at the thought of finally having her own classroom. Student teaching had been extremely rewarding, but she yearned for the chance to be the teacher—the person to whom students and parents turned for guidance. In mid-July the principal called Anita and asked if she would serve on a task force on full inclusion. In his invitation, the principal expressed his strong desire to "involve teachers from the ground up." Their charge was to consider ways to facilitate the school's move away from self-contained special education classrooms and toward full inclusion. Although Anita had not experienced full inclusion in student teaching, she had studied it in her courses; she was flattered to be invited and excited about the challenge.

The task force met in early August, well before the start of school. By the time the meeting was finished, Anita began to sense the difficulty of their task. The other members of the task force talked about "meeting the needs of children" but had very different ideas about what that phrase meant. Moreover, Anita perceived tension between some vocal special education teachers and their general education counterparts.

Issues, Problems, Dilemmas, and Opportunities

Why might special educators and general education teachers view "full inclusion" differently? What educational opportunities might a teacher be able to provide for all students in a class that includes students with special needs compared to teachers in classes without special needs students?

Perceive and Value

Why might the principal have wanted to involve teachers in the inclusion process from the beginning? Although parents are not mentioned here, how might they feel about efforts to include students with special needs in regular classrooms?

Know and Act

If you were Anita, what might you want to know about the students with special needs who were to be included? With whom might you talk to get more information on the situation in this school? Where might you turn for additional information or advice on how full inclusion programs might be constructed fairly and effectively?

Evaluate

How might Anita and the other members of the task force define "success" of a full-inclusion program? Would some outcomes be more important than others? If so, which ones, and why?

ONLINE ACTIVITY

You can find valuable information about programs to assist students online at "A Teacher's Guide to the U.S. Department of Education—Fall 1995." Go to this address: **http://www.ed.gov/pubs/TeachersGuide/**. Some of the resources you will find include

(1) Office of Special Education and Rehabilitative Services Programs (OSERS) (**http://www.ed.gov/pubs/TeachersGuide/pt12.html**), which supports programs that assist in educating children and youth with disabilities, training special education teachers, and conducting research in improved methods of special education and vocational rehabilitation;

(2) Office of Bilingual Education and Minority Languages Affairs (**http://www.ed.gov/pubs/TeachersGuide/pt16.html**), which makes funding available to carry out field-initiated research on students or teachers in bilingual education and to provide for the incorporation of appropriate and effective curriculum and instruction for limited English proficient (LEP) students; and

(3) National Professional Development (NDN) Program (**http://www.ed. gov/pubs/TeachersGuide/pt19g.html**), a nationwide program that helps teachers implement successful programs and practices in their schools and classrooms.

CASE 3

Hans Christian Andersen School

As a building-level administrator, Dr. Barbara Shin has a vantage point from which to recognize issues that most others do not have. She sees both problems and opportunities.

The economic circumstances right now are overshadowing. To have money to do experimental work here is exciting. It is amazing that we have had the support from the school board we've had. If that support should be withdrawn, I think that would just devastate us. . . . Something that concerns me, that didn't concern me until just recently, is the hate groups in the community. That situation could consolidate us and make us stand up even more wholeheartedly for what we believe in, or, it could do damage. I have a tendency to think that external force might strengthen us more than damage us.

Shin is an active professional who tries to stretch beyond her own immediate work life to view the world from others' perspectives. She is well aware that the multicultural gender-fair program at Hans Christian Andersen School might be viewed by some as "politically correct."

Some of the politically correct arguments seem to be based on the idea we will lose the Western point of view. We say we will include more [content], rather than just a literature base that is European in nature. We will bring in the literature of all the cultures within the nation. To us that's becoming educated or multiculturally literate, not just culturally literate in the singular sense.

Shin's background as a teacher shaped the professional knowledge that drives her behavior as an administrator.

Just last night at a meeting someone said to me that a lot of what principals do is based on how they perceive their jobs. I guess you'd have to say that I'm one of the people that falls into the category of seeing myself as instructional leader. I feel really good, because more of my 20 years of experience have been as a teacher than as·an administrator.

Dr. Shin draws on her years of classroom experience to take action or model for both teachers and students how multicultural education can be an integral part of the curriculum. For example, she conducts a "multicultural quiz" for a group of fourth-grade students.

Dr. Shin: What is culture? Give some examples. What does multicultural mean? [Lots of hands go up.] Oh, I'm going to try to give everybody a turn this afternoon, so don't get disappointed if I don't call on you each time. Okay, Russell, I'm going to start with you.

Russell: Many cultures.

Dr. Shin: How simple. Did you know that sometimes grownups get it all confused, and they don't realize that it is very simple; that multicultural means many cultures? Thank you, Russell, that was excellent.

As principal and director of the multicultural gender-fair curriculum project, Dr. Shin is in a position to know how important evaluation of the program can be to people inside and outside the school.

We spent a whole year planning before we jumped into this program. We will go back to the plan itself to see what we've actually accomplished to judge our success. I would say that there must be some concrete results that will show up from all the different ways of gathering information. That's all the way across science, math, writing skills, having a multicultural literature base, that you can see the kids know stories from different cultures, that they're able to talk about them, that they have a common knowledge base that represents diversity. The traditional achievement tests, even though I know they're biased, are still used in the broader picture to measure what we're doing. . . . We are looking at an eclectic approach to assessment. We're going to do some product reviews, portfolios, performance assessment. These will be some of our measures in addition to the standardized tests that are used in the district. . . . Teacher observation and teacher opinion are also very important in transforming the curriculum and in assessing children.

CASE APPLICATION

- Why might Dr. Shin believe it so important for the principal to be present occasionally as a teacher in the classroom?
- Dr. Shin describes the school population as "about one-third American Indian, about one-third African American, and about one-third European American. There are also a few children who are of Asian-American or Hispanic ancestry. About half to two-thirds of our population are served for special needs. . . . About 60% or so receive free or reduced-price lunches."
- How does having such a diverse student body present special challenges and opportunities for teaching and learning?
- Of the four concepts governing educational finance—quality, efficiency, liberty, and adequacy—adequacy has traditionally been at the center of discussions about schools that have a high proportion of low-income students. Why?
- Why might Dr. Shin and others believe that it is desirable to assess student learning using a variety of measures?

10

Curriculum and Instruction

People typically think of *curriculum* as what is taught in school, and *instruction* as the method by which curriculum is delivered. The word *curriculum*, however, encompasses so many ideas that it defies simple description. We use this chapter to discuss some of the more prominent ways curriculum has been defined through educational practice. We explore some of the forces influencing curriculum content and the aims underlying the curriculum—aims that may be stated explicitly or left implicit. We describe ways educators design curriculum. We also describe models of instruction that can be used for a variety of purposes. Finally, we consider factors that determine the effectiveness of classroom instruction.

1 What is curriculum?

2 What forces and change agents affect curriculum content?

3 How are curriculum and instruction planned and organized?

4 What are four general models of instruction?

5 What is effective instruction?

WHAT IS CURRICULUM?

Most people define **curriculum** in terms of what is taught in school. Books are curriculum. Study guides are curriculum. Movies, newspapers, computer programs, board games, animals, and songs can be curriculum. A good working definition of curriculum is the knowledge and skills that schools are held accountable for helping students to master.

There is a "productive uncertainty" of ideas about the content and aims of school programs, however (Schubert, 1986, p. 8). Peter Oliva (1992) observes that *curriculum* has been used to mean a set of subjects, subject content, a program of studies, a set of materials, a sequence of courses, a set of performance objectives, and a course of study. Curriculum can be regarded as everything that goes on within the school, including extra-class activities, guidance, and interpersonal relationships, as well as everything that is taught both inside and outside school that is directed by the school or planned by school personnel. Curriculum can also be described as a series of experiences undergone by learners in school or that which an individual learner experiences as a result of schooling (Oliva, 1992, pp. 5–6).

Americans have a variety of conflicting conceptions about what constitutes curriculum, and thus about what children should or should not be taught in classrooms. The tensions, arguments, and divisions arise in large measure because the population is heterogeneous, and rapid socioeconomic change routinely makes curriculum decisions controversial. Because education is a power reserved to the states, states and localities are left to define curriculum. Beyond some rather vague agreement on the need for students to read, write, and compute, there is considerable variation in people's expectations for how curriculum should be defined.

Who should define the curriculum?

Curriculum is an operative concept outside school as well as inside. Business, industry, churches, prisons, and other organizations provide out-of-school training in topics as diverse as dog obedience, home sales, and natural childbirth. Curriculum is at issue when the agricultural extension agent drops by the rural farmhouse, when children watch Sesame Street and attend Scout meetings, and when people study for a real estate license. Curriculum is not the exclusive province of schools.

■ Explicit and Implicit Curricula

The curriculum contained in policy statements, manuals of procedure, instructional materials, and textbooks that stipulate what and how students are to learn is the **explicit curriculum**. It is a lot like the "public curriculum" of visual images, tours, lectures, and workshops in museums (Vallance, 1995) only more prescriptive. The explicit curriculum expresses in official descriptions of programs, courses, and objectives of study the specific educational expectations held for both teachers and students. Teachers are expected to teach the explicit curriculum; students are supposed to learn it. This is the curriculum for which schools are held publicly accountable.

If the explicit curriculum dominates the public view, another side of the curriculum is unvoiced and often unintended. This side reveals itself in the way teachers present subject matter and in the classroom atmosphere they establish. Philip Jackson (1990, p. 33) calls this curriculum the "hidden curriculum." Elliot Eisner (1985, p. 89) uses the term **implicit curriculum** for essentially the same idea.

Based on observations of teacher–student interactions in elementary classrooms over a period of 2 years, Jackson (1990) perceived a number of institutional expectations that affected a student's success in the classroom. "Trying" was one such expectation taught implicitly, rather than explicitly, through school experiences. If a student "does his homework (though incorrectly), he raises his hand (though he usually comes up with the wrong answer), [and] he keeps his nose in the book during free study period (though he doesn't turn the page very often)," he will likely gain the teacher's approval and be labeled a "model" student (p. 34). Students learn implicitly that mastery of content is not the only road to success in the classroom.

Unofficial routines and rituals of schooling also are part of the implicit curriculum. Teacher behavior, such as calling on students with hands raised while ignoring those who verbalize opinions without permission, is but one of the subtle ways that teachers convey what are considered largely middle-class values.

Another type of implicit curriculum relates to teachers' value orientations and to the subject matter they teach. In case studies of four high school teachers (two English teachers and two history teachers), Sigrun Gudmundsdottir (1991) found that teachers' values seeped into the curriculum through personal interpretations of subject matter and through teaching methods.

For example, when English teachers were presenting *Huckleberry Finn*, one teacher viewed the book as an illustration of "an individual rebelling against conventions," while the other considered it "a book about relationships [between Huck and Jim]" (p. 48). In presenting the book, each teacher selected passages for discussion representative of these ideas, thus creating different "texts" for their students.

What aspects of the explicit curriculum are evident in this photograph? What aspects of the implicit curriculum might you infer?

Null Curriculum

Consequences of school programs are similarly affected by what Eisner (1985) refers to as the **null curriculum**. This is the curriculum that is *not* taught. Our silence on many matters is purported to have a variety of ramifications, not the least of which is a negative effect on students' abilities to examine critically all sides of an issue and to make informed decisions. The intellectual processes and subject matter areas emphasized and neglected by teachers contribute to this condition.

Christine Sleeter and Carl Grant argue that textbook content in particular, "withholds, obscures, and renders unimportant many ideas and areas of knowledge" (1991, p. 97). Their picture and story-line analyses of textbooks

> **Should schools be concerned about aspects of the curriculum that are not taught?**

published between 1980 and 1988 and used in grades 1 through 8 revealed that attention to inequality based on race, sex, disability, and social class left much to be desired. Sleeter and Grant contend that textbooks conveyed an image of a largely middle-class society, devoid of poverty and without great wealth. According to Sleeter and Grant, this tendency to ignore issues of gender, social class, poverty, and disability has the potential for "producing citizens with a shallow social consciousness and narrow sense of history and culture" (p. 101). Such a tendency can alienate from school lower-class children and children of color. Others hypothesize that such curriculum practices reproduce and legitimize existing social-class hierarchies (Apple & Beyer, 1988).

Yet another way that schools convey hidden messages to students is through time schedules for different classes and locations for instruction.

Cultural Awareness

When the New York State Board of Regents set out to shape social studies curriculum for the public schools, its committee acknowledged the contributions of many cultures to the formation of core American values (New York State Social Studies Review and Development Committee, 1991). The Regents appointed a committee of 24 college, university, and public school teachers to review and modify existing social studies syllabi. Their task was to create "a plan for increasing all students' understanding of American history and culture, the history and culture of the diverse groups which comprise American society today, and the history and culture of other peoples throughout the world" (Sobol, 1991, p. 1). In its final report to the board, the committee recommended how social studies curricula should be structured:

> Social studies should not be so much concerned with "whose culture" and "whose history" are to be taught and learned, as with the development of intellectual competence in learners, with

> intellectual competence viewed as having as one of its major components the capacity to view the world and understand it from multiple perspectives. Thus the position is taken that a few fundamental concepts should be the focus of the teaching and learning of the social studies, with applications, contexts and examples drawn from multiple cultural sources, differing perspectives and diverse identity group referents. Multicultural knowledge in this conception of the social studies becomes a vehicle and not the goal. Multicultural content and experience become instruments by which we enable persons to develop their intelligence and to function as human and humane persons. (New York Social Studies Review and Development Committee, 1991, p. 13)

Time devoted to the arts, for example, is substantially less than time devoted to such courses as science and math and communicates to students "what counts" in schools (Eisner, 1992). Moreover, the fact that art teachers are often "floaters"—moving from classroom to classroom—suggests to students that the arts are less permanent and perhaps less important than other courses. Yet if even one generation of students grows up ignorant of architecture, music, paintings, theater, sculpture, dance, poetry, drawing, photography, and graphic and landscape design, the record of human achievement is in jeopardy.

Extracurriculum

Many schools have a well-developed **extracurriculum**, or curriculum that has arisen in and around the core of a student's studies (Berk, 1992). By definition, this extracurriculum is not credit bearing—it is extra, or over and above the required curriculum. Yet it can exert considerable power over students. Students' feelings of self-efficacy, their desire to come to school, their need to belong or be part of a group, and even their performance in other basic curricular areas can be influenced greatly by extracurricular activities.

Sports, band, clubs, study groups, school plays, cheerleading, dance, etc., may fall under the rubric of the extracurriculum. In some schools these activities may be considered "cocurricular" and weighted equally with other academic offerings. In the main, however, most of these activities are viewed as being outside the typical curriculum.

Nevertheless, people make conceptual and policy ties between the curriculum and the extracurriculum. For example, if a student performs poorly on the required curriculum, someone is sure to argue the student should not be allowed to participate in the extracurriculum, at least until there is improvement in her grades. Others will argue the opposite—were it not for the appeal of extracurricular activities, a student with academic problems might be a dropout.

Researchers at the U.S. Department of Education's Office of Research and Improvement (OERI) found a strong connection between extracurricular activities and academic performance. Generally, extracurricular participation rates rose with socioeconomic level, enrollment in an academic curriculum, and attainment of a B+ or better average.

▓ Integrated Curriculum

People across the nation, and in other countries as well, are challenging traditional practices of compartmentalizing subject matter so that teaching and learning bear little resemblance to life outside schools. Instead, they are implementing an **integrated curriculum**, or curriculum that combines concepts and skills from different subject areas (Aceland, 1967). As John Goodlad and Zhizxin Su (1992) note, the ultimate integration of curriculum takes place within the learner—in the learner's mind. The way curriculum is organized aids this process.

Efforts to integrate curricula are occurring in different ways in communities all over the country (Virginia Education Association & The Appalachia Educational Laboratory, 1995). Together, teachers of primary-grade students in a California school plan and teach science, social studies, and foreign language as though distinctions among the subjects were real but not insurmountable obstacles. The teaching team helps students acquire concepts, skills, and values by exploring themes that pervade subject matter. They resist chunking the disciplines by the clock and by the classrooms students occupy. Middle-school teachers in North Carolina take the study of science, social studies, language arts, and mathematics beyond school walls to their community—and even to Disney World—to forge connections in young minds between content acquired and content applied. In other efforts, high school teachers and administrators in Illinois restructure blocks of time in their conventional eight-period day into four periods. They assign staff to interdisciplinary teams, change student entrance and exit requirements for courses, and incorporate an entirely new set of instructional models. All of these programs—regardless of grade level and geographical location—intend to raze artificial barriers that separate subject matters to help diverse students work together to solve real problems.

Emerging technologies give impetus to curriculum integration and to the related topics of interdisciplinary teaching and learning. For example, teachers from across the United States and Canada have begun to work together on the Internet to solve real-life problems by analyzing cases of interdisciplinary teaching and learning (The Hitachi Foundation, 1996). One multimedia Web case is entitled "What Did You Learn in School Today?" It features the day-to-day challenges of a kindergarten teacher. She struggles to complete a six-week plan that allows flexibility in teaching yet conforms to her state's standards of learning. The case involves the teaching of language arts, math, and social studies. It explores issues related to ethnicity, culture, parent involvement, cooperative learning, discipline, use of time, and assessment. (To find out more about this case and teachers' online work visit **http://teach. virginia.edu/go/casecourse**).

WHAT FORCES AND CHANGE AGENTS AFFECT CURRICULUM CONTENT?

In public education there is a profusion of interests at work to shape the curriculum. Historically, some interests have operated close to and directly on the school itself. Others have exercised power indirectly and from a distance,

FIGURE 10.1
**Forces That Shape
the Curriculum**

Which forces and groups are
most influential in shaping
the curriculum in your community's schools?

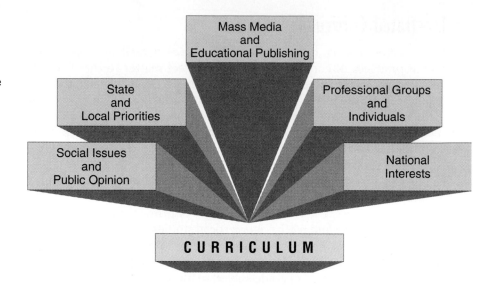

both conceptually and physically. These interests have wielded considerable
authority over what is to be taught and learned. As Figure 10.1 indicates, the
forces that shape the curriculum include, for example, the culture of the community and school, national interests, social issues and public opinion, professional groups and individuals, state and local priorities, and mass media
and educational publishing.

Culture of the Community and School

What takes place in schools is largely defined by community members'
sense of what "should be perpetuated, of what is missing and should be
included, and of what is included but not in the right degree or right way and
should be modified" (Peshkin, 1992, p. 250). According to Alan Peshkin, the
"tangled tapestry of subcultures" within society
make this a challenging task. Community members in a school decide what the language of
instruction should be and which courses should
receive the most emphasis. They also decide
whether there should be a school-wide focus on
a particular area, such as moral instruction, discipline, civic responsibility, or critical thinking.

> To what extent
> should the
> curriculum
> reflect local
> interests and
> values?

As noted in Chapter 8, some school communities have considered race and ethnicity, in particular, when making curriculum decisions.
Concerns about biased views of history led educators in Portland, Oregon,
for example, to develop an Afrocentric curriculum. Students view the past
through the eyes of African Americans.

> School officials in the Oregon city commissioned scholars to write "base-
> line essays" on the contributions of African and American blacks in six
> fields of study: art, language arts, mathematics, science, social studies,
> and music. Teachers are now expected to "infuse" that information
> throughout their teaching. (Viadero, 1990, p. 11)

The National Interest

The Benchmarks for Chapter 3 suggest that the influence of national government on the school curriculum has a long and rich history. Passage of the Environmental Education Act (Public Law 91-516), for example, stimulated the modern environmental education movement (DeBoer, 1991). Vocational education (Smith-Hughes Act of 1917), preschool education (Economic Opportunity Act of 1964), and expanded school access for students with disabilities (Education for All Handicapped Children Act of 1975 and Individuals with Disabilities Education Act, 1990) are funded through federal laws. Laws such as these reflect values about education that are in the national interest.

Federal influence on curriculum development also occurs through funding and exhortation. Between 1994 and 1996, for example, the federal government provided financial assistance to states that submitted plans for ways they might

What kind of curriculum is in the national interest?

help students meet national standards. In 1996, at the second national Education Summit, with leadership from President Clinton, the governors and 49 executives from some of the largest U.S. companies (e.g., IBM, AT&T, Eastman Kodak) pledged to begin asking for academic transcripts from job applicants and to consider a state's educational standards when deciding where to open new plants. The combination of federal, state, and private influences can leverage change in school curriculum simply by their expecting to find evidence of such change in students' transcripts and in the standards that drive curriculum and instruction.

Social Issues and Public Opinion

As noted in Chapter 7, concerns about issues such as teenage childbearing and the spread of AIDS have been the impetus for a number of curricular efforts. Perhaps the most striking and controversial curriculum aimed unabashedly at restructuring society may be that devoted to what is sometimes called *family life education*. Family life education is an integral part of most school programs. It focuses on topics such as personal health and safety, substance abuse prevention, mental health education, human growth and development (including sex education), and HIV-disease prevention. It is probably the one area of the curriculum that is most closely scrutinized by the public. Parents often must sign a permission form for their children to participate in family life offerings.

Family life education programs around the country are alike in that they acknowledge the central role of parents in educating their children. How programs in schools are to be carried out, however, can vary greatly from one district to another. In Fairfax, Virginia, for example, the curriculum for family life education is teacher-centered and highly prescriptive. Those who teach in the program must be selected by their principals and must participate in inservice training "to insure uniform implementation in all schools" (Fairfax County Public Schools, 1991, p. vi). Teachers are given little leeway in how they present curriculum. In a lesson plan designed for sixth graders as a review of basic facts about socially transmitted diseases, the prescriptiveness of the lesson is evident in the note to the teacher found at the beginning of the lesson plan:

> The sixth grade Human Growth and Development unit does not lend itself to open discussion concerning AIDS. Topics of homosexuality and the use of condoms for protection are NOT part of this lesson. Do not deviate from this lesson as presented. Preface all statements as to how the human immunodeficiency virus is transmitted by one of the following statements: "To date scientists believe you cannot get AIDS from . . ." or "Studies have shown that. . . ." (p. 65)

Shreveport, Louisiana, schools have adopted a curriculum for sex education that advocates abstinence. The general line of thought is a familiar one: The more students know, the more curious they become, and the more likely they are to step over some real or imagined line of decency. The challenge for teachers in this situation is to teach junior and senior high school students how to say no.

▨ Professional Groups and Individuals

Curriculum in schools has been influenced over time by professional educators, working collectively or as individuals. Some organizations, such as the National Council of Teachers of Mathematics (NCTM), have developed standards intended to guide reform in schools. The NCTM's *Curriculum and Evaluation Standards for School Mathematics* (1989) comprises 54 value statements. Each is couched in three parts that address (a) what mathematics the curriculum should include, (b) a description of the student activities associated with that mathematics, and (c) instructional examples. Experts assert that the NCTM standards are revolutionary because they "remove computation from its reigning role in the mathematics curriculum and make it serve a more important goal—the development of mathematical thinking" (Association for Supervision and Curriculum Development, 1992, p. 3).

The standards are based on the assumption that "knowing" math means "doing" math. They also recognize the revolution brought about by computers and calculators. The standards set out guidelines for core knowledge, or that knowledge common to all students, as well as special requirements for college-bound students. Standard 3, which follows, addresses how students integrate their knowledge to demonstrate "mathematical power."

Standard 3: Mathematics as Reasoning

In grades 5–8, reasoning shall permeate the mathematics curriculum so that students can—

- recognize and apply deductive and inductive reasoning;
- understand and apply reasoning processes, with special attention to spatial reasoning and reasoning with proportions and graphs;
- make and evaluate mathematical conjectures and arguments;
- validate their own thinking;
- appreciate the pervasive use and power of reasoning as a part of mathematics. (National Council of Teachers of Mathematics, 1989, p. 81)

Figure 10.2 provides an example of a task that reflects this standard.

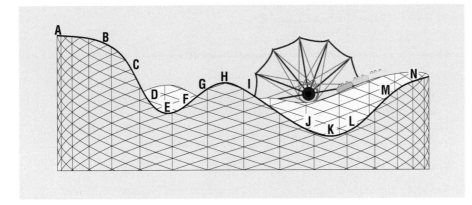

FIGURE 10.2

Sample Problem to Assess Students' Reasoning Skills

Construct a graph without numbers that depicts the speed of the roller coaster at various points on the track.

Note. From *Curriculum and Evaluation: Standards for School Mathematics*, March, 1989 (p. 83), Reston, VA: The National Council of Teachers of Mathematics. Reprinted with permission.

NCTM has also created a companion volume to accompany the standards entitled *Professional Standards for Teaching Mathematics* (National Council of Teachers of Mathematics, 1991). The teaching standards recognize teachers as central to changing mathematics education in the schools. They emphasize, among other factors, the need to shift instruction toward the use of logic and mathematical evidence for verification and away from a reliance on teachers as sources of right answers. The standards also promote teaching practice that encourages conjecture and problem solving. Table 10.1 provides a contact list of professional groups working on national curriculum standards for different subject areas.

Individual teachers also create, select, and transmit curriculum content. Their habits, dispositions, and areas of professional expertise exert powerful influences on what is taught and learned—influences that can be either conservative or boldly innovative. When teachers stick to familiar tools, content, and activities, they operate as conservative—and some believe negative—forces on curriculum (Cuban, 1992). In the 1970s, criticisms of ill-prepared teachers led designers to create what are often referred to as "teacher proof" curricula, or curricula from which students can learn, regardless of the teacher's level of experience, interest, or skill (Grobman, 1970). Today, attitudes toward teachers as professionals are more positive.

> **To what extent should teachers and professional associations determine the curriculum?**

Teachers' creative influences on curricula are many and varied. In language arts or literature-based instruction, for example, teachers who teach with a philosophy of constructivism guide students to define knowledge for themselves, using curricula as stimuli for innovative thinking. These teachers help students select material and act within a social context that molds knowledge but does not determine absolutely what constitutes knowledge (Applebee, 1991; Langer & Applebee, 1986). Teaching in these instances is not a matter of transmitting some objectively formed body of knowledge; it is more a matter of helping students construct and interpret knowledge for themselves.

In other intricate ways, teachers shape what is to be learned by bringing their own personal histories with them into the classroom (Clandinin &

TABLE 10.1   Some Contact Groups for
National Standards

Social Studies	Science
National Council for the Social Studies (NCSS) 3501 Newark St. NW Washington, DC 20016	National Science Education Standards 2101 Constitution Ave. NW, HA 486 Washington, DC 20418
English	**The Arts**
Center for the Study of Reading 174 Children's Research Center 51 Gerty Drive Champaign, IL 61820	Music Educators National Conference (MENC) 1902 Association Drive Reston, VA 22091
Mathematics	**Physical Education**
National Council of Teachers of Mathematics (NCTM) 1906 Association Drive Reston, VA 20091	National Association for Sports and Physical Education 1900 Association Drive Reston, VA 22091

Note. From "Achieving higher standards" by J. O'Neil, 1993, *Educational Leadership, 50*(5), pp. 4–8. Reprinted with permission of the Association for Supervision and Curriculum Development. Copyright ©1993 by ASCD. All rights reserved.

Connelly, 1992). Their personalities, their formal academic preparation, and their experiences are all lived out with students through continual interactions. Teachers—and, in turn, students—become the "texts" for study.

Children's needs can and must dictate the nature of some curricula. Indeed, as students' problems increase in number and/or severity, the standard curriculum may be reduced or modified to make room for special curricular offerings. These curricula and the programs organized to deliver them are organized to fit the students instead of the other way around.

Students' needs and interests also are a major consideration when planning instruction. Teachers and curriculum developers recognize the power of the aphorism that success breeds success. When a curriculum stimulates and holds student attention, the curriculum is likely to be copied, extended, promoted, adapted, and used with other students. Also, in noticeable ways, students influence teachers to behave in certain ways in the classroom; that is, students encourage teachers to emphasize or deemphasize various aspects of the curriculum (Hunt & Sullivan, 1974).

■ State and Local Priorities

State laws and local policies—many promoted by special-interest groups—routinely affect curriculum content (see Chapter 6). State mandates aimed at overhauling school curriculum have resulted in prescribed graduation requirements, an array of state achievement tests, and, in many

VOICES

On the Teacher as Curriculum Maker

Curriculum researchers, D. Jean Clandinin and F. Michael Connelly, perceive the teacher as a curriculum maker—a collaborator with students and researchers in what is to be learned, not merely a purveyor of knowledge established by others.

This literature of teachers' stories and stories of teachers provides an important avenue for conceptualizing the work of teachers as curriculum makers. Learning to listen to the stories teachers tell of their practice is an important step toward creating an understanding of the teacher as curriculum maker. However, we see our task as researchers as moving beyond this step to a second: to create with teachers a story of teachers as curriculum makers. We see this task as a collaborative one in which we participate with teachers in their classrooms and together live out and construct a story of the teacher as curriculum maker and, in this endeavor, imagine the possibility of curriculum reform....(1992, p. 386)

The collaborative living out of researchers', teachers', and children's stories in the classroom changes the curriculum.... In their collaborative endeavor, researcher and teacher see the unfolding plots of the stories and observe them closely. When they tell their mutually constructed story of the teacher as curriculum maker to other teachers and researchers, it invites others to see and examine their stories' plots, scenes, and characters closely. Thus we see the potential for change and growth as other teachers work in their classrooms. To fulfill this agenda calls for not only the creation of a literature that records these stories but also the construction of a method of working with current and prospective teachers and researchers to educate them to the imaginative possibilities of reading this literature (pp. 392–393).

We want to return to a vision of curriculum as a course of life and develop a language of practice in which we think, talk, theorize, and act differently in relation to practice. When we construct the ways in which teachers have experienced our work as curriculum researchers, we realize that we have continued to act out the conduit metaphor, reinforcing the assumption that knowledge is conveyed from outside classrooms to the teachers inside them. This process disallows the use of knowledge that [John] Dewey suggests is "a vehicle for change in our ever-changing environment, in our understanding of the world" (Johnson, 1989, p. 392). We wish to come to know teachers' knowledge as the "very way they construct their reality as they live it through their embodiment, with all its tempos, moods, patterns, and projections. No verbal and intellectualized account of the teacher's beliefs could ever do justice to the experienced reality of this web of experiential processes that constitute the teacher's knowledge-in-process" (p. 393).

CRITICAL THINKING

Why and in what ways might collaborative classroom research change the curriculum? What do the authors mean by "the conduit metaphor" for teachers in relation to curriculum and instruction? What alternative metaphor can you think of that represents the authors' different view? How might you represent visually the "web of experiential processes that constitute the teacher's knowledge-in-process" that Johnson describes? As a teacher, what might be some advantages and disadvantages of being a curriculum maker?

Note. From "Teacher as curriculum maker" by D. J. Clandinin, & F. M. Connelly, (1992). In P. W. Jackson (Ed.) *Handbook of research on curriculum* (pp. 363–401), New York: Macmillan.

In what ways do school curricula reflect state priorities and regional or local interests? What are the other principal sources of influence upon curriculum content?

instances, new textbooks selected to match recommended instructional approaches (Cuban, 1992). In California, for example, when the state adopted a literature-based framework for teaching language arts in 1988, textbook publishers crafted books accordingly. Subsequently, students' poor scores on state and national reading tests in 1995 prompted education officials to revamp their language arts program by combining their literature-based approach with instruction in phonics and basic skills. Delaine Eastin, the state superintendent of schools, notified textbook publishers that materials for the 1996 K–8 adoption needed to reflect California's new approaches to instruction (Diegmueller, 1995b).

State governments and local education agencies are influenced by political action committees, networks of parents, professional education organizations, civic organizations, and religious groups. Each group develops its own education reform agendas. A state or district may prescribe essential elements for all curricula at all grade levels. Some states—Texas for example—issue essential elements for all subjects from preschool through grade 12 (C. Levinson, personal communication, May 20, 1996).

Whose interests should take precedence in states' curricular reform agendas?

The curriculum that students experience in school also often hinges on local geography and community resources. Students at Longfellow Middle School in La Crosse, Wisconsin, for example, explore life on, in, and around the Mississippi River with the help of teachers, and local experts. These include commercial fishermen, officials from the state Department of Natural Resources, and fish and wildlife experts from the National Biological Survey. Students' experiences at the river are the bases for mathematics, science, language arts, and social studies instruction (Pitsch, 1995).

Educational Publishing and Mass Media

Textbooks play an important role in student learning, and the people who select them play an important role in shaping the curriculum (Pinar, Reynolds, Slattery, & Taubman, 1995). Various conservative and liberal watchdog organizations routinely urge people to get involved in textbook selection in their states and communities. Nearly half the states have processes by which curricular materials are evaluated and endorsed at the state level. A state-level endorsement in populous states that keep a tight rein on selection—such as Florida, Texas, and California—can be the difference between success and failure for a particular text and, indeed, for its publisher (Apple, 1993).

State textbook adoption policies have influenced the shape of curriculum for years. According to Michael Apple (1993), these policies originated for several reasons. First, they have been an effort to ensure that school districts purchase books at the lowest possible prices. Second, the state has attempted to protect children from being exposed to poor textbooks by relying on experts to make selections. Third, uniformity among texts at the state level enables the establishment of a minimum standard curriculum throughout the state.

Because textbooks may constitute as much as 70% of the curriculum, some curriculum experts think that textbooks exert the most powerful influence of all on curriculum (Morrison, 1993). They worry about this circumstance because many textbooks lack high quality. They might teach to the "lowest common denominator," or "dumb down" the curriculum; avoid controversy; be pedagogically unsound; or teach inaccurate and erroneous information.

> In an episode that angered educators, scrutiny by an advocacy group in Texas led to the discovery of thousands of errors in the latest U.S. history textbooks. . . . Among the gaffes: One book said President Truman "easily settled" the war in Korea by dropping "the bomb," although nuclear weapons weren't used in Korea, and Eisenhower was president when the armistice was signed. Another said Napoleon won at Waterloo. . . . (Putka, 1992, p. B1)

Protests about textbooks can erupt into community squabbles. Parent groups in Canadian and U.S. schools, for example, protested the use of a K–6 elementary reading series that uses themes such as Halloween to present fiction, nonfiction, and poetry by well-known English, American, and Canadian authors. Curricula based on Halloween are offensive to fundamentalist groups, who contend that they teach children witchcraft (McConaghy, 1992). When such interest-group protests are reported by the mass media, they affect the way textbooks are written.

> **To what extent does the textbook publishing industry determine the curriculum?**

Beyond serving informational and public oversight functions, the media are involved directly in producing their own curricula. Educational programming on public television represents perhaps the most visible and readily accessible forms of curriculum and instruction. The hour-long Public Broadcasting Service (PBS) documentary entitled "On Television: Teach the Children," which first aired in 1992, criticizes television as teacher.

> The primary courses within the TV curriculum, analysts assert, teach expensive lessons in consumption, larded with images of sex, violence, and anti-intellectualism. On occasion, television enhances classroom learning, but TV programming in the U.S. ordinarily consists of "entertainment" fare. (Magee, 1992, p. 9)

Other examples of media-designed and -delivered curricula abound. Chris Whittle's media empire beams Channel One into high school classrooms to educate students about current events and, simultaneously, to hawk commercial products. In 1995 Channel One struck an agreement with Capital Cities/ABC, Inc. to carry ABC daily newscasts to almost 12,000 schools (Reilly, 1995).

Commercial textbook publishers influence the curriculum through the authors they hire and the books and materials they produce. Publishers argue

VOICES

On Student-Centered Instruction

There are many ways for teachers to encourage expression, some quite personal. Nancie Atwell—teacher of adolescents, of writing, and of life—makes personal expression central in her classroom.

I confess. I started out as a "creationist." The first days of every school year I created; for the next thirty-six weeks I maintained my creation. My curriculum. From behind my big desk I set it in motion, managed and maintained it all year long. I wanted to be a great teacher—systematic, purposeful, in control. I wanted great results from my great practices. And I wanted to convince other teachers that this creation was superior stuff. So I studied my curriculum, conducting research designed to show its wonders. I didn't learn in my classroom. I tended and taught my creation.

These days, I learn in my classroom. What happens there has changed; it continually changes. I've become an "evolutionist," and the curriculum unfolds now as my kids and I learn together. My aims stay constant—I want us to go deep inside language, using it to know and shape and play with our worlds—but my practices evolve as eighth graders and I go deeper. This going deeper is research, and these days my research shows me the wonders of my kids, not my methods. But it has also brought me full circle. What I learn with these students, collaborating with them as a writer and reader who wonders about writing and reading, makes me a better teacher—not great maybe, but at least grounded in the logic of learning, and growing. . . .

I didn't intuit or luck into this place, and I didn't arrive overnight. I paved the way through writing and reading about writing, through uncovering and questioning my assumptions, through observing kids and trying to make sense of my observa-tions, through dumb mistakes, uncertain experiments, and, underneath it all, the desire to do my best by my kids.

A lot of the time, doing my best hurt. It means looking hard at what I was doing and asking kids to do. It meant learning—and admitting—that I was wrong. And, most painful of all, it meant letting go of my cherished creation.

I learn in my classroom these days because I abandoned that creation. I had to. When I stopped focusing on me and my methods and started observing students and their learning, I saw a gap yawning between us—between what I did as language teacher and what they did as language learners. I saw that my creation manipulated kids so they bore sole responsibility for narrowing the gap, and my students either found ways to make sense of and peace with the logic of my teaching, or they failed the course. In truth, it was I who needed to move, to strike out for some common ground. I learn in my classroom these days because I moved, because the classroom became a reading and writing workshop, a new territory my students and I could inhabit together.

CRITICAL THINKING

What does Nancie Atwell mean when she calls herself a "creationist" as a novice teacher and later "an evolutionist"? What analogy would you use to describe her new approach to curriculum? What is meant by student-centered instruction, and at what point in her professional development did Nancie Atwell discover it? How might you make teaching and learning a collaborative process in a subject area you plan to teach?

Note. From *In the middle: Writing, reading, and learning with adolescents.* by N. Atwell, 1987 (pp. 3–4), Portsmouth, NH: Boynton/ Cook. Reprinted by permission.

that in fact they do not influence the curriculum as much as do the people who buy the books. In their attempt to read the market, publishers provide what they believe people will buy. And buy they do—textbooks gross nearly $2.16 billion a year (Diegmueller, 1995a).

How are Curriculum and Instruction Planned and Organized?

When planning for instruction, teachers must consider the destination—the aims of education and goals of the curriculum—as well as the best way to reach the destination. As Nancie Atwell (1987) suggests, these decisions cannot be made in a vacuum. To organize curriculum in ways that maximize students' opportunities for success, teachers must also be learners, interacting with students to shape curriculum in ways that meet the students' needs and interests.

Aims of Education

Curriculum and instruction are planned and organized to reflect commitment to specific aims or goals of education. Over the years, differing ideas about the aims of education, roles of teachers and students, and the nature of knowledge have resulted in different orientations toward curriculum. As illustrated in Figure 10.3, orientations include development of cognitive processes; academic rationalism; personal relevance; social adaption, change, and outcomes-based view; and curriculum as technology. The different orientations illustrate how different goals of education influence curriculum development.

Teacher Planning for Instruction

Teacher planning has been described as "the thread that weaves the curriculum, or the *what* of teaching, with the instruction, or how of teaching" (Frieberg & Driscoll, 1996, p. 22). When planning instruction, teachers consider the curriculum, state and local goals and objectives for student learning, instructional strategies for meeting those goals, and means of assessing students' understanding. It is difficult to overestimate the importance of planning how to evaluate student learning and the effectiveness of a lesson.

When identifying goals and objectives, teachers determine what students should learn or be able to do as a result of instruction (e.g., from examples and nonexamples, students should be able to identify similes). Decisions about the desired results of learning help teachers clarify their thinking about methods and materials to use during instruction. Although objectives typically are influenced by state and local mandates, they also are shaped by teachers' perceptions of students' needs and abilities before, during, and after instruction.

Aims of Education	Curriculum Orientation	Roles of Students and Teachers	Examples of Curriculum Content	Examples of Instructional Approaches
Teach students how to learn.	Development of Cognitive Processes	Student-centered: Students think about academic tasks and construct meaningful knowledge in relationship to prior experiences. Teachers mediate and facilitate students' learning.	Thinking skills; study skills; problem-solving skills	Scaffolding; inquiry learning
Impart culture to students,	Academic Rationalism	Teacher-centered: Students receive instruction and demonstrate competencies.	Great ideas; great works of art; literary classics; basic skills	Direct instruction
Help students find self-fulfillment, develop effective learning styles	Personal Relevance	Student-centered: Students and teachers collaborate to create or match curricula to individual and group interests and needs. Teachers provide opportunities for student reflection and self-evaluation.	Opportunities for personal expression; clarification of personal values	Individualized instruction; non-directive teaching
Help students become productive citizens capable of changing the social order.	Social Adaptation, Change, & Outcomes-based view	Teacher-centered: Teachers present facts, issues, problems, and learning challenges for students to act upon or apply in life.	Citizenship; communication skills; environmental, social issues, & job-related skills	Questioning; cooperative learning; project-based learning; internships
Give students the tools they need to master subjects; deliver instruction efficiently.	Curriculum as Technology	Subject-centered: Teachers preestablish developmentally appropriate learning goals, outcomes, objectives, and criteria for assessment for a subject area. Students demonstrate minimum competencies.	Traditional subjects; basic skills	Direct instruction; mastery learning

When planning for instruction, teachers also think about classroom management. By establishing clear rules and routines, teachers minimize confusion and maximize instructional time. This aspect of planning is particularly important at the beginning of the year, when teachers establish patterns, limits, and expectations that often persist for the remainder of the year (Clark & Dunn, 1991).

When thinking about instruction, teachers also consider ways to motivate students. According to Jere Brophy (1987), teachers can achieve this goal by (a) establishing a supportive classroom environment in which students feel comfortable taking intellectual risks, (b) selecting activities at an appropriate level of difficulty "that teach some knowledge or skill that is worth learning," and (c) using a variety of motivational strategies (p. 208). Such strategies include characterizing the lesson to be taught in familiar terms so that students can conceptualize what they will be learning and explaining goals and objectives for a lesson and their relevance to students' personal lives.

FIGURE 10.3 *(opposite)*
Five Aims of Education and Corresponding Curricular Orientations
Which aims of education and curricular orientations interest you the most at this time?

WHAT ARE FOUR GENERAL MODELS OF INSTRUCTION?

There is no single best way to teach all people for all purposes. Professional teachers develop a repertoire of teaching strategies or models that they can use when conditions warrant. As learners vary in needs and abilities, and as goals change, instructional models must change.

Models of teaching explain in broad terms where teachers are going with their students, how they will get there, and how they will know when they

How should decisions be made about what teaching methods to use?

have arrived. However, the tactics involved in implementing particular models—the moment-to-moment adaptations of strategy—can vary according to a teacher's reading of student comments and behaviors. During instruction, for example, teachers might ask themselves a number of questions: Are students attending? Do they understand? Does someone need a question rephrased? Teachers think about such matters and, if necessary, make midcourse corrections or adaptations in their teaching strategies.

Bruce Joyce and Marsha Weil (1996) demonstrate that professional teachers plan for success; they do not leave it to chance. These authors present detailed descriptions of a variety of **instructional models**, explaining the goals for each model, underlying theoretical assumptions, and relevant research supporting the use of a particular model. They also describe the phases of a model, or how a lesson should proceed; teacher and student roles and relationships; recommended ways to respond to what learners say and do during a lesson; and particular materials, personnel, or training necessary for implementing the model.

Joyce and Weil group their models into four "families" based on the models' purposes (see Figure 10.4). The Behavioral Systems Family uses ideas about manipulating the environment to modify students' behaviors. The Social Family capitalizes on people's nature as social beings to learn from and relate to one another. The Information-Processing Family focuses on increasing students' abilities to think—to seek, organize, interpret, and

FIGURE 10.4

Examples of Teaching Strategies that Contribute to a Teacher's Instructional Repertoire

Effective teachers employ strategies and combinations of strategies from all four "families."

Note. Adapted from *Models of Teaching* (5th ed.) by B. R. Joyce, and M. Weil, 1996, Boston: Allyn and Bacon.

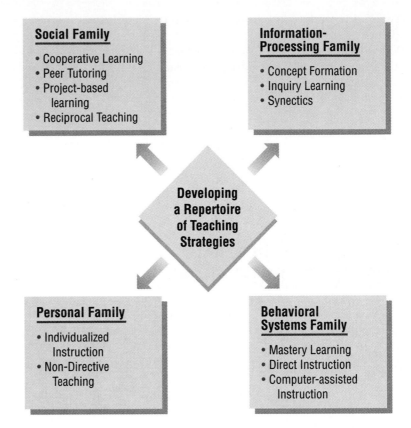

Social Family
- Cooperative Learning
- Peer Tutoring
- Project-based learning
- Reciprocal Teaching

Information-Processing Family
- Concept Formation
- Inquiry Learning
- Synectics

Developing a Repertoire of Teaching Strategies

Personal Family
- Individualized Instruction
- Non-Directive Teaching

Behavioral Systems Family
- Mastery Learning
- Direct Instruction
- Computer-assisted Instruction

apply information both inductively and deductively. The Personal Family encourages self-exploration and the development of personal identity.

Behavioral Systems Family

Mastery learning, one of several behavioral models that has enjoyed widespread use, was developed through the work of Benjamin Bloom (1971), John Carroll (1971), and their colleagues. The basic strategy suggests that student learning is a function of a student's aptitude, his motivation, and the amount and quality of instruction. Instead of defining student aptitude as native ability, proponents of mastery learning define it as the amount of time a student requires to master an objective. Given enough time, the inclination to learn, and instruction fitted to a student's needs, students are thought to be capable of mastering a range of subject matter. Teachers must organize instruction into manageable units, diagnose students' needs with respect to the material, teach in ways that meet those needs, and evaluate progress regularly.

Teachers following Bloom's model select objectives that traverse a hierarchy of simple to complex thought processes (recall, comprehension, application, analysis, synthesis, and evaluation). Bloom's taxonomy of learning objectives has guided the development of many curriculum packages. Table 10.2 shows Bloom's taxonomy and the kinds of tasks teachers must undertake if they are to encourage students to accomplish the objectives.

TABLE 10.2 Bloom's Taxonomy of Educational Objectives

Level	Learner Objectives	Teacher Tasks
1.00 Knowledge	To define, distinguish, acquire, identify, recall, or recognize various forms of information.	To present and/or elicit facts, conventions, categories in ways that enable learners to demonstrate knowledge.
2.00 Comprehension	To translate, transform, give in own words, illustrate, prepare, read, represent, change, rephrase, or restate various forms of information.	To present and/or elicit definitions, words, phrases, relationships, principles in ways that enable learners to demonstrate comprehension.
3.00 Application	To apply, generalize, relate, choose, develop, organize, use, transfer, restructure, or classify various forms of information.	To present and/or elicit principles, laws, conclusions in ways that enable learners to apply what they have learned.
4.00 Analysis	To distinguish, detect, identify, classify, discriminate, recognize, categorize, or deduce various forms of information.	To present and/or elicit elements, hypotheses, assumptions, statements of intent or fact in ways that encourage learners to critically analyze information.
5.00 Synthesis	To write, tell, relate, produce, originate, modify, or document various forms of information.	To present and/or elicit structures, patterns, designs, relationships in ways that encourage learners to form new structures of knowledge.
6.00 Evaluation	To judge, argue, validate, assess, appraise various forms of information.	To present and/or elicit from learners different qualitative judgments.

Note. From *Teacher Development* (p. 57) by R. F. McNergney and C. A. Carrier, 1981, New York: Macmillan.

Like mastery learning, **direct instruction** is a highly structured, teacher-centered strategy. It capitalizes on behavioral techniques such as modeling, feedback, and reinforcement to promote basic skill acquisition, primarily in reading and mathematics. Teachers using this model must set high but not unattainable goals for students. The model prescribes classroom organization and processes that maximize the amount of time students spend on academic tasks at which they can succeed with regularity. Policy emphases on the assessment of students' minimum competency on basic reading and mathematics objectives, rather than complex or advanced learning objectives, have stimulated interest in direct instruction.

Behavioral Objectives In the 1960s and 1970s, Robert Mager (1962) taught educators to write instructional **behavioral objectives**—goal statements, conditions under which learning will occur, and criteria for success. Teaching objectives—and, later, learning objectives—became the backbone of curriculum development, particularly in subject areas in which learning can be measured in quantifiable terms. Statements about what students should know or be able to do after completing a unit of study form the basis of what is taught and how success is judged. As the following example illustrates, outcomes specify the intended result or product of instruction instead of the process of instruction.

An Instructional Behavioral Objective in Mager's Terms

Conditions of Performance:	Given a definition and examples of an adjective as a part of speech,
Behavior:	students will identify adjectives in sentences
Criteria for Performance:	correctly in at least 8 of 10 instances.

Outcomes-Based Education   Another approach associated with behavioral models of instruction is that of **outcomes-based education** (OBE), also known as outcomes-driven developmental model (ODDM) and goal-based education (GBE). This approach is intended to encourage students to achieve outcomes that have real-life applicability. According to William Spady, director of the High Success Network on Outcomes-Based Education, OBE programs have the following characteristics:

1. A clear focus on the outcomes expected.

2. Close articulation of the curriculum with these outcomes.

3. Realistic challenge for students to attain outcome standards.

4. Instructional delivery timed and organized to match student learning levels.

5. Adequate opportunities for students to reach outcome standards.

6. Rewards and grading linked directly to improved performance on outcomes.

7. Support systems for students requiring special assistance.

OBE begins with outcomes and uses a kind of backward planning of instruction.

> Specifying outcomes and setting high performance targets, the thinking goes, would free teachers and administrators to take charge of their schools, envision new strategies for meeting the higher standards, and find innovative ways to guide more children to knowledge and success. (Harp, 1993, p. 19)

But outcomes-based education is proving to be about as controversial as nearly every other reform proposed in recent years, particularly when parents disagree with the outcomes. In Pennsylvania, for example, ex-teacher Peg Luksik organized opposition to the state OBE plan, in large measure because it appeared to reach beyond curriculum and instruction to focus instead on student attitudes and values (Harp, 1993).

Social Family

Instructional models in the social family are intended to help students work together in productive ways to attain both academic and social goals. Teachers serve as guides, encouraging students to express their ideas and to consider others' perspectives as they deal with a variety of problems and issues. Cooperative learning, project-based learning, and reciprocal teaching are just a few examples of approaches to classroom teaching and learning that develop positive school cultures.

Cooperative Learning   **Cooperative learning** is more social in nature than teaching methods in behavioral systems models. Methods for implementing cooperative learning have been articulated by Robert Slavin (1991), Shlomo and Yael Sharan (1989; 1990), and David and Roger Johnson (1991) and their colleague Zhining Qin (1995).

When used as intended, cooperative learning promotes the careful, purposeful formation of heterogeneous groups of students within classrooms to accomplish social, personal, and academic objectives. Cooperative learning has grown in popularity because of its positive effects on student self-esteem, intergroup relations, acceptance of students with academic and physical limitations, attitudes toward school, and ability to work cooperatively (Slavin, 1991).

David and Roger Johnson describe cooperative learning as "learning together." Teachers who use their approach encourage positive interdependence (the idea that the group sinks or swims together), face-to-face interaction among students, individual accountability, the development of social skills, and group processing. Teachers serve as facilitators, observing groups, analyzing problems students have in working together, offering feedback on interaction skills. When necessary, they teach social skills that promote constructive socialization. Students learn constructive ways to deal with controversy and academic disagreements and ways to keep all members verbally involved in the learning process.

Shlomo Sharan (1989; 1990) describes cooperative learning as "group investigation." This means having students work in small groups, with each group taking on a different task. Within groups, students decide what information they need and how to organize and present it. Teachers evaluate students in terms of how they apply and synthesize information and how they make inferences.

Slavin advances a variety of cooperative approaches, sometimes coupled with competition among teams. Student Teams-Achievement Divisions (STAD) has the teacher present a lesson and students work in teams on worksheets or other written material. After one or two presentations and one or two sessions of team practice, students complete independently a quiz or test. Individual scores are based on improvement over previous scores, and team performances are recognized. Teachers can use Jigsaw II, which focuses more on concepts than skills, when students are studying material written in narrative form. Students form teams and receive a common reading to study. Each member of a team becomes an "expert" on one of the topics covered in the reading. Experts from the different teams meet in small groups to master their material and discuss ways to present it to other team members.

While such cooperative strategies have been shown to be more successful in elementary and middle grades, they also work with high school students (Newman & Thompson, 1987). In all of these instances of cooperative learning, teachers plan team formation carefully to encourage not only mastery of subject matter but understanding and acceptance among students as well.

The Education Department of the Metropolitan Opera Guild has created its own cooperative learning model. Teachers can use "Creating Original Opera" to integrate curriculum and to encourage students of all backgrounds and experiences to work collaboratively. The program, designed for students in grades 3 through 6, emphasizes personal responsibility, constructive criticism, and the development of communication skills. Through its emphasis on the formation of an opera company, the program also demands that students work effectively in groups. During an interview, one young actress explained the critical role of cooperation:

> When you act you are part of a company of people putting on the opera. Say like someone forgets their line, and you notice it. Then it is up to you not to make a face or whisper or anything. You have to think fast and make up a new line that your character might say. And that gets the same information said out loud. So imagine that Takisha is supposed to say that she knows the boys are coming, but she forgets her line. Then I have to say, " I think I hear the boys coming," or maybe something like, "We better get going, because this is when the boys usually come to the park." And she should be doing the same thing for me. That's why sometimes when we rehearse you see her or me saying each other's lines. (Wolf, 1994, p. 30)

What model of instruction does this learning activity reflect? How does it fit into Joyce and Weil's four-part classification of instructional models? Why do experts recommend that teachers develop and practice a diverse repertoire of teaching methods?

In 1995 more than 495 classroom teachers and music teachers from more than 250 schools worldwide formed groups of students into opera production companies after participating in the Creating Original Opera Teacher Training Program. Teachers serve as guides or coaches, helping students learn to work within a company structure. Students select a name for their company, then the company's student public relations officers develop a company logo, press release, mailing lists, flyers, posters, invitations, media contacts, and interviews. "While the script and music are being written by the student writers and composers, other company members are beginning to hone their craft—building stage models, wiring lights, applying makeup, working on voice building, etc" (Dik, 1995, p. 9). For information about the Creating Original Opera Program, contact the Metropolitan Opera Guild, 70 Lincoln Center Plaza, New York, NY 10023 (**http://www.operaed.org/coo.htm**).

Other Forms of Peer-Mediated Instruction **Project-based learning** involves students in relatively long-term, problem-based units of instruction. Students pursue solutions to nontrivial problems posed by the students, teachers, or curriculum developers. Students approach the problems by "asking and refining questions, debating ideas, making predictions, designing plans and/or experiments, collecting and analyzing data, drawing conclusions, communicating ideas and findings to others, asking new questions, and creating artifacts" (Blumenfeld, Soloway, Marx, Krajcik, Guzdial, & Palcinsar, 1991, p. 371). Artifacts are concrete, specific products (e.g., models, reports, videotapes, computer programs), representing students' problem solutions. These can be shared with others and critiqued. Feedback from others allows students to reflect on their work and to revise their solutions as needed.

Is peer-mediated instruction as effective as teacher-mediated instruction?

As students deal with real-life problems and issues, they have opportunities to draw on many different curriculum areas, making connections between subject matter disciplines. Also, technology allows students to work with computerized databases to conduct research and with video technology to construct products using computerized design.

Reciprocal teaching is an instructional method used to teach poor readers specific comprehension strategies (Brown & Palincsar, 1989). Teachers present students with written material, which they read together, paragraph by paragraph. While reading, students learn four strategies:

1. predicting what will happen in the next paragraph;

2. formulating questions about the reading;

3. summarizing what has been read; and

4. clarifying word meanings or confusing text.

When introducing the strategies, teachers explain a specific skill, model the skill using a selection of text, then coach students as they try to use the strategy on a paragraph of text. As students take turns demonstrating newly learned skills, the teacher supports their efforts by offering feedback, additional modeling, and coaching. The teacher also encourages students in the group to react to one another's statements by elaborating or commenting on another student's summary, suggesting other questions, commenting on another's predictions, and requesting clarification of material they do not understand (Rosenshine & Meister, 1994). As teacher and students work together, responsibility for much of the work shifts from teacher to students. In this way, teacher and students work cooperatively to bring meaning to text.

> The practice becomes a dialogue: one student asks questions, another answers, and a third comments on the answer; one student summarizes and another comments on or helps to improve the summary; one student identifies a difficult word and the other students help to infer the meaning and give reasons for the inferences they made. (Rosenshine & Meister, 1994, p. 481).

Information-Processing Family

Models in this family stimulate the development of thinking skills such as observing, comparing, finding patterns, and generalizing while also teaching specific concepts or generalizations (Eggen & Kauchak, 1996). Information-processing models are built on the ideas of information-processing theorists and modern constructivists (see Chapter 9). Information-processing models take their cues for instruction from theory that explains how people think.

Forming Concepts and Generalizations   When using the **concept formation** method of instruction, teachers want students to analyze and synthesize data to construct knowledge about a specific concept or idea. A science teacher using concept formation during a unit on plants would likely ask students to (a) examine a variety of plant specimens, (b) place the plants into groups based on structural characteristics, and (c) generate labels for each of the plant groups. The teacher might then provide additional specimens for students to classify. While most of these plants would probably fit existing classifications, students might have to create new categories for some of the plants. In a lesson of this type, students are not passive recipients of information; rather, they are active "creators" or "inventors" of knowledge.

Thinking and Creativity   **Synectics** is a teaching model that seeks to increase students' problem-solving abilities, creative expression, empathy, and insight into social relations. Developed by William Gordon, a businessman from Cambridge, Massachusetts, synectics is designed to "make the familiar strange," or to force distance between the student and the object or subject matter being investigated. Through a series of exercises, students work as a team to stretch and transpose traditional ways of thinking so as to discover new metaphors and to gain new perspectives on topics from a wide range of fields.

Synectics activities begin with a statement of a problem or topic and a series of "stretching exercises," or activities, to familiarize students with using analogies in new ways. A teacher might pose a problem about water pollution, for example, and ask students to consider the effects of pollution and ways they might prevent water pollution. For stretching exercises, students might then brainstorm responses to such questions as "Which is more dangerous to water—chemicals or construction waste? Why?" or "Which is a more powerful agent of change— regulations or education? Why?" (McAuliffe & Stoskin, 1993, p. 23).

> **Can creativity be taught?**

During the next phase of the synectics model, students create direct, personal, and symbolic analogies. In the lesson on pollution, for example, the teacher might help students create direct analogies by saying, "An oil slick is like what animal? Why?" or "Toxic waste is like what machine? Why?" (McAuliffe & Stoskin, 1993, p. 24). Personal analogies call for empathetic identification with a person, plant, animal, or nonliving thing or idea. The teacher might suggest, for example, that students "be" a duck:

> One bright morning while swimming in the bay you suddenly spot something strange sparkling in the water. It is black and shiny. Being a rather curious creature you decide to investigate. Tell what happens to you as you enter the area of the oil spill. Are you saved or lost? Tell your feelings as well as what happens to you. (McAuliffe & Stoskin, p. 25)

After students share their ideas, they develop symbolic analogies involving unusual juxtapositions of ideas. For example, students might think of word combinations, such as "awful beauty," "heavy flight," or "helpful panic" (McAuliffe & Stoskin, 1993, p. 27). By the time students return to their original problem, water pollution, they can think about solving the problem in new and creative ways.

Inquiry Learning   When students engage in **inquiry learning**, they try to answer questions and solve problems based on facts and observations. They think as scientists do while analyzing data and creating and testing theories and hypotheses to expand the conceptual system with which they process information. The Suchman Inquiry Model, one of several ways to structure inquiry lessons, conveys to students that knowledge is tentative.

That is, as new information is discovered and new theories evolve, old ideas are modified or pushed aside.

Teachers using Suchman Inquiry present students with a problem. For example, a biology teacher who has been focusing instruction on prey–predator relationships in the balance of nature might provide students with the following information:

> In the mountains of the Southwest a number of years ago, deer were plentiful, although the population would fluctuate somewhat. There were also wolves in the mountains. Some people from a small town witnessed a wolf pack pull down two of the smaller deer in the herd and were horrified. As a result, the people launched a campaign to eliminate the wolves. To the dismay of many of the people, the years following the elimination of the wolves showed a marked decrease in the population of the deer. Why, when the wolf is the deer's natural predator, should this have happened? (Eggen & Kauchak, 1996, p. 250)

The teacher then guides students through five steps:

1. defining the problem;
2. formulating hypotheses;
3. gathering data;
4. organizing data and modifying hypotheses accordingly; and
5. generalizing about findings.

To save time during the data-gathering phase, rather than students observing animal populations or studying written materials, students ask yes/no questions that are worded so that the answer can be obtained through observation alone. The following dialogue between a student (Steve) and his teacher (Chris) illustrates the way a teacher encourages such inquiry questions:

> Steve: "Does the prey–predator balance have anything to do with the problem?"
>
> Chris: "That's an excellent thought, Steve. We want to try and answer that. Now, if you were out in the woods looking for evidence, what would you look for to try and answer the question?" (Eggan & Kauchak, 1996, p. 263)

When the lesson continues, the teacher continues to guide students as they try to find solutions to problems.

Some curricula, such as the Geometric Supposer—a series of software programs developed at the Education Development Center—are well suited for inquiry lessons. The Supposer has no explicit instructional agenda; that is, it is not programmed to ask questions that will lead students to discover proofs to problems. Instead, students explore the realm of Euclidean plane geometry through problem posing and problem solving. A learner using the Supposer can draw; erase; label; measure angles, perimeters, and areas; change scales; bisect angles; compare angles; repeat figures; make new figures; and so forth. Teachers and students "learn to listen carefully to and assess the quality of one another's arguments," working collaboratively to "make" mathematics (Schwartz, 1989). A screen display for the Geometric Supposer is shown in Figure 10.5.

FIGURE 10.5

Screen Display for the Geometric Supposer

In what three ways might a computer program such as the Supposer complement a standard mathematics textbook?

Note. From *The Geometric Supposer: Triangles*, Pleasantville, NY: Sunburst Communications, Inc. Copyright 1991 by Sunburst Communicators, Inc.

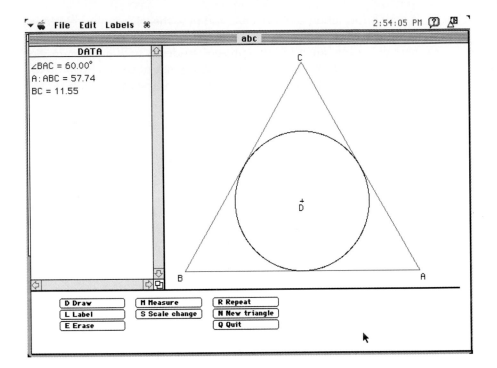

Personal Sources Family

Teachers who use personal models of instruction want to involve students actively in the determination of what and how they will learn. The ultimate goal is to develop long-term dispositional changes rather than short-term instructional effects (Joyce & Weil, 1996). The emphasis is on developing effective learning styles and healthy self-concepts. The nondirective teaching model, based on the work of Carl Rogers (1971) and other advocates of nondirective counseling, is one approach to attaining these goals.

When implementing the **nondirective model**, teachers act both as facilitators and as reflectors. They encourage students to define problems and feelings, to take responsibility for solving problems, and to determine how personal goals might be reached. Problems that the students address may relate to personal, social, or academic issues. When focusing on personal problems, students generally explore feelings about themselves. If considering social issues, students investigate their feelings about others and how their thoughts can influence relationships. Academic concerns generally center around students' feelings about their competence and interests (Joyce & Weil, 1996).

Thus classroom activities are determined by the learner as she interacts with the teacher and with peers. Acting as a facilitator, the teacher follows five steps when employing the nondirective model:

1. The teacher describes the helping situation, and teacher and student agree on procedures for meeting and interacting with one another. During this phase the student may also identify a problem.

2. The teacher, using strategies such as paraphrasing and asking open questions ("Can you say more about that?"), encourages the student to express positive and negative feelings and to clarify the problem.

3. The teacher uses supportive language ("Yes, it is difficult to be alone") to encourage the student to explore the problem and to develop new insight.

4. The teacher clarifies a student's plan for dealing with the problem.

5. The teacher listens as the student explains the actions she has taken and helps the student to consider other things that might be done to solve the problem.

The five phases of the model might occur in one day or across time. Meetings between teacher and student typically are one-on-one, allowing for privacy and time to explore problems and issues important to the student (Joyce & Weil, 1996).

What Is Effective Instruction?

Teachers are students, too. Even the best among them do not always know how or why they are successful. With experience, however, they grow accustomed to not having all the answers and to relying instead on the best information available about teaching and learning—information acquired from successful (and unsuccessful) practice. Because the best have stretched themselves time and again to be creative and technically proficient, they know they can call on their abilities when the need arises. They are not afraid to fail, because they have done that too and have lived to teach and learn another day. A good teacher, like a good student, enjoys the work.

Creative teaching, like creative learning, capitalizes on the inspiration of judgment, sensitivity, and intuitive insight. Stanford professor Elliot Eisner (1991) put it well:

> My work in the arts as a painter made it perfectly clear that cognition, by which I mean thinking and knowing, is not limited to linguistically-mediated thought, that the business of making a picture "that works" is an awesome cognitive challenge, and that those who limit knowing to science are naive about the arts and in the long run injurious to the children whose educational programs were shaped by their ideals. (p. 13)

Technically correct or scientific teaching, like scientific learning, takes advantage of information acquired from careful observation and analysis of phenomena in the surrounding world. This information deals with what goes into teaching and learning, what goes on during the course of instruction, and what results from the delivery of instruction. Social scientists who try to unravel the complexities of teaching and learning often focus on variables such as student characteristics and abilities, teaching behaviors, and measures of students' learning. They seek information that will maximize teachers' chances of being successful.

The ongoing debate about how best to teach reading illustrates well the distinction between technical and creative views of teaching (Matson, 1996).

How should students be taught to read?

Some educators advocate the use of phonics, a systematic method of teaching based on the belief that children learn best when taught small components of words (letters) before being taught larger components (sounds, words, sentences). Specialists diagnose students' weaknesses and prepare prescriptions for remediating

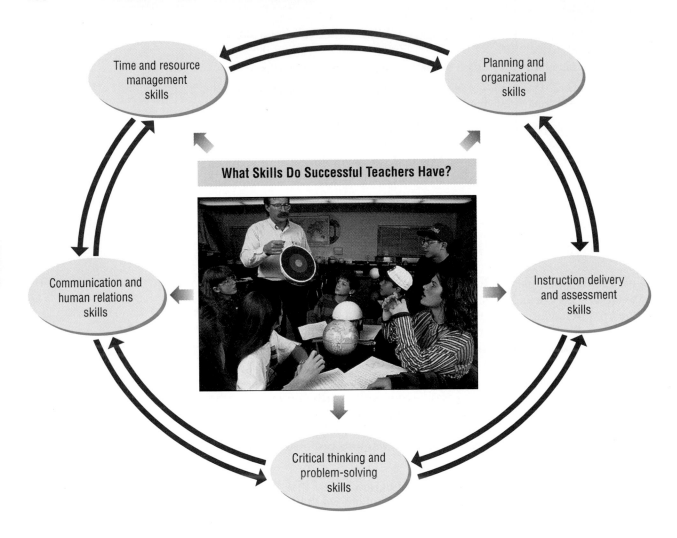

What Skills Do Successful Teachers Have?

FIGURE 10.6

Teachers' Skills

These skills underlie teachers' abilities to understand students, set goals, create learning environments, evaluate student learning, and communicate.

these deficiencies. Reading specialists in laboratories and carefully designed curricular materials aim to develop hierarchies of skills deemed necessary to master the process of reading.

In contrast, advocates of "whole language" do not think that reading should be taught separately from other language arts. Whole language is more an inventive philosophy than a specific method for teaching reading and writing, and whole language advocates contend that teachers should use phonics methods only when they think a child will benefit. Students start with stories and learn sentences, words, and sounds as needed. "The common techniques of whole language teaching—daily journal and letter writing, a great deal of silent and oral reading of real literature, and student cooperation, to name a few—are the philosophy in action" (Gursky, 1991, p. 23).

Good teachers know that science reveals some simple truths about the connection of teaching to learning. Teachers must apply these principles artfully, and on the run, as they construct knowledge applicable to their own unique situations. Attending to both the creative and technical sides of teaching requires that teachers rely on neither creativity nor technical expertise exclusively. Good teachers, like good students, push all their capabilities to the limits to build their knowledge.

The literature on educating teachers is brimming with lists of skills—abilities to use one's knowledge—that one expert or another has advanced as the essential components of teachers' repertoires. As knowledge has grown and as philosophies have changed, programs have required that teacher education students demonstrate far fewer yet more complex skills, such as those described in the sections that follow. Once teachers distinguish themselves as professionals by applying personal, theoretical, and empirical knowledge, they are ready to develop complementary planning and interactive teaching skills, such as those listed in Figure 10.6.

Understanding Students

Good teachers learn about their students so that they can teach in ways that are culturally and developmentally appropriate. Teachers use a variety of methods to understand the influences of students' ages, abilities, and cultural backgrounds to find out what students know, what they can do, how they think, what they value, and what gets in the way of their learning. Teachers can shape their skill of understanding students formally by reading and studying student artifacts, such as tests and projects. They can also informally observe, talk with, and listen to students and their parents.

According to Philip Winne and Ronald Marx (1979), the most frequent, the most critical, and the most generous evaluators of teaching are students. Students watch what teachers do and listen to what teachers say. They take meaning away from their observations, and they assign meaning to what they see and hear. Good teachers understand that when they help students become discerning, reasonable, compassionate adults, they also encourage students to become perceptive, sensible, considerate evaluators of teachers and teaching.

Winne and Marx (1979) argue that people too often overlook students' perceptions in trying to understand how and why teaching works as it does:

> Sometimes, when we have arranged the most stellar teaching imaginable, students do not get the point. And, fortunately, even when we feel we have botched instruction, they often learn in spite of our failure. Why? . . . neither the teacher nor the educational psychologist can fully explain these mismatches of instructional prowess and instructional effectiveness. Perhaps one reason for this gap in the ability to explain effects of teaching stems from neglecting an essential feature of school learning, namely, how students perceive how to learn from teaching. (pp. 210–211)

Research on students' mental activities during instruction has examined factors such as student motivations, beliefs, perceptions, and learning strategies. In one study, sixth graders were shown a videotape of a mathematics lesson in which they had just participated. They were asked to recall what they were thinking at various points during the session. Students proved to be fairly sophisticated thinkers. Besides paying attention to what the teacher was saying, mentally responding to the

To what extent should students be the judges of teacher effectiveness?

teacher's question, and hearing what other students were saying, students also were getting feedback on the correctness of mental responses by listening to the teacher's reaction.

There are great differences, even among able students, in their abilities to demonstrate self-management strategies during instruction (Corno, 1987). Teachers who attempt to understand how students think about learning may be able to fine-tune instruction as needed. They can also give students opportunities to practice strategies for becoming independent learners.

Communicating

At its core, professional teaching is an intellectual enterprise; thus, good teachers are good communicators. They communicate clearly, both verbally and in writing. They transmit information about subject matter and to communicate with parents, administrators, and other teachers. Good teachers also use their skills to communicate expectations for student performance, empathy, positive regard, and willingness to help.

Skillful teachers know how to establish, negotiate, and help students set reasonable goals for learning. Goals typically relate to the development of students' knowledge, skills, and attitudes. Teachers sometimes select goals from existing curricula and match the goals to a student's needs and abilities. This means teachers must help different students accomplish different goals. Sometimes goals are established within a curriculum, and teachers must help all students accomplish the same goals. At yet other times, teachers must help students set their own goals.

Communicating expectations for success and reinforcing success when it occurs are two of the most important functions a teacher serves. Teachers must state their expectations clearly so that students perceive their intent. Teachers also must provide students with feedback about their work, thereby helping students judge their own progress. If feedback is infrequent or unclear, students have no way of knowing whether they have met or exceeded teachers' or their own expectations.

Creating Learning Environments

In addition to understanding students and communicating effectively, good teachers typically plan for teaching and for interacting with students during the course of instruction. As we have noted, planning involves a variety of activities: selecting appropriate content, designing activities that maximize opportunities for students to succeed, and informing parents and other school personnel (e.g., librarians, fine arts teachers, other classroom teachers) of curricular plans so they might help reinforce concepts being taught. Planning also entails arranging the classroom and organizing necessary materials. Good planners provide for student motivation, reinforcement of good work, and management of people, ideas, and resources. Good plans well implemented can inspire students to do their best work.

Effectively implementing one's instructional plans is a subtle blend of art and science (Gage, 1978). Successful teachers adapt general principles of effective teaching to help students engage in meaningful work, to think for themselves, and to succeed. There is no single all-purpose teaching model or strategy; good teachers have many ways of helping students succeed (Fielding & Pearson, 1994).

From her experience of teaching mathematics, Marilyn Burns (1995) offers a set of practical lessons for teachers that seem relevant to the creation of learning environments in all curricular areas:

1. Whatever you do, create a clear structure at the beginning of the year. (Spend the first month helping children learn how to be effective learners.)

2. For sane planning, organize your year into units (whole class lessons; a menu of independent activities for partners, individuals, or groups to work on).

3. Give students choices; this helps to motivate them.

4. Remember that children can often do more than you think they can.

5. Focus on basic facts and emphasize reasoning; these are not mutually exclusive activities.

6. Talk less in class; have children talk more.

7. Want to know what children are learning? Ask them to write about it.

8. Use homework as a vehicle to inform parents about children's learning. (1995, pp. 87–88)

Educators are beginning to realize that one major factor in the creation of powerful learning environments has been largely overlooked: the school schedule. Robert Lynn Canady and Michael Rettig (1995) argue that a well-crafted school schedule can facilitate effective use of time, space, and human and material resources. They also contend that a good schedule can improve the instructional climate and help solve instructional delivery problems. For years Canady has advocated **block scheduling** to encourage longer, uninterrupted periods of instruction and to reduce the loss of time in elementary, middle, and high schools. Meg Sommerfield reports that the practice is catching on—at least "14 percent of high schools nationwide use some form of block scheduling and an extended school year" (1996, p. 1).

Managing Classrooms

Classrooms are often "crowded, competitive, contradictory, multidimensional, simultaneous, unpredictable, public . . . [places where] teachers work with captive groups of students on academic agendas that students have not helped to set" (Weinstein & Mignano, 1993, pp. 5–6). Teachers who understand the complexity of classrooms realize the importance of finding ways to gain students' cooperation and involvement in educational activities. Through careful planning, these teachers also take steps to prevent problems from occurring. **Classroom management**, then, is the collective ability of teachers and students to agree upon and implement a common framework for social and academic interactions (Doyle, 1986; Frieberg, Stein, & Huang, 1995).

What is the key to effective classroom management?

What aspects of effective teaching are evident in this picture? According to the authors, what other knowledge and skills do effective teachers demonstrate?

When organizing the physical setting, effective teachers perform several tasks. They minimize congestion and distractions. They facilitate the types of learning (individualized, cooperative, whole group) they wish to incorporate during the school day. Teachers make sure they have easy access to every student and that students have appropriate access to one another.

Effective classroom managers reduce the complexity of the classroom by making explicit their expectations for behavior. To do so, during the first week of school they establish rules for conduct and procedures for carrying out tasks such as pencil sharpening. These guidelines for behavior are age appropriate, straightforward, and consistent with school rules.

Kounin's classic research (1970) on interactions of teachers and pupils suggests that good classroom managers do not "satiate" students; that is, such teachers prevent boredom by varying learning tasks and by maintaining lesson momentum. They avoid giving too many directions or lengthy explanations. They stop activities when students become restless, and make smooth transitions from one activity to the next. The intent is to maximize student involvement and to minimize disruptions.

When disruptions occur, Kounin suggests strategies that teachers can use to prevent problems from escalating such as "with-it-ness" and "overlapping" behaviors. A teacher who is "with it" seems to have eyes in the back of his or her head. Aware of what is going on, this teacher stops students who are misbehaving and does so in a timely manner. Overlapping, which is a teacher's ability to handle more than one thing at a time, can occur when a teacher who is working with a small group of students also manages a disruption in another part of the room.

Effective classroom managers involve students in self-management to help them learn to monitor their own behavior. If a student is having difficulty staying in his seat, for example, a teacher might help the student observe and record his behaviors to create a level of awareness. Then, over time, the student might gradually assume greater responsibility for his self-control.

◼ Adapting Instruction for Students with Special Needs

In their efforts to help students succeed, effective teachers find ways to capitalize on students' strengths, interests, and related backgrounds. Good teachers also attempt to help students circumvent or compensate for weaknesses in their academic, socioemotional, or physical development. Students with poor fine motor skills, for example, might need access to a computer to complete assignments. Students who have difficulty organizing their thoughts and completing assignments might need to learn self-management and learning strategies.

Lyn Corno (1987) and Philip Winne (1991) think teachers should plan to show students how to take notes from lectures, how to organize their thoughts when writing a paper, and how to monitor and control their concentration during instruction. By providing students with the tools for becoming independent learners, teachers welcome students as "integral, conscious, and rational participants in instructional activities" (Winne, 1991, p. 311). These and other skills, in combination with content knowledge, prepare students to continue learning throughout their lifetimes.

Homework assignments allow students opportunities to practice skills learned in class. When fitted to the needs and abilities of students, homework promotes high rates of success. Appropriate assignments also help children develop self-discipline, responsibility, and a love of learning. When parents are involved in the homework experience, assignments help bridge the connection between schoolwork and the real world (OERI, 1995).

Evaluating Student Learning

Teachers must be able to decide what works in teaching and what does not. Formative assessment is conducted to discover information about students' errors, misunderstandings, understandings, and progress, so that teachers can shape new plans that will improve student performance (Frieberg & Driscoll, 1996). Summative assessment is conducted at the end of a lesson, unit, or course to allow students to demonstrate what they have learned (Frieberg & Driscoll, 1996).

Teachers have access to a variety of information about students. They can use formal measures such as tests and quizzes and informal measures such as questionnaires, interviews, and observations of in-class behaviors. Teachers make judgments daily about students' academic performance, their attitudes and interests, and their ability to work with others. Such information enables teachers to (a) determine what students already know and want to know about topics, (b) plan instruction that is appropriately challenging, (c) motivate student performance, (d) assess progress toward affective and cognitive goals, and (e) communicate progress to others.

Teachers have a responsibility to use the best information available about students before making evaluative decisions. This means assessing students frequently, using procedures that allow students to demonstrate what they can do. After collecting information teachers are obligated to "protect its privacy, recognize the limits of its use in decision making, and not use it to demean or ridicule a pupil" (Airasian, 1996, p. 24).

Measurement and Evaluation   When their offspring are very young, parents begin informally to assess their potential. When children enter school, assessment becomes formalized as **measurement**—the collection of data relevant to personal characteristics—and **evaluation**—interpreting and attaching value to the data. Diagnostic tests are used to identify specific problems, needs, or disabilities to be considered when making placement decisions about individual students. For example, there are tests for identifying hearing impairment, visual-perceptual problems, and coordination problems. Academic progress or lack thereof is gauged most often by **standardized tests**—commercially-prepared tests designed to obtain uniform samples of student behavior. These tests are usually—but not always—multiple-choice, paper-and-pencil tests administered and scored under conditions uniform to all students. Standardized tests do not necessarily measure what should be taught or the levels at which students should perform.

Standardization is important, because it helps equalize opportunities to take a test and to make test scores comparable. The scores students acquire on these tests are estimates of what they know or can do. These scores are imprecise, however, because they are only samples of students' learned behaviors at a particular point in time. Good teachers know that a variety of circumstances, such as testing conditions (e.g., a cold or crowded room), lucky guesses, illness, test anxiety, and disruption at home, can influence how well a child does on a formal assessment (Airasian, 1996). When making judgments about a student's achievement or potential for learning, these teachers are careful to consider both informal (e.g., teacher-made tests, observations) and formal measures of learning. They also must determine that students have had an opportunity to learn content included on formal assessments. In school, the consequences of "measuring up" are significant: results determine the course of one's educational career (U.S. Congress, 1992).

Those who interpret test results have two ways to answer the question, How well did so-and-so do? On a **norm-referenced test**, they compare a student's test score to the scores of other students. On a **criterion-referenced test**, they judge a student's performance by comparing it to some clearly defined criterion for mastering a learning task or skill.

To be useful, scores must be reliable; that is, a student's score today must be the same as or close to a score she would get tomorrow. The score also must generalize to skills similar to those assessed on the test. And if the test is not machine scored, scorers must be able to agree on their estimates of student performance. Test scores also must be valid; that is, they must measure what they are supposed to measure. For example, if a test claims to assess students' understanding of the workings of an internal combustion engine, it should not be a test of their reading ability.

Grading   Teachers often use assessment results to assign grades to students. As we note below, some school systems are beginning to use collections of students' work to describe and report students' progress. Vermont, for example, uses a statewide portfolio assessment consisting of open-ended mathematics questions that emphasize students' problem-solving skills (see **http://cresst96.cse.ucla.edu/index.htm**). But using such methods to replace grades entirely is rare. Most school districts continue to use grades to reward students, report to parents, and provide estimates of students' potential for postsecondary study.

Grades take various forms: the familiar letter grades (A+, A, A–, B+, etc.); pass/fail (P/F) or satisfactory/unsatisfactory (S/U); and numerical values (90–100 = A; 80–89 = B, etc.). Grades are frequently supplemented with teachers' comments or estimates of student effort, attitude, work habits, and the like, to provide a fuller representation of students' performances. These comments might be written directly on report cards.

> **What ethical considerations should guide testing and grading practices?**

Teachers often feel pulled by opposing desires: to use grades to build students' confidence by rewarding effort and progress, and to assign value to students' performances in some "objective" fashion. These sometimes contradictory demands can force teachers to examine their own ethical reasoning with respect to acceptable and unacceptable grading practice. Planning for evaluation and grading early on helps teachers resolve such dilemmas when and if they arise.

Cultural Awareness

Some communities are trying to help all their parents understand how to talk with their children about problems with grades.

UNDERSTANDING:
The Most Important Grade

Tips at
Report Card
Time

If there is a problem at school:

★ SIT DOWN with your child and look over the report card.

★ PRAISE YOUR CHILD. Find at least one good thing: attendance, no tardies.

★ BE CALM! Let your child tell you about his poor grades.

★ ASK how you can help your child do better.

★ ASK what your child can do to make better grades.

★ MAKE A PLAN with your child's teacher and your child to do better.

If you have questions or need help, please contact your child's teacher, guidance counselor, or principal.

Language: Korean

이해
가장 중요한 점수

성적표에
대한 조언

학교에서 문제가 있으면:

★ 성적표를 같이 보며 차분히 자녀와 애기하십시요

★ 자녀를 칭찬하십시요. 결석, 지각이 없었 던것... 등, 적어도 한가지--.

★ 마음을 가다듬고 댁의 자녀로 하여금 왜 성적이 나빴는지 설명하게 하십시요.

★ 어떻게 하면 성적을 올리는데 부모가 도와줄 수 있는지 물어 보십시요.

★ 어떻게 하면 본인이 성적을 올리는데 도움이될지 물어 보십시요.

★ 교사와 의논하여 학업을 올리도록 같이 계획하십시요.

만약 질문 또는 도움이 필요하시면
담임, 상담지도교사 또는 교장에게 연락하십시요.

#45622/Parenting Ed. Center/Korean

Note. From Fairfax County Public Schools, Parenting Education Center. Translated and reprinted by permission of SCAN, National Committee for Prevention of Child Abuse.

■ Providing Authentic Assessment

In recent years, reformers have argued that if schools are to be held accountable for student learning, the instruments of assessment—the tests themselves—must be improved. To many, multiple-choice tests that deemphasize reading, writing, and calculating inhibit learning. Reformers argue that schools need to depend more on authentic assessment: assessment concerned less with students' recognition and recall of facts and more with students' abilities to analyze, apply, evaluate, and synthesize what they know in

FIGURE 10.7

Applying Mathematics to Solve Everyday Problems

Which cereal with milk will have the most protein?

Note. From CORD *Applied Mathematics: Teacher's Guide*, Unit 4, Activity 2: Comparing Breakfast Cereals (p. 33, T-21), Waco, TX: Center for Occupational Research and Development, 1988. Used by permission.

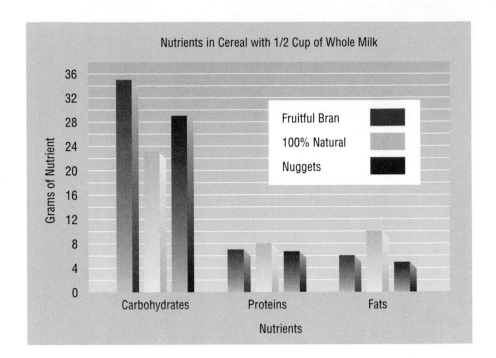

ways that address real-world concerns. Albert Shanker, former leader of the American Federation of Teachers, for instance, argued for the creation of tests that "test for things that are really important: reading, writing, computing, history" ("Shanker Asks," 1989). If this were to happen, of course, it would mean a move away from the use of standardized tests toward some form of authentic assessment.

One effort to promote authentic assessments can be found in the early and continuing work of the Center for Occupational Research and Development (CORD) in Waco, Texas, in conjunction with the Agency for Instructional Technology in Bloomington, Indiana. They have developed and tested curricula for courses that foster cognitive development as it reveals itself in practical application. Figure 10.7 contains an activity from CORD *Applied Mathematics*. This course integrates hands-on laboratory activities, cooperative learning opportunities, and video programs with text materials that teach important math concepts. Instructors emphasize problem-solving and decision-making through workplace applications (CORD Communications, 1996).

More educators are beginning to use portfolios to assess student performance. While there is no standard definition of the term ***portfolio***, and thus no consensus on what should be in one, Judith Arter and Vicki Spandel (1992) have offered this working definition:

> A portfolio is a purposeful collection of student work that tells the story of the student's efforts, progress, or achievement in (a) given area(s). This collection must include student participation in selection of portfolio content; the guidelines for selection; the criteria for judging merit, and evidence of student self-reflection. (1992, p. 36)

A portfolio approach to evaluation has the potential to (a) reveal a range of skills and understandings, (b) encourage student and teacher reflection, (c) illustrate growth over a period of time, and (d) provide some continuity in a child's education from year to year (Vavrus, 1990). People recognize the value of judging students' higher-order thinking skills and practical skills. However, the cost of performance assessment can be immense, both financially and in terms of the time it requires of teachers. Moreover, disagreements over assessment standards will mean that some people do not view such assessments as rigorous (Nuthall, 1992).

Mary Catherine Ellwein (1992, pp. 2, 4) argued persuasively that assessment is a process that is "intertwined with the daily life of teachers" and as much a "state of mind as it is a toolbox." In her efforts to understand teachers' typical evaluative behaviors, she identified two primary activities that teachers use to evaluate: "gathering intelligence" and "kidwatching." By engaging in these activities, teachers learn to understand students in their contexts, determine their strengths and learning strategies, tailor instruction, promote students' awareness of their learning, document their learning and change, and communicate with others connected with the students.

SUMMARY

What is curriculum?

1　Curriculum is generally thought of as knowledge and skills that schools are held accountable for helping students master. The development of curricula is driven by a variety of competing values and philosophies about goals, content, and organization of education programs.

2　Curriculum is an operative concept outside school in business, industry, and private organizations, where training and education are important.

3　Arguments about curriculum arise frequently because the population is heterogeneous, and rapid socioeconomic change routinely makes curriculum decisions controversial.

4　Because education is a power reserved to the states, states and localities are left to define the curriculum. Thus curriculum can be contextually defined. Beyond some rather vague agreement on the need for students to read, write, and compute, there is considerable variation in people's desires and expectations for what the curriculum should deliver.

5　Curricula can be characterized as explicit (visible or public), implicit (unvoiced, often unintended), null (untaught), extra (beyond the required), and integrated (interdisciplinary, thematic, team taught, etc.).

What forces and change agents affect curriculum content?

6　A variety of forces have shaped curriculum through the years, including the culture of the community and school, national interests, social issues and public opinion, professional groups and individuals, state and local priorities, and mass media and educational publishing.

BENCHMARKS

A Sample of Classic Contributions to the Conceptualization of Curriculum and Instruction (1900–2000)

1900–1920   Alfred Binet develops a systematic procedure in France for assessing learning aptitudes. Later, at Stanford University in the United States, Binet's test is revised and a formula for determining IQ added.

Research on teaching concentrates on characteristics of learners and on more and less effective teachers.

In experiments with cats, Edward Thorndike describes the law of effect—that any behavior resulting in satisfaction will tend to be repeated. This and similar work influences development of teaching approaches.

Franklin Bobbitt's *The Curriculum* (1918) marks the birth of curriculum as a professional field of study.

The Commission on the Reorganization of Secondary Education issues its celebrated *Cardinal Principles of Secondary Education* (1918).

1920–1940   In behavioral experiments with dogs, Russian scientist Ivan Pavlov discovers classical conditioning.

Swiss psychologist Jean Piaget describes the stages of cognitive development in children from infancy through adolescence.

Russian Lev S. Vygotsky describes the roles of social learning and language in the cognitive development of children.

W. W. Charters's *Curriculum Construction* (1923) shifts curriculum theorists' focus from content alone to the means for determining curriculum content.

Harold Rugg and Ann Shumaker's *The Child-Centered School* (1928) argues for the involvement of teachers in curricular decisions.

George Counts's pamphlet *Dare the Schools Build a New Social Order?* argues that curriculum and instruction should be less child-centered and more prescriptive, shaping attitudes, developing tastes, and imposing ideas.

1940–1960   Research on teaching begins to concentrate on what teachers do in classrooms rather than on their personal characteristics.

Lewis Terman begins a long-term study of 1,528 gifted American children. This classic study is slated to end in 2010.

In experiments with pigeons and rats, B. F. Skinner develops the concept of operant conditioning, in which learning is based on the consequences of behavior. This work profoundly influences the development of behavioral teaching approaches.

David Wechsler develops the Adult Intelligence Scale, testing different kinds of aptitude, on which the Wechsler Intelligence Scale for Children (WISC-R) is based. This view of learners' abilities shapes teaching approaches.

Humanist psychologists such as Harry Stack Sullivan describe child and adolescent development in terms of interpersonal interaction.

Abraham Maslow describes human motivation in terms of the satisfaction of needs.

Curriculum and teaching reflect concerns for personal development and interpersonal interactions.

1940–1960 cont.	The Harvard Committee on the Objectives of Education in a Free Society publishes *General Education in a Free Society* (1945), a report that questions the appropriateness of curricular materials for high school students who are not college bound.
	Benjamin Bloom publishes a taxonomy of educational objectives for the cognitive domain.
	John Carroll develops the theory of effective instruction, on which mastery learning is based.
	Tyler's *Basic Principles of Curriculum and Instruction* (1949) stimulates the format of curriculum guides, teachers' editions of textbooks, lesson plan books, and evaluation instruments.
1960–1980	Research on primate communication advances the study of human language. Noam Chomsky theorizes that children acquire language through transformational grammar and other deep structures of the brain.
	In human development studies, Erik Erikson describes stages requiring resolutions of psychological crises, and Lawrence Kohlberg describes stages of moral development based on children's responses to moral dilemmas. Dilemmas themselves become teaching materials.
	Research on human memory by R. C. Atkinson and others leads to the development of the information-processing theory of learning. Robert Gagné, Madeline Hunter, and others develop models of direct instruction based on task analysis and information-processing theory.
	Albert Bandura and others describe the behavioral principles of modeling and observational learning.
	J. Kounin and others describe teacher behaviors that relate to teaching effectiveness and efficacious classroom management.
	Robert Mager proposes behavioral objectives stating precisely what students should know or be able to do at the end of a lesson or unit of study.
	Jerome Bruner and others develop discovery learning and instructional models based on cognitive learning theory.
1980–2000	Social and cooperative models of teaching are promoted by individuals such as Robert Slavin, David and Roger Johnson, and Schlomo Sharan.
	Global issues, such as the ecological crisis and economic interdependency, receive increasing attention in curriculum and instruction.
	National standards for curriculum are produced by various professional associations.
	The 1994 Ready-To-Learn Act (Public Law 102-545) establishes Ready-To-Learn Television programs to support educational programming and instructional materials for preschool and elementary schoolchildren and their parents, child care providers, and educators.
	The School-To-Work Opportunities Act of 1994 (Public Law 103-239) provides money to states and communities to develop programs that prepare young people for first jobs and continuing education. The Departments of Education and Labor create a school-to-work home page on the Web (**http:/www.stw.ed.gov**).
	The 1994 Goals 2000: Educate America Act (Public Law 103-227) establishes a new federal partnership to reform the nation's education system through a system of grants to states and local communities.

How are curriculum and instruction planned and organized?

7 Curriculum and instruction relate to the aims of education in five ways: (1) development of cognitive processes, (2) academic rationalism, (3) personal relevance, (4) social adaptation and social reconstruction, and (5) mastery of learning objectives.

8 When planning for instruction, teachers consider a variety of factors: the curriculum, state and local goals and objectives for student learning, instructional strategies for meeting those goals, means of assessing students' understanding, qualities of the learning environment, students' individual needs, classroom management, ways to motivate students, and methods for teaching students learning and self-management strategies.

What are four general models of instruction?

9 The behavioral systems family uses ideas about manipulating the environment to modify students' behaviors. Mastery learning, direct instruction, behavioral objectives, and outcomes-based education are based on this model.

10 The social family capitalizes on people's nature as social beings to learn from and relate to one another. The many forms of cooperative learning, project-based learning, and reciprocal teaching are based on this model.

11 The information-processing family focuses on increasing students' abilities to think—to seek, organize, interpret, and apply information both inductively and deductively. Concept formation, synectics, and inquiry learning are based on this model.

12 The personal sources family encourages self-exploration and the development of personal identity through nondirective teaching methods.

What is effective instruction?

13 Successful teachers exhibit skills of understanding students, setting goals, creating environments conducive to learning, judging those environments, and communicating about teaching and learning to others. Successful teachers also manage classrooms to avoid problems and to handle problems when they arise.

14 Teachers use formal measures such as tests and quizzes and informal measures, such as questionnaires, interviews, and observations of in-class behaviors to judge students' academic performance, their attitudes and interests, and their ability to work with others. Teachers also use authentic assessments concerned with students' abilities to analyze, apply, evaluate, and synthesize what they know in ways that address real-world concerns.

TERMS AND CONCEPTS

behavioral objectives, *p. 391*

block scheduling, *p. 403*

classroom management, *p. 403*

concept formation, *p. 395*

cooperative learning, *p. 393*

criterion-referenced test, *p. 406*

curriculum, *p. 373*

direct instruction, *p. 391*

evaluation , *p. 405*

explicit curriculum, *p. 374*

extracurriculum, *p. 376*

implicit curriculum, *p. 374*

inquiry learning, *p. 396*

instructional model, *p. 389*

integrated curriculum, *p. 377*

mastery learning, *p. 390*

measurement , *p. 405*

nondirective model, *p. 398*

norm-referenced test, *p. 406*

null curriculum, *p. 375*

outcomes-based education, *p. 392*

project-based learning, *p. 394*

reciprocal teaching, *p. 395*

standardized test, *p. 405*

synectics, *p. 396*

teacher planning, *p. 387*

REFLECTIVE PRACTICE

Careful planning does not always prevent problems. On June 22, 1993, Adele Jones, a high school algebra teacher in Georgetown, Delaware, was fired over grades (McCarthy, 1993). Jones had failed 27% of her Algebra II class in 1991–92 and 42% the year before. When the Indian River School Board first announced its decision, some 200-plus students, including some who had failed the course, marched in protest against the dismissal. Jones's colleagues backed her with enthusiasm—43 of 48 signed a letter condemning the board for its action. The Delaware affiliate of the National Education Association paid for a lawyer to take the case to court. Jones claimed to have rebelled against the practice of rewarding students with grades they did not earn; the board interpreted the failure of so many students as an indication of her incompetence.

Issues, Problems, Dilemmas, and Opportunities

Why and for whom is it problematic when large numbers of students fail? Can you think of other situations in which maintaining high academic standards while encouraging all students to succeed becomes a dilemma?

Perceive and Value

Why might the Indian River School Board consider high rates of student failure unacceptable? Can you argue from the board's point of view that high rates of student failure are an indication of teacher failure? In contrast to the board, why might Adele Jones's colleagues be so supportive of her? If you were a parent of one of the students who failed, why might you be angry? Why might you be supportive of the teachers's actions? If you were a student who had been failed, why might you nevertheless support the teachers? What might be the stake of a professional organization such as the NEA or the AFT in this case?

Know and Act

Assume you were the teacher hired to take Ms. Jones's place. What more might you want to know about the definition of failure in this instance and the circumstances that led to so many students failing the course? What might you want to know about the previous teacher's instructional planning, teaching methods, and measurement and evaluation practices? What might you need to do to improve student performance while meeting curriculum goals and the district's curriculum standards? How could you justify your actions to your principal if asked to do so?

Evaluate

How might you determine whether students understood the practical value of the material you were teaching and whether they compared favorably to other students in their mastery of key concepts?

ONLINE ACTIVITY

Authentic assessment is sometimes referred to as "alternative assessment," which denotes assessment that is an alternative to typical standardized measures. Go to the following site on the Web (**gopher://spinoza.cse.ucla.edu:71/11/AltAssessment**) and see what information you can find on alternative assessment in a specific subject area, such as mathematics, language arts, or vocational education, that interests you.

11

Education and the Law

In this chapter we present some differences of opinion about what ought and ought not be done in public schools. The specific types of disagreements described have at one time or another been played out in courts across the land. Specifically, five categories of rights and responsibilities are considered as they have been elaborated by court actions—those of parents, students, teachers, administrators, and school boards.

We have structured this chapter a bit differently from the others. In each general category, vignettes or slices of educational life are presented as they might occur in schools. Some of these situations are similar, but not identical, to cases heard in federal and state courts. Issues and problems follow each vignette. We then provide relevant points of law to help you judge your actions.

In this chapter, then, we encourage consideration of the relevance of the law as it applies in real situations. It is important to note that points of law discussed in this chapter are illustrative, not definitive. Rulings and legal trends sometimes change quickly, thus making it necessary for educators to stay abreast of courtroom events so as to make informed professional decisions.

PROFESSIONAL PRACTICE QUESTIONS

1 What legal principles affect public education?

2 What are parents' rights and responsibilities?

3 What are students' rights and responsibilities?

4 What are teachers' rights and responsibilities?

5 What are the rights and responsibilities of school districts?

WHAT LEGAL PRINCIPLES AFFECT PUBLIC EDUCATION?

The United States Constitution does not mention education. All state constitutions, however, specify that the legislature has the power to establish and maintain free public schools. States' legal control over education is authorized by the 10th Amendment's provision that "powers not delegated to the United States by the Constitution, nor prohibited by it to the States, are reserved to the States respectively, or to the people." Such control must be exercised in a manner consistent with the Constitution's provisions for the basic rights of individuals.

When disputes arise over educational practices or policies, the parties involved make every effort to settle differences at the local level of governance, most always informally before formal entry into the judicial system. Either state courts or the federal judiciary system hear unresolved cases. At the state level, statutes prescribe where cases should be taken and which ones should be heard by the highest court. As Figure 11.1 illustrates, the Supreme Court of the United States is the highest court in the land, beyond which there is no redress. Most cases heard by the Supreme Court are cases in which the validity of a state or federal statute is questioned in light of the federal Constitution or cases in which title, right, privilege, or immunity is claimed under the Constitution (Alexander & Alexander, 1992).

The Supreme Court frequently considers several statutory and constitutional provisions when rendering decisions about educational matters. One is the First Amendment to the Constitution, which contains two clauses

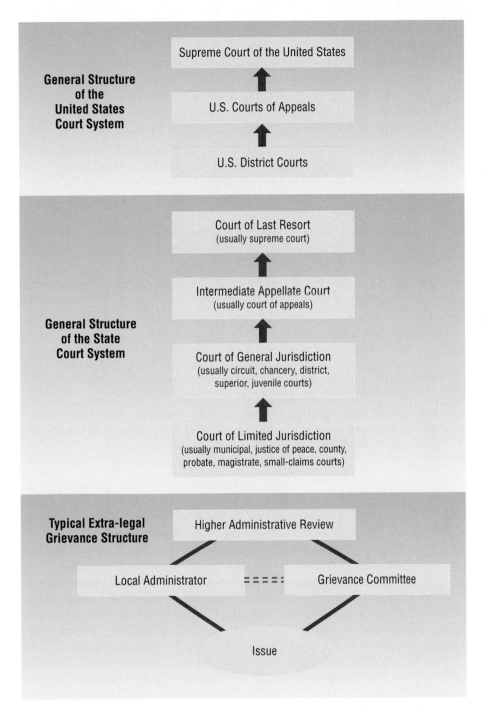

FIGURE 11.1

Levels at Which Disputes Are Heard

In settling disputes, why is it important for the "extra-legal" grievance system to function effectively?

often cited in lawsuits—the **establishment clause** which prohibits recognition of the primacy of one religion and the **free exercise clause** which ensures religious freedom.

- The First Amendment states that

  Congress shall make no law respecting an establishment of religion, or prohibiting the free exercise thereof; or abridging the freedom of speech, or of the press; or the right of the people peaceably to assemble, and to petition the government for a redress of grievances.

This amendment is the basis for a number of lawsuits challenging aid to and regulation of nonpublic schools, public school policies that advance or inhibit religion, and actions that impair expression by teachers and students.

- The Fourth Amendment guarantees citizens that the right

  to be secure in their persons, houses, papers, and effects, against unreasonable searches and seizures, shall not be violated, and no warrants shall issue, but upon probable cause, supported by oath or affirmation, and particularly describing the place to be searched, and the persons or things to be seized.

  When a student's bookbag, locker, or person are searched for illegal or dangerous items, this amendment usually serves as the basis for judgments about the legality of such actions.

- The 14th Amendment is the most widely invoked constitutional provision in school-related cases (McCarthy & Cambron-McCabe, 1992). Section 1 states that

  [N]o State shall make or enforce any law which shall abridge the privileges or immunities of citizens of the United States; nor shall any State deprive any person of life, liberty, or property, without due process of law; nor deny to any person within its jurisdiction the equal protection of the laws.

  This clause—**the equal protection clause**—is significant in litigation related to school finance, the expulsion and suspension of students, the dismissal of teachers, and discrimination on the basis of race, gender, and disabilities.

When disputes relate to contractual situations, Article I, Section 10 of the Constitution typically comes into play. This article states in part that "no State shall . . . pass any . . . ex post facto law, or law impairing the obligation of contracts." Interpretations of this constitutional provision enable the courts to determine the validity of contracts and possible breaches of contracts.

As described in Chapter 6, federal legislation also affects public school policies and practices. Categorical legislation, such as the 1975 Education for All Handicapped Children Act (in 1990, revised as the Individuals with Disabilities Education Act) and the Bilingual Education Act of 1968, protect citizens' constitutional rights and have general application in resolving educational disputes. Figure 11.2 suggests why disputes may arise.

In the scenarios that follow, note that disputes are resolved on the basis of constitutional provisions, state and federal legislation, rules and regulations of state and local boards, and case law (common law) emanating from the judicial system. Note also that Supreme Court decisions have brought some uniformity to educational practices and policies across the land.

WHAT ARE PARENTS' RIGHTS AND RESPONSIBILITIES?

A number of cases decided by the courts have dealt directly with parents' rights and responsibilities as parents and as guardians of their children. As

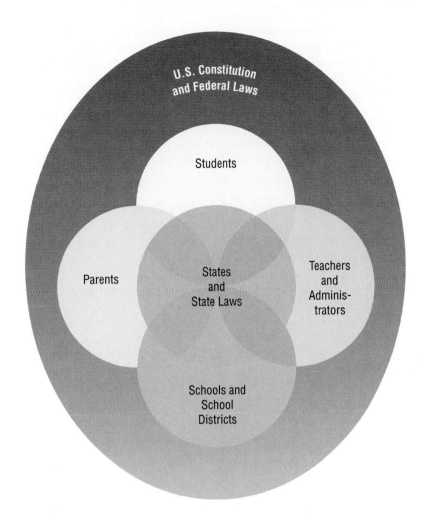

FIGURE 11.2

Groups with Rights and Responsibilities under the U.S. Constitution and Federal Laws

What do overlapping areas in this diagram represent?

the following scenarios suggest, knowledge of such rulings is just as important for teachers as for parents.

A Question of Religious Principle

At the end of the school day, Betty Anne Mason fell into stride with three of her ninth-grade students weaving their way to the locker room. The students—James, Lashanta, and Miranda—were so engrossed in conversation that they didn't notice Betty Anne until they reached the locker room. Normally friendly and outgoing in class, the students seemed suddenly fidgety and nervous when Betty Anne asked good-naturedly if they planned to attend the ninth grade dance Friday night. Miranda muttered something about having to stay home to "do some stuff," then made a beeline for the front door. As Betty Anne turned toward the other two students, James blushed and whispered something to Lashanta who bobbed her head in agreement. "Hey, what's with you guys today?" asked Betty Anne.

"Mrs. Mason," said Lashanta, "I don't know if you heard or not, but there is a meeting at 7:00 tonight after the Bible study session at Miranda's house. A bunch of parents who don't like what is going on here at Walden High are getting together to talk about taking their kids out of school and teaching them at home. Miranda's parents have already told her this is her last week at Walden. Can you believe it?"

As she headed for the principal's office, Betty Anne was upset. Miranda was one of her most promising students. Surely her parents wouldn't try to pull something like this. If they did, wouldn't they be violating the compulsory attendance law? By the time she reached the office, Betty Anne's mind was racing. She headed straight for the principal's office, hoping to get some answers to her questions.

Analysis of "A Question of Religious Principle"   If parents have religious or philosophical objections to a school program, can they exempt their children from school? The Supreme Court's 1972 decision in *Wisconsin v. Yoder* allowed members of the Old Order Amish religious community to exempt their children from school attendance beyond eighth grade, even though home instruction provided by the Amish was not equivalent to instruction in public schools. (The Amish had argued that compulsory attendance in the upper grades would have a detrimental effect on the established way of life in their farm-based, traditional community.) The Court's decision was based on the religious freedom clause of the First Amendment and on evidence that the Amish way of life was an acceptable alternative to formal education (Zirkel, Richardson, & Goldberg, 1995). To hear oral arguments relevant to *Wisconsin v. Yoder*, visit the Web (**http://itg-pc1.acns.nwu.edu/cases/71-354/**).

Litigation since *Wisconsin v. Yoder* suggests that the "Amish exception" cannot be used by parents who wish to exempt their children from schools for philosophical or religious reasons unless evidence suggests that such schooling might destroy their religion. For those dissatisfied with the public schools, however, compulsory attendance requirements may be fulfilled in private, denominational, or parochial schools. In several states, homeschooling is yet another option. To determine the validity of homeschooling, states look at such things as the educational level of parents and the regularity and time of instruction. In many instances, states also administer achievement tests to monitor home instruction.

Cultural Awareness

The relative importance of standardized tests for homeschooled students varies from state to state. Texas, for example, encourages the use of norm-referenced tests but does not require them. In West Virginia, however, children who are taught at home must take standardized tests annually. To continue learning at home, students must attain composite scores at or above the 40th percentile in reading, math, English, grammar, social studies, and science (Data Research, Inc., 1995).

Besides mandating school attendance, most state agencies also require that students be vaccinated against communicable diseases. Sometimes authorities exempt from vaccinations those religious groups whose teachings oppose immunizations as long as the health of others is not endangered. In the event that students are exempted from school because they pose a threat to others' health, schools must provide some type of home instruction for those students.

What are the rights and responsibilities of parents who claim that public school curricula or the public school experience violates their religious principles?

You Can't Spank My Child!

Steve Donovan's face was flushed as he escorted Brian's parents to the door. In his role as principal, he suspected that there might be some backlash from his actions the day before; but, as he had explained to Brian's parents, he had warned Brian several times that if he kept spitting on other students, he was going to be spanked. When Brian repeated the offense yesterday, Steve made good on his promise. Brian's parents were furious. "We know Brian has some behavior problems," they said, "but we sent a note to Brian's teacher telling her that spanking was not to be used as a disciplinary measure. Your behavior was an infringement on our rights as parents, and we're going to see that you don't get away with something like this again!"

> **Can teachers use physical punishment on a child?**

Analysis of "You Can't Spank My Child!" Given that Brian's parents requested formally that their child not be spanked, would a court of law support Steve's actions? In *Ingraham v. Wright* (1977), the Supreme Court ruled that the Constitution does not prohibit the use of corporal punishment in the schools. In so ruling, the Court concluded that cases dealing with corporal punishment should be handled at the state rather than the federal level. Whether Brian's parents have a legitimate complaint, then, depends on state and local school board policies.

In states that allow corporal punishment, parental objection to the practice does not necessarily prevail. In *Baker v. Owen* (1975), a case challenging a North Carolina state law permitting reasonable corporal punishment, the federal district court recognized parents' basic right to supervise the upbringing of their children. The court also recognized the importance of maintaining order in the schools, ultimately deciding that parents' wishes should not interfere with methods chosen by school officials for maintaining discipline.

Some states and localities do have laws requiring written permission from parents before students can be spanked. If there is no state or local regulation to the contrary, however, schools are not required to seek parental permission before administering corporal punishment. Educators must be aware of state laws and board policies banning or restricting the use of corporal punishment in the classroom.

A common restriction is that principals are the only ones who can use corporal punishment, doing so only in the presence of an adult witness. Educators who violate such policies may face monetary fines, dismissal, and even imprisonment (McCarthy & Cambron-McCabe, 1992). Corporal punishment, though often equated with paddling, is more broadly defined as "reasonable physical force used by school authorities to restrain unruly students, to correct unacceptable behavior, and to maintain the order necessary to conduct an educational program" (Data Research, Inc., 1995, p. 135). Sometimes teachers who have demonstrated excessive force when disciplining a student (e.g., throwing a student against a chalkboard and then pulling him upright by his hair) have been dismissed for cruelty or charged with criminal assault and battery.

Michael La Morte (1996) warns teachers working in school systems where corporal punishment is allowed to avoid excessive force and to adhere to local guidelines when administering such punishment. Corporal punishment is unacceptable in most states. Those that allow it do so only as a last resort, to be avoided if at all possible.

Cultural Awareness

About half of the states do not permit the use of corporal punishment. These include Alaska, California, Connecticut, Hawaii, Illinois, Iowa, Maine, Maryland, Massachusetts, Michigan, Minnesota, Montana, Nebraska, Nevada, New Hampshire, New Jersey, New York, North Dakota, Oregon, Utah, Vermont, Virginia, Washington, and Wisconsin. All local school boards in Rhode Island also prohibit corporal punishment (La Morte, 1996). In communities where educators can administer corporal punishment as a last resort, teachers and administrators must follow policy guidelines.

The Fayette County, Tennessee, Board of Education, for example, specifies that students can receive a maximum of three swats with a district-approved paddle. Following are the paddle specifications:

- not less than ⅜ inch nor more than ½ inch thick
- free of splinters
- constructed of quality white ash
- 3 inches wide (except handle) and not more than 15 inches long: grades K–5
- 3½ inches wide (except handle) and not more than 18 inches long: grades 6–12

Parents may exempt their children from paddling by writing a letter to school administrators (Johnston, 1994).

■ Do Some Parents Have Special Rights?

Kenneth and Karen Rothschild, deaf parents of non-hearing-impaired students, used American sign language as their primary means of communication. When the school system denied their request to hire a sign language interpreter for school-sponsored functions, the Rothschilds were forced to obtain their own interpreter at great personal expense. Subsequently, they brought action against the school district and the superintendent for violating section 504 of the Rehabilitation Act of 1973, which prohibits discrimination on the basis of a disability. School officials denied the charge, arguing that they had made good-faith efforts to accommodate the Rothschilds' needs by providing special seating arrangements at all school-sponsored functions.

Analysis of "Do Some Parents Have Special Rights?"   Must a school system provide special services, such as sign language interpreters, to parents who are disabled? In *Rothschild v. Grottenthaler* (1990), the United States Court of Appeals ruled that a public school system receiving federal financial assistance is obligated to provide a sign language interpreter at school district expense to deaf parents attending school-initiated events. In explaining its decision, the court said that without an interpreter, people like the Rothschilds do not have equal opportunity to participate in activities incidental to their children's education. The court also noted that the Rehabilitation Act specifies that access to necessary accommodations for individuals with disabilities should not impose undue financial or administrative burdens on them. Accordingly, the school system was ordered to (a) reimburse the Rothschilds for monies spent on interpreters, and (b) hire an interpreter to assist the Rothschilds at school-initiated activities directly involving their children's academic or disciplinary progress.

WHAT ARE STUDENTS' RIGHTS AND RESPONSIBILITIES?

In *Tinker v. Des Moines Independent Community School District* (1969), the Supreme Court emphasized that students do not lose their rights when they pass through the schoolhouse door. Under the Constitution they continue to be persons "possessed of fundamental rights which the state must respect." Although school authorities are vested with broad powers for the development and implementation of an educational program, then, they must avoid unreasonable, vague, arbitrary actions or actions in direct conflict with students' constitutional rights and freedoms.

■ In God Somebody Trusts

Jack Mills sat at his desk grading papers late one afternoon. He heard singing down the hall in the direction of the principal's office. He recognized the strains of "Onward Christian Soldiers" being sung by what sounded like a fairly large group of students. Students often sang in the building after the final bell; Omega High had many after-school activities. But they did not usually sing hymns. When Ellie Ferro, the sophomore English teacher, stormed into his room, Jack was surprised by her anger.

> **Can students conduct religious practices in school?**

"Jack, the Young Crusaders for Christ are holding a prayer meeting in the auditorium again. Apparently the principal said they could meet there whenever the basketball team was not practicing. It really ticks me off when they get to stay here when nobody else gets to use the building for church meetings. The principal has been cuddling up to those fundamentalists every chance she gets. It isn't fair. I want you to come with me to her office. I think we need to call her on this one."

Analysis of "In God Somebody Trusts"   Jack feels nervous about Ellie's anger, largely because the law on prayer clubs in schools is a mystery to him. Given the number of court cases focusing on the wall of separation between church and state since the mid-20th century, Jack's confusion is understandable. In the tug-of-war over where the lines of separation should be drawn, some argue that the First Amendment's establishment clause prohibits religious observance of any type in schools. Others contend that the Amendment's provisions for free speech, free exercise, and association rights prohibit schools from religious discrimination.

In *Widmar v. Vincent* (1981), the Supreme Court ruled that refusing religious groups access to facilities while allowing other groups use of the same facilities was a violation of students' rights of free speech. Furthermore, the Court deemed college students less impressionable than high school students. As adults, college students could be expected to perceive that the university was neutral in granting permission to a prayer club to meet on public property. With passage of the **Equal Access Act (EAA)** in 1984, Congress indicated that secondary-school students were also mature enough to understand that a school does not condone religion merely by allowing prayer clubs on public property.

The EAA stipulates that secondary public schools accepting federal aid must treat student religious groups in the same way as other extracurricular clubs. That is, if a school allows noncurriculum student groups (e.g., the baseball card collecting club or the chess club) to meet on school property during noninstructional time, other student-initiated groups, regardless of their religious, philosophical, or political views, must have equal access to school premises. In *Board of Education of the Westside Community Schools v. Mergens* (1990), the Supreme Court upheld the constitutionality of the EAA.

Given the Supreme Court's ruling, the sanctioning of any student club not directly tied to the curriculum prohibits schools from discriminating against other student organizations, such as the Young Crusaders for Christ, or even groups having little community support, such as satanists or skinheads. If schools do permit noncurriculum student group meetings during noninstructional time, teachers or other school employees may be present only in a nonparticipatory capacity. Furthermore, meetings may not be coordinated or led by nonschool persons (La Morte, 1996).

Rulings on other major cases dealing with separation of church and state contain implications for educators:

- *West Virginia State Board of Education v. Barnette* (1943)—Educators cannot require students to salute/pledge allegiance to the American flag when those students choose not to for personal or religious reasons.

- *Goetz v. Ansell* (1973)—Requiring students to stand quietly or to leave the room during the pledge of allegiance is unconstitutional. According to the Court, the first action compels an act of acceptance of the pledge over deeply held convictions, while the latter is a benign form of punishment for nonparticipation.

- *School District of Abington Township v. Schempp* (1963)—Prayer and Bible reading in public school classrooms are unconstitutional. However, study of the Bible as part of a secular program of education focusing on its literary and historic value may occur.

- *Wallace v. Jaffree* (1985)—Educators cannot require students to pause for a moment of silence for meditation or voluntary prayer.

- *Lee v. Weisman* (1992)—Prayers at a high school graduation ceremony are unconstitutional. (Since *Weisman*, however, school systems in some states have skirted the ban on prayer at graduation services by allowing students to initiate, plan, and lead invocations.)

> **Does the Lemon test really work?**

Since 1971, Supreme Court justices have often applied the tripartite **Lemon test** (a test emanating from the case *Lemon v. Kurtzman*) when deciding whether specific practices or policies constitute an establishment of religion. Under the Lemon test, each of the following questions must be answered affirmatively to satisfy the Constitution:

1. Does the challenged practice or policy have a secular purpose?

2. Does it have the effect of neither advancing nor inhibiting religious practices? and

3. Does practice or policy avoid an excessive entanglement between government and religion?

How much longer the Lemon test will survive as the yardstick for settling establishment clause disputes is questionable. As Justice Antonin Scalia noted, there are several problems with the Lemon test:

> It is so easy to kill. It is there to scare us (and our audience) when we wish it to do so, but we can command it to return to the tomb at will . . . . For my part, I agree with the long list of constitutional scholars who have criticized *Lemon* and bemoaned the strange Establishment Clause geometry of crooked lines and wavering shapes its intermittent use has produced. (Bureau of National Affairs, 1993)

(To learn more about the Lemon test, visit the Web at **http://www.fac.org/publicat/crossrds/ lem.htm**.)

Cultural Awareness

According to a report released by People for the American Way, a constitutional liberties organization, creationism is making a comeback in public schools (LRP Publications, 1996b). The report indicates that efforts by the religious right have encouraged some school systems either to replace the study of evolution as scientific theory with creationism or to include both theories as part of the science curriculum. Results of efforts to inject creationism in schools include the following:

- In Tangipahoa Parish, Louisiana, teachers must read a disclaimer whenever evolution is presented in written materials.

- In Alabama, the state school board voted 6 to 1 in favor of including a disclaimer in biology textbooks that describes evolution as a "controversial theory some scientists present as a scientific explanation for the origin of living things."

- The state senate in Tennessee voted down a bill that had earlier been approved by Senate and House Education Committees that would have allowed schools to fire any teacher who teaches evolution as fact.

Playing Fairly

At the end of the school day, Mary Ellen, Joe, and David went to the principal's office, where Anne Jeffrey, the assistant principal, handed each of them a sealed envelope addressed to their parents. "As I understand it," she said, "each of you is suspended for three days. This notice of suspension should be given to your parents."

"Are you kidding?" said Joe. "Nobody said anything to me about this. What are the charges against us?"

"Wait a minute," interrupted Mary Ellen. "Does this have anything to do with what happened during lunch today? If it does, this is a bunch of crap. We weren't the ones who started that fight."

"Yeah," said David. "It was that bunch of rednecks. They're always mouthing off and getting in your face. How come they aren't getting suspended? They cause trouble every day! You guys just never see them!"

"Look, I don't want to hear it," said Anne. "The principal asked me to give you these forms and that's it. Now go get on the bus before you get into any more trouble."

"You mean we don't even to get to tell our side of the story?" asked Joe. "Man, this is really wrong!"

Can students ever be denied the right to due process of law?

If you were the teacher of these students, how would you respond to their complaints about the way their suspension was handled?

Analysis of "Playing Fairly"   In *Goss v. Lopez* (1975), the Supreme Court addressed the grievances of Dwight Lopez and several of his peers, who were suspended by the principal for 10 days without being given a hearing—a practice sanctioned by Ohio law. Because the principal did not follow mandated legal procedures, the Court ruled that the students were denied **due process of law**. Specifically, the Court noted that the principal's actions were in violation of the 14th Amendment and subsequently ordered school officials to remove references to the students' suspensions from school records. The Court held that students facing temporary suspension from school must be given oral or written notice of the charges, an explanation of evidence if they disagree with the charges, and an opportunity to present their side of the story. Whenever possible, the notice and hearing are to precede suspension from school (La Morte, 1996).

In instances when student behavior is serious enough to warrant long-term suspension or expulsion, students must be given a written notice describing the charges, time and place of a hearing, and procedures to be followed in the hearing. Students have the right to know what evidence will be presented, who will testify, as well as the substance of such testimony. They also have the right to cross-examine witnesses and to present witnesses to testify on their behalf. Written or taped records of proceedings and the decision of the group conducting the hearing are to be made available to students. Students are also to be made aware of the right of appeal (Fischer, Schimmel, & Kelly, 1995).

Show Me What's in There!

When David Adams, the assistant principal, stepped outside, his attention was drawn to three students walking across the school courtyard. As he moved toward them, he noticed that the boys were looking at a small black bag held by William, one of the students. The bag, a vinyl calculator case, had a suspicious bulge in its side.

When he questioned the boys about where they were going and why they were late to class, William, palming the leather case and hiding it behind his back, responded that his classes had ended and he was on his way home. Curious about what William was hiding, the assistant principal insisted, to no avail, that William show him the object in his hand. "It's nothing," said William. "Leave me alone. You have a search warrant or something?"

After sending the other two boys back to class, David took William to the office and asked an aide to witness his efforts to look at the calculator case. When William refused to let him see it, David pried it out of William's hand, unzipped it, and found marijuana and other drug paraphernalia. David called the police, and William was arrested. As he was being escorted out of the office, William turned to David and said, "You haven't seen the end of this. I know my rights. You can't be searching me or anybody else without a warrant!"

Analysis of "Show Me What's in There!"   Does a school official have the right to search students? The scenario of William follows closely the events as they occurred in a California public school. After being convicted

By what authority do school districts have the right to reasonable search and seizure of students and their property? By what authority can students claim that search and seizure violates their right to privacy?

in juvenile court, William appealed the decision, saying that the evidence against him had been procured via an illegal search and thus should have been excluded from the hearing. In *In re William G.* (1985), the Supreme Court of California agreed, basing its decision on the reasonable suspicion standard set forth in *New Jersey v. T.L.O.* (1985).

In *New Jersey v. T.L.O.* (1985), the Supreme Court stated that school officials are acting not **in loco parentis** (in place of the parents) but as agents of the state when they search students under their authority. While this means that school officials are subject to the Fourth Amendment, the Court ruled that schools are special settings and thus there should be some "easing of the restrictions" normally placed on public authorities when conducting searches. Accordingly, school officials need not obtain a warrant or show "probable cause" when searching a student suspected of violating school rules or the law. Instead, when determining the legality of school searches, school officials can rely on "reason" and "common sense." Tests for determining reasonableness are whether (a) at the inception of the search there are reasonable grounds for suspecting that evidence will be found to prove a student is in violation of the law or school rules; and (b) the scope of the search is reasonably related to the objectives of the search, the age and sex of the student, and the nature of the infraction.

Such guidelines allow for much latitude among courts when interpreting Fourth Amendment rights (McCarthy & Cambron-McCabe, 1992). In the case of William, the court decided that the assistant principal had insufficient grounds for conducting a search. First, the assistant principal had no prior knowledge of William using or selling illegal drugs. Second, suspicion that William was late to class and William's attempt to hide the leather object provided no reasonable basis for a search. Third, William's demand for a warrant merely indicated that he wanted to preserve his constitutional rights (National Organization on Legal Problems of Education, 1988).

In *New Jersey v. T.L.O.*, the situation differed markedly. In this case a student claimed that her Fourth Amendment rights were violated when a school official searched her purse. The student (T.L.O.) was one of two girls sent to the office for smoking in the girl's restroom (a violation of school rules). When questioned by the assistant vice principal, T.L.O. denied having smoked at all. However, when T.L.O. complied with the request to open her purse, the assistant vice principal found marijuana and drug paraphernalia, $40.98 in single dollar bills and change, plus a handwritten note to a friend, requesting that she sell marijuana at school. Subsequently, the school official notified T.L.O.'s mother and the police, and T.L.O., after being advised of her rights, admitted to selling marijuana at the high school.

When the state brought delinquency charges against T.L.O., she claimed that the assistant vice principal had violated her Fourth Amendment rights, and thus evidence from her purse and her confession should be suppressed. The Supreme Court disagreed, saying that the search met the criteria for reasonableness; that is, a teacher had witnessed T.L.O.'s smoking, and thus the school official had a duty to investigate whether a school code had been broken (La Morte, 1996).

Are There Limits on Student Expression?

Students at Kirkwood High School in suburban St. Louis, Missouri, had enjoyed much freedom in the production of the school newspaper. When the students agreed to run an ad for Planned Parenthood, Birthright (an organization concerned with reproductive issues) requested that students run an anti-abortion ad to counteract Planned Parenthood's message. Several parents and local citizens considered such advertisements inappropriate and insisted that principal Franklin McCallie ban the ads from the student newspaper (Conkling, 1991).

Can school administrators censor student publications?

Analysis of "Are There Limits on Student Expression?"   Students had reason to cheer when in 1969 the Supreme Court ruled on *Tinker v. Des Moines Independent Community School District*—a case in which three public school students, suspended for wearing armbands to protest the war in Vietnam, won their court battle. Deciding in favor of the students, the Court declared that public school authorities do not have the right to silence students' political or ideological viewpoints simply because they disagree with students' ideas. Under *Tinker*, only in instances when student behavior could result in disorder or disturbance or interfere with the rights of others may students' verbal or symbolic expression be restricted.

In 1988, the Supreme Court restricted students' First Amendment rights in *Hazelwood School District v. Kuhlmeier* when it ruled that principals could censor school-sponsored publications. The basis for the Court's decision emanated from a case involving students in a high school journalism class who claimed that their First Amendment rights were violated when the principal reviewed their material and removed two stories—one on divorce, the other on three students' experiences with pregnancy—from the school-sponsored newspaper. According to the Supreme Court, a student newspaper does not represent a forum for public expression when it is part of the school curriculum. Thus, school officials can censor material considered inconsistent with the educational mission of the school. This includes material that is ungrammatical, poorly researched, biased or prejudiced, vulgar, or inappropriate for an immature audience.

If schools have clearly established—either through practice or policy—students' rights to control editorial content, the publication is considered an open forum, and restrictions under Hazelwood do not apply. At Kirkwood High School, principal Franklin McCallie firmly believed that the newspaper should be an open forum for student expression. Thus he allowed student journalists to decide what to do about the controversial ads.

Cultural Awareness

Students' freedom of expression can be limited by dress codes imposed by school districts. School officials suspended Jimmy Hines, Jr., a 13-year-old living in rural, north Indiana, for wearing an earring to school. The case posed an unusual contest between family and community values, as Hines contended that he wanted to wear an earring like the one his dad wears. Jimmy's parents argued that the school district's policy violated their son's rights under the due process and equal protection clauses. The Indiana Civil Liberties Union also contended that the district's dress code constituted gender discrimination, because girls were allowed to wear earrings. In *Hines v. Caston School Corporation* (1995), an Indiana appellate court held that the school district's dress code mirrored the community's conservative standards and served to instill discipline in students. The court also rejected the equal protection claim, stating that, without respect to gender, the dress code prohibits all students from wearing jewelry that conflicts with community standards (LRP Publications, 1995).

Treating Different Students Differently— Illegal Discrimination?

As Sam Miller's fifth-grade class lined up to leave the gymnasium, Tyrone grabbed Tony's hat and ran to the end of the line. Tony, a mainstreamed student with emotional disturbance, raced after Tyrone, knocked him to the gym floor, and punched Tyrone hard enough to bloody his nose. When Sam pulled Tony away from Tyrone, Tony swung his fist and hit another child in the stomach. Sam wrapped his arms around Tony's waist and carried him to the back of the gym before he could do any more damage, then sent one of his students to get the principal. This wasn't the first time Tony had exploded, but it was the most serious and dangerous of incidents.

> **Can students with disabilities be expelled for dangerous conduct?**

Sam neared his wit's end. He had talked with the resource teacher about ways to diffuse Tony's anger, but it was sometimes impossible to intervene before Tony's quick temper caused incidents like the one in the gym. In Sam's mind, Tony threatened other students and needed to be disciplined for his misbehavior. Sam decided to ask the principal either to expel Tony or to give him a long-term suspension so that Tony's Individual Educational Plan (IEP) team could have sufficient time to rethink Tony's placement.

Analysis of "Treating Different Students Differently—Illegal Discrimination?"   Can students with disabilities be expelled or given long-term suspensions for dangerous conduct? Disciplining students with disabilities has been a controversial and confusing issue for educators and parents. Under the 1975 Education for All Handicapped Children Act (EAHCA), now called the Individuals with Disabilities Education Act (IDEA), students with disabilities are guaranteed a free and appropriate education. In 1988 the Supreme Court ruled in *Honig v. Doe* that expulsion of students with disabilities for behavior attributable to their disabilities would be a violation of EAHCA provisions (Data Research, Inc., 1995).

The Court did agree, however, that students with disabilities exhibiting behavior dangerous to self or others may be temporarily suspended for up to 10 days if such punishment is the same that would be used for a nondisabled student. During the 10-day period, staff members can review a student's Individualized Education Plan (IEP) and meet with the student's parents to agree on an interim placement. Should parents disagree with a proposed change in placement, the 10-day period also allows school officials to seek court approval of the placement (Russo, 1995; Gorn, 1996).

Cultural Awareness

A number of court cases have helped to clarify legislation designed to protect the rights of individuals with disabilities. Henry Beyer (1989) cited *Irving Independent School District v. Tatro* (1984) as the more enduring of the Supreme Court's decisions helping families obtain "related services" guaranteed by the 1975 Education for All Handicapped Children Act (Public Law 94-142):

> Amber Tatro was an eight-year-old child with spina bifida and a condition which prevented her from emptying her bladder voluntarily. Every three or four hours she needed to have a catheter inserted into her urethra to drain her bladder—clean, intermittent catheterization (CIC), a procedure that she was not yet able to perform by herself. Her Texas public school system argued that CIC was a "medical service" and thus not their responsibility. The Supreme Court, however, ruled that it was a "related service" under 94-142 that must be provided by the school. (p. 54)

▓ Would You Check These Papers for Me?

The terse phone call from Amy Aller's mother, a local lawyer, should have alerted Charles Armstrong to the possibility of an unpleasant parent conference, but Amy was a good student, and as far as Charles knew, she had been quite happy in school. Amy had left school that afternoon a little upset by the low score on her math quiz, but her grades in general were so good that he couldn't imagine one assignment prompting a parent conference; it had to be something else.

As Charles sat facing Mrs. Aller that afternoon, she explained the reason for her conference. Amy was in fact upset—not so much because of her low math score but because of the "unkind" comments about her paper made by classmates. "How did anyone else know Amy's grade on this quiz?" asked Mrs. Aller. Charles shifted uncomfortably in his chair. "I have student helpers who grade papers for me when they finish their work," said Charles. "I guess one of them must have told the others about Amy's paper today. I'm sorry. This has never been a problem before. I'll be sure to say something to my students tomorrow so this type of thing doesn't happen again."

Is posting grades an invasion of students' privacy?

As she stood to leave, Mrs. Aller said, "I like you, Mr. Armstrong, but I want to tell you I don't think you should use this system anymore. I believe it violates the Buckley Amendment. No student should have knowledge of another student's progress in school."

Later that night Charles pulled out his college textbook, read about the Buckley Amendment, and reflected on his conference with Mrs. Aller. If Mrs. Aller was right, did he also violate students' rights of privacy when he displayed some students' papers as examples of good work? What about when he asked students to raise their hands to indicate whether they got something right or wrong on written assignments? Was he in violation of the law when he had students work problems at the board in front of their peers? Charles made a mental note to call the legal advisor to the teachers' organization the next day to get some answers to these questions.

Analysis of "Would You Check These Papers for Me?"   Is it an invasion of privacy when a student checks or corrects a peer's school work? Charles may very well be in violation of the Buckley Amendment when he allows students to grade classmates' papers. Part of the Family Educational Rights and Privacy Act (commonly referred to as the **Buckley Amendment**) prohibits schools from releasing information about a student to third parties without parental or student permission. This ruling suggests that teacher practices such as permitting students to grade or correct other students' papers, reading aloud or posting grades, and asking students to raise their hands if they responded correctly or incorrectly to a problem violate students' rights to privacy, potentially causing students embarrassment or shame (Chase, 1976). To learn more about the Family Educational Rights and Privacy Act, visit the Web (**http://www.epic.org/privacy/education/ferpa.html**).

WHAT ARE TEACHERS' RIGHTS AND RESPONSIBILITIES?

Teachers enjoy a number of rights also extended to students. For example, they may be excused from saluting or pledging allegiance to the flag if such actions violate their beliefs and commitments. However, as with students, there are times when teachers' constitutional rights must be considered in light of important educational goals. Because of the nature of their jobs, teachers usually are held to higher standards of behavior than are ordinary citizens (Imber & van Geel, 1993). The scenarios that follow examine some of the issues decided by the courts in this delicate balance between teachers' rights as citizens and their rights as state employees. The scenarios also suggest some of the responsibilities inherent in teachers' jobs, particularly with regard to student safety.

■ To Join or Not to Join

Megan beamed when she received a contract from the Detroit public schools in July. Although her college advisor had warned her that it might be midsummer or later before anyone heard about their job applications, Megan had been on pins and needles since graduation. For as long as she could remember, Megan had wanted to be a teacher. Now she also had school loans to repay, so she needed to be employed as soon as possible.

A few days after signing her contract, Megan received a letter from the Detroit Federation of Teachers (DFT) describing the benefits of belonging to the professional association and the cost of joining. Megan tossed the letter in the trash, deciding that she would wait until she had some financial stability before spending money she didn't have. During the first week of school, a representative of the DFT announced at a faculty meeting that those who had not paid dues to the DFT needed to do so or risk being dismissed from their jobs. Megan was confused. Perhaps she had misunderstood the announcement. Surely nonmembers of the DFT would not be required to pay dues.

Do teachers have to pay dues to teachers' unions if they are not members?

Analysis of "To Join or Not to Join"   Can teachers who are not union members be required to pay dues to the organization? Federal law recognizes teachers' constitutional right to advocate, organize, and join a teacher union. In many states, teachers also have the right to engage in collective bargaining, a procedure for resolving disagreements between employers and employees. Teachers negotiate with their school boards, usually through their union representative, about such issues as contract hours, salaries, and fringe benefits. There are no constitutional guarantees that school boards must bargain with teachers' unions, however, so restrictions on the scope of bargaining vary greatly from state to state.

By 1991 about 80% of public school teachers belonged to either the National Education Association (NEA) or the American Federation of Teachers (AFT). At the same time, more than half of the states had laws requiring nonmembers of unions to pay dues to the union as a condition of employment. Several Supreme Court rulings uphold the constitutionality of such laws. In a case (*Abood v. Detroit Board of Education*) heard in 1977, Christine Warczak and a number of other teachers challenged a Michigan law requiring teachers who had not become union members within 60 days to pay an amount equal to union dues or face discharge. The teachers argued that because they did not believe in collective bargaining or agree with union activities unrelated to collective bargaining, such a law violated their right to freedom of association as guaranteed in the First and Fourteenth Amendments. The Supreme Court disagreed, noting that union activities benefit every employee, union member or not, thus all should share the cost of the union's collective bargaining activities. The Court also decided, however, that it was a violation of First Amendment rights to require public employees to support financially a union's political activities.

In 1984 the Supreme Court clarified this last portion of the *Abood* decision by ruling in *Ellis v. Brotherhood of Railway Clerks* that a union's nonpolitical publications, conventions, and social activities are sufficiently related to the union's work in collective bargaining to justify the charging of nonunion members for such services. Litigation expenses not involving the negotiation of agreements or settlement of grievances, or charges for general organizing efforts, however, cannot be charged to dissenting employees. In its 1986 ruling in *Chicago Teachers Union, Local No. 1 AFL-CIO v. Hudson*, the Supreme Court also stated that unions must explain the basis for the dues amount, allow a prompt opportunity to contest the fee before an impartial decision maker, and hold in escrow disputed amounts until the parties reach consensus (Fischer, Schimmel, & Kelly, 1995).

There's Got to be a Way to Keep This Job!

Sandra Allen, a second-year teacher, loved her teaching job. With the exception of two or three students who had difficulty controlling their actions, her class was well behaved and motivated to learn. Most students consistently completed assignments on time, and their work was accurate and neat. Sandra knew that parents had been ambivalent about their children having the "new" teacher at school, but their comments during parent conferences indicated that they, too, were pleased with their children's academic progress.

When Sandra received notice in May that she would not be rehired for the upcoming academic year, she felt shocked and angry. Because her principal's midyear evaluation rated Sandra as "above average" or "outstanding" in all categories, Sandra had assumed that her contract would be renewed. She needed only 1 more year of teaching in the system to earn tenure. Surely the school board could not force her out of the system without giving her reasons for doing so, or could it?

Analysis of "There's Got to be a Way to Keep This Job!"   Sandra's story is much like that of David Roth, an assistant professor of political science at Wisconsin State University–Oshkosh, who was hired for a fixed term of 1 academic year. When Roth was notified at the end of the academic term that he would not be rehired for the following year, he went to court, claiming that the decision infringed on his Fourteenth Amendment rights. In ruling on *Board of Regents of State Colleges v. Roth* (1972), the Supreme Court disagreed with Roth's charge, explaining that a probationary teacher does not have the same rights as a tenured teacher.

According to the Court, tenured teachers may not be removed from their positions without specific or good cause, nor may they be dismissed for capricious or arbitrary reasons (e.g., political beliefs and activities). Thus, tenured teachers have a property interest meriting due process protection. In most states, however, the contract of a teacher with probationary status can be terminated at the end of the year (state statute generally specifies a date by which teachers must be notified of such action) without cause. This means that a probationary teacher maintains property interest only for the duration of a 1-year term. However, if the probationary teacher can present evidence to suggest that nonrenewal is in retaliation for exercise of constitutional rights (e.g., freedom of speech), the employer must follow due process (Fischer, Schimmel, & Kelly, 1995).

If the school board resorts to **dismissal** (removing a probationary or tenured teacher before the completion of his contract), the board must provide a notice, hearing, or notification of reasons for dismissal. State statutes typically list broad causes for dismissal, such as incompetency, immorality, unprofessional conduct, and neglect of duty. Lack of funding and a decline in student enrollment may also be just cause for the midyear dismissal of both tenured and nontenured teachers (La Morte, 1996). Many state laws also stipulate that nontenured teachers must be dismissed before tenured teachers, and, among tenured teachers, the least experienced must be dismissed first.

A Line Between Personhood and Professionalism

Jason O'Hara enjoyed his most-popular-teacher status at Baker Middle School. Students, parents, and colleagues respected him for his innovative ideas, sharp wit, and ability to interest students in learning. Now in his fourth year of teaching, Jason had tenure in the school system and was chair of the English department.

> **Can a teacher be dismissed for private conduct?**

When Jason received a note from John Wright, the principal, requesting that he come to the office that afternoon, Jason thought nothing of it. Mr. Wright had been very supportive of Jason and his efforts to upgrade the English curriculum. As he stepped through the office door, however, Jason knew that something was amiss. Mr. Wright, a grim look on his face, handed Jason a two-page letter addressed to the superintendent. The letter, written by a teacher with whom Jason had had a brief homosexual relationship the year before, made explicit the nature of their relationship. Jason read it in stunned silence.

"Jason," said Mr. Wright, "this letter was also mailed to members of the school board. Several of them are really uptight about this. They want to dismiss you for immoral behavior. I think this is going to be an ugly battle. I'll do everything I can to help you, but I think you also need legal assistance. Do you have a good lawyer?"

Analysis of "A Line Between Personhood and Professionalism"

Can a teacher be dismissed for private conduct? As noted in Chapter 2, teachers in earlier times were held to rigid codes of conduct. Those who crossed the line between moral and immoral behavior resigned or were dismissed immediately from their teaching duties. In recent times, however, the line of demarcation has blurred because it is often difficult to get community consensus about what constitutes immoral conduct. Moreover, many educators believe that when the school day ends, what occurs in the privacy of their homes is their own business and should not affect negatively their status as professionals. Those who disagree argue that being a private person does not relieve educators of their duty to serve as role models for children (Sendor, 1992).

VOICES

On Teachers' Freedom of Expression

Court cases such as *Pickering v. Board of Education of Township High School District 205*, heard in 1968, have helped define teachers' rights of freedom of expression on matters of public concern. Marvin Pickering, a tenured teacher, published a letter in a local newspaper that was critical of the school board's efforts to raise new revenue. The board dismissed Pickering on the basis that numerous statements in the letter were false, that he damaged the reputations of board members and administrators, and that such comments would be disruptive to the workplace. The Illinois Circuit and Supreme Courts upheld the board's decision on the grounds that Pickering's letter was "detrimental to the interests of the school system." When the case reached the United States Supreme Court, the courts' judgments were reversed. Justice Thurgood Marshall delivered the Court's opinion:

What we . . . have before us is a case in which a teacher has made erroneous public statements upon issues then currently the subject of public attention, which are critical of his ultimate employer but which are neither shown nor can be presumed to have in any way either impeded the teacher's proper performance of his daily duties in the classroom or to have interfered with the regular operation of the schools generally. In these circumstances we conclude that the interest of the school administration in limiting teachers' opportunities to contribute to public debate is not significantly greater than its interest in limiting a similar contribution by any member of the general public. The public interest in having free and unhindered debate on matters of public importance—the core value of the Free Speech Clause of the First Amendment—is so great that it has been held that a State cannot authorize the recovery of damages by a public official for defamatory statements directed at him except when such statements are shown to have been made either with knowledge of their falsity or with reckless disregard for their truth or falsity. . . . (p. 1737)

In sum, we hold that, in a case such as this, absent proof of false statements knowingly or recklessly made by him, a teacher's exercise of his right to speak on issues of public importance may not furnish the basis for his dismissal from public employment. (p. 1738)

CRITICAL THINKING

The courts have refused to lay down a general standard against which all public statements made by teachers might be measured for protection by the First Amendment. Why would the courts be reluctant to do so? Why do the courts try to balance the need for protecting free speech with the need to ensure harmony among coworkers in the workplace?

Note. From *Pickering v. Board of Education of Township High School District 205*, Will County, Illinois, 391 U.S. 563 (1968).

Ambiguity about what constitutes moral and immoral behavior is reflected by court decisions in different states. In making employment decisions based on a teacher's sexual orientation, courts usually consider "the adverse effect on students or fellow teachers, adversity anticipated within the school system, surrounding circumstances, and possible chilling effects on discipline" (Alexander & Alexander, 1992, p. 586).

Depending on public reaction to Jason's case, then, he may or may not be dismissed from his teaching position. In 1969 the California Supreme Court heard a case (*Morrison v. State Board of Education*) involving a teacher, Marc Morrison, whose circumstances were much like those of Jason. When the superintendent received a letter from a male teacher who had been involved sexually with Morrison the year before, the school board voted to dismiss Morrison on grounds of immoral and unprofessional behavior. The court disagreed with the school board's actions, saying that the board's definition of immoral behavior was dangerously vague and could implicate many educators. Ruling in favor of Morrison, the court also stated that disapproval of an educator's private conduct was insufficient reason for dismissal, particularly when there was no proof that the educator's professional work was affected negatively by the conduct.

Eight years later in a case (*Gaylord v. Tacoma School District No. 10*) heard by the supreme court of Washington, however, the court upheld the dismissal of a teacher who admitted his homosexuality to the vice principal of the school. Based on the fact that at least one student and several teachers and parents had challenged the teacher's fitness to teach, the court held that the teacher's continuance in the system would likely disrupt the educational process.

Such cases end differently in different localities because the U.S. Supreme Court has not yet recognized a constitutional privacy right to engage in homosexual behavior. Based on the 1984 ruling in *National Gay Task Force v. Board of Education of Oklahoma City*, however, teachers have the right to advocate publicly for legalization of homosexuality as long as such activity is not disruptive to the educational process. As indicated in the 1984 ruling in *Rowland v. Mad River Local School District*, advocacy does not include talking with co-workers about personal sexual preferences or those of students. In this case, an Ohio guidance counselor who had been dismissed by the school board for admitting her bisexuality to several members of the staff argued that her First and Fourteenth Amendment rights had been violated. The Court disagreed, saying that the guidance counselor's statements were not protected by the First Amendment because they were not made as a citizen on matters of public concern; rather, the counselor's statements were a matter of private concern. Furthermore, the court held that, absent evidence that heterosexual employees had been or would be treated differently for discussing sexual preferences, nonrenewal of the counselor's contract did not violate the Fourteenth Amendment (Morin, 1991).

■ What Do You Mean I'm Violating Copyright Laws?

During summer vacation, Robert Wells—newly appointed chair of the mathematics department at Central High—videotaped a two-part series on "Mathematics in Today's Workplace" and added it to his growing collection of tapes. Robert's students had responded well to his occasional use of a videotape to illustrate concepts being taught in class. He believed that these newest tapes would be especially effective in the spring, when math analysis students planned projects showing real-life applications of mathematics.

What constitutes fair use?

As he thought about the upcoming inservice program he would conduct for department members, Robert also realized that his videotapes might be an excellent tool for helping others think about ways to vary instruction.

Excited by the prospect, Robert contacted Dorothy James at the media center to see if she would make copies of his videotapes and place them on reserve in the school library. When Dorothy asked Robert if he had permission to videotape the copyrighted television programs, he was caught off guard. "What do you mean?" Robert said. "I'm using these tapes for teaching purposes. Lots of people do that. What's the big deal?"

"I used to think it was okay myself," said Dorothy, "but now I'm not so sure. I'll call central office and see what I can find out. Until we know, we'd better not copy any of those videotapes."

Analysis of "What Do You Mean I'm Violating Copyright Laws?"
Can teachers videotape television programs and use them for educational purposes? Although the Supreme Court has not decided whether it is illegal for teachers to tape television broadcasts on home video recorders for later classroom use, 1981 congressional guidelines for off-the-air taping suggest that such activities may in fact constitute copyright infringement. Guidelines specify that copyrighted television programs may be videotaped by nonprofit educational organizations but that videotapes must be destroyed or erased after 45 calendar days if the institution has not obtained a license for such videotaping. Teachers may use the videotapes with students at school, or with students receiving homebound instruction, one time during the first 10 school days after recording occurs. One additional showing is allowed during the 10-day period, but only for instructional reinforcement. Additional use is limited to evaluation of the videotape's usefulness as an instructional tool (Copyright Information Services, 1992).

In *Encyclopedia Britannica Educational Corporation v. Crooks*, a New York federal district court found a school system guilty of violating fair use standards by engaging in extensive off-the-air taping and replaying of programs broadcast on public television. The court found that such taping interfered with the marketability of producers' films. In 1984, in *Sony Corporation of America v. Universal City Studios*, the Supreme Court ruled that personal videorecording for the purpose of "time shifting" (recording of a program for later viewing), however, did not harm the television market (Fischer, Schimmel, & Kelly, 1995).

Until the Supreme Court decides whether home taping for broader viewing by students in classrooms constitutes fair use of copyrighted materials, teachers are well advised to adhere to congressional guidelines. Another option, of course, is to seek written permission from copyright owners to videotape programs for classroom use.

The Internet offers an exciting array of motion media, music, text material, graphics, illustrations, and photographs for educational purposes. When incorporating others' electronic materials in multimedia projects, however, teachers and students are obligated to act responsibly. To learn more about copyright as applied to multimedia, visit the Web (**http://www.lib. virginia.edu/puboff/ copyright/interp.html**).

Maybe She Is Just a Sickly Child

Theresa chose a desk near the back of the room, not near anyone in particular. She was quiet and somewhat plain in her dress, but her long brown hair was striking. Joan Mason didn't know much about 8-year-old Theresa because Theresa had just moved to town in August. Her permanent records indicated that she was above average in ability. While she had missed a lot of school last year, her grades were about average, maybe a little low in math.

Another parent told Joan that Theresa's mother had been divorced last year and had moved here, at least in part, to get away from her former husband. The family—Theresa's mother and her younger sister; a man she called Jim, whom she described as her mother's friend; and Jim's 17-year-old son—lived in a small ranch house in a nice neighborhood on the outskirts of town.

As Joan worked with Theresa the first few weeks of school, Theresa seldom missed a day of school and kept up with daily assignments. By mid-October, however, things had begun to change. Theresa's attendance became sporadic, and Joan noticed that Theresa often was passive and uncommunicative, both with Joan and with classmates. During seatwork, Theresa chewed her fingernails, her constant gnawing sometimes drawing blood. When Joan talked with Theresa's mother during a parent conference, she did not seem overly concerned by Joan's observations. She indicated that Theresa's behavior at home had not changed and attributed Theresa's recent absences and withdrawn manner to her tendency to be a "sickly child." After the conference, Joan still worried about Theresa, but she didn't know what to do.

What about this situation concerns you? What, if anything, would you do if you were Theresa's teacher?

Analysis of "Maybe She Is Just a Sickly Child."   Educators, unlike physicians, social workers, and law enforcement officers, have a unique opportunity to monitor students' social behaviors, academic progress, and attitudes over time. Some patterns of behavior, especially sudden, dramatic changes, can be a warning sign of something gone awry in a child's life. Teachers need to be particularly alert to patterns of behavior that could indicate that a child is the victim of abuse or neglect.

As defined by the Child Abuse Prevention and Treatment Act, child abuse and neglect include physical or mental injury, sexual abuse or exploitation, negligent treatment, or maltreatment (a) of a child younger than 18 years of age (unless state law specifies a younger age), (b) by any person responsible for a child's welfare, (c) under circumstances that harm or threaten a child's health or welfare.

Sexual abuse is defined as

> [(1)] the use, employment, persuasion, inducement, enticement or coercion of any child to engage in, or assist any other person to engage in, any sexually explicit conduct (or any simulation of such conduct) for the purpose of producing any visual depiction of such conduct, or (2) rape, molestation, prostitution, or other form of sexual exploitation of children, or incest with children. (U.S. Department of Health and Human Services, 1992, pp. 1–2)

As noted in Chapter 7, abuse can occur at any socioeconomic level to both males and females. In every state, educators must report cases of abuse or neglect resulting in physical injury to a child, and, in the majority of states, educators must report instances of emotional, mental, or sexual abuse. Failure to report suspected abuse and neglect constitutes a misdemeanor in most states and, with a few exceptions, teachers are identified among the professionals required to make such reports. Certain behaviors or

TABLE 11.1   Signs of Child Abuse

Signs of Physical Abuse

Consider the possibility of physical abuse when the child:

- has unexplained burns, bites, bruises, broken bones, or black eyes;
- has fading bruises or other marks noticeable after an absence from school;
- seems frightened of the parents and protests or cries when it is time to go home from school;
- shrinks at the approaches of adults; or
- reports injury by a parent or another adult caregiver.

Consider the possibility of physical abuse when the parent or other adult caregiver:

- offers conflicting, unconvincing, or no explanation for the child's injury;
- uses harsh physical discipline with the child; or
- has a history of abuse as a child.

Signs of Neglect

Consider the possibility of neglect when the child:

- is frequently absent from school;
- begs or steals food or money from classmates;
- lacks needed medical or dental care, immunizations, or glasses;
- is consistently dirty and has severe body odor;
- lacks sufficient clothing for the weather;
- abuses alcohol or other drugs; or
- states that there is no one at home to provide care.

Consider the possibility of neglect when the parent or other adult caregiver:

- appears to be indifferent to the child;
- seems apathetic or depressed;
- behaves irrationally or in a bizarre manner; or
- abuses alcohol or other drugs.

Signs of Emotional Maltreatment

Consider the possibility of emotional maltreatment when the child:

- shows extremes in behavior, such as overly compliant or demanding behavior, extreme passivity or aggression;
- is either inappropriately adult (parenting other children, for example) or inappropriately infantile (frequently rocking or head-banging, for example);
- is delayed in physical or emotional development;
- has attempted suicide; or
- reports a lack of attachment to a parent.

Consider the possibility of emotional maltreatment when the parent or other adult caregiver:

- contantly blames, belittles, or berates the child;
- is unconcerned about the child and refuses to consider offers of help for the child's school problems; or
- overtly rejects the child.

Signs of Sexual Abuse

Consider the possibility of sexual abuse when the child:

- has difficulty walking or sitting;
- suddenly refuses to change for gym or to participate in physical activities;
- demonstrates bizarre, sophisticated, or unusual sexual knowledge or behavior;
- becomes pregnant or contracts a venereal disease, particularly if under age 14;
- runs away; or
- reports sexual abuse by a parent or another adult caregiver.

Consider the possibility of sexual abuse when the parent or other adult caregiver:

- is unduly protective of the child, severely limits the child's contact with other children, especially of the opposite sex;
- is secretive and isolated; or
- describes marital difficulties involving family power struggles or sexual relations.

Note. From *Educators, Schools, and Child Abuse,* by D. Broadhurst, © 1994, by permission of the publisher, the National Committee to Prevent Child Abuse, Chicago, Illinois.

signs occurring repeatedly or in combination may cue an educator that child abuse is present in a family (see Table 11.1).

State statutes specify procedures for reporting child abuse or neglect. Many localities also have school board policies and procedures to encourage effective reporting of suspected child abuse. Under the Child Abuse and Neglect Act, educators are assured immunity from civil liability if reports of abuse and neglect are made in good faith.

▉ You Should Have Known Better

Two teachers organized a trip to a museum of natural history for a group of about 50 students ranging in age from 12 to 15 years. When they arrived at the museum, students divided into small groups to tour the museum without supervision. One student, Roberto Mancha, of his own volition joined a group and proceeded with them to the various exhibits. While out of his teacher's sight, Roberto alleged that he was accosted by a group of youths not connected with the school, beaten by them, and as a result, suffered serious injuries. In *Mancha v. Field Museum of Natural History* (1972), Roberto's father initiated action against the school district, the two teachers, and the museum for the injuries suffered by his son at the museum.

Were the teachers negligent? Should they have been expected to supervise students at all times?

Analysis of "You Should Have Known Better"   Suits brought by students injured during school-related activities are the most common type of litigation in education (Imber & van Geel, 1993). A teacher who demonstrates **negligence** (failure to exercise reasonable care to protect students from injury) may be held liable for damages if an injured student can prove the following:

1. the teacher had a legal duty to offer a standard of care that would have prevented the injury from occurring,

2. the teacher did not live up to the standard of care,

3. the teacher's carelessness resulted in harm to the student, and

4. the student sustained an actual injury that could be measured in monetary terms (Imber & van Geel, 1993).

When accused of negligence, a teacher can try to prove that a student's injury was a mere accident, that her action or inaction was not the cause of such injury, and that some other act intervened and was the cause of the injury. Other rejoinders against negligence include contributory negligence, comparative negligence, and assumption of risk (Alexander & Alexander, 1992).

When can a teacher be sued for negligence?

Contributory negligence occurs when the student who was injured failed to exercise the required standard of care for his own safety. When this condition exists, depending on such things as a child's age and mental maturity, the teacher may be absolved from liability. A high school

What are teachers' responsibilities toward children's health and safety? If one of these children were to be injured by another child during recess, can the playground teacher be sued for negligence?

student, for example, who has been taught how to use a power saw and observed to determine that she can operate the machine safely may be guilty of contributory negligence if injured while removing a piece of wood from the machine with her hands—a violation of safety practices that the students have been taught.

In situations in which teacher and student are both held liable for an injury, there may be a charge of **comparative negligence**. Generally, this means that a teacher is held accountable for a proportion of damages commensurate with the degree to which he contributed to the injury. **Assumption of risk**, rarely applicable except in cases of competitive athletics, means that people who are aware of possible risks involved in an activity voluntarily participate, thus agreeing to take their chances.

In *Mancha v. Field Museum of Natural History* (1972), an Illinois court dismissed charges of negligence brought against the school, museum, and teachers. Although the lower courts viewed the teachers' action of letting students tour the museum in an unsupervised group as an intentional act, given the nature of the environment (a museum), it was not an act that teachers should have anticipated would result in harm to a student. In explaining their verdict, the court argued that a museum is very different from a factory, a stone quarry, or a place where there might be dangerous machinery, or a place where there might be a shooting or an assault:

> The Museum in question is itself a great educational enterprise which enables teachers, parents, and children to learn much that could be learned at school. . . . To say that the teachers had a duty to supervise and discipline the entire Museum trip would be to ignore the realities of the situation and to make such trips impossible. (*Mancha v. Field Museum of Natural History*, 1972, p. 902)

However, there have been several cases in which students were injured and educators were found to have breached duty of care:

- A group of students with mental retardation were left unattended for a half hour, and a student received an eye injury when another pupil threw a wooden pointer (*Gonzalez v. Mackler*, 1963).

- A student who was permitted to wear mittens fell while climbing on a jungle gym (*Ward v. Newfield Central School District No. 1*, 1978).

- A student was burned when she and her peers were working on a project for the science fair. The accident occurred when the students tried to light a defective burner that had gone out, and alcohol exploded. Although the teacher had set up the experiment and checked to see that it worked properly, the teacher was not in the room when the students lit the burner. Because the students were not advised to wait until the teacher's return to light the fire and were not personally supervised, the teacher was held liable for negligence (*Station v. Travelers Insurance Co.*, 1974).

WHAT ARE THE RIGHTS AND RESPONSIBILITIES OF SCHOOL DISTRICTS?

Although the courts have consistently asserted that the authority for public education resides in the state legislature, schools for the most part are locally administered. As mentioned in Chapter 6, school boards deal with a variety of educational issues and problems. A number of court cases, in conjunction with federal and state statutes, have clarified the special responsibilities and rights of local school boards.

Balancing Academic Freedom

The school board meeting raged on for several hours. Three English teachers from the high school and a number of parents voiced their opinions about the list of texts used in elective high school literature courses. When the board voted to eliminate 10 texts from the diverse list of 1,285 books, the teachers were enraged. They believed that all of the books were necessary components of a curriculum designed to stimulate debate and broaden student knowledge. Viewing the board's action as an invasion of their First Amendment right to academic freedom, the three English teachers decided to seek legal counsel. They could not believe that a local school board had ultimate authority to determine what textbooks would be used in schools.

> **Do school boards have the power to ban textbooks?**

Analysis of "Balancing Academic Freedom"   Since the U.S. Supreme Court ruling in *Hazelwood School District v. Kuhlmeier* (1988), the Court has indicated a willingness to allow local school boards the final decision regarding the curriculum and the availability of books, films, and materials in elementary and secondary classrooms. However, if school boards' actions contract rather than expand knowledge, judicial intervention is not uncommon (Alexander & Alexander, 1992). When deciding individual cases, the courts usually consider the educational relevance of controversial material, teaching objectives, and the age and maturity of the intended audience.

In *Virgil v. School Board of Columbia County, Florida* (1989), the Supreme Court upheld a local school board's right to remove two readings from the curriculum because of objections to the material's vulgarity and sexual explicitness. Although the Court did not endorse the decision, stating that they seriously questioned how young people could be harmed by reading the masterpieces of Western literature, the Court acknowledged that the school board's decision was reasonably related to "legitimate pedagogical concerns." That is, as in *Hazelwood*, school officials considered the emotional maturity of the intended audience when determining the appropriateness of readings dealing with potentially sensitive topics (Alexander & Alexander, 1992).

How much freedom does a teacher have in the selection of material for her students? In 1989 a Fifth Circuit Court of Appeals ruling held that teachers cannot assert a First Amendment right to replace an official supplementary reading list with their own list of books without first getting administrative approval. Nor may teachers delete parts of the curriculum that conflict with their personal beliefs. A kindergarten teacher, for example, who refuses to teach a unit on patriotic topics may be dismissed by the school board for not covering prescribed material (McCarthy & Cambron-McCabe, 1992).

Teachers do have freedom in selecting teaching strategies, however. Teachers who want to assign controversial materials may usually do so as long as the selected materials are relevant to the topic of study, appropriate to the age and maturity of the students, and unlikely to cause disruption. When a high school psychology teacher in a conservative Texas community was fired for having her students read a masculinity survey from Psychology Today, the court ruled that the school violated the teacher's constitutional rights. In the eyes of the court, there was no evidence that the material caused substantial disruption, and there was no clear, prior prohibition against the use of such materials (Fischer, Schimmel, & Kelly, 1995).

▦ Equal Treatment

Fifteen African-American preschool and elementary students living in a low-income housing project in Ann Arbor, Michigan, brought suit against the board of education for practices they claimed denied them equal educational opportunities. According to the students, their language (African-American English) differed from standard English that was spoken by teachers and used in written materials of the school. The students claimed a violation of Title 20 of the U.S. Code, which provides that no state can deny individuals educational opportunities due to their race, gender, or national origin by failing to overcome language barriers that might inhibit learning (*Martin Luther King, Jr., Elementary School Children v. Michigan Board of Education*, 1979).

Analysis of "Equal Treatment"   Are school boards legally obligated to make special provisions for students who speak "black English"? In its 1954 landmark decision *Brown v. Board of Education of Topeka, Kansas*, the Supreme Court addressed for the first time issues of educational inequality when it repudiated the "separate but equal" doctrine, attempting to put an end to racial segregation in schools. As the courts worked, and continue to work, to effect unitary school systems, many have questioned the quality of educational opportunities for minority-group students in such settings. One area of concern has been classification of students for special services. Sometimes courts and legislatures have directed attention to discriminatory classifications of minority-group students; in other situations, such as those involving linguistic minority-group students, the courts have addressed the absence of student classifications.

In *Lau v. Nichols* (1974), the only Supreme Court decision involving English-deficient students, the Court held that a school district receiving federal aid must provide special instruction for non-English-speaking students whose opportunities to learn are restricted because of language barriers. This

VOICES

On a Perceived Retreat from School Desegregation

In *Missouri v. Jenkins* (1995) the Supreme Court decided that the state of Missouri had no obligation to endlessly fund efforts to correct specific past school discriminations. Charles Russo and Lawrence Rossow (1996) consider the implications of the Court's ruling:

In a stunning, but not entirely surprising, 5–4 reversal, the Supreme Court's ruling in *Missouri v. Jenkins*, spearheaded by the dissent in the earlier suit between the parties, signaled a further retrenchment in the struggle to end racial segregation in the schools. In this, the second action originating in the Kansas City, Missouri, School District (KCMSD) to reach the Court on its merits, the majority held that the federal district court exceeded the bounds of its broad discretion in its mandated desegregation remedy. The trial court had ordered the State of Missouri to pay for both across-the-board salary increases for virtually all personnel and the quality education programs in KCMSD, at a total cost of more than $1.3 billion dollars, because student achievement levels were still at or below national norms at many grade levels.

When coupled with the tentative settlement agreement in *Missouri v. Jenkins* that would free the State from having to pay for Kansas City's elaborate school desegregation program after 1999, the effect of the Court's holding on this bitter eighteen-year dispute remains unclear. Consequently, even though the Court stopped short of dismantling the desegregation program in KCMSD, this decision should be noteworthy for ongoing desegregation actions throughout the Nation. . . . (pp. 1–2)

The majority opinion has caused concern among a number [of] civil rights advocates that run the gamut from despair to cautious optimism. Jesse Jackson was quoted as saying that allowing schools to be financially unequal will create a "Yale track and jail track" for students (Levine, 1995).

Gary Orfield of Harvard University reflected that "We've got a fairly sweeping attack on urban school systems. . . . It encourages people who want to dismantle it to try" (Sanchez & Kaggwa, 1995).

William Taylor, an NAACP lawyer, pointed out that on remand the district court will have to require black students to show how much of the educational deficit was attributable to segregation. Describing the decision as the "It's a Wonderful Life" test, Taylor said, "You'd need a guardian angel to come down to tell what the world would have looked like were it not for segregation" (Frievogel, 1995).

At the same time, there are those who are taking a guardedly optimistic perspective. Arthur Benson, the attorney for the original plaintiffs, thought that O'Connor's concurrence offered some hope. He noted how she opined that the lower courts might still justify a large portion of the school desegregation plan if it were based on improving education for city students rather than desegregative attractiveness for suburban students. . . . Benson even held out the possibility that Judge Clark could justify the salary increases by the need to improve education for students within the district. (p. 11)

CRITICAL THINKING

- Why might some members of our society believe that separate education for children of different races is undesirable, while others seem to be less concerned?

- Why might people interpret the decision in *Missouri v. Jenkins* as a retreat from school desegregation?

- Why is Arthur Benson more optimistic than Jesse Jackson about the decision?

Note. From *Missouri v. Jenkins* redux: The end of the road for school desegregation or another stop on an endless journey? by C. J. Russo & L. F. Rossow, 1996, *West's Education Law Reporter, 103*, 1–12.

particular case centered around the plight of about 1,800 Chinese-American students in San Francisco public schools who spoke little or no English yet were offered no remedial English language instruction or other special compensatory program by the school system. According to the Court, such treatment of students violated Title VI of the **Civil Rights Act of 1964**, which specifies that no one, regardless of race, color, or origin, can be discriminated against or denied participation in programs receiving federal assistance.

Following *Lau*, Congress offered further protection to students when it passed the **Bilingual Act of 1974**, amended in 1988. This act calls for parental involvement in the planning of appropriate educational programs for children with limited English-speaking ability. Neither the Bilingual Act nor Title VI, however, specifies what types of programs are appropriate for addressing the needs of students with limited English-speaking abilities. Types of assistance offered to students who have difficulty understanding standard English vary greatly from state to state.

Since the *Lau* ruling, many cases have been heard by the courts, one of which was *Martin Luther King, Jr., Elementary School Children v. Michigan Board of Education* (1979). As described above, African-American students who protested the use of standard English as the sole medium of instruction brought this suit before the court.

In ruling on the case, the Court acknowledged that Michigan schools had provided special assistance to these and other students through learning consultants, a speech therapist, a psychologist, a language consultant, tutors, and parent helpers. Evidence existed of good faith efforts to meet the needs of students who spoke black English. The Court noted, however, that teachers seemed to lack knowledge about black English and thus were restricted in their ability to educate African-American students. To remedy this, the Court did not order the establishment of a bilingual program, as was done in the Lau case. Instead, the Court required the school board to develop a plan whereby teachers would learn to recognize the home language of students and to use that knowledge to teach reading skills and standard English more effectively.

How Could You Let This Happen to a Student?

When Peter graduated from high school, he sought $500,000 in damages from the San Francisco Unified Schools for failing to provide him with an adequate education. According to Peter, the school system was at fault for his poor skills because it had (a) failed to apprehend his reading disabilities, (b) assigned him to classes in which curricular materials were not geared to his reading level, (c) allowed him to pass from grade to grade without seeing that he mastered basic skills necessary for success at succeeding levels, (d) assigned him to teachers who did not know how to meet his learning needs, and (e) allowed him to graduate without being able to read at the eighth-grade level as required by the Education Code. Moreover, Peter said that his mother had been told that his reading ability was not much below the school's average.

> **Are schools liable for educational malpractice?**

Given the sequence of events, can the school system be held liable for educational malpractice?

Analysis of "How Could You Let This Happen to a Student?"

Although teachers and educational institutions have historically been exempt from legal responsibility and accountability, increasing numbers of educational malpractice claims have forced the courts to deal frequently with issues of academic negligence. A precedent-setting case occurred in California in 1976, when Peter W., the high school graduate described above, accused the school system of negligently and intentionally depriving him of basic skills.

The state appellate court dismissed Peter W.'s suit, contending that there were no explicit "standards of care" by which schools or classroom teachers could be judged negligent in their duties. Besides conflicting ideas about the best way to educate students, the Court noted that there were a variety of physical, neurological, emotional, cultural, and environmental factors that influenced learning yet were beyond a classroom teacher's control. In addition, the Court reasoned that attempts to hold school districts to a "duty of care" in academic matters would likely result in a flood of malpractice suits that would only inhibit their ability to discharge their academic functions (*Peter W. v. San Francisco Unified School District,* 1976).

For the most part, the California court's decision has been followed in educational malpractice litigation. However, in instances when educators have maliciously or intentionally caused injury to children by furnishing false information about a child's learning problems and altering information to cover their actions (*Hunter v. Board of Education of Montgomery County*), or placing a child in a program despite scores showing a placement to be inappropriate (*B. M. v. Montana*), courts have allowed parents to bring action against school officials (Fischer, Schimmel, & Kelly, 1995).

Somebody Will Pay!

Christine Franklin, a 10th-grade student, felt uncomfortable around Andrew Hill, a sports coach and economics teacher at her high school in suburban Atlanta. According to Christine, Hill sexually harassed her by doing such things as asking if she would be willing to have sex with an older man, calling her at home to ask her out, and forcibly kissing her on the mouth in the school parking lot. During Christine's junior year, things got much worse; on at least three occasions, Hill allegedly pressured her into having sex. When Christine reported Hill's actions to school officials, they took no immediate steps to curtail Hill's behavior. By the time Christine had lodged a complaint with the U.S. Education Department's office for civil rights, however, Hill had resigned and the school had adopted a grievance procedure to avoid future violations.

Can students who are victims of sexual harassment sue for damages?

Still angry about the abuse she had suffered at the high school, Christine decided to sue the school district for monetary damages. She argued that Hill's behavior toward her violated Title IX (a law prohibiting schools supported with federal monies from discriminating on the basis of gender). In school officials' eyes, Christine didn't stand a chance in court; they had resolved the problem and it was unlikely to occur again.

Can students who are victims of sexual harassment and other forms of sex discrimination sue for monetary damages?

Analysis of "Somebody Will Pay!"   In 1992, when the Supreme Court heard Christine Franklin's case (*Franklin v. Gwinnett County Public Schools*), the Court ruled unanimously that Christine had suffered sexual harassment. Furthermore, the Court stated for the first time that schools supported by federal funds were susceptible to lawsuit and, in instances of sexual harassment and other forms of sex discrimination, liable for monetary damages to the victims of such mistreatment. What this means for school systems is that more lawsuits will likely be filed against them by individuals alleging discrimination in employment and athletics. Legal experts also predict that this court case will clear the way for monetary damages to victims of race and disability discrimination in schools (Walsh, 1992).

What Kind of Choice Is This?

When the special education teacher and Anita Leopold met at the end of second grade to construct Miranda Leopold's IEP, they agreed that Miranda was at a point where she could benefit academically and socially from interactions with regular education students. Accordingly, they created a plan that would allow Miranda to be mainstreamed into a regular third-grade classroom. With the exception of daily tutorial sessions with a resource teacher, Miranda would experience the regular curriculum for third-grade students.

Anita liked her daughter's new placement. When she learned, however, that Miranda also qualified for the Milwaukee Parental Choice Program, she didn't know what to think. One of the private schools on the choice list focused on art and music, both of which Miranda loved. The idea of sending Miranda to such a school appealed to Anita. When she phoned the school for information about the program, however, Anita learned that the choice school had no resource teacher to help Miranda with her reading skills. Anita was perplexed. Didn't choice schools have to offer the same services to students with disabilities as did the public schools? How could state taxes be used for educational programs that, in a sense, discriminate against certain students? Are choice schools held to the same standards as public schools?

Analysis of "What Kind of Choice is This?"   On March 3, 1992, the Wisconsin Supreme Court voted 4 to 3 to overturn a court of appeals ruling that the Milwaukee Parental Choice Plan was unconstitutional. Established in March 1990, the Choice Plan allowed up to 1,000 low-income students in Milwaukee to receive a voucher worth $2,500 each year to attend certain private, nonsectarian schools in the city. According to Shirley S. Abrahamson, one of the dissenting Justices, the majority opinion on this issue "permits the legislature to subvert the unifying, democratizing purpose of public education by using public funds to substitute private education for public education without the concomitant controls exerted over public education" (*Davis v. Grover*, 1992).

Participating private schools do not have to meet the same standards as do public schools in the Milwaukee Parental Choice Plan. This fact has been troubling to many. Julie Underwood (1991) noted that "quality assurances" in the Choice Plan ensure that participating schools operate as private schools and that one of the following occur: at least 70% of the student body advances one grade level per year; average attendance rate is at least 90%; at least 80% of the pupils show "significant" educational progress; or at least 70% of the pupils' parents meet school criteria for active involvement in the program.

Such criteria omit requirements for the provision of services to students such as Miranda, who may have special learning needs. Minimal standards for participating private schools mean that schools may deny admission to students with disabilities if the school determines that it cannot accommodate students' needs. Thus "large numbers of students with disabilities are effectively proscribed from participation in a publicly funded choice plan" (Mead, 1995).

Since *Davis v. Grover*, the Supreme Court has ruled unanimously that parents of students with learning disabilities may be eligible for tuition reimbursement if they send their children to private schools for special help, even if the schools are not approved by the local school district (*Florence County School District Four v. Carter,* 1993). Such litigation will surely redefine the relationship between public and private schools in the years ahead.

SUMMARY

What legal principles affect education?

1 States' legal control over education is authorized by the Tenth Amendment.

2 When educational disputes arise, the parties involved make every effort to resolve differences at the local level. Most cases heard by the Supreme Court of the United States, the highest court in the land, are cases in which the validity of a state or federal statute is questioned.

What are parents' rights and responsibilities?

3 In many states, parents may exempt their children from attending school if they meet certain requirements for providing education at home.

4 The legality of corporal punishment varies from state to state and district to district.

5 Public schools receiving federal financial assistance must afford special educational assistance to students categorized as having special learning needs.

BENCHMARKS

Selected Supreme Court Cases on School-Related Issues

1943	*West Virginia State Board of Education v. Barnette.* Requiring students to salute or pledge to the American flag becomes unconstitutional.
1963	*School District of Abington Township v. Schempp.* Prayer and Bible reading in public school classrooms become unconstitutional.
1969	*Tinker v. Des Moines Independent School District.* Students do not lose their constitutional rights and freedoms when they pass through the schoolhouse door.
1971	*Lemon v. Kurtzman.* States may not provide direct aid for secular services to parochial schools, including teacher salaries and instructional materials.
1974	*Lau v. Nichols.* School districts receiving federal aid must provide special instruction for non-English-speaking students whose opportunities to learn are restricted because of language barriers.
1975	*Goss v. Lopez.* Students may not be suspended from school without a hearing.
1977	*Ingraham v. Wright.* The U. S. Constitution does not prohibit the use of corporal punishment in the schools. *Abood v. Detroit Board of Education.* It is constitutional for states to require nonmembers of unions to pay union dues as a condition of employment.
1981	*Widmar v. Vincent.* Refusing religious groups equal access to public facilities while allowing access to other groups is a violation of students' freedom of speech.

What are students' rights and responsibilities?

6 As long as the school building is available for use by other noncurriculum clubs, and as long as the school does not sponsor or conduct club meetings, religious clubs are permissible on school grounds.

7 Students cannot be suspended or expelled without due process.

8 School searches must be guided by "reason" and "common sense"; that is, at the inception of the search, there must be reasonable grounds for suspecting that evidence will be found to prove a student is in violation of the law or school rules, and the scope of the search must be reasonably related to the objectives of the search, the age and sex of the student, and the nature of the infraction.

9 School officials can censor school-sponsored student-produced material that they consider inconsistent with the educational mission of the school.

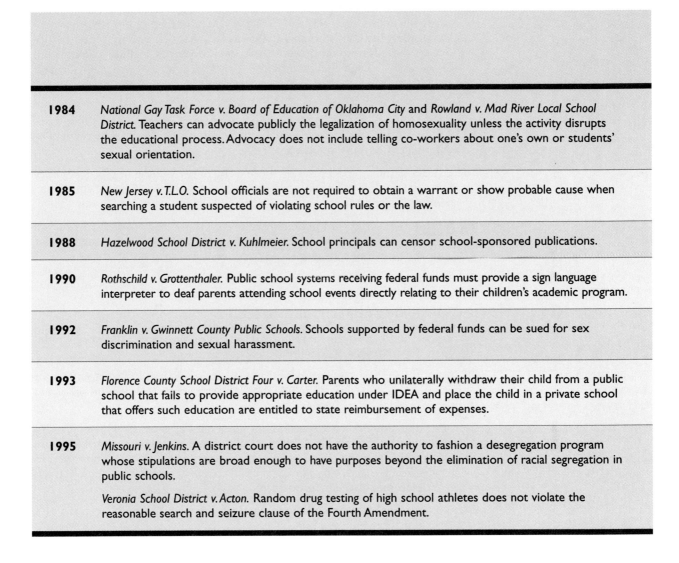

1984 *National Gay Task Force v. Board of Education of Oklahoma City* and *Rowland v. Mad River Local School District.* Teachers can advocate publicly the legalization of homosexuality unless the activity disrupts the educational process. Advocacy does not include telling co-workers about one's own or students' sexual orientation.

1985 *New Jersey v. T.L.O.* School officials are not required to obtain a warrant or show probable cause when searching a student suspected of violating school rules or the law.

1988 *Hazelwood School District v. Kuhlmeier.* School principals can censor school-sponsored publications.

1990 *Rothschild v. Grottenthaler.* Public school systems receiving federal funds must provide a sign language interpreter to deaf parents attending school events directly relating to their children's academic program.

1992 *Franklin v. Gwinnett County Public Schools.* Schools supported by federal funds can be sued for sex discrimination and sexual harassment.

1993 *Florence County School District Four v. Carter.* Parents who unilaterally withdraw their child from a public school that fails to provide appropriate education under IDEA and place the child in a private school that offers such education are entitled to state reimbursement of expenses.

1995 *Missouri v. Jenkins.* A district court does not have the authority to fashion a desegregation program whose stipulations are broad enough to have purposes beyond the elimination of racial segregation in public schools.

Veronia School District v. Acton. Random drug testing of high school athletes does not violate the reasonable search and seizure clause of the Fourth Amendment.

10 Schools can institute dress codes.

11 Schools cannot expel students with disabilities for behavior attributable to their disabilities; however, schools may temporarily suspend students with disabilities who exhibit behavior dangerous to self or others.

12 Schools cannot release information about a student to third parties without parental or student permission, except in the event of an emergency.

What are teachers' rights and responsibilities?

13 Teachers may be required to share in the cost of the union's collective bargaining activities even though they do not belong to the union.

14 Tenured teachers cannot be dismissed without specific or good cause. Teachers with probationary status, however, generally have no constitutional right to due process when their contract is terminated at the end of the school year.

15 The Supreme Court has not yet recognized a constitutional privacy right to engage in homosexual behavior. Teachers do have the right to advocate publicly for legalization of homosexuality as long as such activity is not disruptive to the educational process. Advocacy does not include talking with co-workers about sexual preference.

16 Until the Supreme Court decides whether home videotaping for broader viewing by students in classrooms constitutes fair use of copyrighted materials, teachers are well advised to adhere to Congressional guidelines. Another option is to seek written permission from copyright owners to videotape programs for classroom use.

17 Educators must report cases of abuse or neglect resulting in physical injury to a child, and, in most states, educators must report instances of emotional, mental, or sexual abuse.

18 Educators are expected to demonstrate care that a reasonable and prudent person would take when supervising students. When unusual dangers exist, special caution must be employed to prevent injury or harm to students.

What are the rights and responsibilities of school districts?

19 School boards generally have the right to determine curriculum to be taught, even if teachers disagree with the board's decision.

20 School districts receiving federal aid must provide special instruction for non-English-speaking students whose opportunities to learn are restricted because of language barriers.

21 Educational malpractice suits do not fare well in the courts. However, educators cannot maliciously or intentionally injure children by furnishing false information about a child's learning problems and altering information to cover their actions, or by placing a child in a program despite scores showing a placement to be inappropriate.

22 Public schools can be sued for sexual harassment and other forms of sex discrimination.

23 The relationship between public and private schools may be redefined in the future in cases involving the funding of school choice programs.

TERMS AND CONCEPTS

assumption of risk, *p. 442*
Bilingual Act of 1974, *p. 446*
Buckley Amendment, *p. 432*
Civil Rights Act of 1964, *p. 446*
comparative negligence, *p. 442*
contributory negligence, *p. 441*
dismissal, *p. 435*
due process of law, *p. 427*

Equal Access Act (EAA), *p. 424*
equal protection clause, *p. 418*
establishment clause, *p. 417*
free exercise clause, *p. 417*
in loco parentis, *p. 428*
Lemon test, *p. 425*
negligence, *p. 441*

REFLECTIVE PRACTICE

Lexington, North Carolina, September 26, 1996—First grader Johnathan Prevette is accused of sexual harassment of a classmate. Johnathan kissed a female classmate on the cheek, and the girl's mother charged sexual harassment. The superintendent suspended Johnathan from school.

If Jane Ottinger, a teacher at Lincoln Middle School, had read this headline in her Sunday paper a year ago, she would have believed that it was some kind of cruel joke. Since when did a little boy kissing a little girl become sexual harassment?

But that was before she had lived through what was to become known as the Amy Christopher Incident. Amy was a bright, pretty girl in Jane's sixth-grade class. Mr. and Mrs. Christopher argued that the boys in Amy's class had treated her so badly that she had become an emotional wreck. When the Christophers complained to Jane about the behavior, Jane went immediately to the principal and recounted her conversation with them. The principal said that he would handle the matter and that Jane should be alert to signs of inappropriate behavior but not to worry too much. As nearly as Jane could remember, he said something like, "The hormones begin to rage about this time in kids' lives. Sometimes the boys, and the girls too, get carried away. This is natural. Although the school does not want and would never condone such behavior, you need to understand that some parents are fanatics who blow everything out of proportion. Flirting and teasing are part of life in the sixth grade."

Six months later the Christophers moved to another school district. Their move was accompanied by a front-page story in the local paper, in which they were quoted as saying that they "had complained repeatedly to the teacher and school officials about the sexual harassment of their daughter and other children, but gotten no results."

Now, some four months later, when Jane read the story about little Johnny she felt sad. Had times changed so much since she was a child? Where would all these claims and counterclaims end?

Issues, Problems, Dilemmas, and Opportunities

How do issues such as the Amy Christopher Incident offer opportunities for teaching and learning? How do incidents of possible sexual harassment impede learning?

Perceive and Value

If you were Amy's parents, what might you say to your daughter's teacher and principal if you suspected other children of sexual harassment? If you were Amy's teacher, what would you think of the principal's response?

Know and Act

If you were a teacher faced with a situation like that presented by Amy Christopher, what more would you want to know? Assuming that you reported incidents between students and told your principal about parents' concerns, what more—if anything—might you do? Rank the activities on page 454 in the order in which you might undertake them. Explain your reasoning.

- Weave prevention of sexual harassment throughout the curriculum.

- Train peer leaders in awareness and prevention, and use them to teach workshops for other children.

- Provide students with safe avenues to report harassment.

- Involve parents in lessons and homework on sexual harassment (LRP Publications, 1996a, p. 3).

Evaluate

Examine your own perceptions about sexual harassment. What standards guide your assessment of acceptable and unacceptable behaviors among young people? Examine a school's faculty handbook. Does it mention sexual harassment among students? If so, what does it communicate?

ONLINE ACTIVITY

Go to Oyez Oyez Oyez, a Web resource of the U.S. Supreme Court (**http://oyez. at.nwu.edu/oyez.html**). There you will find a link entitled "Index of Cases by Date Decided." When you click on this link, you will find summaries of cases dealing with religious establishment, gender equality, freedom of expression, and so on. Scroll to cases decided in 1987, and click on "Edwards v. Aguillar" (religious establishment). This case dealt with a Louisiana law entitled the "Balanced Treatment for Creation Science and Evolution Science in Public School Instruction Act." The law prohibited the teaching of the theory of evolution in the public schools unless that instruction was accompanied by the teaching of creation science, a Biblical belief that all forms of life appeared abruptly on Earth at about the same time. Schools were not forced to teach creation science, but if either topic was to be addressed, evolution or creation, teachers were obligated to discuss the other as well.

The Court decided the case in a 4 to 3 vote (with 2 abstentions). Find out the results and explain their reasoning.

Nancy Willard, a specialist in computer law and education law, has created a Web site (**http://www.erehwon.com/k12aup/**) to help K–12 school systems develop effective Internet policies and practices. School districts everywhere are moving quickly to provide Internet access for their students and employees. With such access comes unfiltered information and opportunities to communicate with people from around the world.

Willard's site evaluates some of the basic constitutional issues, as well as educational issues, that arise in the context of K–12 acceptable use policies for Internet access. She bases her analysis on past court decisions in other environments. "Use of the Internet in the K–12 environment is so new that there are no court cases that are directly on point." Visit the site and read the "Student Acceptable Use Template." What kind of restrictions might a school legally place on student access to the Internet?

12

Comparative
and Global
Education

We are a country of immigrants. Even though we have slowly and reluctantly begun to recognize some historical native influences, we have been and continue to be shaped by the values and lessons of life that people bring with them to this land. At about the time we begin to slip unconsciously into ethnocentric self-satisfaction, some individual from another country or international group makes us realize that people everywhere share a lot of the same dreams and fears. When we pay attention we often learn much about people who live

FIGURE 12.1 *(opposite)*

**Selections from
An Immigrant Calendar**

This figure shows major holidays for selected months, celebrated in the countries of origin of New York City's largest immigrant groups. What approach does Newcomers High School take to the education of immigrants?

outside our borders and who speak languages other than or in addition to English. We learn a lot about ourselves, too.

We use this chapter to explore how education in other countries and cultures can be relevant to our own classroom experiences in the United States. In doing so, we discuss how people around the globe experience a kind of interdependence and how educators can enhance awareness of global links. We examine educational systems in seven other nations, describing briefly how educators handle problems and opportunities similar to those we face. We conclude by considering the advantages and disadvantages of making educational comparisons between and among countries.

PROFESSIONAL PRACTICE QUESTIONS

1 How is comparative education relevant to classroom teachers?

2 How can we enhance global awareness?

3 What can we learn about education from other countries?

4 What factors should we consider when making international comparisons?

HOW IS COMPARATIVE EDUCATION RELEVANT TO CLASSROOM TEACHERS?

We can urge ourselves to be more open, less parochial, and more global in our views, but the inhabitants of Newcomers High School in the New York City borough of Queens do so every day. Newcomers High—a school devoted to meeting the special needs of immigrant children—opened its doors to about 60 immigrant students in September 1995. Less than a year later, staff at Newcomers were educating nearly 600 students who spoke some 20 languages and came from more than 40 countries. The world literally comes to the door of Newcomers High.

Imagine what it must feel like to face a group of 30 high school students who have just assembled in the middle of the most populous city in the country. You must be able to communicate with them, to say nothing of being able to teach them. Diversity of language, thought, religion, custom, and values just might stretch a teacher to rethink the meaning of the word *education*. Figure 12.1 contains examples of some major holidays celebrated by students at Newcomers High School.

At Newcomers High School, teachers and administrators try to provide students with the skills necessary to function effectively in mainstream schools and in the larger community. Students participate in an orientation program, for example, that focuses on such basic skills as how to make change and how

456

January

1 New Year's Day
  Independence Day
   (Haiti)
  Founding Day of Republic
   of China (Taiwan)
2 Day of the Ancestors
   (Haiti)
6 Day of the Kings
   (Dominican Republic)
  Epiphany (Greece)
7 Christmas (Russia)
13 New Year (Russia)
15 Shabebarat (Pakistan)
26 Republic Day (India)
31 Lunar New Year's Day
   (China, Korea, Taiwan,
   Vietnam)

February

1 Beginning of Ramadan
5 Constitution Day
   (Mexico)
21 Martyrs Day
   (Bangladesh)
23 Anniversary of the
   Republic (Guyana)
27 Independence Day
   (Dominican Republic)
28 Fat Tuesday

March

1 Ash Wednesday
  Independence Movement
   Day (Korea)
2 Eid al Fitr
8 International Women's
   Day (Russia)
17 St. Patrick's Day
   (Ireland)
20 Feast of San Jose
   (Colombia)
21 Benito Juarez's Birthday
   (Mexico)
23 Pakistan Day
25 Independence Day
   (Greece)
26 Independence Day
   (Bangladesh)
29 Youth Day (Taiwan)

April

1 Children's Day (Taiwan)
5 Arbor Day (Korea)
  Tomb Sweeping Day
   (Taiwan)
9 Palm Sunday
  Day of Valor (Philippines)
14 Good Friday
  Pan American Day
15 Festival of Passover
  Pahela Baishakh-First Day of
   Bangla Year (Bangladesh)
16 Easter
17 Easter Monday
23 Easter (Russia)
25 Liberation Day (Italy)
27 Holocaust Memorial Day

May

1 Labor Day (Bangladesh,
   Colombia, Ecuador,
   Greece, Haiti, Ireland,
   Italy, Mexico, Philippines,
   Poland, Russia, Taiwan)
  May Day (China, Pakistan)
  Orthodox Easter (Greece)
3 Anniversary of the
   Constitution (Poland)
4 Independence Day (Isreal)
5 Children's Day (Korea)
  Cinco de Mayo-Battle
   of Puebla (Mexico)
9 Victory Day WWII (Russia)
10 Eid-al-Adha
18 Flag Day (Haiti)
23 Labor Day (Jamaica)
29 Ascension Day (Colombia)
30 Muslim New Year

June

2 Dragon Boat Festival
   (Taiwan)
4 Whit Sunday
5 Whit Monday (Ireland)
8 Ashura
12 Independence Day
   (Philippines)
15 Corpus Christi
19 Sacrado Corazon
   (Colombia)
  Labor Day
   (Trinidad & Tobago)
26 Ascension del Senor
   (Colombia)

July

1 Communist Party
   Anniversary (China)
4 U.S. Filipino Friendship
   Day (Philippines)
5 Caribbean Day (Guyana)
17 Constitution Day (Korea)
20 Independence Day
   (Colombia)
24 Simon Bolivar Day

August

1 Army Day (China)
5 National Day (El Salvador)
7 August Bank Holiday
   (Ireland)
  Freedom Day (Guyana)
  Battle of Bojaco (Colombia)
  Independence Day (Jamaica)
8 Birth of Mohammed
10 Independence Day (Ecuador)
14 Independence Day
   (Pakistan, India)
15 Feast of the Assumption
  Ferragosto (Italy)
  Liberation Day (Korea)
16 Restoration of Independence
   (Dominican Republic)
20 Holiday of the Perfect
   Moment (Bangladesh)
21 Corpus Christi (Colombia)
29 Janmastmi (India,
   Bangladesh)
31 Independence Day
   (Trinidad & Tobago)

September

6 Defense Day (Pakistan)
8 Chusoc (Korea)
9 Mid-Autumn Festival
   (Taiwan)
11 Death of Quaid-e-Azam
   (Pakistan)
15 Independence Day
   (El Salvador, Guatemala,
   Costa Rica)
16 Independence Day (Mexico)
24 Virgin de la Mercedes
   (Dominican Republic)
25 Rosh Hashanah
28 Confucius' Birthday (Taiwan)
30 Republic Day
   (Trinidad & Tobago)

October

1 National Day (China)
3 National Foundation Day
   (Korea)
4 Yom Kippur
10 Double Tenth National Day
   (Taiwan)
12 Columbus Day
17 National Heroes Day
   (Jamaica)
23 Diwali (India)
25 Taiwan's Retrocession Day
   (Taiwan)
30 October Bank Holiday
   (Ireland)
31 Chiang Kai-Shek's Birthday
   (Taiwan)

November

1 All Saints Day
2 Day of the Dead
   (Mexico, El Salvador)
5 First Cry of Independence
   (El Salvador)
7 State Holiday (Russia)
  National Day (Bangladesh)
9 Birthday of Allama Iqba
   (Pakistan)
11 National Independence Day
   (Poland)
12 Sun Yat-Sen's Birthday
   (Taiwan)
13 Cartagena Independence Day
   (Colombia)
30 National Heroes Day
   (Philippines)

December

5 Discovery of Haiti (Haiti)
12 Virgin de Guadalupe
   (Mexico)
  Constitutional Day (Russia)
16 Victory Day (Bangladesh)
18 First Day of Chanukah
25 Christmas Day
  Shab-e-Maira (Pakistan)
26 Boxing Day
  St. Stephen's Day (Ireland)
30 National Hero Jose Riza Day
   (Philippines)

to use the subway system. To stay competitive with students in mainstream schools, enrollees attend classes in core content areas that are taught in their home languages. For about 9 hours each week, students also attend English as a Second Language (ESL) classes that focus on listening, writing, reading, and speaking skills. In the different classes students work individually and cooperatively on a variety of assignments.

The program at Newcomers High School includes learning opportunities for parents as well. At least one afternoon a week, the school offers ESL classes for parents. Several times during the school year, parents may also attend information sessions that focus on such issues as immigration laws, as well as local, state, and national laws.

The International Baccalaureate Organization (IBO), a nonprofit educational foundation based in Switzerland, takes another approach to making comparative education relevant to teachers and students around the world. Founded in the 1960s, the IBO grew out of international school efforts to establish a common curriculum and university entry credentials for geographically mobile students. International educators also hoped that a shared academic experience that emphasized critical thinking and exposure to a variety of viewpoints would foster tolerance and intercultural understanding among young people.

The IBO's diploma program for students in their last two years of high school and the middle years program for students ages 11 to 16 are offered in English, French, and Spanish. Both programs seek to enhance international understanding and academic excellence.

> The desired profile of the IBO student is that of a critical and compassionate thinker, an informed participant in local and world affairs who values the shared humanity that binds all people together while respecting the variety of cultures and attitudes that makes for the richness of life. (International Baccalaureate Organization, 1996)

The IBO provides curriculum and assessment development, teacher training and information seminars, electronic networking, and other educational services to 630 participating schools in more than 80 countries around the world. For more information on the history, governance, curriculum, and member schools of the IBO, visit the Web (**http://www.ibo.org**).

Teachers in the United States can create a classroom climate in which understanding of other cultures is either fostered or undermined. Teachers must prepare students from all ethnic, cultural, economic, and ability backgrounds to address problems they will face in the world at large. The challenge is to construct education in a global context, within which can be placed the more familiar ethnic, local, or disciplinary strands of thinking. (See Figure 12.2 for an internet-based resource that allows teachers and students around the world to interact with one another.)

HOW CAN WE ENHANCE GLOBAL AWARENESS?

Students at Our Lady of the Westside, a largely African-American Catholic school in inner-city Chicago, participate in an arts education program that encourages the idea of making cultural connections around the world through music and dance.

> [T]hey are practicing traditional Indian dance to the high-pitched accompaniment of an Indian flute, a drum and a sitar.... At the center of the

Global SchoolNet Foundation
Linking Kids Around the World

GSN Navigation Help
MAIN INDEX
Alphabetical Listing of Contents
SEARCH by Keyword or Concept

COOL! Stuff
Worth Looking At!
Win Eudora Pro 3.0 Site License!
Check it Out!

Visit the *NEW*
Global Schoolhouse®
sponsored by Microsoft®
Join the Global Schoolhouse
Community!

Projects Registry
sponsored by Walden University
Best Curriculum Projects on the Net!
K12 Opportunities
Free Stuff, Conferences, Contests,
Training & Special Web Sites.

International Schools
CyberFair 97!
sponsored by MCI, Cisco
& Network Solutions
Share & Unite! Register Now!
Entries due by March 7, 1997!

ThinkQuest
sponsored by Advanced
Network & Services
$1 Million in Prizes Available!
Proposals due by Feb 28, 1997!

Desktop Video Conferencing
sponsored by Canon Visual
Communications Systems
CU-SeeMe Users Can Visit Us at 192.215.2.3

Harnessing the Power of the Web
Also Available on CD! A Step-by-Step,
Easy to Follow, Web Tutorial!
NEW *Four Ways to Earn Graduate Extension Credit!*

Jane Goodall Institute
Youth and Education Programs,
Parks and Sanctuaries

Where on the Globe is Roger?
sponsored by MCI Foundation
NEW Join the Peace Pal Project!

CalWeb:
The California Web Project

Our WWW Contest
Next Drawing March 31, 1997!

Our Articles
Integrating Internet into the Classroom

News & Discussion Lists
Updates & Opportunities

Honors & Awards
Special Recognition for Our Hard Work!

Sponsorship Info
Meet Our Partners or Become One!

Learn More About the Global SchoolNet Foundation
We give you a reason to be connected!

Partnerships Are Very Important to Global SchoolNet!

The Global SchoolNet Foundation has repeatedly partnered with leaders in the communications industry,
including: Aldea Communications, Advanced Network & Services, CERFnet, Cisco Systems, MCI
Corporation, Microsoft, National Science Foundation, Pacific Bell, NBC and ABC World News to use
information technology to reform the classroom and to change the world!

dancing children is the guest instructor, dancer Pranita Jain. Wrapped in a saree—six yards of loose-fitting purple cloth—Jain wears a thick black braid down her back, and, at mid-forehead, the red powdered dot worn by many Indian women—the Hindu symbol for a third, meditative eye. The children, dressed in school uniforms of crisp blue oxford shirts and starched pants or skirts, also wear the forehead marks: Theirs are fuzzy red stickers, each in a different shape. 'The eye sees what is inside of you,' says Ricky Wallace, a round-faced 9-year-old. 'It sees what you feel.' (Foltz-Gray, 1995, pp. 58–59)

The extent to which these children recognize their connections to other countries and people of the world constitute an estimate of their **global awareness**. Such awareness is important, as Tye and Tye (1992) observe, because the welfare of the United States is tied to the welfare of other countries by economics, the environment, politics, culture, and technology. When there is unusual activity on the New York stock market, people watch to see what effect it will have in Tokyo, Bonn, and London. Acid rain, depletion of the ozone layer, ocean pollution, and disposal of nuclear waste are multinational concerns. The fall of the Soviet Union and reorganization of Eastern Europe have had reverberations in military spending, labor policies, capital investment, and, most immediately, in the immigration of children into the classrooms of the world.

As more people travel and work in countries other than those in which they were born, and as more people employ the dramatic advances in communications technology, the interplay of cultures increases. In some instances increased contact leads to competition and conflict. In other cases, familiarity breeds cooperation, for different people realize that they must work together if they are to survive and prosper. Everywhere, people call upon schools to promote technical skills to communicate and wisdom to use these technological skills for enhancing mutual understanding. Schools around the world must help tomorrow's adults learn languages, understand cultures, and use a host of electronic communication systems in order to function in today's world. A global society is no longer the pipedream of the futurist. It is an idea that people define each day as they reach around the world with their computers and fax machines.

> **What are the implications of joining education and technology on a global scale?**

Unfortunately it is difficult to discuss global challenges and the potential of modern education without using grandiose language—the kind that glazes people's eyes. The simple truth, however, is that the implications of joining education and technology on a global scale are nothing short of breathtaking.

Tye and Tye (1992) argue that a global perspective, aided by technology, forces people to consider problems that cut across national boundaries. Educators who think about the world also cultivate students' abilities to decenter and to view the world from others' perspectives. Elise Boulding (1988) noted that this process has occurred naturally for years through voluntary associations referred to as "nongovernmental organizations", or **NGOs**. These transnational associations—groups such as churches, scouts, farmers, chambers of commerce, physicians, athletes, and educators—grew in number from 176 in 1909 to more than 18,000 in the mid-1980s. They all advance agendas that focus on problems and issues of common interest, regardless of national borders.

Futures For Children (FFC) is an INGO (or International NGO) with its homebase in Albuquerque, New Mexico. For nearly 40 years the organization has worked to improve the well-being of children and communities by helping people help themselves. For example, they offer leadership programs for young Native Americans in New Mexico, Arizona, North Dakota, and Oregon. The FFC Leadership Program encourages young people to

- work in their communities to discover their leadership abilities;

- carry out projects in their communities;

- build relationships with adults whom they respect;

- choose and achieve a fund-raising goal to assist the next group of students; and

- meet and share experiences on a regular basis.

Why is global awareness important? What are some implications of joining education and technology on a global scale?

FFC also collaborates with four sister organizations that work in more than 150 communities in Central and South America. The FFC counselors and volunteers build schools, hospitals, roads, bridges, water sanitation systems, latrines, and wells and offer cholera prevention education programs, agricultural improvements, and small business development in Medellin, Colombia; Tegucigalpa, Honduras; San Jose, Costa Rica; and Oaxaca, Mexico.

For educators to enlarge their views of the world, or to think globally and encourage their students to do the same, the basic curriculum and instruction in most schools must change. Change with regard to a school's attention to global education must overcome a number of obstacles or competing demands. Historically, school leaders have not considered global perspective to be very important. Teachers' limited time is already devoted to existing curricula, standardized testing, and accreditation demands. Moreover, leadership is essential if people are to attend global issues, and in many districts there is no leadership.

When a critical mass of educators think globally, however, they can make global thinking come alive for students. For example, in one school—along with engaging in regular activities, such as using library materials and listening to guest speakers—teachers and students instituted a simple set of special projects and materials:

- a set of folk literature, poetry, and music from around the world for grades 1 and 2;

- a collection of books dealing with cultural commonalities among families of the world for grades 7 and 8;

- an endangered species unit for the middle grades;

- a special global education section in the school library; and

- an all-school display of "Our Earth" that represented interdisciplinary work at all grade levels (Tye & Tye, 1992).

A more elaborate example of what can be done to foster international perspectives in students can be found on the Internet at a site called MayaQuest.

On April 24, 1995 at 10:52 A.M., 12-year-old Sierra Gaitan was on hand as archaeologists uncovered an important hieroglyphic text at Caracol, a

VOICES

On Teaching Abroad

Sheryl Cohen and Jennifer Post, U.S. and Canadian citizens respectively, were colleagues at the Colegio Bolivar in Cali, Colombia. The school—a pre-kindergarten through 12th-grade private, bicultural, bilingual American school—enrolls nearly 1,200 students, the vast majority of whom are Colombian nationals. Sheryl taught third grade; Jenn taught high school English. Both have recently resumed their careers in the United States and Canada. Why did they decide to teach in Colombia? How were their experiences both disappointing and rewarding?

JENN: I had been teaching in Canada for 8 years and felt like I needed new challenges. I had always traveled, but I wanted to be more than just a tourist for a couple of weeks. I also wanted to live and work in a non-English-speaking country.

SHERYL: I was burned out after 5 years of teaching in an inner-city Los Angeles school. I had just enrolled in a master's program at Pepperdine and turned 30—I needed a change. I also wanted to improve my Spanish and learn more about the Spanish culture. I went to a job fair, and the principal from Colegio Bolivar sold me on the school.

Sheryl Cohen

JENN: My first year, I had problems with differences between the culture I was used to and my new Colombian culture. For example, my conceptions of truth, fairness, and sharing differed greatly from those of my students. I thought students were cheating, they thought they were sharing. I had to build into my teaching strategies techniques to minimize shared work so I could get an account of what an individual knew independently of the group.

Classroom management also differed from Canadian schools. The idea of quiet work did not exist. My students talked all the time—constant mumbling. What I perceived as rudeness, they perceived as normal. I never felt as though I bonded with my students, largely because they saw me as an outsider, which, of course, I was. They did not confide in me, and I missed that in students.

I loved the idea of rising to the challenge in Colombia. Creative writing was especially exciting. The natural poetry of the Spanish language helped my students be excellent writers. The quality of work done by second-language learners in my traditional introductory British literature class was incredible.

Mayan site deep in the Belize jungle. Sierra studied the glyphs, conversed with the archaeologists, offered her interpretation and then had to leave in a hurry. The bell rang, signaling the end of her 4th hour class at Como School in St. Paul, Minnesota. She logged off the computer and let the next class connect to Central America. (MayaQuest, no date)

The MayaQuest project, developed by the Minnesota Education Computing Consortium (MECC), engages an online audience to help explain the ninth-century collapse of the ancient Mayan civilization. Sierra Gaitan and her 7-year-old brother were among students across the country who followed this adventure. Contact **MayaQuest@InforMNs.k12.mn.us** by e-mail for more information and visit the Web site (**http://www.mecc.com/mayaquest.html**).

I could see that my Colombian students were far better prepared to work in the global marketplace than are my Canadian students. The material I covered at Bolivar was much more difficult than I can cover in Canada.

SHERYL: While the opportunity was there to work with others on my grade level, I felt isolated from teachers above and below me. For example, I remember how much my third-grade students liked my reading of *Charlie and the Chocolate Factory*. When a fourth-grade teacher found out I was reading the book, she really got upset. She was going to teach it to my students the following year, and she thought I had destroyed the chance for her to motivate them. I had no idea of what she or the other teachers in fourth grade taught. This was different from my experience in Los Angeles schools.

Despite the lack of communication across grade levels, my creative freedom as an elementary teacher in Colombia was unlimited. I could try new programs, new techniques; my principal always encouraged and supported me. I had only 16 children in my class. I gave my students a lot of personal attention—I knew them very well. My kids were much more affectionate than my students in

Jennifer Post

the United States. The younger children were affectionate, but that changed as they grew older. Even though the official language of instruction was English, my Spanish improved dramatically. A child would come to me and say in Spanish "I want to say [something] in English" so I told them how to say it. We talked in Spanish about how to talk in English. While my kids in LA spoke Spanish at home and at school, I did not teach in Spanish, nor did I encourage them to use their Spanish. My own Spanish wasn't good enough, and it was always a struggle to find resources to support ESL speakers. In Cali, a city that was not a tourist destination, the minute I walked out of the school gate, my world was in Spanish.

CRITICAL THINKING

What challenges did Sheryl Cohen and Jennifer Post encounter when working with students and colleagues in Colombia? What unexpected opportunities arose during their teaching experiences in Colombia?

Note. From S. E. Cohen & J. Post, personal communications, April 10, 1996.

Not only teachers and interesting curricula foster attention to global issues; money and jobs also fuel interest in international and worldwide issues. Business leaders have been among the more vocal parties in encouraging schools to think globally, for they view schools as vital to the production and maintenance of the workforce that will be called upon to compete in a wider world.

An example of one state's commitment to the connection between schooling and competitiveness in the global marketplace can be found in South Carolina, where the state established special schools to train workers, free of charge, for any company that agrees to create new jobs in the area. Workers with no experience learned to use such tools as the metric system, computers, and blueprints. Such efforts have given South Carolina an edge, especially in attracting internationally owned corporations such as Michelin and other European high-end machining and high-technology manufacturing firms. BMW, the 46th German company to invest in South Carolina's Spartanburg County and the 76th to invest in the state, is one of the highest profile plants in the area. A billboard alongside interstate highway 85 in South Carolina includes the BMW logo and the message, "Soon the world will know South Carolina craftsmanship." By 1994 the plant's initial 520 workers, including fewer than 30 Germans, had turned out their first vehicle. The company projected that by the end of the decade the plant would employ a total of 2,000 workers (Harrison, 1994; Evanoff, 1995).

The real challenge for American public education is to educate workers today for careers and jobs they will fill tomorrow. In other words, educators must identify and teach knowledge and skills now, in hopes of preparing students for a future they can only vaguely imagine. If you were asked to identify knowledge and skills deemed critical for today's students to master, what would you say?

> **For what kind of future should American schools prepare students?**

WHAT CAN WE LEARN ABOUT EDUCATION FROM OTHER COUNTRIES?

The concept of **international comparative education** suggests that (a) problems of educational development are common in many societies; and (b) by studying education in different societies, educators develop new insights into these societies, and they derive innovative understanding of their own society, as well (Thomas, 1990). The discourse in this country on multicultural education, for example, has been framed in purely American terms. International comparative perspectives have largely been missing. This is unfortunate, because the United States is not the only country that is experiencing or has experienced the phenomenon of being home to a diversity of cultural groups within its national borders. Nor is the United States the only country addressing problems that arise from close interaction among diverse cultural groupings. In many instances, the problems Americans face are not unique to U.S. society. People in other countries face them too, often with considerable success. Their experiences can help us reflect on our own assumptions and actions in ways that would be impossible without a point of comparison.

With the North American Free Trade Agreement (NAFTA), the General Agreement on Tariffs and Trade (GATT), the European Union (EU), and other multinational pacts, multicultural understanding becomes increasingly important for all people and all nations. Indeed the ancient Greeks recognized the importance of learning about and from others. For Plutarch, people who studied life's lessons wherever they found them demonstrated their strength of character. Thucydides suggested that people who learn from others may prepare themselves to avoid some of life's pitfalls and to capitalize on success.

Education in Canada

Had it not been for a week's worth of television reports and newspaper headlines in the United States in 1995, many Americans might have missed completely the struggle to keep Canada united as one nation. The rebellion of French-speaking Canadians, centered in Quebec, nearly split the country in two with a secession vote. Yet we Americans appeared inured to the troubles of our best trading partner and most trusted military ally. One wonders if we could pass a multiple-choice quiz on basic facts on Canada. If asked, could we explain why the propagation of culture through schooling matters so much in Canadian society?

What makes the propagation of culture through schooling a problem in any country?

Canada's land mass makes it the second-largest country in the world. Its economy is diverse and successful. Nearly two thirds of the population live in metropolitan areas along the border with the United States. Some 60% of Canada's population live in 2 of its 12 provinces and territories—English-speaking Ontario and French-speaking Quebec. Until recently, Canada had one of the highest birth rates in the industrialized world. Canada has been a refuge, a home for immigrants from around the world (Berg, 1995).

Although Canada is a federal state, provincial governments control education. Canada has neither a national system of education nor a central office of education. Each province has its own Ministry of Education, headed by an elected minister. In all provinces schools are operated by local boards of education; the degree of decentralization varies across provinces. Both provincial governments and local governmental units fund the educational enterprise. Typically, children start school at age 6 or 7. They must attend for at least 10 years, or until the age of 15 or 16. The organization of school levels (elementary, middle, high) varies by province, with some using a system of 7 years in elementary, 2 in middle, and 3 in high school. Others use a 7–5, 8–4, or, as in Quebec, a 6–5–2 system. The school year runs between 180 and 200 days per year.

Promotion through the elementary grades is more or less automatic. At the secondary level variation exists among the provinces, but most use the credit system, with children taking varying levels of courses to accumulate credits for graduation. Students in British Columbia, Alberta, and Quebec must pass a graduation diploma examination. Many schools offer general and advanced levels of diplomas. An average of more than 60% of high school graduates go on to some form of postsecondary education (Berg, 1995).

The Canadian educational system, like many others in modern economic states, faces the challenges of the information age and an increasingly competitive global economy. Consequently, many Canadian educators recognize the need to improve and make relevant the kind and quality of education young people receive. Movements for teacher accountability, strengthening basic skills education, accommodating increasing cultural diversity, and addressing gender inequality characterize current Canadian education reform.

Because Canada has 12 systems of education, it is not surprising that the response to these demands has been piecemeal. Efforts to define the role of education in a complex society and to determine priorities will consume educators, parents, and government officials into the next century. An estimated two-thirds of the jobs created between 1989 and 2000 will require a minimum of 12 years of schooling, and about 40% will require more than 16 years of school (Berg, 1995).

Canadian schools have reflected the cultural similarities among Canadians as well as the deep division that exists between French speakers and English speakers in Quebec. In 1977 Bill 101 was passed into law, with support of the Parti Quebecois, a separatist party in Quebec. The bill established French as the only official language in the province and imposed many restrictions on the use of English or any other language in business and education. French was the only language allowed to be displayed by businesses on outdoor signs. Language police from the Office de la Langue Francaise were appointed to ensure that businesses were not violating the law. A ruling of the Supreme Court of Canada has since eased such restrictions.

Bill 101 had a profound effect on education in Quebec, because all (non-anglophone and even some anglophone) immigrants to Quebec had to attend French language schools. The bill was an attempt by the government of Quebec to preserve the prominence of francophones in the province in the face of the increasing number of immigrants entering the province since 1990, the majority of whom spoke no French. The Montreal Catholic School Commission which operates more than 300 schools in Montreal has considered an outright ban on any language but French in its schools. (Public schools in Quebec are designated as either Protestant or Catholic and are supported financially by the government.) This ban would include all school-sponsored activities, as well as speech in the halls and on schoolyards. Offenders would be transferred to other schools, and repeat offenders would be expelled.

Many educators in the United States, particularly those in the West and Southwest, would have difficulty reading about events in Quebec schools without drawing parallels between their situation and the English-only movement in California. How are the positions of students with English as their primary language similar to and different from one another in the two countries? How do the positions of the language-minority students compare in both countries?

To be sure, if we relied only on the sensational events in Quebec, we would have a drastically skewed perception of life in Canadian schools. Education in the provinces and territories reflects the diversity of the nation. You can test this assertion by visiting some Canadian schools online (**http://www.edunet.ie/links/canada.html**).

Education in Mexico

The images of Mexico we receive from movies, television, and the popular press seem to alternate between extremes: culturally rich, socially warm, and humanly inviting versus stunningly poor, socially archaic, and openly hostile to outsiders. Both suggest that image exists largely in the eye of the beholder.

The United States of Mexico is a country of 31 states that shares its borders with the United States of America, Guatemala, and British Honduras. The nation has one of the highest population growth rates in the world. Population density varies greatly among the states. The capital, Mexico City, and one of its neighboring states account for more than 22% of the total population. Mexico City is the second largest city in the world, with 24 million people. Over-

What effects does the United States have on education in Mexico?

all the Mexican population is becoming more urbanized: the percentage of the population living in urban areas increased from 42% in 1950 to 71% in 1990. The Mexican economy has been hit by a series of economic crises in the past several decades that have resulted in a continued and radical uneven distribution of wealth. High expectations surround the signing of the NAFTA agreement, which reduces Mexico's trade barriers with Canada and the United States of America.

Spanish is the official language of Mexico, although more than 93 languages and dialects are present (Reyes, 1995). Nearly one million Mexican citizens do not speak Spanish, and 10% are illiterate.

Since 1993 the state governments have controlled the running of preschools, primary and secondary schools, and teacher-training institutes, except in the Federal District. This decentralization of power represents a major shift in education policy.

In 1992 the length of compulsory education was increased from six to nine years. The Mexican education system is structured in a 6–3–3 configuration: six years of primary school; three years of lower secondary school; and either passing of an entrance examination to gain entry to three years of upper secondary school (*bachillerato*) leading to a higher education qualification, or transferring to a three- or four-year technical school.

Mexican schools contain a large percentage of overage students in each grade because of students repeating grades and/or dropping out and then re-enrolling in school. Overage students account for up to 30% of enrollment in some grades, particularly in the fifth and sixth grades. Because overage students inflate enrollment numbers in elementary schools, pupil–teacher ratios are high, at 30 to 1. Many Mexican students do not advance to the upper secondary school level. According to the 1990 census, only 54% of the 20- to 24-year-olds in Mexico had completed ninth grade. Among 40- to 44-year-olds, only 25% had completed ninth grade (Reyes, 1995).

David Lorey (1995) has argued that by far the most serious problem at the basic level of education is the high and persistent dropout rate—a consequence of family poverty. "Only about 50% of entering students at any level complete their studies. In rural areas of the country, approximately 75% of school children do not finish the first six years of primary education" (1995, p. 1).

The rapid increase in the number of school-age children has placed a heavy burden on the educational system nationwide. Overall, the emphasis of national basic-education programs has been on access rather than on relevance or quality (Lorey, 1995). There has been a demand to accommodate an additional 500,000 students per year since 1950, although this trend has slowed since the mid-1980s. Since 1978, on average, 42 classrooms have been added to the public education system each day. This expansion of the educational system has not been equal in all regions of Mexico; the northern part of Mexico and Mexico City attain high enrollment ratios, but states in the southeast regions have lower rates (Reyes, 1995). Twenty-three percent of Mexican elementary schools are one-teacher schools, and 15% do not offer all six grades. Although accommodations are made for students with special needs, only about 10% of such students enroll.

Mexico is engaged in a major national effort to improve the quality of education, with special emphasis at the elementary level. This effort includes attention to factors that contribute to the large numbers of overage students in classrooms. As Mexico's economy becomes more globalized, the country will not be able to rely as heavily on workers in the manufacturing sector to provide long-term economic health and stability. If they are to compete successfully, Mexicans—like many of the rest of us—must develop and expand the numbers of people who are educated for managerial, technical, and research positions.

Cultural Awareness

Lynda Leyba is in her third year of teaching at Columbus Elementary School, a bilingual elementary school in Columbus, New Mexico. Ms. Leyba was a high school rodeo queen, active in 4-H and Future Farmers of America (FFA) while growing up in Las Vegas, New Mexico. The district hired her to teach in  Columbus Elementary primarily because she speaks Spanish. Just speaking Spanish, however, is no guarantee that teaching will be smooth sailing. Says Lynda Leyba,

> The lack of books is a problem, because we are supposed to be teaching in Spanish for part of the day. But the only thing that we have in Spanish are the readers. All the other materials are in English, so that is a problem. All of the teachers here at Columbus in grades kindergarten through 3 have an instructional assistant to help out with different things. My aide this year is really wonderful. She helps out a great deal. She teaches the Spanish reading to the students, because I am not as fluent. I can speak the language, and I understand it, but I don't know how to teach it. (Herbert & McNergney, 1996, p. 3)

Berliner and Biddle (1995) describe an interesting example of how Mexico has collaborated with Ford Motor Company to produce such workers.

> [A] decade ago the Ford Motor Company set up a new engine plant in Chihuahua, Mexico, that employed workers with few technical skills—indeed, many of them were high school dropouts. The plant set up its own skills-training program and provided good job security; and it now leads the world in automotive-engine productivity. (p. 88)

The message from this Mexican program and others like it is clear, according to Berliner and Biddle: "If schools are truly to serve the needs of business, it appears they should concentrate less on skill training and more on the values that students will need when they enter the workplace" (p. 89).

Mexico, and its neighbor in the United States, New Mexico, have some strong educational bonds (Herbert & McNergney, 1996a; 1996b). For example, each day, children cross the border from Palomas, Mexico, to attend public schools in Columbus and Deming, New Mexico, free of charge. About 90% of the 450-plus students, grades kindergarten through 12, hold dual citizenship because they were born in the United States. The other 10% hold only Mexican citizenship. All, however, call Mexico home.

The decision to allow young people from a border town to attend U.S. schools at taxpayers' expense is unparalleled anywhere else in our country. School districts in Texas, California, and Arizona, for example, abide by strict residency and tuition requirements, which prohibit such practice. The unique situation in Deming School District serves as an example of how communities on opposite sides of an international border can cooperate to promote a common educational culture. Can you imagine why people on both sides of the border might support this venture?

Education in Japan

Critics of American education often hail Japan as an example to be emulated. The Japanese, they argue, demand educational excellence, and they get it. At the same time, others contend that Japan's schools foster conformity and reward obedience. Our knowledge of and feelings about Japanese education most often are mixed.

Japan is a country of more than 3000 islands in East Asia, with a population of more than 125 million. This densely populated country of city dwellers is ethnically homogeneous (with only 1% minorities). Tokyo, the capital, is the largest city in the world, with more than 28 million inhabitants.

From the time of its defeat in World War II until 1990, Japan enjoyed extraordinary economic success. Between 1990 and 1994, however, land values fell dramatically and industrial giants, such as Nissan, closed factories, as car production fell about 22%. While Japanese citizens struggled with the realities of increasing unemployment and the social problems accompanying it, they continued to place a high priority on the development of a well-educated and skilled populace (Desmond, 1996).

The modern education system in Japan began to form with the introduction of the Fundamental Law of Education in 1947. Subsequent amendments and reforms to the Fundamental Law of Education have articulated the most important educational objectives in Japan as being (1) the development of broad-minded, healthy, creative individuals; (2) the rearing of the spirit of freedom, self-reliance, and public awareness; and (3) the education of the Japanese individual to live in the global human society (Kanaya, 1995). These aims of education reflect a set of strongly held cultural values.

Structurally, the Japanese education system closely resembles the American system. The vast majority of Japanese students attend public schools in mixed-ability classrooms. Unlike the United States, there is no external examination scheme in Japan—no public or private testing service that creates, sells, distributes, and scores a set of examinations common to students across the country. Internal, school-system assessments determine promotion and certification of completion. Students at all levels wear uniforms. They begin school at age 6, attending elementary schools (grades 1–6) with an average pupil–teacher ratio of 20 to 1. After completion of elementary school, students attend a 3-year lower-secondary school, with 50-minute class periods and an average pupil–teacher ratio of 17.4 to 1. Nearly all lower-secondary school students study English as a foreign language.

Although not compulsory, 96% of the children who complete lower-secondary school attend upper-secondary school. Some 70% of these students attend public school, the remainder pay to attend private schools. In upper-secondary schools, 75% of the students pursue a general, academic course of study, and the remainder enroll in specialized (streamed) tracks, such as technology, foreign languages, and computers. Students with special needs can complete secondary school by correspondence. Since 1988, some students with special needs can attend credit-system upper-secondary schools, or schools that award diplomas for courses taken instead of requiring students to pass a graduation examination. Thirty-four percent of Japanese upper-secondary school graduates continue in higher education after passing a competitive entrance examination (Kanaya, 1995).

At the end of the school day, many young people in Japan attend a private after-school class. Classes may be of two types: **okeiko-goto** (enrichment classes in areas such as music, the arts, and physical education) and **juku** (supplementary classes in academic subjects). Together, *juku* and *okeiko-goto* are a multi-million-dollar industry. *Okeiko-goto* often begin during children's elementary years and may continue throughout their lives. *Juku*, however, are taken exclusively during children's elementary and secondary years. *Juku* classes help young people keep up with the demanding school curriculum, provide remedial instruction in areas of weakness, and prepare students for various entrance exams.

Juku range from classes of one to three students meeting in a teacher's home to multiple schools all over the country with dozens of classes at each site. Classes meet two to three times a week and may last two to three hours or more. Unlike teachers in the public schools, *juku* teachers often group their students by ability rather than by

What are the purposes of *okeiko-goto* and *juku* classes in Japan? What might be some advantages and disadvantages of Japanese educational practices from an American perspective? from a Japanese perspective?

grade level. Phases of drill and individual assistance by the teacher also are common in *juku* schools. Some people contend that the instruction young people receive in these settings closes the "sensitive gap" between what is learned in public schools and what students must know to move up the educational ladder (Harnisch, 1994). Presumably, as in other cultures, this gap represents the difference between explicit curriculum (what is set forth for public consumption) and the implicit curriculum (the more subtle but quite powerful adult expectations of student performance).

How does Japan's educational system compare to the United States' system?

There are different perspectives on what transpires in Japanese public schools. Some reports suggest that schools demand intense rote learning and conformity (Desmond, 1996). Other studies suggest that teachers in the public schools generally function more as facilitators and "knowledge guides" than dispersers of information and facts. Teachers are described as believing that students must construct knowledge, not merely receive it from teachers (Sato and McLaughlin, 1992). Professor Harold Stevenson and James Stigler demonstrate the constructivist approach with the following example of a fifth-grade mathematics class:

> The teacher walks in carrying a large paper bag full of clinking glass. Her entry into the classroom. . . . by the time she has placed it on her desk, the students are regarding her with rapt attention. What's in the bag? She begins to pull out items, placing them one by one on her desk. She removes a pitcher and a vase. A beer bottle evokes laughter and surprise. She soon has six containers lined up on her desk. . . . The teacher, looking thoughtfully at the containers, poses a question: 'I wonder which one would hold the most water?' This leads to a great deal of experimentation on the part of the students—filling and measuring with buckets and cups of water. Groups of students record their results. Finally the teacher returns to the question she posed at the beginning of the lesson: Which container holds the most water? She reviews how they were able to solve the problem, and points out that the answer is now contained in the bar graph on the board [which she constructed from their results]. (Stevenson & Stigler, 1992, pp. 177–178).

School governance and finance in Japan are shared across three levels. The Ministry of Education, Science, and Culture prescribes the curriculum as a basic framework at each level of schooling, including instructional objectives, content, and standard time allotment, and allocates financial aid. Municipalities each have a five-member board of education, who prepare guidelines for curricular development. Individual schools organize their own detailed instruction according to government-designed courses of study and guidelines (Kanaya, 1995).

Japanese educators face many serious issues. These include declining enrollments in schools overall, increasing enrollments of non-Japanese students in some schools, an increase in the number of working mothers, a move from the 6-day workweek to the 5-day workweek, and the need to teach emerging global issues (T. Kanaya, 1995).

As Berliner and Biddle (1995) have noted, the mass media frequently compare American public education to Japanese education, resulting in a distorted view of both systems. Many news reports proclaim the Japanese system superior in producing higher achievement among its students. These reports often suggest that Japanese students attend school more days per year than do American students and produce higher mathematics and science test scores. Much emphasis also has been placed on Japanese schools' adherence to national standards that are enforced through nationwide examinations.

But these "facts" can be misleading. When eighth-grade American students' mathematics abilities were compared to their Japanese counterparts who had been exposed to similar curricula, American students' scores were found to match or exceed those of the Japanese students (Westbury, 1992). Although Japanese students spend more days in school than do American students (240 days and 180 days, respectively), the difference in the amount of academic instruction is not profound (Stevenson & Stigler, 1992). A typical school year in Japan includes 65 to 70 afternoons of either free time or nonacademic activities. Three or four days a year also are devoted to cleaning the school (Goya, 1993). Japanese students enjoy longer lunch periods and breaks between classes than do American students. Entrance into upper secondary school requires passing an examination but it is a test of elimination. If there are 300 freshman slots and 304 students apply, the test is given to eliminate 4 students. Passing scores can be as low as 5% (Goya, 1994).

Education in India

India, a nation of nearly 900 million people, in addition to being the world's largest democracy, may be the most culturally and ethnically diverse country in the world. It is in a region known historically for its tolerance of diversity; nonetheless, regional and ethnic tension continue. Because the language of commerce and of instruction in India is English while more than a dozen regional languages (such as Hindi, Urdu, and Tamil) and local dialects are used in everyday speech in all but the major cities, the nation offers unique opportunities to educate others about diversity. Bilingualism is the norm, and trilingualism is common.

The Indian constitution set forth in 1950 directs the government to provide free and compulsory education for all children up to age 14. It also provides for equal educational opportunity and protection of religious and linguistic minority groups. The school system, which varies from state to state, is generally organized as 2 to 3 years of private kindergarten (beginning at about age 3), followed by 10 years of private or public basic education, perhaps followed by 2 years of private or public higher secondary education, and then perhaps followed by 3 years of tuition-free higher education. School holidays include 20 religious festivals from Hindu, Muslim, Christian, Sikh, Parsi, and Jain traditions.

In 1986 the federal parliament adopted its National Policy for Education and Policy of Action, which have served as the bases for the development of the National Curriculum for Elementary and Secondary Education. The intent of the common core is to cut across subject areas and to promote "India's common cultural heritage, egalitarianism, democracy and secularism, equality of the sexes, protection of the environment, removal of social barriers, observance of the small family norm, and the encouragement of a scientific outlook" (Bordia, 1988, p. 351). In advancing this agenda, the central government makes explicit the need to encourage attention to similarities among Indians, not to exploit their differences.

The realities of schooling in India often vary considerably from the official intent and formal proclamations. Enrollment rates are greater in the cities than in the rural areas and greater for boys than for girls, especially girls from disadvantaged groups (people of low castes, tribal people, and religious minorities). In 1990 to 1991, the enrollment rate in primary schools was reported as 115% for boys and 86% for girls (Theobald, 1995). (Boys exceeded 100% because under- and overage children attended school.) Theobald notes that enrollment figures are especially important, because they determine the number of teachers assigned, the number of books provided, and the number of classrooms available—all of which typically are insufficient. Nonattending students should be removed from the rolls, but this rarely happens. "Participation is therefore much lower than many of the raw statistics would lead one to believe" (Theobald, 1995, p. 144).

What are the preconditions for universal literacy in any society?

Improvements in Indian teaching methods are difficult to effect, in part because classes often have more than 50 students. Many students are plagued by poverty (some 45% of the country live below the poverty line and another 20% barely above it). "[T]he young teacher inevitably succumbs to the advice of older colleagues and settles into a pattern of delivering sermons and a stylized catechism of question-and-answer exchanges" (Taylor, 1991, p. 331).

One method used to control teachers is to threaten them with transfers. Indian teachers are government employees, so they are subject to transfer by the authorities. Not surprisingly, teachers resist the practice. Amrik Singh, for example, argues that threatening teachers with transfers is wrong:

> I have lived in London for almost three years. At no stage did I ever hear of any teacher being transferred from one school to another. . . . Nobody in London argued, as we do in India, that teachers, if posted to a particular school, tend to go out of hand, and are difficult to control unless there is the constant threat of transfer. This mode of thinking is typically Indian and typically bureaucratic. Transfers are made not because of educational reasons but because someone in authority thinks that this is the way to control teachers. To put it another way, teachers are equated with other government servants. This is wrong in principle. . . . Teachers are a category by themselves. There is something unique about them. Their job is different from a 10-to-5 job which those working for government are obliged to do. Their job specifications are different and the kind of skills and attitudes that they should have are different. Teaching is a profession and it is the demands of the profession which are of greater importance than bureaucratic procedures. (1996, p. 24)

In India, as in many countries, the professionalization of teaching is a major concern. Singh's letter suggests that when teachers view their assignments as careers, not merely as jobs, they expect to exercise a degree of control over their professional lives. These expectations often conflict with government responsibilities of oversight. Differences in expectations of officials at local and regional levels can confuse and frustrate even the most well-meaning people in a system.

The KATHA school was founded in a New Delhi, India, slum by Geeta Dharmarajan in 1990. She believes that children's mothers can help their children succeed by becoming empowered themselves. How might this belief be expressed in the KATHA school curriculum?

Life can be especially difficult for women and girls in India, because they have been forced historically to play the role of caregiver and often denied formal education in the process. The KATHA school in Delhi is one example of an organization created specifically to address their problems. Some 600 students—Hindus, Muslims, Christians, Jains, Parsis, and others—learn to work together on common literacy and life skills necessary for survival. The school began as a creche, or nursery for babies. The teachers care for babies and thus free the older girls to get an education in the Girl/Child Program, a program designed to address gender oppression in the slums of Delhi. The mothers come for classes and learn how to cook, bake, and sell their wares to support their families. Teachers provide the women not only with life skills but also with the confidence necessary to earn a living for themselves and their children (McNergney, Regelbrugge, & Harper, 1997).

Education in the United Kingdom

Children between ages 5 and 16 in the United Kingdom (England, Scotland, Wales, and Ireland) must attend school. At 16, students take main secondary school examinations. Advanced-level examinations typically follow after a further two years of schooling and constitute the entrance standard for higher education. Publicly supported schools often are called "state schools," "government schools," or "council schools" (run by borough government councils) to differentiate them from the privately funded schools, called "public schools." (Note the completely opposite meaning of the term *public* as it is used in the United States.)

Schools are organized into two or three tiers. The two-tier system is composed of primary schools (ages 5 to 11), occasionally subdivided into infant (ages 5 to 7) and junior (ages 7 to 11), and secondary schools (ages 11 to 16 or 18), which resemble American comprehensive high schools. The three-tier system, used only in England, consists of first schools (ages 5 to 8 or 9), middle schools (ages 8 to 12 or 9 to 13), and upper schools, which usually are nonselective (ages 12 or 13 to 16 or 18). Churches help operate some primary and secondary schools even though these schools are supported by public funds (Booth, 1988).

The United Kingdom is characterized by great ethnic and cultural diversity. More than half of London's 10 million inhabitants were born outside Great Britain. Immigrant settlement has not been limited to London; many immigrants have settled in other cities, towns, and villages.

Unlike schools in the United States, those in England include religious education (RE) as a core subject. The focus of RE is on the officially established Church of England. With the diversity of cultures and religions in schools, the practice has not been without its critics. In January 1996 more than 1,500 junior school students in 40 schools were withdrawn from RE courses by their Muslim parents ("Muslim parents," 1996). The boycott, one of the largest mass exercises to date, was prompted by parents' concern over the dominance of Christianity in RE syllabuses taught by non-Muslims. Parents worried that their children would

> **How does the existence of a state religion affect education in any country?**

receive inaccurate information about Islam and be confused by other faiths introduced in religious classes.

One creative educational response to the changing culture in the United Kingdom can be found in the work of the Association for Science Educators Multicultural Education Working Party, chaired by Kabir Shaikh (Thorp, 1991). This group identified a range of teaching methods designed to incorporate issues of race and equality in science teaching. They came up with these methods to emphasize the "potential of science to enhance the curriculum by drawing on the richness and diversity of cultures and on the practice of science, now and throughout history . . . (and) the powerful role of science teaching for combating racism and prejudice in society" (Thorp, 1991, p. 5). Figure 12.3 shows an activity that is part of this new curriculum, which also reflects an emphasis on global awareness.

Until recently, the British educational system had a long tradition of noninterference by the central government. In 1988, however, the Education Reform Act emphasized two themes in the education of all students in the British system: back to the basics and the link between education and the economy (Judge, 1989). The act was followed by pressure for a national curriculum and teacher accountability (i.e., the alignment of teaching performance with the curriculum). It also promoted the idea of giving parents a greater voice

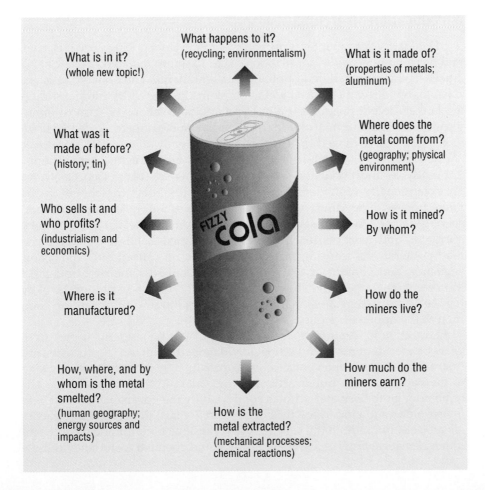

FIGURE 12.3

Activity from the "Cola Can Curriculum"

What science instruction could be planned on the basis of this activity? How might issues of race and ethnicity enter into such a plan? What do you think are some advantages and disadvantages for teachers and students working in this way?

Note. From *Race, equality and science teaching: An active INSET manual for teacher educators* (p. 125) by S. Thorp (Ed.), 1991, London: The Association for Science Education. Adapted by permission.

in managing schools and stimulated the creation of a new system of national compulsory and universal examinations. As Liz Bondi (1991) observed, the shift in mood in the British system from expansion and optimism to one of retrenchment and redefinition has mirrored the mood in the United States. The reasons for this shift have largely to do with demographic changes, public disenchantment, and a shortage of public funds to support education.

The United Kingdom hopes to improve student learning by infusing technology into the curriculum. In Scotland, for instance, national educational guidelines for students ages 5 to 14 resulted in an environmental studies program that actively involves students in problem-solving situations. According to results from a cross-national case-study project sponsored by the Organization for Economic Co-Operation and Development, primary schools implement the technology curriculum in various ways. In one rural school, for example, student tasks include activities such as constructing a lookout tower and observation platform using only recycled materials and designing a model of an earth-moving machine that could clear a level path for a new airport runway. Among teachers' objectives are to make learning practical and to create an interdisciplinary approach that incorporates contributions from teachers of art, design, and home economics ("A Global Revolution," 1996).

Education In Denmark

Denmark offers an interesting contrast to the United Kingdom. It is small and has a homogeneous population of slightly more than 5 million. Danish citizens exhibit open, liberal politics and sentiments. They have one of the most highly developed social welfare systems in the world. Immigration is a relatively recent phenomenon in Denmark. Since about 1970, most immigrants have come from Turkey and the Indian subcontinent. Recently, however, people have moved to Denmark from virtually all over the world.

The Danish Ministry of Education takes an activist, interventionist approach to educational and social problems. Yet schools in Denmark have an exceptionally high degree of local control, similar to schools in the United States. The Ministry of Education sets school objectives, but local schools decide how to meet them. Individual schools determine their own curricula, and teachers teach however they please. Highly experienced teachers write the learning materials. There is no control over the scope, sequence, and content of textbooks. While Danish is the first and most important language, English is widely spoken and at a very high level by the well-educated professional classes. Classes taught in English are common at the upper-secondary level.

Education in Denmark is free and compulsory for students from 7 to 16 years of age. Students attend school for 20 more days than U.S. students, but their school day is somewhat shorter. Approximately 90% of the students go to the **Folkeskole**, or public school as it is called in the United States. The remainder go to "private" schools supported by the government. Most 3- to 6-year-olds go to kindergartens. For the first 7 years, the Folkeskole teaches all subjects. In grades 8 through 10, the Folkeskole is comprehensive except in mathematics, English, German, physics, and chemistry; students in these courses attend either basic or advanced classes. Grade 10 in the Folkeskole is optional, after which students enter various forms of vocational–technical education and commercial training programs or attend a gymnasium—a higher preparatory course of study.

Evaluation of student progress in Danish schools is quite different from that in other countries. Children do not take end-of-the-year examinations in primary education and receive no grades for the first seven years of compulsory education. Students enrolled in grades 8 through 10 receive marks generally based on a scale of 1 to 10. Students in grades 9 and 10 also take a "leaving examination" at the end of the year. Exams are optional, and there is no cut-off score or minimal mark that a student must receive in order to pass. The relatively casual nature with which examinations are given and used ensures the promotion of most students (Jansen & Kreiner, 1995).

To handle the diversity of student needs in classrooms, the Danish have increasingly relied on special education services. About 12.5% of students enrolled in Danish public schools receive special education services; twice as many boys as girls are in this group. Overall, approximately 13% of children are referred for behavioral problems, 14% for intelligence problems, 6% for speech impairments, 7% for sensory or physical impairments, and 60% for learning problems. The majority of students with learning disabilities receive support in Danish, particularly in reading. Special education services also are extended to adults with physical and mental disabilities (Jansen & Kreiner, 1995).

During their professional training program, future teachers become qualified to teach Danish and two special subjects of their choosing at all levels in primary and secondary education. For this reason, it is possible for Danish teachers, working together in teams, to follow the same group of students throughout their 9 or 10 years in the Folkeskole. The "class teacher", or lead teacher, for the team is generally the same person throughout this period of time (Bjerg, et al., 1995). The lead teacher is usually a teacher of Danish or mathematics and serves as the primary link between students, parents, and the school (McAdams, 1993).

Students are involved in planning the content of lessons and making decisions about classroom issues. A pupil council at each school makes recommendations to the school board on matters of schoolwide concern. The school board at each Folkeskole includes five to seven parents elected by parents of children enrolled in the school. Two teacher representatives, two students, a member of the municipal council, and the lead teacher participate as nonvoting members of the board (McAdams, 1993).

Like people of other nations, the Danes seek to prepare students to be qualified technically to function effectively in society. They also try to socialize young people to the importance of common moral concepts and social solidarity (Florander, 1988). Like many Western countries, Denmark has lost unskilled jobs in recent years. As a consequence, the Danes are eager to boost the knowledge and skills of citizens to remain economically competitive in the emerging European Union.

For this reason, education of adults is also a priority in Denmark. Evening schools are common, and they cover a wide range of subjects. To reduce the expense of such courses, the state awards a grant to approved evening schools. Educational offerings for adult immigrants are required by the 1990 Open Education Act and are financed through counties' education budgets. Courses focus on Danish language, Danish culture, and Danish social conditions (Jansen & Kreiner, 1995).

Education in Singapore

The Republic of Singapore, a city-state on the southern tip of continental Southeast Asia, is considered the world's laboratory for experiments in social engineering. It is a multicultural society, comprising people of Chinese (77%), Malay (14%), Indian (7%), and Eurasian (2%) ancestries. Just under 3 million people inhabit the 231 square miles of Singapore (Gopinathan, 1994). The city-state, with one of the highest living standards in Asia, bills itself as the Switzerland of Asia, the Gateway to the Future. Singapore is a city of business opportunity and a hub of high-tech development. The government tries to assure all citizens that, no matter what their ethnic or cultural background, they are first and foremost Singaporean.

Singapore consists mainly of immigrants and their descendants. While Singapore was a British colony, Singaporean education required English as the language of government and advanced schooling. The system also fostered ethnic segregation and had separate schools taught in Chinese, Tamil, and Malay. Since Singapore's establishment as a republic in 1965, however, life has changed. Today, most tourists to Singapore know that it is illegal to chew gum (actually, it is illegal to import chewing gum) and that extinguishing a cigarette on the sidewalk can draw a large fine. But few realize that the Singaporean educational system has developed innovative approaches to multicultural education. For example, even though Singapore maintains four official languages, the government has unified the English- and non-English-speaking schools (Chinese, Malay, and Tamil) into a single educational system. The unification of schools, undertaken in the late 1950s, was viewed by leaders as an essential ingredient in their strategy to build a nation with its own unique identity.

> **Would other countries' solutions for multilingual education work for the United States?**

By 1968, as a result of a strong family planning program and a large investment in school facilities and teacher education, all children of primary-school age were enrolled in school. In 1973, educational authorities required all students to know English as either their first or second language and to know one other major language of the community. In the 1980s, authorities backed off this overly ambitious goal. Most students try to become bilingual, and many seek the English track as a first choice because of the access it offers to jobs and higher education (Thomas, 1988).

Singaporean teachers from Anderson Secondary School work together to develop multicultural curricula for their students. Why are multicultural curriculum and instruction so important to these Southeast Asian teachers?

Cultural Awareness

Singaporean schools track, or "stream," students early in their educational careers. Children's placements are influenced heavily by their proficiency in English and their mother tongue (Chinese, Malay, or Tamil). The following explanations to parents for streaming are provided by the Ministry of Education.

Q. How is my child streamed?

At the end of Primary 3, the school will advise you on your child's progress in his studies. This will provide you with an idea of his strengths and inclinations. He will then go on to Primary 4. At the end of Primary 4, your child will be assessed on his performance in English, the mother tongue, and mathematics. Based on this assessment, the school will recommend to you the stream which your child should attend in Primary 5.

Q. Is streaming really necessary?

The purpose of streaming is to place your child in a language stream for which he is most suited so that he completes primary education successfully. The school will be keeping a record of your child's abilities and inclinations and will be in a good position to advise you on the language stream he should continue his primary education in.

Q. Do I, as a parent, have a say as to which language stream my child goes to?

Your child's teachers and principal will advise you on the stream that matches your child's ability. You will, however, have the final say as to which language stream you wish your child to be in when he enters Primary 5.

Q. What are the differences between these language streams?

At the end of Primary 4, if your child does very well in English, the mother tongue, and mathematics, he will be recommended for the EM1 stream, in which he will learn English and the mother tongue at a higher level (i.e., Higher Chinese, Higher Malay, or Higher Tamil . . .). The majority of pupils will be recommended for the EM2 stream, which teaches English and the mother tongue. . . . The principals will decide on the pupils who will need additional lessons in English . . . or the mother tongue. . . .

If your child is less able to cope with languages and mathematics, he will be recommended for the EM3 stream, offering English and the mother tongue at basic proficiency level. The teaching of the mother tongue will emphasize oral/aural skills, reading, and listening comprehension as well as conversation.

Parents of children recommended for the EM3 stream in Primary 5 will also be able to opt for the ME3 stream for their children. Schools will provide ME3 classes if there is sufficient demand for them. Pupils in the ME3 stream will study the mother tongue (at Higher Chinese, Higher Malay, or Higher Tamil) and basic English. The teaching of English will emphasize oral/aural skills, reading, and listening comprehension as well as conversation. The language of instruction for all school subjects in the ME3 stream will be the mother tongue.

Q. Can my child switch streams halfway?

At primary 5, in the orientation stage, teachers will have further opportunities to know your child's ability, interest, and aptitude. Transfers between streams is possible at the end of Primary 5. These will be decided by the principal on the basis of your child's progress.

Q. Will my child be transferred out of his school as a result of Primary 4 streaming?

It is intended that all pupils will remain in the same school until they complete primary education. However, some reorganization may be necessary if there are insufficient pupils to form classes in a stream in certain schools. Visit the Ministry of Education online for more information (see **http://www.moe.ac.sg**).

In Cape Town, South Africa, students leave Queen's Park High School. Their diversity reflects modest progress toward racial integration following the abolishment of apartheid. What educational challenges does South Africa face?

Primary schools teach basic skills for 6 years. The curriculum of the first 2 years of secondary school is the same for all students and varies only slightly in the last 2 years. At the end of the 4th year, examinations screen students for a preuniversity course of study, followed by more examinations to screen for admission to postsecondary education. Students are tracked as early as the third grade. The schools operate multiple language streams in the same building to encourage interaction among students and to promote a feeling of national unity (Thomas, 1988).

Unlike the United States, in Singapore there are close relationships among government, industry, and secondary and postsecondary education. Annual surveys estimate workforce needs, and the schools and informal educational organizations respond with programs to fill those needs. These connections are especially important to a country that has few natural resources and must depend on the talents of its people for its place in the world.

Education in South Africa

Under the leadership of Nelson Mandela, South Africa continues to make news. In 1996 a court ruled that a white school in an Afrikaner town 180 miles north of Johannesburg had to admit three black students it had tried previously to bar (Associated Press, 1996). In doing so, the court knocked down what many believed was one of the most blatant challenges to South Africa's first constitution that promised equal rights.

South Africa is one of the most multicultural societies in the world. From 1949 to 1991, the structure of society was shaped by an official policy of **apartheid** (pronounced "a·par·tate" or "a·par·tite"), or separation of the races.

VOICES

On the Bond Between Schools and Society

Professor Saravanan Gopinathan (1994) of the National Institute of Education, Nanyang Technological University, points to the influence of Singapore's first prime minister, Lee Kuan Yew, on the formation of the present school system. Lee Kuan Yew served as prime minister for almost 4 decades, and he foresaw early in his tenure the importance of the bond between schools and society.

If in the four different languages of instruction, we teach our children four different standards of right and wrong, four different ideal patterns of behavior, then we will produce four different groups of people and there will be no integrated coherent society. What is in the balance is the very foundation of our society. For if we are not to perish in chaos caused by antagonisms and prejudices between watertight cultural and linguistic compartments, then you have to educate the right responses amongst our young people in school.

CRITICAL THINKING

Is Lee Kuan Yew's view as expressed here appropriate only for a nation that is just beginning to define itself, or do such "right responses" also exist in stable, enduring democracies, such as the United States? If there are such right responses in the United States, what might they be? If there are no right responses, on whom or what do American educators rely for guidance? Do you know what right responses Lee Kuan Yew might have had in mind? How could you find out?

Note. From "Speech" by L. K. Yew, December 9, 1959, *Straight Times*, p. 1.

This meant that blacks lived in "homelands," "black states," and segregated "townships" outside the major cities. Under apartheid, whites were not allowed to enter the townships without permission, and nonwhites were not permitted to stay overnight in white urban areas without special permission. People had to carry passes at all times. Schools for whites got money, facilities, and teachers, while black schools were, for the most part, neglected.

Although the United States is marked by a history of slavery, it is difficult for most Westerners to imagine how a policy such as apartheid could be justified in recent history anywhere in the world. The former language of apartheid in South Africa, however, must sound hauntingly familiar to western ears: The ultimate goal of apartheid was to create "a mosaic of peoples, each with a separate national identity. They will be politically independent but economically interdependent" (King, 1988, p. 600).

The open challenge to segregated education began in 1976 to 1977 with riots in Soweto, a black township outside Johannesburg (Lemmer, 1993). This revolt was triggered by an attempt to impose instruction in Afrikaans (an amalgam of Dutch, French, German, African, and Malay) instead of English (King, 1988). The apartheid legislation was repealed in 1991, initiating what promises to be a dramatic restructuring of society, including a restructuring of the segregated education system that has supported it. A new constitution was adopted in 1993, opening the door to free elections in which all South Africans may participate. In daily life, however, segregation continues to be reinforced by great disparities in wealth, personal attitudes, and historically separate and unequal education systems.

Almost all South African school systems are organized with 4 years of junior primary, 3 of senior primary, 3 of junior secondary, and 2 of senior secondary. Schools have been oriented toward the western view of a liberal education, that is, students are to be well grounded in history, languages, mathematics, the sciences, and the arts. Teaching typically is teacher-centered, and learning is passive, with a heavy emphasis on rote and academics. As such, education has been perceived as irrelevant to black children, who generally live bleak lives. School is compulsory for whites until age 16, Asians until 15, coloureds until age 14. School attendance is not yet compulsory for black South Africans. Figure 12.4 shows the distribution of students by race.

For 10 years or more prior to the election of Nelson Mandela, blacks in large numbers boycotted schools and destroyed school property. The morale and authority of black teachers was seriously damaged. Many black students literally forgot how to learn and how to study. Influential black leaders fear that the crisis in education may have cost the nation a generation of young people (Hartshorne, 1990). The government is in the process of reconceptualizing the school system from top to bottom in an effort to clarify the legal status of different categories of schools and to establish national norms and standards for governance, finance, and the effectiveness of schooling (Committee to Review the Organization, Governance and Funding of Schools, 1995).

FIGURE 12.4

Composition of Primary and Secondary School Enrollment in South Africa, 1994

What student groups are minorities in South Africa? How does minority status differ in South Africa compared to the United States?

Note. From *Education and Manpower Development* (p. 4) by J. P. Strauss, S. J. Plekker, J. W. W. Strauss, and H. J. van der Linde. Copyright 1994, Research Institute for Education Planning, Bloem Fontein. Reprinted by permission.

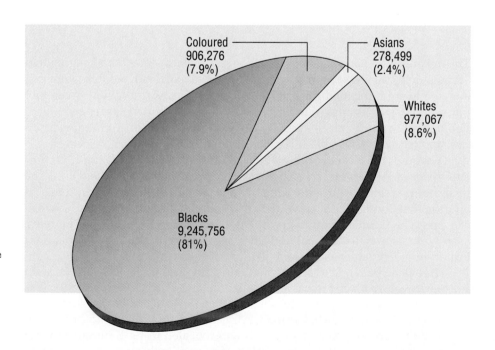

Coloured
906,276
(7.9%)

Asians
278,499
(2.4%)

Whites
977,067
(8.6%)

Blacks
9,245,756
(81%)

Cultural Awareness

Today in South Africa some black students find themselves in formerly all-white schools. They live in a period of disequilibrium between a stage of apartheid and an ensuing stage of mutual social and educational development, not yet defined clearly in thought or practice. Black, white, and so-called coloured students can be seen in the same buildings, but they are not often seen or heard talking, laughing, or working together outside classrooms. In other words, the system has begun to desegregate, but students within these schools are not yet working and living together as friends.

All students come to school with assumptions and preconceptions about one another. They attend classes together, wear the same school colors, and cheer for school teams. Yet, as a high school senior at Westerford High School explains, students often choose not to associate across racial lines:

> Although we have open schools, we still find that the black children sort of group around and form friendships with the blacks, and the same with the coloureds and the white children. And this is not because people set out to exclude themselves. I think because we've been so divided, we don't know enough about each other to understand one another. It is easy to talk about acceptance and tolerance of each other's differences. But if we don't understand each other's cultures, how can we really accept them, let alone respect them?

You can see and hear this young woman speak on the Web in an offering entitled *Project Cape Town: Education and Integration in South Africa*. To find the site, enter the following address: **http://curry.edschool. Virginia.EDU/go/capetown/**.

WHAT FACTORS SHOULD WE CONSIDER WHEN MAKING INTERNATIONAL COMPARISONS?

Americans always seem to be asking, "How are we doing, educationally speaking, compared to people in other nations?" The question too often forces discussion into a descending spiral of invidious comparisons—a series of attempts to make the United States look better, or worse, than other countries by examining test scores, dollars spent on education, and other factors. Measures of academic achievement and school funding can be enlightening when used appropriately, but they do not represent the only points of international comparison—or even the best ones.

The Big Dog Syndrome

Gerald Bracey (1996) believes that international comparisons of schooling are often abused. With a kind of my-dog's-bigger-than-your-dog mentality, people compare, often inappropriately, educational systems around the world. Bracey wonders why people feel obliged to portray U.S. schools in such a negative light in international comparisons or on domestic indicators. His answer is simple and persuasive: People are out to make a political or ideological point by making unfair comparisons of groups of students and misinterpreting results.

> **What might be valid and valuable in international comparisons of education?**

> [M]any of the results in international comparisons have been for mathematics, a subject in which it is typically reported that American students, in general, perform terribly. The data, taken together, however, reveal that many students perform quite well relative to students even in mathematics and in even the highest scoring nations in mathematics. (1996, p. 10)

United States students also consistently perform well in reading. Studies conducted on students in 31 countries revealed that American 9-year-olds finished second only to Finland, 22 points out of first place on a 600-point scale identical to that of the SAT. American 14-year-olds tied for eighth place. The high-ranking countries were so tightly bunched together that no statistical differences were found among the 2nd- and 11th-place nations (Bracey, 1996, p. 9).

Cynthia Patrick and Robert Calfee call such comparisons a "textbook case of hype." To them, the truly unfortunate consequence of this practice means that people are "so busy trying to make the case that schools have gotten worse that they've overlooked the more critical issue: how to prepare our students for the future" (1996, p. C4).

But can international assessments ever be done well, that is, in such a way as to help nations improve their schools? Robert Mislevy (1995) thinks so, but he also believes they can never be comprehensive enough to provide "the right answers" about how best to educate young people.

> No single index of achievement can tell the full story and each has its own limitations. We increase our understanding of how nations compare by increasing the breadth of our vision. [My] answer to people who want comparative standings is to give them comparative standings—lots of them: in different topics, at different ages, with different kinds of tasks. (1995, p. 419)

Most comparisons are based on survey data, which cannot prove a cause-and-effect relationship (Mislevy, 1995). Surveys only reveal associations that are worth investigating in studies that can tell us about effects of policies and instructional approaches. One must be careful about comparing different samples of students that appear similar on the surface but really are quite different from one another. For example, the percent of students in their last year of high school can vary from as high as 75% in the United

States to as low as 9% in Iran. Choosing a specific age group to compare across countries, such as all 13-year-olds, also can be problematic. Only 20% of U.S. eighth-grade students take algebra, but nearly 80% of Japanese students enroll in algebra. Ian Westerbury (1992) found that in the Second International Mathematics Study (SIMS), the top 20% of U.S. 13-year-old students who had taken algebra had an average similar to the top 20% of Japanese students.

Mislevy notes that the strictly timed, no-talking-no-help format tasks of most international assessments favor students and nations where such assessments are common. "An American student excused from gym class to take a pencil-and-paper test may have a different motivation for doing well than a 'champion of the school' selected to take the same test in Korea" (1995, p. 422). If a Belgian student learns early on to answer only if he is sure, not to guess at answers, and an American student learns from an early age to guess to obtain a higher score, then the student from Belgium is likely to have fewer wrong answers than the American.

The French teach mathematics without the constant reviewing that characterizes U.S. teaching methods. The Japanese divide students into academic and nonacademic tracks at much older ages than do schools in the United States. The Poles teach chemistry, biology, and physics together from grade 6 on; they do not switch subjects each year, as schools in the United States typically do (Gladwell, 1991). Some countries organize mathematics into units of algebra, geometry, trigonometry, and calculus and offer them from the seventh grade onward. The kind of calculus taught to seventh graders in another country is not the calculus taught to U.S. students in an AP calculus course. If students were tested on mathematics at age 13, 15, and 17, people might draw different conclusions about their mathematical prowess because of their nation's curricular organization.

Any international comparison of achievement must account for students' opportunities to learn the material on which they are tested. Achievement relates positively to money spent to create opportunities. If students in different countries do not have opportunities to learn the same things at the same time or by the same age, we must question the value of comparing these students in terms of academic achievement. When spent wisely, money can create many opportunities for students to learn. Figure 12.5 contains comparative information on national spending on education.

For some time now, critics of U.S. public education have used international comparisons to condemn U.S. schools. Others have dismissed these comparisons as mean spirited and wrong headed. Lawrence Stedman argues for a more balanced perspective.

> Our students have been world class in some subjects at certain ages. [Citing Bracey, 1993, he argues] This message should be repeated frequently so it can penetrate a national media that often ignores the good news about U.S. schools. We must not shy away from the harsh realities, however. There are deep and long-standing problems in U.S. educational achievement. The international assessments are not so flawed that we can afford to ignore the often poor position of U.S. students. (1994, p. 30)

FIGURE 12.5

**Government Spending
for Education**

In this sample, Finland ranks
first in the world in terms
of government support for
education. How does the
United States rank? What
factors influence nations'
comparative spending on
education?

Note. From *The Condition of Education 1995* (Table 54–1, p. 393) by
U.S. Department of Education,
1995. Washington, DC: U.S.
Government Printing Office.

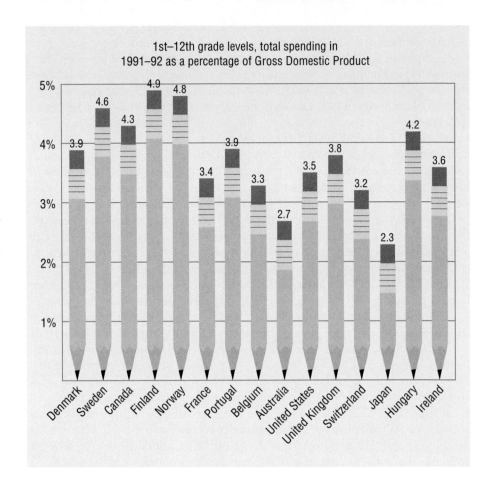

1st–12th grade levels, total spending in
1991–92 as a percentage of Gross Domestic Product

Comparisons That Foster a Global View

Concepts of global and comparative education need not be restrictive.
They can stretch far beyond the narrow focus of the big dog syndrome to
address commonalities among people, regardless of where they live. People
are naturally curious about what it is we share as a result of our humanness.
Are there activities in which we all engage that make us more alike than we
are different from one another? How and what can we learn about ourselves
by learning about others who live in markedly different cultures? Questions
such as these stimulate us to look well beyond our familiar surroundings to
investigate life in other places.

Some studies of teaching and learning across cultures suggest how much
educators share, regardless of where they live and work. For example, the
educational construct of "wait-time" has been investigated in many settings
in many international contexts and with different kinds of students.

Professor Mary Budd Rose (1986) originated the concept of wait-time as
a way to describe the pauses in a classroom teacher's verbal activity. One type
of wait-time occurs when a teacher asks a question of a student and then waits
for a student to respond. The other type occurs after the student responds. If
a teacher can learn to wait for at least 3 seconds before filling the void with her

talk, then the quantity and quality of students' responses increase dramatically, regardless of where in the world these events take place.

Graham Nuthall and his colleague Adrienne Alton-Lee from New Zealand explored how students think about tests—in particular, achievement tests in science and social studies (1995). When students were asked to describe how they got their answers and to recall experiences and activities that were relevant to the formulation of those answers, the students described using direct knowledge, deduction and inference, and plain old guessing— much like students everywhere. As the following exchange between an interviewer and 10-year-old Jan suggests, students often remember events that surrounded learning long after the events occur. Students are also more or less likely to take the word of their peers in class discussions.

> Interviewer: Where did you learn that?
>
> Jan: Last year, Mr. B. said, does anyone know what mercury is? And Tony put up his hand and said . . . Oh, no! . . . Mr. B. said, what's in a thermometer? And Tony put up his hand and said it was mercury. And it was right, and since then I have remembered.
>
> (The researchers' original recording of the event shows that Jan's memory was essentially correct. But when she was asked if she remembered what she thought at the time, her recollection was more complicated.)
>
> Jan: I thought, you [Tony] have got to be wrong. I thought mercury was sort of a jewel or something like that. Or just a planet.
>
> Interviewer: So you thought he was wrong?
>
> Jan: Mm. I thought it was ink or water. (1995, pp. 196–97)

Jan went to school in a New Zealand community, but she might as well have been from San Diego, Cleveland, or Albany. Like other students around the world, she could visualize past classroom events and transport herself back in time to reconstruct the interactions. Many learning principles and teaching strategies do have cross-cultural validity.

Other studies of classroom interactions point to common concerns among educators working around the globe, while highlighting culture-based differences in the ways they respond to those concerns. Research on the evaluative behaviors of Asian teachers, for example, suggests that they, like their American counterparts, learn much by watching their students. Their learning differs, however, in important ways from that of American teachers particularly when interpreting students' mistakes.

> For Americans, errors tend to be interpreted as an indication of failure in learning the lesson. For Chinese and Japanese, they are an index of what still needs to be learned. These divergent interpretations result in very different reactions to the display of errors—embarrassment on the part of American children, calm acceptance by Asian children. They also result in differences in the manner in which teachers utilize errors as effective means of instruction. (Stigler & Stevenson, 1991, p. 27)

Ernest Boyer (1992) identified eight fundamental characteristics that bind all people together as teachers and learners. Boyer suggested that these characteristics might even serve as the core of a curriculum for global/ comparative studies.

BENCHMARKS

Developments in International Education

1940s　United Nations Educational, scientific, and Cultural Organization (UNESCO) is founded to broaden the base of education throughout the world and to encourage cultural interchange.

The International Telecommunication Union (ITC) becomes a part of the United Nations to promote international cooperation in telecommunications.

1960s　National Academy of Education (NAE) is founded to stimulate research in education and includes a division in comparative education.

International Baccalaureate Organization (IBO) and the Institute of International Education are founded in the United States for international teacher education and the study of comparative education.

1970s　Telecommunications satellites, cable television, information processing, and fiber-optic technologies are developed for commercial use.

1980s　European Center for Higher Education (ECHE) implements new programs to increase student mobility across national education systems and to develop databases to facilitate transnational exchange of information.

The Internet becomes a loosely organized, research-based network of computer users at major universities in Europe and the United States. The world's first distance learning collaborations are set up based on telecommunications and computer technologies.

1990s　National Security Education Act triples federal spending on undergraduate study abroad, overseas graduate research, and grants to support programs in international studies.

UNESCO begins efforts to standardize educational credential reporting, licensing, and certification.

The Internet expands to colleges, businesses, governments, individual users, and elementary and secondary schools in more than 65 countries.

1. As human beings we share the mysteries of the life cycle—birth, growth, and death. We do so, of course, without fully understanding or appreciating how these phenomena are alike and different from culture to culture.

2. We all use symbols to express feelings and ideas. Language, both written and spoken, shapes how we think and behave.

3. The aesthetic forms a kind of universal language that transcends words. We connect with others through music, dance, painting, sculpture, and a host of visual arts.

4. So far as we know, we are unique among living creatures in our abilities to recall the past and to anticipate the future. This sense of time is not uniform from culture to culture, but the present we occupy allows us to look forward and back at the same time.

5. Every person belongs to groups. Some memberships are assigned, some are freely chosen. Some memberships are brief, others last a lifetime. People are social beings.

6. We are all connected to planet Earth. For some of us the direct connections are more apparent—living and working on a farm as opposed to dwelling in a city. Regardless of the immediacy of our connections, we all depend on the natural world for our survival.

7. Work occupies our lives. We all produce, and we all consume. We all must take to survive, but we all must give back if people are not only to survive but to prosper.

8. Although we must meet our basic human needs for food, shelter, etc., people everywhere want more from life. In every corner of the globe, we can find people searching for a larger purpose in life.

Boyer's eight fundamental characteristics do not begin to exhaust the list of people's commonalities. Certainly we can think of others that unite people generally around the globe, and teachers and students more specifically. We might be surprised, for example, to find out how teachers and students think about the concept of learning. How rich and varied are their definitions? How strongly do they hold their perceptions? Do these perceptions change over time and across borders?

SUMMARY

How is comparative education relevant to classroom teachers?

1 Teachers in the United States often teach immigrants and their children. Immigrants' languages, cultural mores, and other factors require that teachers be attuned to life in other countries.

How can we enhance global awareness?

2 Teachers can enhance global awareness—the recognition among people that they are connected to other countries and people of the world—by attending to the concept in any or virtually all subject-matter domains.

3 Nongovernmental organizations (NGOs) also cultivate people's abilities to view the world from others' perspectives. These transnational associations—groups such as churches, scouts, farmers, chambers of commerce, physicians, athletes, and educators—focus on problems and issues that transcend national borders. The number of NGOs is increasing.

What can we learn about education from other countries?

4 International comparative education suggests that problems of educational development are common across societies, and that by studying education in different societies, people develop new insights into these societies and an improved understanding of their own society.

5 People in nations as different from one another as Canada, Mexico, Japan, India, the United Kingdom, Denmark, Singapore, South Africa, and the United States can learn much from one another about teaching and learning.

What factors should we consider when making international comparisons?

6 International comparisons of education systems can serve useful educational purposes. As we examine conceptions of students, teaching, and learning in other countries, we can better understand, and in some instances change, our own practices. Because of differences in measures, students being compared, and the contexts in which education occurs, comparisons among the school systems of the world must be undertaken with care.

7 People are bound to one another by many fundamental characteristics, including—but not limited to—their use of symbols, their appreciation for aesthetic forms, and their ability to recall the past and to anticipate the future.

TERMS AND CONCEPTS

apartheid, *p. 480*
Folkeskole, *p. 476*
global awareness, *p. 460*
international comparative
    education, *p. 464*

juku, *p. 470*
NGO, *p. 460*
okeiko-goto, *p. 470*

REFLECTIVE PRACTICE

Newcomers High School teacher Diana Cabot discusses the challenges of teaching physical education to Newcomers students:

> I was born and raised in Queens and graduated from Newtown High School. Students there speak many languages, so I was used to being around people from different cultures. English is my primary language, but I also speak Spanish. Many of my students speak Spanish, but some do not, so I try to speak English only. One of the biggest challenges I face as a classroom teacher is how to deal with the different languages. I teach physical education, and one thing I have be concerned about is safety. To be sure students understand the rules, I try to use a lot of visuals when I teach. I even bring in a T-shirt and pants to show them what they are supposed to wear for class.

I also have to find out about students' cultures. Girls from the Indian cultures, for example, must wear long-sleeved blouses. I am concerned that they might get too hot during aerobics and dehydrate, so I keep an eye on them. They can't have contact with males either, so in the beginning when we had coed classes that was difficult. I had to work with them separately while someone else taught the boys.

I learn about students' religions too. Recently, for example, some of my students were celebrating Ramadan, and they were fasting. I was concerned that they would be too weak to do anything physical, so I had them help me with attendance. I would tell them to do as much as they could but to sit down if they got tired and I would excuse them, because I wasn't sure who was or wasn't fasting. So I had to get parents' permission to excuse students from some of the activities. It's a learning experience. Every time somebody says, "Oh, I can't do this," I do some research to find out about religious holidays or cultural expectations. Of course, sometimes students are shy, and they won't say anything. They will just take a zero rather than participate. So I ask them questions or talk to their teachers to find out if what I am doing conflicts with their religion.

The biggest challenge for students is probably the language. We do a lot of group work here. I assign students to groups, because if I allow them to pick their own partners, students work only with the people they know. I want them to communicate with others. They tend to be shy, so I mix the language groups. My goal is not only for students to learn physical skills but also to learn English. If they don't understand each other they can't do the work.

Issues, Problems, Dilemmas, and Opportunities

Ms. Cabot notes several challenges—both for her and her students—in the physical education classes at Newcomers High School. List them, and rank them in terms of their likely importance from Ms. Cabot's point of view.

Perceive and Value

Assume a point of view other than Ms. Cabot's. For example, imagine yourself as a student in a physical education class at Newcomers High School. Imagine that you do not speak English, or at least not very well. How might you feel? Why? What might you be most worried about in the class? Why? Do you hold any personal values that might make you more or less successful in this class? What values might you share with Ms. Cabot?

Know and Act

Suppose you are co-teaching with Diana or serving as a teaching assistant in her class. How might you help her (a) get to know the students better; (b) communicate better with all the students; (c) modify curriculum and instruction appropriately and comfortably for both herself and the students; and (d) infuse a coherent multicultural approach into the program? How might you help the students to (a) know one another better; (b) communicate better with each other and with you and Diana; and (c) succeed in meeting curriculum goals in culturally appropriate contexts?

Evaluate

In what ways specifically could you evaluate the effectiveness of each possible solution or strategy you identified? What criteria could you and Diana use to determine the success of your program?

ONLINE ACTIVITY

Visit the Global SchoolNet Foundation (**http://www.gsn.org**). This exciting Web site links students and teachers around the world. You will find school curriculum projects which include the International Cyber Fair 96, where people enter and share the best of their online work. You will also find collaborative projects among students. Visitors to the site can "travel" the globe with Roger and a group of students. There are news and discussion lists, contests, articles on a wide variety of topics, and many opportunities to link with others around the world to advance global understanding. There is even a service called "Globalink"—a translation company that facilitates multilingual communications.

13

Teaching Futures in a Changing World

Only soothsayers predict the future with assurance, but we need no special powers to conclude that two broad trends in teaching are certain. First, the days of teaching in self-contained classrooms are over. Professional educators of tomorrow will know where and how to connect with many others who share resources and an interest in educating young people. Educators will depend more on each other and on people with special knowledge and talents. They will cooperate and collaborate to solve educational problems and create new educational opportunities.

Second, professional educators will have greater opportunities to construct their own careers. They will assume new roles and take on new tasks, redefining their jobs and themselves in the process. Teachers will conduct classroom research; create curriculum; participate in school- and system-level decision making; design, implement, and report evaluations of educational progress; work with other service providers in the context of their communities; and master technology. No single skill will be more important for educators than the ability to think on one's feet.

In this chapter we describe how forces in society, often outside the control of teachers themselves, affect their professional lives. We explain how one influence in particular—technology—seems almost to be shifting the educational foundation under our feet. We also describe how collaborative networks of people can transform teaching, learning, and the professional development of educators. Finally, we look forward to teachers preparing themselves to continue learning as they work, and in doing so constructing a promising future for themselves and their students.

PROFESSIONAL PRACTICE QUESTIONS

1 What trends are changing teachers' professional roles?

2 How are new links to technology changing the foundations of education?

3 How are collaborative networks transforming teaching and learning?

4 How are collaborative networks transforming the professional development of teachers?

5 How can professional educators prepare for the future?

WHAT TRENDS ARE CHANGING TEACHERS' PROFESSIONAL ROLES?

Continuing calls for reform challenge teachers to raise the performance of all students by providing a world-class education. When people discuss how to encourage such performance, they agree more on general principles than on specific actions to take. People emphasize different factors they consider critical for ensuring high student performance, such as goals, standards, instructional objectives, curriculum, measurable outcomes, minimum competence, or opportunities to learn. While everyone touts the importance of working together to improve education for children, teachers are most instrumental in defining collaboration and determining ways to enhance student performance.

■ Trends Toward National Goals and Standards

In 1989 and 1990 Presidents Bush and Clinton and other political leaders established the first National Education Goals (see Chapter 1). Prompted by public dissatisfaction with "low levels of student performance, increasing global economic competition, and consistently poor showings on international assessments," the creators of the Goals sought to rally national attention to achieving high-performance education results (National Education Goals Panel, 1994, p. 12). The values and attitudes driving their efforts are epitomized in the quote from Vince Lombardi that appears above the introduction to the 1994 National Education Goals Report: "If you're not keeping score, you're just practicing" (p. 13).

On March 26 to 27, 1996, President Clinton and 40 of the nation's governors met in Palisades, New York, for the second national Education Summit. Their task was to advance progress on improving academic **standards**, or the benchmarks against which student progress can be judged. They also addressed how student assessment should proceed and how technology should be used in the public schools. They were joined by a select number of chief executive officers (CEOs) from major corporations who believe they have a stake in the success of the nation's schools.

Despite some disagreements, the governors agreed to develop and establish—within 2 years—internationally competitive standards, assessments to measure progress toward meeting them, and accountability systems of consequence (Lawton, 1996a). The 49 CEOs committed themselves to establishing—within a year—new hiring standards that require applicants to demonstrate academic achievement through such school-based records as transcripts and diplomas. Christopher Cross, long-time civil service employee and highly respected president of the Council for Basic Education, was quoted as saying "I think there's a good deal of facile commitment to standards and not a lot of understanding of what that means" (Lawton, 1996a, p. 23).

At the time the National Education Goals were conceived, with the exception of mathematics, no subject area had national standards to suggest a common focus in education. The push to set demanding expectations for students in grades kindergarten through 12 has since resulted in the development of national standards in a number of academic areas. In the 1994 to 1995 academic year alone, final versions of national standards were released for civics and government, geography, health, social studies, and physical education. National standards for history also were developed, but controversy erupted over their content, and they had to be redrafted.

Will national goals and standards raise academic standards nationwide?

The standards themselves were formulated by nonprofit, professional associations of educators and were designed to be used on a voluntary basis. The federal government, however, underwrote the cost of creating many of these documents and provided financial incentives to states that implemented them. Figure 13.1 shows an example of standards taken from the national physical education standards as applied to sixth graders.

FIGURE 13.1

Example of National Standards

When students fail to reach benchmarks such as those at right, you have several choices. For example, you might change the standard, alter your teaching to support success, enlist others who might help students succeed, or simply accept the results. With which of these options might you begin, and why?

Note. From *Moving into the Future: National Standards for Physical Education* p. 52 by National Association for Sport and Physical Education, 1995, Oxon Hill, MD: AAHPERD.

The following is taken from the national physical education standards as applied to sixth graders:

Standard:
Achieves and maintains a health-enhancing level of physical fitness.

The emphasis for the 6th-grade student will be to:
- Participate in moderate to vigorous physical activity in a variety of settings.
- Monitor intensity of exercise.
- Begin to develop a strategy for the improvement of selected fitness components.
- Work somewhat independently with minimal supervision in pursuit of personal fitness goals.
- Meet the health-related fitness standards as defined by a Fitnessgram (a physical fitness test).

Sample Benchmarks:
1. Keeps a record of heart rate prior to, during, and after vigorous physical activity.
2. Participates in fitness-enhancing organized physical activities outside of school (e.g., gymnastics clubs, community-sponsored youth sports).
3. Engages in physical activity at the target heart rate for a minimum of 20 minutes.
4. Correctly demonstrates activities designed to improve and maintain muscular strength and endurance, flexibility, and cardiorespiratory functioning.

Assessment Example:
Group project-observational record

Students, working in small groups, are asked to design a "fitness video" depicting exercises or activities appropriate for each component of health-related fitness. The group presentation will include a verbal description of each fitness component as well as a demonstration of the selected exercises or physical activity . The group may choose a class presentation or an actual video.

Many school districts have made special efforts to draft academic standards that would be congruent with national standards. One educator, Assistant Superintendent Charles Hill in Putnam Valley, New York, created a Web site on the Internet to facilitate his school district's efforts. The site, hailed by many as "one of the best on the Web," includes links to the professional groups responsible for the voluntary content area standards, drafts of their standards, and relevant journal articles and government documents (Sommerfeld, 1996). The site can be accessed on the Web (**http://putwest.boces.org/standards.html**). Online discussions of goals and standards often touch on the issues described in the following sections.

Outcome-Centered Learning   Critics of existing education programs, especially business leaders, frequently voice concern about the need to demonstrate results in education. Outcome-centered learning considers the products of learning as a reflection of students' time spent in school. The argument for the idea is simple: The nation must be able to assess student progress systematically, that is, to evaluate student performance across locales and over time. This is the only way of knowing (a) how well or how poorly students are performing, (b) what might be done to improve weak results, and (c) whether various reform measures actually make any difference.

As noted in Chapter 10, the focus on educational outcomes or products is not new. In the 1920s efforts were made to apply scientific principles to education problems and to assess these applications by examining students' work. Accountability has always been associated with demands to demonstrate evidence of student competence—test scores, compositions, times clocked in races. What makes recent emphases on accountability different from past efforts is the role of the teacher. Today's teachers assume greater responsibility for student competence and exert more influence over the kinds of outcomes used to assess students as opposed to relying so heavily on tests created outside schools. The intent is to enhance the authenticity of student evaluations.

How are teachers' and students' roles changing in today's classrooms? What trends in curriculum standards and assessment might account for those changes?

At the local level, students' outcomes are also measured through teacher-made and standardized tests. Educators may use test results to make instructional and placement decisions and also to compare performances of students from school to school and from district to district. In some localities, testing data are used to rate classroom teachers. Under a plan approved in 1996 by the Baltimore, Maryland, school board, teachers whose students do not improve on tests or assignments are required to undergo training in the district's professional development department. Should students' scores not climb by the third year, teachers can be dismissed ("Performance-Based Ratings," 1996). As mentioned in Chapter 10, schools across the nation supplement information from objective tests with samples of student work, portfolios, demonstrations, and other student products so as to measure not only what students know but also what they can do and how they reason.

> **Will accountability for national standards cause schools to "teach to the test"?**

National Assessments of Educational Progress (NAEP)

Student assessments such as the National Assessments of Educational Progress (NAEP) have become benchmarks of the reform process in the United States. The NAEP is a congressionally mandated set of tests developed by the Educational Testing Service. Since 1969, the NAEP has been administered nationally to samples of students in grades 4, 8, and 12 to measure their knowledge and skills in a variety of subject areas.

Education reformers view the NAEP as a stimulus to change in teaching practice. Yet some people have criticized the NAEP as useful only for comparing trends in students' performance over time rather than for measuring students' actual abilities in subjects such as mathematics (Glaser & Linn, 1992). In 1992 the NAEP mathematics tests required students to spend as much as 5 minutes to solve individual problems and to use words and pictures to explain their answers. Results were disappointing, but most educators agree that these will improve in time as new standards take hold

(Viadero, 1993). (Figure 13.2 shows the overall national reading proficiency by grade in 1992 and 1994.) Teachers need time and support to bring curriculum and instruction in line with new expectations, and the tests themselves must reflect the importance of what is to be taught and learned (Koretz, 1995).

In 1996 the National Assessment Governing Board approved plans for an NAEP civics and government test to be administered in 1998 that is based on the national standards (Lawton, 1996b). An improved NAEP system may eventually include local and state assessments, international comparisons, and explicit links between assessments, curricula, teaching, and professional development for teachers (Technical Subgroup for the National Education Goals Panel, 1992).

The Minimum Competency Movement   If school is designed for all of society's children, is there some common body of knowledge and minimal level of learning that can and should be expected of all students? Those who answer this question affirmatively support minimum competency programs, or curriculum and instruction geared toward the successful completion of **minimum competency tests**. These tests are designed to assess the lowest acceptable levels of student performance.

The minimum competency movement began in the 1970s as a reaction against (a) what some have perceived as a diminished emphasis on content and academic rigor in schools; (b) the practice of social promotion—promoting children through the grades to keep them with their agemates even if they could not keep pace academically; and (c) decreasing performance in the use of public funds to foster **literacy**—defined most often as scores on tests of reading, writing, and calculation. The minimum competency movement has advanced an agenda for educational and social change. "Minimums" are often defined in terms of what some adults believe children will need to know and be able to do in order to get and keep a job in later life. By concentrating on

FIGURE 13.2

Overall National Reading Proficiency by Grade— NAEP 1992 and 1994

The pattern of improvement in reading proficiency across grade—older students are more proficient than younger students—might be explained in at least two ways: (1) the longer you stay in school, the more you learn; (2) weaker students drop out over time, leaving stronger students taking the examinations. If such a pattern were evident in your school, how might you begin to explore the relative power of each explanation?

Note. From National Center for Education Statistics, National Assessment of Educational Progress (NAEP), **http://www. ed.gov/NCES/naep/**

*Significant decrease between 1992 and 1994

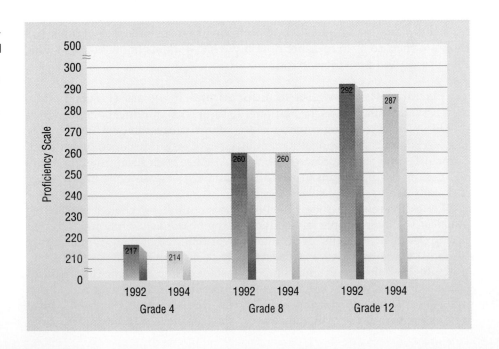

the "minimums" in curriculum, proponents intend to raise—indirectly—maximum standards (Lerner, 1991). The movement promotes curriculum, instruction, and evaluation that prepare students for the future. This means emphasis on technology in the workplace and concentration on basic skills.

Advocates of minimum competence want to help children from poverty-stricken areas, shortchanged by poor schools, receive the preparation they need to build secure futures. They often define security in terms of job skills and self determination.

Is a focus on minimum competency a disservice to students?

Many states have developed lists of minimum competencies for students. Arizona, for example, has developed lists of skills in seven subjects for the 8th and 12th grades. The following skills are examples from Arizona's list of 87 skills in health for 8th-grade students.

- Identifies personal care practices. Example: washing hands before eating, brushing teeth.

- Communicates symptoms of his/her physical illness.

- Lists some of the ways communicable diseases are transmitted.

- Identifies and describes a variety of foods.

- States the importance of eating breakfast and describes a healthful breakfast (Oliva, 1992, p. 122).

Critics contend that the minimum competency movement has led to an overemphasis on **"high stakes tests"**—tests used to evaluate school performance, that determine students' grade promotion, graduation, and access to specific fields of study. High-stakes testing, critics argue, limits the curriculum to simplistic ideas. Even in the lower grades, more stimulating and potentially more important subject matter has been dropped from the curriculum in favor of training for tests in basic skills (Madaus & Kellaghan, 1992).

Opportunity-To-Learn Standards   Critics of minimum competency tests have advanced the concept of **opportunity-to-learn (OTL) standards**. OTL standards are meant to hold schools accountable for giving students a fair chance to succeed by providing them with appropriate support—books, materials, machines, teachers, time to learn, and other tools.

For a school to meet an opportunity-to-learn standard, it must provide a sufficient quantity and quality of resources, practices, and the conditions necessary for student success. Responsibility to meet such standards, proponents argue, must fall not only to schools but to districts and to states as well. Students must be given the opportunity to learn by the adults who run the educational systems if students are to be held accountable for their performance later in life.

As Andrew Porter (1995) has observed, however, the OTL standards are strictly voluntary; they will not be used to hold states or localities accountable.

If they have any influence on school improvement, it will be through persuasion provided by visions of good education practice and information from OTL indicators on progress [viz., evidence of resources devoted to creating favorable conditions for learning] schools are providing toward school improvement. (Porter, 1995, p. 27)

▦ Trends Toward Comprehensive Curriculum and Assessment

Evolving educational standards emanating from changes in the public's expectations will stimulate reform of curriculum, methods of teaching and learning, and processes of assessment. These reforms will occur slowly in some places and rapidly in others; when viewed together they will constitute a noticeable trend in the way teachers will perform their jobs.

Many educators recognize that curricular reform requires more than continually adding information to courses of study. Processes of curriculum integration must blend old and new material, form links between concepts, structure content so students will make connections in their minds, organize people and ideas by themes, and team students and teachers.

Reformed educational systems will look different from one another; but the integration of knowledge, people, and thinking—not the mere addition of information to the curriculum—is likely to be a common attribute among systems. Students who will graduate in 2004 from Maryland schools, for example, will be expected to pass a battery of 10 tests: three in English, three in social studies, and two each in mathematics and science. Exams for each content area will assess students' abilities to work with others, communicate, use technology, and think critically. The notion behind the new tests is to hold all students, regardless of which school they attend, to the same high standards (Lawton, 1996).

Concerns about student progress have prompted educators to rethink time-honored practices of defining achievement solely or even mainly in terms of standardized achievement tests. Tests that yield information on students' abilities to pick "right" and "wrong" answers will diminish in importance in the years ahead. In their place, educators want to develop a **comprehensive assessment** of student progress that will provide information on students' capacities for reasoning, thinking divergently, and solving problems creatively.

Are integrated curricula and comprehensive, authentic assessments feasible?

To be useful, such a comprehensive assessment will need to reflect more accurately the kinds of challenges students will face in real life than do multiple-choice tests of knowledge acquisition. A truly comprehensive assessment will provide estimates of students' abilities to complete a variety of life's tasks and to function effectively in many contexts. To develop such an assessment for a future that is, at best, difficult to predict is a challenging task, but it is also a task that teachers—in collaboration with other professionals—will undertake.

New authentic assessment, or assessment that is connected to what students must be able to do in the real world and thus is connected directly to instruction in schools, will allow teachers to assert their roles as assessment experts. Educators will place less emphasis on having outside measurement experts create tests, which separates assessment from teaching. Consequently, assessment will more often emphasize having teachers identify logical student outcomes, communicate expectations for student performance, and tie evaluation directly to instruction (Stiggins, 1994).

Just as she teaches continually, the teacher who demonstrates comprehensive, authentic methods of assessment will be engaged continually in processes of assessment. She will teach material, and she will create opportunities for students to demonstrate their mastery of that material in various ways. For example, if students are studying the compass points, the teacher might have them playing games on the playground that require them to demonstrate their knowledge of direction by moving from place to place; she might turn them loose on a football field with compasses in hand and maps to be charted; or she might put them at computers with opportunities to "travel" from place to place on the globe. In any or all instances, she will observe their abilities to perform their tasks. She might also have students judge the difficulty of the problems they face and estimate their own understanding of these problems, while she makes the same judgments. As processes of assessment and teaching become more comprehensive and authentic, then, they also will become more interrelated than they have been.

Trends Toward Education for Diversity

Standards are uniform, but children are different. If they are to achieve the same or similar outcomes, children need different levels and kinds of support. Increasingly, in the years ahead, teachers will be called upon to make informed decisions about students' needs and abilities and to deliver support fitted to individual and group needs. In addition to developing multicultural curricula and instructional approaches (see Chapter 8), for example, educators will plan interventions for gender equity and adaptations for mainstreamed students with disabilities.

Gender Sensitivity Training   One trend prevents gender bias in the classroom and offers **gender sensitivity training** to students. Gender-fair education provides curricula that avoid sex-role stereotyping and promotes equal educational opportunities for girls and women. Standard textbooks now draw attention to women's relevant contributions. Teachers routinely encourage girls to take and to master mathematics and science courses throughout their educational careers. Education texts avoid the generic use of male terms.

A number of educators have created curricula that avoid sex role stereotyping and identify opportunities for girls and women to take advantage of all their possibilities for education. The *Civitas* curriculum offers the following objectives for gender sensitivity training.

The citizen should be able to:

1. explain the similarities and differences between men's and women's political participation throughout American history.

2. explain how the changing roles that have been deemed appropriate for men and women have affected their participation in American politics.

How can gender-fair education be provided in all classrooms? What role can gender sensitivity training play in addressing problems of gender bias?

3. explain how the effects of public policies vary by gender, affecting men and women differently.

4. take, defend, and evaluate positions on constitutional and public policy issues regarding gender and political participation. (Quigley & Bahmueller, 1991, p. 258)

Overall, *Civitas* examines gender from three frames of references—conceptual, historical, and contemporary—suggesting directions for sharply defined study. The conceptual frame draws attention to such factors as the basis for past exclusion of women from politics, the role of feminism, arguments for and against changing women's roles in society, women's changing place in politics, and women's relatively small role in the exercise of formal political power. The historical perspective emphasizes the place of women in politics at the founding of the nation, the beginning of women's political activism, the campaign for women's suffrage, and the various phases of the feminist movement. The contemporary perspective looks out on gender issues as they have been articulated in the 1990s, including wage inequality and job segregation, and considers women in politics in present-day America.

How far should schools go in attempting to ensure gender equity?

Civitas is constructed to be sensitive to the raging controversy over multicultural issues in the social sciences. The writers and editors have tried to respond to critics of other curricula who have argued that too often Western values and European contributions to the United States and to the world have been overstressed. Certainly, the gender section of the curriculum, and other sections, are geared toward change.

Equity between males and females might be realized as people adopt a more caring attitude toward others. Nel Noddings (1984, 1992), Madeline Grumet (1987), and others have argued that society's prevailing conceptions of gender will be changed only by "transforming" what and how children are taught about caring and ethics.

> I have argued for a curriculum aimed at producing people who will not intentionally harm others; a transformed structure of schooling that will encourage the development of caring relations; a moral education that emphasized maternal interests in preserving life, enhancing growth, and shaping acceptable children; and the development of a morality of evil that should help all of us understand and control our own tendencies toward evil. (Noddings, 1992, p. 678)

Teaching All Students in Inclusive Classrooms   As described in Chapter 9, the inclusion movement in special education has encouraged the teaching of children with disabilities in general education classrooms instead of teaching them in self-contained classrooms or facilities. Inclusion carries the force of law and considerable public support. At the same time, disagreement abounds about which settings are most appropriate for which students and about how to provide instruction for students with disabilities in inclusive classrooms.

Cultural Awareness

Some disabilities—for example, blindness—affect not only the person with the visual impairment but the people with whom that person interacts—indeed, the culture in which that person resides.

Visual impairments seem to evoke more awkwardness than do most other disabilities. Why are we so uncomfortably aware of blindness? For one thing, blindness is visible. We often do not realize that a person has impaired hearing, for example, until we actually talk to him. The person with visual impairment, however, usually has a variety of symbols—a cane, thick or darkened glasses, a guide dog. Another possible reason for being self-conscious around people who are blind is the role that eyes play in social interaction. Poets, playwrights, and songwriters have long recognized how emotionally expressive the eyes can be for people who are sighted. We all know how uncomfortable it can be to talk with someone who does not make eye contact with us. Think of how often we have heard someone say or have ourselves said that we prefer to talk "face to face" on an important matter, rather than over the telephone. We seem to rely a great deal on the expressiveness of people's eyes to judge how they are responding to what we are saying. (Hallahan & Kauffman, 1997, p. 354)

As a classroom teacher you will face the following. First, teaching children with disabilities requires that you understand the needs and abilities of all students as fully as possible. Students' characteristics may well dictate what they can accomplish and how they are to be taught. Second, you must set tasks or objectives that are worthwhile and that students with disabilities can accomplish. All students may not be able to achieve all of the same objectives at the same level of proficiency. Third, you must fit instruction to individuals' goals, needs, and strengths. This means more than simply varying the amount of work or the amount of learning time; you may also need to structure teaching and assignments for special students in different ways. Fourth, you will have to assess students in ways that allow them to demonstrate what they know and can do. This means relying less on standard measures of learning for students with disabilities and more on alternative assessments of what they have learned.

Trends Toward Character Education

As crime and violence have increased in society, so too have calls for teachers to transmit moral values to children. If parents fail in their responsibilities, the argument goes, teachers must teach basic values.

Clarifying or teaching values, sometimes referred to as **character education**, has become highly controversial since the 1960s. According to Professor

Thomas Likona, the values clarification teaching of the 1960s and 1970s "led students to believe whatever values they had were O.K., as long as they were clarified, even if it was shoplifting or Satanism" (Viadero, 1992, p. 12). Likona believes that students were misled when teachers opened lessons on values by saying that there is no right or wrong answer. Instead, teachers need to say that there may be more than one answer and that students must be prepared to support their answers with sound moral reasoning.

Character education, or "moral education," has detractors, but the movement to return values teaching to the standard curriculum is gaining momentum. With violence increasing in society, particularly among the young, and with the problems of dysfunctional families, more educators, politicians, and citizens are pushing for a curriculum that teaches the difference between right and wrong.

How far should schools go in teaching moral values?

Hugh Sockett (1992) contends that teachers help students think about right and wrong and how to behave ethically through example. But how teachers do so is largely a mystery.

> We do not know the ways in which teachers generally confront such basic issues as racial prejudice and sexism or what their curriculum strategies look like. We do not know the extent to which teachers are more or less influenced by their religious persuasions when they teach, nor the precise extent to which state mandates or local community values inhibit moral teaching. Nor do we know to what extent teachers feel their integrity is compromised by any conflict between their world view in moral terms and the practices of the school in which they work. (p. 562)

Like everyone else, teachers are driven by their own convictions about right and wrong. Teachers' beliefs, however, may carry greater moral suasion than do those of most adults, because teachers have more opportunities to influence young people. Teachers also must create a climate that fosters personal and social responsibility in the young.

Many values regarded as appropriate for character education relate to living in a democracy. If a democracy is to function successfully, citizens must demonstrate a collective sense of civic responsibility. For communities to "work" properly, individuals must be willing to sacrifice some of their personal autonomy for the good of the group.

To give students a sense of belonging and to encourage them to participate in the responsibilities of community, state, and nation, a number of schools have developed curricula to encourage volunteerism, or **service learning**. Joseph Kahne and Joel Westheimer (1996) contend that service learning programs fall into two general categories: those that encourage the goal of change and those that foster the goal of charity. Change programs encourage students to adopt a moral stance of caring, a political view of the value of reconstructing society, and an intellectual stance on the importance of engaging in experiences that transform the way people think. Charity programs are organized around the moral principle of giving, the political ideal of performing one's civic duty, and the added intellectual value of gaining experience from engaging in service activities.

In many instances, volunteer groups such as the 300-member service club at Fallston High School in Harford County, Maryland, perform their services outside school hours and receive no credit, awards, or certificates of appreciation from their school. Individual service projects, such as tutoring peers or younger children or working with residents in nursing homes, foster communication and intergenerational understanding. Group service projects, such as repairing bleachers or cleaning up the local park, help students learn to plan and cooperate with others to get a job done. Students who volunteer also become more responsible and develop more favorable attitudes toward the people they work with than do other young people.

Should schools make service learning mandatory?

Service learning often includes environmental stewardship. From instructional units that teach students about water conservation in the West, to programs that educate young people about controlling soil erosion in the Midwest, to curriculum aimed at raising consciousness about acid rain in the East, science and social studies teachers work to sensitize young people to the importance of preserving the delicate balance of forces in their environment. Schools regularly encourage student participation in such activities as Arbor Day, recycling programs, and wildlife preservation projects. In so doing, schools play an important but indirect role in educating parents about environmental issues.

Education about the environment incorporates the teaching of values and problem-solving approaches to ethical dilemmas as well as to practical ones. Figure 13.3, for example, shows different points of view about resource management in a Wisconsin curriculum.

HOW ARE NEW LINKS TO TECHNOLOGY CHANGING THE FOUNDATIONS OF EDUCATION?

New teacher roles also are emerging through new links to technology. As schools develop capacities to deliver video, audio, data, and text to classrooms through electronic media, teachers face multiple challenges beyond the problems of operating the machinery. They must use technology both as a means of direct instruction that focuses on basic skills and as a way to help students construct their own knowledge and develop a deep understanding of the subject matter. Teachers must also teach students to use technology for themselves. Computers often are used only for drill and practice or as rewards for students who finish their "real work" early. In some schools, lack of funds limits access to computers. Even with an ample supply, the challenge is to use computers in ways that actually help students to think and learn.

Most experts agree that some basic conditions must exist if computers are going to be used effectively to link students with information and people in the larger world. Computers must be available in sufficient number so that work stations can be provided for every two to three students. Teachers need training and opportunities to use computers if they are going to help students use them. Teachers also need time to restructure their curricula around computers if the machines are going to be used for anything other than drill and practice. Teachers will have difficulty integrating technology with classroom instruction when students must go to a lab to access a computer.

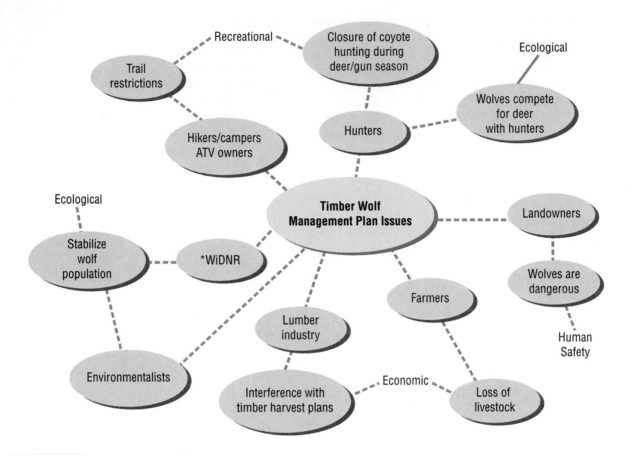

FIGURE 13.3

An Issue Web: Wolves in Wisconsin

What are some curricular goals and learning objectives that an issue web like this would support?

Note. From "Science Related Social Issues in the Elementary School: The Extended Case Study Approach" by J. M. Ramsey and M. Kronholm, 1991, *Journal of Science Education, 3*(2), p. 6. Reprinted by permission.

*Wisconsin Department of Natural Resources

Mark and Cindy Grabe (1996) have identified five themes that describe the different uses of technology in classrooms. When students use technology to study a particular content area, and the technology is secondary to learning the content, then the technology has been "integrated into content-area instruction." As teachers encourage students to learn to apply general-purpose software, such as word-processing programs, they are using a "tools approach" to technology instruction. The Grabes also write of using technology to promote "an active role for students." By "active" they mean the mental behavior of students as they use technology to construct meaning for themselves or to solve complex problems. Technology also can be used to facilitate "an integrated or multidisciplinary approach" to teaching and learning involving a broad range of skills. Finally, technology can enhance interactions among students, providing the benefits of "cooperative learning."

Internet and the World Wide Web

Tools for active, multidisciplinary cooperative uses of technology in instruction include the Internet. The **Internet** is a global telecommunications network that began as a military effort to ensure communications in case of a nuclear attack. Sometimes referred to as the "information superhighway," the Internet now carries both public and private/commercial information to an estimated 30 million people—a number that grows daily. More than 5,000 smaller networks are connected to each other via the Internet by **modem** (a device that allows one to connect a computer to a network using special software and a regular telephone line), through direct fiber-optic or copper links, and/or over radio and light waves.

Judi Harris (1994) points out that there are four basic ways to exchange information on the Internet: (1) person-to-person; (2) person-to-group; (3) person-to-computer program; and (4) person-to-information archive. Each type of connection is made possible through different kinds of telecomputing tools.

Electronic mail (e-mail) is the most popular application of the Internet. Users can send e-mail to individuals or to groups of individuals at the same time. Teachers often establish a mailing list, or **listserv**, that allows them to send a message to all of their students in a class at the same time with a single keystroke.

News Groups are electronic message services that post to servers locally, regionally, nationally, and/or internationally. People subscribe to a news group to gain access to the messages and to post their own messages. News groups are widely used in education.

A **file transfer protocol (FTP)** lets people move, or "download," files from computers anywhere on a network to their own computers. A teacher might locate files of pictures, documents, or raw data at NASA and wish to use them with her students in a science class studying outer space. She might use an FTP to capture the files, put them on her computer, and use them whenever she or the students need them.

The **World Wide Web** (also called the "Web" or WWW) is a subset of the Internet. The Web consists of tens of thousands of documents that often have text and still images, as well as audio and video. These documents are called **hypermedia**.

With appropriate software and an Internet connection, one can access virtually any of the Web's documents. The range of information accessible on the Web is remarkable. One can "travel" to points all around the world, as well as find some truly phenomenal educational resources (see Pathways to School Improvement at **http://www.ncrel.org/sdrs/pathways.htm**). Getting information from the Web requires no permission, and users can also share what they have with the rest of the world.

A **Web browser** is the software that enables the user to retrieve and see what is on the Web. Popular browsers include Netscape, Mosaic, and Lynx. A **home page**, the first page of a Web document, is much like a textbook's table of contents. Besides indicating who or what organization has posted the document, the page suggests what might be found within the Web site.

Distance Learning

Televised instruction has been a fact of life for decades, but new technology designed to promote **distance learning** provides possibilities for teachers and students to connect with each other and to make content areas and topics come alive by communicating interactively over long distances. In its most advanced form, distance learning allows people to interact with one another

VOICES

On an Internet-Based Course for Teachers

In 1996, seven universities across the United States and Canada collaborated to offer an Internet-based course for teachers on interdisciplinary teaching and learning. Both the curriculum and instruction were designed to alter radically the foundations of education.

Participants in a 1996 Internet-based course on interdisciplinary teaching and learning.

Students concentrated on cases or problems of interdisciplinary teaching and learning in elementary, middle, and secondary schools across North America. Course contents were delivered via the Internet (World Wide Web, video conference, discussion groups, and electronic mail), videotape, and print materials. The purpose of the course was to prepare teachers to collaborate across disciplines so that they might address issues of teaching and learning as they occur in our culturally diverse world. The course also promoted the use of new technologies.

Mary Sudzina, Associate Professor, University of Dayton: "My course evaluations suggest this was an experience in true collaboration for inservice teachers. They came from different schools and different disciplines, yet they worked together on some common tasks. Because students' analyses and the cases they wrote were posted at the Web site, they got to see what other people at other places thought about the same problems. This was a self-affirming experience for them. When people work alone they often think they are off base in some way. But here they learned they were more like other people than they

Mary Sudzina

as if they were in the same room. Students can see and hear teachers, and teachers can answer students' questions and react to students' comments instantaneously. These features are especially useful when students are located in geographically remote areas.

The Star Schools Program, established by the Department of Education in 1988, has awarded more than $125 million to schools using distance learning. You can learn more about the program on the Internet (**http://gopher.ed.gov/prog_info/StarSchools/whatis.html**). The purpose of the Star Schools Program is to encourage improved instruction in mathematics, science, and foreign languages, as well as other areas, such as literacy skills and vocational education. The program uses telecommunications to teach underserved populations, including low-income and nonliterate stu-

were different. They saw themselves in a professional light."

JoAnn Haysbert, Associate Professor, Hampton University: I like the idea that Hampton students have opportunities to engage in teaching and learning with students from other academic and geographical environments. Students across the sites have exchanged ideas and in so doing have learned from each other. My students have liked being a part

JoAnn Haysbert

of the new era of technology. They have engaged in dialogue on the Internet with students about common problems teachers face. I think they feel more of a partnership with students in other places because of their concentration on common issues. I have also observed them preparing in a different way from students who don't work with others across the country. They have a greater enthusiasm for fine-tuning their views on an issue.

I have heard them saying they needed to consider what students in other places might think. My students really try to consider points of view of others in the class."

CRITICAL THINKING

According to Sudzina and Haysbert, why was it beneficial for their students to be linked to students at home and at other institutions? How might teachers in the field use technology in a similar way to improve their teaching? What frustrations might they encounter in their efforts? Would you consider using the Internet as a means of communicating with other teachers? Why or why not? Visit the Internet-based course (**http://teach.virginia.edu/ go/casecourse**).

When you arrive at the site, you will find, among other things, a scene from a multimedia Web case on the traditional Native American unit in kindergarten. Can you identify any potentially troubling issues in this scene, that is, issues to which you might have to respond if you were a teacher in the situation?

Note. From M. Sudzina and J. Haysbert, personal communications, April 22, 1996.

dents; students with limited English proficiency, and students with disabilities. By the mid-1990s, about 1.6 million students in all states, the District of Columbia, and the territories had enrolled in courses in math, science, foreign language, and other subjects funded in part by Star School grants. In addition, thousands of teachers had taken courses and participated in staff development programs offered through the Star Schools Program. Regional partnerships exist in cities and states across the nation.

Distance learning projects are especially important for many small, isolated school districts that, because of cost constraints, have had to exclude all but basic-level courses from their curriculum. As financial support goes down and state education standards go up, distance learning offers attractive possibilities for making connections with people and ideas.

Cultural Awareness

Beyond the direct and expected benefits of Star Schools, notes Northwest Regional Educational Laboratory (NWREL) evaluator Kim Yap, the stakeholders identified a number of "spin-off" results. Perhaps the most surprising spin-off, Yap says, is Star Schools' far-reaching impact on communities. Yap asserts,

> The services that distance education offers. . . have really enhanced rural viability. A lot of parents told us that Star Schools allowed them to stay in a rural area. They didn't have to move into more populated areas in order to give their children the educational opportunities they need for their future. Ultimately, these choices have bearing on rural stability and economic development.

> [Parents say] that because Star Schools allow their children to compete academically with students in more metropolitan areas, the rural school—and in turn, the rural community—is more attractive. If parents are prevented from fleeing remote areas, so are the small businesses that many of them own. (Northwest Regional Educational Laboratory, 1994, p. 1)

■ Telecommunications Capabilities in the Schools

Kenneth Green of the Center for Educational Studies at Claremont Graduate School in Claremont, California, directs a national research project focused on the use of information technology in higher education. In addition to the increasing use of electronic mail, computer classrooms, computer simulations, and CD-ROM-based materials, he found that educators displayed a growing interest in the Internet and the World Wide Web.

> The 1995 data indicate that about 6% of all college courses currently tap into Web-based resources to support instruction. Three-fourths of the respondents (76.5%) indicate that "providing Internet/WWW training" will be a "very important" computing priority for their campuses over the next 3 years. Similarly, three-fourths (75.1%) report that Netscape, a widely used Internet browser, will be "very important" in their campus technology planning. Using Internet resources for instruction is a "very important" priority for more than two-thirds (71.5%) of the responding campuses, while more than half (50.3%) view Web pages for individual classes and courses as being "very important" over the next 2 to 3 years. (Green, 1996, p. 2)

To understand how technology is changing the foundations of education, we need to know how and where technology is being used. Do educators and their students enter the "information age" when they enter schools, or do they drop back in time, technologically speaking? As illustrated in Figure 13.4, a growing number of students have access to computers at home and at school. Is the "technology revolution" touching everyone or only those in wealthy areas and in certain geographic regions of the country? How is technology affecting the formation, acquisition, and use of knowledge?

A survey of telecommunications conducted for the U.S. Department of Education tapped a national sample to yield some partial answers to these questions (Heaviside, Farris, Malitz, & Carpenter, 1995). The results suggest that in the mid- to late-1990s, public elementary and secondary schools have been scrambling to use technology in a variety of ways.

Nearly three-fourths of schools reported having some type of telecommunications capabilities (computer networks or cable/broadcast television). Schools most often cited funding as the major barrier in the acquisition or use of advanced telecommunications, resulting in inadequate or outdated equipment and too few access points in the buildings. Most schools that reported having computers with telecommunication capabilities did not have them in classrooms. This fact may say as much about educational priorities and knowing how to use computers instructionally as it does about availability of equipment. While three-fourths of public schools had access to some kind of computer network, only half had access to a wide-area network—35% had access to the Internet, and 14% had access to other wide-area networks, such as America OnLine.

In the southeastern United States, schools were about twice as likely to report statewide telecommunications plans than were schools in the other regions of the country. Smaller schools, those with enrollments of less than 300 students, were less likely to be on the Internet than were larger schools. For the 35% of the public schools that had Internet access, e-mail was the most widely available service. The Internet capabilities of e-mail, news groups,

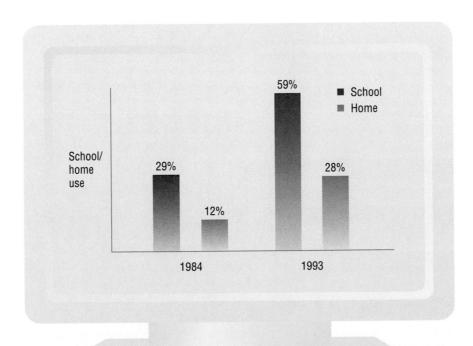

FIGURE 13.4

Student Use of Computers

The percentage of students using a computer at school more than doubled between 1984 and 1993, increasing from 29 to 59 percent. Twenty-eight percent of students used a computer at home in 1993, up from 12 percent in 1984. Why is it so important for access to computers to be higher in schools than in homes?

Note. From *Indicator of the month: Student use of computer* by U.S. Department of Education, December, 1995, Washington, DC: U.S. Government Printing Office.

resource location services, and graphical user interface were more often available for teachers and administrators than for students. (See Figure 13.5.)

There are important educational, cultural, and economic reasons why schools are likely to promote telecommunications technologies as learning tools—tools to be placed in the hands of students. As Al Rogers (1995) argues, chief among these reasons are the preservation and extension of democracy.

> Since the days of Gutenberg, the publishing of information has been an autocratic enterprise. . . . Information—its formation, transmission, and interpretation—was controlled by a tiny handful of people. They determined what constituted "news," "good taste" or "political correctness" and generally what was deemed to be "important." (Rogers, 1995)

In contrast, Rogers characterized the Internet as a way to give millions of people direct access to information that flows freely across national borders and around the world. For example, within hours of Boris Yeltsin's successful resistance of a *coup d'etat* in Moscow in 1991, the president of the Russian Republic issued a decree of defiance, seizing authority from the central government. His decree was flashed around the world on the Internet to tens of thousands of computers on college campuses, businesses, homes, and schools. The message went directly from Moscow to the people of the world—"unfiltered, unedited, without the benefit of selection or commentary, interpretation, or embellishment" (Rogers, 1995).

In short, technology in the hands of ordinary people is democratizing the foundations of education. Technology brings opportunities for a person anywhere with a computer and a telephone line to make, acquire, interpret, and apply knowledge. (If you visit the AskERIC Virtual Library at **http://ericir. syr.edu** you can see just how quickly and easily knowledge is available to those who seek it online.)

FIGURE 13.5

How the Internet Is Used

Why might teachers have to learn how to use the Internet when they already have a telephone at their fingertips and a library nearby?

Note. From "How the Internet is Used," 1993, *Education Week, 12*(40), p. 3. Copyright 1993 by *Education Week.* Reprinted by permission.

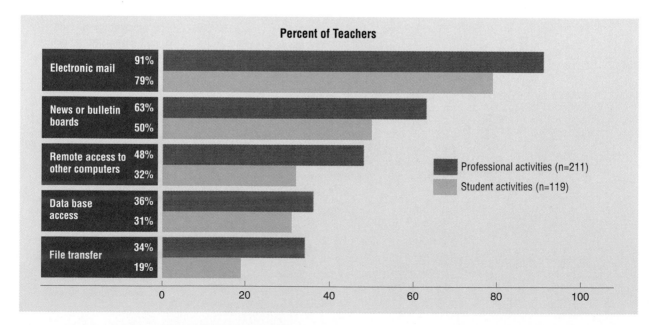

But what price must people pay for this new freedom? With increasing opportunities for people to make themselves public electronically comes the

Could the Internet have a negative impact on education?

necessity of sorting the "good" information from the "bad." The kind of quality control exercised in traditional publishing does not exist in electronic communication and publication, except in a few instances. Moreover, issues of censorship that have been settled legally and practically in traditional publishing must be reexamined with regard to the new communication technologies. Are the creators and managers of the Internet to censor materials? Are school leaders to control what is appropriate and inappropriate for young people to read, see, and hear online? Who will decide?

Teachers will change the foundations of education when they begin to use technology to learn how students learn. When teachers work with students to gather, analyze, and display data, teachers can learn much about student thinking, which can inform teaching. As Glen Bull, president of the Society for Information Technology and Teacher Education (SITE), observes, simultaneous interaction with print, video, and audio media may constitute the most dramatic advancement in civilization since the invention of movable type—an advancement that will actually change the way students think. For example, while symbolic representations work best for some algebraic analyses, graphical representations are better for others. The computer permits the use of either or both, as they might appear designed and redesigned by experts and students. As teachers watch and listen to students think, both will learn to make technology work with curriculum.

By its very nature, technology forces people to look forward, to anticipate not only what is important at the moment but what is likely to be important later. When teachers consider how technology is being used on college campuses, they can get a sense of what their own elementary and secondary students will need to know and be able to do when they get to college.

How ARE COLLABORATIVE NETWORKS TRANSFORMING TEACHING AND LEARNING?

Collaborative networks are groups of people gathered voluntarily to help each other explore and advance particular educational issues. Such groups are at the hub of efforts to improve the education of targeted student groups, such as students at risk of school failure. One innovative approach is to form "learning communities" that provide children with rich experiences and connect their schools with the children's experiences, their culture, and their community. This approach is part of Stanford Professor Henry Levin's **Accelerated Schools** program. Instead of trying to remediate perceived deficiencies in children's learning abilities, Levin encourages educators to capitalize on students' strengths, giving at-risk students the kind of rich and challenging instruction typically reserved for gifted and talented children.

This notion of viewing all children as deserving of and benefiting from the same approach that had been reserved exclusively for those who were labeled gifted and talented was certainly a strange perspective a decade ago when the Accelerated Schools Project was launched. At the time, the standard fare for children in at-risk situations was to immerse them in remedial experiences that emphasized basic skills and repetitive drills in a simplified curriculum. The result was that the longer they attended school, the farther they lagged behind the mainstream in their academic development. (Levin, 1996, p. 3)

For Levin, collaboration is important in the process of transforming a school into an Accelerated School: 80% of the staff must agree on the concept before he will work with them. He encourages them to "take stock" of what they are doing and to form a "deep vision" for the future (Brandt, 1992). Always, the adults who run schools must ask themselves a simple question: Is this what we would want for our own children? The answer to the question can spur people to behave in new and creative ways.

Levin argues that people must begin changing schools by developing a deep vision of the future. Sometimes this process can takes weeks or months. This vision is not often found in the typical mission statement of a school— a document that, according to Levin, frequently lacks vision. Instead, he wants to help people work together to develop a set of beliefs that drive their daily behavior.

> We ask people to select working cadres, typically no more than eight or nine people. And the real work goes on when these small groups start to do research. . . . The first school I worked in—this is a school with 600 kids, 90% minority, very poor—they had 17 parents come to back-to-school night—and 7 of them left after they ate. If you ever saw teachers who had no faith in parents, there they were. The next year, as they were planning another back-to-school night they said, "We don't agree with you—we don't believe we can get parents interested—but we'll test it by adding to our notice for back-to-school night that there will be a short presentation on 'How to Help Your Child Succeed with Homework.'" Well, 175 parents showed up. We had to run out for more coffee and doughnuts. (Brandt, 1992, p. 23)

When Beth Keller and Pilar Soler (1996) investigated the effects of the Accelerated Schools philosophy on teachers' beliefs and practices, they found changed attitudes, but they did not know how these attitudes might have filtered into classroom life. Teachers they surveyed reported changes in how they conceptualized teaching styles, expectations for students, accountability, collaboration, reflection, and participation. The investigators also noted that teachers viewed the principal's support and encouragement as crucial to the success of translating the philosophy into action.

Developing Schools

Partnerships involving university researchers and government support stimulate the development of innovative programs, such as the **America 2000** schools. In 1991 the **New American Schools Development Corporation (NASDC)**—a private, nonprofit, tax-exempt organization formed by

American business leaders and the Bush administration—sponsored a national competition for "break the mold" schools. These newly conceptualized schools were to serve as models that would lead the nation into the 21st century and restore American education to world preeminence.

In July 1992, NASDC selected 11 out of 686 design teams' proposals for further refinement and field testing and, upon approval, nationwide implementation between 1995 and 1997. Eventually, nine plans formed the nucleus of NASDC.

> **Could "break the mold" schools be models for public schools?**

One plan, Roots and Wings, was based in four elementary schools in Lexington Park, Maryland. The brainchild of researchers at Johns Hopkins University, officials in the Maryland Department of Education, and teachers and administrators at the four schools, the plan called for students to engage in problem solving, hands-on activities, and teamwork. Work in groups was to be based on abilities and interests rather than age. Those who had trouble keeping up with their schoolwork would not be retained; instead, they would receive tutoring, family support services, and other help to master content. Special "World Lab" projects, simulations rooted in real-world contexts, would be used to encourage students to work collaboratively to solve a variety of problems. Designed to take the place of existing science and social studies curricula, projects were intended to be long range and multidisciplinary, drawing heavily on the use of computers and other technologies (Olson, 1993).

By 1995 the designs had been tested in 155 schools in 18 states (Olson, 1995a). The New American Schools Development Corporation has held showings of their school designs from Memphis to Miami and from Philadelphia to Seattle. NASDC negotiated the creation of large numbers of their schools in Cincinnati; Dade County, Florida; Los Angeles; Memphis; Philadelphia; Pittsburgh; San Diego; Seattle; and the states of Kentucky, Maryland, and Vermont (Olson, 1995b).

Targeting Students at Risk

There are other collaborative strategies for teaching children at risk. Since the 1970s James B. Comer of Yale University and his colleagues have been working with teachers, principals, parents, and community members to help children at risk to beat the odds and succeed. Comer uses a collaborative process to create programs that foster child development. He calls the process the "School Development Program."

Comer's strategy has been tried and found successful in some of the toughest schools in Washington, D.C.; Camden, New Jersey; Brooklyn; Dade County; Chicago; Dallas; Detroit; New Orleans; and many other communities. David Squires and Robert Kranyik (1995/1996) characterize the Comer approach as a form of site-based management, in which teams of professionals engage in "no-fault problem solving" and "consensual or collaborative decision making." In other words, people do not blame one another for problems; they work together to solve them.

When Dallas adopted Comer's approach in 10 schools, they called it "School-Centered Education" to convey the idea that it was their own special adaptation. They used principals, teachers, and parents to help train others in the approach. They redirected resources to local schools from the central office and restructured the central office staff to focus on providing services to schools. The lesson in the Dallas experience—and in other places, as well—is that success depends heavily on public ownership of the ideas. People in the school community need to "own" the ideas if they are to take root and grow.

Cultural Awareness

Comer schools encourage practical ways of building community. Advocates stress the importance of people considering others' points of view. When students, teachers, parents, administrators, and other community members talk and listen to each other, they gain a deeper understanding of what they want from their schools. Through the discussions they become better prepared to take individual or collective action. They also build the bonds of community that are essential to effective schools. (Leighninger & Niedergang, 1995)

Collaborative networks also are transforming teaching and learning in American high schools. In 1984 to 1985, for example, Theodore Sizer of Brown University organized the **Coalition of Essential Schools**, with nine member schools. Sizer's intent was to build and maintain viable networks of parents, students, and educators who could transform high schools into better places to teach and learn. By 1996, 232 schools were members of the Coalition, and another 271 "planning schools" intended to apply for membership (Coalition of Essential Schools, 1996). Most of the schools were public and 18 were private. Each school defines for itself what constitutes a "good school," but the coalition of all schools expresses allegiance to nine common principles, shown in Figure 13.6.

One challenge for Essential Schools is to link or integrate everything from curricula to people. In their effort to live up to the motto Less is more, Essential Schools encourage high school teachers who view themselves as subject matter specialists to think about stripping down their own discipline to essentials and linking instruction between the disciplines. Coalition members advocate "adopting common themes or aligning parallel courses, either separately or in teams" (Cushman, 1993b, p. 4), and then combining the content of two or more courses—for instance, linking history, literature, government, and the arts in an American studies course (Cushman, 1993a).

When studying five Coalition high schools in four states, Patricia Wasley and her colleagues (Wasley, King, & Louth, 1995) found that the Coalition strategy involved the whole school in discussion about how to help students, but not without a price. "While more are now engaged, there is more conflict, as the various beliefs and attitudes between the various stakeholders in the group are revealed" (p. 219). Teachers examined the relationship of their own

FIGURE 13.6

Principles of Essential Schools

If you were asked to rank by importance the attributes of an Essential School listed at left, what would be your top two or three?

Note. From *Horace's School: Redesigning the American High School* by T. R. Sizer, Boston: Houghton Mifflin.

The Essential School should

✓ focus on helping adolescents learn to use their minds;

✓ have a simple mission requiring students to master essential skills and knowledge;

✓ help all students strive for the same goals, but vary means according to students' needs;

✓ personalize teaching and learning;

✓ be guided by the metaphor of student as worker, not teacher as deliverer of instruction;

✓ prepare students to exhibit their language and mathematical skills;

✓ set a tone that communicates expectations, trust, and decency; use incentives; and encourage parents to collaborate;

✓ help staff think of themselves first as generalists and next as specialists; and

✓ provide for planning time, competitive salaries, and per-pupil costs of no more than 10% above traditional schools.

---

work to student learning, and faculty did more teaming than they had before they joined the Coalition.

Should all students be exposed to the same basic curriculum?

Strategies for involving parents and community members in an Essential School run the gamut of possibilities: sponsoring evening study groups in which adults explore the same educational issues, holding public exhibitions of student work, paying parents as classroom aides, organizing parent advisory groups, holding small-group sessions with the principal, publishing a newsletter, encouraging the local newspaper to cover educational issues, and so forth (Cushman, 1993a, p. 7).

In late 1993 Sizer and his colleagues received a $50 million grant from philanthropist Walter Annenberg. In 1996 the Coalition collaborated with the Annenberg Institute for School Reform to extend its work.

Increasing Parental Involvement

Collaborative approaches must involve parents to succeed. Children's futures are inextricably linked to their parents. When parents take an interest in their children's progress—when parents hold high but reasonable expectations for their children's performance and support them by meeting basic needs, good things happen: Students' school attendance improves, their self-esteem and achievement spiral upward, and their long-term prospects for living successful, productive lives increase.

Educators work to forge and maintain strong ties to families. The most obvious connections can be seen in the thousands of parent–teacher organizations across the country. The most famous, the National Parent Teacher Association (National PTA), celebrated its 100th anniversary in 1996. In 1896, when Alice McLellan Birney founded the organization as the National Congress of Mothers in Washington, D.C., she did so with refreshing clarity of purpose: "Let us have no more croaking as to what cannot be done; let us see what can be done" (National PTA, 1995–1996). What had to be done was to establish and tend lines of communication between home and school. The PTA and other such organizations sanctioned connections between families and schools; they made it appropriate and possible for adults in and out of the educational system to work together for children.

Too often, however, it is difficult to meet and work with the parents and guardians of children most in need of a strong home–school support network—single parents, those working at more than one job, those pulled in so many directions by so many problems that they are struggling just to survive. Often there is no easy way to solve these problems, but there is a place where teachers can find ideas about structuring time and have opportunities to encourage parents' participation in their children's educational lives. The **National Parent Information Network (NPIN)** is an online service supported by the ERIC Clearinghouses on Elementary and Early Childhood Education (ERIC/EECE) at the University of Illinois and on Urban Education at Columbia University (ERIC/CUE). NPIN provides access to information about raising and educating children and focuses on providing high-quality, easy-to-understand parenting. It is especially designed to reach out to and train low-income parents and people who work collaboratively with them to support children. See the NPIN home page (**http://ericps.ed.uiuc.edu/npin/ npinhome.html**). The NPIN Web site contains information on where to locate special services for children, the pros and cons of requiring uniforms in public schools, how to administer medication to children, what might be done to care for children on snowy days when school is out, research on the benefit of magnet schools, how older men fare as fathers, names and telephone numbers of people and organizations who promote children's and parents' issues, and more.

How ARE COLLABORATIVE NETWORKS TRANSFORMING THE PROFESSIONAL DEVELOPMENT OF TEACHERS?

The Holmes Group, an association of education deans from 93 research universities, has concentrated on reforming teacher education while others have worked to change life in elementary and secondary schools. Chief among the Holmes Group's initiatives has been a call for the establishment of "professional development schools." A **professional development school (PDS)** is a school devoted to the development of both novice and experienced professionals.

> In such schools, experienced teachers, conscious of membership in a profession, help teach and induct new members. Also, by pulling together and demonstrating their know-how, by questioning their

assumptions and routines, by taking part in research and development projects, they keep on learning to teach. They contribute their experience and wisdom to the profession's systematic fund of knowledge. (Holmes Group, 1995, p. vi)

William Johnson (1990) likens the notion of a professional development school to the image of the teacher promoted by John Dewey as an "interpreter of culture to active children, not the scientific classroom manager guiding children through hierarchically organized curricula" (1990, p. 584). Paul Dixon and Richard Ishler call the professional development school movement "the inventing of a new institution mixing the best of theory, research, and practice at the precollege level and among teacher preparatory programs" (1992, p. 28). The concept of a professional development school is very similar to what others have called a "professional practice school" (Levine, 1992).

How are new collaborative networks for teachers extending collegiality beyond school walls? What other collaborative networks are transforming American education?

Texas Tech, five schools in the Lubbock Independent School District, and Texas's Region 17 Education Service Center formed a professional development school in 1991. This PDS melds ideas from both the Holmes Group and the Accelerated Schools model. The PDS houses student teachers and students participating in other field experiences. Some elementary preservice courses are taught in one of the participating elementary schools, and public school teachers help teach these courses. Cadres of professors, school faculty, and service unit representatives are organized to address the PDS goals, which range from offering "family and health services as a natural extension of the school" to altering the "organizational structure and culture of the school" (Holmes Group, 1992).

Why is there not more collaboration between universities and public schools?

Researchers at the Center for Research on the Context of Teaching at Stanford University suggest that "teachers' professional communities—be they academic departments, schools, or teacher networks—are powerful mechanisms for stimulating innovation, reflection, experimentation, and reform" (McLaughlin & Talbert, 1993, p. 3). Despite many encouraging and highly visible attempts to foster collaboration between universities and public schools, however, people are probably more likely to read about such efforts than to experience them.

Advancing Subject Area Studies

Collaborative networks for teachers as professionals also focus on content areas and mutual professional development through collegial activities. In 1985 and 1986 the Ford Foundation targeted more than $6 million to 11 cities across the United States to establish collaborative networks of mathematics teachers, school administrators, and mathematicians from colleges and universities and industry. These 11 cities were Cleveland, Durham, Los Angeles, Memphis, Minneapolis-St. Paul, New Orleans, Philadelphia, Pittsburgh, St. Louis, San Diego, and San Francisco. Since 1990 four more cities have been added to the group—Dayton, Ohio; Columbus, Georgia; Worcester, Massachusetts; and Milwaukee, Wisconsin.

The networks have attempted to break teacher isolation and encourage professionalism by providing activities such as industrial internships for teachers, symposia, workshops, dinner meetings, and site visits (Wisconsin Center for Education Research, 1992). They have also funded trips to conferences and professional meetings for teachers.

Evaluation of the collaboratives' activities suggest that of the approximately 3,000 high school mathematics teachers in the original sites, about 20% have become frequent participants in activities offered at their sites. More than 80% of those teachers thought that the network had enriched their professional lives and that, in fact, they were valued by a larger community (Webb & Romborg, in press).

Enhancing Collegiality Among Educators

John Goodlad and others at the University of Washington have led efforts to institutionalize some new opportunities for teachers to interrelate as colleagues with common interests and to function cooperatively. Goodlad and his colleagues established the **National Network for Educational Renewal**, consisting of some 15 universities and 50 to 60 partner schools. The intent of this network is to simultaneously renew schools and teacher education. This means shifting the focus of reform from the management aspects of teaching and learning to the moral and political dimensions of the teaching profession itself (R. Soder, personal communication, August 24, 1993). Members of the National Network for Educational Renewal agree to address three goals:

> (1) to promote exemplary performance by universities in their role of educating educators; (2) to promote exemplary performance by schools in their role of educating the nation's young people; and (3) to promote constructive collaboration between schools (and their districts) and universities in assuring exemplary performance of overlapping mutual self-interests. (Goodlad, 1990, p. 324)

If educators are to pool their energies in creative ways for the good of students, Catherine Lugg and William Boyd argue that schools must organize themselves to encourage collegial interaction.

> We need to restructure our schools, following a "communitarian" rather than a bureaucratic model, if we are to make them better places for making connections between adults and young people. As an antidote to the fragmentation and depersonalization of our traditional "factory model" of schooling, our big schools need to be restructured into schools within schools, with teachers and students organized into "teams" of manageable size that work (and play) together for sustained periods of time—perhaps staying together as teams for two or three years so that strong interpersonal relationships can flourish. (1993, p. 253)

HOW CAN PROFESSIONAL EDUCATORS PREPARE FOR THE FUTURE?

It would be natural for educators to be overwhelmed by the complexity and pace of our rapidly changing world. There is so much to know, so much to do. Faced with the diversity of interests that contend for attention in public education, it would be easy to take one of two actions: leap headfirst into the maelstrom of problems or sit back, paralyzed with indecision. But professionals chart another course. They distinguish themselves from nonprofessionals in two important ways: by what they know and by what they know how to do. Those who continue to grow do so by participating in collaborative networks for the purposes shown in Figure 13.7, by building their store of knowledge and refining their repertoire of skills.

> **Can collaborative networks contribute to the professionalization of teaching?**

Using Professional Knowledge

Both informal and formal sources of knowledge inform the successful practice of teaching. The formal knowledge base of a profession exists in books, periodicals, and other writings. This knowledge serves as a foundation for teacher education programs, as a basis for licensure and certification examinations, and as a benchmark by which teachers gauge their own practice. The informal knowledge base is an uncodified body of knowledge that exists in the minds and hearts of those who practice the profession. For many teachers this personal source of knowledge can be richer and more immediately applicable than the recorded knowledge (Clandinin & Connelly, 1996).

The formal knowledge base for teaching consists of two general kinds of knowledge: theory-driven conceptions of effective teaching, and results of empirical research. These two kinds of knowledge often complement each other. Theory helps to explain how teaching and learning occur; research provides results of observations or experiments that help to explain relationships between teaching and learning. The most useful theories for educators explain what teachers should do and why (Joyce & Weil, 1996).

For example, Jean Piaget formulated a theory of intellectual development that has implications for guiding teachers' actions. (See Chapter 9.) He described intellectual development in terms of stages (sensorimotor, preoperational, concrete operational, formal operational). In his theory, the teacher's role is threefold: (1) to create environments where children can spontaneously construct knowledge for themselves in ways that match their stages of cognitive development, (2) to assess children's thinking, and (3) to organize group activities for social interaction among children (Wadsworth, 1978).

Other research and theory guide the use of different teaching strategies. Teachers who understand and can articulate the relationship between knowledge and practice demonstrate that they are ready to do their best and to do better as their knowledge improves. (One way to improve your knowledge

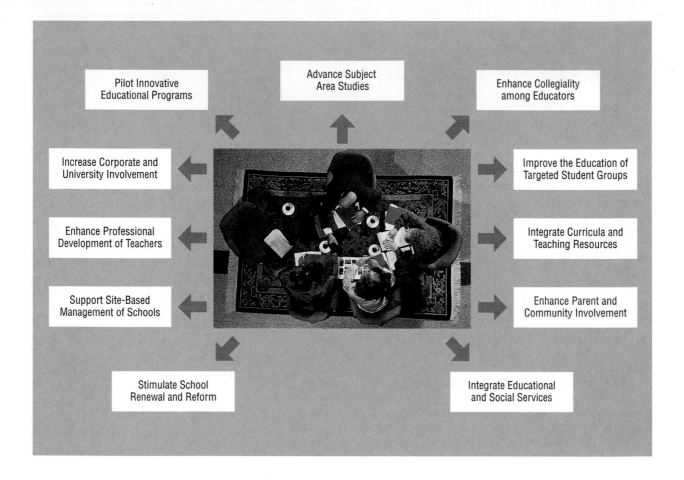

FIGURE 13.7

Uses of Collaborative Networks

People are more likely to collaborate when they have reasons to do so and opportunities for working together. What barriers, other than time and opportunity, might restrict collaboration among teachers? What other factors might enhance the likelihood of collaboration?

about education is to visit the National Library of Education online (**http://www.ed.gov/NLE**).

Harold Mitzel (1960) first described the empirical research on teaching in a way that made it accessible to practitioners. He gave us a way to think and talk about the knowledge underlying our field so that we could apply it and participate in its development. Mitzel depicted a set of four instructional variables to describe teaching and learning as interrelated activities. These instructional variables include presage characteristics, teaching processes, student products, and instructional contexts.

Presage characteristics are the characteristics of teachers that are said to presage, or precede, acts of teaching—for example, teachers' personalities and background knowledge. Teaching process variables are demonstrated by teachers during a lesson—the questions they ask, the feedback they provide, and the like. Student product variables are student outcomes measured by tests, demonstrations, applications of knowledge, and other measurable indications of learning. Instructional context variables are factors outside the classroom that impinge on teaching and learning, such as school leadership, money spent on education, and children's home environments. The relationships among these variables are shown in Figure 13.8.

Herbert Walberg (1991) summarized some 8,000 studies of teaching and learning in elementary and secondary schools to provide an overview of

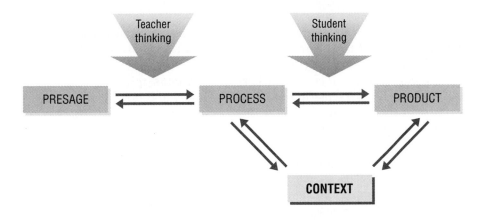

FIGURE 13.8

Model for Describing Research on Teaching

Research on teaching cannot be conducted without the help and cooperation of lots of people—teachers, students, parents, administrators. What factors might influence your willingness to participate in research studies either as an investigator or as the subject of investigation?

Note. Adapted from "Teacher Effectiveness: Criteria of Teacher Effectiveness" by H. E. Mitzel, 1960. In *Encyclopedia of Educational Research* (3rd ed.) (pp. 1481–1486) by C. S. Harris (Ed.) Copyright 1960 and renewed 1988, by American Research Association. Used by permission of Macmillan Publishing Company.

more and less effective educational practices. Using a statistical process of calculating "effect sizes," he revealed the relative power of different instructional behaviors to boost student achievement. For instance, Table 13.1 shows the greater effectiveness of using manipulative materials in the teaching of mathematics over problem-solving approaches and the new math of the 1960s and 1970s.

As Thomas Good and Jere Brophy (1994) have noted, current research builds on findings that indicate how important teachers are when it comes to stimulating student learning. This new research also focuses on the role of the student and recognizes that students do not passively receive or copy input from teachers.

> Instead they actively mediate it by trying to make sense of it and to relate it to what they already know (or think they know) about the topic. This is precisely what we want them to do, because unless students build representations of the new learning, "making it their own" by paraphrasing it in their own words and considering its meanings and implications, the learning will be retained only as relatively meaningless and inert rote memories. (1994, p. 414)

The teachers best prepared to face the future are those armed not only with empirical and theoretical knowledge but with practical knowledge of teaching, as well. This knowledge is constructed through teachers' own

TABLE 13.1 Effects of Mathematics Methods

Method	Number of Studies	Effect Size	Graphic Representation of Effect Size
Manipulative materials	64	1.04	.xxxxxxxxxx
Problem solving	33	0.34	.xxxx
New mathematics	134	0.24	.xx

Note. From *Effective Teaching: Current Research* (p. 58) by Hersholt C. Waxman and Herbert J. Wahlberg (Eds.), 1991, Berkeley, CA: McCutchan. Copyright 1991 by McCutchan Publishing Corporation, Berkeley, CA 94702. Permission granted by the publisher.

experiences. In many ways practical knowledge held tacitly by teachers is far ahead of theory and research. Teachers have always constructed their own knowledge by intuiting or experiencing what it takes to work with others to help them learn.

Researchers who focus on teachers' and students' thinking try to explain how teachers make sense out of what they know and how their knowledge influences their actions. Greta Morine-Dershimer (1990, 1992) and her colleagues suggest using concept maps—ways of organizing ideas about a particular topic so that relationships among subtopics can be displayed visually—to describe how teachers construct their own knowledge about effective teaching. As shown in Figure 13.9, a teacher's concept map is organized in concentric fashion. The farther a concept is from the hub, the less central it is to the teacher's thinking about effective teaching (Saunders & Tankersley, 1990).

Successful teachers possess both general and specific teaching knowledge but apply their knowledge differently with different students. Jere Brophy and Mary McCaslin (1992) underscore the importance of teaching to individual students' needs in a series of studies they did on teachers' perceptions of and strategies for dealing with "problem students" (students exhibiting unsatisfactory achievement, personal adjustment, or classroom behavior). Teachers who had been identified by their principals as less successful in

FIGURE 13.9

Construction of Knowledge About Effective Teaching: A Concept Map

What thoughts about planning seemed most important to this teacher?

Note. From "Choosing Among Alternatives for Tracing Conceptual Change" by G. Morine-Dershimer, S. Saunders, A. Artiles, M. Mostert, M. Tankersley, S. Trent, and D. Nuttycombe, 1992, *Teaching and Teacher Education, 8*(5/6), p. 473. Reprinted by permission from Elsevier Science Ltd., Pergamon Imprint, Oxford, England.

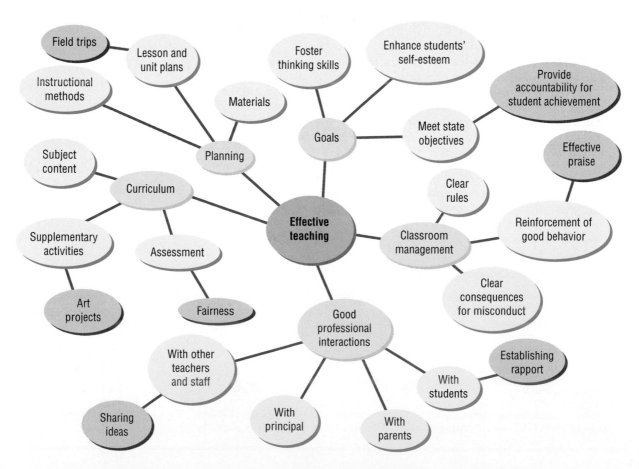

VOICES

On What Teachers Need to Know About Themselves to Be Successful

Old ways of thinking about teaching and about change in the way schools operate seem inadequate in these professionally challenging times. Deborah Meier (1992), educator and founder of the celebrated Central Park East Elementary School in New York City, suggests the kinds of lessons that teachers must learn if they are to serve students to the best of their abilities.

Since I began teaching, some twenty-five years ago, I have changed the way I think about what it means to be a good teacher. Today it is clear that since we need a new kind of school to do a new kind of job, we need a new kind of teacher too.

The schools we need require different habits of work and habits of mind on the part of teachers—a kind of professionalism within the classroom few teachers were expected to exhibit before. In addition, to get from where we are now to where we need to be will require teachers to play a substantially different role within their schools as well as in public discourse. Teachers need to relearn what it means to be good in-school practitioners, while also becoming more articulate and self-confident spokespeople for the difficult and often anxiety-producing changes schools are expected to undertake. If teachers are not able to join in leading such changes, the changes will not take place.

The lessons drawn from sixteen or more years of school experience as a student remain largely intact and dictate the way most people handle their role as teachers. This is hardly surprising. Many of those who enter teaching hope to do unto others what the teachers they knew and loved did unto them. . . . [I]n most cases the constraints of the job, plus old habits and a kind of societal nostalgia for what school "used to be like," make teachers part of the broader inertia that makes fundamental change hard to implement.

The habits of schooling are deep, powerful, and hard to budge. No public institution is more deeply entrenched in habitual behavior than schools—and for good reason. Aside from our many years of direct experience as students, we have books, movies, television shows, advertisements, and myriad other activities, games, and symbols that reinforce our view of what school is "supposed" to be.

If I could choose five qualities to look for in prospective teachers they would be: (1) a self-conscious reflectiveness about how they themselves learn and, maybe even more, how and when they do not learn; (2) a sympathy toward others, an appreciation of their differences, an ability to imagine their "otherness"; (3) a willingness to engage in, better yet a taste for, collaborative work; (4) a desire to have others [with whom] to share some of one's own interests; and (5) a lot of perseverance, energy, and devotion to getting things right.

CRITICAL THINKING

Meier speaks of the "often anxiety-producing changes schools are expected to undertake." What specific changes do you think she has in mind? How do you think you would measure up on Meier's five qualities? Has she left out any important qualities? If so, which ones?

Note. From "Reinventing teaching" by D. Meier, 1992, *Teachers College Record, 93*(4), 594–609. Reprinted by permission.

dealing with "problem students" described those students as underachievers, low achievers, aggressive, defiant, distractible, immature, shy, or rejected by peers. Brophy and McCaslin found no magic formula for teaching problem students, but they did identify some notable differences between successful and unsuccessful teachers. Typically, successful teachers demonstrated more willingness to become personally involved with students, showed more confidence in their own abilities to help the students improve their behaviors, and were better able to articulate strategies for helping students to change their behavior and increase their learning.

What teachers need to know about teaching is also closely allied to their disciplines. It is not enough to possess general teaching knowledge at the expense of content knowledge any more than it is to know the content and be ignorant of teaching. To teach mathematics successfully, for example, a teacher must master the subject matter but must also possess the teaching knowledge necessary for creating environments where students can learn mathematics. This blending of content knowledge and teaching knowledge has been called **pedagogical content knowledge** (Shulman, 1986).

Reflecting on Professional Practice

Throughout this text we have encouraged the idea that the best preparation for a future in teaching is to learn from work on the job. Those who can reflect intelligently on practice have the greatest chance of continuing to progress as teachers. Reflection is also a springboard toward greater professional self-determination. Reflection is the basis of the five steps of professional practice that this text teaches and tries to model.

In any field, professionals *perceive* problems and opportunities, because they are awake—they are mentally alert to what is going on around them.

Competent and respected professionals also can articulate their *values* in relation to the values of others they work with and serve. Values drive actions, and professionals must be prepared to deal with differences in values in constructive ways.

In addition, professionals possess some specialized knowledge that nonprofessionals do not. Professional educators *know* their content, and they know how to communicate in ways that students will understand and accept. They possess a great deal of knowledge about teaching and learning. Exceptionally talented teachers, both experienced and novice, also often know when they need to know more. They become lifelong learners in pursuit of their development as professionals.

Acting on the basis of one's perceptions, values, and knowledge is the bread-and-butter of professional life. Professionals continually apply their knowledge and perform their skills in ways that nonprofessionals cannot.

Finally, professionals *evaluate* their actions to determine their effectiveness and to plan for the future. People who can reflect intelligently on their practice—and who enjoy doing important work as best they can—turn jobs into careers.

Teachers are students too. Even the best among us do not always know how or why we are successful. With experience, however, we grow accustomed to not having all the answers and to relying, instead, on the best information available about teaching and learning—information acquired from successful and unsuccessful practice. No matter how professionally capable or personally adept teachers become, we will never single-handedly teach our students all that they need to know and be able to do. Nor can we anticipate all of the problems students will face. We must learn to work together with others, to work democratically, if we hope to maximize our effects. And the most important people with whom we must learn to collaborate are the students. By working together we model for students what we hope they in turn will model for others. We also transmit a set of democratic values that is the cultural bedrock of our society.

The best teachers stretch themselves time and again to be creative and technically proficient; they know they can call on their abilities when the need arises. They are not afraid to fail, because they have done that too and have lived to teach and learn another day. A good teacher, like a good student, gains power from doing the work.

SUMMARY

What trends are changing teachers' professional roles?

1 The role of teacher is changing because of public attention to a variety of educational factors—performance standards, goals, instructional objectives, curriculum, measurable student outcomes, concepts of minimum competence and comprehensive assessment, as well as students' opportunities to learn the material for which they will be held accountable.

2 Minimum competency tests and other high-stakes tests focus educators and the lay public on educational outcomes, or what students know and can do. Some people argue that if such tests are to be used to hold students accountable, then school systems must be held accountable for providing opportunities for students to learn.

3 There are several notable efforts to change how students are taught and assessed: integrating curriculum rather than simply adding more information; assessing students' skills, knowledge, and attitudes using comprehensive measures; and making assessment reflect what students must be able to do and how they will need to behave in real life if they are to be successful.

4 A number of other trends also promise to alter the role of teacher, including gender issues, inclusion of students with disabilities in general education classrooms, and attention to the character education of children in the forms of service learning and environmental education.

How are new links to technology changing the foundations of education?

5 Technology can be integrated into content area instruction or taught as tools to perform tasks. Technology can promote an active role for students by encouraging them to use technology to construct meaning for themselves and to solve complex problems. Technology also can be used to facilitate an integrated or multidisciplinary approach to teaching and learning involving a broad range of skills. Technology can enhance interactions among students, providing the benefits of cooperative learning.

6 Technology in the hands of ordinary people is democratizing the foundations of education, because technology brings opportunities for a person anywhere with a computer and a telephone line to make, acquire, interpret, and apply knowledge. Technology also forces people to look forward, to anticipate not only what is important at the moment but what is likely to be important later.

How are collaborative networks transforming teaching and learning?

7 Collaborative networks of parents, educators, business leaders, government bureaucrats, etc., are at the hub of efforts to improve the education of targeted student groups, such as students at risk of school failure. Other collaborative networks intent on changing current educational practice target schools and subject matter areas.

How are collaborative networks transforming the professional development of teachers?

8 Professional development schools represent one approach to advancing the development of teachers. These organizations are meant to function much as teaching hospitals in the medical field, or to be places where novice and experienced professionals work together to demonstrate and share their expertise.

9 Collaborative networks for teachers as professionals also focus on content areas and mutual professional development through collegial activities. These networks try to break teacher isolation and encourage professionalism by providing activities such as industrial internships for teachers, symposia, workshops, dinner meetings, site visits, conferences, and professional meetings for teachers.

How can professional educators prepare for the future?

10 Professional teachers prepare themselves to continue learning by steeping themselves in the foundational knowledge base of the profession—knowledge that emanates from many sources, including theory, research, and practice.

11 The teachers best prepared to continue learning on the job are those who can reflect on their work. Reflection means recognizing issues, taking perspectives or examining values, calling up relevant professional knowledge upon which to base one's actions, taking such actions, and evaluating their effects.

TERMS AND CONCEPTS

Accelerated Schools, *p. 513*
America 2000, *p. 514*
character education, *p. 503*
Coalition of Essential Schools, *p. 516*
collaborative network, *p. 513*
comprehensive assessment, *p. 500*
distance learning, *p. 507*
electronic mail (e-mail), *p. 507*
file transfer protocol (FTP), *p. 507*
gender sensitivity training, *p. 501*
high stakes test, *p. 499*
home page, *p. 507*
hypermedia, *p. 507*
Internet, *p. 506*
listserv, *p. 507*
literacy, *p. 498*
minimum competency test, *p. 498*
modem, *p. 507*

National Network for Educational
    Renewal, *p. 520*
National Parent Information
    Network (NPIN), *p. 518*
New American Schools Develop-
    ment Corporation (NASDC)
    p. 514
news groups *p. 507*
opportunity-to-learn (OTL)
    standards, *p. 499*
pedagogical content knowledge,
    p. 526
professional development school,
    p. 518
service learning, *p. 504*
standards, *p. 495*
Web browser, *p. 507*
World Wide Web, *p. 507*

REFLECTIVE PRACTICE

In the following case, Sarah, a classroom teacher, attends a faculty meeting on teachers' use of lab computers. After reading this case, apply the steps of professional practice as outlined in the questions that follow.

> After students left for the day, Sarah returned to her classroom, exhausted and frustrated. She wondered what she might do to minimize the difficulty she experienced when conducting a structured computer activity. She wasn't sure how to remedy that with all the other demands on her time. Tom Howard doubled as the computer coordinator. He had already been generous with his time, and she didn't feel right about asking for more. Sarah wished there were other support for teachers.

> As she was straightening her classroom and preparing to return to the computer lab, the intercom came to life with a squeal and a thump. Mr. Greenway addressed the faculty:

> "Good afternoon teachers! Our faculty meeting will begin promptly in 10 minutes. Refreshments are available in the conference room. Please come now and grab a bite to eat so that we can begin and end on time."

> Sarah had forgotten there was a meeting this afternoon. All she wanted to do was to go home and relax before dinner. She had planned to do some errands and make a couple of calls to parents, which would consume most of her evening. . . .

Mr. Greenway began the meeting soon after Sarah arrived by reading a letter from a parent, praising teachers for providing a nurturing environment for students at Andrew Jackson. As the meeting continued, Sarah struggled to keep her mind focused on the topic of discussion until Mr. Greenway mentioned a concern about the computer lab.

"It has come to my attention that the computers in the lab are being used inappropriately. When we were asked last year to identify our greatest need, everyone agreed on more computers for instruction. As all of you know, funding for the three computers needed to complete the lab was provided in large part by the PTA. Now that we have the computers we asked for, it is time that we begin integrating them into our instructional program, not using them for fun and games."

Mr. Greenway continued: "Specifically, I want each grade-level team to meet in the next couple of weeks to establish goals for using computers to supplement instruction. I will be working with Tom and a few others to develop inservice programs to address some existing training needs. All faculty will be expected to attend. When you do develop computer-related projects, be sure to showcase them when parents visit. Products developed by children on computers should be set out for parents to see on PTA nights and on other special occasions. If you are not taking your class to the lab on a weekly basis, do so. There is a schedule on the lab door. Just sign up for an open block. Finally, when you take your class to the lab, you should be prepared to teach a lesson that makes meaningful use of the applications available on those computers. I do not want to hear of teachers taking their classes to the lab to play while they grade papers. The computer lab was set up at great expense to function as an educational resource to our students. It was not intended to be a video arcade."

Immediately Sarah recalled Mr. Harris's visit to the lab. (He was the father of one of her students.) She drove home after the meeting, worried that Mr. Harris had complained to Mr. Greenway about students playing games on the computer. If so, Sarah wondered, what, if anything, she should do to rectify the situation. She also wondered what counted as "instructional use" of computers. Would Mr. Greenway perceive keyboarding as frivolous activity? Sarah felt like a first-year teacher all over again.

Note. From "The webs we weave" by F. Becker 1996. In *Contemporary Issues: Interdisciplinary teaching and learning.* Washington, DC: The Hitachi Foundation. [Online] Available: **http://curry.edschool.Virginia.EDU/go/casecourse**.

Issues, Problems, Dilemmas, and Opportunities

Identify as many problems and issues as you can in this brief episode, and try to group them as "chronic" and "acute." Chronic problems tend to persist and are not easily resolved, while acute problems require immediate attention.

Perceive and Value

Think about this situation from Sarah's point of view. Why might she feel like a first-year teacher again? What, specifically, might Sarah be thinking as she muses about the need for "other support" for teachers?

Think about the situation from Mr. Greenway's point of view. Why might Mr. Greenway be so concerned about making "meaningful use of the applications available on [the] computers"? And why is he so concerned about showcasing students' work?

If you were Mr. Harris or the parent of another child in Sarah's room, what might lead you to think that too much time is spent playing games on the computers? As a parent, what actions might you take if you were concerned about this possibility?

Know and Act

What would Sarah need to know to address the problems you identified as acute? How could she best obtain the information she would need to address those problems effectively?

Assume that you are Sarah. What might you do to address the problem you identified as most acute, and what rationale would you develop for your action? Answer in first person, as if you were Sarah (e.g., "I would call Mr. Harris and invite him to our classroom as soon as possible").

Evaluate

What might be some positive and negative consequences of the particular actions you identified in the previous paragraph? For instance, if you immediately invited Mr. Harris to your classroom, and your students or you were unprepared for his visit, his perceptions might go from bad to worse. On the other hand, if Mr. Harris came to your class and saw the students working together on computers to study some interesting and important content, his impressions might improve.

Use the case as the basis for an essay in which you (1) tie your judgments to your actions, (2) consider that most actions typically have both positive and negative consequences, and (3) speculate on several different ways to judge success.

ONLINE ACTIVITY

Conduct a search on the Web for any one or more of the Terms and Concepts listed in this chapter. In all but a few instances you will find direct references to the terms. In those few for which you find little or no direct reference, you will want (1) to narrow your search, using more specific key words (as in the case of *home page*); or (2) add another word to modify a term (e.g., add *educational* to *standards*). In one or maybe two instances, you will find no relevant reference—can you guess with which terms you might come up empty-handed? How else might you seek online information on these terms?

Learning how to work effectively to involve parents in school activities is a critical part of a teacher's job. Regardless of how experienced they may be, professional teachers cannot be expected to have all the necessary ideas for forming and maintaining successful collaborations with parents. Go to the NPIN homepage **http://ericps.ed.uiuc.edu/npin/npinhome.html** and identify some specific Internet resources for parents and for those who work with parents.

CASE 4

Newcomers High School

I *see people coming to this country aspiring to become somebody, to help themselves and to help people around them. The biggest challenge for me as a teacher is to make their life easier, better than it was for me.*

Constantin Parv, a former Rumanian speed skater, immigrated to the United States in 1989. He began almost immediately coaching gymnastics and shortly thereafter teaching as a substitute in physical education classes in the New York City public schools. He now teaches full time at Newcomers High School in the borough of Queens.

Newcomers High School has an unusual mission: to serve as an academy for new Americans, easing their transition into life in the United States. In order to enroll at Newcomers, a student must not have resided in this country for more than 1 year. The school opened in the fall of 1995 with approximately 60 students. By the spring of 1996, the enrollment approached 600 students.

Perhaps because Constantin Parv immigrated recently to the United States, he *recognizes issues* unique to the special character of Newcomers' student body.

I *have a class where students are coming from countries that don't have formal physical education programs. They don't know about playing ball or working together. They can't handle free play. I have to be formal and emphasize rules and routines.*

Parv has little difficulty *taking others' perspectives* who have recently arrived in this country.

I *want to see these students succeeding in New York. I want them to be familiar, to be at home. That means they must be able to communicate well, to function properly in any New York high school. They should feel at home in their country.*

No doubt Parv's own highly disciplined training for international athletic competition, under the tutelage of demanding coaches, helped form his beliefs about teaching and learning. He worries, however, that the conception

of *professional knowledge* that governs his new life as a teacher in the New York schools may cost him his job.

When I came here I took those NTE tests. In Rumania and other countries you have to take special tests in physical education. There is a specific test for each kind of teacher. The main point is to be a physical education teacher. I don't think it is fair for all teachers to have to take the same test. Why don't other teachers have to do what I'm doing on the bars, in judo, and gymnastics? Other teachers don't have to do what I do.

Parv, like teachers everywhere, relies heavily on his own conception of professional knowledge to guide his actions.

Teaching cannot work unless you have a disciplined class. A teacher must know how to manage the class. Discipline and routine is part of managing and teaching the class.

Regardless of how he performs on standardized tests of teaching knowledge, Parv must still be able to *take action* to help his students succeed in his classes.

These kids coming to us are not familiar with our techniques. When you teach in an American program, most kids are already familiar with our methods. As a teacher I have to take my time and explain, explain, explain.

For Parv, the *evaluation* of teaching and learning must be done almost exclusively in terms of student understanding. He does not expect all students to excel athletically in his classes; however, he does want them to understand what they are supposed to do and why.

Kids at Newcomers learn as fast as kids anywhere in New York. The only difference is that they are not familiar with our techniques. I have to take my time so they comprehend what they are supposed to do.

CASE APPLICATION

■ What factors might Constantin Parv consider as he selects curriculum and adapts instruction to fit his students' needs?

■ What special legal constraints—restrictions outside normal or typical expectations —if any, might come into play in a place like Newcomers High School?

■ If you taught at Newcomers High School, how might you encourage attention to global and comparative educational issues?

■ Constantin Parv stresses the importance of students learning to speak English. "That's the bottom line: If you speak English you are going to speak to society." If you taught mathematics, chemistry, physical education, or any other subject at Newcomers High School, would you also be willing to assume some responsibility for teaching English in the context of your classes? Why or why not?

■ If you taught at Newcomers High School, would you define the success and failure of your efforts any differently than if you taught in a typical or mainstream high school elsewhere in the nation? If so, how might you define successful teaching in this unusual setting?

APPENDIX

The Praxis Series: Professional Assessments for Beginning Teachers™

From Preparation Through Performance

The Praxis Series offers assessments for each stage of the beginning teacher's career, from entry into teacher education to actual classroom performance.

Praxis I tests skills in reading, writing, and mathematics that all teachers need, regardless of grade or subject taught.

Praxis II measures candidates' knowledge of the subjects they will teach.

Praxis III judges teaching skill in the classroom through the use of local assessors.

Praxis I	Praxis II	Praxis III
Academic Skills Assessments	Subject Assessments	Classroom Performance Assessments

Designed with State Licensing Requirements in Mind

The Praxis Series provides nationally available tests in a choice of formats. The series' built-in flexibility helps states meet specific licensing requirements for beginning teachers and other educational professionals. The series integrates current tests with newly developed assessments to measure key areas of competence.

Research Based

Each assessment is founded on extensive research, including analysis of tasks considered important for beginning teachers. These job analyses involved thousands of teachers, teacher educators, administrators, and educational policymakers.

Note. From *21st century teacher assessments*. Educational Testing Service, 1992. Princeton, NJ: Author.

Innovative Assessment Formats

In addition to multiple-choice questions, many tests in the series feature candidate-constructed-response questions, requiring examinees to produce their own answers.

The computer-based assessments introduce *adaptive testing*. The computer creates a unique test geared to the test-taker's performance level. The computer-based assessments also allow candidates to use *built-in calculators and word processors.*

The Classroom Performance component recognizes the unique nature of every teacher and every teaching situation. It uses an *integrated framework* of criteria reflecting the complex nature of teaching. This component includes a training program to prepare local assessors to make informed judgments about beginning teachers' performance.

Cost-Saving Validation Procedures

Before new tests are assembled, ETS submits all questions to multistate validation panels. Because ETS underwrites the cost of these studies, states save both time and money. Since only questions validated by these panels of practicing professionals are assembled into tests, states can be confident that all questions in all tests have been approved for use.

A closer look . . .

PRAXIS I: Academic Skills Assessments

Should entry-level teachers be able to determine the main point of the reading selection? Organize ideas clearly and effectively? Interpret tables and graphs?

ETS analyzed surveys from almost 3,000 teachers, teacher educators, administrators and other professionals to determine what skills they considered important for beginning teachers.

Based on their comments and extensive research, ETS has created Academic Skills Assessments in reading, writing, and mathematics.

These tests, designed to be taken early in the candidate's college career, determine that prospective teachers have the enabling skills they need for their profession.

Praxis I offers two testing formats, both of which are linked to a new, computer-delivered structural package.

Computer-Based Academic Skills Assessments

- Computer delivered—expands range of question types to include multiple response, highlighting, fill-ins, reordering, and candidate-constructed response

- Computer adaptive—tailors tests to suit candidates' performance

- Technologically advanced—includes built-in calculator and word processor

- Flexible administration—scheduled to accomodate candidates' needs.

Pre-Professional Skills Tests (PPST)

- Paper-and-pencil format requires no special equipment

- Convenient scheduling, administered eight times a year

- Revised and linked to job analysis

LearningPlus™—Computer-Delivered Instructional Package

To help teacher candidates who may need to improve certain basic academic skills and to help increase access to the profession, ETS has developed a new computer-delivered instructional package—**LearningPlus™: Computer-Based Learning of Skills and Strategies.**

Based on contemporary learning theory and research identifying important enabling skills for entry level teachers, LearningPlus™ is individualized to match each student's needs:

- Covers skills in reading, writing, and mathematics tested in Praxis I

- Leads candidates to specific lessons through diagnostic skills profiles

- Provides 20 to 30 hours of instruction in each subject

- Focuses on strategies for learning, ways of organizing knowledge, and development of skills

- Links instruction to both the revised Pre-Professional Skills Tests and the new Computer-Based Academics Skills Assessments

Here's How It Works . . .

1. A familiarization program introduces students to computer and mouse functions and to the built-in assistance of a calculator and word processor.

2. Students then take a diagnostic skills profile.

3. Students are directed to computer-delivered lessons in specific areas as needed. They are led through learning programs that gradually remove instructional assistance as students' skills improve.

4. Immediate feedback lets students decide if they're ready for the actual test or need to review certain skills.

5. Students may receive between 20 and 30 hours of instruction in each of the three areas—reading, writing, and mathematics.

6. Lessons are modular. Students take only those identified by diagnostic skills profiles.

7. Many different examples are included. Candidates can review one skills area a number of times without repeating material.

8. Materials may be used in a learning lab.

9. Practice tests help candidates decide when they are ready for the actual test.

More than 70 subjects covered . . .

PRAXIS II: Subject Assessments

ETS offers states new modular Subject Assessments for measuring teaching candidates' understanding of the subjects they will teach.

These tests give states great flexibility in meeting their individual licensing requirements.

- Before beginning development of these new tests, ETS considered state licensing content area requirements.

- Teachers, teacher educators, and other professionals were involved throughout the evolution of the individual assessments.

- Test developers were guided by results of extensive job analysis.

- Constructed-response modules target skills and knowledge difficult to assess through multiple choice tests. They allow candidates to demonstrate in-depth understanding and reinforce the importance of writing within the teaching profession.

- Modular subject area tests give states maximum flexibility.

For example:

The Spanish Assessment features a 2-hour multiple-choice core and two optional candidate-constructed response modules—productive language skills and pedagogy. In the Mathematics Assessment, the 2-hour multiple-choice core is supported by four optional modules—multiple-choice advanced content; proofs, models, and problems (levels 1 and 2); and pedagogy.

The optional modules in each area give states maximum flexibility in tailoring their assessments to meet their specific licensure requirements.

- The content core is central to each nationally available subject assessment.

- Optional modules focus on particular aspects of the subject or on ways of teaching the subject.

- Modular options differ from test to test. For example, in addition to a 2-hour multiple choice core in social studies, a state might choose one or more candidate-constructed-response modules covering analysis, interpretation, and how to teach the subject.

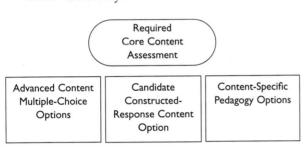

Required Core Content Module

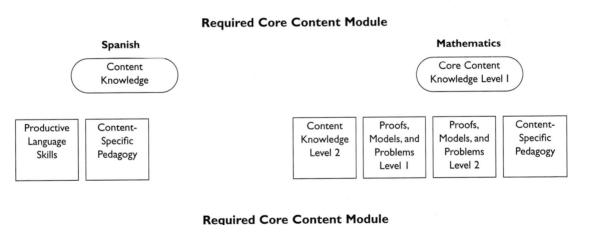

Required Core Content Module

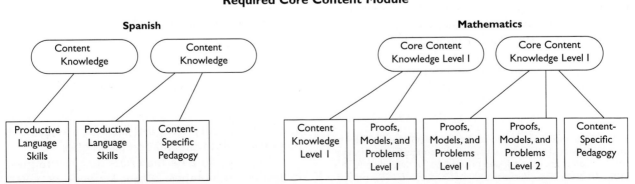

- ETS is underwriting the costs of multistate validity studies for these new assessments.
- Expanded and improved study guides will offer test-taking tips, test-content specifications, and sample questions.

Modular Subject Assessments* Available for Adoption:

- Art
- Biology
- Chemistry
- Elementary Education
- English Language, Literature, and Composition
- French
- General Science
- Mathematics
- Music
- Physical Education
- Physical Sciences
- Physics
- Principles of Learning and Teaching
- Spanish
- Social Studies

Combinations of assessments—for example, Biology and General Science—are also possible.

Subject Area Tests Cover a Wide Range of Topics

Many additional subject assessments are available for adoption. Covering subjects from Audiology through Technology Education, these tests may combine questions on subject knowledge and items covering content-specific pedagogy.

Specialties, such as Teaching English as a Second Language, and non-teaching specialties, including School Guidance and Counseling, School Psychologist, and School Social Worker, are also available.

*Some of the candidate-constructed-response modules in these tests were developed jointly by Educational Testing Service and the California Commission on Teacher Credentialing (CTC) in the Content Area Performance Assessment (CAPA) project.

Core Battery Tests

Tests covering Communication Skills, General Knowledge, and Professional Skills are available. These multiple-choice tests may be used together, individually, or in combination with other subject assessments.

ETS Field Marketing Representatives will work with state licensing boards to create a system of tests suited to state licensing requirements.

Teaching for student learning . . .

Praxis III: Classroom Performance Assessment

ETS has responded to increasing state emphasis on teachers' performance in the classroom and one criterion for licensing.

The development of the performance assessment has been guided by a conception of teaching that reflects the complexity of the classroom environment, sensitivity to individual student needs, awareness of multicultural issues, differing requirements for different subjects, and an understanding of teaching. The assessment recognizes the need for teachers to be judged on their ability to make thoughtful decisions, then put them into action.

Through job analysis, research reviews, and extensive discussions with educators drawn from the entire educational spectrum, the ETS development team and a group of practicing educators created a comprehensive performance assessment that

- provides training for local assessors;
- uses a framework of criteria and assessment strategies to judge beginning teachers in an in-school setting; and
- combines in-class assessment with documentation and pre- and post-observation interviews.

Training Local Assessors

The foundation of the performance assessment is the training program.

The ETS training program introduces local assessors to state-accepted criteria, assessment methods, and documentation techniques.

Use of up-to-date materials and techniques, including videotapes, allow trainees to make judgments about observed behaviors and to confirm their judgments through expert critiques.

Beginning teachers benefit from the use of consistent framework, orientation to the criteria, and state-determined feedback.

National Scope . . . Adapted for Individual States

ETS has spent more than five years developing this comprehensive system for the testing and licensing of beginning teachers. Advisory committees of teachers, teacher educators, administrators, professional organizations, and many other constituencies offered their candid evaluations of current testing programs and their ideas about teacher licensing assessments.

The methodologically advanced test formulas are based on the latest research. The participation of thousands of teaching professionals in extensive job analysis has ensured assessments that accurately reflect the skills required of beginning teachers.

What this means for the states . . .

- Assessments based on job-relevant knowledge and skills

- Test-development expertise of seasoned teachers and key educators

- Flexibility, with options designed to fit the licensing needs of states concerned with the competence of entry-level teachers

- Commitment to minority representation at every stage of development and validation

- Ongoing review by external committees

- A new academic skills instructional package that opens doors to those who may need additional preparation

- Cost savings through ETS-conducted multistate validity studies.

The Praxis Series Users Chart (as of April 15, 1995)

The Praxis Series is responsible for the development, administration, scoring, and reporting of its tests. Policies regarding their use or the setting of qualifying scores are established by the score users or score recipients. Questions about the development and administration of the Praxis Series tests should be addressed to The Praxis Series Office. Questions regarding admission, certification, or other requirements should be addressed to the appropriate state agency, association, or organization office. Please note that the requirements are periodically revised. The requirements of individual colleges and school districts may differ from state requirements. The Praxis Series is not responsible for incorrect information that examinees may receive from agencies that require its tests. Please note that the first digit in each test code indicates the session during which the test is offered.

NTE CORE BATTERY TESTS	AR	CA	CT	DE	DC	FL	HI	ID	IN	KS	KY	LA	ME	MD	MN
General Knowledge (10510)								●	●		●	●	●	●	
Communication Skills (20500)								●	●		●	●	●	●	
Professional Knowledge (30520)	●					★		●	●	●	●	●	●	●	

PRINCIPLES OF LEARNING AND TEACHING	AR	CA	CT	DE	DC	FL	HI	ID	IN	KS	KY	LA	ME	MD	MN
PLT: Grades K–6 (30522)							●								
PLT: Grades 7–12 (30524)							●								

MULTIPLE SUBJECTS ASSESSMENT FOR TEACHERS	AR	CA	CT	DE	DC	FL	HI	ID	IN	KS	KY	LA	ME	MD	MN
Content Knowledge (10140)		●													
Content Area Exercises (20151)		●													

PRAXIS 1: ACADEMIC SKILLS ASSESSMENTS	AR	CA	CT	DE	DC	FL	HI	ID	IN	KS	KY	LA	ME	MD	MN
Pre-Professional Skills Tests: Mathematics (10730)	●			●	●	★	●			●			●		●
Pre-Professional Skills Tests: Reading (10710)	●			●	●	★	●			●			●		
Pre-Professional Skills Tests: Writing (20720)	●			●	●	★	●			●			●		●
Computer-based Test: Mathematics	x		●	x	x	★	x						x		x
Computer-based Test: Reading	x		●	x	x	★	x						x		x
Computer-based Test: Writing	x		●	x	x	★	x						x		x

PRAXIS 11: SUBJECT ASSESSMENTS & NTE SPECIALITY AREA TESTS	AR	CA	CT	DE	DC	FL	HI	ID	IN	KS	KY	LA	ME	MD	MN
Accounting (PA) (10791)															
Agriculture (10700)											●				
Agriculture (CA)(10900)		●													
Agriculture (PA) (10780)			●												
Art: Content Knowledge (10133)							●								
Art: Content, Traditions, Criticism, & Aesthetics (20132)		●	●				●								
Art Education (10130)	●		●						●		●			●	
Art Making (20131)		●	●												
Audiology (10340)															
Biology (10230)				●					●					●	
Biology: Content Essays (30233)		●		★			★				★				
Biology: Content Knowledge, Part 1 (20231)				★	●		●				★				
Biology: Content Knowledge, Part 2 (20232)					●		★								
Biology: Pedagogy (30234)				★	●		★								
Biology & General Science (10030)	●								●		●	●		●	
Business Education (10100)	●	●	●				●		●		●	●		●	
Chemistry (10240)				●					●					●	
Chemistry: Content Essays (30242)		●	●	★											
Chemistry: Content Knowledge (20241)				★	●		★				★				
Chemistry, Physics, & General Science (10070)	●										●	●		●	
Communication (10800)															
Computer Literacy/Data Processing (10650)															
Cooperative Education (10810)															

MS	MO	MT	NE	NV	NJ	NM	NY	NC	OH	OK	OR	PA	RI	SC	TN	VA	WV	WI	ASHA	CAE	DDDS	NASP	NASW
●		●			●	●	○	●				●	●		●	●				●			
●		●				●	○					●	●		●	●				●	●		
●	●	●	●			●	○	●	●		●	●	●	●	●	●					●		

MS	MO	MT	NE	NV	NJ	NM	NY	NC	OH	OK	OR	PA	RI	SC	TN	VA	WV	WI	ASHA	CAE	DDDS	NASP	NASW
							★																
							★																

MS	MO	MT	NE	NV	NJ	NM	NY	NC	OH	OK	OR	PA	RI	SC	TN	VA	WV	WI	ASHA	CAE	DDDS	NASP	NASW
							●																
							★																

MS	MO	MT	NE	NV	NJ	NM	NY	NC	OH	OK	OR	PA	RI	SC	TN	VA	WV	WI	ASHA	CAE	DDDS	NASP	NASW
★			●	●				●	●	●					●		●	●		●	●		
★			●	●				●	●	●					●		●	●		●	●		
★			●	●				●	●	●					●		●	●		●		●	
★			x	x				x		x					x		x	x		x			
★			x	x				x		x					x		x	x		x			
★			x	x				x		x					x		x	x		x			

MS	MO	MT	NE	NV	NJ	NM	NY	NC	OH	OK	OR	PA	RI	SC	TN	VA	WV	WI	ASHA	CAE	DDDS	NASP	NASW
											●												
	●														●								
											●												
												●											
											★												
											★												
●	●				●			●	●		●	●			●	●							
											★												
●								●	●									●					
●	●								●			●			○	●							
								●			●				★								
				★				●			●				★								
				●							●												
				★				●			●				★								
●			●						●			●		●	●								
●	●		●	●				●	●		●			●	●	●							
●	●								●			●			○	●							
								●			●				★								
						●		●			●				★								
●			●						●			●		●	●								
												●											
●																							
												●											

PRAXIS II: SUBJECT ASSESSMENTS & NTE PROGRAMS SPECIALITY AREA TESTS	AR	CA	CT	DE	DC	FL	HI	ID	IN	KS	KY	LA	ME	MD	MN
Data Processing (PA) (10792)															
Early Childhood Education (10020)	●				●	★			●		●	●		●	
Earth Science: Content Knowledge (20571)															
Earth/Space Science (20570)			●	★					●						
Economics (20910)									●						
Education in the Elementary School (20010)	●					★			●		●	●		●	
Education of Students with Mental Retardation (10320)						★			●			●			
Education Leadership: Administration & Supervision (10410)	●										●	●			
Elementary Educ.: Content Area Exercises (20012)				★	●		★								
Elementary Educ.: Curriculum, Instruction, & Assessment (10011)				★	●	★	●								
English Language & Literature (10040)	●								●		●	●		●	
English Language, Lit., & Composition: Content Knowledge (10041)			●	★	●	★	●				★				
English Language, Lit., & Composition: Essays (20042)		●	●	★							★				
English Language, Lit., & Composition: Pedagogy (30043)				★	●		●								
Environmental Education (10830)															
Foreign Language Pedagogy (10840)															
French (10170)	●		●		●				●		●	●		●	
French: Content Knowledge (10173)							●								
French: Linguistic, Literary, & Cultural Analysis (30172)		●													
French: Productive Language Skills (20171)		●	●				●								
General Science (10430)			●						●						
General Science: Content Essays (30433)		●		★			★								
General Science: Content Knowledge, Part 1 (10431)					●		●								
General Science: Content Knowledge, Part 2 (10432)				★	●		★				★				
Geography (20920)									●						
German (20180)		●	●				●		●		●	●		●	
German: Content Knowledge (20181)															
Government/Political Science (20930)									●						
Health & Physical Education (10850)															
Health Education (10550)	●		●						●						
Home Economics Education (10120)	●	●	●				●		●		●	●		●	
Introduction to the Teaching of Reading (10200)	●	●		★					●						
Italian (10620)			●												
Japanese (10660)															
Latin (10600)			●												
Library Media Specialist (10310)	●								●		●	●		●	
Marketing Education (10560)	●														
Marketing (PA) (10793)															
Mathematics (10060)	●		●			★			●		●	●		●	
Mathematics: Content Knowledge (10061)				★	●		●				★				
Mathematics: Pedagogy (20065)				★	●		●								
Mathematics: Proofs, Models, & Problems. Part 1 (20063)		●		★	●						★				
Mathematics: Proofs, Models, & Problems. Part 2 (30064)		●													
Music Education (10110)	●		●						●		●	●		●	
Music: Analysis (20112)		●													
Music: Concepts & Processes (30111)		●					●								
Music: Content Knowledge (10113)							●								
Office Technology (10980)															
Office Technology (PA) (10794)															
Physical Education (10090)	●					★			●		●	●		●	
Physical Education: Content Knowledge (10091)			●				●				★				
Physical Ed.: Movement Forms—Analysis & Design (30092)		●	●				●				★				

MS	MO	MT	NE	NV	NJ	NM	NY	NC	OH	OK	OR	PA	RI	SC	TN	VA	WV	WI	ASHA	CAE	DDDS	NASP	NASW
												•											
	•							•	•		•	•		•	•	•							
	•							•				•		•	•	•							
															•								
•	•							•	•			•		•	•	•							
•								•	•		•			•		•							
•				•	•			•			•			•	•								
				•																			
				•																			
•	•													•	○	•							
					•			•			•	•			★								
				•				•			•				★								
				•				•			•				★								
												•											
												•											
•	•			•	•			•	•		•			•	•	•							
											★												
											★												
											★												
				•					•														
				★				•			•				★								
				★	•			•			•				★								
				★	•			•			•				★								
															•								
•	•				•			•			•					•							
											★												
															•								
												•											
•								•	•		•	•		•	•								
•	•							•	•		•	•		•	•	•							
												•		•									
•	•							•	•				•	•	○	•							
				•	•			•			•				★								
				•				•			•				★								
				•							•												
											•												
•	•				•			•			•	•		•	•	•							
											★												
											★												
											★												
															•								
												•											
•	•								•					•	○	•							
				•	•			•			•				★								
				•				•			•				★								

PRAXIS II: SUBJECT ASSESSMENTS & NTE PROGRAMS SPECIALITY AREA TESTS	AR	CA	CT	DE	DC	FL	HI	ID	IN	KS	KY	LA	ME	MD	MN
Physical Ed.: Movement Forms—Video Evaluation (20093)			●												
Physical Science: Content Essays (20482)		●		★			★								
Physical Science: Content Knowledge (20481)				★	●		●								
Physical Science: Pedagogy (30483)				★	●		★								
Physics (10260)			●						●					●	
Physics: Content Essays (30262)		●	●	★											
Physics: Content Knowledge (10261)				★			★					★			
Pre-Kindergarten Education (10530)									●						
Psychology (20390)									●						
Reading Specialist (10300)	●														
Safety/Driver Education (10860)															
School Food Service Supervisor (10970)															
School Guidance & Counseling (20420)	●					★	●								
School Psychologist (10400)	●										●				
School Social Worker (10210)						★									
Secretarial (PA) (10795)															
Social Studies (10080)	●					★			●		●	●		●	
Social Studies: Analytical Essays (20082)		●		★											
Social Studies: Content Knowledge (10081)				●	★	●	★	●				★			
Social Studies: Interpretation of Materials (20083)		●										★			
Social Studies: Pedagogy (30084)				★	●		●								
Sociology (20950)									●						
Spanish (10190)	●								●		●	●		●	
Spanish: Content Knowledge (10191)			●				●				★				
Spanish: Linguistic, Literary, & Cultural Analysis (30193)		●													
Spanish: Pedagogy (30194)					●		★								
Spanish: Productive Language Skills (20192)		●	●		●		★				★				
Special Education (10350)	●		●		●	★	●				●			●	
Special Education: Application of Core Principles Across Categories of Disability (10352)															
Special Education: Knowledge-based Core Principles (10351)							★								
Special Education: Preschool/Early Childhood (10690)															
Special Education: Teaching Students with Behavioral Disorders/Emotional Disturbances (20371)					★										
Special Education: Teaching Students with Learning Disabilities (20381)															
Special Education: Teaching Students with Mental Retardation (20321)															
Speech Communication (10220)	●								●		●			●	
Speech–Language Pathology (10330)	●														
Teaching Deaf and Hard-of-Hearing Students (10270)	●								●						
Teaching English as a Second Language (20360)					●		●								
Teaching Speech to Students with Language Impairments (10880)															
Teaching Students with Emotional Disturbance (10370)						★			●						
Teaching Students with Learning Disabilities (10380)						★			●						
Teaching Students with Orthopedic Impairments (10290)															
Teaching Students with Physical and Mental Disabilities (10870)															
Teaching Students with Visual Impairments (10280)	●														
Technology Education (10050)	●	●	●				●		●		●			●	
Theatre (10640)															
Vocational General Knowledge (10890)															
World & U.S. History (10940)															

MS	MO	MT	NE	NV	NJ	NM	NY	NC	OH	OK	OR	PA	RI	SC	TN	VA	WV	WI	ASHA	CAE	DDDS	NASP	NASW
											●												
				★																			
				★				●							★								
●	●							●				●			○	●							
											●				★								
					●						●				★								
				●										●	●								
								●			●	●											
												●											
															●								
●				●				●	●		●			●	●								
●						●		●	●		●			●	●							●	
															●								●
												●											
●	●								●			●		●		●							
					●			●			●												
				●	●			●			●												
								●			●												
															●								
●	●								●					●	○	●							
				●	●			●			●				★								
											★												
								●			●				★								
●	●							●			●			●	●								
											★												
											★												
				★							●				●								
●	●			●	●			●			●				●	●							
●	●			●	●			●	●		●			●	★					●			
●								●				●	●	●									
								●	●														
				★								●											
●								●	●					●		●							
								●	●					●		●							
														●									
												●											
								●	●		●	●		●	●								
●	●				●			●			●	●		●	●	●							
															●								
												●											
				●											●								

GLOSSARY

A

Accelerated Schools: schools designed to speed up the learning of economically disadvantaged students, based on the work of Henry Levin.

accreditation: the review and approval of education programs by outside experts.

aesthetics: the branch of philosophy concerned with beauty.

Afrocentric curriculum: educational program that places African culture and history at the center of what students are expected to learn, illustrating the important role that Africa has played in the development of Western civilization.

alternative certification: approval to teach without having participated in a traditional, state-approved teacher education program.

alternative school: any school operating within the public school system that has programs addressing the specific needs or interests of targeted student groups.

America 2000 schools: experimental schools designed to achieve the National Education Goals.

American Federation of Teachers (AFT): political organization of 800,000 members devoted to the advancement of educational issues and affiliated with the American Federation of Labor/Congress of Industrial Organizations (AFL/CIO). The organization has sponsored such projects as Dial-A-Teacher and Learning Line. It has also supported teacher internship programs, adopt-a-school programs, and national conferences for paraprofessionals and other school personnel.

apartheid: separation of the races.

at-risk students: children who are unlikely to complete high school; have failed one or more grades; are enrolled in special education classes; speak a language other than English; and/or are affected adversely by life- and health-threatening factors, such as poverty, disease, abuse and neglect, substance abuse, teenage pregnancy, and physical violence.

attention-deficit/hyperactivity disorder (ADHD): a neurobiologically based disorder characterized by inappropriate levels of inattention, impulsivity, and hyperactivity.

apprenticeship: practical work experience under the supervision of skilled workers in the trades and the arts.

assimilation: the process of educating and socializing a population or group to make it similar to the dominant culture.

assumption of risk: implicit responsibility when people who are aware of possible risks involved in an activity voluntarily participate, thus agreeing to take their chances.

authentic assessment: assessment concerned less with students' recognition and recall of facts and more with students' abilities to analyze, apply, evaluate, and synthesize what they know in ways that address real-world concerns.

axiology: a branch of philosophy that seeks to ascertain what is of value.

B

behavioral objectives: objectives that describe conditions for teaching and learning, what is to be learned, and criteria for success.

behaviorism: a philosophical orientation based on the belief that human behavior is determined by forces in the environment that are beyond human control rather than by the exercise of free will.

Bilingual Act of 1974: a law requiring parental involvement in the planning of appropriate educational programs for children with limited English-speaking ability.

bilingual education: instruction in both English and a student's native language.

black codes: conduct codes established by southerners that allowed African Americans to hold property, to sue and be sued, and to marry, but forbade them to carry firearms, to testify in court in cases involving European Americans, or to leave their jobs.

block grant: money provided in a lump sum for several education programs in a locality.

block scheduling: organizing class schedules typically to provide longer instructional periods during the school day.

Blue-Backed Speller: Webster's *American Spelling Book*, first published in 1783.

Brown v. Board of Education: the Supreme Court case that determined that segregation of students by race is unconstitutional and that education is a right that must be available to all Americans on equal terms.

Buckley Amendment: part of the Family Educational Rights and Privacy Act that prohibits schools from releasing information about a student to third parties without parental or student permission.

Bureau of Indian Affairs (BIA): a governmental agency established to, among other activities, oversee education programs for Native Americans.

C

career ladder: incentive program designed to acknowledge differences in the skills of teachers.

categorical grant: funding for an education program designed for a particular group and a specific purpose (e.g., bilingual education).

central office staff: superintendents and their associates and assistants.

certification: recognition by the state that a teacher has met minimum standards for competent practice.

character education: a curricular approach driven by personal relevance that focuses on clarifying or teaching values.

charter school: independent public schools supported by state funds but freed from many regulations and run by individuals who generally have the power to hire and to fire colleagues and to budget money as they see fit.

Chautauqua movement: an adult education movement that began in the late 1800s and led to the establishment of civic music associations, correspondence courses, lecture-study groups, youth groups, and reading circles.

chief state school officer: the chief administrator of the state department of education and the head of the state board of education, sometimes referred to as the state superintendent or the commissioner of education.

Child Abuse Prevention and Treatment Act: passed by Congress in 1974 to provide financial support to states that implemented programs for identification, prevention, and treatment of instances of child abuse or neglect.

Civil Rights Act of 1964 (Title VI): a law that specifies that no one, regardless of race, color, or origin, can be discriminated against or denied participation in programs receiving federal assistance.

classroom management: the collective ability of teachers and students to agree upon and implement a common framework for social and academic interactions.

Coalition of Essential Schools: alternative high schools serving targeted students through school-based educational reform initiatives; based on Theodore Sizer's work.

cognitive development theory: the study of changes in children's mental functioning over time.

cognitivism: a philosophical orientation based on the belief that people actively construct their knowledge of the world through experience and interaction rather than through behavioral conditioning.

collaborative network: a group of people who have come together voluntarily to help each other explore and advance specific educational issues.

collective bargaining: the negotiation of the professional rights and responsibilities of workers (e.g., teachers) as a group.

collegiality: relationships based on a sharing of power.

Committee of Fifteen: a committee that addressed the curriculum of elementary schools in 1895. Its curriculum focused on "the five windows of the soul"—grammar, literature and art, mathematics, geography, and history. It believed the role of school to be an efficient transmitter of cultural heritage through a curriculum that was graded, structured, and cumulative.

Committee of Ten on Secondary School Studies: a committee established by the NEA in 1892 to standardize high school curricula.

common school: tax-supported school established in colonial times to allow all boys and girls to have 3 free years of education focused on reading, writing, arithmetic, and history; predecessor of public schools.

comparative negligence: situations in which teacher and student are both held liable for an injury.

compensatory education program: a program that provides children from low-income families with additional education opportunities beyond those offered in a school's standard program to compensate for factors (e.g., teachers, curricula, time, and materials) missing in young people's lives.

comprehensive assessment: assessment that measures students' capacities for reasoning, thinking divergently, and solving problems creatively.

concept formation: a method of instruction teachers use when they want students to analyze and synthesize data to construct knowledge about a specific concept or idea.

conflict mediation: training in problem solving, in which teachers provide opportunities for students to practice skills in negotiating and mediating differences among themselves. Students learn to state what they want; state how they feel; state the reasons for their wants and feelings; summarize their understanding of the other person's wants, feelings, and reasons; invent three optional plans to resolve the conflict; and choose a plan and shake hands.

constructivism: a view of knowledge as constructed or built up by individuals acting within a social context that molds knowledge but does not determine absolutely what constitutes knowledge.

contributory negligence: failure of a person who is injured to exercise the required standard of care for her own safety.

cooperative learning: a teaching model that encourages heterogeneous groups of students to work together to achieve such goals as mastery of subject matter and understanding and acceptance of one another.

cosmology: the study of nature and origin of the cosmos, or universe.

Council of Chief State School Officers: a non-policy-making organization composed of leaders of state departments of elementary and secondary education in the 50 states, the District of Columbia, the Department of Defense Dependents Schools, and 5 U.S. extra-state jurisdictions—Virgin Islands, Puerto Rico, Northern Mariana Islands, Guam, and American Samoa.

criterion-referenced test: a test by which a student's performance is judged by comparing it to some clearly defined criterion for mastering a learning task or skill. The quality of a student's performance is measured against an absolute standard.

cultural literacy: shared information or common knowledge of a culture supposedly needed to function fully in that culture.

cultural pluralism: a state in which people of diverse ethnic, racial, religious, and social groups maintain autonomous participation within a common civilization.

culture: the sum of the learned characteristics of a people (e.g., language, religion, social mores, artistic expression, sexual behavior), which may be tied to geographical region. Culture also can be used in a "micro" sense to describe more conceptually discrete groups of people—cultures within cultures, subcultures, or microcultures.

curriculum: what is taught inside and sometimes outside school.

D

dame school: educational program for boys and girls, run by local women in a colonial community, that typically focused on rudimentary reading skills.

developmentally appropriate instruction: instruction geared to the needs and abilities of students.

direct instruction: highly structured, teacher-centered strategy capitalizes on such behavioral techniques as modeling, feedback, and reinforcement to promote basic skill acquisition, primarily in reading and mathematics.

discrimination: differential treatment associated with labels.

dismissal: removal of a probationary or tenured teacher before the completion of his contract.

distance learning: the capacity for teachers to communicate interactively with students, colleague or with one another over long distances.

district power equalization: a relationship between state and local government in which localities establish the tax rate for educational spending and the state guarantees a set amount of money proportional to local revenue.

due process of law: mandated legal procedures designed to protect the rights of individuals.

E

early intervention: providing care and support from the prenatal period through the first years of life to enable children to enter school ready to learn.

Education for All Handicapped Children Act (Public Law 94-142): federal law that requires all states to provide a free and appropriate public education to children with disabilities between the ages of 5 and 18. Education is to be planned through an individualized education program (IEP) and carried out in the least restrictive environment.

Education Consolidation and Improvement Act (ECIA): the 1981 act of Congress that consolidated many education programs into two major programs (Chapter One and Chapter Two).

electronic-mail (e-mail): messages sent and received via computers.

Elementary and Secondary Education Act (ESEA) of 1965: the single most comprehensive extension of federal involvement in education, which resulted in policy-making power shifting to the federal level. The Act provided funds to alleviate the effects of poverty through a variety of programs. It supported school libraries, the purchase of textbooks and other instructional materials, guidance, counseling, health services, and remedial instruction. It also established research centers and laboratories to advance educational practice.

emergency certification: certification granted temporarily until requirements and standards required for becoming a practicing teacher are met.

English Academy: a school established in Philadelphia in 1749 by Benjamin Franklin that emphasized the acquisition and application of knowledge thought to be most useful to the modern man.

English as a Second Language (ESL): an instructional program designed to teach English to speakers of other languages.

epistemology: a branch of philosophy concerned with the nature of knowledge or how we come to know things.

Equal Access Act: a 1984 law passed by Congress that recognizes that secondary-school students are mature enough to understand that a school does not condone religion by merely allowing prayer clubs on public property.

equal educational opportunity: access to the resources, choices, and encouragement each student needs to achieve his or her fullest potential through education, regardless of race, color, national origin, gender, disability, or socioeconomic status.

equal protection clause: Section 1 of the Fourteenth Amendment, which prevents states from making or enforcing laws which abridge the privileges or immunities of citizens of the United States; deprive people of life, liberty, or property without due process of law; or deny equal protection of the laws.

essentialism: a philosophical orientation that acknowledges the existence of a body of knowledge that all people must learn if they are to function effectively in society.

establishment clause: the clause in the First Amendment prohibiting Congress from making laws respecting the establishment of religion or prohibiting the free exercise of religion.

ethics: a branch of philosophy concerned with issues of morality and conduct.

ethnicity: a term for describing a group of people with a common tradition and a sense of identity that functions as a subgroup within the larger society; membership is largely a matter of self-identification.

ethnocentric: unable to see and understand society from points of view different from one's own.

Eurocentric: of curriculum and/or teaching, depicting Europe as the cradle of Western culture.

evaluation: interpreting and attaching value to data relevant to people, programs, teaching, and learning.

exceptional learner: child who has a special ability or disability that sets him apart from other children.

exclusion act: act, based on race, passed by Congress to stop unwanted immigration.

existentialism: a philosophy that emphasizes the subjectivity of human experience and the importance of individual creativity and choice in a nonrational world.

explicit curriculum: curriculum contained in policy statements, manuals of procedure, instructional materials, books, and other printed matter that explicate what and how students are to learn.

extracurriculum: non-credit-bearing activities, such as debate club and cheerleading, that are over and above the required curriculum.

F

file transfer protocol (FTP): a means for moving, or "downloading," files from computers anywhere on a network to a specific computer.

flat grant: a uniform or variable grant provided by the state to the school districts.

Folkeskole: a Danish public school.

formative assessment: evaluation conducted for the purpose of shaping, forming, and improving knowledge and performance.

for-profit school: school that does not have tax-exempt status because it is run by a company to make money.

foundation program: a program by which the state guarantees school districts a certain amount of money for educational expenditures and determines what proportion of that cost should be shouldered by localities.

free exercise clause: a clause in the First Amendment prohibiting Congress from making laws abridging the freedom of speech or of press or the right to peaceably assemble or to petition the government for a redress of grievances.

Freedman's Bureau: a government-sponsored organization established 1 month before the end of the Civil War to provide food, medicine, and seed to destitute southerners.

full inclusion: teaching students with disabilities in regular general education classrooms throughout the day in their neighborhood schools.

full-service school: a school that attempts to meet basic needs of students by providing such things as food, clothing, showers, medical care, and family counseling.

full state funding: payment by the state of all educational expenses of school districts through a statewide tax.

funding equity: equal amounts of financial support for students, regardless of where they live.

G

gender bias: discriminatory treatment, often subtle or unconscious, that unfairly favors or disfavors individuals because they are females or because they are males.

gender sensitivity training: use of curricula that avoid sex-role stereotyping and the creation of educational opportunities for females to take advantage of all their possibilities for education.

giftedness: the potential for high performance due to strengths in one or more of the following areas: general intellectual ability, specific academic aptitude, creative or productive thinking, leadership ability, ability in the visual or performing arts, and psychomotor ability.

global awareness: the recognition of people's connections to other countries and peoples of the world

H

habits of mind: the shared skills, attitudes, and values transmitted by custom or convention from one generation to the next.

Head Start: the first major early childhood program subsidized by the federal government; provides comprehensive services to low-income 3- and 4-year-olds and their families.

hearing impairment: degree of deafness; uncorrectable inability to hear well.

hidden passage: educational activities that provided slaves with the intellectual power to escape bondage and to make lives for themselves after the Civil War.

high stakes test: test used to evaluate school performance that determine students' grade promotion, graduation, and/or access to specific fields of study.

Hispanic: having Spanish colonial origins or being Spanish-speaking.

holding power: the ability to keep students in school until they receive a high school diploma or an equivalency certificate.

home page: the first page of a Web document.

hornbook: an instructional material used during colonial days. Letters, numerals and other information were affixed to a piece of wood and transparent material from the horns of cattle was put over the top to serve as a protective layer.

humanism: a philosophy that, in terms of education, calls for respect and kindness toward students and developmentally appropriate instruction in liberal arts, social conduct, and moral principles.

hypermedia: documents that consist of text and still images, as well as audio and video.

I

idealism: a philosophy that suggests that ultimate reality lies in consciousness or reason.

implicit curriculum: the unvoiced and often unintended lessons influenced by teachers' value orientations.

Improving American Schools Act: reauthorizes and revamps the Elementary and Secondary Education Act. Legislation includes Title 1, professional development and technical assistance programs, safe and drug-free schools and communities provision, and provisions promoting school equity.

incentive program: program that offers outside incentives for good attendance and good grades.

Indian Self-Determination and Educational Assistance Act: the decision by Congress in 1975 to terminate federal reservations for Native Americans.

individualized education program (IEP): a plan approved by parents or guardians that spells out what teachers will do to meet students' individual needs.

Individuals with Disabilities Education Act (IDEA): a 1990 act of Congress that amended the Education for All Handicapped Children Act by changing the term *handicapped* to *with disabilities* and by extending a free and appropriate public education to every individual between 3 and 21 years of age, regardless of the nature or severity of her disability.

induction program: program that provides special assistance, mentoring from experienced colleagues, and feedback on teaching performance to beginning teachers in the first 1 to 3 years on the job.

information processing theory: theory about how people think (what kinds of strategies they use to approach tasks and the mental effort that goes into the tasks).

in loco parentis: a term meaning "in place of the parent" that suggests that educators possess a portion of a parent's rights, duties, and responsibilities.

inquiry learning: answering and solving problems by analyzing data and creating and testing theories and hypotheses to expand the conceptual system with which one processes information.

institution: an established organization having an identifiable structure and a set of functions meant to preserve and extend social order.

instructional models: deliberate, explicit, complete plans for teaching that can be fitted to students and objectives.

integrated curriculum: curriculum that combines concepts and skills from different subject areas so that they are mutually reinforcing.

intelligence quotient (IQ): score calculated by dividing an individual's mental age by his or her chronological age and multiplying the result by 100.

intermediate educational unit (IEU): collaborative organization maintained by separate districts to provide educational services (e.g., joining together to construct and maintain a technical training center for students).

international comparative education: the study of education in different societies to develop new insights into these societies and to derive innovative understanding of one's own society.

Internet: an electronic network having the capacity to span the globe.

interpersonal power: the ability to influence others due to one's position in an organization or one's personal attributes (e.g., possession of special knowledge or skills).

J

juku: after-school classes offered to elementary and secondary students in Japan to help them keep up with the demanding school curriculum.

K

kindergarten: educational program for young children; first established by Friedrich Froebel in 1837.

L

land grant school: public school established through federal assistance, the first of which was provided by the Northwest Ordinance of 1785.

language disorder: receptive, expressive, or language processing problem; and/or difficulty with the meaning of words (semantics), the sequential organization of words according to their relationship to each other (syntax), and/or the purpose of or uses for language.

latchkey child: child who is without adult supervision for several hours each day.

Latin grammar school: the first formal type of secondary school in the colonies, established in Boston in 1635 for boys from 9 to 10 years of age who could read and write English.

learning disability: a disorder in one or more of the basic psychological processes involved in understanding or in using language, spoken or written, which may manifest itself in an imperfect ability to listen, think, speak, read, write, spell, or do mathematical calculations.

Lemon test: a tripartite test used to decide whether specific practices or policies are an establishment of religion.

license: a certificate that indicates a teacher has demonstrated minimal teaching competence.

limited English proficient (LEP): a categorization of students who are qualified for instruction in English as a Second Language.

listserv: a mailing list that allows a person to send a message to a group of individuals with a single keystroke.

literacy: one's ability to read, write, and calculate.

local property taxes: taxes on land and improvements firmly attached to the land (e.g., fences, barns) and on personal property, such as automobiles.

local school board: the primary policy-making body for public schools, composed of elected or appointed public servants.

Lyceum: out-of-school program, such as a reading circle or debating club, designed to improve the education of children and adults.

M

magnet school: an alternative school within a public school system that draws students from its whole district instead of drawing only from their own neighborhood and that offers a curriculum based on a special theme or instructional method.

Marxism: a philosophy based on Karl Marx's belief that the human condition is determined by forces in history that prevent people from achieving economic freedom and social and political equality.

mastery learning: one of several behavioral models that suggest that, given enough time, the inclination to learn, and instruction fitted to a student's needs, students are capable of mastering a range of subject matter.

McGuffey reader: book first produced in 1836 by William Holmes McGuffey to teach literacy skills and to advance the Protestant ethic through stories and essays.

measurement: the collection of data from individual students from a variety of sources (e.g., tests and quizzes, interviews, questionnaires, observations of in-class behaviors).

mental retardation: significantly subaverage intellectual function [an IQ standard score of 70 to 75 or lower], existing concurrently with related limitations in two or more of the following applicable adaptive skills areas: communication, self-care, home living, social skills, community use, self-direction, health and safety, functional academics, leisure, and work.

mentoring program: support system aimed at enhancing academic success and self-esteem of at-risk students; also, a program to help new teachers.

merit pay: an incentive program designed to encourage teachers to strive for outstanding performance by rewarding such practice.

metacognitive skills: methods for monitoring and controlling one's own thinking; thinking about thinking.

metaphysics: the branch of philosophy that focuses on the study of reality.

minimum competency test: test designed to assess the lowest acceptable level of student performance.

minority: a term that carries both a quantitative meaning (e.g., a group or subgroup in society that is identifiably fewer in number than another group) and/or a political connotation (e.g., the relative political power or influence that perceptions of a group exert in society).

mission school: school established by priests to convert Native Americans to Catholicism.

modem: a device that allows one to connect a computer to a network, using special software and an ordinary telephone line.

monitorial method: a method devised by Lancaster for teaching large groups of students, by which a master teacher instructed monitors, and they, in turn, instructed younger children.

moral development: changes, relating to age and intelligence, in the way an individual makes reasoned judgments about right and wrong.

multicultural education: a reform movement designed to bring about educational equity for all students, including those from different races, ethnic groups, social classes, ability, and gender.

multiple intelligences: a large number of cognitive abilities, each slightly different from the next, that constitute one's intellectual ability.

N

National Assessment of Educational Progress (NAEP): a congressionally mandated battery of achievement tests operated by the Educational Testing Service to assess the effects of schooling.

National Association for the Advancement of Colored People: established in 1934, this was the first nationwide special-interest group for African Americans.

National Association for the Education of Young Children (NAEYC): one of the largest professional associations for early childhood educators.

National Board for Professional Teaching Standards (NBPTS): a nonprofit organization charged with the task of creating a national system of certification to be used to designate truly outstanding teachers.

National Center for Education Statistics (NCES): an arm of the executive branch responsible for collecting and analyzing education statistics for the nation.

national certification: recognition for individual teachers, based on a national sample.

National Congress of Parents and Teachers (PTA): the largest volunteer education organization in the United States; it has long supported legislation at the state and national levels designed to benefit children.

National Defense Education Act (NDEA): a federal law passed in 1958 to provide funds for upgrading the teaching of mathematics, science, and foreign languages and for establishing guidance services.

National Education Association (NEA): an organization with 2 million members who are guided by the vision of enabling students to develop themselves as people, to practice human relations skills, to learn how to be economically productive citizens, and to be responsible for their community and nation. It was instrumental in creating the National Council for Accreditation of Teacher Education (NCATE), a national organization that monitors the quality of collegiate teacher education programs.

National Education Goals: national goals established by President George Bush and the 50 governors in 1989 to ensure readiness for school, high school completion, student achievement and citizenship, excellence in science and mathematics, adult literacy and lifelong learning, and safe, disciplined, and drug-free schools. Extended by President Clinton in 1994 to include teacher education and parental involvement.

National Governors' Association: a coalition of state chief executives.

National Network for Educational Renewal: a network consisting of universities and partner schools designed to simultaneously renew schools and teacher education.

National Parent Information Network (NPIN): an online service for parents that provides information about raising and educating children.

negligence: failure to exercise resonable care to protect students from injury.

New American Schools Development Corporation (NASDEC): a private nonprofit, tax-exempt organization formed by American business leaders and the Bush administration.

news groups: electronic message services that post to servers locally, regionally, nationally, and/or internationally.

NGO: international nongovernmental organization that advances agenda focused on problems and issues of common interest, regardless of national interest.

nondirective model: a teaching strategy in which teachers act as facilitators and as reflectors to encourage students to define problems and feelings, to take responsibility for solving problems, and to determine how personal goals might be reached.

nongraded classroom: a classroom in which children are grouped heterogeneously by ability, sometimes with students of various ages.

normal school: educational program established in the 1800s dedicated solely to training teachers so that they could perform according to high standards, or "norms."

norm-referenced test: a test used to compare the quality of a student's performance to that of other students.

null curriculum: the curriculum that is not taught in schools.

O

okeiko-goto: enrichment classes in such areas as music, the arts, and physical education that people in Japan may continue throughout their lives.

ontology: the study of nature, existence, or being.

opportunity-to-learn standards: standards meant to hold schools accountable for giving students a fair chance to succeed by providing them with appropriate support—books, materials, machines, teachers, time to learn, and other tools.

outcomes-based education: education that concentrates first on what students are to acquire or to be able to do as a result of the activities in which they engage.

P

parochial school: school established by one of various religious groups to inculcate their beliefs and ideas in children.

pedagogical content knowledge: the particular teaching knowledge necessary to impart content knowledge.

perennialism: a philosophy that exalts the great thoughts and accomplishments of the past for their own sake and for what they can offer to future generations.

per-pupil expenditure: money allocated for educational services divided by the number of pupils to be served.

philosophy: a set of ideas about the nature of reality and about the meaning of life.

Plessy v. Ferguson: the 1896 Supreme Court case that legalized separate but equal public facilities for African-Americans and served to legalize school segregation.

portfolio: a purposeful collection of student work that tells the story of the student's efforts, progress, or achievement in (a) given area(s).

practical knowledge: knowledge constructed through teachers' own experiences about what works with students in classrooms.

pragmatism: a philosophical method that defines the truth and meaning of ideas according to their physical consequences and practical value.

Praxis Series: an examination battery that purports to assess skills and knowledge at each stage of a beginning teacher's career from entry into teacher education to actual classroom performance.

primer: textbook for children designed to impart rudimentary reading skills that also reflected the religious values of the colonies.

principal: the person responsible for managing a school at the building level.

private school: nonprofit, tax-exempt institution governed by a board of trustees and financed through private funds, such as tuitions, endowments, and grants; sometimes called for-profit schools.

professional development school: a school where university and public school people work together to explore problems of teaching and learning.

professional teachers: people who possess specialized knowledge about education.

progressive taxation: taxes, such as income taxes, that require people to pay more as they earn more.

progressivism: a movement aimed at using human and material resources to improve the American's quality of life as an individual; in schools this meant focusing on the needs and interests of students rather than on those of teachers. The movement was characterized by a willingness to experiment with methods of teaching and learning.

project-based learning: the involvement of students in relatively long-term, problem-based units of instruction that allow students to pursue solutions to problems posed by students, teachers, or curriculum developers.

psychometric perspective: the belief that intelligence can be measured with tests.

psychosocial development: changes relating to age and intelligence in the way an individual's social and emotional needs are met through relationships with others.

pull-out program: program in which individual students are removed from regular classes for a period of time each day for special instruction.

R

race: a classification that is not typically chosen but instead assigned by others; defined most often by physical characteristics.

realism: a philosophy that suggests that objects of sense or perception exist independently of the mind.

reciprocal teaching: an instructional method used to teach poor readers specific comprehension-monitoring strategies.

reciprocity agreement: a pact by which professional licensure for educational practice in one state makes one eligible for licensure in another state.

regressive taxation: method of taxing citizens that requires those with limited incomes to spend a greater percentage of their income on taxes than wealthy people spend.

remediation: curriculum designed to correct students' weaknesses.

retention: nonpromotion from one grade to the next at the expected time because of school failure.

S

scaffolding: a method of teaching in which a teacher provides assistance, guidance, and structure to enhance student learning and self-regulation.

school-based budgeting: allocating resources at the building level rather than at the level of central administration.

school-based management: involving people at the school level directly in making decisions about teaching and learning, budgeting, and hiring personnel.

school choice: the idea that people should be free to choose schools for their children.

school district: a state-defined geographical area assigned responsibility for public instruction within its borders.

school governance: establishing and overseeing the structure and functions of public education.

school restructuring: efforts to encourage site-based management.

self-esteem: the value or sense of worth an individual places on his own characteristics, abilities, and behaviors.

seminary: academy for girls that was the primary means for advancing the educational skills of future teachers.

service learning: learning that results from volunteer work performed outside school hours.

site-based management: the involvement of people at the school level in decisions about teaching and learning, budgeting, and hiring personnel.

social promotion: the passing of children to successive grades to keep them with others of their age, regardless of their past performances or academic abilities.

social reconstructionism: a philosophy based on the belief that people are responsible for social conditions and can improve the quality of human life by changing the social order.

socioeconomic status: a combination of one's income, occupation, values, education, and lifestyle.

Socratic method: teaching through inquiry and dialogues in which students discover and clarify knowledge.

special interest group: people who coalesce around particular interests and try to exert pressure for the advancement of their causes.

speech impairment: fluency disorder (such as stuttering), articulation disorder (abnormality in the production of sounds), voice disorder (such as hoarseness or hypernasality—too many sounds produced through the nose), and/or delayed speech.

standardized tests: assessment through tests, often multiple-choice, paper-and-pencil tests, administered and scored under conditions uniform to all students.

standards: benchmarks against which progress can be judged.

state board of education: regulatory agency that controls standards for educational practice in most states and advises governors and legislators about the conduct of educational business.

state education department (SED): a bureaucracy that acts as an advisor to the executive and legislative branches of a state government. An SED is organized to carry out a state's education business, including regulating or overseeing elementary and secondary schools and colleges' and universities' conduct of teacher and administrator preparation.

state standards boards: commissions established to regulate professional practice in education that either have final authority or serve only in advisory capacity to policymakers.

student–teacher ratio: an estimate of average class size, calculated by dividing the total number of students in a school by the total number of staff (often including noninstructional staff).

student teaching: a field experience in which preservice teachers plan, organize, and provide instruction to students full time over a period of weeks.

summative assessment: assessment designed to inform a summary decision, for example, an assessment of a teacher's strengths and weaknesses to be used to make decisions about such matters as tenure and termination of contract.

superintendent of schools: executive officer of the local school board, appointed by the board.

synectics: a teaching model that seeks to increase students' problem-solving abilities, creative expression, empathy, and insight into social situations.

T

teacher planning: consideration of such things as curriculum, state and local goals and objectives for student learning, instructional strategies for meeting those goals, and methods for assessing students' understanding.

teacher portfolio: a compilation of products displaying a teacher's knowledge and skills, such as teacher-created tests and videotapes of one's own teaching.

teacher-proof curricula: curricula that minimize the role of those who transmit them to students.

teacher union: a confederation of educators joined politically to advance their cause.

tenure: a continuing contract that guarantees a teacher's employment unless just cause for termination can be demonstrated.

Thomism: a philosophy based on the writings of Saint Thomas Aquinas that suggests that reality is an ordered world created by God that humans can come to know. Life is temporary, and humans strive for eternity with God.

Title I: one of the largest federally funded education programs for at-risk elementary and secondary students; begun in 1965 as the first bill of President Johnson's War on Poverty.

Title IX: a provision of the 1972 Education Amendments Act that guarantees that individuals may not be excluded on the basis of sex from any education program or activity receiving federal financial assistance.

tracking: a process of segregating students by ability.

tuition tax credit: a provision that allows a taxpayer to subtract educational costs from taxes owed.

tuition tax deduction: a provision that allows a taxpayer to subtract educational costs from taxable income before computing taxes.

U

universal schooling: educating all citizens for the common good.

V

visual impairment: degree of blindness; uncorrectable inability to see well.

voucher: scrip used to purchase education for one's child.

W

Women's Educational Equity Act (WEEA): a 1974 law that expanded programs for females in mathematics, science, technology, and athletics; mandated nonsexist curriculum materials; implemented programs for increasing the number of female administrators in education and raising the career aspirations of female students; and extended educational and career opportunities to minority-group, disabled, and rural women.

Web browser: the software that enables a person to retrieve and see what is on the World Wide Web.

World Wide Web: a subset of the Internet consisting of tens of thousands of multimedia documents.

Y

Year-round school: educational program that runs through the summer months as well as during the academic year.

Z

zero-based budgeting: a process of budgeting that requires all expenditures to be justified each fiscal year.

REFERENCES

Chapter I

A new voice for teachers. (1992, May/June). *Teacher Magazine*, p. 10.

American Association of Colleges for Teacher Education (AACTE). (1985). *A call for change in teacher education.* Washington, DC: Author.

Association of Teacher Educators (ATE). (1986). *Visions of reform: Implications for the education profession.* Reston, VA: Author.

Barber, L.W. (1990). Self-assessment. In J. Millman & L. Darling-Hammond (Eds.), *The new handbook of teacher evaluation: Assessing elementary and secondary school teachers* (pp. 216–228). Newbury Park, CA: Sage.

Brandt, R.M. (1990). *Incentive pay and career ladders for today's teachers: A study of current programs and practices.* Albany, NY: State University of New York Press.

Carnegie Forum on Education and the Economy, Task Force on Teaching as a Profession. (1986). *A nation prepared: Teachers for the 21st century.* New York: Author.

Choy, S.P., Bobbitt, S.A., Henke, R.R., Medrich, E.A., Horn, L.J., & Lieberman, J. (1993). *America's teachers: Profile of a profession.* Washington, DC: U.S. Department of Education.

Clark, D.L., & McNergney, R.F. (1990). Governance of teacher education. In W.R. Houston, M. Haberman, & J. Sikula (Eds.), *Handbook of research on teacher education: A project of the Association of Teacher Educators* (pp. 101–118). New York: Macmillan.

■ Campbell, D.M., Cignetti, P.B., Melenyzer, B.J., Nettles, D.H., Wyman, R.M. (1997). *How to develop a professional portfolio: A manual for teachers.* Boston: Allyn and Bacon.

■ Corcoran, T.B. (1995, June). Helping teachers teach well: Transforming professional development. *CPRE Policy Briefs.* New Brunswick, NJ: Rutgers University.

■ Darling-Hammond, L. (1995, Summer). The condition of teaching in America. Resources for restructuring. New York: National Center for Restructuring Education, Schools, and Teaching, Teachers College, Columbia University.

■ Darling-Hammond, L., & Dilworth, M. (1996, January). Working paper. In L. Darling-Hammond, M.E. Dilworth, M. Bullmaster, M.S. Lewis, & C.J. Graddy (Eds.), *Educators of color.* Washington, DC: Office of Educational Research and Improvement, National Alliance of Black School Educators, and Phi Delta Kappan.

■ Daugherty, R.F. (1995). *A report from the 1994 Sallie Mae symposium on quality education.* Washington DC: Sallie Mae.

Dilworth, M.E. (1990). *Reading between the lines: Teachers and their racial/ethnic cultures.* Washington, DC: ERIC Clearinghouse on Teacher Education and American Association of Colleges for Teacher Education.

Dimensions: The teacher's work week. (1990, February 7). *Education Week*, p. 3.

Ducharme, E.R. (1993). *The lives of teacher educators.* New York: Teachers College Press.

Duke, D.L., & Stiggins, R. J. (1990). Beyond minimum competence: Evaluation for professional development. In J. Millman & L. Darling-Hammond (Eds.), *The new handbook of teacher evaluation: Assessing elementary and secondary school teachers* (pp. 116–132). Newbury Park, CA: Sage.

■ Feistritzer, C.E. (1996). *Profile of teachers in the U.S.* Washington, DC: National Center for Education Information.

Fenstermacher, G.D. (1990). Some moral considerations on teaching as a profession. In J.I. Goodlad, R. Soder, & K.A. Sirotnik (Eds.), *The moral dimensions of teaching* (pp. 130–151). San Francisco: Jossey-Bass.

Freudenberger, H.J. (1975). The staff burnout syndrome in alternative institutions. *Psychotherapy: Theory, Research, and Practice, 12*, 73–82.

■ Fisher, R., & Ury, W. (1991). *Getting to yes: Negotiating agreement without giving in* (2nd ed.). New York: Penguin.

Gerard, D.E., & Hussar, W.J. (1991). *Projections of education statistics to 2002.* Washington, DC: National Center for Education Statistics.

Gold, Y., & Roth, R.A. (1993). *Teachers managing stress and preventing burnout: The professional health solution.* London: Falmer Press.

Gursky, D. (1992, April 1). Separating the 'stars' from the 'quitters,' professor predicts urban teachers' success. *Education Week*, pp. 6–7.

■ Herbert, J.M., & Keller, C.E. (in press). A case study of an effective teacher in an inner-city mainstreamed classroom. In R.F. McNergney & D. Keller (Eds.), *Images of integration.* New York: Garland Press.

Holmes Group. (1986). *Tomorrow's teachers.* East Lansing, MI: Author.

■ Interstate New Teacher Assessment and Support Consortium. (1996, Spring). The INTASC newsletter returns. *INTASC in Focus, 1* (1), 1.

■ Jarchow, E., McKay, J.W., Powell, R., & Quinn, L.F. (1996). Communicating personal constructs about diverse cultures: A cross-case analysis of international student teaching. In D.J. McIntyre & D.M. Byrd (Eds.), *Preparing tomorrow's teachers: The field experience, teacher education yearbook IV* (pp. 178–196). Reston, VA: the Association of Teacher educators; and Thousand Oaks, CA: Corwin Press.

■ Kelley, C., & Odden, A. (1995, September). Reinventing teacher compensation systems. *CPRE finance briefs.* New Brunswick, NJ: Rutgers University.

Lawton, M. (1991, July 31). Teach for America: Salvation or "disservice"? *Education Week*, pp. 26-27.

■ Lewis, M.S. (1996, February). Supply and demand of teachers of color. *ERIC Digest.* Washington, DC: ERIC Clearinghouse on Teaching and Teacher Education.

Lortie, D.C. (1975). *School teacher: A sociological study.* Chicago: The University of Chicago Press.

■ Louis Harris and Associates, Inc. (1995). *The Metropolitan Life survey of the American teacher 1984-1995: Old problems and new challenges.* New York: Metropolitan Life Insurance Company.

National Association of State Directors of Teacher Education and Certification (NASTEC) Joint Standards and Middle Level Committee. (1992). *Promoting systemic change in teacher education and certification: NASDTEC outcome-based standards and portfolio assessment.* Dubuque, IA: Kendall-Hunt.

■ National Commission on Teaching & America's Future (1996). *What matters most: Teaching for America's future.* New York: National Commission on Teaching & America's Future.

■ National Council for the Accreditation of Teacher Education. (1995). *Standards, procedures and policies for the accreditation of professional education units*, 1995. Washington, DC: NCATE.

National Education Association. (1992). *The status of the American public school teacher*, 1990-91. Washington, DC: Author.

■ National Education Association. (1995). *1994-95 estimates of school statistics.* Washington, DC: Author.

National Governors' Association. (1986). *Time for results: The governors' 1991 report on education.* Washington, DC: Author.

■ NEA Today. (1994, October). The new interest in bargaining. *NEA Today, 13* (3), 12–13.

Ogle, L.T., Alsalam, N., & Rogers, G.T. (1991). *The condition of education 1991: Volume 1, elementary and secondary education.* Washington, DC: U.S. Department of Education, National Center for Educational Statistics.

■ Richardson, J. (1995a). Court orders Tennessee to equalize teacher salaries. *Education Week, 14* (23), 16.

■ Richardson, J. (1995b). Critics target state teacher-tenure laws: Calif. governor seeks to dismantle system. *Education Week, 14* (23), 1, 13.

Romer, R. (1991). Foreward. In *National Education Goals Panel, Executive summary: The national education goals report* (p. 1). Washington, DC: National Education Goals Panel.

- Rowan, B. (1994, August-September). Comparing teachers' work with work in other occupations: Notes on the professional status of teaching. *Educational Researcher*, 23 (6), 4–17.

Stinnett, T.M. (1969). Teacher education, certification, and accreditation. In E. Fuller & J.B. Pearson (Eds.), *Education in the states: Nationwide development since 1900* (pp. 381–438). Washington, DC: National Education Association of the United States.

- *Teacher Magazine* (1995a). Controversial corps regroups, 6 (5), 11.
- *Teacher Magazine* (1995b). National certification now a reality, 6 (5), 10.
- Tryneski, J. (1996). *Requirements for certification of teachers, counselors, librarians, administrators for elementary and secondary schools* (61st ed.). Chicago: University of Chicago Press.

Warren, D. (Ed.). (1989). *American teachers: Histories of a profession at work*. New York: Macmillan.

- U.S. Department of Education. (1994). *Public elementary teachers' views on teacher performance evaluations*. Washington, DC: U.S. Government Printing Office.
- U.S. Department of Education. (1995). *Digest of education statistics, 1996*. Washington, DC: U.S. Government Printing Office.
- U.S. Department of Education. (1996a). *The condition of education, 1996*. Washington, DC: U.S. Government Printing Office.
- U.S. Department of Education. (1996b). *Digest of education statistics, 1996*. Washington, DC: U.S. Government Printing Office.

Chapter 2

- Ambrose, S.E. (1996). *Undaunted courage: Meriwether Lewis, Thomas Jefferson, and the opening of the American West*. New York: Simon & Schuster.

Barman, J., Hebert, Y., & McCaskill, D. (1986). *Indian education in Canada* (Vol. I). Vancouver: University of British Columbia.

Barnard, H. (1857, March). The public high school. *The American Journal of Education*, pp. 185–189.

Berlin, I. (1974). *Slaves without masters: The free negro in the antebellum South*. New York: Vintage.

Best, J.H. (Ed.). (1962). *Benjamin Franklin on education*. New York: Teachers College Press, Columbia University.

Blum, J.M., McFeely, W.S., Morgan, E.S., Schlesinger, A.M., Jr., Stampp, K.M., & Woodward, C.V. (1989). *The national experience: A history of the United States* (7th ed.). San Diego: Harcourt Brace Jovanovich.

Boyd, W. (Ed.). (1962). *The Emile of Jean Jacques Rousseau*. New York: Bureau of Publications, Teachers College, Columbia University.

Bullock, H.A. (1967). *A history of Negro education in the South: From 1619 to the present*. Cambridge, MA: Harvard University Press.

Coleman, M.C. (1993). *American Indian children at school, 1850–1930*. Jackson: University Press of Mississippi.

Cremin, L.A. (1970). *American education: The colonial experience, 1607-1783*. New York: Harper & Row.

Cremin, L.A. (1980). *American education: The national experience, 1783-1876*. New York: Harper & Row.

Cross, B.M. (1965). *The educated woman in America: Selected writings of Catharine Beecher, Margaret Fuller, and M. Carey Thomas*. New York: Teachers College Press, Columbia University.

Deighton, L.C. (Ed.). (1971). *The encyclopedia of education* (Vol. 9). New York: Macmillan Company and The Free Press.

Dolan, J.P. (1985). *The American Catholic experience: A history from colonial times to the present*. Garden City, NY: Doubleday.

Douglass, F. (1882). *Life and times of Frederick Douglass*. Hartford, CT: Park.

Douglass, F. (1974). Frederick Douglass describes his self-education (c. 1830). In S. Cohen (Ed.), *Education in the United States: A documentary history* (Vol. 3) (pp. 1624–1625). New York: Random House.

Downs, R.B. (1978). *Friedrich Froebel*. Boston: Twayne.

Edwards, P. (Ed.). (1972). *Encyclopedia of philosophy* (Vol. 7). New York: The Macmillan Company and The Free Press.

Elsbree, W.S. (1939). *The American teacher: Evolution of a profession in a democracy*. New York: American Book.

Emerson, R. W. (1884). *Lectures and biographical sketches*. Cambridge, MA: Riverside.

Flynn, G. (1971). *Sor Juana Ines de la Cruz*. New York: Twayne.

Fogel, D. (1988). *Junipero Serra, the Vatican, and enslavement theology*. San Francisco, CA: Ism.

Ford, P.L. (Ed.). (1899). *The New England primer*. New York: Dodd, Mead.

Franklin, B. (1842). *Memoirs of Benjamin Franklin* (Vol. 1). New York: Harper & Brothers.

- Franklin, J.H. (1980). *From slavery to freedom: A history of negro Americans* (5th ed.). New York: Alfred A. Knopf.

Gay, P. (Ed.). (1964). *John Locke on education*. New York: Bureau of Publications, Teachers College, Columbia University.

Gutek, G.L. (1968). Pestalozzi and education. New York: Random House.

Hahner, J. (1976). *Women in Latin American history*. Los Angeles: University of California.

- Hallahan, D.P., & Kauffman, J.M. (1997). *Exceptional children: Introduction to special education* (7th ed.). Boston: Allyn and Bacon.

Hewett, F.M., & Forness, S.R. (1984). *Education of exceptional learners* (3rd ed.). Boston: Allyn and Bacon.

Jefferson, T. (1931). Report of the commissioners appointed to fix the site of the University of Virginia. In R.J. Honeywell (Ed.), *The educational work of Thomas Jefferson* (pp. 248–260). Cambridge, MA: Harvard University Press.

Kaestle, C.F. (1983). *Pillars of the republic: Common schools and American society, 1780–1860*. New York: Hill and Wang.

Kauffman, J. (1981). Introduction: Historical trends and contemporary issues in special education in the United States. In J.M. Kauffman & D.P. Hallahan (Eds.), *Handbook of special education* (pp. 3–23). Englewood Cliffs, NJ: Prentice-Hall.

Krug, E.A. (1964). *The shaping of the American high school, 1880–1920*. New York: Harper & Row.

Lannie, V.P. (1968). *Public money and parochial education: Bishop Hughes, Governor Seward and the New York school controversy*. Cleveland, OH: Press of Case Western Reserve.

Mann, H. (1974). On the employment of female teachers, 1884. In S. Cohen (Ed.), *Education in the United States: A documentary history* (pp. 1315–1317). New York: Random House.

Mann, L. (1979). *On the trail of process: A historical perspective on cognitive processes and their training*. New York: Grune & Stratton.

Manuel, H.T. (1965). *Spanish-speaking children of the Southwest: Their education and the public welfare*. Austin: University of Texas Press.

Pestalozzi, J.H. (1898). *How Gertrude teaches her children* (2nd ed.). Syracuse, NY: C.W. Bardeen.

Reigart, J.F. (1969). *The Lancasterian system of instruction in the schools of New York City*. New York: Arno Press & The New York Times.

Riesman, D. (1954). *Individualism reconsidered*. Glencoe, IL: Free Press.

Rury, J.L. (1989). Who became teachers?: The characteristics of teachers in American history. In D. Warren (Ed.), *American teachers: Histories of a profession at work* (pp. 9–48). New York: Macmillan.

- Spacks, P.M. (1995). *Boredom: The literary history of a state of mind*. Chicago: The University of Chicago Press.

Steinhardt, M.A. (1992). Physical education. In P.W. Jackson (Ed.), *Handbook of research on curriculum* (pp. 964–1001). New York: Macmillan.

The Sun. (1833a, December 19). p. 2.

The Sun. (1833b, December 20). p. 3.

Tocqueville, A. (1840). *Democracy in America: Part the second, the social influence of democracy* (H. Reeve, Trans.). New York: J. & H.G. Langley.

Tyack, D. (1967). *Turning points in American educational history*. Lexington, MA: Xerox College.

Ulich, R. (1968). *History of educational thought*. New York: D. Van Nostrand.

Zitkala-Sa. (1921). *American Indian stories*. Washington, DC: Hayworth.

Chapter 3

Adams, L.L. (1977). *Walter Lippann*. Boston: Twayne Publishers.

Agee, J., & Evans, W. (1960). *Let us now praise famous men* (2nd ed.). New York: Ballantine.

Alba, R.D. (1991). *Ethnic identity: The transformation of white America*. New Haven, CT: Yale University Press.

Ayres, L.P. (1909). *Laggards in our schools*. New York: Charities publication committee.

Bennett, C.I. (1990). *Comprehensive multicultural education* (2nd ed.). Boston: Allyn and Bacon.

Bestor, A.E. (1953). *Educational wastelands: The retreat from learning in our public schools*. Urbana, IL: University of Illinois Press.

Blum, J.M., McFeely, W.S., Morgan, E.S., Schlesinger, A.M., Jr., Stampp, K.M., & Woodward, C.V. (1989). *The national experience: A history of the United States* (7th ed.). San Diego: Harcourt Brace Jovanovich.

Bond, H.M. (1934). *The education of the Negro in the American social order*. New York: Prentice-Hall.

Bossert, S.T. (1985). Effective elementary schools. In R.J. Kyle (Ed.), *Reaching for excellence* (pp. 39–53). Washington, DC: U.S. Government Printing Office.

Brinkley, D. (1988). *Washington goes to war*. New York: Alfred A. Knopf.

Brown, C.L., & Pannell, C.W. (1985). The Chinese in America. In J.O. McKee (Ed.), *Ethnicity in contemporary America: A geographical appraisal* (pp. 195–216). Dubuque, IA: Kendall/Hunt.

Callahan, R.E. (1962). *Education and the cult of efficiency*. Chicago: University of Chicago Press.

Carlson, R.A. (1975). *The quest for conformity: Americanization through education*. New York: John Wiley and Sons.

Carnegie, D. (1936). *How to win friends & influence people*. New York: Simon and Schuster.

Carnegie Forum on Education and the Economy (1986). *A nation prepared: Teachers for the 21st century, the report of the task force on teaching as a profession*. New York: Carnegie Corporation.

Cole, J.Y. (1979). *For Congress and the nation: A chronological history of the Library of Congress*. Washington, DC: Library of Congress.

Commission on the Reorganization of Secondary Education. (1918). *Cardinal principles of secondary education* (Bulletin No. 35). Washington, DC: U.S. Government Printing Office.

- Consortium for Policy Research in Education. (1996). *Public policy and school reform: A research summary*. Philadelphia: University of Pennsylvania.

Cremin, L.A. (1988). *American education: The metropolitan experience*. New York: Harper & Row.

Cuban, L. (1984). *How teachers taught: Constancy and change in American classrooms 1890–1980*. New York: Longman.

Dabney, C.W. (1969). *Universal education in the South: Vol. II*. New York: Arno Press & The New York Times.

- Daily Report Card. (1995, Oct. 20). Bilingual ed: *Transition or "bog"?* Available online at: http://www.utopia.com/mailings/reportcard/DAILY.REPORT.CARD156.html#Index6.

- Daily Report Card. (1996, June 26). *Children and television, watching television: The new racial divide*. Vol. 6, No. 58. Available online at: http://www.utopia.com/mailings/reportcard/DAILY.REPORT.CARD218.html#Index10.

- Day, J.C. (1996). *Population projections of the United States by age, sex, race, and Hispanic origin: 1995 to 2050*. U.S. Bureau of the Census, Current Population Reports, pp. 25-1130. Washington, DC: U.S. Government Printing Office.

Degler, C.N. (1959). *Out of our past: The forces that shaped modern America*. New York: Harper & Row.

Du Bois, W.E.B. (1904). *The souls of black folk*. Chicago: A.C. McClurg.

Ebenstein, W. (1954). *Today's ISMS*. Englewood Cliffs, NJ: Prentice-Hall.

Education Amendments of 1972 (PL 92-318) (1972 June 23). *United States Statutes At Large*, Volume 86, pp. 373–375.

Edwards, J. (1991). To teach responsibility, bring back the Dalton Plan. *Phi Delta Kappan*, 72 (5), 398–401.

Efron, S. (1990, April 29). Few Viet exiles find U.S. riches. *Los Angeles Times*, p. 1.

Franklin, J.H. (1967). *From slavery to freedom* (3rd ed.). New York: Alfred A. Knopf.

Fuchs, L.H. (1990). *The American kaleidoscope: Race, ethnicity, and the civic culture*. Middletown, CT: Wesleyan University Press.

Goodman, J.M. (1985). The Native American. In J.O. McKee (Ed.), *Ethnicity in contemporary America: A geographical appraisal* (pp. 195-216). Dubuque, IA: Kendall/Hunt.

Gould, J.E. (1961). *The Chautauqua movement*. Albany: State University of New York Press.

Halberstam, D. (1979). *The powers that be*. New York: Alfred A. Knopf.

- Hallahan, D.P., & Kauffman, J.M. (1997). *Exceptional learners: Introduction to special education*. (7th ed.). Boston: Allyn and Bacon.

Harris, K.A. (1984). *Profiles of Detroit's high schools: 1975 to 1984*. Detroit: Detroit School District, U.S. District Court Monitoring Commission.

Jackson, H.H. (1977). *A century of dishonor: A sketch of the United States government's dealings with some of the Indian tribes*. St. Clair Shores, MI: Scholarly Press. (Original work published 1880)

- James, W. (1899). *Talks to teachers on psychology: And to the students on some of life's ideals*. New York: Henry Holt and Company.

Jencks, C., Smith, M., Acland, H., Bane, J.J., Cohen, D., Gintis, H., Heyns, B., & Michelson, S. (1972). *Inequality: A reassessment of the effect of family and schooling in America*. New York: Basic Books.

Kauffman, J.M. (1981). Historical trends and contemporary issues in special education in the United States. In J.M. Kauffman & D.P. Hallahan (Eds.), *Handbook of special education*. Englewood Cliffs, NJ: Prentice-Hall.

Kliebard, H.M. (1986). *The struggle for the American curriculum, 1893–1958*. Boston: Routledge & Kegan Paul.

- Kunen, J.S. (1996, April 29). The end of integration. *Time*, 147(118) pp. 39–45.

Lazarus, E. (1888). *The poems of Emma Lazarus: Vol. 1*. Boston: Houghton Mifflin.

Link, A.S., & Catton, W.B. (1963). *American epoch: A history of the United States since the 1890s*. New York: Alfred A. Knopf.

Lodge, H.C. (1891). The restriction of immigration. *North American Review*, pp. 27–36.

Massachusetts Commission on Industrial and Technical Education. (1906). *Report of the Commission on Industrial and Technical Education*. Boston, MA: Wright & Potter.

McCorry, J.J. (1978). *Marcus Foster and the Oakland public schools: Leadership in urban education*. Berkeley: University of California Press.

Minzey, J.D., & LeTarte, C. (1979). *Community education, from program to process to practice: The schools' role in a new educational society*. Midland, MI: Pendell.

Murphy, J. (1990). The educational reform movement of the 1980s: A comprehensive analysis. In J. Murphy (Ed.), *The educational reform movement of the 1980s* (pp. 3–55). Berkeley, CA: McCutchan.

National Commission on Excellence in Education. (1983). *A nation at risk: The imperative for education reform*. Washington, DC: U.S. Department of Education.

- Nifong, C. (1996, August 6). Hispanics and Asians change the face of American South. *Christian Science Monitor*, sec. 1, p. 4.

Orfalea, G. (1988). *Before the flames: A quest for the history of Arab-Americans*. Austin: University of Texas Press.

Painter, N.I. (1977). *Exodusters: Black migration to Kansas after Reconstruction*. New York: Alfred A. Knopf.

Parkhurst, H. (1922). *Education on the Dalton Plan*. New York: Dutton.

Peabody, E.P. (1886). *Sara Winnemucca's practical solution of the Indian problems: A letter to Dr. Lyman Abbot of the "Christian Union."* Cambridge, MA: John Wilson and Son.

Powell, A.G., Farrar, E., & Cohen, D.K. (1985). *The shopping mall high school: Winners and losers in the educational marketplace*. Boston: Houghton Mifflin.

Raven, S., & Weir, A. (1981). *Women in history*. London: Weidenfeld and Nicolson.

Rice, J.M. (1969). *The public-school system of the United States*. New York: Arno Press.

Riis, J.A. (1890). *How the other half lives*. New York: Charles Scribner's Sons.

■ Staff. (1995, November). Equity for the education of women and girls: Did you know? Tarrytown, NY: The Marymount Institute for the Education of Women and Girls. *Equity Newsletter*, 1(2), p. 9

Travers, R.M. (1983). *How research has changed American schools: A history from 1840 to the present*. Kalmazoo, MI: Mythes.

Tyack, D., & Hansot, E. (1982). *Managers of virtue*. New York: Basic Books.

U.S. Bureau of the Census. (1975). *Historical statistics of the United States: Colonial times to 1970 (Part 1)*. Washington, DC: U.S. Government Printing Office.

U.S. Bureau of the Census. (1990). *Statistical abstract of the United States* (110th ed.). Washington, DC: U.S. Government Printing Office.

■ U.S. Bureau of the Census. (1996, April). *Current population reports: Consumer income. Income, poverty and valuation of noncash benefits: 1994* Table B–6. Washington, DC: U.S. Department of Commerce, Economics and Statistics Administration.

U.S. Bureau of Indian Affairs. (1974). Government schools for Indians (1881). In S. Cohen (Ed.), *Education in the United States: A documentary history* (Vol. 3, pp. 1754–1756). New York: Random House.

U.S. Department of Education, Office of Educational Research and Improvement. (1900). *The condition of education, 1990* (Vols. 1–2). Washington, DC: U.S. Government Printing Office.

■ U.S. Department of Education (1996a). *Digest of education statistics, 1996*. Washington, DC: U.S. Government Printing Office.

■ U.S. Department of Education (1996b). *The condition of education, 1996*. Washington, DC: U.S. Government Printing Office.

Washington, B.T. (1907). *The future of the American Negro*. Boston, MA: Small, Maynard.

Chapter 4

Achebe, C. (1968). *Things fall apart*. London: Heinemann Educational Books.

Adler, M. (1982). *The Paideia proposal: An educational manifesto*. New York: Macmillan.

■ Apple, M. (1995). *Education and power*. New York: Routledge.

Asante, M.K. (1987). *The Afrocentric idea*. Philadelphia: Temple University Press.

Asante, M.K. (1992). Learning about Africa. *Executive Educator, 14*(9), 21-23.

Banks, J.A. (1994). *Multiethnic education: Theory and practice* (3rd ed.). Boston: Allyn and Bacon.

Bestor, A. (1985). *Educational wastelands: The retreat from learning in our public schools* (2nd ed.). Urbana: University of Illinois Press.

Bloom, A. (1987). *The closing of the American mind*. New York: Simon and Schuster.

Brameld, T. (1950). *Patterns of educational philosophy: A democratic interpretation*. New York: World Book.

Brown, R.G. (1991). *Schools of thought*. San Francisco: Jossey-Bass.

■ Bryk, A.S., Lee, V.E., & Holland, P.B. (1993). *Catholic schools and the common good*. London: Harvard University Press.

Buber, M. (1970). *I and thou* (W. Kaufman, Trans.). New York: Charles Scribner's Sons. (Original work published 1937)

■ Clark, C.M. (1995). *Thoughtful teaching*. London: Cassell.

Clark, C.M., & Peterson, P.L. (1986). Teachers' thought processes. In M.C. Wittrock (Ed.), *Handbook of research on teaching* (3rd ed.) (pp. 255-296). New York: Macmillan.

Clive, J. (1989). *Not by fact alone: Essays on the writing and reading of history*. Boston: Houghton Mifflin.

Cohen, S., & Hearn, D. (1988). Reinforcement. In R.F. McNergney (Ed.), *Guide to classroom teaching* (pp. 43-66). Boston: Allyn and Bacon.

Corbin, H. (1993). *History of Islamic philosophy*. London: Kegan Paul International.

■ Council for Exceptional Children. (1996). CEC supports educators with disabilities. *CEC Today, 3*(2), 11.

Counts, G.S. (1928). *School and society in Chicago*. New York: Harcourt, Brace.

Dewey, J. (1916). *Democracy and education: An introduction to the philosophy of education*. New York: Macmillan Company.

Durant, W. (1961). *The story of philosophy: The lives and opinions of the great philosophers*. New York: Simon and Schuster.

Eisner, E.W. (1992). Curriculum ideologies. In P.W. Jackson (Ed.), *Handbook of research on curriculum* (pp. 302-326). New York: Maxwell Macmillan International.

Ewert, G.D. (1991). Habermas and education: A comprehensive overview of the influence of Habermas in educational literature. *Review of Educational Research, 61*(3) 345-378.

Fakhry, J. (1983). *A history of Islamic philosophy* (2nd ed.). New York: Columbia University Press.

Fenstermacher, G. D. (1986). Philosophy of research on teaching: Three aspects. In M.C. Wittrock (Ed.), *Handbook of research on teaching* (3rd ed.) (pp. 37-49). New York: Macmillan.

■ Fine, M. (1987). Silencing in public schools. *Language Arts, 64*(2), 157-174.

Friere, P. (1970). *Pedagogy of the oppressed*. New York: The Seabury Press.

Fukuyama, F. (1992). *The end of history and the last man*. New York: The Free Press.

Gerber, P.J. (1992). Being learning disabled and a beginning teacher and teaching a class of students with learning disabilities. *Exceptionality, 3*(4), pp. 213-231.

■ Giroux, H.A. (1984). Public philosophy and the crisis in education. *Harvard Educational Review, 54*(2), 186-194.

Green, T. (1976). Teacher competence as practical rationality. *Educational Theory, 26*, 249-258.

■ Haberman, M. (1995). *Star teachers of children in poverty*. West Lafayette, IN: Kappa Delta Pi.

Hirsch, E.D., Jr. (1987). *Cultural literacy: What every American needs to know*. Boston: Houghton Mifflin.

■ Hirsch, E.D., Jr. (1996). *The schools we need and why we don't have them*. New York: Doubleday.

Hirsch, E.D., Jr., Rowland, W.G., Jr., & Stanford, M. (Eds.). (1989). *A first dictionary of cultural literacy: What our children need to know*. Boston: Houghton Mifflin.

Holtom, D.C. (1922). *The political philosophy of modern Shinto: A study of the state religion of Japan*. Chicago: University of Chicago Libraries.

Hunt, D.E. (1987). *Beginning with ourselves: In practice, theory, and human affairs*. Cambridge, MA: Brookline Books.

Hutchins, R.M. (1936). *The higher learning in America*. New Haven: Yale University Press.

James, W. (1899). *Talks to teachers on psychology: And to students on some of life's ideals*. New York: Henry Holt.

James, W. (1907). *Pragmatism and four essays from The Meaning of Truth*. New York: Longmans, Green and Co.

King, M.L., Jr. (1964). *Stride toward freedom: The Montgomery story*. New York: Harper and Row.

Kneller, G.F. (1971). *Introduction to the philosophy of education* (2nd ed.). New York: Wiley.

Lesko, N. (1988). *Symbolizing society: Stories, rites, and structure in a Catholic high school*. New York: Falmer Press.

Morine-Dershimer, G. (1990, April). *To think like a teacher*. Vice-presidential address presented at the annual meeting of the American Educational Research Association, Boston.

Nietzsche, F. (1924). *On the future of our educational institutions*. New York: Macmillan.

Nietzsche, F. (1961). *Thus spake Zarathustra: A book for everyone and no one*. (R.J. Hollingdale, Trans.). New York: Penguin. (Original work published 1883)

Noddings, N. (1984). *Caring: A feminine approach to ethics & moral education*. Berkeley: University of California Press.

O'Neill, W.F. (1981). *Educational ideologies: Contemporary expressions of educational philosophy*. Santa Monica, CA: Goodyear.

Organ, T.W. (1974). *Hinduism: Its historical development*. Woodbury, NY: Barron's Educational Series.

Paley, V. (1979). *White teacher*. Cambridge: Harvard University Press.

Rambachan, A. (1992). *The Hindu vision*. Delhi: Motilal Banarsidass.

Rickover, H.G. (1963). *American education—A national failure: The problem of our schools and what we can learn from England.* New York: E.P. Dutton.

Robinson, F. (1990, November 18). Learning the new age way. *The Washington Post Education Review*, pp. 9-11.

Rorty, R. (1991). *Objectivity, relativism, and truth: Philosophical papers: Vol 1.* Cambridge: Cambridge University Press.

Sartre, J.-P. (1947). *Existentialism.* New York: Philosophical Library.

Schön, D.A. (1987). *Educating the reflective practitioner: Toward a new design for teaching and learning in the professions.* San Francisco: Jossey-Bass.

Shulman, L.S. (1987). Knowledge and teaching: Foundations of the new reform. *Harvard Educational Review, 57,* 1-22.

Skinner, B.F. (1971). *Beyond freedom and dignity.* New York: Alfred A. Knopf.

Sleeter, C.E., & Grant, C.A. (1993). *Making choices for multicultural education: Five approaches to race, class, and gender* (2nd ed.). New York: Merrill.

Snelling, J. (1987). *The Buddhist handbook: A complete guide to Buddhist teaching and practice.* London: Century.

Westbrook, R.B. (1991). *John Dewey and American democracy.* Ithaca, NY: Cornell University Press.

Winkler, K.J. (1994). An African writer at a crossroads *The Chronicle of Higher Education, XL*(19), A9, A12.

X, M. (1965). *The autobiography of Malcolm X.* New York: Grove Press.

Chapter 5

■ Achilles, C.M. (1996). Students achieve more in smaller classes. *Educational Leadership, 53,* 76–79.

■ Ackerman, R., Donaldson, G.A., Jr., & Van der Bogert, R. (1996). *Making sense as a school leader: Persisting questions, creative opportunities.* San Francisco: Jossey-Bass.

■ Alexander, K.L., & Entwisle, D.R. (1996) Schools and children at risk. In A. Booth & J.F. Dunn (Eds.), *Family-school links: How do they affect educational outcomes?* (67–88) Mahwah, NJ: Lawrence Erlbaum.

American Political Network. (1992, September 15). *Daily Report Card,* Note 8 of 8, p. 13.

■ Ames, N.L. (1996). Creating secure school environments through total school reform: The Harshman story. *Middle School Journal, 2*(3), 4–13.

Bainbridge, W.L., & Sundre, S.M. (1992, October 14). What parents really look for in a school. *Education Week,* p. 27.

Baltzell, D.C., & Dentler, R.A. (1983). *School principal selection practices: Five case studies.* Cambridge, MA: Abt Associates. (ERIC Document Reproduction Service No. ED 319 107)

Barnes, H. (1991, October). Learning that grows with the learner. An introduction to Waldorf education. *Educational Leadership,* pp. 52–54.

Barth, R.S. (1990). *Improving schools from within: Teachers, parents and principals can make the difference.* San Francisco: Jossey-Bass.

■ Bellm, D. (1996). At the table: Child care teachers and providers speak out at the White House. *Young Children, 51* (3), 36–37.

■ *Blackboard Bulletin.* (1995, November). LaGrange, IN: Pathway.

■ Boyer, E.L. (1995). *The basic school: A community for learning.* Princeton, NJ: Carnegie Foundation for the Advancement of Teaching.

Bradley, A. (1992, November 18). Reforming Philadelphia's high schools from within. *Education Week,* pp. 1, 17–19.

Brown, S.M. (1992, Fall). The choice for Jewish dayschools. *Educational Horizons,* pp. 45–52.

Bryant, D.M., Clifford, R.M., & Peisner, E.S. (1991). Best practices for beginners: Developmental appropriateness in kindergarten. *American Educational Research Journal, 28*(4), 783–803.

Callahan, R.E. (1962). *Education and the cult of efficiency: A study of the social forces that have shaped the administration of the public schools.* Chicago: University of Chicago Press.

■ Carson, C.C., Huelskamp, R.M., & Woodall, T.D. (1993). Perspectives on education in America. *The Journal of Educational Research, 86*(5), 259–310.

Commission on Jewish Education in North America. (1991). *A time to act.* Lanham, MD: University Press of America.

Cushman, K. (1990, Summer). The whys and hows of the multi-age primary classroom. *American Educator,* pp. 28–32.

■ David, J.L. (1995/1996). The who, what, and why of site-based management. *Educational Leadership, 53*(4), pp. 4–9.

Deal, T.E., & Peterson, K.D. (1991, June). *The principal's role in shaping school culture.* Washington, DC: U.S. Department of Education.

■ Decker, L.E., Gregg, G.A., & Decker, V.A. (1995). *Teacher's manual for parent and community involvement.* Fairfax, VA: National Community Education Association.

■ Dennebaum, J.M., & Kulberg, J.M. (1994). Kindergarten retention and transition classrooms: Their relationship to achievement. *Psychology in the Schools, 31*(1), 5–12.

■ Dornbusch, S.M., & Glasgow, K.L. (1996). The structural context of family–school relations. In A. Booth & J.F. Dunn (Eds.), *Family–school links: How do they affect educational outcomes?* (pp. 35–44) Mahwah, NJ: Lawrence Erlbaum.

Eaton, W.E. (Ed.). (1990). *Shaping the superintendency: A reexamination of Callahan and the cult of efficiency.* New York: Teachers College Press.

■ Eccles, J.S., & Harold, R.D. (1996). Family involvement in children's and adolescents' schooling. In A. Booth & J.F. Dunn (Eds.), *Family–school links: How do they affect educational outcomes?* (pp. 3–34) Mahwah, NJ: Lawrence Erlbaum.

Feistritzer, C.E., Quelle, F., & Bloom, I. (1988). *Profile of school administrators in the U.S.* Washington, DC: National Center for Education Information.

Fichter, F.H. (1958). *Parochial school: A sociological study.* Notre Dame, IN: University of Notre Dame Press.

Figueroa, D.L. (1992, December 2). Federal joint venture offers job training to troubled students. *Washington Post,* p. 3.

Finn, J.D., & Achilles, C.M. (1990). Answers and questions about class size: A statewide experiment. *American Educational Research Journal, 27*(3), 557–577.

■ The Focused Reporting Project. (1995). *School reform in Long Beach.* Atlanta, GA: Southern Education Foundation.

Ford, R. (1995). Critical perspective on the case of Hans Christian Andersen School. *Guide to foundations in action: Videocases of teaching and learning in multicultural settings* (pp. 161–174). Boston: Allyn and Bacon.

■ Gamoran, A. (1996). Student achievement in public magnet, public comprehensive, and private city high schools. *Educational Evaluation and Policy Analysis, 18*(1), 1–18.

Glass, G.V. (1988). *At last—A better way to measure class size: A step-by-step guide for local associations.* Washington, DC: National Education Association.

■ Glass, T.E. (1992). *The 1992 study of the American school superintendency.* Arlington, VA: American Association of School Administrators.

Glazer, N. (1992, March 18). Do we need big-city school superintendents? *Education Week,* p. 36.

■ Grubb, W.N. (1996). The new vocationalism: What it is, what it could be. *Phi Delta Kappan, 77*(8), 535–546.

Gursky, D. (1992, September 16). Where school's spirit is a "sense of community." *Education Week,* pp. 1, 14–15.

■ Guskey, T.R. & Peterson, K.D. (1995/1996), The road to classroom change. *Educational Leadership, 53*(4), 10–14.

Gutiérrez, R., & Slavin, R.E. (1992). Achievement effects of the nongraded elementary school: A best evidence synthesis. *Review of Educational Research, 62*(4), 333–376.

■ Hadley, W.H. (1996). Teacher preparation and certification in middle grades education. *Journal of Instructional Psychology, 23*(1), 21–25.

■ Hanushek, E.A. (1995). Moving beyond spending fetishes. *Educational Leadership, 53*(3), 60–64.

Harp, L. (1993, February 24). Advocates of year-round schooling shift focus to educational advantages. *Education Week,* pp. 1,17.

■ Hartzell, G.N. (1995). *New voices in the field: The work lives of first-year assistant principals.* Thousand Oaks, CA: Corwin Press.

Hill, D. (1993, February). Teach your children. *Teacher Magazine,* pp. 16–23.

Holmes, C.T. (1989). Grade level retention effects: A meta-analysis of research studies. In L.A. Shepard & M.L. Smith (Eds.), *Flunking grades: Research and policies on retention* (pp. 16–33). London: Falmer Press.

■ Homeschooling. (1996, March). *Teacher Magazine, 7*(7), 9.

Hostetler, J.A., & Huntington, G.E. (1992). *Amish children: Education in the family, school, and community* (2nd ed.). Orlando, FL: Holt, Rinehart and Winston.

House, E. (1974). *The politics of educational innovation.* Berkely, CA: McCutchan.

Hoy, W.K., & Miskel, C.G. (1991). *Educational administration: Theory, research, and practice.* New York: McGraw-Hill.

■ Judson, G. (1996, February 1). Education company banned from Hartford schools. *New York Times, 5,* p. B3.

■ Kalson, S. (1996, June 4). The world's best child care: The Reggio Emilia schools in Italy help children find answers to their questions. *Pittsburgh Post Gazette,* p. A–8.

■ Kennedy, J. (Ed.), (1996). Making all schools charter schools is more likely to change systems. *R & D Watch, 1*(2), 4.

■ Lareau, A. (1996). Assessing parent involvement in schooling: A critical analysis. In A. Booth & J.F. Dunn (Eds.) *Family–school links: How do they affect educational outcomes?* Mahwah, NJ: Lawrence Erlbaum. 57–66.

■ Lee, V.E., Smith, J.B., & Croninger, R.G. (1996). Restructuring high school helps improve student achievement. *WCER Highlights, 8*(1), 4, 5, 9.

Leithwood, K., Steinbach, R., & Begley, P. (1992). Socialization experiences: Becoming a principal in Canada. In F.W. Parkey & G.E. Hall (Eds.), *Becoming a principal: The challenges of beginning leadership* (pp. 284–307). Boston: Allyn and Bacon.

Levine, D. (1991). Creating effective schools: Findings and implications from research and practice. *Phi Delta Kappan, 72*(5), 389–393.

Mansnerus, L. (1992, November 1). Should tracking be derailed? *New York Times,* Sect. 4A, pp. 14–16.

National Association for the Education of Young Children & the National Association of Early Childhood Specialists in State Departments of Education (NAECS/SDE) (1991). Guidelines for appropriate curriculum content and assessment in programs serving children ages 3 through 8. *Young Children, 46*(1), 21–38.

■ National Association of Elementary School Principals. (1994). *Best Ideas from America's blue ribbon schools: Vol. 2.* Thousand Oaks, CA: Corwin Press.

■ National Association of Secondary School Principals. (1996). *Breaking ranks: Changing an American institution.* Reston, VA: NASSP.

Natriello, G. (1990). Intended and unintended consequences: Purposes and effects of teacher evaluation. In J. Millman & L. Darling-Hammond (Eds.), *The new handbook of teacher evaluation: Assessing elementary and secondary school teachers* (pp. 35–45). Newbury Park, CA: Sage.

Nazario, S.L. (1992, June 16). Move grows to promote failing pupils. *Wall Street Journal,* p. B1.

New York City Public Schools. (1992, February 10). *Qualities of the New York City schools chancellor.* Facsimile of an unofficial document.

■ New York City Public Schools, Division of Strategic Planning/Office of Educational Data Services. (1995, October 31). *Annual pupil ethnic census city-wide by school level.*

■ Norton, M.S., Webb, L.D., Dlugosh, L.L., & Sybouts, W. (1996). *The school superintendency: New responsibilities, new leadership.* Boston, MA: Allyn and Bacon.

■ Oakes, J. (1995). More than meets the eye: Links between tracking and the culture of schools. In H. Pool & J.A. Page (Eds.), *Beyond tracking: Find success in inclusive schools.* Bloomington, IN: Phi Delta Kappa Educational Foundation.

Olson, L. (1990, May 16). Education officials reconsider policies on grade retention. *Education Week,* p. 1, 13.

Olson, L. (1992, October 7). New approaches blurring the line between public and private schools, *Education Week,* p. 1.

■ Ordovensky, P. (1996). What makes an excellent school? *USA Today,* p. D19–20.

■ Parks, D., & Barrett, T. (1994). Principals as leaders of leaders. *Principal, 74*(2), 11–12.

Pate-Bain, H., Achilles, C.M., Boyd-Zaharias, J., & McKenna, B. (1992). Class size does make a difference. *Phi Delta Kappan, 74,* 253–256.

Penkowsky, L.B. (1991, winter/1992, spring). Teacher feature: Real life examples of integrating academic skills in vocational education. *The Journal of the National Association of Vocational Education Special Needs Personnel,* pp. 66–69.

Phelan, P., Davidson, A.L., & Cao, H.T. (1992). Speaking up: Students' perspectives on school. *Phi Delta Kappan, 73*(9), 695–704.

■ Ponessa, J. (1996). Catholic school enrollment continues to increase. *Education Week, 15*(30), 5.

■ Pool, H., & Page, J.A. (Eds.). (1995) Introduction. *Beyond tracking: Finding success in inclusive schools.* Bloomington, IN: Phi Delta Kappa Educational Foundation.

■ Popham, J.W. (1995). School-site assessment: What principals need to know. *Principal, 75*(8), 38–40.

■ Raymond, A. (1996). "The basic school"—Important step for school improvement. *Teaching K–8, 26*(4), 42–46.

■ Rumberger, R.W. (1995). Dropping out of middle school: A multi-level analysis of students and schools. *American Educational Research Journal, 32*(3), 583–625.

Shepard, L.A., & Smith, M.L. (1989). Flunking grades: A recapitulation. In L.A. Shepard & M.L. Smith (Eds.), *Flunking grades: Research and policies on retention* (pp. 214–236). New York: Falmer Press.

■ Sommerfeld, M. (1993). School of life. *Teacher Magazine, 4*(5), 8–9.

■ Sommerfeld, M. (1995). Under the big top. *Educational Week, 15*(14), 22–29.

Tift, C. (1990, June). *Rural administrative leadership handbook.* Portland, OR: Northwest Regional Educational Laboratory.

Til, W.V., Vars, G.F., & Lounsbury, J.H. (1967). *Modern education for the junior high school years* (2nd ed.). Indianapolis: Bobbs-Merrill.

Toch, T. (1991, October 20). Lost in class: How oversize schools fail our students. *Washington Post,* pp. C1, C2.

The tracking wars: Is anyone winning? (1992). *The Harvard Education Letter, 8*(3), 1–4.

U.S. Department of Education. (1993). *Announcement: New report.* Washington, D.C.: Office of Educational Research and Improvement.

■ U.S. Department of Education (1995). Characteristics of the 100 largest public elementary and secondary school districts in the United States: 1992–93. Washington, D.C.: U.S. Government Printing Office.

■ U.S. Department of Education. (1996a). *Digest of education statistics, 1996.* Washington, D.C.: U.S. Government Printing Office.

■ U.S. Department of Education. (1996b). *The condition of education, 1996.* Washington, D.C.: U.S. Government Printing Office.

■ U.S. Department of Education. (1996c). *NAEP 1994 trends in academic progress.* Washington, D.C.: U.S. Government Printing Office. Available electronically at http://www.Ed.gov/NCES/naep/

■ Viadero, D. (1996). School for thought. *Teacher Magazine, 7*(3), 18–20.

Wagner, M.B. (1990). *God's schools: Choice and compromise in American society.* New Brunswick, NJ: Rutgers University Press.

Walsh, D.J., Ellwein, M.C., Eads, G.M., & Miller, A. (1991). Knocking on kindergarten's door: Who gets in? Who's kept out? *Early Childhood Research Quarterly, 6,* 89–100.

■ Walsh, M. (1996). Edison posts high marks in inaugural year. *Education Week, 15*(36), 1, 10–11.

Welsh, P. (1990, September 16). Fast-track trap: How "ability grouping" hurts our schools, kids and families. *Washington Post,* p. B1.

- Zill, N. (1996). Family change and student achievement: What we have learned, what it means for schools. In A. Booth & J.F. Dunn (Eds.), *Family–student links: How do they affect educational outcomes?* (139–176). Mahwah, NJ: Lawrence Erlbaum.

Chapter 6

AAUW Educational Foundation and the National Education Association. (1992). *The AAUW report: How schools shortchange girls: A study of major findings on girls and education.* Washington, DC: Authors.

Appalachia Educational Laboratory. (1990). Rural school finance, fiscal policies for rural schools, a conference summary [Special issue]. *The Link, 9*(4).

Bales, R.F. (1954). In conference. *Harvard Business Review*, No. 32, 41–49.

Barnard, C.I. (1938). *The function of the executive.* Cambridge: Harvard University Press.

Becker, G.S. (1964). *Human capital: A theoretical and empirical analysis, with special reference to education.* New York: Columbia University Press.

Berliner, D.C. (1992, February). *Educational reform in an era of disinformation.* Paper presented at the annual meeting of the American Association of Colleges for Teacher Education, San Antonio, TX.

Berliner, D.C. & Biddle, B.J. (1995). *The manufactured crisis: Myths, fraud, and the attack on America's public schools.* Reading, MA: Addison-Wesley.

Berryman, S.E., & Bailey, T.R. (1992). *The double helix of education and the economy: Executive summary.* New York: The Institute on Education and the Economy, Teachers College, Columbia University.

Bowers, D.G., & Seashore, S.E. (1966). Predicting organizational effectiveness with a four-factor theory of leadership. *Administrative Science Quarterly, 11*, 238–264.

Bracey, G.W. (1991). Why can't they be like we were? *Phi Delta Kappan, 73*(2), 105–117.

- Bradley, B. (1996). Toward civic-minded media. *Media Studies Journal, 10*(1), 40–41.

Burrup, P.E., & Brimley, V. (1982). *Financing education in a climate of change.* Boston: Allyn and Bacon.

Campbell, R.F., Cunningham, L.L., Nystrand, R.O., & Usdan, M.D. (1990). *The organization and control of American schools* (6th ed.). Columbus, OH: Merrill.

Carson, C.C., Huelskamp, R.M., & Woodall, T.D. (1991). *Perspective on education in America* (3rd draft). Albuquerque, NM: Sandia National Laboratories.

Chubb, J.E., & Moe, T.M. (1990). *Politics, markets, and America's schools.* Washington, DC: The Brookings Institute.

- Clune, W.H. (1995). Educational adequacy: A theory and its remedies. *University of Michigan Journal of Law Reform, 28*(3), 481–491.

Cohn, E., & Geske, T.G. (1990). *The economics of education* (3rd ed.). Oxford: Pergamon Press.

- Darling-Hammond, L., & McLaughlin, M.W. (1995). Policies that support professional development in an era of reform. *Phi Delta Kappan, 76*(8), 597–604.

Education Writers Association. (1989). *Wolves at the schoolhouse door: An investigation of the condition of public school buildings.* Washington, DC: Author.

- Elam, S.M., & Rose, L.C. (1995). The 27th annual Phi Delta Kappan/Gallup Poll of the public's attitudes toward the public schools. *Phi Delta Kappan, 77*(1), 41–56.

- Elam, S.M., Rose, L.C., & Gallup, A.M. (1996). The 28th annual Phi Delta Kappan/Gallup Poll of the public's attitudes toward the public schools. *Phi Delta Kappan, 78*(1), 41–59.

Feistritzer, C.E., Quelle, F., & Chester, D.T. (1989). *Profile of school board presidents in the U.S.* Washington, DC: National Center for Education Information.

Fiedler, F.E. (1967). *A theory of leadership effectiveness.* New York: McGraw-Hill.

- Friedman, M. (1955). The role of government in education. In R.A. Solo (Ed.), *Economics and the public interest* (pp. 123–144). New Brunswick, NJ: Rutgers University Press.

Friedman, M. (1995, June 23). *Public schools: Make them private,* Washington, DC: CATO Institute.

Griffiths, D.E. (Ed.). (1959). *Administrative theory.* New York: Appleton.

Guthrie, J.W., Garms, W.I., & Pierce, L.C. (1988). *School finance and education policy: Enhancing educational efficiency, equality, and choice.* Englewood Cliffs, NJ: Prentice-Hall.

- Hanushek, E. (1989). Expenditures, efficiency, and equity in education: The federal government's role. *The American Economic Review, 79*, 46–51.

Hedges, L.V., Laine, R.D., & Greenwals, R. (1994). Does money matter? A meta-analysis of studies of the effects of differential school inputs on student outcomes. *Educational Researcher, 23*(3), 5–14.

Hentschke, G.C., Dembowski, F.L., Faux, J.H., Hansen, S.J., Kehoe, E., Meno, L., Murphy, M.J., Vigilante, R.P., & Yagielski, J. (1986). *School business administration: A comparative perspective.* Berkeley, CA: McCutchan.

Hoy, W.K., & Miskel, C.G. (1991). *Educational administration: Theory, research, and practice.* New York: McGraw-Hill.

Kozol, J. (1991). *Savage inequalities: Children in America's schools.* New York: Crown.

- Leithwood, K.A. (1992). The move toward transformational leadership. *Educational Leadership, 49*(5), 8–12.

Levin, H.M. (1980). Educational vouchers and social policy. In J.W. Guthrie (Ed.), *School finance: Policies and practices* (pp. 235–263). Cambridge, MA: Balinger.

Levin, H.M. (1987, June). *Finance and governance: Implications of school-based decisions.* Paper presented at the National Advisory Committee of the Work in America Institute, New York.

- Lindle, J.C. (1996). Lessons from Kentucky about school-based decision making. *Educational Leadership, 53*(4), 20–23.

- Lindsay, D. (1994) Schoolhouse rot. *Education Week, 13*(39), 27–33.

McCormick, K. (1984). These tried-and-true alliances have paid off for public schools. *The American School Board Journal, 10*, 24–26.

Miller, J.A. (1993, April 21). Budget greeted with mixed reviews, predictions Congress will change it. *Education Week*, p. 23.

National Association of Manufacturers. (1993). *Tap your workers' potential.* Washington, DC: Author.

- National Association of State Boards of Education. (1996, January). *State education governance at-a-glance.* Alexandria, VA: National Association of State Boards of Education.

National Organization for Women Legal Defense and Education Fund. (1993, Fall). *NOW LDEF challenges St. Louis board of education.* (p. 2) NOW Legal Defense and Education Fund.

- National School Boards Association. (1995, December). *Education vital signs.* Alexandria, VA: National School Boards Association.

Odden, A. (1984). Financing educational excellence. *Phi Delta Kappan, 65*(5), 311–318.

Olson, L., & Bradley, A. (1992, April 29). Boards of contention. *Education Week/Special Report*, pp. 2, 3, 5, 7, 9, 10.

Putka, G. (1991, May 15). Whittle develops plan to operate schools for profit. *Wall Street Journal*, p. B8.

Pyhrr, P. A. (1973). *Zero-base budgeting: A practical management tool for evaluating expenses.* New York: John Wiley & Sons.

Richardson, J. (1992, May). Who benefits? School/business partnerships. *Education Reporter*, pp. 1, 2, 7.

- Sadowski, M. (1995, March/April). The numbers game yields simplistic answers on the link between spending and outcomes. *The Harvard Education Letter, 11*(2), 1–4.

Schultz, T.W. (1981). *Investing in people: The economics of population quality.* Berkeley: University of California Press.

Sergiovanni, T.J., Burlingame, M., Coombs, F.S., & Thurston, P.W. (1992). *Educational governance and administration.* Boston: Allyn and Bacon.

Spring, J. (1991). *American education: An introduction to social and political aspects* (5th ed.). New York: Longman.

Stearns, T.M., Hoffman, A.N., & Heide, J.B. (1987). Performance of commercial television stations as an outcome of interorganizational linkages and environmental conditions. *Academy of Management Journal, 30,* 71–90.

Stogdill, R.M. (1981). Traits of leadership: A follow-up to 1970. In B.M. Bass (Ed.), *Stogdill's handbook of leadership* (pp. 73–97). New York: Free Press.

Thro, W.E. (1990). The third wave: The impact of the Montana, Kentucky and Texas decisions on the future of public school finance reform litigation. *Journal of Law & Education, 19*(2), 219–250.

■ Tovey, R. (1995). Despite the promises, school choice can worsen racial and social class inequities. *The Harvard Education Letter, 11*(3), 1–3.

■ United States General Accounting Office. (1995, September). *School finance: Trends in U.S. education spending.* Washington, DC: Author.

■ U.S. Advisory Commission on Intergovernmental Relations. (1995, February). *Significant features of fiscal federalism: Vol. 1. Budget processes and tax systems.* Washington, DC: U.S. Government Printing Office.

■ U.S. Department of Education (1996a). *Digest of education statistics, 1996.* Washington, DC: U.S. Government Printing Office.

■ U.S. Department of Education (1996b). *The condition of education, 1996.* Washington, DC: U.S. Government Printing Office.

■ U.S. Department of Education (1995a). *Indicator of the month: Public school district funding differences.* Washington, DC: U.S. Government Printing Office.

■ U.S. Department of Education (1996a). *Education policy issues: Statistical perspectives. Use of school choice.* Washington, DC: U.S. Government Printing Office.

U.S. Department of Education. (1989). *Making sense of school budgets.* Washington, DC: Office of Educational Research and Improvement.

Verstegen, D. (1990). Efficiency and economies-of-scale revisited: Implications for financing rural school districts. *Journal of Education Finance, 16,* 159–179.

Verstegen, D., & McGuire, C.K. (1991). The dialectic of reform. *Educational Policy, 5*(4), 386–411.

Ward, J.G. (1992). Schools and the struggle for democracy: Themes for school finance policy. In J.G. Ward & P. Anthony (Eds.), *Who pays for student diversity?* (pp. 241–250). Newbury Park, CA: Corwin Press.

Webb, L.D. (1990). New revenues for education at the state level. In J.K. Underwood & D.A. Verstegen (Eds.), *The impacts of litigation and legislation on public school finance: Adequacy, equity, and excellence* (pp. 27–58). New York: Harper & Row.

■ Weiss, C. (1995). The four 'I's of school reform: How interests, ideology, information, and institution affect teachers and principals. *Harvard Educational Review, 65*(4), 571–592.

West, P. (1993, April 21). Educators say technology program comes up short. *Education Week,* p. 25.

Williams, J. (1992). The politics of education news. In R.F. McNergney (Ed.), *Education research, policy, and the press: Research as news* (pp. 177–200). Boston: Allyn and Bacon.

Zaleznick, A. (1977). Managers and leaders: Are they different? *Harvard Business Review, 55*(3), 67–78.

Chapter 7

■ Applebome, P. (1996, June 6). Aid plan that inspired Clinton is a success. *The New York Times,* p. A20.

■ Balli, S.J. (1996, Winter). Family diversity and the nature of parental involvement. *The Educational Forum, 60,* pp. 149–155.

■ Barr, R.D., & Parrett, W.H. (1995). *Hope at last for at-risk youth.* Boston: Allyn and Bacon.

■ Carnegie Corporation of New York. (1995, Winter). Full-service schools: Ideal as reality. *Carnegie Quarterly, 40*(1), 9.

■ Casper, L.M., Hawkins, M., & O'Connell, M. (1994). *Who's minding the kids?* Washington, DC: U.S. Department of Commerce, Bureau of the Census.

■ Centers for Disease Control and Prevention. (1996, June). *HIV/AIDS surveillance report.* Atlanta, GA: Author.

Children's Defense Fund. (1992). *The state of America's children 1992.* Washington, DC: Author.

Children's Defense Fund. (1995). *Facts and figures.* Available online at http://www.tmn.com/cdf/facts. html#uschildren.

■ Children's Defense Fund. (1996, April 9). *Child gun deaths up 94 percent.* Washington, DC: Author.

Cohen, D.L. (1993b, April 21). Perry Preschool graduates show dramatic new social gains at 27. *Education Week,* pp. 1, 16–17.

■ Coles, A.D. (1996). Kindergarten cops: A partnership between a Los Angeles elementary school and the city's much-maligned police force reaps benefits for both parties. *Teacher Magazine, 15*(27), 37–38.

Creighton, L.L. (1991, December 16). Silent saviors. *U.S. News and World Report,* pp. 80–89.

■ Diver-Stamnes, A. (1995). *Lives in the balance: Youth, poverty, and education in Watts.* Albany: State University of New York Press.

■ Dryfoos, J.G. (1994). *Full-service schools: A revolution in health and social services for children, youth, and families.* San Francisco: Jossey-Bass.

Finn, C.E., Jr. (1991). *We must take charge: Our schools and our future.* New York: Free Press.

■ Fried, R.L. (1995). *The passionate teacher: A practical guide.* Boston: Beacon Press.

Gallup Organization, Inc. (1991). *Teenage suicide study executive summary.* Princeton, NJ: Author.

Garbarino, J., Dubrow, N., Kostelny, K., & Pardo, C. (1992). *Children in danger.* San Francisco: Jossey-Bass.

■ Girls' substance abuse. (1996). *Education Week, 15*(38) 7.

■ Gladding, S.T. (1996). *Counseling: A comprehensive profession* (3rd ed.) (p. 389) Englewood Cliffs, NJ: Prentice-Hall.

Green, J. (1991, October 13). This school is out: At Harvey Milk, a high school for gay students, lessons are taught in grammar, algebra and survival. *The New York Times Magazine,* pp. 32, 33, 36, 59, 60, 68.

Groopman, J.E. (1993, March 8). T.B. or not T.B.? *The New Republic,* pp. 18–19.

■ Harp, L. (1994, September). Who's minding the children? *Education Week, 14,* 28–33.

Hewlett, S.A. (1991). *When the bough breaks: The cost of neglecting our children.* New York: Basic.

■ Jalongo, M.R., Isenberg, J.P., & Gerbracht, G. (1995). *Teachers' stories: From personal narrative to professional insight.* San Francisco: Jossey-Bass.

■ Johnson, M., & Gomez, D. (1995, April). *Big buddies/little buddies: Fostering an ethic of care in an elementary classroom* Paper presented at the annual meeting of the American Educational Research Association, San Francisco.

■ Kann, L., Warren, W., Collins, J.L., Ross, J., Collins, B., & Kolbe, L.J. (1993). Results from the national school-based 1991 Youth Risk Behavior Survey and progress toward achieving related health objectives for the nation. *Public Health Reports, 108,* Supplement 1, pp. 47–55.

■ Kozol, J. (1995). *Amazing grace.* New York: Random House.

■ Landau, S., Pryor, J.B., & Haefli, K. (1995). Pediatric HIV: School-based sequelae and curricular interventions for infection prevention and social acceptance. *School Psychology Review, 24*(2), 213–229.

■ Lawton, M. (1995, May). Suicide rate among youths soaring, C .D.C. reports. *Education Week, 14*(32), 5.

■ Leighninger, M., & Niedergang, M. (1995). Good news at Fairbanks Elementary. *Education: How can schools and communities work together to meet the challenge?* Pomfret, CT: Topsfield Foundation.

■ Louis Harris and Associates, Inc. (1996). *The Metropolitan Life survey of the American teacher, 1996: Students voice their opinions on: Violence, social tension and equality among teens, part I.* New York: MetLife.

■ Macfarlane, E. (1995, May). Parent involvement does make a difference in student achievement. *The ERIC Reader* (pp. 1–2) Bloomington, IN: ERIC Clearinghouse on Reading, English, and Communication.

McCarthy, M.M., & Cambron-McCabe, N. (1992). *Public school law: Teachers' and students' rights* (3rd ed.). Boston: Allyn and Bacon.

Merina, A. (1993, February). Stopping violence starts with students. *NEA Today*, pp. 4–5.

Mitchell, E. (1991, May 20). One man's Taylor-made tuition. *Time*, p. 62.

■ Mullet, J.H., & Groves, C.C. (1996, March). Second chance university. *American School Board Journal*, pp. 23–25.

National Commission on Children. (1991). *Beyond rhetoric: A new American agenda for children and families*. Washington, DC: Author.

■ National Research Council. (1993). *Understanding child abuse and neglect*. Washington, DC: National Academy Press.

■ Neuman, S.B., Hagedorn, T., Celano, D., & Daly, P. (1995, Winter). Toward a collaborative approach to parent involvement in early education: A study of teenage mothers in an African-American community. *32*(4), 801–827.

Panel on High-Risk Youth, Commission on Behavioral and Social Sciences and Education, National Research Council. (1993). *Losing generations: Adolescents in high-risk settings*. Washington, DC: National Academy Press.

Phelps, L., & Bajorek, E. (1991). Eating disorders of the adolescent: Current issues in etiology, assessment, and treatment. *School Psychological Review, 20*(1), 9–22.

Portner, J. (1993, June 16). Prevention efforts in junior high found not to curb drug use in high school. *Education Week*, p. 9.

Reynolds, B. (1993, June 12). Throwaway children are nation's secret scandal. *USA Today*, p. 11A.

■ Riley, R. (1996, March 7). *Riley Touts National Read, Writing Partnership as Reading Report Card is Issued* Available online at http://inet.ed.gov/PressReleases/03-1996/readfin.html.

■ Ross, S.M., Smith, L.J., Casey, J., & Slavin, R.E. (1995, Winter). Increasing the academic success of disadvantaged children: An examination of alternative early intervention programs. *American Educational Research Journal, 32*(4), 773–800.

Sanderson, C.A., & Wilson, S.N. (1991). Sexuality education in schools: Planning the future. *Curriculum Review, 30*(5), 3–7.

■ Sidel, R. (1996). *Keeping women and children last: America's war on the poor*. New York: Penguin.

■ Smith, T., Polloway, E., Patton, J., & Dowdy, C. (1995). *Teaching students with special needs in inclusive settings*. Boston: Allyn and Bacon.

■ Strapp, L. (1996). Teen parenting: One school system's efforts to help mothers and their babies. *Equity and Excellence in Education, 29*(1), 86–90.

■ *Teacher Magazine* (1995, February). Free breakfasts for all, *6*(5), p. 9

Tonks, D. (1992, December/1993, January). Can you save your students' lives? Educating to prevent AIDS. *Educational Leadership*, pp. 48–54.

U.S. Bureau of the Census. (1994a). *Statistical abstract of the United States*. Washington, DC: U.S. Government Printing Office.

U.S. Bureau of the Census. (1994b). *Marital status and living arrangements*. Washington, DC: U.S. Government Printing Office.

■ U.S. Bureau of the Census. (1995). *Statistical abstract of the United States*. Washington, DC: U.S. Government Printing Office.

■ U.S. Bureau of the Census. (1996). *Income and poverty: 1994*. Available online at http://www.census. gov/hhes/income/povregn.html.

U.S. Department of Education. (1993). *Reinventing Chapter 1: The current Chapter I program and new directions, final report of the National Assessment of the Chapter 1 Program*. Washington, DC: Author.

U.S. Department of Education (1994). *Condition of education 1994*. Washington, DC: U.S. Government Printing Office.

■ U.S. Department of Education (1995a). *Indicator of the month: Crime in the schools*. Washington, DC: U.S. Government Printing Office.

■ U.S. Department of Education (1995b). *Indicator of the month: Welfare recipiency, by educational attainment*. Washington, DC: U.S. Government Printing Office.

■ U.S. Department of Education (1995c). *National education longitudinal study of 1988: Two years later: Cognitive gains and school transitions of NELS: 88 eighth graders*. Washington, DC: U.S. Government Printing Office.

■ U.S. Department of Education (1996). *Digest of education statistics 1996*. Washington, DC: U.S. Government Printing Office.

■ U.S. Department of Health and Human Services (1996, January/February). Teen births decline. *Public Health Reports, 3*(1), 95.

Viadero, D. (1994, December 14). Table talk. *Education Week, 14*(15), 35–37.

■ Viadero, D. (1996). Title 1 students show gains. *Education Week, 15*(31) 10.

Waxman, H.C. (1992). Introduction: Reversing the cycle of educational failure for students in at-risk environments. In H.C. Waxman, J. Walker de Felix, J.E. Anderson, & H.P. Baptiste, Jr. (Eds.), *Students at risk in at-risk schools: Improving environments for learning* (pp. 1–9). Newbury Park, CA: Corwin Press.

Chapter 8

Asante, M.K. (1991). The Afrocentric idea in education. *The Journal of Negro Education, 60*(2), 170–180.

■ Banks, J.A. (1996). The historical reconstruction of knowledge about race: Implications for transformative teaching. In J.A. Banks (Ed.), *Multicultural education, transformative knowledge, and action: Historical and contemporary perspectives* (pp. 64–87). New York: Teachers College Press.

■ Banks, J.A. (1997). Multicultural education: Characteristics and goals. In J.A. Banks & C.A. McGee Banks (Eds.), *Multicultural education: Issues and perspectives* (3rd ed.) (pp. 3–28). Boston: Allyn and Bacon.

■ Banks, J.A., & Banks, C.A. (Eds.). (1995). *Handbook of research on multicultural education*. New York: Macmillan.

■ Bennett, C. I. (1995). *Comprehensive multicultural education: Theory and practice* (3rd ed.). Boston: Allyn and Bacon.

Bernstein, R. (1990, October 14). In U.S. schools: A war of words. *The New York Times Magazine*, pp. 44–47.

Bourdieu, P., & Passeron, J.C. (1977). *Reproduction: In education, society, and culture*. Beverly Hills, CA: Sage.

■ Bradley, A. (1996, March 13). Unconventional wisdom: Two distinguished African-American educators dissent from the progressive ideology of contemporary school reform. *Education Week, 15*(25), 34–43.

Bullivant, B.M. (1993). Culture: Its nature and meaning for educators. In J.A. Banks & C.A. McGee Banks (Eds.), *Multicultural education: Issues and perspectives* (2nd ed.) (pp. 29–47). Boston: Allyn and Bacon.

Caplan, N., Choy, M.H., & Whitmore, J.K. (1991). *Children of the boat people: A study of educational success*. Ann Arbor: University of Michigan Press.

■ Carey, N., & Farris, E. (1996, March). *Racial and ethnic classifications used by public schools*. Washington, DC: National Center for Education Statistics, Office of Educational Research and Improvement, Department of Education.

■ Caudell, L.S. (1996). Research review. *NW Education, 1*(1), 31–34.

■ Chevigny, G.G. (1996). *The Nation, 262*(9), 16–21.

Cooper, K.J. (1992, November 27). Broadening horizons: Afrocentrism takes root in Atlanta schools. *Washington Post*, p. A1.

Deck, S.L. (1991, November 14). A young teacher corps faces old battles. *The Declaration—A Weekly Newsmagazine*, pp. 6–7.

■ Gay, G. (1995). Curriculum theory and multicultural education. In J.A. Banks & C.A. Banks (Eds.), *Handbook of research on multicultural education* (pp. 25–43). New York: Macmillan.

■ Gollnick, D.M. (1995). National and state initiatives for multicultural education. In J.A. Banks & C.A. Banks (Eds.), *Handbook of research on multicultural education* (pp. 44–64). New York: Macmillan.

■ Grant, C.A., & Gomez, M.L. (1996). *Making schooling multicultural: Campus and classroom*. Englewood Cliffs: Prentice-Hall.

■ Harrison, R., & Bennett, C. (1995). Racial and ethnic diversity. In R. Farley (Ed.), *State of the union: America in the 1990s: Vol. 2. Social trends*. New York: Russell Sage Foundation.

■ Herbert, J.M., & McNergney, R.F. (1996). *The case of Columbus, New*

Mexico: Educational life on the border. Washington, DC: American Association of Colleges for Teacher Education and ERIC Clearinghouse on Teaching & Teacher Education.

Hill, D. (1990, June/July). A theory of success and failure. *Teacher Magazine*, pp. 40–45.

Hollins, E. (1982). The Marva Collins story revisited: Implications for regular classroom instruction. *Journal of Teacher Education, 33*(1), pp. 37–40.

■ Johnson, D.W., Johnson, R., Dudley, B., Ward, M., & Magnuson, D. (1995). The impact of peer mediation training on the management of school and home conflicts. *American Educational Research Journal, 32*(4), 824–844.

Kamen, A. (1991, August 12). The Cambodians: A temple anchors community. *Washington Post*, p. A9.

Kleinfeld, J. (1995). Critical perspective on the case of Hans Christian Andersen School. In *Guide to foundations in action: Videocases: Teaching and learning in multicultural settings* (pp. 191–208). Boston: Allyn and Bacon.

■ Kunen, J.S. (1996). The end of integration. *Time, 147*(18), 38–45.

Lach, M.C. (1992). Essay: An inner-city education. *Scientific American, 266* (1), p. 151.

■ Louis Harris and Associates, Inc. (1996). *The Metropolitan Life survey of the American teacher: 1996: Students voice their opinions on violence, social tension and equality among teens, part I.* New York: Author.

■ Manning, M.L., & Baruth, L.G., 1996. *Multicultural education of children and adolescents* (2nd ed.). Boston: Allyn and Bacon.

Marshall, S. (1992, December 24). Louisiana ruling draws fire. *USA Today*, p. A3.

Matute-Bianchi, M.E. (1991). Situational ethnicity and patterns of school performance among immigrant and nonimmigrant Mexican-descent students. In M.A. Gibson & J.U. Ogbu (Eds.), *Minority status and schooling: A comparative study of immigrant and involuntary minorities* (pp. 205–248). New York: Garland.

McDonnell, L.M., & Hill, P. (1993). *Newcomers in American schools: Meeting the educational needs of immigrant children.* Washington, DC: RAND Corporation.

Meek, M. (1992, Fall). The peacekeepers: Students use mediation skills to resolve conflicts. *Teaching Tolerance*, pp. 46–52.

■ Morin, R. (1995, October 8). A distorted image of minorities. *Washington Post*, pp. A1, A27.

Mosle, S. (1993, August 1). Scissors, not sermons. *Washington Post Education Review*, p. 5.

National Education Association. (1993, February). Stopping violence starts with students. *NEA Today*, pp. 4–5.

New York State Social Studies Review and Development Committee. (1991). *One nation, many peoples: A declaration of cultural interdependence.* Albany, NY: New York State Education Department.

Nieto, S. (1992). *Affirming diversity: The sociopolitical context of multicultural education.* New York: Longman.

■ Oei, T. & Lyon G. (1996). In our own words. *Teaching Tolerance, 5*(2), 46–59.

Office of Federal Statistical Policy and Standards. (1978). *Statistical policy handbook.* Washington, DC: U.S. Department of Commerce.

Ogbu, J.U. (1991). Immigrant and involuntary minorities in comparative perspective. In M.A. Gibson & J.U. Ogbu (Eds.), *Minority status and schooling: A comparative study of immigrant and involuntary minorities* (pp. 3–36). New York: Garland.

■ Phillips, W. (1993). Introduction. *Partisan Review, 60*(4), 509.

■ Ponessa, J. (1995). NEA backing for gay month sparks firestorm. *Education Week, 15*(8), 3.

■ Porter, R.P. (1995). The New York City study. *READ Perspectives, 2*(2), 1–5.

Pratt, R.A. (1992). *The color of their skin: Education and race in Richmond, Virginia 1954–89.* Charlottesville: University Press of Virginia.

Quality Education for Minorities Network. (1991, March 4). *Multicultural education.* Washington, DC: QEM Network.

■ Ramirez, J.D. (1992, Winter/Spring). Executive summary. *Bilingual Research Journal, 16*: 1–245.

Ravitch, D. (1990, November 29). We can teach cultural history—or racial hate. *New York Daily News*, p. 30.

■ Searle, J.R. (1993). Is there a crisis in American higher education? *Partisan Review, 60*(4), 693–708.

■ Sleeter, C.E. (1993). Multicultural education: Five views. *Education Digest, 58*(7), 53–57.

■ Sleeter, C.E., & Grant, C.A. (1994). *Making choices for multicultural education: Five approaches to race, class, and gender* (2nd ed.). Englewood Cliffs, NJ: Merrill/Prentice-Hall.

■ Steele, S. (1990). *The content of our character: A new vision of race in America.* New York: Harper Perennial.

■ Steel, M. (1995, spring). New colors: Mixed-race families still find a mixed reception. *Teaching Tolerance, 4*(1), pp. 44–49.

Terkel, S. (1992). *Race: How blacks and whites think and feel about the American obsession.* New York: New Press.

■ Ungar, S. (1995). *Fresh blood: The new American immigrants.* New York: Simon & Schuster.

■ U.S. Bureau of the Census. (1996, February). *How we're changing: Demographic state of the nation: 1996.* Washington, DC: U.S. Government Printing Office.

U.S. Department of Commerce, Census Bureau. (1994). *Statistical abstract of the U.S.* (114th ed.). Washington, DC: Author.

■ U.S. Department of Education. (1996, June). *Announcement: NCES releases proceedings of the Conference on Inclusion Guidelines and Accommodations for limited English proficient students in the National Assessment of Educational Progress.* Washington, DC: U.S. Government Printing Office.

■ Viadero, D. (1996, April 10). Culture clash: When teachers and students come from different backgrounds, researchers say, they may end up not speaking the same language. *Education Week, 15*(29), 39–42.

Villegas, A.M. (1991). *Culturally responsive pedagogy for the 1990s and beyond.* Princeton, NJ: Educational Testing Service.

Vobejda, B. (1991, September 23–29). The changing face of America: Racial and ethnic shifts are remixing the melting pot. *Washington Post*, pp. 6–7.

■ Westside Prep. '60 Minutes' crush *The Bell Curve.* (1995, September 26). *Chicago Defender, 11*, 1.

■ Words that hurt: Chicago exhibit forces kids to confront prejudice. (1996, May/June). *Teacher Magazine*, p. 13.

■ Wright, L. (1994, July 25). One drop of blood. *The New Yorker.* New York: The New Yorker Magazine, Inc., pp. 46–55.

Chapter 9

AAUW Educational Foundation and the National Education Association. (1992). *The AAUW report: How schools shortchange girls: A study of major findings on girls and education.* Washington, DC: Authors.

Abramowitz, R.H., Petersen, A.C., & Schulenberg, J.E. (1984). Changes in self-image during early adolescence. In D.Offer, E. Ostrov, & K. Howard (Eds.), *Patterns of adolescent self-image* (pp. 19–28). San Francisco: Jossey-Bass.

American Association on Mental Retardation. (1992). *Mental retardation: Definition, classification, and systems of support* (9th ed.). Washington, DC: Author.

■ Arnett, J. (1994/1995). The fun (and danger) of reckless behavior. *Counseling and Human Development Newsletter, 14*(1), 1–3.

Avery, P.G., & Walker, C. (1993). Prospective teachers' perceptions of ethnic and gender differences in academic achievement. *Journal of Teacher Education, 44*(1), 27–37.

Bempechat, J., London, P., & Dweck, C.S. (1991). Children's conceptions of ability in major domains: An interview and experimental study. *Child Study Journal, 21*(1), 11–35.

Berg, C.A. (1992). Perspectives for viewing intellectual development throughout the life course. In R.J. Sternberg & C.A. Berg (Eds.), *Intellectual development* (pp. 1–15). Cambridge: Cambridge University Press.

■ Brooks-Gunn, J., Graber, J.H., & Paikoff, R.L. (1994). Studying links between hormones and negative affect: Models and measures. *Journal of Research on Adolescence, 4*(4), 469–486.

Bouchard, J.J., Jr., Lykken, D.T., McGue, M., Segal, N., & Tellegen, A. (1990). Sources of human psychological differences: The Minnesota study of twins reared apart. *Science, 250*, 223–228.

■ Cameron, J., & Pierce, W.D. (1994, Fall). Reinforcement, reward, and intrinsic motivation: A meta-analysis. *Review of Educational Research, 64*(3), 363–423.

Ceci, S. J., & Ruiz, A. (1993). Transfer, abstractness, and intelligence. In D. Detterman & R. J. Sternberg (Eds.), *Transfer on trial: Intelligence, cognition, and instruction* (pp. 168–191). Norwood, NJ: Ablex.

Children's Defense Fund. (1992). *The state of America's children 1992.* Washington, DC: Author.

■ Clark, C.M. (1995). *Thoughtful teaching.* London: Cassell.

Cohen, D.L. (1993, April 7). New study links lower I.Q. at age 5 to poverty. *Education Week*, p. 4.

Cremin, L.A. (1957). *The republic and the school.* New York: Teachers College Press.

■ Daily Report Card. (1996, June 19). Single-sex classes: A return to the turn of the century? Available online at http://www.utopia.com/mailings/reportcard/DAILY.REPORT.CARD217.html#Index2.

■ Davydov, V.V. (1995, April). The influence of L.S. Vygotsky on education theory, research, and practice. *Educational Researcher, 24*(3), 12–21.

Elliott, E., & Dweck, C.S. (1988). Goals: An approach to motivation and achievement. *Journal of Personality and Social Psychology, 54*, 5–12.

Erikson, E.H. (1980). *Identity and the life cycle.* New York: Norton.

■ Fine, M. (1995). *Habits of mind: Struggling over values in America's classrooms.* San Francisco: Jossey-Bass.

Finkel, D. (1993, June 13). The wiz. *Washington Post Magazine*, pp. 8–13, 22–27.

■ Friend, M., & Bursuck, W.D. (1996). *Including students with special needs: A practical guide for classroom teachers.* Boston: Allyn and Bacon.

Gardner, H. (1993). *Multiple intelligences: The theory in practice.* New York: Basic Books.

■ Gardner, H. (1995, November). Reflections on multiple intelligences: Myths and messages. *Phi Delta Kappan, 77*(3), 200–209.

Gardner, H., & Hatch, T. (1989). Multiple intelligences go to school: Educational implications of the theory of multiple intelligences. *Educational Researcher, 18*(8), 4–10.

Gartner, A., & Lipsky, D.K. (1989). *The yoke of special education: How to break it.* Rochester, NY: National Center on Education and the Economy.

Gilligan, C. (1982). *In a different voice: Psychological theory and women's development.* Cambridge, MA: Harvard University Press.

Gilligan, C., & Attanucci, J. (1988). Two moral orientations: Gender differences and similarities. *Merrill-Palmer Quarterly, 34*, 223–237.

Guilford, J.P. (1988). Some changes in the structure-of-intellect model. *Educational and Psychological Measurement*, 48, 1–4.

■ Hallahan, D.P., & Kauffman, J.M. (1997). *Exceptional children: Introduction to special education* (7th ed.). Englewood Cliffs, NJ: Prentice-Hall.

Hammill, D.D., Leigh, J.E., McNutt, G., & Larsen, S. (1988). A new definition of learning disabilities. *Learning Disability Quarterly, 11*(3), 217–232.

■ Hansen, D.T. (1996, January). Teaching and the moral life of classrooms. *Journal for a Just and Caring Education, 2*(1), 59–74.

Henry, S.L., & Pepper, F.C. (1990). Cognitive, social, and cultural effects on Indian learning style: Classroom implications. *Journal of Educational Issues of Language Minority Students, 7*, 85–97.

■ Herrnstein, R.J., & Murray, C. (1994). *The bell curve.* New York: Free Press.

Hilliard, A. G., III. (1990). Back to Binet: The case against the use of IQ tests in the schools. *Contemporary Education, 61*(4), 184–189.

■ Jenkins, J., Zigmond, N., Fuchs, L., Fuchs, D., & Deno, S. (1993). Special education in restructured schools: Findings from three multi-year studies. *Phi Delta Kappan.*

Kauffman, J.M. (1990). Restructuring in sociopolitical contest: Reservations about the effects of current reform proposals on students with disabilities. In J.W. Lloyd, N.M. Singh, & A.C. Repp (Eds.), *The regular education initiative: Alternative perspectives on concepts, issues, and models* (pp. 57–66). Sycamore, IL: Sycamore.

■ Keating, D.P. (1984). The emperor's new clothes: The "new look" in intelligence research. In R.J. Sternberg (Ed.), *Advances in the psychology of human intelligence: Vol. 2* (1–45) Hillsdale, NJ: Erlbaum.

■ Kohn, A. (1996, Spring). By all available means: Camero and Pierce's defense of extrinsic motivators. *Review of Educational Research, 66*(1), 1–4.

Kuralt, C. (1992, May 29). *Sunday morning.* (CBS). Transcript from: Livingston, NJ: Burrelle's Information Services.

■ Lawton, M. (1995). More children becoming overweight, study finds. *Education Week, 15*(6), 6.

■ Lawton, M. (1996). Effort to improve diet, exercise of students results in some gains. *Education Week, 15*(27), 14.

Leff, L. (1992, April 5). The learning curve: Inside an American high school. *Washington Post*, pp. A1, A22, A23.

■ Lepper, M.R., Keavney, M., & Drake, M. (1996, Spring). Intrinsic motivation and extrinsic rewards: A commentary on Camero and Pierce's meta-analysis. *Review of Educational Research, 66*(1), 5–32.

■ LoVette, O.K., & Jacob, S. (1995). Why do so many high achieving high school students dislike school? *NASSP Bulletin, 79*(575), 70–75.

Lyons, N.P. (1993). Luck, ethics, and ways of knowing: Observations on adolescents' deliberations in making moral choices. In A. Garrod (Ed.), *Approaches to moral development: New research and emerging themes* (pp. 133–154). New York: Teachers College Press.

■ Magik, P.J. (1995). Disability culture. *The Disability Rag and Resource, 16*(5), 7.

■ Marsh, H.W., Chessor, D., Craven, R., & Roche, L. (1995). The effects of gifted and talented programs on academic self-concept: The big fish strikes again. *American Educational Research Journal, 32*(2), 285–319.

Mwamwenda, T.S. (1992). Comment: Universality of formal operational thought. *Perceptual and Motor Skills, 78*(2), 78.

National Association of State Boards of Education (NASBE) Study Group on Special Education. (1992). *Winners all: A call for inclusive schools.* Alexandria, VA: National Association of State Boards of Education.

Page, R. M. (1990, September/October). Loneliness and adolescent health behavior. *Health Education*, pp. 14–17.

Palmer, J.M., & Yantis, P.A. (1990). *Survey of communication disorders.* Baltimore, MD: Williams & Wilkins.

■ Pogrow, S. (1995). Making reform work for the educationally disadvantaged. *Educational Leadership, 52*(5), 20–24.

■ Pollina, A. (1995). Gender balance: Lessons from girls in science and mathematics. *Educational Leadership, 53*(1), 30–33.

Power, F.C., Higgins, A., & Kohlberg, L. (1989). *Lawrence Kohlberg's approach to moral education.* New York: Columbia University Press.

Renzulli, J.S. (1982). Dear Mr. and Mrs. Copernicus: We regret to inform you. . . . *Gifted Child Quarterly, 26*, 11–14.

Rierdan, J., & Koff, E. (1991). Depressive symptomology among very early maturing girls. *Journal of Youth and Adolescence, 20*, 415–25.

Rutherford, F.J., & Ahlgren, A. (1990). *Science for all Americans.* New York: Oxford University Press.

Sadker, M., & Sadker, D. (1993, March). Fair and square? *Instructor*, pp. 45, 46, 67, 68.

Schmidt, P. (1993, May 26). Seeking to identify the gifted among L.E.P. students. *Education Week*, pp. 1, 12–13.

Spearman, C. (1927). *The abilities of man.* New York: Macmillan.

Sprinthall, N.A., & Sprinthall, R.C. (1990). *Educational psychology: A developmental approach* (5th ed.). New York: McGraw-Hill.

Sternberg, R.J. (1988). *The triarchic mind: A new theory of human intelligence.* New York: Viking.

■ Sternberg, R.J. (1996, March). Myths, countermyths, and truths about intelligence. *Educational Researcher, 25*(2), 11–16.

Sternberg, R.J., & Detterman, D.K. (Eds.). (1986). *What is intelligence?: Contemporary viewpoints on its nature and definition.* Norwood, NJ: Ablex.

Sutherland, P. (1992). *Cognitive development today: Piaget and his critics*. London: Paul Chapman.

■ U.S. Department of Education (1993). *National excellence: A case for developing America's talent*. Washington, DC: U.S. Government Printing Office.

■ U.S. Department of Education (1995a). *Education policy issues: Statistical perspectives: Extracurricular participation and student engagement*. Washington, DC: U.S. Government Printing Office.

■ U.S. Department of Education (1995b). *Statistics in brief: Who can play? An examination of NCAA's Proposition 16*. Washington, DC: U.S. Government Printing Office.

■ U.S. Department of Education (1995c). *Seventeenth annual report to Congress on implementation of the Individuals with Disabilities Education Act*. Washington, DC: Author.

■ U.S. Department of Education (1996). *NCES releases the educational progress of women*. Washington, DC: U.S. Government Printing Office.

U.S. Department of Health, Education, and Welfare. (1977, August 23). *Federal Register, 42*(163), 42478.

■ Viadero, D. (1996, January). Expert testimony. *Teacher Magazine*, pp. 24–25.

Wolf, B., Pratt, C., & Pruitt, P. (1990). *Human exceptionality: Society, school and family* (3rd ed.). Boston: Allyn and Bacon.

Yussen, S.R., & Kane, P.T. (1985). Children's conception of intelligence. In S.R. Yussen (Ed.), *The growth of reflection in children* (pp. 207–241). Orlando, FL: Academic Press.

Chapter 10

■ Aceland, R. (1967). *A move to the integrated curriculum*. Exeter, England: University of Exeter.

■ Airasian, P.W. (1996). *Assessment in the classroom*. New York: McGraw-Hill.

Apple, M.W. (1993). *Official knowledge*. New York: Routledge.

Apple, M.W., & Beyer, L.E. (1988). Social evaluation of curriculum schooling. In L.E. Beyer & M.W. Apple (Eds.), *The curriculum: Problems, politics, and possibilities* (pp. 334–349). Albany: State University of New York Press.

Applebee, A.N. (1991). Environments for language teaching and learning. In J. Flood, J. Jensen, & J.R. Squire (Eds.), *Handbook of research on teaching the English language arts* (pp. 549–558). New York: Macmillan.

Applebee, A.N., & Purves, A.C. (1992). Literature and the English language arts. In P.W. Jackson (Ed.), *Handbook of research on curriculum* (pp. 726–748). New York: Macmillan.

Arter, J.A., & Spandel, V. (1992). NCME instructional module: Using portfolios of student work in instruction and assessment. *Educational Measurement, 11*, 36–44.

Association for Supervision and Curriculum Development. (1992, January). What the NCTM standards say. *Curriculum Update*, p. 3.

■ Atwell, N. (1987). *In the middle: Writing, reading, and learning with adolescents* (pp. 3–4). Portsmouth, NH: Boynton/Cook.

■ Berk, L.E. (1992). The extracurriculum. In P.W. Jackson (Ed.), *Handbook of research on curriculum* (pp. 1002–1043). New York: Macmillan.

Bloom, B. (1971). Mastery learning. In J.H. Block (Ed.), *Mastery learning: Theory and practice* (pp. 13–28). New York: Holt, Rinehart & Winston.

Blumenfeld, P., Soloway, E., Marx, R., Krajcik, J., Guzdial, M., & Palcinsar, A. (1991). Motivating project-based learning: Sustaining the doing, supporting the learning. *Educational Psychologist, 26*(3 & 4), 369–398.

Brophy, J. (1987). On motivating students. In D.C. Berliner & B.V. Rosenshine (Eds.), *Talks to teachers* (pp. 201–245). New York: Random House.

■ Brown, A.L., & Palincsar, A.S. (1989). Guided, cooperative learning and individual knowledge acquisition. In L.B. Resnick (Ed.), *Knowing, learning, and instruction: Essays in honor of Robert Glaser* (pp. 393–451). Hillsdale, NJ: Lawrence Erlbaum.

■ Burns, M. (1995). The 8 most important lessons I've learned about organizing my teaching year. *Instructor, 105*(2), 86–88.

■ Canady, R.L., & Rettig, M.D. (1995). The power of innovative scheduling. *Educational Leadership, 53*(3), 4–10.

Carroll, J.B. (1971). Problems of measurement related to the concept of learning for mastery. In J.H. Block (Ed.), *Mastery learning: Theory and practice* (pp. 29–46). New York: Holt, Rinehart & Winston.

Clandinin, D.J. & Connelly, F.M. (1992). Teacher as curriculum maker. In P.W. Jackson (Ed.), *Handbook of research on curriculum* (pp. 363–401). New York: Macmillan.

Clark, C.M., & Dunn, S. (1991). Second-generation research on teachers' planning. In H.C. Waxman & H.J. Walberg (Eds.), *Effective teaching: Current research* (pp. 183–201). Berkeley, CA: McCutchan.

Corno, L. (1987). Teaching and self-regulated learning. In D.C. Berliner & B.V. Rosenshine (Eds.), *Talks to teachers* (pp. 249–266). New York: Random House.

■ Corno, L. (1995). The principles of adaptive teaching. In A.C. Ornstein (Ed.). *Teaching: Theory into practice*. Boston: Allyn and Bacon.

Cuban, L. (1992). Curriculum stability and change. In P.W. Jackson (Ed.), *Handbook of research on curriculum* (pp. 216–217). New York: Macmillan.

DeBoer, G.E. (1991). *A history of ideas in science education: Implications for practice*. New York: Teachers College Press.

■ Diegmueller, K. (1995a). Buy the book. *Education Week, 15*(8), 3–11.

■ Diegmueller, K. (1995b). California plotting new tack on language arts: State to wed phonics and whole language. *Education Week, 14*(38), 1, 12.

■ Dik, D.A. (1995). *Overseas school advisory council project #4-93: Two year project of special merit, final rept, December, 1995*. New York: Metropolitan Opera Guild.

Doyle, W. (1986). Classroom organization and management. In M.C. Wittrock (Ed.), *Handbook of research on teaching* (3rd ed.) (pp. 392–431) New York: Macmillan.

■ Eggen, P.D., & Kauchak, D.P. (1996). *Strategies for teachers: Teaching content and thinking skills* (3rd ed.). Boston: Allyn and Bacon.

Eisner, E. W. (1985). *The educational imagination: On the design and evaluation of school programs* (2nd ed.). New York: Macmillan.

Eisner, E.W. (1991, September). What the arts taught me about education. *Art Education*, pp. 11–19.

Eisner, E.W. (1992). The misunderstood role of the arts in human development. *Phi Delta Kappan, 73*(8), 591–595.

Eisner, E.W., & Vallance, E. (1974). *Conflicting conceptions of curriculum*. Berkeley, CA: McCutchan.

Ellwein, M.C. (1992). Research on classroom assessment meanings and practices. *Commonwealth Center News, 5*(1), 2, 4.

Fairfax County Public Schools. (1991). *Family life education: Human growth and development, grades 5–6*. Fairfax, VA: Office of Curriculum Services, Fairfax County Public Schools.

■ Fielding, L.G., & Pearson, R.D. (1994). Reading comprehension: What works. *Educational Leadership, 51*(5), 62–68.

■ Frieberg, H.L., & Driscoll, A. (1996). *Universal teaching strategies* (2nd ed.). Boston: Allyn and Bacon.

■ Frieberg, H.L., Stein, T.A., & Huang, S. (1995). Effects of a classroom management intervention on student achievement in inner-city elementary schools. *Educational Research and Evaluation, 1*(1), 36–66.

Gage, N.L. (1978). *The scientific basis of the art of teaching*. New York: Teachers College Press.

■ Goodlad, J.I., & Su, Z. (1992). Organization of the curriculum. In P.W. Jackson (Ed.), *Handbook of research on curriculum* (pp. 327–344). New York: Macmillan.

Grobman, H. (1970). *Developmental curriculum projects: Decision points and processes*. Itasca, IL: Peacock.

Gudmundsdottir, S. (1991). Values in pedagogical content knowledge. *The Journal of Teacher Education, 41*(3), 44–52.

Gursky, D. (1991, August). After the reign of Dick and Jane. *Teacher Magazine*, pp. 22–29.

Harp, L. (1993, September 22). Pa. parent becomes mother of "outcomes" revolt. *Education Week*, pp. 1, 19–21.

■ The Hitachi Foundation. (1996). UVA's real-world approach to teacher training. *Education Today, 7*(3), S3.

Hunt, D.E., & Sullivan, E.V. (1974). *Between psychology and education*. Hinsdale, IL: Dryden Press.

Jackson, P.W. (1990). *Life in classrooms*. New York: Teachers College Press.

Johnson, D., & Johnson, R. (1991). *Learning together and alone* (3rd ed.). Englewood Cliffs, NJ: Prentice-Hall.

■ Johnson, M. (1989). Embodied knowledge. *Curriculum Inquiry*, 19(4), 361–377.

■ Joyce, B., & Weil, M. (1996). *Models of teaching* (5th ed.). Boston: Allyn and Bacon.

Kounin, J.S. (1970). *Discipline and group management in classrooms*. New York: Holt, Rinehart and Winston.

Langer, J.A., & Applebee, A.N. (1986). Reading and writing instruction: Toward a theory of teaching and learning. In E.Z. Rothkopf (Ed.), *Review of research in education: Vol. 13* (pp. 171–194). Washington, DC: American Educational Research Association.

Magee, M. (1992). *On television: Teach the children* (Study guide & transcript). Kent, OH: PTV.

Mager, R.F. (1962). *Preparing instructional objectives*. Palo Alto, CA: Fearon.

■ Matson, B. (1996). Whole language or phonics? Teachers and researchers find the middle ground most fertile. *The Harvard Education Letter*, 12(2), 1–3.

■ McAuliffe, J., & Stoskin, L. (1993). *What color is Saturday? Using analogies to enhance creative thinking in the classroom*. Tucson, AZ: Zephyr Press.

McCarthy, C. (1993, July 3). Firing the messenger. *Washington Post*, p. A23.

McConaghy, T. (1992). A witch hunt bedevils a Canadian reading series. *Phi Delta Kappan*, 73(8), 649.

■ Morrison, G.S. (1993). *Contemporary curriculum K–8*. Boston: Allyn and Bacon.

National Council of Teachers of Mathematics. (1989). *Curriculum and evaluation standards for school mathematics*. Reston, VA: Author.

National Council of Teachers of Mathematics. (1991). *Professional standards for teaching mathematics*. Reston, VA: Author.

New York State Social Studies Review and Development Committee. (1991). *Executive summary of the report of the New York State Social Studies Review and Development Committee*. New York: State Education Department and the University of the State of New York.

Newman, F.M., & Thompson, J.A. (1987). *Effects of cooperative learning on achievement in secondary schools: A summary of research*. Madison, WI: National Center on Effective Secondary Schools.

Nuthall, D.D. (1992, May). Performance assessment: The message from England. *Educational Leadership*, pp. 54–57.

■ Office of Educational Research and Improvement (OERI) (1995, October). *Announcement: Helping your child with homework*. Washington, DC: U.S. Department of Education.

Oliva, P.F. (1992). *Developing the curriculum* (3rd ed.). New York: HarperCollins.

■ Peshkin, A. (1992). The relationship between culture and curriculum: A many fitting thing. In P.W. Jackson (Ed.), *Handbook of research on curriculum*. (pp. 248–267). New York: Macmillan.

■ Pinar, W.F., Reynolds, W.M., Slattery, P., Taubman, P.M. (1995). *Understanding curriculum: An introduction to the study of historical and contemporary curriculum discourses*. New York: Peter Lang Publishing, Inc.

■ Pitsch, M. (1995, February). Life on the Mississippi. *Teacher Magazine*, 6, 14–15.

Putka, G. (1992, February 12). Readers of latest U.S. History textbooks discover a storehouse of misinformation. *Wall Street Journal*, CCXIX(30), B1.

■ Qin, Z., Johnson, D.W., & Johnson, R.T. (1995). Cooperative versus competitive efforts and problem solving. *Review of Educational Research*, 65(2), 129–144.

■ Reilly, R.M. (1995). Channel One is said to gain full access to Capital Cities–ABC News programs. *Wall Street Journal*, CCXXVI (14), B1.

■ Rogers, C. (1971). *Client centered therapy*. Boston: Houghton Mifflin.

Rosenshine, B., & Meister, C. (1994). Reciprocal teaching: A review of the research. *Review of Educational Research*, 64(4), 479–530.

Schubert, W.H. (1986). *Curriculum: Perspective, paradigm, and possibility*. New York: Macmillan.

Schwartz, J.L. (1989). Intellectual mirrors: A step in the direction of making schools knowledge-making places. *Harvard Educational Review*, 59(1), 51–61.

Shanker asks end to some standard tests. (1989, October 29). *Washington Post*, p. A13.

Sharan, S. (1990). Cooperative learning and helping behavior in the multi-ethnic classroom. In H.C. Foot, M.J. Morgan, & R.H. Shute (Eds.), *Children helping children* (pp. 151–176). New York: John Wiley & Sons.

Sharan, Y., & Sharan, S. (1989). Group investigation expands cooperative learning. *Educational Leadership*, 47(4), 17–21.

Slavin, R.E. (1991). Synthesis of research on cooperative learning. *Educational Leadership*, 48(5), 71–82.

Sleeter, C.E., & Grant, C.A. (1991). Race, class, gender, and disability in current textbooks. In M.W. Apple & L.K. Christian-Smith (Eds), *The politics of the textbook* (pp. 78–110). New York: Routledge.

Sobol, T. (1991). *Memorandum to members of the New York Board of Regents*, June 13.

■ Sommerfield, M. (1996). More and more schools putting block scheduling to test of time. *Educational Week*, 15(35), 1, 14.

■ U.S. Congress, Office of Technology Assessment. (1992). *Testing in American schools: Asking the right questions* (OTA-SET-519). Washington, DC: U.S. Government Printing Office.

■ Vallance, E. (1995). The public curriculum of orderly images. *Educational Researcher*, 24(2), 4–13.

Vavrus, L. (1990). Put portfolios to the test. *Instructor*, 100(1), 48–50.

Viadero, D. (1990, November 28). Battle over multicultural education rises in intensity: Issue is what kind, not whether. *Education Week*, pp. 1, 11, 13.

■ Virginia Education Association & The Appalachia Educational Laboratory. (1995, April). *Interdisciplinary units with alternative assessments: A teacher-developed compendium*. Washington, DC: U.S. Department of Education, Office of Educational Research and Improvement.

Weinstein, C.S., & Mignano, A.J. (1993). *Elementary classroom management: Lessons from research and practice*. New York: McGraw-Hill.

Winne, P.H. (1991). Motivation and teaching. In H.C. Waxman & H.J. Walberg (Eds.), *Effective teaching: Current research* (pp. 210–230). Berkeley, CA: McCutchan.

Winne, P.H., & Marx, R.W. (1979). Perceptual problem solving. In P.L. Peterson & H.J. Walberg (Eds.), *Research on teaching: Concepts, findings, and implications* (pp. 210–230). Berkeley, CA: McCutchan.

■ Wolf, D.P. (1994). *An assessment of "Creating Original Opera,"* Cambridge, MA: Performance Assessment Collaboratives for Education.

Chapter 11

■ *Abood v. Detroit Board of Education*, 431 U.S. 209, 97 S.Ct. 1782 (1977).

Alexander, K., & Alexander, M.D. (1992). *American public school law* (3rd ed.). St. Paul, MN: West.

Baker v. Owen, 395 F. Supp. 294 M.D.N.C. (1975).

Beyer, H.A. (1989, September). Education for All Handicapped Children Act: 1975–1989. A judicial history. *Exceptional Parent*, pp. 52–54, 56, 58.

■ *B.M. by Berger v. State of Montana*, 649 P.2d 425 (Mont. 1982).

Board of Education of the Westside Community Schools v. Mergens, 496 U.S. 226 (1990).

Board of Regents of State Colleges v. Roth, 408 U.S. 564 (1972).

■ *Brown v. Board of Education of Topeka, Kansas*, 349 U.S. 294, 75 S.Ct. 753 (1955).

Bureau of National Affairs. (1993). Lamb's Chapel and John Seigerwald, petitioners v. Center Moriches Union Free School District et al. *The United States Law Week*, 61(46), 4549–4554.

Chase, C.I. (1976). Classroom testing and the right to privacy. *Phi Delta Kappan, 58*, 331–332.

- *Chicago Teachers Union, Local No.1 v. Hudson*, 475 U.S. 292, 106 S.Ct. 1066 (1986).

Conkling, W. (1991, November/December). The big chill. *Teacher Magazine*, pp. 46–53.

Copyright Information Services. (1992). *The official fair-use guidelines: Complete texts of four official documents arranged for use by educators* (3rd ed.). Friday Harbor, WA: Author.

- Data Research, Inc. (1995). *1995 deskbook encyclopedia of American school law*. Rosemount, MN: Author.

Davis v. Grover, 480 N. W. 2d 460, (Wis. 1992).

- *Ellis v. Brotherhood of Railway Airline and S.S. Clerks*, 466 U.S. 435, 104 S.Ct. 1885 (1984).

- *Encyclopedia Britannica Educational Corporation v. Crooks*, 542 F.Supp. 1156 (W.D. N.Y. 1982).

Fischer, L., Schimmel, D., & Kelly, C. (1995). *Teachers and the law* (4th ed.). White Plains, NY: Longman.

Florence County School District Four v. Carter, U.S. Lexis 7154, 62 U.S L.W. 4001 (S.C., 1993).

- *Franklin v. Gwinnett Country Public Schools*, 112 S.Ct. 1028 (1992).

- Frievogel, W.H. (1995, June 13). KC school case ruling curbed: Judge went too far, court says. *St. Louis Post Dispatch*, 1A.

- *Gaylord v. Tacoma School District No. 10*, 88 Wa.2d 286, 559 P. 2d 1340 (1977).

Goetz v. Ansell, 477 F.2d 636 (2nd Cir. 1973).

Gonzalez v. Mackler, 241 N.Y.S.2d 254 (N.Y. App. Div. 1963).

- Gorn, S. (1996). *What's hot, what's not: Trends in special education litigation*. LRP.

Goss v. Lopez, 419 U.S. 565, 95 Ct. 729, 42 L.Ed.2d 725 (1975).

Gursky, D. (1992, February). Spare the child? *Teacher Magazine*, pp. 17–19.

Hazelwood School District v. Kuhlmeier, 484 U.S. 260 (1988).

- *Hines v. Caston School Corporation*, 63 USLW 2799 (Ind. App. 1995).

Imber, M., & van Geel, T. (1993). *Education law*. New York: McGraw-Hill.

- *Honig v. Doe*, 484 U.S. 305, 108 S.Ct. 592 (1988).

- *Hunter v. Board of Education of Montgomery Country*, 425 A.2d 681 (Md.App.1981), aff'd in part and rev'd in part on other grounds, 439 A.2d 582 (Md.App.1982).

Ingraham v. Wright, 430 U.S. 651, 97 S.Ct 1401, 51 L.Ed.2d 711 (1977).

In re William G., 221 Cal. Rptr. 118 (1985).

Irving Independent School District v. Tatro, 468 U.S. 883, 104 S.Ct. 3371, 82 L.Ed.2d 664 (1984).

- Johnston, R.C. (1994). Policy details who paddles students and with what. *Education Week, 14*(11), 5.

- La Morte, M.W. (1996). *School law: Cases and concepts* (5th ed.). Boston: Allyn and Bacon.

Lau v. Nichols, 414 U.S. 563 (1974).

Lee v. Weisman, 69 U.S.L.W. 4723 (1992).

Lemon v. Kurtzman, 403 U.S. 602, 91 S.Ct. 2105, 29 L.Ed.2d 745 (1971).

- Levine, S. (1995, June 15). Jackson objects to court ruling. *Palm Beach Post*, p. 18a.

- LRP Publications. (1995). District can ban males from wearing earrings to school. *Your School and the Law, 25*(8), 9.

- LRP Publications. (1996a, May). Five ways to prevent peer sexual harassment. *Your School and the Law, 26*(5), 10.

- LRP Publications. (1996b, May). PFAW report: Creationism is making a comeback. *Your School and the Law, 26*(5), 10

Mancha v. Field Museum of Natural History, 283 N.E.2d 899 (Ill. App. 1972).

Martin Luther King, Jr., Elementary School Children v. Michigan Board of Education, 473 Federal Supplement, 1371 (1979).

McCarthy, M.M., & Cambron-McCabe, H. (1992). *Public school law: Teachers and students' rights* (3rd ed.). Boston: Allyn and Bacon.

- *Missouri v. Jenkins*, 115 S.Ct. 2038, 132 L. Ed. 2d 63 [100 Ed. Law Rep. [506]] (1995).

- Mead, J.F. (1995). Including students with disabilities in parental choice programs: The challenge of meaningful choice. *West's Education Law Reporter, 100*, 463–496.

Morin, C.M. (1991). *Summary of cases relating to the rights of gay/les-bian public employees*. Washington, DC: National Education Association.

- *Morrison v. State Board of Education*, 1 Cal.3d 214, 82 Cal.Rptr. 175, 191, 461 P. 2d.375, 391 (1969).

- *National Gay Task Force v. Board of Education of Oklahoma City*, 729 F.2d 1270 (10th Cir. 1984), aff'd by divided court, 470 U.S. 903 (1985).

National Organization on Legal Problems of Education (1988). *Education Law Update 1987–1988*. USA: Author.

New Jersey v. T.L.O., 221 Cal. Rptr. 118 (1985).

Peter W. v. San Francisco Unified School District, 131 Cal.Rptr. 854 (1976).

- *Rowland v. Mad River Local School District, Montgomery County, Ohio*, 730 F.2d 444 (6th Cir. 1984).

- Russo, C.J. (1995). *The yearbook of education law 1995*. Topeka, KA: National Organization on Legal Problems of Education.

- Russo, C.J., & Rossow, L.F. (1996). *Missouri v. Jenkins* redux: The end of the road for school desegregation or another stop on an endless journey? *West's Education Law Reporter, 103*, 1–12.

Rothschild v. Grottenthaler, 907 F. 2nd, 286, (1990, June 27).

- Sanchez, M., & Kaggwa, L. (1995, June 18). Left, right, put spin on cases: Rulings on affirmative action will intensify debate. *Kansas City Start*, B1.

- *School District of Abington Township v. Schempp*, 374 U.S. 203, 300,83 S.Ct 1560, 1620 (1963).

Sendor, B. (1992, January). The teacher as a private person. *American School Board Journal*, p. 18.

- *Sony Corporation of America v. Universal City Studios, Inc.*, 464 U.S. 417 (1984) *reh'g denied*, 465 U.S. 1112 (1984).

Station v. Travelers Insurance Co., 292 So.2d 289 (La. Ct. App. 1974).

Tinker v. Des Moines Independent Community School District, 393 U.S. 503, 89 S.Ct. 733, 21 L.Ed.2d 731 (1969).

Underwood, J.K. (1991). *Choice Wisconsin style*. Madison: Wisconsin Center for Educational Policy.

U.S. Department of Health and Human Services. (1992). *Child abuse and neglect: A shared community concern*. Washington, DC: Clearinghouse on Child Abuse and Neglect Information.

Virgil v. School Board of Columbia County Florida, 862 F.2d 1517 (1989).

Wallace v. Jaffree, 427 U.S., 38 (1985).

Walsh, M. (1992, March 4). Students claiming sex harassment win right to sue: Ruling holds schools to workplace standard. *Education Week*, pp. 1, 24.

Ward v. Newfield Central School District No. 1, 412 N.Y.S.2d 57 (N.Y. App. Div. 1978).

West Virginia State Board of Education v. Barnette, 319 U.S. 624; 642 (1943).

Widmar v. Vincent, 454 U.S. 263 (1981).

Wisconsin v. Yoder, 406 U.S. 205 (1972).

- Zirkel, P.A., Richardson, S.N., & Goldberg, S.S. (1995). *A digest of Supreme Court decisions affecting education* (3rd ed.). Bloomington, IN: Phi Delta Kappa Educational Foundation.

Chapter 12

- Associated Press. (1996, February 17). Court orders S. African school to admit blacks. *The Washington Post*, p. A28.

- Berg, D.L. (1995). Canada. In T.N. Postlethwaite (Ed.), *The encyclopedia of comparative education and national systems of education* (2nd ed.) (pp. 180–189). Oxford: Pergamon Press.

- Berliner, D.C., & Biddle, B.J. (1995). *The manufactured crisis: Myths, fraud, and the attack on America's public schools*. Reading, MA: Addison-Wesley.

- Bjerg, J., Callewaert, S., Elle, B., Mylov, P., Nissen, T., & Silberbrandt, H. (1995). Danish education, pedagogical theory in Denmark and in Europe, and Modernity. *Comparative Education, 31*(1), 31–47.

Bondi, L. (1991). Choice and diversity in school education: Comparing developments in the United Kingdom and the USA. *Comparative Education, 27*(2), 125–34.

Booth, C. (1988). United Kingdom. In T.N. Postlethwaite (Ed.), *The encyclopedia of comparative education and national systems of education, Second* (2nd ed.) (pp. 691–698). Oxford: Pergamon Press.

Bordia, A. (1988). India. In T.N. Postlethwaite (Ed.), *The encyclopedia of comparative education and national systems of education* (pp. 350–358). Oxford: Pergamon Press.

Boulding, E. (1988). *Building a global civic culture: Education for an interdependent world*. Syracuse, NY: Syracuse University Press.

■ Boyer, E. (1992). Educating in a multicultural world. In D. Bragaw & W.S. Thomson (Eds.) *Multicultural education: A global approach* (pp. 48–53). New York: The American Forum for Global Education.

■ Bracey, G. W. (1996). International comparisons and the condition of American education. *Educational Researcher, 25*(1), 5–11.

■ Committee to Review the Organization, Governance and Funding of Schools. (1995, August 31). *Report of the committee to review the organization, governance and funding of schools*. Pretoria: Department of Education.

■ Desmond, E.W. (1996). The failed miracle. *Time, 147*(17), 60–64.

■ Evanoff, T. (1995, March 13). Trade schools are often strong lures for industry. *The Virginian-Pilot* (Norfolk) [Online]. Available: NEXIS Library: File: BUSDTL.

Florander, J. (1988). Denmark: System of Education. In T. Husen & T.N. Postlethwaite (Eds.), *The International encyclopedia of education: Research and studies: Vol. 3* (pp. 1354–1360). New York: Pergamon Press.

■ Foltz-Gray, D. (1995). World & rhythms. *Teaching Tolerance, 4*(1), 58–61.

■ Gladwell, M. (1991, December 2–8). Apples plus 4 oranges equals 1 uproar over math skills. *The Washington Post Weekly Edition*, p. 33.

■ A global revolution in science, mathematics and technology. (1996, April 10). *Education Week, 15*(29), Special Forum Section, 1–8.

■ Goya, S. (1993). The secret of Japanese education. *Phi Delta Kappan, 75*(2), 126–129.

■ Goya, S. (1994). Japanese education: Hardly known facts. *The Education Digest, 59*(8), 8–12.

■ Harnisch, D.L. (1994). Supplemental education in Japan: Juku schooling and its implication. *Journal of Curriculum Studies, 26*(3), 323–334.

■ Harrison, B. (1994, October 19). Survey of North American business locations. *The Financial Times* [Online]. Available: NEXIS Library: File: FINTME.

Hartshorne, K. (1990). Post-apartheid education: A concept in process (opportunities within the process). In R. Schrire (Ed.), *Critical choices for South Africa: An agenda for the 1990s*, Oxford: Oxford University Press, 168–185.

■ Herbert, J.M., & McNergney, R.F. (Eds.). (1996a). *The case of Columbus, New Mexico: Educational life on the border*. Washington, DC: American Association of Colleges for Teacher Education.

■ Herbert, J.M., & McNergney, R.F. (Eds.). (1996b). *The case of Deming, New Mexico: International public education*. Washington, DC: American Association of Colleges for Teacher Education.

■ International Baccalaureate Organization (1996) *Welcome to the International Baccalaureate Organization* [online]. Available: http://www.ibo.org/ Geneva, Switzerland.

■ Jansen, M., & Kreiner, S. (1995). Denmark. In T.N. Postlethwaite (Ed.), *The encyclopedia of comparative education and national systems of education* (2nd ed.) (pp. 31–47). Oxford: Pergamon Press.

Judge, H. (1989, June). Is there a crisis in British secondary schools? *Phi Delta Kappan, 70*(10), 813–815.

■ Kanaya, T. (1995). Japan. In T.N. Postlethwaite *International encyclopedia of national systems of education* (pp. 482–488). New York: Elsevier Science.

■ Kaplan, R.D. (1996). *The ends of the earth: A journey at the dawn of the 21st century*. New York: Random House.

King, E.J. (1988). South Africa. In T.N. Postlethwaite (Ed.), *The encyclopedia of comparative education and national systems of education*, (2nd ed.) (pp. 600–605). Oxford: Pergamon Press.

Lemmer, E.M. (1993). Educational renewal in South Africa: Problems and prospects. *Compare, 23*(1), 53–62.

■ Lorey, D.E. (1995, March–April). Education and the challenges of Mexican development. *Challenge*, 38:51–55.

■ MayaQuest. (undated). *Back by popular demand—MayaQuest '96: Students around the country log onto the Internet, lead expedition into Central America*. Minneapolis, MN: MayaQuest Interactive Expedition.

■ McAdams, R.P (1993). *Lessons from abroad: How other countries educate their children*. Lancaster, PA: Technomic.

■ McNergney, R.F., Regelbrugge, L.A., & Harper, J.P. (1997). Multicultural education in a global context. In J. McIntyre & D.M. Byrd (Eds.), *Teacher education yearbook*, pp. 7–25. Thousand Oaks, CA: Corwin Press.

■ Mislevy, R.J. (1995). What can we learn from international assessments? *Educational Evaluation and Policy Analysis, 17*(4), 419–437.

■ Muslim parents boycott religious classes. (1996, January). *The Times Educational Supplement*, p. 3.

■ National Center for Education Statistics. (1995). *The condition of education, 1995*. Washington, DC: U.S. Department of Education, Office of Educational Research and Improvement.

■ Nuthall, G., & Alton-Lee, A. (1995). Assessing classroom learning: How students use their knowledge and experience to answer classroom achievement test questions in science and social studies. *American Educational Research Journal, 32*(1), 185–223.

■ Patrick, C.L., & Calfee, R.C. (1996, April 7). A textbook case of hype. *The Washington Post*, p. C1.

■ Regelbrugge, L., & Moultrie, L. (1995). The role of diversity in sustainable community development. *Issues and Views*, p.2.

■ Resnick, L.B., & Nolan, K.J. (1995). Where in the world are world-class standards? *Educational Leadership, 52*(6), 6–10.

■ Reyes, M.E. (1995). Mexico. In T.N. Postlethwaite (Ed.), *International encyclopedia of national systems of education* (2nd ed.) (pp. 643–652). New York: Elsevier.

■ Rowe, M. (1986). Wait time: Slowing down may be a way of speeding up! *Journal of Teacher Education, 37*, 43–50.

■ Roy, D.A. (1991). A foundation for the future. *The Hitachi Foundation 1991 Annual Report*. Washington, DC: The Hitachi Foundation.

■ Sato, N., & McLaughlin, M.W. (1992). Context matters: Teaching in Japan and the United States. *Phi Delta Kappan, 73*(5), 359–366.

■ Singh, A. (1996). Don't transfer teachers. *The Hindustan Times, 72*(69), 9.

■ Stedman, L. (1994). Incomplete explanations: The case of U.S. performance in the international assessment of education. *Educational Researcher, 23*(7), 24–32.

■ Stevenson, H.W., & Stigler, J.W. (1992). *The learning gap: Why our schools are failing and what we can learn from Japanese and Chinese education*. New York: Summit.

■ Stigler, J.W., & Stevenson, H.W. (1991, Spring). How Asian teachers polish each lesson to perfection. *American Educator*, pp. 20–30.

■ Taylor, W.H. (1991). India's national curriculum: Prospects and potential for the 1990s. *Comparative Education, 27*(3), 325–344.

■ Theobald, D. (1995, June). Investing in grandchildren: Basic education in the Indian sub-continent. *Asian Affairs, 26* (Part 2), 141–151.

Thomas, R.M. (Ed.). (1988). *Oriental theories of human development*. New York: Peter Lang.

Thomas, R.M. (Ed.) (1990). *International comparative education: Practices, issues, & practices*. Oxford: Pergamon Press.

Thorp, S. (Ed.).(1991). *Race, equity, and science teaching*. London: Lavenham Press.

■ Thurow, L.C. (1996, April 7). Preparing students for the coming century. *The Washington Post: Education Review, 119*(124) pp. 1, 4, 30.

■ Tye, B.B., & Tye, K.A. (1992). *Global education: A study of school change*. Albany, NY: State University of New York Press.

■ Westbury, I. (1992). Comparing American and Japanese achievement: Is the United States really a low achiever? *Educational Researcher, 21*(5), 18–24.

Chapter 13

■ Becker, F. (1996). The webs we weave. In *Contemporary issues: Interdisciplinary teaching and learning*. [Online]. Available: http://curry.edschool.Virginia.EDU/go/casecourse/. Washington, DC: The Hitachi Foundation.

Brandt, R.S. (1992). On building learning communities: A conversation with Hank Levin. *Educational Leadership*, 50(1), 19–23.

Brophy, J, & McCaslin, M. (1992). Teachers' reports of how they perceive and cope with problem students. *The Elementary School Journal*, 93(1), 3–68.

Clandinin, D.J., & Connelly, F.M. (1996). Teachers' professional knowledge landscapes: Teacher stories—stories of teachers—school stories—stories of schools. *Educational Researcher*, 25(3), 24–30.

Coalition of Essential Schools. (1996, April 3). *Information on member schools*. Providence, RI: Coalition of Essential Schools.

Cushman, K. (1993a). Essential collaborators: Parents, school, and community. *Horace*, 9(5), 1–8.

Cushman, K. (1993b). What's essential? Integrating the curriculum in essential schools. *Horace*, 9(4), 1–8.

Dixon, P.N., & Ishler, R.E. (1992). Professional development schools: Stages in collaboration. *Journal of Teacher Education*, 43(1), 28–34.

Glaser, R., & Linn, R. (1992). *Assessing achievement in the states: The first report of the National Academy of Education Panel on the Evaluation of the NAEP Trial State Assessment—1990 Trial Assessment*. Stanford, CA: National Academy of Education.

Good, T.L., & Brophy, J.E. (1994). *Looking in classrooms* (6th ed.). New York: HarperCollins.

Goodlad, J.I. (1988, October). Studying the education of educators: Values-driven inquiry. *Phi Delta Kappan*, 70(2), 105–111.

Goodlad, J.I. (1990). *Teachers for our nation's schools*. San Francisco: Jossey-Bass.

Grabe, M., & Grabe, C. (1996). *Integrating technology for meaningful learning*. Boston: Houghton Mifflin.

Green, K.C. (1996, January). *The 1995 national survey of desktop computing in higher education: Technology use jumps on college campuses*. Encino, CA: The Campus Computing Project.

Grumet, M. (1987). Women and teaching: Homeless at home. *Teacher Education Quarterly*, 14(2), 39–46.

Hallahan, D.P., & Kauffman, J.M. (1997). *Exceptional learners: Introduction to special education* (p. 354). Boston: Allyn and Bacon.

Harris, J. (1994). *Way of the ferret: Finding educational resources on the internet*. Eugene, OR: International Society for Technology in Education.

Heaviside, S., Farris, E., Malitz, G., & Carpenter, J. (1995, February). *Advanced telecommunications in U.S. public schools, K–12*. Washington, DC: U.S. Department of Education.

Holmes Group. (1992). Texas Tech and Lubbock schools start 5-school PDS collaborative. *The Holmes Group Forum*, 7(1), 12–13.

Holmes Group. (1995). *Tomorrow's schools of education*. East Lansing, MI: The Holmes Group.

Johnson, W.R. (1990). Inviting conversations: The Holmes Group and tomorrow's schools. *American Educational Research Journal*, 27(4), 581–588.

Joyce, B.R., & Weil, M. (1996). *Models of teaching*. Boston: Allyn and Bacon.

Kahne, J., & Westheimer, J. (1996). In the service of what? The politics of service learning. *Phi Delta Kappan*, 77(9), 593–599.

Keller, B.M., & Soler, P. (1996). The influence of the Accelerated Schools philosophy and process on classroom practices. In C. Finnan, E.P. St. John, J. McCarthy, & S.P. Slovacek (Eds.), *Accelerated schools in action: Lessons from the field* (pp. 273–290). Thousand Oaks, CA: Corwin Press.

Koretz, D. (1995). The quality of information from NAEP: Two examples of work done in collaboration with Leigh Burstein. *Educational Evaluation and Policy Analysis*, 17(3), 280–294.

Lawton, M. (1996a). Board approves plans for NAEP civics test. *Education Week*, 15(25), 6.

Lawton, M. (1996b). States move to toughen exit exams: Educators, employers, seek to set bar higher. *Education Week*, 15(22), 1, 23.

Leighninger, M., & Niedergang, M. (1995). *Education: How can schools and communities work together to meet the challenge? A guide for involving community members in public dialogue and problem solving*. Pomfret, CT: Topsfied Foundation.

Lerner, B (1991, March). Good news about American education. *Commentary*, pp. 19–25.

Levin, H.M. (1996). Accelerated schools : The background. In C. Finnan, E.P. St. John, J. McCarthy, & S.P. Slovacek (Eds.), *Accelerated schools in action: Lessons from the field* (pp. 3–23). Thousand Oaks, CA: Corwin Press.

Levine, M. (Ed.). (1992). *Professional practice schools: Linking teacher education and school reform*. New York: Teachers College Press.

Lugg, C.A., & Boyd, W.L. (1993, November). Leadership for collaboration: Reducing risk and fostering resilience. *Phi Delta Kappan* 75, 253–256.

Madaus, G.F., & Kellaghan, T. (1992). Curriculum evaluation and assessment. In P.W. Jackson (Ed.), *Handbook of research on curriculum* (pp. 119–156). New York: Macmillan.

McLaughlin, M.W., & Talbert, J.E. (1993). *Contexts that matter for teaching and learning*. Stanford, CA: Center for Research on the Context of Secondary School Teaching.

Mitzel, H.E. (1960). Teacher effectiveness. In C.W. Harris (Ed.), *Encyclopedia of of educational research* (3rd ed.) (pp. 1481–1486). New York: Macmillan.

Morine-Dershimer, G. (1990, October). *Choosing among alternatives for tracing conceptual change*. Paper presented at the annual meeting of the Northeast Education Research Association, Ellenville, NY.

Morine-Dershimer, G. (1992, April). *Patterns of interactive thinking associated with alternative perspectives on teacher planning*. Paper presented at the annual meeting of the American Educational Research Association, San Francisco.

National Association for Sport and Physical Education. (1995). *Moving into the future: National standards for physical education* (p. 52). Oxon Hill, MD: AAHPERD.

National Education Goals Panel. (1994). *The national education goals report 1994*. Washington, DC: U.S. Government Printing Office.

National PTA. (1995–1996). *National PTA 100 Years* [Online]. Available: http://www.pta.org.

Noddings. N. (1984). *Caring: A feminine approach to ethics and moral education*. Berkeley: University of California Press.

Noddings. N. (1992). Gender and the curriculum. In P.W. Jackson (Ed.), *Handbook of research on curriculum* (pp. 659–686). New York: Macmillan.

Northwest Regional Educational Laboratory. (1994, May). The power and potential of distance education. *Northwest Report*, p. 1.

Oliva, P.F. (1992). *Developing the curriculum* (3rd ed.). New York: HarperCollins.

Olson, L. (1993, April 21). Off and running. *Education Week*, pp. 4–12.

Olson, L. (1995a). Could I interest you in a late-model school design? *Education Week*, 14(35), 33.

Olson, L. (1995b). NASDC discloses 11 jurisdictions for model schools. *Education Week*, 14(23), 3.

Performance-based ratings. (1996). *Education Week*, 15(17), 4.

Porter, A.C. (1995). The uses and misuses of opportunity-to-learn standards. *Educational Researcher*, 24(1), 21–27.

Quigley, C.N., Bahmueller, C.F. (Eds.). (1991). *Civitas: A framework for civic education*. Calabasas, CA: Center for civic education.

Rogers, A. (1995, January 4). *Global literacy in a Gutenberg culture*. [Online]. Available: http://www.gsn.org/gsn/articles/article. gutenberg.html.

Saunders, S., & Tankersley, M. (1990). *En route to conceptions of effective teaching: Preservice teachers' concept maps*. Paper presented at the annual meeting of the Northeast Educational Research Association, Ellenville, NY.

Shulman, L.S. (1986). Paradigms and research programs in the study of teaching. In M.C. Wittrock (Ed.), *Handbook of research on teaching* (3rd ed.) (pp. 3–36). New York: Macmillan.

Simon, S.B., Howe, L.W., & Kirschenbaum, H. (1972). *Values clarification: A handbook of practical strategies for teachers and students*. New York: Hart.

Sizer, T.R. (1992). *Horace's school: Redesigning the American high school*. Boston: Houghton Mifflin.

Sockett, H. (1992). The moral aspects of the curriculum. In P.W.

Jackson (Ed.), *Handbook of research on curriculum* (pp. 543–569). New York: Macmillan.

- Sommerfeld, M. (1996). Web site on K–12 standards efforts launched. *Education Week*, 15(26), 9.
- Squires, D.A., & Kranyik, R.D. (1995/1996). The Comer program: Changing school culture. *Educational Leadership*, 53(4), 29–32.

Stiggins, R.J. (1994). *Student-centered classroom assessment.* Upper Saddle River, NJ: Prentice-Hall.

Technical Subgroup for the National Education Goals Panel. (1992). *Gauging high performance: How to use NAEP to check progress on the National Education Goals.* Washington, DC: Author.

Viadero, D. (1992, November 25). Survey finds young people more likely to lie, cheat, steal. *Education Week*, p. 5.

Viadero, D. (1993, September 8). Students fall short on "extended" math questions, analysis finds. *Education Week*, p. 16.

Wadsworth, B. (1978). *Piaget for the classroom teacher.* New York: Longman.

Walberg, H.J. (1991). Productive teaching and instruction: Assessing the knowledge base. In H.C. Waxman & H.J. Walberg (Eds.), *Effective teaching: Current research* (pp. 33–62). Berkeley, CA: McCutchan.

- Wasley, P.A., King, S.P., & Louth, C. (1995). Creating coalition schools through collaborative inquiry. In J. Oakes & K.H. Quartz (Eds.), *Creating new educational communities.* Ninety-fourth yearbook of the National Society for the Study of Education, Part 1, (pp. 202–223). Chicago, IL: National Society for the Study of Education and University of Chicago Press.
- Webb, N.L., & Romberg, T.A. (in press). *Collaboration as a process of reform: The urban mathematics collaborative project.* New York: Teachers College Press.

Wisconsin Center for Education Research. (1992). Collaboration breaks mathematics teacher isolation and builds professionalism. *WCER Highlights*, 4(1), 1–2.

NAME INDEX

SUBJECT INDEX